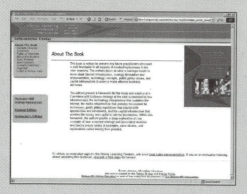

Internet Marketing: Building [...] ***Economy Website***—For studen[...] [...]nclude chapter overviews and quizzes to help them master essential concepts and competencies. For instructors, there is a link to the MarketspaceU website where they can download sample syllabi, lecture notes, PowerPoint slides, and other multimedia materials.

marketspaceU (www.marketspaceU.com)—Instructors in the e-commerce field continually confront the challenge of staying current with industry events. Securing fresh classroom material and staying on the cutting edge of theory and practice are among the most important and time-consuming of instructor duties. MarketspaceU solves these problems by offering outstanding instructor support, including regular case updates, news feeds, PowerPoint case timelines, and video segments. Instructors will also find lectures (including teaching notes and PowerPoint slides), sample syllabi, and multimedia materials for each chapter.

E-Commerce PowerWeb – Online access to current full-text articles, quizzing and assessment, validated links to relevant material, interactive glossaries, weekly updates, and interactive web exercises.
http://www.dushkin.com/powerweb

Internet Marketing

Building Advantage in the Networked Economy

Second Edition

Rafi A. Mohammed

Marketspace, a Monitor Group Company

Robert J. Fisher

R.A. Barford Professor in Marketing
Communications
Richard Ivey Business School
University of Western Ontario

Bernard J. Jaworski

Markets Chair, Monitor University
Marketspace, a Monitor Group Company

Gordon J. Paddison

Senior Vice President, Worldwide
Interactive Marketing and Business
Development
New Line Cinema

McGraw Hill Irwin
marketspaceU

Boston   Burr Ridge, IL   Dubuque, IA   Madison, WI   New York   San Francisco   St. Louis
Bangkok   Bogotá   Caracas   Kuala Lumpur   Lisbon   London   Madrid   Mexico City
Milan   Montreal   New Delhi   Santiago   Seoul   Singapore   Sydney   Taipei   Toronto

The McGraw·Hill Companies

INTERNET MARKETING: BUILDING ADVANTAGE IN A NETWORKED ECONOMY
Published by McGraw-Hill/Irwin, a business unit of The McGraw-Hill Companies, Inc.,
1221 Avenue of the Americas, New York, NY, 10020. Copyright © 2004, 2002 by Marketspace,
LLC, a member of Monitor Company Group, LP. All rights reserved. No part of this
publication may be reproduced or distributed in any form or by any means, or stored in a
database or retrieval system, without the prior written consent of Marketspace, LLC, including,
but not limited to, in any network or other electronic storage or transmission, or broadcast for
distance learning.
Some ancillaries, including electronic and print components, may not be available to
customers outside the United States.

This book is printed on acid-free paper.

6 7 8 9 0 CCW/CCW 0 9 8 7

ISBN-13: 978-0-07-253842-7
ISBN-10: 0-07-253842-2

Publisher: *John E. Biernat*
Associate sponsoring editor: *Barrett Koger*
Editorial coordinator: *Scott Becker*
Marketing manager: *Kimberly Kanakes*
Media producer: *Craig Atkins*
Project manager: *Natalie J. Ruffatto*
Senior production supervisor: *Michael R. McCormick*
Coordinator freelance design: *Artemio Ortiz Jr.*
Supplement producer: *Betty Hadala*
Senior digital content specialist: *Brian Nacik*
Cover design: *JoAnne Schopler*
Typeface: *10/12 New Baskerville*
Compositor: *Black Dot Group*
Printer: *Courier Westford*

Library of Congress Cataloging-in-Publication Data

Internet marketing: building advantge in the networked economy/Rafi Mohammed . . . [et al.].—
2nd ed.
    p. cm.
  Rev. ed. of: Internet marketing/Rafi Mohammed . . . [et al.]. c2002.
  Includes bibliographical references and index.
  ISBN 0-07-253842-2 (alk. paper)
  1. Internet marketing. I. Mohammed, Rafi. II. Internet marketing. III Title.
HF5415.1265.I565 2004
658.8'4—dc21

2002043195

www.mhhe.com

Dedications

To Sachiko, Shakil, Selina, Morgan and Liza, I very much appreciate your love, support and friendship. Love, Rafi

To the memory of my mother, Shirley A. Fisher (1928–2001). R

To Mary, Ryan, Katie and Meredith, thank you for all your support and love, you make my life truly enjoyable. Bernie

With love to Atsuko, Gordon

About the Authors

Rafi A. Mohammed is a business strategy thought leader and business advisory consultant in the Cambridge office of Marketspace, a Monitor Group Company. Since joining Monitor in 1998, he has worked on media, new economy, broadband, and online service marketing/development strategy issues. At Marketspace, he focuses on media strategy and pricing issues. Prior to joining Monitor in 1998, he started a media strategy consulting practice in Los Angeles and worked on deregulatory issues at the Federal Communications Commission in Washington, D.C. As a teacher in Cornell University's economics department, Dr. Mohammed was awarded a fellowship in recognition of his teaching skills and contributions to teaching excellence.

Dr. Mohammed has a Ph.D. in economics from Cornell University and holds economics degrees from the London School of Economics and Boston University. His academic research has focused on media and business strategy topics. He has published an article on strategic bundling in the *Rand Journal of Economics*, a leading academic economics/strategy journal, and is a co-author of MarketspaceU's recent *e-Commerce* textbook. He was appointed a Batten Fellow of Strategy at the University of Virginia's Darden School of Business in 2001.

Robert J. Fisher is the R.A. Barford Professor in Marketing Communications at the Richard Ivey Business School at the University of Western Ontario. He was previously a member of the faculty of the University of Southern California.

Dr. Fisher's research focuses on joint decision making by managers and consumers. His recent work examines the effects of cooperative decision-making strategies in new product development teams composed of engineering and composed marketing managers. His research has been published in journals including the *Journal of Marketing, Journal of Consumer Research, Journal of Applied Psychology, Journal of Services Marketing* and *Journal of Product Innovation Management*. He is on the editorial board of the *Journal of Marketing, Journal of Consumer Research,* and *Psychology & Marketing*. He served as editor for a special issue in *Psychology & Marketing* on social desirability bias.

Dr. Fisher has extensive industry experience and has consulted for a variety of major corporations in the automotive, financial services, and nonprofit sector. He has also written a variety of case studies on marketing management and Internet marketing and has received several teaching awards. He enjoys teaching courses at the executive, MBA, Ph.D. and undergraduate levels.

Bernard J. Jaworski is one of the founding members and senior leaders of Marketspace, a Monitor Group company. He previously was the Jeanne and David Tappan Marketing Fellow and a tenured, full professor of Marketing at the University of Southern California. He also served on the faculty at the University of Arizona and was a visiting professor at Harvard Business School. He has lectured widely on the topics of marketing strategy, sales force management, branding, and e-commerce. From 1994 to 1999, he was dean of Texas Instruments' University. He is among the most widely published authors in the top marketing journals. Most recently, he was rated as one of the top 50 most published authors in top marketing journals. A recent University of Colorado study ranked Dr. Jaworski as the second most productive marketing scholar—as evidenced by publications in the four most highly regarded marketing journals. He is the recipient of both teaching and research awards. In 1997, he received the Golden Apple Award as the MBA teacher of the year at USC. He is one of a few two-time winners of the prestigious Alpha Kappa Psi award for best marketing practice article published in the *Journal of Marketing*. In February 2002, Dr. Jaworski (along with his co-author Ajay Kohli) was awarded the first-ever Sheth Foundation/*Journal of Marketing* Award for their 1993 article, "Market Orientation: Antecedents and Consequences." The award honors the *Journal of Marketing* article that, six to 10 years after its publication, has made the greatest long-term contribution to the field of marketing.

He has co-authored four e-commerce textbooks: *e-Commerce*, *e-Commerce: Casebook*, *Internet Marketing*, and *Introduction to e-Commerce*. He currently serves on the review board of the *Journal of Marketing, Journal of Marketing Research, Journal of Business-to-Business Marketing, Asian Journal of Marketing*, and other journals.

Gordon J. Paddison is senior vice president of worldwide interactive marketing and business development at New Line Cinema, an AOL Time Warner Company.

Mr. Paddison is credited as "one of the first interactive marketers at a major studio," according to *The Hollywood Reporter*. As the executive responsible for online and wireless content, promotions, and publicity behind New Line's motion pictures, Mr. Paddison has captured the industry's attention with his creative campaigns behind the *Austin Powers* and the *Lord of the Rings* series, converting online buzz into significant ticket sales. With the studio's award-winning *Lord of the Rings* website, Paddison engaged the pre-existing Tolkien fan base and expanded the word-of-mouth to the general audience. According to selected theater exit polls, more than 40 percent of the opening weekend audience said they learned about the first *Rings* movie from the Web promotions.

In addition to his well-known achievements with the *Austin* and *Rings* series, Paddison created the Web's consumer-focused guerilla marketing campaigns for films as diverse as *Blade, Blow, Thirteen Days, The Cell, Final Destination, Boogie Nights, Lost in Space, Pleasantville, Rush Hour, Magnolia*, and the re-release of *Gone With The Wind*, among many others.

Mr. Paddison manages all interactive media strategy, planning, campaign analysis and creative design, in addition to overseeing New Line's online promotional and advertising programs with America Online. He was named in *Entertainment Weekly*'s 2001 "IT List" as one of the top 100 people in show business. Mr. Paddison was also chosen by *Variety* as a member of the trade paper's "The *Digital* Dozen," a list of twelve individuals who will have a strong hand in shaping a new wired Hollywood.

Contributing Authors for This Edition

Katherine Jocz

Bruce Weinberg

Jon Davis

Kate Bernhardt

Craig Thompson

We are very grateful to the co-authors of the first edition who worked so hard under very tight deadlines to create the core foundation of this textbook.

George Eliades	Javier Colayco
David Bennion	Christian M. Dippon
Aileen Cahill	Toby Thomas
Mark Pocharski	Yannis Dosios
Leo Griffin	Ives Moraes
Marco Smit	

About MarketspaceU

MarketspaceU is a community of award-winning academics and talented business practitioners dedicated to developing managers for the networked economy. We are part of Marketspace, a Monitor Group company, founded in 1998 as a multimedia enterprise to provide advice on, research about, and analysis of the impact of new media and technology on businesses. Marketspace activities include consulting to freshly minted dot-coms, as well as to Global 1000 companies, and providing networked-economy insights to the public through a variety of media, including Web, television, and print.

Drawing upon the resources at Marketspace and at other Monitor Group companies, as well as from a network of academic institutional partners and CEO visionaries, marketspaceU brings together the diverse talents of practitioners, management consultants, academic experts, and writers.

Preface

This book is the result of a multiyear effort to understand how the Internet has affected the function of marketing. For the various authors of the text, this has meant a combination of classroom instruction, design of MBA coursework, client interaction in a wide variety of industries, geographies, and settings, reading of emergent academic literature, and immersion in the popular media. The book is very much a work in progress. We are living in a period during which the field of marketing is undergoing a fundamental reexamination of its core principles and doctrine. It is an exciting time, and we are fortunate to be able to share our journey with you.

The goals of the book are:

- To develop a general framework—in this case, a seven-stage process—to enable the design of Internet marketing programs.
- To illustrate that Internet marketing programs must be integrated with an overall marketing effort. Often the effectiveness of Internet marketing can only be understood in concert with traditional marketing efforts.
- To focus on the "best of" both academic theory and the practice of Internet marketing.
- To illustrate tools that work in practice.
- To provide an entertaining and thoughtful read.

Why This Particular Book?

While there are a multitude of books in the market that have the words "Internet marketing" in their titles, we believe that our book is truly innovative and distinctive. No Internet marketing text on the market today creates a framework to help students and practitioners understand how to think about and implement Internet marketing. Most books have good descriptions of some Internet marketing tools. However, they do not show the reader how to take these tools and make Internet marketing actually work in an integrated way. To use a simple analogy, Internet marketing books currently on the market are like cookbooks that list only the ingredients for a complex dinner. While our book comprehensively lists the ingredients, one key advantage is that we actually show the reader how to create the complex dinner.

Our four-stage, demand-centric framework shows readers how to use the Internet to create intense and profitable relationships with their customers. In addition to comprehensively discussing the key levers that marketers can use to create relationships, we focus on two primary forces that the Internet brings to marketing—individualization and interactivity. We label these two forces the 2Is. We discuss in detail how these 2Is influence key marketing levers and how these forces can be leveraged to create intense relationships with customers. An important chapter of our book illustrates an integrative framework that details exactly what levers should be used to advance customers through differing intensity relationship levels. We also have a chapter that shows the reader how to create an integrative marketing plan. Throughout the book, we illustrate these concepts by applying the framework to eBay.

The Role of New Line Cinema

One exciting feature of the book is the application in Chapter 14 of the core principles to New Line Cinema's *The Lord of the Rings: The Fellowship of the Ring*. One of the most extraordinary Internet marketers of this generation, Gordon Paddison, worked closely with us to illustrate how New Line was able to integrate its entire online and offline marketing effort for this very successful film. In particular, we were able to use our Marketspace Matrix (introduced in Chapter 1 as a key framework for the design of marketing programs) to highlight the film's marketing campaign.

The choice of the New Line example was motivated by two goals:

- To provide an interesting example for readers to follow throughout the book. Readers are more prone to learn if the examples in each chapter are engaging and enjoyable.
- To intrigue the readers and academics. To the best of our knowledge, there has been no trade or textbook that has been written in conjunction with a leading industry player. This association will clearly illustrate to the reader that in addition to providing innovative academic thought on Internet marketing, our framework and ideas are applicable to a leading media company.

Approach

We believe the true insights for long-term competitive advantage will be generated by deep observation of both new and established businesses wrestling with the challenges of online marketing and general business strategy. Thus, we take a militantly field-based and practitioner-based perspective on this work. This is not to say that marketing theory is irrelevant. Existing and emergent concepts from leading academics do apply. However, the Internet marketing literature is just emerging and has yet to occupy a significant number of pages in our leading journals. We do anticipate that this will change in the next few years. In the meantime, we believe that practice is ahead of theory, and we must "mine" the practice of Internet marketing for the new ideas.

We also believe that the concepts and ideas must be actionable within firms. Some of the concepts and frameworks have already been tested with our clients; others have yet to be tested. However, we want to make sure that these ideas are road-tested across the globe and in a variety of industries. We make this commitment to you as we move forward into future editions of this book.

New for This Edition

One of the key revisions in this edition is our desire to more fully incorporate Internet marketing levers and strategies currently being used. Gordon Paddison, leveraging his position near the center of Internet marketing, incorporated his experiences into many of the core chapters. The end-of-the-chapter eBay examples have been completely revised. All exhibits and website listings have been updated, and student Web activities have been added to key core chapters. In this edition, we opted to omit the chapter on corporate strategy. Also, we significantly restructured the market research chapter into a new chapter focusing on leveraging customer information through technology. We also swap the humorous, yet highly informative, *Austin Powers* chapter from the first edition, for a new chapter on the marketing campaign for the film *The Lord of the Rings: The Fellowship of the Ring*. This chapter highlights the intense and creative strategy behind the *Lord of the Rings* marketing campaign and focuses on the state-of-the-art Internet marketing levers that were used. In addition, significant revisions were made in the following chapters:

Chapter 2—Framing the Market Opportunity. This chapter was completely reorganized and a new digital photography example was used throughout it.

Chapter 3—Marketing Strategy in Internet Marketing. We include a new section on segmentation prioritization, resource allocation, and timing. A new Drill-Down titled "Under What Conditions Should a Firm Incorporate Internet Marketing into its Marketing Plan?" was added. Several new examples were used throughout the chapter.

Chapter 4—Customer Experience. The Experience Hierarchy model was significantly revised. Examples were revised throughout the chapter.

Chapter 5—Customer Interface. This chapter now appears earlier in the book so that students can dive deeper into the Internet earlier. Actionable design tips and principles were added throughout the chapter.

Chapter 6—Customer Relationships. We added discussions on situational and enduring involvement and further developed discussions on privacy, trust, and the relationship between loyalty and relationships. Examples were updated and revised throughout the chapter.

Chapter 7—Product. This chapter was completely revamped in an effort to clearly relate product and the Internet. A new framework classifies Internet products and services into digitizable goods and services, retail/distribution services, and product augmentations. A discussion on product dynamics, including product life cycle, early-mover advantages, and the importance of innovation has been added. The section on new-product development more closely focuses on how the Internet has changed product development.

Chapter 8—Pricing. The structure of basic pricing has been divided into two categories—retail pricing strategies and basic pricing strategies. Enhanced discussions on bundling and fairness were added. Finally, the chapter outlines a new price-setting framework, the Pricing Pentagon.

Chapter 9—Communication. The chapter describes new online marketing levers that have become more prevalent since the first edition. The communications process is now directly linked to strategic targeting and positioning. The six-step marketing communication process has been significantly revised.

Chapter 10—Community. One of the key changes in this chapter is a significant revision of the Three-Level Macro Approach, which has been renamed the Three Stages of Community. The Four-Stage Micro Approach has also been significantly revised and renamed the Community Growth Path. New Drill-Downs and examples were added.

Chapter 11—Distribution. A discussion on infomediaries was added to make the chapter more consistent with the latest thinking on online distribution types. An expanded discussion of mixed mode channels was added. New examples also appear.

Chapter 12—Branding. This revised chapter includes an expanded discussion of a promotional program's effect on branding, a discussion of top Internet brands, and an expanded discussion of brand associations and negative brand equity.

Chapter 13—Designing the Marketspace Matrix. The key principles of the Marketspace Matrix have been significantly revised. The chapter now includes an enhanced discussion on the strategic aspects relating to the matrix—segmentation, target marketing, and positioning.

Chapter 16—Metrics. The chapter now provides more detail on specific metrics commonly used in marketing management. It has been significantly restructured so as to be more tightly integrated with the overall structure of the book. It introduces a new metrics framework that focuses on financial and other metrics of overall marketing performance, customer metrics, and metrics for the implementation of the marketing program. Finally, the chapter focuses on linking all metrics to financial performance.

User's Guide

Textbook Navigation

Because networked-economy businesses operate in rich-media or new-media environments, we have endeavored to make this book a rich information environment. You will see that every chapter has a variety of standard features that augment the text. You can count on these to enrich your understanding of the material covered, to introduce new and often controversial perspectives, and to provide greater detail on topics of current and future salience. Look for these features as you read:

- *Drill-Downs and Sidebars:* These highlighted sections provide deeper explorations of topics that appear in the text by taking a focused approach to issues that some readers will find essential at a level of detail inappropriate to the main body of our work. For example, not every reader will want to explore the intricacies of collaborative filtering or viral marketing, but many will find these additional materials useful. Think of Drill-Downs and sidebars as hypertext—there when you need them, out of your way when you don't.

- *Point–Counterpoints:* These segments acknowledge the reality that many debates in networked-economy businesses—such as whether profits matter or whether Internet company valuations are rational—remain unresolved. Rather than take an artificial approach to these issues and present the "right" answers, we make the case for and against. Of course, we do have our points of view, and you will find these clearly indicated.

- *POVs (Points of View):* Throughout the chapters, we have included sidebar commentary from leading practitioners in the networked economy—people who have invented new business approaches, developed new network architectures, created major Web brands, and influenced policy in the field. These comments are excerpted from articles published in leading periodicals.

- *Sound Bytes:* Marketspace has invested heavily in media and video products that lend unique insights into the networked-economy. These interviews are transcribed excerpts from our ongoing research and videotaped conversations with thought leaders in the field including Netscape co-founder Marc Andreessen, Ethernet inventor Bob Metcalfe, and the creators of ICQ instant messaging, Yair Goldfinger and Sefi Vigiser. These interviews give fresh, up-to-date, and exclusive perspectives on the state of play in our field. Longer streaming-video excerpts are available on our website at *http://www.marketspaceu.com,* and full interviews are available on videotape for purchase.

- *eBay case study:* At the end of every chapter, we visit one company, eBay, that the networked-economy and old-economy companies alike have come to admire as one of the leading firms of the new millennium. Despite a competitive landscape that includes big players such as Yahoo! and Amazon, eBay continues to dominate the online auction space. eBay serves as a case study to which we apply the ideas and concepts presented in each chapter. We show exactly how these ideas apply, and we help you see the ideas in action in ways that have created substantial value for a company doing business in the real world.

Supporting Materials

To facilitate the teaching of the book content, we realize that instructors need teaching support materials. In our effort to assist instructors, we have developed a comprehensive support package that includes materials available in print and on the Web.

- *Introduction to e-Commerce.* This textbook lays out a comprehensive foundation for students to understand both the strategy and infrastructures underlying the field of e-commerce. With chapters on market opportunity, business plans, customer interface, marketing communications and branding, implementation, and metrics, we provide the reader with the ability to formulate a solid strategic plan for leading an online company. We then explain the four infrastructures—technology, media, capital, and public policy—that will influence a company's strategy. With knowledge of both e-commerce strategy and infrastructures, the student will understand how the online environment works, how it is different from—and similar to—the pre-Internet business environment, and how to leverage the knowledge that has been gained into a successful company.

- *e-Commerce.* This textbook provides an in-depth review of strategy formulation in the networked economy. The reader is guided through a multistep process that includes focused coverage of market opportunity analysis, building a business model, designing customer interface, implementation, and metrics. Underlying this strategy foundation are network infrastructure and the convergence of new and old media. An eBay case study throughout the book demonstrates how the text concepts can be applied to a leading new-economy firm.

- *e-Commerce Casebook.* Available for purchase separately, our casebook complements our textbook and charts an educational course through the key practical issues in the new economy business landscape. Case studies— long used in clinical psychology, medical, and business school programs— are designed to facilitate a dialogue, or more appropriately, a healthy debate on the alternative solutions to a particular problem. Today, there are precious few case studies that illustrate "what works" in the networked economy, and in our casebook we have assembled a unique and comprehensive selection that is directly relevant to the new economy.

- *Online Instructor Assistance.* We have designed and written material to help faculty using our textbook to teach an Internet marketing course or module. Our online instructor resources (available at *www.mhhe.com/marketspace*) offers a concise summary of each chapter's key themes, classroom questions (and answers) that highlight those themes and spur lively classroom debates, and relevant student project assignments (and answers) designed to reinforce key learning points in each chapter. The *Internet Marketing* materials provide teaching tips and suggestions for presenting each chapter, PowerPoint slides for each of the chapters (10–15 slides per chapter), suggested test/discussion questions for each chapter, and suggested exercises and associated websites that illustrate the chapter content.

- *MarketspaceU Multimedia Materials.* We draw upon the extensive professional media capabilities of the Marketspace media group and of our partners to let the networked economy speak for itself.

  - The Marketspace media archives contain over 100 focused, broadcast-quality interviews with leading CEOs, investors, inventors, and implementers, conducted at leading conferences around the world. Streaming-video excerpts are available on our website at *http://www.marketspaceu.com,* and full interviews are available on videotape for purchase.

  - We have captured Professors Rayport and Jaworski in a series of "Dot-com Debates" on live and lively issues in the new economy. Does profit matter? Do the valuations make sense? Who's got it better, dot-com startups or dot-coms backed by bricks-and-mortar giants? Does segmentation matter on the Web? Tune in by visiting us at *http://www.marketspaceu.com* as Dr. Rayport and Dr. Jaworski provide an educational—and entertaining—Point–Counterpoint discussion.

- *Our Cases.* Our library includes cases written for top business schools and our own cases written by our team of scholars and practitioners. Case studies—long used in clinical psychology, medical, and business school programs—are designed to facilitate a dialogue, or more appropriately, a healthy debate on the alternative solutions to a particular problem.

Today, there are precious few case studies that illustrate "what works" in the new economy. Our casebook provides a unique and comprehensive selection of cases that are directly relevant to the new economy. The interesting challenge in crafting cases on new-economy firms is that the "solution" seems to be changing as rapidly as the practitioner is able to diagnose the problem. We use the term "seems" since there are some basic strategy principles that *do* last the test of time. Our intent is to challenge your thinking—and debate with your classmates, colleagues, or friends—about the lasting principles that will emerge in the new economy.

- *Case Dashboards at MarketspaceU.com.* For each case, we offer an enhanced multi-media teaching note to supplement teaching notes from the case publisher in order to keep instructors informed on the cases and in control in the classroom. Each dashboard provides regularaly updated support materials: a quick summary of the case (including a summary of significant development since the date it was written), key articles, teaching aids (e.g., a timeline of company developments, ways to teach the case), discussion questions and focused point–counterpoint debates, and real-time news updates. There is also a link to the case publisher (e.g., Harvard Business School) so that instructors can order the original teaching notes and other material.

- *Lecture Dashboards at MarketspaceU.com.* For each textbook chapter, we offer both enhanced PowerPoint slide decks designed to capture key chapter themes and insights. These slide decks offer visual aids to assist instructors who are using our textbook to teach an e-commerce course or module. Similar to the case dashboards, we provide 24/7 news feeds on themes related to the lectures as well as streaming videos with various new-economy leaders.

- *Our Syllabi.* For instructors using our textbook to teach an Internet marketing course or module, we offer three types of suggested syllabi (all case format, all lecture format, combination case/lecture format) to use for their course.

  - All-Case Teaching Format. For instructors using an all-case format, we offer a syllabus that outlines a 13-week course structure that specifies suggested course timing, class session summaries, recommended cases that illustrate important e-commerce themes, and class preparation questions.

  - All-Lecture Teaching Format. For instructors using an all-lecture format, we offer a syllabus that outlines a 13-week course structure that specifies suggested course timing, class session summaries, and class preparation questions.

  - Combination Case/Lecture Format. For instructors using a combination case/lecture format, we offer a syllabus that outlines a 13-week course structure that specifies suggested course timing, class session summaries, recommended cases to augment textbook based lectures, and class preparation questions.

- *McGraw-Hill/Irwin Website.* McGraw-Hill/Irwin continues its leading role in providing excellent support to instructors in higher education. Instructors using our textbook to teach an e-commerce course or module are able to access the McGraw-Hill/Irwin website (*www.mhhe.com/marketspace*) for sample syllabi—for different approaches to teaching the material; descriptions of how to use the various pedagogical features—such as the POVs, Point–Counterpoints, and videos; suggested test/discussion questions for each chapter; guidelines for different types of projects; and PowerPoint slides for each of the chapters (10 to 15 slides per chapter).

For Faculty

The changes taking place in the networked economy have both energized the classroom and brought a new set of challenges to faculty teaching in this space. Students have unprecedented access to sources of information and data as well as a greater range of experiences—from investments in e-commerce companies to their own startup battle-scars—so support for teachers in the classroom has advanced from a blackboard or two to a multimedia tool kit to make lessons more immediate.

These developments make the job of staying on top of the networked economy and effectively conveying its lessons more difficult. Given the speed of change, how can we prevent being blindsided by late-breaking developments? Since the "old war horse" cases often no longer work, what *can* we repurpose, and where do we turn for new frameworks?

- Our *Internet Marketing* textbook provides a strong knowledge foundation to help chart your course through the new economy.
- Our other textbooks, casebooks, and stand-alone cases raise the key issues to show how e-commerce knowledge is applied in the business world and to drive productive discussions.
- Our teaching support materials give you unequaled confidence in the classroom. Our teaching notes outline the issues and chart the questions; our case updates give you real-time intelligence on the case, timelines of case developments, key articles, and focused point–counterpoint questions.
- Our articles and forums provide in-depth insights on what academic and business leaders are thinking and doing.
- Our extensive media library of interviews provides the first—and the last—word on networked-economy issues from the men and women who are driving it.

For Students

You are riding the wave of a technological revolution that is changing the way the economy operates. Businesses, entrepreneurs, governments, academic institutions, nonprofit organizations—they all are scrambling to hire students that understand, can operate in, and can lead in the networked economy.

- Our *Internet Marketing* textbook provides a strong networked economy knowledge foundation.
- Our case studies show how networked-economy knowledge is applied in the business world.

- Our articles and forums provide in-depth insight on what academic and business leaders are thinking and doing.

Acknowledgments

As with the first edition, writing the second edition has been a very intense, stressful, and productive period of our lives. However, we cannot emphasize how much fun we have had. While much of the fun was around brainstorming and coming up with new insights, we had a great crew working with us and the interaction of such diverse personalities really made this experience enjoyable.

We are fortunate to have worked with an outstanding team who helped to make the preparation of this book possible. While we acknowledge specific contributions on a chapter-by-chapter basis, we want to take the time to thank our colleagues in Marketspace, a Monitor Group company, who worked tirelessly to write and rewrite this book. Katherine Jocz is a great colleague to work with. Kathy willingly took on the greatest challenges and always delivered outstanding work. Jon Davis and Kate Bernhardt also made outstanding contributions to the second edition. We are grateful to Bruce Weinberg and Craig Thompson for their work on the new Customer Information Systems chapter in this second edition. Leo Abbett added a great deal of fun and humor to this second edition with his outstanding cartoons. We are very appreciative of JoAnn Kienzle's hard work on managing the page-proof process. We sincerely thank Marie Claire Guglielmo for her management, friendship, and great sense of humor.

We also must extend our deep gratitude to our colleagues who worked so hard on the first edition: Javier Colayco, George Eliades, David Bennion, Ives Moraes, Toby Thomas, Mark Pocharski, Chris Dippon, Leo Griffin, Yannis Dosios, Ben Monnie, Marco Smit, and Aileen Cahill. Bob Lurie, Felice Kincannon, Eric Paley, and Dan Kim contributed important insights and helped craft the core of the first edition.

Jenny Johnston and Jennifer Sturak did an outstanding job copyediting the chapters under very tight deadlines.

We are very grateful to Steve Szaraz, Michael Yip, Russell Schwartz, Wendy Rutherford, Victoria Shaw, Marian Thomas, Stephanie Yang, Craig Alexander, David Ruben, Allison Reese, Kimberly Basile, Kristia DeRoche, Ryan Jones, Max Kalehoff, and Heather Kuehnel for their tremendous efforts in getting this book completed!

Patrick DeGraba, Chris Maxwell, Sarah Maxwell, Bradley Miller, Jim Burrows, and Dick Rapp provided intellectual stimulation as well as outstanding references for the pricing chapter.

Many other people took exceptionally good care of us during the many weeks that we spent in Los Angeles working on the first and second editions of this textbook. Many thanks to Chris Denton and the crew at MR CHOW for the outstanding cuisine, great times, and excellent tables. We also are most grateful for the hospitality of Cormac O'Modhrain and his outstanding staff at the Park Hyatt Los Angeles. Specifically, we would like to sincerely thank Ann Joyce and Andrew Lovette for their tremendous efforts in making us feel at home.

Special thanks to THE AGENT, Rafe Sagalyn.

We also want acknowledge the editorial support at McGraw-Hill/Irwin of Rob Zwettler, vice president and editor-and-chief; Barrett Koger, associate sponsoring editor—marketing; and Scott Becker, editorial coordinator—marketing. We also would like to thank our good friend and strong supporter, Gary Bauer, for his efforts on our behalf.

Finally, none of this would have been possible without the generous support and enthusiasm of Mark Fuller, Joe Fuller and Mark Thomas, cofounders and leaders of the Monitor Group, and our leader, the czar of Marketspace, Jeffrey Rayport.

Brief Contents

Contents

Marketing Strategy in Internet Marketing 85

CHAPTER 3

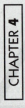

Customer Experience   129

CHAPTER 4

CHAPTER 5

Customer Interface 159

CHAPTER 6

Customer Relationships 199

CHAPTER 7

Product   237

CHAPTER 8

Pricing 275

CHAPTER 11

Distribution   443

CHAPTER 1

Introduction to Internet Marketing

This chapter provides an overview of the core concepts covered in the text. It begins with a discussion of the ways in which the Internet has irrevocably transformed the field of marketing through the introduction of new products, new audiences, and new strategies for reaching those audiences. Traditional marketing methods are still highly relevant in the networked economy. But firms must also consider a host of new and innovative marketing methods now at their disposal, such as dynamic pricing and banner advertisements.

The Internet marketing process occurs in seven stages. The process begins with framing the market opportunity, then moves to formulating the marketing strategy, designing the customer experience, crafting the customer interface, designing the marketing program, leveraging customer information through technology, and evaluating the results of the marketing program as a whole. The section that discusses marketing program design also introduces the concept of the Marketspace Relationship Levers Matrix (Marketspace Matrix for short)—a simplifying framework that illustrates the levers that the Internet marketer may choose to use at each stage of the customer relationship.

This chapter also introduces two other concepts that alter the playing field of modern marketing: individualization and interactivity. In contrast to the one-way mass promotion that characterizes much of modern marketing, Internet marketing enables firms to engage in individual, personalized dialogue with their customers. The chapter concludes with a discussion of the changing role of marketing professionals in this new environment.

QUESTIONS

Please consider the following questions as you read this chapter:

1. What is Internet marketing?
2. What is the narrow view versus the broad view of Internet marketing?
3. What are the seven stages of Internet marketing?
4. What are the four stages of the customer relationship?

With substantive input from George Eliades, Steve Libenson, and Aboud Yaqub

5. What are the six classes of variables in the Internet marketing mix?

6. What is the Marketspace Matrix?

7. How do interactivity and individualization come into play in the design of the marketing program?

8. What are the critical success factors for the Internet marketing professional?

Introduction

At its core, the mission of marketing is to attract and retain customers. To accomplish this goal, a traditional bricks-and-mortar marketer uses a variety of marketing variables—including pricing, advertising, and channel choice—to satisfy current and new customers. In this context, the standard marketing-mix toolkit includes such mass-marketing levers as television advertising, direct mail, and public relations, as well as customer-specific marketing techniques such as the use of sales reps.

With the emergence of the Internet and its associated technology-enabled, screen-to-face interfaces (e.g., mobile phones, interactive television), a new era of marketing has emerged. Well-respected academics and practitioners have called for new rules and urged debate about fundamental tenets of marketing, including segmentation, mass marketing, and regionalized programs.[1] At the other extreme, pundits and academics alike have argued that both the basic building blocks of marketing strategy and the pathways to competitive advantage have remained the same.[2]

The approach taken in this textbook falls between these polar views.[3] That is, new levers have been added to the marketing mix, segments have been narrowed to finer gradations, consumer expectations about convenience have forever been altered, and competitive responses happen in real time. In short, these are new, exciting changes that have a profound impact on the practice of marketing. At the same time, some of the fundamentals of business strategy—seeking competitive advantage based on superior value, building unique resources, and positioning in the minds of customers—have remained the same.

The intent of this text is to provide a clear indication of what has changed and what has not changed. At the same time, the text would not be complete (indeed, might not be actionable from the standpoint of business practice) if it did not propose a broader framework for understanding the practice of Internet marketing. Frameworks such as the 4Ps of marketing or the "five forces" of competitive analysis are important because they provide easy-to-remember, simplifying structures for complex problems. They also serve as guides to managerial action. Thus, understanding the five forces enables firms to comprehensively map their competitive environment while simultaneously identifying specific actions for their managers (e.g., reduce buyer power by increasing the number of buyers). This opening chapter provides a simple seven-stage framework for Internet marketing. But first it offers a brief review of the basics of marketing and the scope of Internet marketing.

Definition and Scope of Internet Marketing

It is perhaps best to begin with the basic American Marketing Association definition of marketing:

> Marketing is the process of planning and executing the conception, pricing, promotion, and distribution of ideas, goods, and services to create exchanges that satisfy individual and organizational goals.[4]

The Basics: What Is Marketing?

The definition summarized above has four critical features. These are:

Marketing Is a Process. A process is a particular method of doing an activity, generally involving a series of steps or operations. The classical marketing approach involves four broad steps: market analysis, market planning, implementation, and control.[5] Market analysis involves searching for opportunities in the marketplace, upon which a particular firm—with unique skills—can capitalize. Market planning requires segmentation, target market choice, positioning, and the design of the marketing mix (also termed the 4Ps, or marketing program). Market implementation includes the systems and processes to go to market with the marketing program. Finally, marketing control refers to the informal and formal mechanisms that marketing mangers can use to keep the marketing program on course. Analysis, planning, implementation, and control collectively provide a process for marketing managers to follow in the design and execution of marketing programs.

It Involves a Mix of Product, Pricing, Promotion, and Distribution. Strong marketing programs do not involve one action, such as the design of a great product. Rather, the most successful marketing programs involve mixing the ingredients of marketing to deliver value to customers. This mixing entails blending the right amounts of the 4P ingredients, at the right time, and in the right sequence. Too often, marketing programs fail because they allocate too many (or too few) resources in an uncoordinated way. How often have you seen a hot new Christmas toy advertised—but not found it on the shelf? In the Internet environment, this translates into significant problems with order fulfillment at the most pressing times of the year.

It Is About Exchange. Marketing is not successful unless two parties exchange something of value. The buyer may exchange time, money, or services, while the seller must exchange something of value to the buyer. The traditional retail context provides the simplest illustration of this principle. A given consumer exchanges money for a particular good or service. However, exchange also occurs in a wide variety of contexts, many of which are nonmonetary. These include bartering, volunteering services, and political donations.

It Is Intended to Satisfy Individual and Organizational Needs. The aim of marketing is to provide a satisfactory outcome for both the firm and the customer. Firms can have highly satisfied customers if they provide services for free. However, those organizations are not likely to have a long life. The key to modern marketing is simultaneously satisfying the customer, the firm, and its shareholders. In the long run, the firm must have a positive cash flow or show a clear path to profitability for investors to maintain confidence.

What Is Internet Marketing?

If traditional marketing is about creating exchanges that simultaneously satisfy the firm and customers, what is Internet marketing?

> Internet marketing is the process of building and maintaining customer relationships through online activities to facilitate the exchange of ideas, products, and services that satisfy the goals of both parties.[6]

This definition can be divided into five components:

A Process. Like a traditional marketing program, an Internet marketing program involves a process. The seven stages of the Internet marketing program process are framing the market opportunity, formulating the marketing strategy, designing the customer experience, crafting the customer interface, designing the marketing program, leveraging customer information through technology, and evaluating the results of the marketing program as a whole. These seven stages must be coordinated and internally consistent. While the process can be described in a simple linear fashion, the marketing strategist often has to loop back and forth during the seven stages.

Building and Maintaining Customer Relationships. The goal of marketing is to build and create lasting customer relationships. Hence, the focal point shifts from finding customers to nurturing a sufficient number of committed, loyal customers.[7] Successful marketing programs move target customers through three stages of relationship building: awareness, exploration, and commitment. It is important to stress that the goal of Internet marketing is not simply building relationships with online customers. Rather, the goal is to build offline as well as online relationships. The Internet marketing program may well be part of a broader campaign to satisfy customers who use both online and offline services.

Online. By definition, Internet marketing deals with levers that are available in the world of the Internet. However, as noted previously, the success of an Internet marketing program may rest with traditional, offline marketing vehicles. Consider, for example, the recruiting and job-seeking service Monster.com. Monster's success can be tied directly to the effectiveness of its television advertising and, in particular, its widely successful Super Bowl ads several years ago.[8]

Exchange. At the core of both online and offline marketing programs is the concept of exchange. In the networked economy, firms must be very sensitive to cross-channel exchanges. That is, an online marketing program must be evaluated according to its overall exchange impact—not just the online exchange impact. Hence, online marketing may produce exchanges in retail stores. Firms must be increasingly sensitive to these cross-channel effects if they are to measure the independent effects of online and offline marketing programs.

Satisfaction of Goals of Both Parties. One of the authors of this book is a loyal user of the website weather.com. Each morning he checks the weather in his city, as well as the weather in cities he will be traveling to during the week. He is clearly satisfied with and loyal to the site. To the extent that weather.com can monetize this loyalty—most likely, in the form of advertising revenue—both parties will be satisfied. However, if the firm is unable to meet its financial obligations to employees, suppliers, or shareholders, then the exchange is unbalanced. Customers are still happy, but the firm is unable to sustain its revenue model. Both parties must be satisfied for exchange to continue.

While the hype of Internet marketing has died down, it is clear that Internet marketing is here to stay and should be an important component of any marketer's arsenal. In addition to providing advertising competition to traditional advertising mediums (e.g., television, radio, print), the Internet has opened up a new window for marketers. During weekdays, Internet consumption exceeds all other media consumption for at-work users. Daytime on the Internet is prime time for at-work users.[9]

For certain product types, the Internet has become an essential component of marketing strategy. J.D. Power and Associates, a consumer research firm, says that 62 percent of new-car buyers research cars on the Internet before making a purchase. For auto manufacturers with affluent demographics, such as BMW and Volvo, as many as 85 percent of their customers research cars on the Internet. As will be discussed later in the text, BMW produced its own online film series. By mid-2001, the site had received 11 million film views with an additional 15,000 people viewing the films daily. Volvo, in partnership with AOL, launched its new S60 sedan exclusively online. Between October 15, 2000, and March 15, 2001, the campaign's duration, more than 2 million unique users visited Revolvolution.com. More than 250,000 people opted-in to Volvo's e-mail database, and 45,000 people configured cars online and requested a quote from a local dealer (the requests included names, phone numbers, and e-mail addresses). Volvo estimates that its Internet promotion drove 27,000 customers to its dealers' show rooms.

A Narrow View Vs. a Broad View

The discussion on the previous page raises the question of how broadly one should define the scope and impact of Internet marketing programs. Consider Exhibit 1.1. Cell 1 represents a situation in which the marketing effort is online (e.g., viral marketing, banner ads) and the sales revenue is realized online. Online marketing clearly produces online-based revenue. Then look at Cell 2. Here, the online marketing effort has led to revenue increases offline; visiting Gap's online store results in more sales to the traditional Gap retail store. Cell 3 shows the reverse effect. That is, traditional offline marketing activities (e.g., Amazon billboard, Monster Super Bowl ad) drive traffic and purchases at the website. Cell 4 shows how traditional advertising (e.g., television ads for Gap retail stores) drives the traffic and purchases at the retail store.

A narrow view of Internet marketing would be that it focuses principally on Cell 1. Advocates of this view would argue that it is only in this quadrant that one can truly measure and attribute the effects of Internet marketing—other cells (or the spillover effects) should not be counted. On the other hand, it could be argued that Cells 1, 2, and 3 should be counted as part of the overall Internet marketing effort. After all, the firm would realize lower total revenue if the cross-channel marketing effects did not occur. Hence, these cross-channel impacts should be considered part of Internet marketing. This text strongly advocates the broad view of Internet marketing. The overall efforts of marketing—all four quadrants—need to be coordinated and managed in an integrated way.

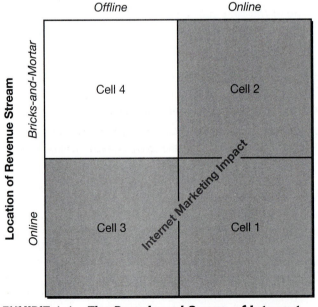

EXHIBIT 1.1   The Broadened Scope of Internet Marketing

Drill-Down

Common Myths Associated with Internet Marketing

Myth 1: Customers Behave Online as They Do Offline

- Marketers assumed that they can reach customers online in the same manner in which they reached them offline: with one-way broadcast messages.
- As more online marketers began vying for the customer's attention and as click-through rates declined, companies developed more obtrusive, untargeted advertising, thinking that consumers would be more willing to pay attention.
- Marketers operated under the assumption, "He who shouts the loudest will be heard."

Our Point of View on Myth 1:

- Firms must gauge the degree of interactivity to which their audience will most likely respond. Customer responses fall into three categories:
  - **Active.** Customer takes the lead in seeking out or spreading product information. Example: Microsoft's Xbox. Customers actively search for product information and reviews. Xbox customers have created numerous product/community websites.
  - **Interactive.** Some dialogue between customer and marketer. Example: Cannondale. Cannondale offers customers interactive tools to assist with bike model selection. Such tools augment and/or replace salesforce interactions in the exploration stage of the customer relationship.
  - **Reactive.** Customer has limited means of responding to marketer at the moment when the message was sent. Example: Coca-Cola. Coke has been experimenting with new ad formats that have the potential to boost brand awareness and sales.

Myth 2: Segmentation No Longer Matters Online

- After the promise of achieving one-to-one marketing faded, the pendulum swung so far that marketers are largely ignoring segmentation.
- Many websites are designed to achieve specific objectives, without consideration for the segment of users they are likely to attract.
- Some marketers assume that the active nature of Internet users renders any type of online segmentation useless.

Our Point of View on Myth 2:

- Segmentation *does* matter; the Internet opens new ways to segment customers.
  - Demographics, psychographics, purchasing habits, browsing habits, usage occasions, and relationship archetypes are all segmentation possibilities.

Myth 3: Online Personalization Is a Waste of Time and Money

- The Internet promised marketers the ability to reach customers on a one-to-one basis.
- Industry estimates reveal that nearly 50 percent of all customer relationship management projects are considered failures, as they fail to generate tangible benefits for companies and customers alike.

Our Point of View on Myth 3

- Personalization *does* matter, but only if it enhances the user experience and drives business results.
  - Travelocity, the online travel agency, reportedly converts its targeted e-mail recipients to shoppers at a rate twice as high as its non-targeted mass e-mail offers.

The Seven Stages of Internet Marketing

Exhibit 1.2 provides an overview of the seven stages of Internet marketing: framing the market opportunity, formulating the marketing strategy, designing the customer experience, crafting the customer interface, designing the marketing program, leveraging customer information through technology, and evaluating the results of the marketing program.

Stage One: Framing the Market Opportunity

Stage One involves the analysis of market opportunities and an initial first pass of the business concept—that is, collecting sufficient online and offline data to establish the burden of proof of opportunity assessment. Let us say, for example, that you are running a major dot-com business such as Amazon.com. The senior management team is continually confronted with go/no-go decisions about whether to add a new business unit or develop a new product line within that existing business unit. What mechanism do they put in place to evaluate these opportunities?

In this second part of the Internet marketing process, a simple six-step methodology helps evaluate the attractiveness of the opportunity (see Exhibit 1.3). The six steps include: seeding the opportunity, specifying unmet or underserved customer needs, identifying the target segment, declaring the company's resource-based opportunity for advantage, assessing opportunity attractiveness, and making the final go/no-go decision. The final go/no-go choice is often a corporate or business-unit decision. However, it is very important to stress that marketing plays a critical role in this market opportunity assessment phase. Chapter 2 provides a more detailed review of the opportunity framing process by applying its concepts to the online book industry.

In order for the firm to make an informed choice about the opportunity, the management team needs to obtain a sufficient picture of the marketplace and a clear articulation of the customer experience that is at the core of the opportunity. Thus, during the market opportunity assessment phase, the firm also needs to collect sufficient market research data (see Chapter 15).

Stage Two: Formulating the Marketing Strategy

Internet marketing strategy is based upon corporate, business-unit, and overall marketing strategies of the firm. This set of linkages is shown in Exhibit 1.4. The marketing strategy goals, resources, and sequencing of actions must be tightly aligned with the business-unit strategy. Finally, the overall marketing strategy includes both offline and online marketing activities. As Exhibit 1.4 illustrates, even for pure-play online businesses such as Amazon's tools and hardware group, two of the four cells of activity (Cells 1 and 3 of Exhibit 1.1) must be coordinated in a systematic go-to-market strategy. This will be covered in greater depth in Chapter 3.

Stage Three: Designing the Customer Experience

Firms must understand the type of customer experience that needs to be delivered to meet the market opportunity. The experience should correlate

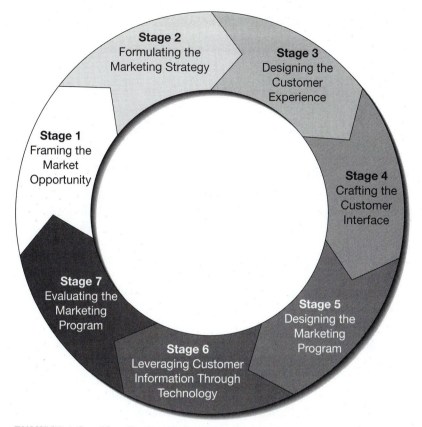

EXHIBIT 1.2   The Seven-Stage Cycle of Internet Marketing

with the firm's positioning and marketing strategy. Thus, the design of the customer experience constitutes a bridge between the high-level marketing strategy (Stage Two) and the marketing program tactics (Stage Five). This articulation and design of the desired online customer experience is the focus of Chapter 4.

Stage Four: Crafting the Customer Interface

The Internet has shifted the locus of exchange from the marketplace (i.e., face-to-face interaction) to the marketspace (i.e., screen-to-face interaction). The key difference is that the nature of the exchange relationship is now mediated by a technology interface. This interface can be a desktop PC, sub-notebook, personal digital assistant, mobile phone, wireless applications protocol (WAP) device, or other Internet-enabled appliance. As this shift from people-mediated to technology-mediated interfaces unfolds, the senior management team is confronted with a growing number of interface design considerations. What is the look-and-feel, or context, of the interface? Should the interface include commerce activities? How important are communities to the business model? To capture these design considerations, Chapter 5 introduces the 7Cs Framework. The 7Cs are a rigorous way to understand the interface design choices that confront senior managers as they implement their marketing programs online.

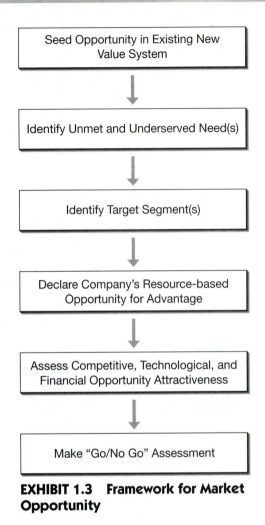

EXHIBIT 1.3   Framework for Market Opportunity

Stage Five: Designing the Marketing Program

Upon completion of Stages One through Four, the firm should have a clear strategic direction. The firm has made a go/no-go decision on a particular option. Moreover, it has decided upon the target segment and the specific position that it wishes to own in the minds of the target customer. Stage Five entails designing a particular combination of marketing actions (termed levers) to move target customers from awareness to commitment. The framework used to accomplish this task is the Marketspace Matrix. Simply put, the Internet marketer has six classes of levers (product, pricing, communication, community, distribution, and branding) that can be used to create target customer awareness, exploration, and, it is hoped, commitment to the firm's offering. However, prior to discussion of the Marketspace Matrix, the stages of the customer relationship and the associated classes of levers that can be employed must be defined.

Building and Nurturing Customer Relationships.   A relationship can be defined as a bond or connection between the firm and its customers. This bond can originate from cognitive or emotional sources. The connection

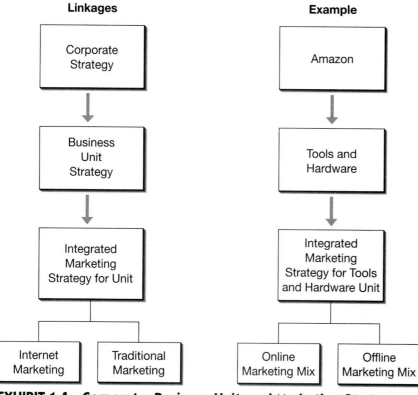

EXHIBIT 1.4   Corporate, Business-Unit, and Marketing Strategy

may manifest itself in a deep, intense commitment to the brand (e.g., membership in the Harley-Davidson HOG club) or a simple, functional-based commitment (e.g., regular use of weather.com). Whether defined as a function or an organization-wide culture, marketing is responsible for acquiring and retaining target customers.[10] In this process, successful marketers manage to move desirable customers from awareness through exploration and, finally, commitment. Once customers reach commitment, the firm is in a position to observe their behavior patterns and determine which customers to nurture and which customers to terminate (or serve at a lower level of cost). Managing this building and pruning process is one of marketing's key tasks. The four stages of customer relationships are briefly outlined below (see Exhibit 1.5).

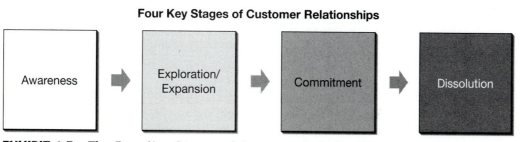

EXHIBIT 1.5   The Four Key Stages of Customer Relationship

Awareness.   When customers have some basic information, knowledge, or attitudes about a firm or its offerings but have not initiated any communications with the firm, they are in the awareness stage. Consumers become aware of firms through a variety of sources, including word-of-mouth, traditional marketing such as television advertising, and online marketing programs such as banner ads. Awareness is the first step in a potentially deeper relationship with the firm. However, as one can imagine, awareness without action is not in the best interests of the firm.

Exploration/Expansion.   In the exploration/expansion stage, the customer (and firm) begin to initiate communications and actions that enable an evaluation of whether or not to pursue a deeper connection. This stage is also likely to include some trial on the part of the customer. Exploration/expansion is analogous to sampling songs, going on a first date, or test-driving a car. In the online world, exploration/expansion may take the form of frequent site visits, some e-commerce retail exchanges, and possibly even the return of merchandise. It may include phone call follow-ups on delivery times or e-mails about product inventory. The exploration/expansion stage may take only a few visits or perhaps years to unfold.

Commitment.   In this context, commitment involves feeling a sense of obligation or responsibility for a product or firm. When customers commit to a website, their repeated, enduring attitudes and behaviors reflect loyalty. Commitment is a state of mind (e.g., I strongly prefer Amazon.com over Barnes & Noble.com) as well as a pattern of behavior (e.g., nine out of 10 of my book purchases are made through Amazon). One direct measure of commitment to a particular site is the extent to which the individual has invested in customizing the site (e.g., creating a personalized page on weather.com).

Dissolution.   Not all customers are equally valuable to the firm. In an industrial marketing context, managers often refer to the 80/20 rule of profitability. That is, 20 percent of customers provide 80 percent of the profit. By implication, therefore, a large number of customers are unprofitable or have high cost to serve. Firms should segment their most valuable and least valuable customers. The most valuable customers may be identified based on profit, revenue, and/or strategic significance (e.g., a well-regarded customer may not be profitable but opens the door to new accounts). The firm does not want this set of customers to terminate the relationship. Unprofitable, nonstrategic customers are a different matter. Often it is in the best interests of the firm to terminate the relationship or encourage this set of customers to disengage from the firm. Chapter 6 provides a much more thorough review of these four stages.

The four stages vary by the intensity of the connection between the firm and the customer (see Exhibit 1.6). Intensity of connection may be defined as the degree or amount of connection that unfolds between the firm and its target customers. Three dimensions capture intensity:

1. The frequency of the connection: How often does the customer visit the site?

2. The scope of the connection: How many different points of contact does the customer have with the firm?

3. The depth of contact: How thoroughly is the customer using the site?

A customer might visit a website such as Amazon on a regular basis, but only to purchase books. This visitor would have a high level of frequent contact but a low level of scope. Another customer might visit Amazon frequently but not stay on the site for a long duration or engage in deeper connections such as writing reviews, commenting on products, or communicating with other Amazon users. This customer would have high frequency but low depth. In all cases, relationship intensity is correlated with the stage of the relationship (see Exhibit 1.6).

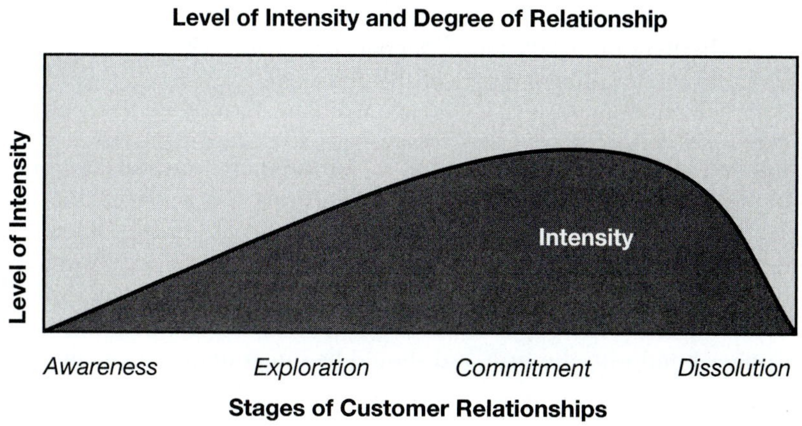

Level of Intensity and Degree of Relationship

EXHIBIT 1.6   The Four Key Stages of Customer Relationships by Level of Intensity

The Internet Marketing Mix.   The traditional 4Ps of marketing are product, price, promotion, and place/distribution. All four of these choices are part of the Internet marketing mix, plus two new elements: community and branding. Community is the level of interaction that unfolds between users. Certainly, the firm can encourage community formation and nurture community development. However, community is about user-to-user connections. Branding is a critical component of building long-term relationships on the Internet. Thus, rather than view branding as a subcomponent of the product, it is developed here as a moderating variable upon the levers—product, pricing, communication, community, distribution, and branding.

Product.   The product is the service or physical good that a firm offers for exchange. A wide range of product forms is being offered on the Internet, including physical goods (e.g., clothing), information-intensive products (e.g., *The Wall Street Journal* online), and services (e.g., online grocers). Frequently, the offerings are a combination of all three forms. In the course of building customer relationships, the firm can use a variety of product levers to build enduring customer relationships. Product packaging is often used to build customer awareness, upgrades and complementary services enable customers to explore a deeper connection, and customized offerings strengthen commitment. The key point is that specific product levers can be used to encourage a stronger connection. Chapter 7 further develops the process by which product levers can move customers through the four stages.

Pricing.   Price is an increasingly important marketing lever. Chapter 8 highlights core pricing theory, traditional pricing levers, and new pricing options afforded by the Internet. Traditional levers include such potential choices as tiered loyalty programs, volume discounts, subscription models, and targeted price promotions. The Internet has created an entirely new category of pricing tools for new-economy firms to use, including dynamic pricing strategies.

Communication.   Chapter 9 defines marketing communication as an activity that informs one or more groups of target customers about the firm and its products. This text takes a broad view of market communication to include all types of firm-level communications, including public relations, the use of sales representatives, and online advertising. Advertising and other forms of communication such as television and direct mail can make target customers aware of a firm's offerings. However, marketing communication can also encourage exploration, commitment, and dissolution. For example, viral marketing (where one user informs another user about a site through e-mails) often leads to exploration of a firm's offerings by new customers. Permission marketing (where customers opt to receive communications from the firm) is intended to encourage commitment to the firm. Both offline and online communication levers can encourage customers to build a stronger bond with the firm and should be integrated into any marketing program.

Community.   Community is a set of interwoven relationships built upon shared interests that satisfies those needs of its members that are not attainable individually. One of the unique aspects of the Internet is the speed with which communities can be formed. Equally important is the impact that these communities can have on the firm. A critical question confronting Internet marketers is how communities should be leveraged to build deep customer relationships. Communities can be leveraged to build awareness (e.g., user-to-user communication to make others aware of a product promotion), encourage exploration (e.g., user groups discussing which automotive options to purchase—or not to purchase), and commitment (e.g., bonds between users lead to deepening involvement with the site). Chapter 10 addresses the community levers that can be employed to nurture customer relationships.

Distribution.   The Internet is simultaneously a completely new form of commerce—a revolution in how customers and firms interact—and a distribution channel for the firm's products. With respect to the role as a distribution channel, the Internet has the power to shift customers to a new channel—or to use the Internet channel in combination with other channels (e.g., search the Internet and then purchase at the retail store). Distribution levers include the number of intermediaries (both online and offline), the breadth of channel coverage, and the messaging from the channels. Broad levels of distribution impact both customer awareness and the potential for more customer exploration of the firm and its offerings. Chapter 11 tackles the issue of distribution levers and their impact on customer relationships.

Branding.   Branding plays two roles in marketing strategy. First, branding is an outcome or result of the firm's marketing activities. Marketing programs affect how consumers perceive the brand, and hence its value. Second, branding is a part of every marketing strategy; each marketing activity is enhanced if the brand is strong, or suppressed if the brand is weak. Thus, a strong advertising program for Travelocity.com is likely to produce better results than a strong advertising program for a site with a weaker brand, such as Travel.com. Branding levers work in concert with other marketing levers to produce positive financial and/or customer results for the firm. Chapter 12 provides an in-depth discussion of these two branding roles.

In sum, the Internet marketing mix comprises six classes of levers. Exhibit 1.7 uses a cloud metaphor to show how branding mixes with each of these elements to produce an interactive effect. This interactive, or multiplier, effect of the brand can be positive or negative. Importantly, this does not mean that the other mix elements do not interact, because they do. However, branding is unique insofar as it is both a lever and an outcome of marketing actions.

Individualization and Interactivity. The previous section provided an overview of the six variables in the Internet marketing mix. However, simply specifying that the firm is able to manage these six classes of variables in an online environment does not do full justice to the uniqueness of the Internet environment. Two very important concepts need to be introduced to fully understand the profound implications that the Internet has for business. These two concepts are individualization (or customization) and interactivity.

Customers expect to have a personal experience with the firm, but broadcast approaches send the same messages to all members of the target audience. The Internet enables the firm to engage in customer-specific actions—a broadcast to an audience of one. Equally important, the customer can control the degree of customization by taking action to set the level of

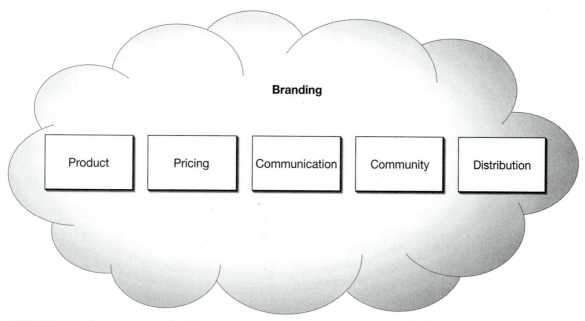

EXHIBIT 1.7   Internet Marketing Mix

customization he or she desires. Hence, the amount of individualization can be controlled either by the firm or by the customer.

Interactivity is defined as the extent to which a two-way communication flow occurs between the firm and customers. The Internet enables a level of customer dialogue that has not previously been experienced in the history of business. Certainly, customers could have conversations with retail store clerks, sales reps, or managers; however, it was not possible at the scale that the Internet affords. Hence, the fundamental shift is one from broadcast media such as television, radio, and newspapers to one that encourages debate, exchange, and conversation.

Exhibit 1.8 shows how the 2Is (interactivity and individualization) affect the design of all of the levers of the Internet marketing mix. Pricing can be both interactive and individualized—indeed, that is the essence of dynamic pricing. So can market communications; that is the purpose of real-time customer service on the Internet. Furthermore, products and services can be designed in real time by the customer, maximizing both interactivity and customization. This level of custom dialogue has revolutionized marketing. To capture this revolution, each of the lever chapters (Chapters 7–12) includes a discussion of how these two forces influence the design of each marketing-mix element.

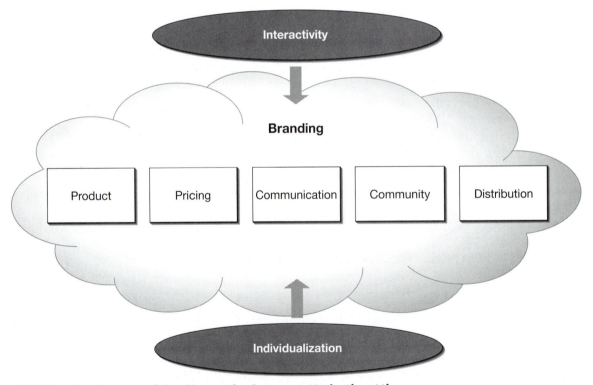

EXHIBIT 1.8   Impact of the 2Is on the Internet Marketing Mix

The Marketspace Matrix.   Having touched upon customer relationships, the Internet marketing mix, and the 2Is, attention now turns to the Marketspace Matrix. Exhibit 1.9 illustrates the key cross-tabulation that needs to be managed by the Internet marketing team. The design of the marketing program— or, to put it differently, the process of filling in the relationship-levers matrix—must be guided by a series of principles. Chapter 13 provides an overview of the integration of this matrix, and introduces design principles that relate to the crafting of an integrated marketing mix. However, this discussion would be incomplete without a case study. Chapter 14 uses this matrix to illustrate the marketing campaign for New Line Cinema's 2001 film, *The Lord of the Rings: The Fellowship of the Ring*.

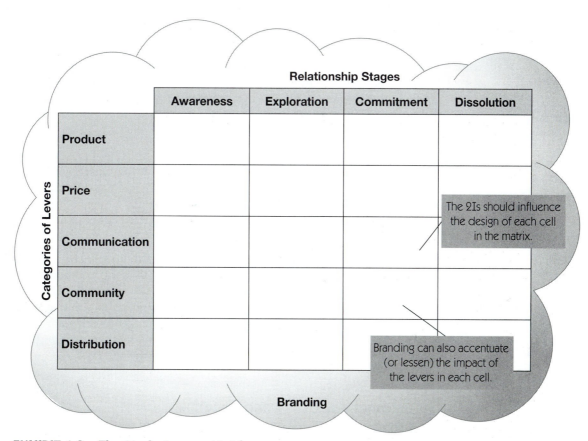

EXHIBIT 1.9   The Marketspace Matrix

Stage Six: Leveraging Customer Information Through Technology

In a customer-centric environment, firms have to make and act on three key decisions: (1) strategically select what markets to pursue (marketing research); (2) learn more about customers and devise strategies to acquire target customers (database marketing); and (3) assess the long-term profitability of customers and retain key customers (customer relationship management). Firms can use technology to obtain, organize, analyze, and utilize customer-relevant information, which can reduce the uncertainty associated with each of the three major types of decisions.

Stage Seven: Evaluating the Marketing Program

This last stage involves the evaluation of the overall Internet marketing program. This includes a balanced focus on both customer and financial metrics. Chapter 16 begins with a review of traditional offline customer metrics, continues with a new model of online customer metrics, and ends with a suggested integrative customer-metrics approach. This model emphasizes the importance of capturing the cross-platform behaviors that are observed by customers. Within this context, the chapter also discusses some of the challenges, complexities, and pitfalls of tracking customer behavior across channels. Chapter 16 also includes a discussion of financial metrics used to track the success of marketing programs.

To this point, this introductory chapter has focused on the process of marketing—not the characteristics of the people who must drive the program. The next section considers the roles and responsibilities of Internet marketing executives.

Critical Success Factors for Internet Marketing Executives

Marketers have always been in the business of anticipating and managing change, and technology has been their principal tool for managing it. The Internet presents an adaptive challenge for the marketing executive. Today's Internet marketing executive must have all the traditional skills of the offline marketing professional, but must place extra emphasis on some of them to account for the new economy. These critical new skills include customer advocacy and insight, integration, balanced thinking, and a willingness to accept risk and ambiguity.[11]

Customer Advocacy and Insight

An insatiable curiosity for customers and marketplaces is a necessity for today's marketing professional. This innate curiosity fuels an individual's desire to transform mounds of customer data into meaningful and actionable insights, which in turn become a platform for advocacy. Because the Internet enables a much greater degree of interaction with customers, designing and promoting these interactions around customers' needs and progressively gaining deeper insights are critical components of creating positive customer experience. A true customer advocate will be looking to provide demonstrable added value to each customer interaction to form the basis for a meaningful relationship. As both customer behaviors and enabling technologies simultaneously evolve, a deep understanding of customer needs should serve as the guidepost driving marketing decisions. Marketing professionals will need to strategically collect information from many disparate sources, create insightful customer mosaics, and effectively translate them into marketing strategies and tactics.

Integration

The Internet represents both a new channel and a new communications medium. The networked-economy marketing professional needs to have an integrated or holistic view of the customer and the enterprise in order to create a uniquely advantaged strategic plan. In today's multichannel environment, a consistent message and experience must be maintained across customer touchpoints in order to create a consistent brand image. Beyond strategy, a marketing manager must fundamentally understand how to integrate these new tools into the overall marketing mix. Managers who are able to design their marketing plan in a highly integrated fashion are more likely to capitalize on the synergies between marketing elements, and thus drive greater effectiveness.

Balanced Thinking

An Internet marketing professional needs to be highly analytical and very creative. Culling specific customer insights from a veritable fire hose of data is critically important for networked-economy managers. It requires understanding the dynamic tension between one-to-one marketing and mass marketing and being able to strike a strategic balance between them. It also requires determining the appropriate customer data requirements. Internet marketing professionals must also be technologically savvy. Understanding the strategic and tactical implications of the Internet, leveraging the rapid learning environment and accelerated decision-making process it creates, and then creatively applying the insights gleaned from analysis are critical success factors for all Internet marketing professionals.

Passion and Entrepreneurial Spirit

Although very hard to objectively assess, passion, or fire in the belly, is what will differentiate leaders from followers in the networked economy. Trying to change the status quo is never easy, and only people with conviction and passion will be heard over the din of the inevitable naysayers. Successful marketing managers use this passion to fuel their entrepreneurial instincts and vision, creating "bleeding edge" tools as they lead their teams to success.

Willingness to Accept Risk and Ambiguity

In the networked economy, Internet marketing professionals need to retool themselves and their companies to enter into a new era of customer-centric marketing. The Internet has enabled customers to have much more information and many more choices than ever before, thus shifting the balance of power toward the customer and creating the need for a whole new set of "pull"-based marketing tools. Successful Internet professionals need to rely on marketing tools that work in an extraordinarily dynamic environment. Having the courage to try new things is the key to developing breakthrough Internet marketing. The risk and ambiguity of managing in such uncharted territory is tremendous, and the most successful Internet marketers will be willing to play at the edges.

Today's online marketing professionals must have the basic skill set of the offline marketing professional. But they must also react more quickly and manage more information and channels in order to stay one step ahead of the competition. The skill set has not changed tremendously, but the tools need to be applied with more vigor and sometimes with greater speed. Successful Internet marketers will build their business models and value propositions around a deep understanding of customer needs—not around the product.

EXHIBIT 1.10   The New Rules of Marketing for the Global Digital World

The New Rules

1. Target segments of one, and create virtual communities.

2. Design for customer-led positioning.

3. Expand the role of branding in the global portfolio.

4. Leverage consumers as co-producers through customization.

5. Use creative pricing in the Priceline.com world.

6. Create anytime/anyplace distribution and integrated supply chains.

7. Redesign advertising as interactive and integrated marketing, communication, education, and entertainment.

8. Reinvent marketing research and modeling as knowledge creation and dissemination.

9. Use adaptive experimentation.

10. Redesign the strategy process and supporting organizational architecture.

Source: Wind, Jerry, and Vijay Mahajan. 2001. *Digital Marketing*. This material is used by permission of John Wiley & Sons, Inc.

Overview of the Chapters

The following chapter summaries are broken down into the seven divisions of Internet marketing. The aim of the overview is to provide a simple roadmap of the book (see Exhibit 1.11). A more thorough discussion of concepts and new frameworks for Internet marketing will come in the following chapters.

Part I: Framing the Market Opportunity

The first task of the Internet marketer is to assess new market opportunities. Chapter 2 provides a detailed explanation of the process marketers use to evaluate the viability of opportunities from the perspective of the individual firm. An analysis of marketing opportunities should be performed using rich data on the competitors, customers, and industry.

Chapter 2—Framing the Market Opportunity. "Where will the business compete?" This is a fundamental question any firm must address. Ideally, location is chosen according to where customer needs are, where there are few or no competitors, where there is a large financial opportunity, and

Point–Counterpoint

New Rules or Old Rules?

Internet marketing executives must have all of the skills of the traditional marketer plus a set of new capabilities. This naturally leads to the question of how "new" Internet marketing really is. Is Internet marketing as simple as extending the marketing mix into the online world? Or is there something new—perhaps radically new— about the online environment?

Those who believe that something is radically new point to a number of basic conceptual and process changes in marketing programs, perhaps best summarized by two of the world's leading marketers, Jerry Wind and Vijay Mahajan. In a recent book, these authors identify 10 new rules for marketing in the online environment (see Exhibit 1.10).[12] Two rules are particularly notable. The first is the ability to deliver on the promise of one-to-one marketing. While the concept of one-to-one marketing has been around for a decade or so, the technology is now in place to segment "markets of one." The second is the fundamental shift from a supply-side world to a world that is demand-side.

Opponents of this view argue that it overstates the differences between traditional and online marketing, and point out several key marketing concepts that carry over into this new environment. First, the concept of segmentation is still at the core of marketing. On the demand side, clusters of consumers will emerge with the same attitudes and behavior patterns; from a supply-side perspective, it is best to aggregate these similar demand patterns to reduce costs and provide the best value to customers. Second, marketing is ultimately a process of positioning the offering in the mind of customers. Certainly, there has been a shift to customer-led positioning and real-time coproduction, but the positioning concept itself remains largely the same. Third, the successful ingredients of a marketing program include traditional levers such as product, pricing, and advertising. Yes, the process has become more interactive and more individualized, but the master mixer concept still remains.

where the company is well positioned to fulfill the customer need. Obviously, it is very difficult to find all of these elements in one locale. Hence, a firm should follow a rigorous approach—such as the six-step process outlined in this chapter—to isolate market opportunities.

Part II: Formulating the Marketing Strategy

The second stage of an Internet marketing program is to specify strategy. This process consists of an analysis of market opportunity (Chapter 2) and a careful assessment of how the potential marketing strategy reinforces corporate and business-unit strategies. Hence, this section begins with a discussion of the component parts of corporate and business-unit strategy and leads into a look at how marketing strategy must be aligned with the business strategy. Chapter 3 examines two marketing strategy formulation pathways: one for pure-play online firms and one for the integrative firms with both online and offline distribution channels. A discussion of segmentation, target-market choice, and positioning sets the stage for the design of the marketing program in stage three.

Chapter 3—Marketing Strategy in Internet Marketing.   Three components of marketing strategy—segmentation, target-market selection, and positioning— still apply in the online environment. However, is it also clear that developing an overall online/offline marketing strategy is more complicated for

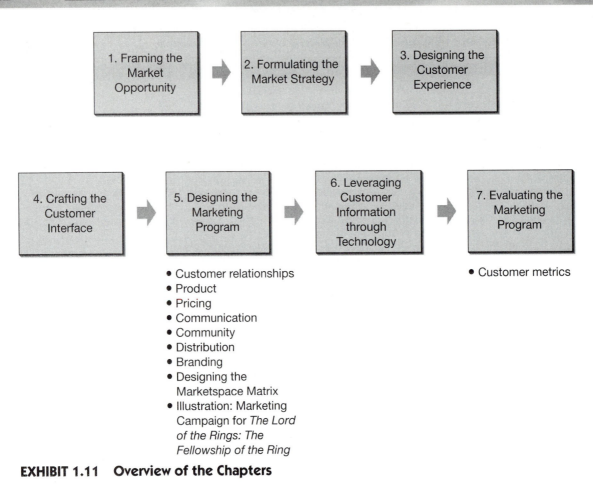

EXHIBIT 1.11   Overview of the Chapters

bricks-and-mortar firms because they have the added issue of integrating their offline business with their online business. This chapter concentrates on how business-unit strategy is connected to and drives marketing strategy by describing the basic concepts of marketing strategy, then comparing the marketing strategy process of pure online firms with traditional bricks-and-mortar firms that have decided to move online. The conclusion highlights the ways in which the marketing strategy process is influenced by four key forces in the online marketplace.

Part III: Designing the Customer Experience

Once the firm has decided upon a positioning of its offering, it must figure out the corresponding customer experience that it has to create. The customer experience articulation process can be viewed as a bridge between the high-level positioning strategy and the tactics of the marketing program.

Chapter 4—Customer Experience.   This chapter explores the concept of customer experience by discussing its seven key attributes, then defining the four stages that customers travel through during their relationship with a firm and its site: functional, intimate, internalized, and evangelical. Since the evangelist group is such an important group, particular attention is paid to how firms can leverage this customer group in the marketplace. The chapter concludes with a discussion on how a firm can best design a winning customer experience.

Part IV: Crafting the Customer Interface

This section of the book focuses on website design. In particular, seven basic design variables (the 7Cs) can be used to build an online customer experience. It is important to recognize that this chapter focuses on online design considerations; some marketing programs may choose to integrate a discussion of both online interfaces and traditional bricks-and-mortar design considerations at this point.

Chapter 5—Customer Interface. The purpose of this chapter is to introduce the concept of a technology-mediated customer interface. This interface can be a desktop PC, subnotebook, personal digital assistant, cell phone, WAP device, or other Internet-enabled appliance. Within a technology-mediated customer experience, the user's interaction with the company shifts from the traditional face-to-face encounter to a screen-to-face encounter. As this shift from people-mediated to technology-mediated interfaces unfolds, it is important to consider the types of interface design considerations that confront senior management. What is the look-and-feel, or context, of the site? Should the site include commerce activities? How important are communities to the business model? These design considerations are captured in the 7Cs Framework. The 7Cs are a rigorous way to understand the interface design choices that confront senior managers as they implement their business models.

Part V: Designing the Marketing Program

This section covers the heart of the Internet marketing program. A comprehensive discussion of building and nurturing customer relationships (Chapter 6) precedes an in-depth description of the Internet marketing mix's six components: product, pricing, community, communication, distribution, and branding (Chapters 7–12). In Chapter 13, the Marketspace Matrix is introduced as a way to integrate a firm's supply-side choices (e.g., the six elements) and the demand-side requirements of target customers (e.g., the four stages). Chapter 13 also introduces several principles for the design of an integrative marketing program. Finally, Chapter 14 provides an in-depth discussion of how the Marketspace Matrix applies to the successful online (and offline) marketing of the blockbuster film *The Lord of the Rings: The Fellowship of the Ring*.

Chapter 6—Customer Relationships. This chapter introduces a customer-centric approach to Internet marketing, emphasizing how firms can use the Internet to increase customer awareness, encourage customers to explore and expand the depth of client/company interaction, and create customers committed to the firm and its products. The circumstances under which the firm may want to dissolve or end its relationship with some customers is discussed next. An illustration of how interactivity and individualization—the 2Is—are fundamental to building close buyer/seller relationships leads to a discussion of how eBay develops online relationships.

Chapter 7—Product.   Recognizing that a broad body of knowledge about products already exists, the purpose of this chapter is to explain how the Internet affects the development and marketing of products today. As appropriate, additional networked-economy technologies such as customer databases and computer telephony integration are touched upon. Also discussed are the details of developing products, the marketing levers available to manage the offering, and how some of these levers can further customer relationships.

Chapter 8—Pricing.   This chapter examines the wide assortment of old and new pricing tools available to firms. Additionally, the chapter provides a framework to help managers decide which pricing strategy is best for their product. The effects of the 2Is on traditional pricing levers, as well as the role of the 2Is in creating a new category of pricing called dynamic pricing, are also discussed. A key section of the chapter showcases how various pricing levers can be used to move consumers through each of the four consumer relationship stages. Lastly, the chapter discusses eBay's pricing levers.

Chapter 9—Communication.   Consumers are rapidly adopting hybrid shopping models—they might research a product via one channel, purchase via another, and request product support through a third. Therefore, firms must develop communication methods that are integrated across channels and that work together with synergy to move customers from awareness toward commitment. The key market communication levers that companies can use to create customer relationships are brought out in this chapter. This is followed by a discussion of how the 2Is of the Internet encourage the progress of relationships between firms and their customers.

Chapter 10—Community.   The values of online community are easy to recognize. For instance, members typically benefit from the increased ability to share resources and information. But what of the benefits for the firm that sponsors a community? How else is value specifically created and transferred throughout a community? More important, how can community be built to create committed members and, ultimately, committed customers? These questions are explored in Chapter 10.

Chapter 11—Distribution.   One of the most fundamental debates of the networked economy is whether the Internet is simply another channel of distribution or a business revolution in and of itself. On the one hand, it seems unlikely that all consumers will eventually buy personal computers, clothing, books, and groceries over the Internet. Some segment of consumers will always want to touch, feel, hear, smell, or taste the merchandise before they buy. Therefore, the Internet channel will never be attractive to every single customer in every single segment of the market. Yet while the Internet might not replace traditional commerce, it is impossible to overstate the impact it will have (and, indeed, has already had) on distribution. The purpose of this chapter, then, is to review the impact of the Internet distribution channel, review the levers that are available to Internet marketers, and discuss how distribution choices can affect the movement of target customers through each of the four stages.

Chapter 12—Branding.   The chapter begins with some fundamentals— namely, the definition of brand and a discussion of what types of brands exist. The effects of the 2Is on branding are also examined; so is the concept of brand equity, how it is measured, and how it can be created. Then, a seven-stage process is introduced to guide firms in the development of strong brands. Finally, the principles of branding developed within the chapter are applied to the strategies of competing entities: Citibank Online versus Bank of America Online Banking, and CBS MarketWatch.com versus Bloomberg.com.

Chapter 13—Designing the Marketspace Matrix.

Chapter 13 begins with an integrative summary of the design of the marketing program. The Marketspace Matrix is then introduced as the integration tool that enables marketers to visualize their entire marketing program. With this visual display, the marketer is able to observe allocation of resources, the timing of individual levers, the sequencing of levers, and overall program consistency. This chapter also introduces 15 new principles that help guide the development of the overall integrated program.

Chapter 14—Design of the Marketing Program for The Lord of the Rings.

This chapter reviews a highly successful interactive marketing campaign—the marketing campaign for New Line Cinema's 2001 film, *The Lord of the Rings: The Fellowship of the Ring*. The campaign integrated offline and online levers to produce a creative, interactive campaign that advanced a large segment of people through the relationship stages and into the commitment stage. The campaign used a wide variety of creative interactive marketing levers, and also created a thriving online community.

Part VI: Leveraging Customer Information Through Technology

This section shows how firms can use technology to better understand and leverage their customers through market research, database marketing, and customer relationship management.

Chapter 15—Customer Information Systems.

This chapter focuses on three key types of decisions that customer-centric marketers have to make: (1) deciding which markets they should pursue, (2) learning more about their customers and how to activate key customer segments, and (3) understanding the long-term profitability of their customers (which customers should they better serve, which customers they should weed out, etc.). These decisions are typically made under conditions of uncertainty; however, the chapter offers some insight into how marketers can use technology to make decisions that are better informed.

Part VII: Evaluating the Marketing Program

How well did the marketing program do? Did it deliver on its objectives? This section introduces new metrics that can be used to track the success of the online marketing program. These metrics reflect customer actions as well as critical financial metrics that need to be assessed.

Chapter 16—Metrics.

This chapter proposes an approach to measuring both customer and business performance metrics for online firms. It begins with a review of traditional offline customer metrics, then introduces a new model of online customer metrics. This model emphasizes the importance of capturing the cross-platform behaviors that are observed by customers; with this in mind, some of the challenges, complexities, and pitfalls of tracking customer behavior across channels are examined. The chapter concludes with an application of the chapter's key concepts to the example of eBay.

Summary

1. What is Internet marketing?

Internet marketing is the process of building and maintaining customer relationships through online activities to facilitate the exchange of ideas, products, and services that satisfy the goals of both parties.

2. What is the narrow view versus the broad view of Internet marketing?

The narrow view holds that Internet marketing focuses specifically on online marketing efforts, and that sales revenue is realized online as well. The broad view notes that revenue for the overall firm would not be realized if cross-channel marketing efforts did not occur, and therefore that these cross-channel impacts should be considered part of Internet marketing.

3. What are the seven stages of Internet marketing?

The seven stages are (1) framing the market opportunity; (2) formulating the marketing strategy; (3) designing the customer experience; (4) crafting the customer interface; (5) designing the marketing program; (6) leveraging customer information through technology; and (7) evaluating the results of the marketing program.

4. What are the four stages of the customer relationship?

The four stages are:
1. *Awareness* (the degree to which the customer has some basic information, knowledge, or attitudes about a firm or its offerings, but has not initiated any communications with the firm)
2. *Exploration/Expansion* (when customer and firm begin to initiate communications and actions that enable an evaluation of whether to pursue a deeper connection)
3. *Commitment* (when customer and firm feel a sense of obligation or responsibility to each other)
4. *Dissolution* (isolation of the most valuable customer group, and disconnection with the least valuable customers)

5. What are the six classes of variables in the Internet marketing mix?

The six variables are product, pricing, communication, community, distribution, and branding.

6. What is the Marketspace Matrix?

The Marketspace Matrix is a framework illustrating the levers that the Internet marketer may choose to use at each stage of the customer relationship. These levers are the six classes of variables mentioned in Question 5, and the customer relationship stages mentioned in Question 4.

7. How do interactivity and individuality come into play in the design of the marketing program?

Interactivity is the extent to which two-way communication flow occurs between the firm and customers; individuality refers to a consumer's personal experience with the firm. Both affect the design of the levers of the Internet marketing mix—price, market communications, and products and services.

8. What are the critical success factors for the Internet marketing professional?

The critical success factors are:
1. *Customer advocacy and insight:* Marketing professionals need to strategically collect information from many disparate sources, create insightful customer mosaics, and effectively translate them into marketing strategies and tactics.

2. *Integration:* Marketing professionals need to have an integrated or holistic view of the customer and the enterprise in order to create a uniquely advantaged strategic plan.

3. *Balanced thinking:* Marketing professionals need to be highly analytical and very creative in order to understand the strategic and tactical implications of the Internet.

4. *Willingness to accept risk and ambiguity:* Marketing professionals need to retool themselves and their companies to enter into a whole new era of customer-centric marketing.

[1] Wind, Jeffrey, and Vijay Mahajan. *Digital marketing: Global strategies from the world's leading experts*. New York: John Wiley & Sons 2001. Kelly, Kevin. 1998. *New rules for the new economy*. New York: Viking.

[2] Porter, Michael E. 2001. Strategy and the Internet. *Harvard Business Review* 79: 63–78.

[3] There is clearly uncertainty in the field about how best to deal with the emergence of technology-enabled and technology-enhanced interfaces. Deighton, John. 1996. The future of interactive marketing. *Harvard Business Review* 74: 4–15; and Achrol, Ravi S., and Philip Kotler. 1999. Marketing in the network economy. *Journal of Marketing* 63: 146–163.

[4] Dictionary of marketing terms.

[5] See, for example, Pride, William, and O.C. Ferrell. 2000. *Marketing*. New York: Houghton-Mifflin, and Kotler, Philip. 2000. *Marketing management: Analysis, planning, and control*. Englewood Cliffs: Prentice-Hall.

[6] Imber, Jane, and Betsy-Ann Toffler. 2000. *Dictionary of marketing terms*. 3rd ed. Barrons Business Dictionaries

[7] Oliver, Richard. 1999. Whence customer loyalty. *Journal of Marketing* 63: 33–44.

[8] Rayport, Jeffrey. 2000. Monster.com. Case No. N9-800-304. Boston: Harvard Business School Publishing.

[9] Online Publishers Association / MBIQ Media Consumption Study, November 2001

[10] There is an interesting debate that is unfolding in the marketing literature. The debate is whether marketing is simply a function within the firm or whether it is a philosophy (and associated set of activities) that permeates all levels and functions of the firm. As Peter Drucker once noted "marketing is too important to be left to the marketing function." The consensus emerging is that "marketing" is both a function and a philosophy or orientation that guides organization-wide activities. For further reading, see Moorman, Christine, and Roland Rust. 1999. The role of marketing. *Journal of Marketing* 63: 180–197; Greyser, Stephen. 1997. Janus and marketing: The past, present, and prospective future of marketing. In *Reflections on the futures of marketing*, ed. Donald R. Lehmann and Katherine Jocz. Cambridge: Marketing Science Institute, 3–14; Webster, Frederick E., Jr. 1992. The changing role of marketing in the corporation. *Journal of Marketing* 56: 1–17.

[11] This section was largely based on interviews with two well-regarded Internet executives: Dennis Troyanos and Cathy Shemmer.

[12] Wind, Jerry, Vijay Mahajan and Yoram Wind. 2000. *Digital marketing: Global strategies from the world's leading experts*. New York: John Wiley & Sons.

Framing the Market

Opportunity

One of the most exciting and creative challenges for senior managers is identifying and evaluating new revenue opportunities. New opportunities offer the promise of alternative sources of revenue and associated cash flow. This is an exciting activity, but also a serious one: Opportunity analysis must be based upon a rigorous, thoughtful methodology that not only identifies the opportunity but also provides a rationale for why the firm can be successful.

In Chapter 2, we describe a six-step process that identifies the window of opportunity, or the hole in the market, that may be available to firms. Importantly, this analysis is a blend of understanding the unmet need in the context of forces unfolding in the marketplace (such as competitive offerings or the emergence of new leapfrog technologies) and within the firm itself (the firm's capabilities to deliver the needs, for instance).

Framing the Market
Opportunity

In Chapter 1, we discussed high-level strategy and the associated types of decisions. This chapter adds a level of granularity and detail in order to answer the first key question that a company must address: "Where will the business compete?" Ideally, it is an area where customer needs are not fully met, there are few or no competitors, there is a large financial opportunity, and the company is well positioned to fulfill customers' needs either on its own or through partnerships. Obviously, meeting all these criteria is difficult. Hence, a firm needs to follow a rigorous approach—such as the one outlined in this chapter—to isolate market opportunities.

Market-opportunity analysis is an essential tool for those who plan to launch businesses, whether startups or new ventures within an existing business. While it does not guarantee a venture's success, the process of thinking through the conditions that define opportunity attractiveness increases the likelihood of pursuing a solid idea. Not doing opportunity analysis, or doing it poorly, increases a venture's chance of failure.

This chapter examines two key questions: "Where will the business compete?" and "How will it succeed?" Regardless of the reasons for seeking online business opportunities, the successful company defines its **"marketspace"**—our word for the online equivalent of a physical-world marketplace— early in the business development process. By defining the intended marketspace, the company identifies its potential customers and competitors. This marketspace may change as the company and the market evolve, but a clear initial definition is necessary to develop the business model.

This chapter proposes a framework for market-opportunity analysis and reviews some of the tools that can be used. A lot of this spadework is actually iterative. Depending on the degree and tolerance for risk and the burden of proof required by a particular organization, these analyses will be deepened and refined as the company develops and launches a market offering. This is discussed in subsequent chapters.

This chapter introduces a six-step process: (1) investigating an opportunity in an existing or new value system, (2) identifying unmet or underserved needs, (3) determining target segments, (4) assessing resource requirements to deliver the offering, (5) assessing the attractiveness of the opportunity, and (6) making an educated go/no-go decision.

Co-authored by Toby Thomas, Mark Pocharski, Kate Bernhardt, and Jon Davis

QUESTIONS

Please consider the following questions as you read this chapter:

1. What is the framework for market-opportunity analysis?
2. Is market-opportunity analysis different in the networked economy?
3. What are the three basic value types?
4. How do marketing managers identify unmet or underserved needs?
5. What determines the specific customers the company is to pursue?
6. Who provides the resources to deliver the benefits of the offering?
7. How do marketing teams assess the attractiveness of the opportunity?
8. How does a firm prepare a go/no-go assessment?

Market-Opportunity Analysis in the Networked Economy

Before deeply exploring market-opportunity analysis for the networked economy, consider whether it should differ from an analysis in more traditional sectors. Some authors and analysts believe that opportunity analysis in the marketspace requires a different approach, as the reasoning below outlines.

Competition Occurs Across Industry Boundaries Rather Than Within Industry Boundaries

Web-enabled business models can operate across traditional industry boundaries because they lack the constraints of physical product manufacturing or service delivery. Consequently, these businesses can more accurately match value creation from the customer's perspective. For example, in one visit customers on Carpoint (*www.carpoint.msn.com*) can research new and used vehicles, purchase a car and an extended warranty, apply for financing, and obtain insurance. Because Carpoint is part of the MSN network, visitors can also get traffic reports or information on an upcoming car show. In both traditional and networked-economy businesses, a firm that limits opportunity assessment to narrow definitions of industry or value systems could miss important market opportunities.

Competitive Developments and Responses Are Occurring at an Unprecedented Speed

Advances in technology and the adoption of creative business models are occurring rapidly. During the browser wars between Microsoft and Netscape in the late 1990s, each firm introduced a new version of its product approximately every six months. Telecommunications and the handheld computer market are other industries whose product development cycles move extremely quickly. Market-opportunity assessments must be continually refreshed by keeping abreast of important trends or discontinuous events that could redefine opportunity attractiveness.

Competition Occurs Between Alliances of Companies Rather Than Between Individual Companies

Many technology-based products rely heavily on complementary products. For example, Web businesses rely on browser technology; browsers depend on operating systems, PCs, and modem technologies. Furthermore, the networked nature of the Web means that several companies can easily ally to create a seamless offer. Companies can often find themselves in **co-opetition**[1] with each other—i.e., they are both competitors and collaborators. For example, BizBuyer.com and Staples.com compete as suppliers of products such as computers and photocopiers to small and medium-sized businesses, yet they are also partners. Staples.com customers can use Bizbuyer.com to source business services such as Web design and consulting from an extensive supplier network. In assessing the resources necessary to succeed, managers must examine both internal and external possibilities, rather than assume the company must perform alone. In addition to the traditional make-or-buy decision, a company now has a third option: ally. And because many companies today create vast networks of partners, the real challenge is managing these networks effectively.

Consumer Behavior Is Still in the Early Stages of Being Defined; Thus It Is Easier to Influence and Change Consumer Behavior

Most modern marketing textbooks emphasize the value of being customer-focused. This means that businesses must analyze customer needs, define products that meet those needs, and implement defendable strategies. In traditional businesses, competitive battles are frequently fought over a well-defined set of consumer behavior patterns (e.g., shopping in grocery stores). In the networked economy, however, new software and hardware tilt the landscape of consumer behavior. Companies introduce products leading to new behavior and new customer requirements. The challenge is listening closely enough to today's customers to develop insights about opportunities without being lulled into simply meeting defined needs. To state the obvious, customers don't know what they don't know. The company's task is to define new experiences based on insights into how customers are acting today and why.

Consider, for example, the emergence of file-sharing services such as Napster, Gnutella, KaZaA, and Morpheus, which enabled members of those networks to search, share, and copy MP3 music files. Shortly after it was introduced in fall 1999, Napster dramatically influenced consumer behavior in the music industry. When, in spring 2000, a new use of Napster emerged—the swapping of not just MP3 files but any file format, including games, movies, software, and spreadsheets—file sharing became a way of life for many people who certainly "didn't know what they didn't know" only a few months previously. With Napster in the lead, other file-sharing services emerged to take advantage of the new market. And even although Napster suffered dramatically due to copyright infringement lawsuits, it may live on as a paid subscription service in its new home as part of the Bertelsmann media empire. It revolutionized consumer media consumption and the recording industry as well. Another interesting example is PayPal (*www.paypal.com*), which capitalizes on the evolution of e-mail and wireless transactions. PayPal eases financial transactions by enabling users to send funds via e-mail, wireless devices, and the Internet for a small fee. Its success led to eBay's acquisition and promotion of a similar service.

Industry Value Chains, or Systems, Are Rapidly Being Reconfigured

The Internet allows businesses to reconfigure customer interaction by such means as allowing 24/7 interactions, increasing the level of information throughout the value chain, and eradicating or significantly reducing the cost of stages in the value chain. Examples of this online reengineering are easy to find. Freemarkets.com constructed a reverse auction for business-to-business (B2B) markets and eliminated many of the costly process steps of finding product price quotes. Another prominent example of value chain reengineering exists in the job placement/executive recruiting industry. In the past, companies tried to fill positions by advertising to and recruiting job seekers, who were primarily in a responsive mode. With the emergence of websites such as Monster, 6FigureJobs.com, CareerBuilder, and HotJobs, the job market has become a two-way exchange, with employers searching résumé databases and job seekers searching postings of open positions. This reengineering has greatly enhanced the access and reach that individuals can have in this marketplace.

Obviously, many existing companies, as well as startups, begin opportunity framing from a base of experience about a market or a technology. This experience base may enable a management team to accelerate through one or more of the six steps. Regardless of where a company enters the opportunity-framing process, satisfying all six steps should create a sufficient base of knowledge and perspective to frame a winning business model and establish a solid foundation for making a well-informed go/no-go decision.

Whether you choose to spend a day, a month, or a year examining a market opportunity, the framework presented in this chapter provides a useful way to discuss whether and how to pursue an opportunity in the marketspace. As mentioned earlier, the degree of analytic due diligence needs to be commensurate with the relative level of risk, and this iterative process should become increasingly rigorous over time.

Market-Opportunity Analytic Framework

Our framework for market-opportunity analysis consists of five investigative stages followed by a go/no-go decision. It is important to note that these stages are not necessarily sequential, and, depending on the situation, a company could step into this process at any point. In addition, this is an iterative process. For initial due diligence, an organization might go through each stage at a very high level and then, if the idea merits it, return and refine the analysis. Often, companies put a time limit on the analysis that is commensurate with the magnitude of the decision they need to make. Exhibit 2.1 lists the steps that firms should satisfy in order to frame market opportunity, as well as the benefits of each step. When they are taken together, these six steps constitute a sound market-opportunity analysis:

Step 1: Investigate opportunity in an existing or new value system.

Step 2: Identify unmet or underserved needs.

Step 3: Determine target customer segments.

Step 4: Assess resource requirements to deliver the offering.

Step 5: Assess competitive, technological, and financial attractiveness of opportunity.

Step 6: Conduct a go/no-go assessment.

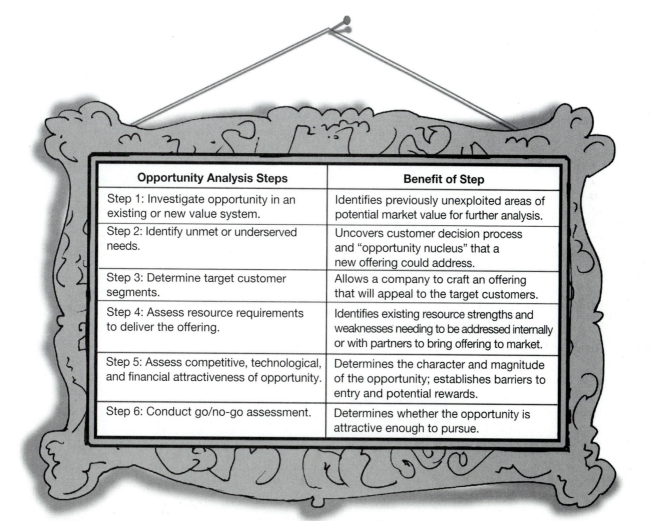

Opportunity Analysis Steps	Benefit of Step
Step 1: Investigate opportunity in an existing or new value system.	Identifies previously unexploited areas of potential market value for further analysis.
Step 2: Identify unmet or underserved needs.	Uncovers customer decision process and "opportunity nucleus" that a new offering could address.
Step 3: Determine target customer segments.	Allows a company to craft an offering that will appeal to the target customers.
Step 4: Assess resource requirements to deliver the offering.	Identifies existing resource strengths and weaknesses needing to be addressed internally or with partners to bring offering to market.
Step 5: Assess competitive, technological, and financial attractiveness of opportunity.	Determines the character and magnitude of the opportunity; establishes barriers to entry and potential rewards.
Step 6: Conduct go/no-go assessment.	Determines whether the opportunity is attractive enough to pursue.

EXHIBIT 2.1   Framework for Market Opportunity

Step One: Investigate Opportunity in an Existing or New Value System

Opportunity identification and analysis is anchored in an existing or new value system—the playing field. The **value system** can be thought of as the entire chain of suppliers, distributors, competitors, buyers, and intermediaries that bring an existing offering to market. In the networked economy, the starting point for opportunity identification often is someone who believes that a value system can be reinvented. This value system becomes the anchor for framing the opportunity. Then, one can identify customers, current market players, and economic activities to harness, redirect, or create.

The first step in framing the business opportunity is to broadly identify the arena where the new company will participate. The purpose is to declare both what is in and what is out of the business-model consideration set. For our purposes, the business arena is typically defined within or across an industry value chain, or a value system. Businesses are made up of discrete collections of individual and organizational activities that work together to create and deliver customer benefits via products or services. These integrated activities describe a value chain. Value chains are linked within an industry or, in the networked-economy environment, across industries to create a value system. A value system is an interconnection of processes and activities within and among firms that creates benefits for intermediaries and end consumers.[2] Value is created from the first inputs through to the end: customer purchase, usage, and disposal activities.

Start the exploration by looking for a set of activities ripe for positive transformation, either within a firm or across activities conducted by multiple firms. Within a firm, there may be ways to create value. After all, a firm is made up of a series of connected activities that result in the creation of an end product or the delivery of a service. From purchasing inputs to manufacturing, to marketing and sales, to product delivery, to after-sales support, all of the activities make up a value chain that is contained within one company. In addition, there are supporting activities necessary to ensure a company's viability, from financial planning and control to employee recruiting and training, to research and development. Just as many of these activities are interconnected within one company, there are also connections with other companies or with consumers. Both the activities within a firm (the value chain) and those connecting firms with other firms and customers (the value system) are potential candidates for networked-economy value creation. Furthermore, there may be value chain opportunities across related industries.

Three Basic Value Types

Firms should look at the value system with a lens that yields ideas about new business possibilities. Specifically, a firm looks for one of three things: trapped value that can be liberated, new-to-the-world value that can be created, or a hybrid of trapped and new-to-the-world value (see Exhibit 2.2).

Trapped Value.   Networked-economy companies often unlock **trapped value** by creating either more efficient markets or more efficient value systems.

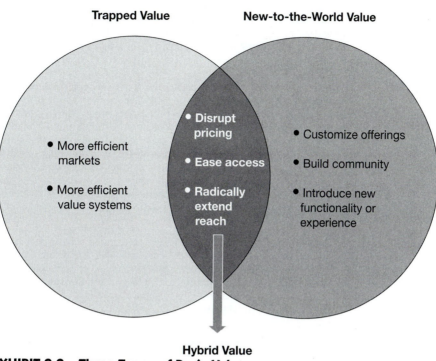

EXHIBIT 2.2   Three Types of Basic Value

Create More Efficient Markets. By lowering search and transaction costs, the market is more efficient—customers can buy what's best for them at a lower net cost. For example, Bizbuyer.com brings together suppliers and buyers of products and services for small and medium-size businesses. Customers submit a proposal request, and qualified suppliers give quotes. The entire transaction can be arranged over the Web. LendingTree Inc. (*www.lendingtree.com*) is a consumer mortgage website that also creates a more efficient market. The consumer fills out a single loan application, LendingTree requests bids from participating banks, and the consumer receives loan packages from competing banks, all within 48 hours. CircleLending (*www.circlelending.com*) is another business that creates a more efficient market, by bringing a new group of lenders and borrowers together. Because it recognized that 4 percent of the $1.5 trillion consumer credit market ($60 billion dollars) was in the form of person-to-person loans, it structures and monitors loans among friends and family members.

Create More Efficient Value Systems. Compressing or eliminating steps in a current value system can result in saved time or cost. For example, General Electric started using the Internet in 1994, when its GE Plastics division distributed technical documentation to engineers over the Web. Based on this early success, GE rolled out other Web initiatives in its heavy and light manufacturing, financial services, and transportation and broadcasting units. These initiatives were designed to create value by decreasing overhead costs.

New-to-the-World Value. In addition to reconfiguring existing value chains to release trapped value, companies can look to create new-to-the-world

---

Point–Counterpoint

Which Is Better? Analysis (Ready, Aim, Fire) Vs. No Analysis (Fire, Ready, Aim)

During the height of the dot-com boom, a debate began over whether market-opportunity assessment is helpful, valueless, or even harmful. That debate continues today, as companies struggle to balance their need to capture market share with their need to maintain fiscal discipline. Many still argue that speed, not precision, is critical. A basic economic force referred to as network economics is at work in many marketspace businesses. Businesses with network economics capitalize on first-mover momentum—rapidly connecting with and locking in large numbers of customers—the "Fire, Ready, Aim" strategy. It is then extremely difficult for competitors to catch up, and a cycle is created in which the large customer base provides lower costs. This allows the first mover to win more customers at a faster rate than its competitors, and the cycle continues.

Another argument for the Fire, Ready, Aim approach is that despite the stock market correction that curtailed many dot-com initiatives, it may turn out to be true that the networked economy is nascent, a place where old rules no longer apply and no one really understands the forces that drive the market. Consequently, companies are better off learning by doing. Finally, some argue even more vociferously that market analysis is a waste of time because a company will end up further behind, having passed up major market opportunities while performing the analysis.

However, a different, more traditional point of view is gaining ground. It says that the Fire, Ready, Aim approach actually limits a company's potential. While speed is important, the real goal is to reach critical mass with key customer segments in as short a time as practical—the "Ready, Aim, Fire" strategy. All the potential channel blind alleys, time-intensive partner negotiations, and customer complaint black holes inevitably bog down companies if they don't sort out a clear opportunity path from the start. Although a company may feel it is moving quickly by not assessing its opportunity, it is likely generating more heat than light. Furthermore, in some cases second and third movers actually survive longer and perform better than pioneers. They can capitalize on the mistakes and the groundwork done by others and capture more mind and market share for less effort. The classic example of the success of a "fast follower" is Microsoft, whose Windows interface was modeled on the graphic user interface that had first been introduced to consumers by Apple. Microsoft was able to build on Apple's features, functionality, and design conventions, and quickly moved well ahead in the marketplace.

---

benefits. These new benefits can enhance an existing offer or become the basis for a new offer. There are at least three ways companies can create **new-to-the-world value:** customize offerings, build community, and introduce new-to-the-world functionality or experience.

Customize Offerings. With the digital flexibility and economic advantages of the Internet, companies can allow customers to customize products or services. Companies can also make their products more attractive by removing features that customers do not value. Yahoo! exemplifies both dimensions. By personalizing news and stock quotes through its My Yahoo! function, it created value for customers who previously had to navigate through one-size-fits-all news and information services. This personalized page contains just a small subset of available information, but it is information that is relevant to the individual user. Within the financial services industry, Quicken.com's My Finances page allows individuals to manage their banking online and customize stock quotes, news, and alerts.

Build Community. The Internet enables efficient community building, as seen in the explosion of chat rooms on myriad topics, as well as public and private communities. Closed-community websites like MyFamily.com seek to bring together the far-flung modern family by enabling conversation, picture sharing, recipe exchanges, etc. An interesting open-community site is Zeal.com, where users discuss and rate websites. Participants are called Zealots and receive points and recognition for the quality and quantity of their reviews. The site welcomes new Zealots and assigns them mentors to help guide them through the community. Natural communities can be leveraged in many ways, including enhancing the effectiveness and impact of viral marketing. A very important aspect of community is that website visitors create value above and beyond that which is provided by the host. Chapter 10 contains a detailed perspective of community and its role in the new economy.

Introduce New-to-the-World Functionality or Customer Experience. The convergence of communications, computing, and entertainment—as well as the ever-changing form and functionality of access devices—is making new experiences possible. One of them is Internet telephony through services such as Dialpad (*www.dialpad.com*) and Net2Phone (*www.net2phone.com*). People still make most telephone calls over traditional landlines, but Internet telephony is likely to become a part of everyday life. Another development enabled by new technology is digital photography, with products and services that run the gamut from the cameras themselves to photo CDs and online storage and print facilities. While traditional photography still dominates the market, more than 8.3 million digital cameras will be sold by the end of 2002, only six years after Kodak introduced the first consumer digital camera in 1996.

Hybrid Value. Can a company simultaneously unlock trapped value and create new benefits? It certainly seems possible—look at Amazon.com. Not only has it eliminated steps and reduced hassle in book shopping, it introduced extra services and functionality to enhance the experience. Through collaborative filtering technology from Net Perceptions, readers can browse, get recommendations (either from other readers or based on their previous orders) and pay with 1-Click checkout. Amazon has changed how people think about shopping in product categories such as books, music, and toys. It has also significantly disrupted the retail book industry's pricing structure because of its everyday discounts on publishers' list prices.

Hybrid value, as the term connotes, is most powerful when the synergistic effects of both trapped and new-to-the-world value can be combined. There are three distinct mechanisms by which a company can create hybrid value: disrupting pricing, enabling ease of access, or extending its market reach.

Disrupt Current Pricing. In addition to making markets more efficient, this value-unlocking activity changes current pricing-power relationships. Customers can gain influence over pricing and capture part of the vendor's margin when they have more information about relative vendor performance, a deeper understanding of vendor economics, or insight into the vendor's current supply–demand situation. By providing customers with these types of information and demystifying vendor economics, a networked-economy company gives customers greater negotiating power. MySimon (*www.mysimon.com*) and BizRate (*www.bizrate.com*) are two popular services that help shoppers find a product's lowest price by searching various websites. They add additional value by providing reviews from others who have purchased the product, thus matching the right product with the right price. This type of unbiased information provides a transparency in the retail industry that significantly impacts pricing as well as the basis for competition.

Enable Ease of Access. This entails enhancing the access points and the degree of communication between relevant exchange partners. Abebooks.com created one of the largest networks of independent booksellers. Customers now have a single point of access for hundreds of booksellers around the world, making it easier to find rare, used, and out-of-print books. Another way access is improved is by using the Internet as a channel. The discount retailer Target, well known for its stores, recently added Target.com as a sales channel. The website offers many of the same products as its offline channels, but with the convenience of online shopping.

Radically Extend Reach. Companies can extend the boundaries of an existing market or create a new market by delivering cost-effective reach. This includes enabling collaboration among multiple people across locations and time. In the networked world, people are working together more efficiently and more effectively. Keen Inc. (*www.keen.com*) created a market by building a virtual advice marketplace where anyone can advertise his or her advice services on subjects such as managing your love life or choosing a career. Customers go to the website, choose an adviser, and connect to that adviser for a per-minute fee. Keen and the adviser share the revenues. The distance-learning and online-education industries are growing quickly by radically extending their reach. Educational institutions were historically constrained by the physical limitations of campuses, buildings, and the number of faculty members. Today, websites such as the ones for the University of Maryland's UMUC Distance Education program (*www.umuc.edu/distance*) and Digital-Think (*www.digitalthink.com*) are expanding both reach and scope by offering customized classes to students and executives, and the prestigious Massachusetts Institute of Technology has committed to making all of its courses available online, at no cost to the user, by 2011.

Sound Byte

Releasing or Creating Value Through the Internet: Heidi Roizen, Managing Director, Mobius Venture Capital

"Is there an inherent advantage in being on the Net? Is there profit we squeeze out of the physical channel by being on the Net? Is there added customer value we can bring in the improvement of the relationship? So you're looking for something that makes the online world superior to the physical world, and then you can make those investments."

Value Discussion

To find the location in a value system or value chain where a company should focus its development activities, there are two simple dimensions to first consider: horizontal or vertical plays. In the business world, horizontal plays improve functional operations that are common *across* multiple industries and types of value systems. In the software world, horizontal players typically improve functional areas such as accounting and control, customer service, inventory management, and standard computer-aided design/computer-aided manufacturing (CAD/CAM) applications. In the consumer world, horizontal plays reflect common consumer activities such as paying taxes.

Vertical plays, on the other hand, focus on creating value *within* activities that are central to a particular business. One example is Covisint, an online consortium made up of auto manufacturers (including DaimlerChrysler, Ford, General Motors, Nissan, and Renault) and technology companies (including Commerce One and Oracle), which facilitates transactions of materials for the automotive supply chain. These vertical plays are often industry-specific, serving such groups as the steel industry, the chemical industry, or the auto industry. There are, of course, niches within each industry, so there may be vertical niches (e.g., automotive parts distributor website versus supply-chain website in the automotive industry).

At its most extreme, a white-sheet exercise (a thorough analysis beginning from a blank slate) would systematically look for and evaluate the trapped and new-value potential across all functions and activities pursued by businesses and consumers. More typically, a group of managers is familiar with or interested in a particular horizontal function or vertical activity. The challenge is to map out the major sets of activities related to that horizontal function or vertical business. The group should then consider a series of questions designed to guide the knowledgeable manager in uncovering trapped value or recognizing the opportunity for new-value creation.

The guiding questions include the following:

- Is there a high degree of asymmetric information between buyers and sellers or colleagues at any step in the value system that traps value?
- Are significant amounts of time and resources consumed in bringing people together to make a transaction or to complete a task?
- Do customers view activities (e.g., shopping across a variety of categories) as more collapsed than industry participants do?
- Are key participants in an activity able to collaborate effectively and efficiently at critical stages in a process?
- Do people have access to the advice and information necessary to maximize their effectiveness or the ability to extract maximum benefits from a given activity?
- Are people not participating in an activity due to privacy or other concerns?

While identification of hot spots in a value system is a necessary starting point, the process is not sufficiently developed to make the leap from identification to creation of the value proposition or the business model. At this point the manager has a general outline of where the opportunity may lie in terms of business and customer activities. The next step is to specify the nature of that opportunity from a customer's perspective. As the manager begins to specify the opportunity, its potential should become more apparent.

Step Two: Identify Unmet or Underserved Needs

New-value creation is based on doing a better job of meeting customer needs. What do customers do today that frustrates them? What aren't they doing, consciously or unconsciously, that could bring benefits? What can be fixed, even if customers do not know it is broken? What customer needs will the new business serve? Are these needs currently being met by other companies in the market, and if so, why will customers choose the new business over the competition? Customers will switch only if the new company does a better job of meeting some set of needs and effectively communicates its value proposition. This step of the opportunity-analysis framework describes the uncovering of an "**opportunity nucleus,**" a set of unmet or underserved needs.

Customer Decision Mapping Process

The customer decision mapping process is an organizing framework to help managers look systematically for unmet or underserved needs. It maps the customers' activities and choices in accessing a specific experience within a value system, and then lays out the series of steps from awareness to purchase, through use, and afterward. Mapping the **customer decision process** may help generate new ideas about unmet or underserved needs. For example, examining the process that people go through to buy books might identify the fact that people rely on recommendations from others. Jeff Bezos of Amazon.com identified this need (and saw its applicability to other products as well) and created a feature where customers can read reviews and comments from others while they browse the website. Amazon, therefore, is harnessing the power of personal recommendations and making it easy for customers to get the information necessary to make a purchase.

Before looking for unmet or underserved needs, senior managers should map out the customer decision process. When properly answered, the following questions will help to structure that process.

- What steps does a typical customer go through in the decision process?
- Where does the customer get information?
- Who gets involved, and what roles do they play?
- Are there any distinct activities or significant paths that different customers go through?
- Where does the process take place?
- How much time does the overall process take? How much time is associated with individual steps? Does the customer move through the entire process at once or take breaks?
- What product category and competitors do customers consider along the way?
- What choices do customers not consider? What choices are they unaware of?
- Which customers are not participating in this customer decision process for a specific value system? Why not?

Of course, not all businesses involve purchases just by consumers. Access to CNN's website is free for users but is paid for by advertisers, so the business has two sets of customers. In this case it is worthwhile to develop two customer decision processes, one for visitors (who use the site, but do not purchase from it) and one for advertisers (who purchase ad space on the website).

Exhibit 2.3 sets out the customer decision map for buying a camera, showing how someone chooses among various alternatives. Some decision processes are highly linear, while others may have multiple pathways or loop-backs. Each process is organized into three broad categories: prepurchase, purchase, and postpurchase.

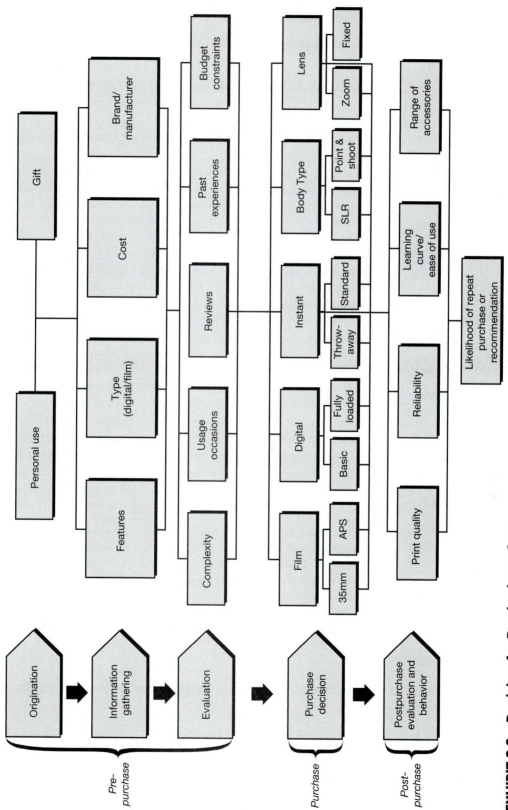

EXHIBIT 2.3   Decision for Purchasing a Camera

Revealing Unmet or Underserved Needs.   Having identified the steps in the customer decision process, the management team can begin to uncover unmet or underserved needs. The following questions can help identify these needs:

- What are the series of activities or steps of the customer decision process in which a customer participates to receive an experience?
- What is the nature of the ideal experience the customer wishes to receive, both functionally and emotionally? How does it vary step by step in the activity?
- How closely does the actual experience compare to the customer's view of the ideal? What are the key frustration points? What actions (also called "compensating behaviors") does the customer take to overcome these frustrations? How successful has the customer been, and why? What underserved needs do you observe, regardless of whether the customer is conscious of them?
- Does the experience customers seek vary according to their environment? (Environment factors might include how often they participate in the activity, with whom they participate, where they use the product or service, or their role in an organization.)
- What are customer beliefs and associations about carrying out this activity? How do they view their relative competence and role? How positively or negatively do they view the current set of company offerings?
- What barriers block some or all participation by potential customers? What would potentially block adoption of an online activity?
- What are the online opportunities to enhance or transform the customers' experience? What will be the most important drivers for getting customers to adopt an online activity in this value system?
- How do the customers define value for critical steps in the process? Would they be willing to pay for certain elements of that value?

Uncovering these needs may be as straightforward as having conversations with a number of customers, or as complex as creating observation opportunities to watch customers in action and identify behaviors of which they may be unaware. Immersion in the customer decision process is the most effective way to reveal opportunities for a better way of doing things. As a result, it is highly likely that in-depth customer research will be required to gain the level of insight required to create compelling customer value. Chapter 15 discusses a broad spectrum of research approaches and the effect of the Internet on these techniques.

Step Three: Determine Target Customer Segments

The act of choosing and identifying priority customers leads to a preliminary understanding of the firm's target segments. Who are these customers, and what makes them attractive to pursue? What experiences do they seek? What would the company need to offer them? What barriers would the company need to overcome to get these customers to participate in an offering? The company should develop an initial sketch of these customers to both shape the business concept and estimate the size of the opportunity. This knowledge is essential as the company determines the nature and size of its offer.

Sound Byte

Customer Research May or May Not Be Useful; Avie Tevanian, Senior Vice President of Software Engineering, Apple Computer Inc. "We do a lot of market research. We survey buyers of our computers either when they're at the store if we can or with follow-up after they register. It helps us to understand if we're building the right things, what they'd like to see us do. And we do a lot of standard market research like that to get a lot of things. For example, one of the reasons we moved to five colors in the iMac from the original bondi blue is because we had a lot of customer feedback. They love bondi blue, but they wish they could pick their color.

"Now, I will also say that we're careful to not build all of our products just based on customer feedback. And the reason for that is because customers are great at telling us what those incremental improvements are—going from one color to five, things like that. But they're not particularly good at seeing what's possible beyond that because they don't always understand what technology is enabling. So they can't tell us build an iMac that will let me build home movies because they don't know that the technology now exists to put those all together. So we do that ourselves, and we think we get it right. So far, we're doing OK. But no customer feedback is going to tell us to do this: We're going to do it anyhow because we think it's right."

Drill-Down

Empathic Design[3]

All companies, particularly technology companies, rely on innovation to survive. A natural choice is to rely on customers to tell you their needs and ways to better serve them. The problem is, customers are particularly bad at doing that. They rarely are able to imagine or describe innovations.

One solution is to use empathic design, a set of techniques described by Dorothy Leonard and Jeffrey Rayport in a *Harvard Business Review* article titled, "Spark Innovation Through Empathic Design." Two things distinguish empathic-design research techniques from those used in traditional market research: (1) they are based around observation (watching consumers) rather than inquiry (asking consumers), and (2) unlike traditional lab-based usability testing (which typically involves observing consumers using a product in a laboratory), empathic-design research is conducted in the environment where consumers would commonly use the product.

Empathic design is not a substitute for traditional research, but it can yield five types of information that are not ordinarily revealed by traditional techniques:

- Triggers of use: What circumstances cause people to use a product?
- Interactions with the users' environment: How does the product fit with users' idiosyncratic environments and habits?
- User customization: Do users redesign the product to fit their needs? If so, how?
- Intangible product attributes: Intangible attributes may be important in creating an emotional franchise with the consumer.
- Unarticulated user needs: Observation can discover unarticulated user needs that can be easily fulfilled.

Different people notice different things, so the use of a small team with a diverse set of skills (e.g., interface design, product management, etc.) may bring up otherwise unnoticed subtleties. The team should observe and record the subjects' normal behavior. The team should also take detailed notes of observations and minimize interruptions or interference with the subject. Photographs, videos, and sketches can all help the team to record what it finds.

A common criticism of the innovative ideas that can emerge from empathic design is, "But users didn't ask for that." This is precisely the point of the exercise. By the time that customers ask you for an innovation, they will be asking your competitors, too.

Determining Target Customers

The discussion thus far has been about where a company is likely to play in the value system, how customers go through the decision-making process, and potential areas for value creation. The next part of this discussion will focus on the specific customers whom the company plans to pursue. Companies need to develop a sense for the types of customers they ultimately seek to serve. This understanding allows a company to assess opportunity attractiveness at a high level and to focus on crafting an offering that will appeal to the target customer.

The value proposition, or value cluster, is just such a customer-specific offering. Designing the value cluster has three distinct components: (1) the choice of target customer segment(s), (2) a selection of focal customer-driven benefits to offer, and (3) a reason for customers to believe—the rationale for why this particular firm and its partners can deliver the value cluster significantly better than its competitors can.

In analyzing the outcome of the customer decision process, companies are likely to identify subsets of customers with very different patterns of behavior, underlying needs, and drivers of behavior. **Segmentation** is the process of grouping these customers based on their similarities. Once the different segments have been identified, the company must determine the segments (or customers) it will target in order to further refine the type of opportunity the company will seek to capture. Of course, the digital play that a company has in mind may radically change how customers act in this value system. Hence, a company would look for segments that both disproportionately benefit from some change in the status quo and those more predisposed to adopt an entirely new product or service.

Drill-Down

Image-Elicited Narratives

The primary determinants of consumer behavior are unconscious. Projective techniques that use image-elicited narratives are geared toward uncovering these hidden motivations and knowledge. In these methods, participants are asked to use images (magazine photos, pictures from their own albums, and so on) or objects they find meaningful to help them describe deeply-held concepts they have about a brand or product. After all, if consumer behavior is determined subconsciously, then even the most willing research participant and the best direct questions are unlikely to elicit meaningful insights. Market-research techniques that utilize projective and metaphoric tools enable consumers to identify symbols that identify their behavioral drivers and to develop a comfortable vocabulary for describing their motivations, decision-making processes, and other subconscious behaviors.

In his book *Strategic Brand Management: Building, Measuring, and Managing Brand Equity*, Kevin Lane Keller identifies seven premises on which these elicitation techniques are based:[4]

1. Most human communication is nonverbal.

2. Thoughts often occur as nonverbal images.

3. Metaphors are essential units of thought and the key mechanism for viewing consumer thoughts and feelings and for understanding consumer behavior.

4. Sensory images provide important metaphors.

5. Consumers have mental models—interrelated ideas about a market experience—that represent their knowledge and behavior.

6. Hidden or deep structures of thought can be accessed.

7. Emotion and reason are forces that commingle in the minds of consumers.

So how does this type of consumer research exercise work? Participants are asked, "What are your thoughts and feelings about this experience or product?" They are then asked to collect pictures and objects that capture these thoughts and feelings or display the exact opposite of these thoughts and feelings. Each participant returns about a week later to discuss his or her collection of pictures with a trained interviewer in a two-hour session. During that interview, the participant describes each picture, as well as any pictures that he or she searched for but was unable to obtain. Next, the participant organizes the pictures and describes those that portray the opposite of his or her thoughts and feelings. Finally, with the help of a graphic artist, the participant and the interviewer build a collage with the selected images. A careful examination of this collage can shed light on the participant's thoughts and associations.

continued

To illustrate the output of these sessions, consider the result of a pantyhose study.[5] Twenty pantyhose-wearing women were asked, "What are your thoughts and feelings about buying and wearing pantyhose?" The pictures they selected included fence posts encased in plastic wrap, twisted telephone cords, and steel bands strangling trees. These images are relatively easy to interpret: Pantyhose are tight and inconvenient. However, other images showed another mind-set. For example, one woman selected a photograph of flowers resting peacefully in a vase. The discussion with the interviewer revealed that the flowers referred to the fact that wearing the product made her feel thin and tall. Further discussions revealed that pantyhose made women feel they had longer legs, and that this was important because men think long legs are sexy. Hence, a desired experience from wearing pantyhose is to feel sexy around men. A traditional research method would have great difficulty revealing this type of thought process.

The new frontiers of marketing research are exploring the use of brain scans, which would allow interviewers to see how people think and where thoughts take place inside the brain. Messages with a negative effect on respondents lead to activity in an area of the brain associated with negative feelings. In contrast, messages that lead to positive feelings stimulate activity in a different part of the brain. By massaging their marketing messages, companies may at some point be able to create messages that activate only areas of the brain associated with positive feelings. This technique is still in development but has great potential to further revolutionize the way market research is conducted.

Approaches to Market Segmentation

There are many approaches to segmentation, and the best way to segment a market is an often-debated topic. The decision depends on the value system that the opportunity is centered upon, how the customer can and will make decisions within that value system, and what action the company is likely to take. Before a practical approach to segmentation for the networked economy is described, it is important to briefly review the different ways that a market (and customers) can be segmented. Academic literature and textbooks often cite the following segmentation approaches:[6]

- *Demographic (or "firmographic").* For individuals, the demographic approach includes grouping by age, gender, occupation, ethnicity, income, family status, life stage, Internet connectivity, and browser type. In a firmographic approach, companies are segmented based on number of employees, online or offline status, company size, job function, and purchasing process.
- *Geographic.* Country/region/city, city size, density (urban, suburban, rural), ISP domain, etc.
- *Behavioral.* Online shopping behavior, offline shopping behavior, Web usage, website loyalty, prior purchases, etc.
- *Occasion (or situational).* Routine occasion, special occasion, time (time of day, day of week, holidays), location (from home, on the road), event (while writing a business plan, when shopping), trigger (out of supply), etc.
- *Psychographic.* Lifestyle (thrill-seekers, fun lovers, recluses), personality (laid-back, Type A, risk takers), affinity (community builders, participants, outcasts), etc.
- *Benefits.* Convenience, economy, quality, ease of use, speed, information, selection, etc.

- *Beliefs and attitudes.* Brand beliefs (networked economy, old fashioned), attitudes toward the category, channel effectiveness beliefs, beliefs about themselves (technically savvy), etc.

Exhibit 2.4 provides a more comprehensive listing of variables, with illustrations. Over time, segmentation has evolved from the use of more actionable "customer external" variables (age, income, geography) in the 1960s and 1970s to more meaningful "customer internal" variables (needs, attitudes) in the 1980s and 1990s. Still, neither set of variables is sufficient on its own to fully define a segment. The difficulty comes with selecting the segmentation approach and the variables that most effectively describe and reflect the nature of the opportunity being analyzed.

Segmentation Type	Description	Examples of Variables
Geographics	Divides market into geographical units	Country, region, city
Demographics	Divides market based on demographic values	Age, gender, income, education
Firmographics	Divides market based on company-specific variables	Number of employees, company size
Behavioral	Divides market based on how customers actually buy and use the product	Website loyalty, prior purchases
Occasion (Situational)	Divides market based on the situation that leads to a product need, purchase or use	Routine occasion, special occasion, part of day
Psychographics	Divides market based on lifestyle and/or personality	Personality (laid-back, type A), lifestyle
Benefits	Divides market based on benefits or qualities sought from the product	Convenience, economy, quality

EXHIBIT 2.4   Segmentation Approaches

Actionable and Meaningful Segmentation

Unfortunately, most segmentation efforts fail to deliver on the intended objective—to be both useful and insightful. The segments are often either easy to recognize but do not provide much insight into customer motivations (actionable, but not meaningful), or they generate real insight on customers but are difficult to address (meaningful, but not actionable). The goal of market segmentation is to identify the combination of marketplace variables that will generate **actionable** and **meaningful segmentation** of customers.

Actionable Segmentation.   To be actionable, segmentation must be consistent with how a company can go to market, and must be able to be sized and described. A segmentation is actionable if meets the following criteria:

- The segments are easy to identify.
- The segments can be readily reached.
- The segments can be described in terms of their growth, size, profile, and attractiveness.

Meaningful Segmentation. To be meaningful, segmentation must help explain why customers currently behave—or are likely to behave—in a specific way. A segmentation is meaningful if it meets certain criteria:

- Customers within a segment behave similarly, while customers across segments behave in different ways.
- It provides some insight into customers' motivations.
- It corresponds to the set of barriers that customers face when they buy or use a product or service.
- It corresponds with how customers currently (or could) buy or use the product or service.
- It correlates to differences in profitability or cost to serve.
- The segments and/or their differences are large enough to warrant a different set of actions by your company.

eBay, the online auction market leader, provides a good illustration of the value of segmentation and how it can be both actionable and meaningful. The company looked at its core auction market—collectibles and odds and ends sold by individuals and mom-and pop businesses—and saw that there were more market segments to be served with greater economic returns. It used income (affluent), lifestyle (luxury), trigger (need to have), behavioral (regular online usage), and benefits (convenience) as categories to segment the market. These are all variables readily found through research services. As a result, eBay partnered with the most respected offline auction house, Sotheby's, to create a premier version of the original eBay platform. Similar segmenting exercises resulted in the launch of other eBay variants, including eBay Motors and eBay Travel, as well as a push to attract bigger businesses to use eBay to sell excess inventory and older versions of current products. eBay's growth into a multibillion-dollar company is a testament to the power of effective segmentation.

The Right Blend of Segmentation Variables

Finding the right blend of segmentation variables that are both actionable and meaningful is difficult; in practice, a company is often forced to trade one variable for another. In the online world, this trade-off is easier than in the offline world because firms can quickly collect data that are both actionable and meaningful. Through a registration form that asks customers for basic demographic information (such as income, gender, age, and zip codes) or through real-time tracking of customer click streams on both search data and final purchase behavior, online companies have access to a rich source of segmentation data.

"Clickographics," the observation of an online customer's behavior using click-stream data, is an interesting example of a behavioral variable that tends to be highly meaningful and actionable. Server logs can capture every step a customer takes while surfing a company's website. Careful click-stream analysis allows a company to identify and communicate with its target customers. Amazon.com, one of the most successful online retailers at effectively merchandising its goods online, keeps track of all of its customers' purchases. Based on the purchases of other people who bought the same book as a given customer, Amazon.com suggests that this customer may also like books X, Y, and Z. Amazon.com's suggestions are meaningful variables because they present books that customers with similar tastes have purchased. The segment is also actionable because the website can offer these suggestions in real time to all customers, both old and new.

Often, an intersection—or combination—of demographic, geographic, situational, and behavioral variables will create a market segmentation that is both actionable and meaningful. Typical variables to consider include intersections of user demographics, life stage, purchase occasion, and online behavior. The end result is a segmentation scheme that tends to favor one factor or another, such as online holiday purchasers (more occasion based), first-time users (more behavior based), or graduating high school seniors from affluent neighborhoods (demographics and geography). Psychographic variables or attitudinal variables in isolation are rarely recommended as a basis for a segmentation; these approaches often maximize meaningful dimensions but are rarely actionable, and therefore are rejected by managers. It would be difficult for high-end retailer Ashford.com to identify a customer as a high achiever before or as he or she interacts with the website. Rather, a company may need to look at prior purchase data (other luxury brands purchased on sale) and the path taken into the site (click-through from mySimon.com) to determine the likelihood that this customer would shop for a Rolex watch at a bargain price. The point is to use the more observable information to generate insight on the motivation, not the other way around.

Point–Counterpoint

Which Is Better? Online Consumer Tracking Vs. a Holistic View

In the online world, there is no lack of data. Click-stream information reveals purchase patterns, online habits, basic demographics, and often a host of other consumer information. But is this information sufficient to define new business opportunities?

Many argue that studying past and real-time behavior will yield enough information about customers to enable managers to determine the best variety of services. The Web enables companies to watch customers interacting in real time with their products with a high degree of precision and allows them to intervene while the customer is still in the buying process—the Holy Grail of marketing. Procedures like collaborative filtering allow real-time suggestive selling. An example is Amazon.com's success at cross-selling to customers.

An alternative view is that data based on click streams provide an insufficient picture of the reasons customers behave the way they do. In other words, click-stream analysis explains what customers do, but not why they do it. A total customer view brings together consumer behavior and insights about motivations for that behavior. This view considers the behavior as well as the customer context and environment, the functional and emotional desired experiences of the customer, and the customer's beliefs and associations about the product, service, and current purveyors of the offering. Without a total customer view, managers are unlikely to generate real insight into key customer groups. Companies such as DoubleClick seem to have been responding to this concern by trying to merge their online data sets with behavioral data gathered offline.

Segmentation Variables About the Customers

To gain some insight into what variables to use, businesses can ask the following questions about their customers:

- Who are they? Where do they live? What do they do for a living? How busy are they? What else do they do? What do they like to do in their spare time? How much spare time do they have?

- What is their purchase process?

- When and where do they shop? What else do they buy? How much did they pay for the product? How often do they buy? To which channels do they have ready access?

- From where do they get their information? Is there anyone else who influences the purchase or use of the product? If so, who?

- What is their usage process? What external factors affect their product use? When do they use the product? How often do they use the product? For which occasions are the products purchased or used? Are these occasions frequent or episodic?

- Where do they use the product? What setting are they in? How often are they in this setting?

- Is the purchase or usage planned? What happens to them if they do not purchase the product?

EXHIBIT 2.5   Segmentation Variables

Segmentation Variables About the Microeconomics

To gain insight into what variables to use, businesses can ask the following questions about the microeconomics:

- What are the major cost drivers? Are they related to physical proximity? Are they affected by time?

- Are there major learning-curve effects? Are they scale sensitive? Are they scope sensitive?

The world of digital photography and its evolution from the traditional photography industry provides a good example of how to apply market segmentation. There have been a number of digital disruptions of traditional businesses—e-books to the print industry and MP3 files to the recording industry are two recent examples—but the photography and film business stands out. The industry is in the midst of a tumultuous shift from traditional photography (i.e., cameras requiring film and chemical-based development facilities to create pictures) to digital photography (i.e., cameras that digitally store images that can then be downloaded to PCs, e-mailed to friends, and printed on computer printers or at professional development facilities). Camera and film companies that define their business solely within the confines of the traditional photography market are likely to be left behind or become disintermediated as others move in to fill digital photographers' needs.

Until recently, most amateur and professional photographers had to go to film developers to view their pictures, to the cheers of Kodak, Fuji, and local and national developers that developed slides and prints. With the advent of digital cameras, however, the landscape changed dramatically. Suddenly photographers could download pictures to their PCs, burn them onto CDs, e-mail them to friends and family, and perhaps most profoundly, delete pictures that they had no use for, bypassing any development costs. With this shift came a host of new players. Storage manufacturers pushed their CDs, memory sticks, and other devices to store gigabytes of photos; online developers emerged to turn these digital files into prints; and hardware manufacturers cranked out cameras to feed the demand for new cameras.

Traditional photography companies such as Kodak needed to change their strategies in order to seize opportunities represented by the emergence of digital photography. They needed to ask questions such as: How do we segment the market? Which segments should we be most interested in? How big is the opportunity likely to become?

They might also identify segmentation variables that, when combined with other variables, correlate to customer motivations, barriers, use habits, and profitability. Certain combinations of variables would generate insight. For Kodak, the list could include these variables:

- *Occasion (or situation)*. The purchase occasions for digital cameras (self-consumption, gift, etc.) are indications of customers' buying motivation, the degree of research invested in the buying process, and their relative price sensitivity. Furthermore, the intended purpose for acquiring and mastering a digital camera is likely to vary considerably across these occasions.

- *Demographics*. The higher-education system in the United States helps create people's lifelong media and learning habits. Many higher-education programs require students to own laptop computers for class use and assignments. In fact, computers are being introduced at earlier and earlier stages of the education system. Thus, education and age are both proxy variables for technological adoption. Education has historically been highly correlated with technological adoption, while age has been a reliable predictor. People older than 40 did not grow up with computers and other technologies as part of everyday life, and therefore have a low adoption rate for new technologies.

Combining these variables yields distinct, actionable, and meaningful segments of the market to whom Kodak can sell digital cameras. Exhibit 2.6 illustrates the segmentation that emerges from this analysis. The vertical axis divides the population into demographic groups based on age and degree of comfort with computers. The horizontal axis shows purchase occasions (reasons for buying), along with the intended usage occasion. (This segmentation also assumes that purchasing power increases with age.) Cross-tabulating the two axes and blocking some of the subsegments together creates a matrix of behaviorally distinct segments.

The digital-camera example illustrates the value of going beyond "business or pleasure?" as a market segmentation variable for this market. First, the purchase reason is very important. Are customers buying the camera for themselves, and therefore likely to have a much greater level of insight into exactly what they want? Or is it a gift that is intended as a thoughtful sentiment to the recipient? The reason a consumer is buying a digital camera—for work, for special occasions, or simply because they like electronic toys—may indicate a consumer's relative price sensitivity, overall interest, and involvement with the purchase. By understanding the role that hardware and software play in the lives of people considering buying a digital camera, Kodak can develop specific products and services to serve the needs of very distinct segments.

Choice of Focal Customer Benefits

A business articulates a value proposition or cluster when it specifies the key benefits that will be delivered to a certain target segment. The benefits need to be relevant, important, and parsimonious. Conventional marketing and business-strategy textbooks often recommend that firms focus on one or two critical benefits. The examples often cited include Volvo (which emphasizes safety), Southwest Airlines (which emphasizes convenience and low prices), or the Four Seasons (which emphasizes outstanding service). As the proponents of segment focusing would agree, firms that attempt to compete on more than one benefit create two basic problems. The first, on the demand side, is that customers are confused by the company's messages. The second, on the supply side, is that systems must be uniquely constructed to deliver certain benefits. Choosing two highly conflicting benefits (such as fast delivery and low price) will lead to compromises in the development of strategy— the classic "stuck in the middle"—and average performance on two benefits, while other firms deliver high performance on a single benefit.

Three specific classes of criteria should be used to assess a company's value proposition:

- *Customer Criteria.* Multiple criteria can be used to assess to what degree the target customer values the position. Do target customers understand the proposition or cluster? Is it relevant to their needs? Is it believable?

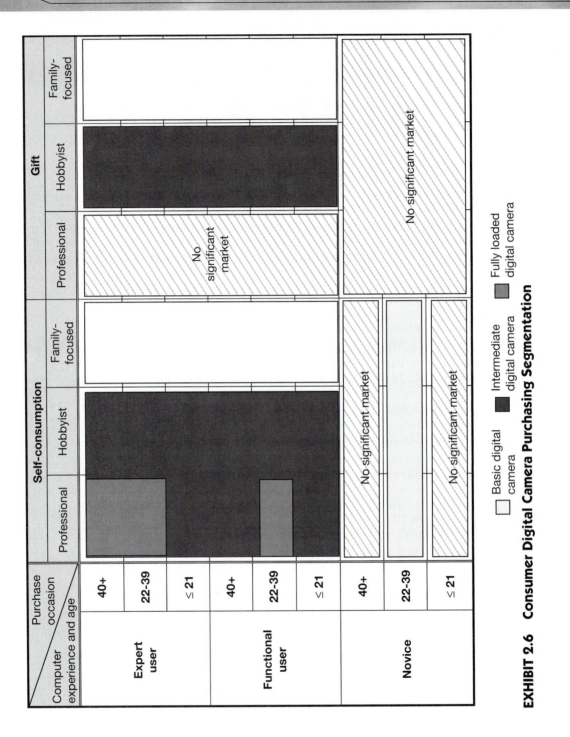

EXHIBIT 2.6   Consumer Digital Camera Purchasing Segmentation

Is it perceived as unique or as indistinguishable from other propositions or clusters? Will it provoke action on the part of the target customer?

- *Company Criteria.* Will the organization rally around the proposition? Does the company have the resources or capabilities to own this cluster? Will it block or facilitate the eventual move to additional vertical markets?

- *Competitive Criteria.* Are there competitors attempting to hold a similar proposition or cluster? Will competitors allow the focal company to own the stated cluster in the market? Can current competitors match this cluster? How easy is it for future competitors to match this cluster?

Market Mapping and Target Customers

With a set of actionable and meaningful dimensions identified, managers can construct a basic marketing map to show the segment's size, ideal media, growth rate, and financial attractiveness. For Kodak, some of the digital-camera segments noted in Exhibit 2.6 are small. For instance, the segment for fully loaded digital cameras is limited to professional photographers who need to keep up with trends in their industry and are also computer literate and able to afford the higher-priced cameras and accessories to support the shift to a digital photography platform. On the other hand, basic digital cameras, as gifts or self-purchases, appeal to the family-focused segment that represents 49 percent of consumer photographers. This is partly due to the basic cameras' low entry price and ease of use. The market mapping process focuses management's attention on the segments that can produce most meaningful results.

As in many markets, consumers have a choice as to how they want to receive information, from broadcast to print. Once again, the purchase and usage occasions, along with the user demographics, indicate that only some segments are well suited for digital cameras. For example, someone who has never used a computer and is not interested in learning how to use one is not going to be a candidate for a digital camera in the near future. The market mapping process can extend beyond the single illustrated map. Once one market map has been created, you can map multiple dimensions within its framework. For instance, the frame of Exhibit 2.6 could be used to map competitors, prioritize segments, or aid the decision process in other ways.

These simple maps are important tools for several reasons. First, the maps identify the location of the money and the relative opportunities in the market. Second, a clear representation of the opportunity's location makes it easier to select initial target segments and to lay out a game plan for sequencing the approach to other segments in the future. Third, maps provide structure for synthesizing additional information and insight. Fourth, the segmentation can help identify future shifts in market definition and opportunity.

It is often as important to identify those who are unlikely to find the idea attractive as it is to find likely target segments. It is also important to communicate who is "in" or "out" to potential collaborators to minimize the negative response that could otherwise ensue. The Kodak example illustrates this concept well.

A final note is in order. Some analysts have argued that online businesses no longer need to focus on demographics or other traditional criteria because the online world enables them to track consumer behavior in real time. Hence, this behavior by itself combines both actionability and meaningfulness. To some degree, this argument is correct because behavior data (and an e-mail address) are sufficient information to initiate interaction with current customers. However, standard demographic data are still highly relevant in the online world for three reasons. First, the online firm can more effectively sell advertising. Second, the firm will know where to place its own offline advertising to attract customers. Third, for companies with both bricks-and-mortar and online operations, this picture of the customer will foster more effective activation of channels, product mix choices, and other marketing mix decisions.

Step Four: Assess Resource Requirements to Deliver the Offering

Examining the distinct capabilities the company would need to bring to a new offering—through its own resources and those of potential partners—helps gauge the degree of alignment between the opportunity and the company's capabilities. A company must bring a set of distinct resources to win in the market. Without them, the company will not have the advantages it needs to generate cash flow. Having determined the initial customer focus of the business, a firm is then ready to make a first attempt at describing the business concept. At this step, the company should stake out what experience and benefits **the offering** will provide and what capabilities and technology will be needed to deliver the benefits of the offering. While the offering and the means to deliver its benefits will be revisited and refined many times, understanding these details will be a vital part of the company's rationale for success in this endeavor.

Point–Counterpoint

Does Segmentation Really Matter?

There are some who have begun to question whether segmentation applies in the online world. Because the online world enables consumers to customize products, services, and information, the segmentation concept has given way to individualization, they say.

Proponents of this direct approach use terms such as "1:1," "segment of one," or "one-to-one" marketing. Furthermore, they argue that Web businesses such as eBay often attract an exceptionally wide variety of customers who weigh buying criteria (such as low price, most convenient buying method, best online information and reviews, or broadest selection) quite differently. Hence, it is foolish to attempt to cluster these widely divergent groups. Rather, customization enables firms to uniquely meet the needs of each customer. Additionally, they argue, the back-office supply systems and infrastructure can easily accommodate every type of customer. Finally, multiple storefronts—even individual storefronts—can be constructed in real time. (Amazon.com's homepage, which is tailored for each customer, is an excellent example. Exhibit 2.7 shows the differing Amazon homepages for two customers who visited the website at exactly the same time.)

Proponents of segmentation argue that all Web storefronts, by definition, already segment the market. That is, if a given Web storefront simultaneously attracts selected customers and repels certain customers, it is segmenting the market. By disregarding these segments and focusing exclusively on 1:1 marketing, the company misses the fundamental economics of which classes of customer are most profitable or least profitable. For example, Buy.com offers some of the lowest prices on a wide variety of products. It is not clear that the store explicitly targets a particular customer segment; however, the store's focus on prices is likely to attract the most price-sensitive customers.

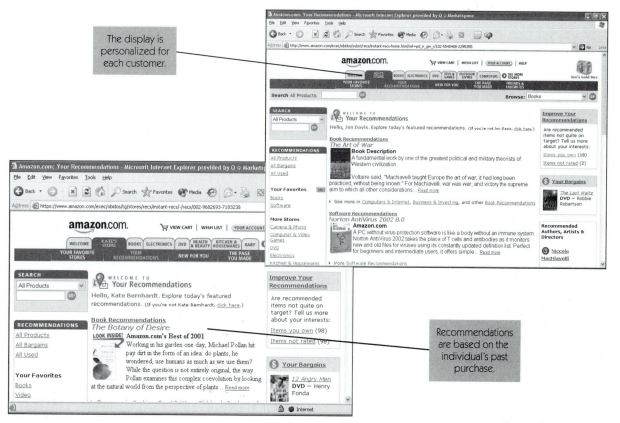

The display is personalized for each customer.

Recommendations are based on the individual's past purchase.

EXHIBIT 2.7   Amazon.com Homepage for Two Different Customers

Courtesy of *www.amazon.com*

Company Resources

Before spending a great deal of time crafting a specific business model to support a concept, the management team should identify at least three or four resources or assets that it can leverage in the online space. These resources should be central to delivering new benefits or unlocking trapped value—the core of the company's value story. These resources should also hold the promise for advantage, considering the current and prospective players in the targeted space. With three or four such resources, the management team will have the beginnings of a robust business.

In this step, the team will already have a strong understanding of the following:

- The selected value system in which the company will be participating
- The key stages of the customer decision process and the benefits sought or value trapped at each stage
- The target customer segments

Looking across these insights, the management team should identify which winning resources it can bring to bear, create, or provide through business partnerships. A **resource system** is a discrete collection of individual and organizational activities and assets that, when taken together, create organizational capabilities. These capabilities allow the company to serve customer needs. Resources that a company can bring to bear can be grouped into three classifications:

- *Customer-Facing.* Customer-facing resources include brand name, a well trained sales force, and multiple distribution channels.
- *Internal.* These resources are associated with the company's internal operations. Examples include technology, product development, economies of scale, and experienced staff.
- *Upstream.* These resources are associated with a company's relationship to its suppliers. Examples include partnerships with suppliers and the degree of operational seamlessness between the company and its suppliers.

Partners

On its own, a company may not be able to bring all of the resources necessary to deliver value to its target segments. In opportunity assessment, a company must be realistic about any capability gaps. If the gaps are insurmountable, the company should not proceed; if the gaps can somehow be closed, it must find a way to do so. Partnering is often an effective alternative to building or acquiring the capability. Networked-economy companies find partnerships particularly relevant because their offerings span traditional value-system boundaries. The Internet abounds with affiliate partnerships, in which complementary sites drive traffic to each other and share the revenue generated by that traffic. In fact, effective partnering can be an important source of competitive advantage. Barnes & Noble.com's exclusive marketing deal with AOL is one example; Amazon.com's use of Net Perceptions for collaborative filtering is another. A partnership may transform more than the two businesses involved—as was the case with the merger of AOL and Time Warner, a $106.2 billion deal that created one of the largest media companies ever. These two companies brought complementary assets to the merger: AOL's direct customer access and deep online experience coupled with Time Warner's extensive content and traditional business experience and acumen creating new opportunities for both.

Characteristics of a Successful, Unique Resource System

The Resource System.   The value proposition and offering specification are critical steps in defining the resource system of the company.[7] The resource system shows how a company must align its internal systems (and partners) to deliver the benefits of the value proposition or cluster. Conventional wisdom suggests that the factor that sets highly successful companies apart from lesser companies is not simply the value proposition but the choice of actions and assets that are used to deliver the value proposition. These actions include the selection of capabilities and activities that uniquely deliver the value proposition.[8]

The prevailing logic is that unique activities, tied to the value proposition, lead to a competitive advantage. However, four important modifications must be made to the resource-system logic in order to apply it to the online marketplace. The actions to take now not only include the selection of capabilities and activities to deliver the value proposition uniquely, they also involve the supply of all the resources needed to make the capabilities and activities a reality. The four modifications are listed below:

- *Shift from Physical World to Virtual-and-Physical World.*[9] The first key modification is to shift from activities and capabilities in the physical world to a combination of marketplace and marketspace capabilities. Resource systems, for many companies, are a combination of the physical and virtual asset bases.

- *Shift from Activities to Capabilities*. Capabilities are the higher-order skills and assets of the company. Capabilities are typically supported by a cluster of resources that build and differentiate one or more of a company's capabilities. Resources[10] may take various forms; they might be physical assets (such as warehouses or server farms) or intangible assets, such as Yahoo!'s brand name or Priceline's patents on its business model. Activities might also be considered resources. For example, eBay might argue that it is better at running auctions than a competitor would be.

- *Shift from Supply-Side Focus to Demand-Side Focus*. Many activity systems focus heavily on the internal capabilities of the firm. This may seem reasonable, but what is more appropriate is the initial focus on the benefits desired by targeted customer segments. The desired benefits should largely dictate the choice of capabilities.

- *Shift from Single to Multifirm Systems*. A key aspect of the online environment is the need for partnerships. Resource systems require capabilities that must be in place and ready to use in order to win various markets. These capabilities may reside in the firm, need to be developed in-house or acquired in the open market, or accessed through strategic partnerships and alliances.

Specifying a Resource System.   With these four modifications in mind, we examine the steps in the construction of a resource system.

1. Identify core benefits in the value proposition or cluster.

2. Identify capabilities that relate to each benefit. Linking the capabilities that are required to deliver a particular customer benefit helps define the resource-system requirements.

3. Link resources to each capability. After the capabilities are identified, the firm can identify the resources that deliver against each of these requirements. These are the key assets, activities, actions, and partnerships or alliances that create the firm's capability.

4. Identify to what extent the firm can deliver each capability. This requires a close internal look at the company to determine whether it has all the necessary capabilities, or whether it must outsource and/or partner with others.

5. Identify partners who can complete capabilities.

Assessing the Quality of a Resource System.   A number of criteria can be used to assess the quality of the resource system.

- *Uniqueness of the System*. Uniqueness refers to the extent to which the organization provides benefits, capabilities, and activities that are different from those of competitors. Is the company providing benefits that the customer might not be able to obtain otherwise?

- *Links Between Capabilities and Benefits*. Does each capability support the delivery of a customer benefit? Is the support strong or weak?

- *Links Among Capabilities in the System.* How well do the capabilities and activities complement and support one another? Are there tight linkages between the capabilities and activities? Are they consistent with the overall value cluster?

- *Links Among Resources.* Are the specific resources mutually reinforcing? Are they complementary? Are they consistent with the various benefits?

- *Links Between Virtual-World and Physical-World Business Systems.* Does the online resource system support or conflict with the offline system?

- *Sustainable Advantage.* Is the resource system difficult to replicate? Possessing a unique but easily copied resource system will deliver only a fleeting advantage to a firm. Sustained high profits will come only from a sustainable competitive advantage. The ease with which a resource system can be imitated may depend on a number of factors.[11]

Combining the benefits to be delivered along with the way in which the company will deliver them creates the overall business concept. With the high-level understanding in mind, the attractiveness of the opportunity from financial, technical, and competitive points of view can be assessed.

Step Five: Assess Competitive, Technological, and Financial Attractiveness of Opportunity

There is little point in targeting a new business concept, even to a meaningful and easy-to-reach segment, if the opportunity is not attractive. There are nine factors in four areas that can be used to determine the character and magnitude of the opportunity.

- *Competitive Intensity.* Factors that relate to overall competitive intensity can be expressed in a competitors map that includes (a) the number and identity of competitors along with their respective (b) strengths and weaknesses at delivering benefits.

- *Customer Dynamics.* Elements that frame the overall customer dynamics of the market are (a) the level of unmet need, or magnitude of unconstrained opportunity, (b) the level of interaction between major customer segments, and (c) the likely rate of growth.

- *Technology Vulnerability.* Technology vulnerability includes (a) the impact of the penetration of enabling technologies and (b) the impact of new technologies on the value proposition.

- *Microeconomics.* The microeconomics of the opportunity include (a) the size/volume of the market and (b) the projected level of profitability.

Competitive Intensity

Identify Competitors. To measure competitive intensity, a company obviously needs to identify the competitors it will face. In the discussion of value systems, a company's key competitors would have been identified, and "white space" opportunities (those in which there is no apparent competition) would have been isolated. At this step, the task is to develop a better understanding of the threats and opportunities associated with various participants.

For online businesses, identifying competitors is easier in some ways, but it also has challenges that do not exist offline. On one hand, the firm can simply use search engines to begin identifying competitors (although generic searches may deliver thousands of "relevant" pages), then visit the websites of these potential competitors to gain an understanding of their offerings. On the other hand, competition in the marketspace typically occurs across traditional industry boundaries. No matter what online business you are in, there is a good chance that Microsoft, AOL Time Warner, or both are competitors.

In the online world, companies that one would not consider direct competitors (because they do not offer a similar or competing product) can become indirect competitors because they are reaching and attracting the same customers, or because they are developing a technology, platform, or offering that might compete with your offering.

Simply put, **direct competitors** are rivals in the same industry. In his book *Competitive Strategy*, Michael Porter defines these firms as offering products or services that are "close substitutes" for each other.[12] For example, Barnes & Noble.com and Amazon.com are direct competitors; both offer books to customers. Direct competitors reach and compete for the same customers. **Indirect competitors** contain two categories of companies:

- *Substitute Producers.* Porter defines substitute producers as companies that, though they reside in different industries, produce products and services that perform the same function.[13] Keen.com and Britannica.com are substitute producers. Keen.com is a switchboard that connects people with questions to individuals who can answer them knowledgably. Britannica.com offers answers to a wide range of questions through its online encyclopedia.

- *Adjacent Competitors.* Adjacent competitors do not currently offer products and services that are direct substitutes, but they have the potential to quickly do so. For example, adjacent competitors may have a relationship with a company's current customers. In the games market, Microsoft was known for its MSN GameZone, where players from novices to experts would congregate. But until it introduced the Xbox, its own game hardware system, it didn't compete with the other major hardware suppliers, Sony and Nintendo. Adjacent competitors might also use a similar technology or platform or have similar activity systems. The entrance of Apple's iPhoto service makes it an adjacent competitor to a traditional photography company, such as Kodak.

A useful tool for identifying direct and indirect competitors is the profiling approach illustrated in Exhibit 2.8, which shows the radar screen for Kodak. The screen consists of three concentric circles.[14] The innermost circle contains the set of customer activities that are central to the industry being examined. In Kodak's case, these include purchasing a camera, purchasing film, taking pictures, downloading and choosing pictures to print, printing and receiving pictures, sharing pictures, storing them on a CD, and purchasing accessories. Kodak faces competition in each of these areas. The middle circle contains Kodak's direct competitors. For example, in the "purchase camera" step, competitors include Fuji, Sony, Nikon, and Olympus. In the "downloading and choosing pictures to print stage," Kodak faces offline and online players, including Ofoto, PhotoAccess, PhotoWorks, Shutterfly, and Snapfish. Finally, the outermost circle contains Kodak's most notable indirect competitors, Intel and Hewlett Packard. In the "purchase camera" stage,

HP and Intel do not offer cameras, but they do provide accessory hardware products that are targeted to the same customer groups; the hardware products conceivably could be leveraged toward offering cameras in the future.

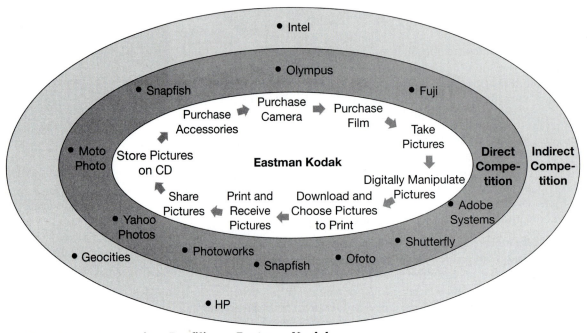

EXHIBIT 2.8   Competitor Profiling—Eastman Kodak

Competitor Maps.   Current and prospective competitors can significantly shape the nature of a company's online opportunity. Previous steps identified the customer segments that the company wants to target and the competitors (direct and indirect) that a company may face. To assess competitive intensity, the firm needs to map the competitors to the target segments. In other words, a business needs to define where current competitors are participating and determine their effectiveness in delivering benefits to target customers. This analysis will help the company do the following:

- Demarcate any white space (underserved areas) in the market and, conversely, the most competitive areas.
- Identify the companies the company will compete against and gain preliminary understanding of their strengths.
- Spot companies that could be potential collaborators—in other words, companies that might offer a critical capability or unique access to customers at a specific stage of the customer decision process.

The competitor mapping of segments can also be used to record the relative strengths and weaknesses of current competitors and their offerings at each relevant cell in the map. Ultimately, the customer seeks specific benefits. Assessing the current players' performance in meeting the customer standard will tell whether there is potential for a company to move in and win. Understanding current competitor capabilities will also indicate the height of competitive hurdles a company may face in its selected space.

Customer Dynamics. After assessing competitor vulnerabilities, the firm next needs to turn its attention to the customer dynamics of the market and how they create, accelerate, and sustain unit demand. When analyzing customer dynamics, three central factors must be considered.

Unconstrained Opportunity. This is the amount of white space in the marketplace. Markets with a high degree of trapped or relatively untapped new-to-the-world value are particularly prized. Note the explosive growth of eBay in the online auctions space. The number of goods that individuals wanted to buy and sell, combined with the relatively arcane auction system in which they found themselves trading, signaled a massive opportunity. (There is a detailed case study on eBay at the end of this chapter.)

Segment Interaction. This is the level of reinforcing activity that generates more purchase and usage. Companies that have member-influencing-member dynamics—also called "viral dynamics"—can quickly capture much of the opportunity. For example, through its self-serve customer-feedback offering, Zoomerang.com, MarketTools created a geometric viral effect. Each member can send a feedback survey to 30 customers, who then experience the Zoomerang offering and decide whether to write their own survey and send it on to 30 of their customers, and so on. Blue Mountain Arts (*www.bluemountain.com*) used the same principle to build a successful online greeting card business. When people received e-greetings, they often went to the website and sent online cards to friends of their own, thus accelerating Blue Mountain's interaction within and across a variety of customer segments. So successful was this segment interaction, with an active user community of more than 12 million people, that Excite@Home paid $780 million for it in 1999. With the drop in advertising sales on the Internet, however, Blue Mountain Arts' potential languished, and it was sold to rival American Greetings for $35 million only two years later.

Growth. Growth usually refers to the percentage of annual growth of the underlying customer-unit market. Markets with high expected growth represent significant opportunities for players. For example, Onvia.com, which informs small businesses about available government contracts, can benefit from the high rate of growth in the small-business sector—the fastest growing sector of the economy. Onvia benefits from a growth "three-fer": a growing number of small businesses, penetration of existing small businesses, and a growing number of services that small businesses require.

Technology Vulnerability. Beyond the competitive arena, the company must make a high-level judgment on the concept's vulnerability to technology trends, both in the penetration of enabling technologies and in the impact of new technologies on the value proposition.

Technology Adoption. Is there sufficient penetration of the technologies (e.g., cable modems, scanners) that enables the customer to take advantage of or participate in the offering? What penetration is necessary to make the offering financially viable? When is the minimum penetration likely to be met? Is there an introductory version that could be upgraded as technology penetration increases?

Impact of New Technologies. What new technologies could radically alter the economics of delivering an offering or require adjustment of the actual features and functionality of an offering? How likely is it that your target population or competitors will use these technologies?

The pace and discontinuity of technological change make forecasting the future particularly challenging, and it is not our intent to provide an exhaustive treatment of the subject here.[15] Fortunately, several rules of thumb about technological development can guide entrepreneurs. One of them is that computers will continue to increase in power. Moore's Law, which states that the number of transistors per computer chip doubles every two years, forecasts the exponential pace at which processing power increases. Our definition of what a computer is will also probably change. It is not far-fetched to speculate that soon, many mechanical devices will be computerized. Many believe these devices will all be connected by a vastly larger Internet. George Gilder, the technology forecaster for whom Gilder's Law is named, predicts that total bandwidth of communications systems will triple every 12 months for the foreseeable future. The challenge for entrepreneurs is to understand what these macrotrends will mean for their proposed businesses.

Microeconomics. This section has assessed the magnitude of the opportunity from a competitive perspective (how easy it is to enter the space and to differentiate the company from competitor offerings), from the perspective of customer dynamics (how unit demand is created, accelerated, and sustained), and from a technology standpoint. The firm now needs to assess the level of financial opportunity. Two factors—market size and profitability—are critical to this task.

Market Size. This is the dollar value of all of the sales generated in a particular market. Opportunities with a large market size are very attractive, because winning even a small piece of the pie may correspond to a significant revenue flow. For example, a large number of competitors emerged in the online travel industry in response to the huge size of the U.S. business and vacation travel market, estimated at $582 billion. However, sales generated in a particular market represent today's actual market size. What really needs to be determined to accurately assess an opportunity is the *future* potential. This is especially important for online ventures with new-to-the-world benefits, offerings, business models, and pricing. Offline market size is not necessarily indicative or even proportional to online market size. There are many forecasting techniques available, and due to the high degree of uncertainty, it is highly advisable to collect as much consumer and market data as possible and forecast the market size using multiple techniques. Feel confident if the estimates are of the same order of magnitude. If not, the underlying assumptions and key drivers need to be explored and a healthy dose of logic applied.

Profitability. This is the profit margin that can be realized in the market. Markets with high profit margins are attractive because they can generate high levels of profit with moderate sales volume. For example, eBay's auction market provides a highly attractive opportunity partly because it generates profit margins in excess of 80 percent.[16] The breadth of inventory that a retailer such as Lands' End is able to have online, including out-of-season items, generates additional sales revenues and increases profitability.[17]

Metcalfe's Law; Bob Metcalfe, Founder, 3Com

"Metcalfe's Law says that the value of the network, of any network, grows as the square of its number of users—and I did not call it Metcalfe's Law but I'm not fighting. . . . In 1980 I had a slide which I was using to promote Ethernet, and this slide showed the value of the network growing as the square. Every time you add a user, not only do you add value to that user, but then that user is valuable to all the other users that are already there. So the value of the network is the number of users times the number of users: n^2. And so I have this slide and I was arguing that, after a critical point—there is a critical mass point—connectivity begins to feed on itself, and the network becomes an enormously winning proposition. We've seen it happen with the Ethernet and we've seen it happen with the Internet."

Drill-Down

Network Economics

Network economics[18] is a fundamental driving force in the networked economy. This law of economics states that users of network products tend to value those products more (because they get more utility from them) when there are a large number of users. In fact, the value of a product to each of its users increases with the addition of each new user. Telephones are an example of a product subject to network economics. The first purchaser of a telephone had no use for it—it was impossible to call anyone. The second purchaser made the telephone valuable for the first purchaser (they could now call each other), and the third purchaser increased the utility of the telephones purchased by the other two. (It was now possible to make conference calls!)

Named after Bob Metcalfe, the inventor of the network technology known as Ethernet, **Metcalfe's Law** states that the value of a network to each of its members is proportional to the number of other users (which can be expressed as $\frac{n^2 - n}{2}$). The near-universal adoption of Windows as a PC operating system is another good example of network economics. The more users who adopted Windows, the more software companies that wrote Windows compatible products, making Windows more and more valuable to its users.

In many cases, however, computers with Windows are not connected to a network, so why does this product benefit from network economics? Windows users may or may not be physically networked together, but they do operate in a form of community. They use software written for the Windows operating system, and they share files with each other. These activities make Windows subject to network economics.

Network economics has a profound impact on the equilibrium states of the markets in which it operates. Because users tend to prefer products that already have many users, strong companies tend to get stronger (this is known as positive reinforcement) and weak companies weaker (negative reinforcement). As a result, markets with many competing technologies tend to converge on one product standard.

An important aspect of the assessment of market size and profitability is determining how the company will generate revenue. What are the opportunities for monetizing the value creation? Consider typical sources of revenue in the networked economy: advertising revenue, referrals, affiliate program fees,[19] customer subscriptions, and the purchase of products and services.

In the case of Kodak, the emergence of digital photography has important consequences for the bottom line. For digital cameras to succeed, you need to have willing buyers and sellers. Kodak's Photography Group works directly with the fickle and often enigmatic mass customer, accounting for 60 percent of its revenue and 70 percent of its profits—in effect, it is the very core of the Kodak business. A shift to digital photography is both an opportunity and a threat to this business. For example, families with digital cameras take 60 percent more pictures, but take 33 percent fewer film photographs. Meanwhile, only 20 percent of digital photographs taken are developed. Exhibit 2.9 shows the implications of the shift to digital photography to a unit like Kodak's Photography Group. A worst-case scenario complete consumer shift to digital photography would result in a 50 percent loss in revenue per household. This figure emphasizes the importance of market opportunity analysis to a company that, like Kodak, is in the midst of a shifting business environment.

	Traditional Film	Film + Digital	Fully Digital	Key Assumptions
# Photos Taken	100	160	300	• For easy comparison, assume 100-photo base for average family.
# Film Photos Developed	100	67	0	
# Digital Photos Developed	0	18	54	• Revenue/Film Print assumes $8.99 per 24 exposures.
Revenue/Film Print	$0.37	$0.37	$0.37	• Revenue/Digital Print assumes 50 cents per exposure.
Film Print Revenue	$37.46	$25.10	$0.00	
Film Revenue	$17.00	$11.39	$0.00	• Film revenue assumes $3.99 for 24 exposures.
Revenue/Digital Print	$0.50	$0.50	$0.50	• Families with digital cameras take 60% more pictures, but take 33% fewer film photographs.
Digital Print Revenue	$0.00	$9.00	$27.00	
Total Revenue per Household	$54.46	$45.49	$27.00	• Only 20% of digital photos taken are developed.
% Profit Loss vs. Film Only	0%	16%	50%	

EXHIBIT 2.9 Calculation of Per-Household Consumer Film Revenue

Kodak stands to lose as much as 50% of its film revenue in a fully digital photography world

To assess the overall opportunity attractiveness, managers must rate each factor separately *and* as part of a whole. Whether a particular factor helps, has no effect on, or hinders the overall market opportunity, the manager must try to gauge the magnitude of its impact. Look across all factors to see the overall effect, because these effects may be multiplicative and not additive. For Kodak, it is not enough to simply map the digital-camera market. It should also look at the entire digital-photography value chain and see where it makes sense to find other opportunities along the chain (see Exhibit 2.10). This is reflected in Kodak's string of recent investments and partnerships (Exhibit 2.11). Exhibit 2.12 shows a snapshot, so to speak, of Kodak's overall market opportunity in digital photography. While the weighting includes a negative factor in technological vulnerability, an assessment of Kodak's opportunity yields generally positive or neutral values, suggesting that it is well placed to succeed in the digital photography market.

The value of this exercise is in thinking about all the pluses and minuses. The objective is to determine if this situation is a poor, moderate, good, great, or gigantic opportunity.

Step Six: Conduct Go/No-Go Assessment

Action standards are measurements a company establishes as a hurdle for investment or other resource allocation decisions. Ideally, these action standards are established before assessing an opportunity and applied broadly, thus creating a set of objective and universal metrics. Many organizations, such as General Electric, have a well established set of go/no-go decision tools and enabling processes. In essence, this phase presents the business case for why an opportunity is or is not worth pursuing.

	Capture	Store and Retrieve	Enhance	Repurpose	Share
Film Value Chain: Products and services	• Still Cameras • Film • Batteries	• Commercial processing • Negatives	• Commercial processing • PictureMaker kiosks	• Commercial processing • PictureMaker kiosks	• Reprints • Albums
Virtual Value Chain: Products and services	• Digital cameras • Webcams • PDA cameras	• Memory sticks • Flash cards • CDs • PC hard drive • Home inkjet printer • Inkjet paper • Inkjet ink • Commercial processing • Online upload and development • PDA	• Commercial processing • PC software • Online software • PictureMaker kiosks	• Commercial processing • PC software • Online software • PictureMaker kiosks	• Reprints (online services, printers) • Online albums • E-mail • Diskettes • Flash cards • Memory sticks • PDA

EXHIBIT 2.10   Photography Value Chain

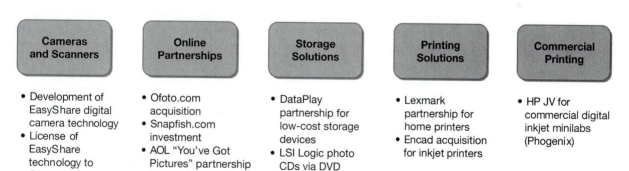

Cameras and Scanners	Online Partnerships	Storage Solutions	Printing Solutions	Commercial Printing
• Development of EasyShare digital camera technology • License of EasyShare technology to Olympus • Investment in PictureVision scanners and servers	• Ofoto.com acquisition • Snapfish.com investment • AOL "You've Got Pictures" partnership • PhotoAlley.com investment • iFilm.com investment • MyFamily.com investment • Partnership with CVS.com and Kmart photofinishing • Partnership with Circuit City for creating and sharing prints • Partnership with Freeserve, largest ISP in the UK	• DataPlay partnership for low-cost storage devices • LSI Logic photo CDs via DVD players	• Lexmark partnership for home printers • Encad acquisition for inkjet printers	• HP JV for commercial digital inkjet minilabs (Phogenix)

EXHIBIT 2.11   Notable Investments and Partnerships, 2000–2001

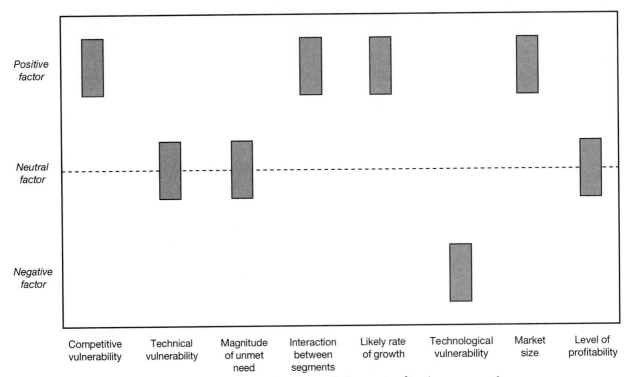

EXHIBIT 2.12   Kodak's Digital Photography Overall Opportunity Assessment

At this point, the management team should have a clear picture of the market opportunity. Its members should be able to describe the value system for the industry and have a strong sense for how intervention into this value system and the customer decision process could create new benefits, enhance existing ones, or unlock value trapped in the current system. The team should be able to clearly identify the customer segments that it will be targeting and support its determination with data or strong hypotheses about the underserved or unmet needs of one or more of these customer segments. This understanding provides the basis for creating a high-level value proposition and determining capabilities that the team can bring to bear to participate successfully in the business. The examination of potential competitors enhances the team's thinking about where to participate in the identified market and what to bring to the opportunity.

The management team should then craft an "opportunity story"—in essence, the rough outline of the business plan. The opportunity story should do the following:

- Briefly describe the target segment(s) within the selected value system.
- Articulate the high-level value proposition.
- Spell out the expected elements of customer benefits (this chapter has focused on functional benefits; however, needs can be emotional or self-expressive).
- Identify the critical capabilities and resources needed to deliver the customer benefits.
- Lay out the critical reasons to believe that the identified capabilities and resources will be a source of advantage over the competition.

- Categorize the critical capabilities (and supporting resources) as in-house, build, buy, or collaborate.
- Describe how the company will monetize the opportunity (i.e., how it will capture some portion of the value that it creates for its customers).
- Provide an initial sense for the magnitude of the financial opportunity for the company.
- Identify critical underlying assumptions that must be true in order for this opportunity to materialize in the marketplace.
- Identify risk factors associated with pursuing the opportunity.

The team now must decide whether to proceed to defining the specific value proposition and designing a business model. This should be the first of several go/no-go decision gates. If it hasn't already done so, the team should define the criteria to be met before members will feel comfortable proceeding to the next step of the business development process. At each successive decision gate, the clarity of the proposition should become more refined and the action standards for proceeding more rigorous.

If uncertainty remains around one or more of the gating questions, the management team must judge whether additional analysis would remove uncertainty or if there are ways to proceed while revisiting the areas of greatest concern. The team should not proceed too far down the path toward business model development if members cannot reach a consensus on passing these initial gates. At this point in the process, there remains a high degree of uncertainty, and the team must be willing to place a bet by allocating resources to this opportunity.

Conducting a rigorous market opportunity assessment is an important tool for managers to identify areas where their company can compete and thrive. While companies may have varying tolerances for following each step in precise detail, failing to adequately evaluate a market opportunity can result in misallocated resources or product blind alleys. The Drill-Down titled "E-Books: The Market Opportunity That Wasn't (Yet)" examines the rise and fall of the e-book—a promising technology, certainly, but one still in search of a market.

eBay Example

History of the Firm

According to company lore, the idea for eBay came from founder Pierre Omidyar's wife, who wanted to trade Pez dispensers with other collectors over the Internet. In truth, Omidyar had been pondering an Internet auction venture before he was even aware of Pez mania.[20] "I had been thinking about how to create an efficient marketplace—a level playing field, where everyone had access to the same information and could compete on the same terms as anyone else."[21] After writing the code for the website, Omidyar launched eBay from his home in mid-1995. The concept of an Internet marketplace where individuals could buy and sell collectibles caught on so quickly that by the end of the year, eBay was getting a few thousand hits daily.[22] Even more impressive, the website was profitable from its inception (see Exhibit 2.13).

Drill-Down

E-Books: The Market Opportunity That Wasn't (Yet)

During the dot-com boom, with its "land grab" and "Internet time" imperatives, systematic market-opportunity analysis often fell victim to frenzied bandwagon-jumping. As a result, countless businesses, and even entire industries, boldly set sail with only the vaguest understanding of their markets—and inevitably sank when those hoped-for markets failed to materialize.

The market for electronic books, or e-books, is a good example. In 2000, several large publishers, including Random House (AtRandom) and Time Warner (iPublish.com), launched separate units devoted to producing digital books that could be read on desktop computers or portable devices. Despite lackluster e-book sales, the publishers, like so many people, were convinced that the Internet had "changed everything" for their industry. It wasn't a question of whether electronic books would supplant the traditional paper-and-print models. It was simply a matter of when.

But it was one thing to envision a digital future; another to build a business around it. Publishers ended up trying to identify their market opportunities more or less on the fly. Should e-books cost less than paperbacks, or more? Should some titles be released exclusively as e-books? Should they be timeless classics by big-name authors or new works by up-and-coming writers, designed to appeal to a younger, more tech-savvy audience? Should they be fiction or nonfiction? Standard length or shorter? Full or condensed versions of existing volumes? Should they feature enhanced digital content, such as hyperlinks?

Various publishers tried one or several of these approaches. AtRandom, for example, started out intending to publish short-format nonfiction works by high-profile authors that would come out a month before the print versions. Then it tried standard-length niche and Internet-related offerings that were released simultaneously as e-books and trade paperbacks. When neither approach worked, it folded, in November 2001. A month later iPublish, which aimed to uncover brand-new authors via online submissions and layperson reviews, bit the dust due to lagging sales. Throughout the fledgling e-books industry, it was the same story: Many firms either scaled back or closed up entirely.

In fact, by 2002, it seemed that only one book-industry segment had identified a viable near-term e-book market: educational publishers. With a natural distribution channel (highly wired universities), content that benefited from online searching, real-time updating and other digital enhancements (textbooks), and a tech-friendly target market (students), educational publishers had a significant leg up on their mass-market counterparts. Of course, many analysts still believe that the future of the publishing industry belongs to e-books. But until a host of technical, economic, and cultural issues are worked out—and until would-be e-publishers apply more forethought and rigor to their market-opportunity analyses—it seems that future is still a long way off.

Still, Omidyar knew that in order to grow his business to its full potential, he would need help. In 1996, he hired recent Stanford Business School graduate Jeff Skoll to co-lead his management team. He also sought venture-capital funds. "I was looking for a strategic partner," he explained. "We did not care about the money; we wanted someone that could help build the company."[23] He found it in Benchmark Capital, which paid $5 million for a 22 percent stake in eBay in 1997.

Benchmark helped Omidyar recruit a top-tier management team, including a seasoned chief executive officer. The choice was Meg Whitman, a former executive at Hasbro Inc., The Walt Disney Co., Procter & Gamble, and the flower delivery service FTD. Whitman brought considerable brand expertise,

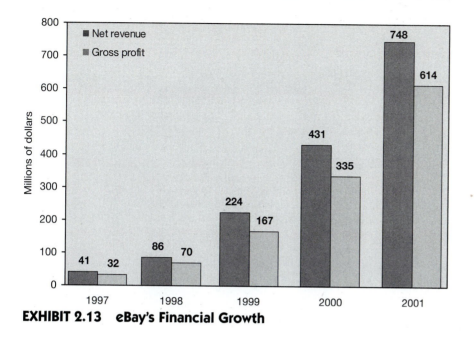

EXHIBIT 2.13   eBay's Financial Growth

the holistic thinking of a strategy consultant, and a strong sense of company ethos. Her goals at eBay, as she put it, were "to develop the work ethic and culture of eBay as a fun, open and trusting environment and to keep the organization focused on the big-picture objectives and key priorities."[24]

eBay went public in September 1998 at $18 a share. By early March 1999, the stock was trading at approximately $282 per share. The company's market capitalization had surpassed that of even Amazon.com, making it the world's most valuable Internet retailer.[25]

In 2001, eBay traded $9.3 billion worth of goods—equivalent to roughly 20 percent of all consumer e-commerce that year and the lion's share of the online auction market (see Exhibit 2.14). More than $1 billion of that total was estimated to come from autos alone, a category that did not even exist on eBay two years earlier.[26] Meg Whitman attributes most of the achievement to eBay's trusted online community.

> "eBay wouldn't exist if it wasn't for our community. . . . At eBay, our customer experience is based on how our customers engage one another. They rarely deal with the company. . . . The only thing we can do is to influence customer behavior by encouraging them to adopt certain values. Those values are to assume that people are basically good, to give the people the benefit of doubt, and to treat people with respect."[27]

—Meg Whitman, eBay CEO

Framing the Market Opportunity

Looking at eBay through the lens of the market opportunity framework sheds light on why eBay has been successful and why it is engaged in certain market segments (and not in others).

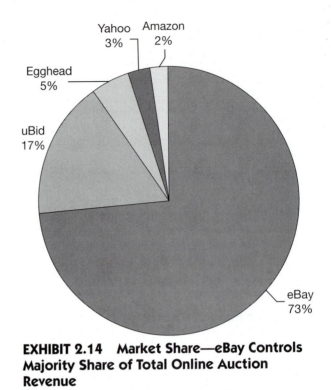

EXHIBIT 2.14   Market Share—eBay Controls Majority Share of Total Online Auction Revenue

Investigate Opportunity in an Existing or New Value System

Pierre Omidyar could not have imagined just how large (or how quickly) the online auction business would grow when he created eBay in 1995, but he knew that Internet technology could be used to create a forum to exchange collectibles and other items efficiently. History shows his instincts were good. Today, the online auction business is huge—eBay, which commands more than 80 percent[28] of the online person-to-person auction market, posted gross merchandise sales (the value of goods sold on eBay and Half.com) totaling $2.7 billion in the fourth quarter of 2001. Clearly Omidyar, by providing people with the tools to buy and sell goods and creating a centralized meeting place, formed the nucleus of a company from which tremendous value could be unlocked.

Identify Unmet or Underserved Needs

Having created the core eBay platform, the next step in framing the business opportunity was to broadly identify the business arena in which the firm participates. Initially, eBay was one of only a few auction websites, and its merchandise was generally small, low-priced items. Now there are hundreds of auction websites ranging from single-niche auction websites to auction aggregators to traditional bricks-and-mortar auction houses who have added websites to their client offerings.

Exhibit 2.15 illustrates some of the areas of potential value release or generation. One way that eBay makes markets more efficient, or releases trapped value, is by aggregating suppliers and buyers at its website, reducing search and transaction costs for both. eBay also releases trapped value by creating more efficient markets and value systems within the auction industry. In fact, some feel that eBay is too good at making efficient markets—in the original collectibles and antique categories, for instance, eBay has created such an efficient market that average selling prices declined 30 percent from March 2001 to March 2002.[29]

Value Type	How	Extent
Trapped	• Create more efficient markets	●
	• Create more efficient value systems	◐
Hybrid	• Disrupt market pricing	●
	• Enable ease of access	●
	• Radically extend reach	●
New	• Customize offerings	◔
	• Enable community building	◐
	• Introduce new functionality or experience	◐

EXHIBIT 2.15   eBay—Defining the Value System

Adding hybrid value—allowing a consumer to harvest the synergistic effects of releasing trapped value while creating new-to-the-world value—has been a key driver of eBay's in-market success. eBay has clearly disrupted market pricing by providing the ability to sell (or buy) virtually anything with detailed product information in real time. This shift gives consumers much more influence over the pricing of products and enables them to capture a portion of the traditional auctioneer's margin. eBay enables ease of access by significantly enhancing the communication between trading partners. A prospective buyer has the seller's contact information and is encouraged to e-mail them with questions, in contrast to a traditional auction in which the seller is unknown to the buyer. The Internet, of course, extends the reach of eBay well beyond that of traditional auctioneers.

Exhibit 2.16 illustrates the purchase process of a traditional auction and indicates numerous areas of unmet or underserved needs. The purchase process is broken into three main areas: prepurchase (including steps such as determining what is being sold and where one can purchase these items), purchase (attending or participating in the auction), and postpurchase (primarily disbursement of funds). There were a plethora of needs that were not addressed or were served poorly by the traditional auction market, on which eBay subsequently capitalized. For example, there was no notification process, and if a

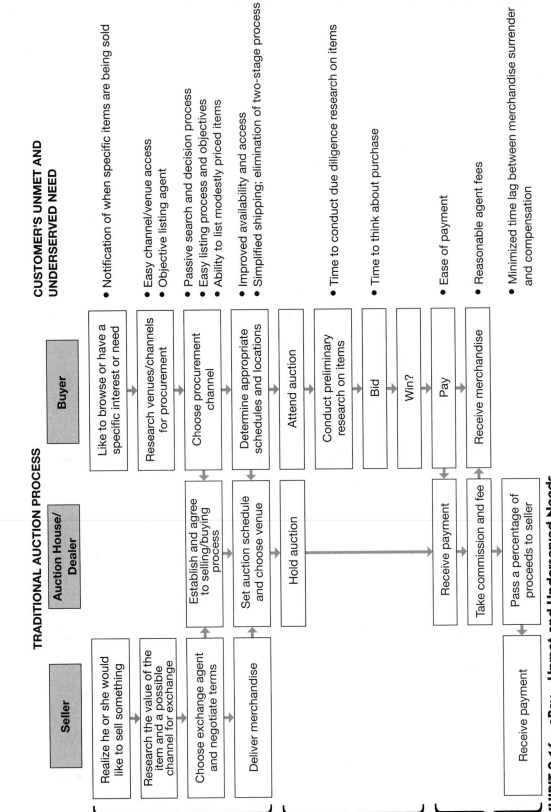

EXHIBIT 2.16   eBay—Unmet and Underserved Needs

TRADITIONAL AUCTION PROCESS

Seller

- Realize he or she would like to sell something
- Research the value of the item and a possible channel for exchange
- Choose exchange agent and negotiate terms
- Deliver merchandise
- Receive payment

Auction House/ Dealer

- Establish and agree to selling/buying process
- Set auction schedule and choose venue
- Hold auction
- Receive payment
- Take commission and fee
- Pass a percentage of proceeds to seller

Buyer

- Like to browse or have a specific interest or need
- Research venues/channels for procurement
- Choose procurement channel
- Determine appropriate schedules and locations
- Attend auction
- Conduct preliminary research on items
- Bid
- Win?
- Pay
- Receive merchandise

CUSTOMER'S UNMET AND UNDERSERVED NEED

- Notification of when specific items are being sold
- Easy channel/venue access
- Objective listing agent
- Passive search and decision process
- Easy listing process and objectives
- Ability to list modestly priced items
- Improved availability and access
- Simplified shipping; elimination of two-stage process
- Time to conduct due diligence research on items
- Time to think about purchase
- Ease of payment
- Reasonable agent fees
- Minimized time lag between merchandise surrender and compensation

customer wanted a specific item, he or she had to continually keep abreast of the auctions (with the exception of an auction house's top-tier clients). Also, it was very difficult for sellers to get objective assessments of an item's value, and only relatively expensive treasures were accepted for sale. Customers needed improved availability and access to the dealer, less cumbersome and time-consuming listings, researching processes, and time to carefully consider their purchase decisions. Finally, customers needed easier and more expeditious payment mechanisms as well as more reasonable dealer fees.

Determining Target Segments

The next step in the analysis of eBay's market opportunities is to better understand its target customers, those whose needs it would strive to serve, by breaking down the market into meaningful and actionable segments and then identifying the segments of highest priority. Selecting variables (in this case, demographics and behavior) can help segment the auction services market, as follows:

- *Demographics.* A consumer's income correlates with the discretionary income he or she may have to spend on collectibles and other popular auction items. Income is also a leading indicator of a prospective customer's relative price sensitivity. Age and income are also proxy variables for Internet adoption.

- *Behavior.* A customer's historical response to promotions is a proxy for identifying customers who enjoy the pursuit of a deal and/or the act of deal making. This may also be an indicator of a customer's relative price sensitivity. If you consider that consumers in the United States are exposed to thousands of advertising messages daily, many of which include promotions of some type, then consumers with a disproportionately high response or redemption history could be driven by an underlying motivation that causes them to actually seek out promotions, while the segment with a lower redemption rate may be more passive and certainly less motivated by promotional activity. The underlying assumption is that these motivated promotion seekers will be highly attracted to the wheeling-and-dealing environment provided by eBay.

Combining these variables can yield distinct, actionable, and meaningful segments of the market to which eBay could offer its online auction services. Exhibit 2.17 illustrates the market segmentation. It also indicates the target segments of primary, secondary, and tertiary priority for eBay, as well as those segments that were not priorities. eBay clearly started off by focusing on the active frugal collectors, and its initial product assortment was well suited for these segments.

eBay's purchase of the auction house Butterfield & Butterfield, its partnership with Sothebys, and its launch of eBay Premier are clear attempts to expand its customer base into the "active deal makers with means" segment. This subbranding portfolio strategy is implemented as a site-within-a-site concept. It has augmented both the product portfolio as well as the buyer services within the premier site. Here, the website lists items such as $80,000 tapestries and offers a five-year guarantee of authenticity and a 30-day money-back guarantee. Once eBay successfully expands into this second-tier customer segment, it may want to consider adding some features and

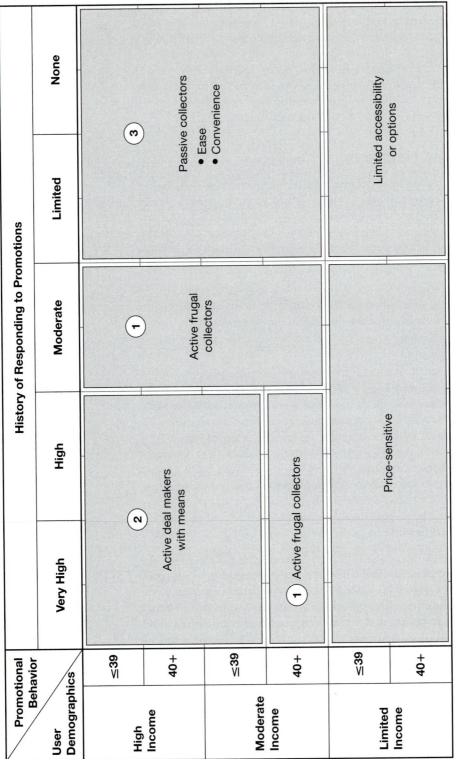

EXHIBIT 2.17   Potential eBay Customers: Identifying Key Customer Segments

① = **Top priority**
② = **Medium priority**
③ = **Low priority**

functionalities to its site and adjust its business model to facilitate and deliver even greater ease and convenience within the auction services industry in order to attract consumers in the tertiary segment.

eBay is also growing its business by expanding its highly successful business model into other industries where similar consumer benefits would match unmet or, in some cases, unarticulated need. With eBay Motors, it developed the strategy and application of its business model for the automotive industry. In essence, eBay's core competencies are matching buyers and sellers, facilitating the deal-making process, listening to customers and responding to their needs, and introducing a meaningful level of ease and convenience into an otherwise inefficient market. In late 1998, eBay managers noticed people were selling not just die-cast toy cars, but actual automobiles. Today eBay is the nation's biggest car dealer, with more than $1 billion in sales of cars and car parts in 2001. It currently operates eBay Motors as a completely separate but complementary brand.

Assess eBay's Resources

The next step is to look at eBay's resource system and determine how to leverage it to its greatest advantage. This can be divided into the following three groupings:

Customer-Facing Resources

eBay's greatest resource in this category is its online presence, represented by the original eBay site, Half.com, and the handful of eBay verticals that are all tied together to create the overall eBay user experience. The common thread is ease of use and customer-friendly features. They also have the shared benefit of strong network effects. The fact that more items are listed on eBay than anywhere else attracts buyers, which in return attracts more sellers. This self-serving cycle is perhaps eBay's greatest asset, outside of its actual Web structure.

Internal Resources

eBay's greatest internal resource is its human assets. Were it not for the few individuals who noticed an uptick in auto-related items while sifting through the enormous amount of data generated by eBay's auctions back in 1998, eBay may never have created eBay Motors or received the significant revenue driven by that business. This points out another important internal eBay resource: data. By tracking listings, sales, message board traffic and other inputs from eBay's operations, eBay is poised to create new features and customer experiences that lead to untapped opportunities.

Upstream Resources

While eBay doesn't have suppliers like traditional retailers (after all, one of the beauties of eBay's business model is that it doesn't have a traditional cost of goods sold since it never takes ownership of the items sold through its many websites), its "suppliers" are its buyers and sellers, without whom all business would stop immediately. Think of the famous tagline, "When E.F. Hutton speaks, people listen," but with a twist: When people speak, eBay listens. By continuing to listen to its buyers and sellers, eBay puts itself in position to provide them with everything they need to be successful.

Assess Opportunity Attractiveness

Competitive intensity is just one of the factors to consider while assessing overall opportunity attractiveness for eBay. Exhibit 2.18 provides a preliminary rating of these factors for eBay in 2002. For example, eBay has a number of positive factors: a large and growing market, high profitability, interaction between customer segments, and the ability to deliver against many unmet and underserved customer needs. At this point, its Achilles' heel is technology. The website faces intermittent stability problems. Although eBay hired the shogun of information technology, Maynard Webb, and has built backup systems, the website still has occasional outages and will need to meet the ever-increasing demands of a huge and dynamic inventory and heavy visitor traffic.

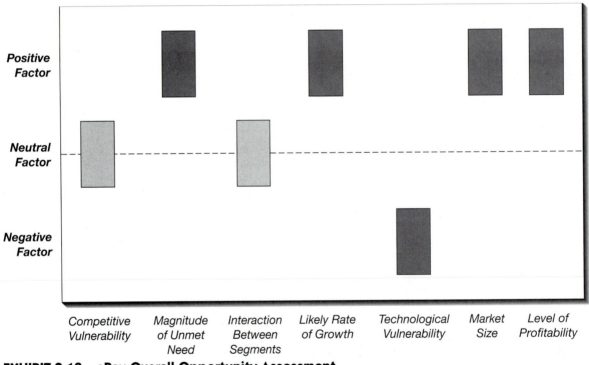

EXHIBIT 2.18   eBay Overall Opportunity Assessment

Summary

1. What is the framework for market-opportunity analysis?

The market-opportunity analysis framework consists of five main investigative stages, as well as a final assessment of the opportunity and a go/no-go decision. The five main stages are: (1) investigate opportunities in an existing or new value system, (2) identify unmet or underserved needs, (3) determine the target customers, (4) assess resource requirements to deliver the offering, and (5) assess competitive, technological, and financial attractiveness.

2. Is market-opportunity analysis different in the networked economy?

Market-opportunity analysis in the networked economy is distinctive in the following five areas: (1) competition occurs across industry boundaries rather than within industry boundaries, (2) competitive developments and responses are occurring at an unprecedented speed, (3) competition occurs between alliances of companies rather than between individual companies, (4) consumer behavior is still in the early stages of being defined, thus it is easier to influence and change consumer behavior, and (5) industry value chains or systems are rapidly being reconfigured.

3. What are the three basic value types?

Firms should look at the value system as a lens that yields ideas about new business possibilities. Specifically, a firm is looking for one of the following: (1) trapped value to be liberated, (2) new-to-the-world value to be introduced, or (3) hybrid value, a combination of trapped and new-to-the-world value.

4. How do marketing managers identify unmet or underserved needs?

New-value creation is based on doing a better job of meeting customer needs. Customers will switch from their old supplier only if the new company does a better job of meeting some set of needs. The customer decision process is an organizing framework to look systematically for unmet or underserved needs. The process maps the activities and the choices that customers make in accessing a specific experience within a value system. The customer decision process lays out the series of steps, from awareness to the purchase experience and through the usage experience. The process of generating a map of the customer decision process may help to generate new ideas about unmet or underserved needs.

5. What determines the specific customers the company is to pursue?

To be effective and efficient, it is essential for the company to know which customer groups are most attractive, which groups the company should pursue, which groups the company should not emphasize, and what offerings to present to which target segment. Customer segmentation, or the grouping of similar customers in order to better serve their needs, must be both actionable (consistent with how the company can take action in the market) and meaningful (correlating to differences in how customers will behave). Simple market maps profiling the segments will identify where the money is, how well competitors serve the segments, and where underserved customers reside.

6. Who provides the resources to deliver the benefits of the offering?

Having determined the initial customer focus of the business, the company should stake out the capabilities and technology needed to deliver the benefits of the offering. The management team should identify at least three or four resources or assets that make up a winning resource system that it can bring to bear, create, or provide through business partnerships. This resource system is central to delivering new benefits or unlocking trapped value, the core of the company's value story, and should hold the promise for measurable advantage when compared with the current and prospective players in the targeted marketspace. A resource system is a discrete collection of individual and organizational activities and assets that, when combined, create organizational capabilities. These capabilities allow the company to serve customer needs.

On its own, a company may not be able to bring all the necessary resources to deliver value to its target segments. In opportunity assessment, a company must be realistic about any missing capability gaps. Partnering may be an effective alternative to building or acquiring the capability. The potential partners for a company can be grouped into two categories: complementors and traditional partners.

7. How do marketing teams assess the attractiveness of the opportunity?

There are nine factors in four areas that marketing teams can assess to determine the character and magnitude of the opportunity:

- *Competitive intensity:* Competitor mapping that shows (1) direct and indirect competitors and (2) their strengths and weaknesses.
- *Customer dynamics:* Levels of (3) unconstrained opportunity, (4) segment interaction, and (5) the likely rate of growth.

- *Technology vulnerability:* Impact of (6) the penetration of enabling technologies and (7) new technologies on the value proposition.
- *Microeconomics:* Estimate of the (8) size or volume of the market and (9) level of profitability.

8. How does a firm prepare a go/no-go assessment?

An opportunity story may be thought of as the first draft of a business plan. The story should articulate the value proposition and the target customers. It should demonstrate the benefits to these customers and the way in which the company will monetize the opportunity. It should estimate the magnitude (in financial terms) of the opportunity, identify the key capabilities and resources, and finally, discuss the reasons to believe. In other words, the story should tell why the company's capabilities will create a competitive advantage for the new business in serving its target customers.

The management team must decide whether to proceed to defining the specific value proposition and designing a business model. This should be the first of several go/no-go decision gates. The team should define the criteria to be met in order to feel comfortable in proceeding to the next step of the business development process. If uncertainty remains about one or more of the gating questions, the management team must judge whether additional analysis would remove uncertainty or if there are ways to proceed while revisiting the areas of greatest concern. The team should not proceed too far down a path toward business model development if it cannot reach a consensus on passing these initial gates.

Activities for Students

1. Choose a product or service and prepare a market mapping exercise for it. What variables would you use to meaningfully segment the market? What are the high-priority segments? Do you think the provider of the product or service is doing a good job targeting those segments? Why or why not?
2. Pick a company that has used both meaningful and actionable segmentation steps online. Demonstrate how the effort met both criteria.
3. Take a closer look at the e-book market, described briefly in the Drill-Down titled, "E-Books: The Market Opportunity That Wasn't (Yet)." Prepare a market-opportunity analysis of this product. Present an argument based on whether you think e-books may still find their market niche.

Key Terms

co-opetition	customer decision process	direct competitors
value system	segmentation	indirect competitors
trapped value	actionable segmentation	
new-to-the-world value	meaningful segmentation	
hybrid value	the offering	
opportunity nucleus	resource system	

Endnotes

[1]Brandenburger, Adam M., and Barry J. Nalebuff. 1996. *Co-opetition.* New York: Currency Doubleday.

[2]Interested readers could learn more about value chains and value systems in the following cited reference: Porter, Michael E. 1985. *Competitive advantage: Creating and sustaining superior performance.* New York: The Free Press; London: Collier Macmillan.

[3]This sidebar is summarized from the following article: Leonard, Dorothy, and Jeffrey F. Rayport. 1997. Spark innovation through empathic design. *Harvard Business Review* November–December, 102–13.

[4]Keller, Kevin Lane. 1998. *Strategic brand management: Building, measuring and managing brand equity.* Upper Saddle River, NJ: Prentice Hall, 317–18.

[5]Pink, Daniel H. 1998. Metaphor marketing. *Fast Company*, April, 214.

[6]Kotler, Philip. 2000. *Marketing management*. 10th ed. Upper Saddle River, NJ: Prentice Hall, Chapter 9.

[7]Value chains are company-specific activities that range from raw materials acquisition through to after-sale customer service (see Porter, Michael E. 1985. Competitive advantage. New York: The Free Press, 37). Activity systems are largely derived from the value chains but focus on the key themes and associated activities that are the most important in the delivery of a differentiated value proposition. Additionally, activity systems focus heavily on the links between activities, reflecting the need to interweave the activities as a network rather than a linear chain. This work was an important influence on the evolution of our resource system perspective.

[8]Porter, Michael E. 1996. What is strategy? *Harvard Business Review* November–December, 61–78.

[9]Rayport, Jeffrey F., and John J. Sviokla. 1995. Exploiting the virtual value chain. *Harvard Business Review* November–December, 75–85.

[10]For an excellent discussion of the resource-based view of the firm, read the article by Collis, David J., and Cynthia A. Montgomery. 1995. Competing on resources: Strategy in the 1990s. *Harvard Business Review* July–August, 118–28.

[11]*ibid*

[12]Porter, Michael E. 1980. *Competitive strategy*. New York: The Free Press, 5.

[13]*Ibid*, 23

[14]For more information on the E66 diagram, please see Sawhney, Mohanbir. 1999. Making new markets, *Business 2.0* (May): 116–21.

[15]Interested persons should refer to these references for further reading: Foster, Richard N. 1986. *Innovation: The attacker's advantage*. New York: Summit Books, and Christensen, Clayton M. 1997. *The innovator's dilemma: When new techniques cause great firms to fail*. Boston: Harvard Business School Press.

[16]Simons, David. 1999. What's the deal: The true cost of marketing. I*ndustry Standard*, 2 December.

[17]*Internetweek.com*, Y2Ks Winner's and Losers. December 18, 2000.

[18]Shapiro, Carl, and Hal R. Varian. 1999. *Information rules*. Boston: Harvard Business School Press. This book contains an excellent and detailed examination of network economics.

[19]Rayport, Jeffrey F., and Jaworski, Bernard J. 2000. *e-Commerce*, McGraw-Hill/Irwin MarketspaceU, Chapter 4.

[20]Bunnel, David. 2000. *The eBay phenomenon*. New York: John Wiley & Sons, p. 22.

[21]Pierre Omidyar's introduction in Kaiser, Laura Fisher, and Michael Kaiser. 1999. *The official eBay guide*. New York: Fireside/Simon & Schuster, p. xv

[22]Stross, Randall. 2000. eBoys. New York: Crown Publishers, p. 50.

[23]Pierre Omidyar's introduction in Kaiser, Laura Fisher, and Michael Kaiser. 1999. *The official eBay guide*. New York: Fireside/Simon & Schuster, p. xv.

[24]See: *http://pages.ebay.com/community/aboutebay/overview/management.html*.

[25]Porter, Kelley. 1999 *eBay, Inc*. 28 September 1999. Boston: Harvard Business School Publishing.

[26]Schonfeld, Erich. 2002. eBay's Secret Ingredient, *Business 2.0*, March.

[27]Temptest, Nicole. 1999. *Meg Whitman at eBay Inc*. (revised 1 October 1999). Boston: Harvard Business School Press, pp. 5–6.

[28]Hof, Robert D. 2001. The People's Company, *BusinessWeek*, 3 December.

[29]Schonfeld, Erich. 2002. eBay's Secret Ingredient, *Business 2.0*, March.

Formulating the Marketing Strategy

Part I provides a detailed methodology for the go/no-go decision of the market opportunity. If the firm gives a "go" decision, next it must carefully craft the high-level components of marketing strategy: target market selection and positioning. This is the focus of Chapter 3.

Market-opportunity analysis can be at a very high level of abstraction, or it can be very granular in its detail. As noted in Chapter 2, market-opportunity analysis should include a discussion of how to segment the market and the specific choice of target segment. If the market-opportunity analysis is detailed and thorough, then a large portion of the strategist's time would shift to the exact positioning strategy of the offering and the detailed development of the marketing program (Part V). Chapter 3 also introduces the various marketing strategy processes and choices for pure-play and traditional firms. This discussion is important because, in the case of the latter set of firms, the marketing strategy choices need to take into account the existing positioning of product offerings. To be concrete, what the bricks-and-mortar store J.Crew does has significant implications for what its online store, jcrew.com, can do with its positioning, marketing program, and brand. We explicitly consider these two alternative marketing strategy pathways in Chapter 3.

Marketing Strategy in Internet Marketing

This chapter discusses how business-unit strategy is linked to marketing strategy and how these links affect the alignment of goals, resources, and activities within the firm. This chapter also explores the basic concepts of marketing strategy while discerning how the marketing strategy process of pure online companies differs from that of traditional bricks-and-mortar (BAM) firms that have decided to move online. A key message of the chapter is that the three components of traditional marketing strategy—segmentation, target market selection, and positioning—still apply in the online environment. However, marketing strategy development is more complicated for BAM firms because they face the unique issue of integrating an existing offline business with a newer online business. The chapter concludes with a discussion of how the marketing strategy process is changing in the online marketplace.

QUESTIONS

Please consider the following questions as you read this chapter:

1. What is marketing strategy?

2. What is an effective segmentation? How does traditional segmentation change for BAMs moving online?

3. What factors should be considered when evaluating segment attractiveness? How does traditional targeting change for BAMs moving online?

4. What are the traditional positioning strategies? How does traditional positioning strategy change for BAMs moving online?

5. How does the Internet affect marketing strategy?

Introduction

The preceding chapters have provided an overview of business-unit strategy and market opportunity analysis. This chapter focuses on the links between business-unit strategy and marketing strategy—in particular, how

---

Co-authored by Javier Colayco. With substantive input from Steve Libenson and Aboud Yaqub.

good marketing strategy is influenced by business-unit strategy. The chapter begins by broadly discussing the links between business-unit strategy and marketing strategy. This discussion focuses on the four types of alignment that must be considered and managed to successfully integrate the two levels of strategy.

Following this discussion is a basic review of **marketing strategy**, which clarifies and defines its traditional building blocks: segmentation, target market selection, and positioning. Importantly, the section also explains how the traditional marketing process remains generally the same when applied by pure-play online firms—but differs markedly when applied by BAM firms. Because BAMs already have existing business-unit strategies, marketing strategies, and marketing tactics, their online marketing strategies will need to take different factors into account. Consider, for example, the Old Navy retail store. Old Navy operates under a well-defined corporate strategy, a well-regarded marketing program, and a positioning message that caters to fashion-forward but cost-conscious families with young children. As Old Navy expands online, it faces a number of new marketing strategy issues such as:

- Is the online retail clothing segment similar to or different from the offline segment?
- Should oldnavy.com target the same customers as Old Navy retail stores, a subset of the same customers, or new customers?
- How should oldnavy.com position its site?

BAMs face the unique issue of making key marketing strategy moves within the context of existing marketing and business-unit strategies. The complexities of these choices will also be explored in this chapter. Finally, the key points of the chapter will be applied to eBay. Because the remainder of this book discusses eBay's marketing choices in more detail, this chapter will examine these choices at their highest level.

How Is Business-Unit Strategy Linked to Marketing Strategy?

Microsoft CarPoint

In examining the links between business-unit strategy and marketing strategy, it might be helpful to start with an example. Consider the case of Microsoft CarPoint (*www.carpoint.com*). Launched in 1996, CarPoint's goal was to own the largest share of auto-related sales and transactions on the Internet. CarPoint spotted two key opportunities: (1) the opportunity to give consumers who were dissatisfied with the offline car-buying process a new way to purchase a car, and (2) the opportunity to capitalize on the trend of using the Internet for retail transactions.

The CarPoint strategy was to become an automobile portal where consumers could undertake extensive research and refine their search for a new car. In terms of customer research opportunities, CarPoint offered videos, prices, independent reviews, and side-by-side auto comparisons. CarPoint also offered a free referral service that sent consumers to a nearby auto dealer. Local dealers paid CarPoint for these qualified leads, and a CarPoint lead was much more valuable than a person simply walking into the dealership off the street. CarPoint users would enter the dealership having fully researched the vehicle; all that was left in the buying process was to test-drive the car. CarPoint's goal was to generate a car sale for every $100 that the dealer invested.

How did CarPoint think that it would win in the competitive purchase environment, and what were the underlying strategic activities in which it engaged in order to deliver these benefits? First, it should be noted that CarPoint (now called MSN Autos) has a number of unique assets:

1. It is the most popular car-buying site. In 2002, over 6 million unique users visited CarPoint every month. CarPoint leads generate $8 billion in auto sales a year.

2. As the most popular car-buying site, CarPoint is able to further leverage the consumer information gained to enhance its value to subscribing dealers.

3. As a Microsoft property, CarPoint enjoys exclusive, free placement on Microsoft Web properties, including the MSN network (the most popular destination on the Web, attracting 210 million unique visitors each month) and Microsoft's homepage.

4. In a field crowded with competitors, CarPoint benefits (from both a consumer and a dealer standpoint) from the strength of the Microsoft brand.

As the auto market evolved, so did CarPoint's services. To encourage customer stickiness, CarPoint offered ownership services that allowed customers to register their vehicles at no cost. Registered owners received service reminders, recalls, repair estimates, and local dealer information. CarPoint also began targeting the used-car market; aside from used-car information, customers were able to access used-car inventories from dealers in their area. CarPoint also enhanced its B2B services with DealerPoint, a customer management tool that helps dealers manage and follow up on Internet sales leads from any Internet referral system (including CarPoint's competitors). The goal of this software was to help dealers manage the Internet sales process, respond to customer enquiries, and cut the average per-car selling costs. In addition, CarPoint sold to dealers customer information such as the makes, models, and accessories of greatest interest to customers.

So how does CarPoint compete from a marketing strategy perspective? As already noted, CarPoint targets new-car buyers, used-car buyers, car dealers, and car manufacturers. CarPoint promotes itself to new-car customers as the one-stop meta-site for new car information; the hope is that once customers have researched a car, they have a strong incentive to take advantage of CarPoint's car-buying service. Similarly, CarPoint positions itself to used-car buyers as a meta-site for used-car information and, just as importantly, a listings service for used-car inventory available at local dealers. For car dealerships and manufacturers, CarPoint promotes itself as the most visited auto-buying site. Finally, leveraging Microsoft's software expertise, CarPoint has created software for dealers to use to manage Internet-related sales leads. Thus, CarPoint's strategy focuses on being the best available auto information site for consumers and converting that into revenue-producing activities such as offering qualified leads and insights on customer behavior.

Ultimately, this positioning strategy is well aligned with CarPoint's business strategy of leveraging its consumer popularity to sell banner advertising, leads, and customer information. The key message here is that effective marketing strategy, as in the case of CarPoint, relates to business strategy through good alignment. Marketing strategy needs to be consistent with the firm's business strategy, goals, and resources in order to be effective.

The Link: Business Strategy Directs Choices of Marketing Strategy

Business strategy, then, should relate to marketing strategy by providing good direction, guidance, and benchmarks for alignment. In the case of CarPoint, it is clear that the firm's strategic focus on providing the best information, value, and inventory was derived from a combination of market-facing choices (e.g., the design of the website, wide variety of information, and customer stickiness) and back-office activities (e.g., lead-generation process, updated auto and inventory information). These broad choices for competitive advantage provided a clear umbrella under which the marketing strategy could be implemented. Once the broad business strategy parameters were set, the choice of positioning and associated marketing mix could more appropriately be set.

A marketing strategy works most effectively when it is highly aligned and consistent with the business strategy. But how, specifically, should a marketing strategy be aligned with business strategy? And in this regard, how should success and progress be measured in this alignment?

Criteria to Assess Alignment between Business and Marketing Strategy

There are four organizational dimensions along which marketing strategy needs to be aligned and integrated with business strategy in order for the two strategies to work optimally. Exhibit 3.1 shows that the fit between the two levels of strategy will be enhanced if there is **alignment** of each strategy's goals, resources, activities, and implementation plans.

Goal Alignment.   At issue in this dimension is whether the strategic and financial goals of the business unit are consistent with the strategic, financial, and customer goals specified by the managers of the marketing strategy. For example, if CarPoint's business strategy looks to rapidly expand into new business segments (e.g., the used-car market), senior marketers within Car-Point should ask if the marketing strategy goals are directly supportive of the business strategy effort. Very often, even a well-intentioned company can misalign goals due to (a) rapidly changing business strategy, (b) poor communication between the senior leaders of the business unit and marketing, or (c) lack of process checkpoints to ensure that the strategy and marketing efforts are in sync.

Resource Alignment.   Assuming the firm has goal alignment, the next question to ask is whether the resources of the business unit and the resource allocation of the marketing unit are consistent. At the beginning of each fiscal year, the business unit develops a budget for how resources will be allocated across various activities, functions, and programs. Within this broader budgeting process, resources are allocated to the marketing organization. The issue here is whether the business unit has provided sufficient resources for a particular marketing program or effort to be effectively implemented.

Consider a possible CarPoint situation in which the business unit has specified performance targets for the used-car segment. At the same time, assume that CarPoint has held constant the marketing budget from the prior fiscal year. On the marketing side, let us also assume that there is no plan in place to hire a marketing manager for the used-car segment, nor is there a line item in the marketing budget for sufficient market resources to go after this segment. In this case, there is an observable disconnect between the nature and degree of the resources allocated from the business unit and the effective implementation of a marketing program.

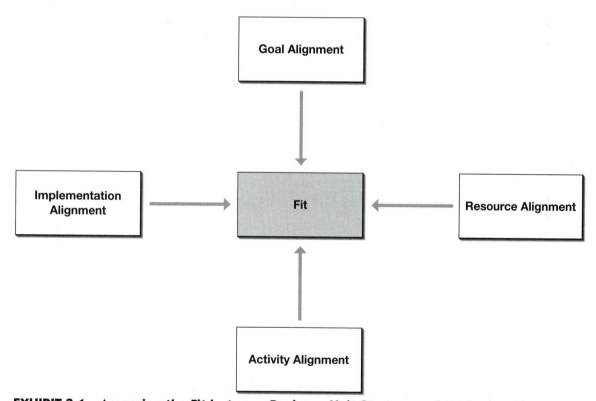

EXHIBIT 3.1   Assessing the Fit between Business-Unit Strategy and Marketing Strategy

Activity Alignment.   Activity or function alignment speaks to the issue of whether the business-unit activities (e.g., human resources allocation for hiring, choice of website design) reinforce the downstream choice of marketing strategy. Put differently, this alignment asks if a firm's activities— order fulfillment, market communications, customer service, and pricing— work together with the marketing effort to provide a consistent offering to customers.

It is important to note that the activities of the business unit need to work together in a complementary way with other organizational units in order for the firm to most effectively go to market. In this particular case, the question is whether the activities at the business-unit level are interlocking with the activities within the marketing unit.

Implementation Alignment.   It is entirely possible that the goals, activities, and resources of the business-unit strategy and marketing strategy are aligned, but the collective strategies are not executed well in the market. This could be due to poor implementation when going to market. Thus, even if the strategies are sound, there could be problems related to timing—for instance, correctly sequencing the marketing program with vendor product availability, or correctly timing the allocation of business-unit resources to effectively implement marketing programs. Thus, significant problems can arise from poor implementation even if the other three dimensions are aligned.

The key message in this section is that business-unit strategy and marketing strategy need to be synchronized. Even in the most well-intentioned firms, a misalignment of goals, resources, activities, or implementation can hamper optimal execution of either strategy. The firm must continually monitor the consistency and fit between these two strategies. Having established the importance of alignment, we now turn to marketing strategy, its key concepts and processes, and how it will differ in various online scenarios.

Marketing Strategy: A Basic Review

Key Concepts in Marketing Strategy

Traditionally, marketing strategy consists of segmentation, targeting, and positioning. This strategy is then supported by the marketing program, which involves decisions related to the marketing mix—price, product, promotion, and distribution (see Exhibit 3.2). All of these decisions are interdependent and interrelated—which makes it difficult to describe the process by which managers make these decisions. For example, marketing managers must sometimes start from a blank slate; in early startup companies, the customer base has often not yet been segmented, target customer segments have not yet been well identified, a positioning message has not yet been established, and the product has not yet been fully developed. In this instance, the marketing strategy might consist of a comprehensive process of segmentation, target market selection, and positioning, then leveraging the rest of the marketing mix. In another example, such as that of a BAM moving online, the product may have already been designed and a minimum price point established. The distribution channel may also be constrained by the firm's distinctive competencies. Accordingly, the marketing managers focus their efforts on the positioning strategy, then communications, and finally the target market. Each decision context is unique.

While the marketing strategy process will differ according to context—for example, the process will not be the same for an online firm as it is for a BAM—senior managers will need to be familiar with the following key concepts in planning any Internet marketing strategy, regardless of how their companies are positioned. Below, the three key concepts in marketing strategy—segmentation, targeting, and positioning—are broadly defined. While not directly related to marketing strategy, the concept of marketing mix is also briefly discussed.

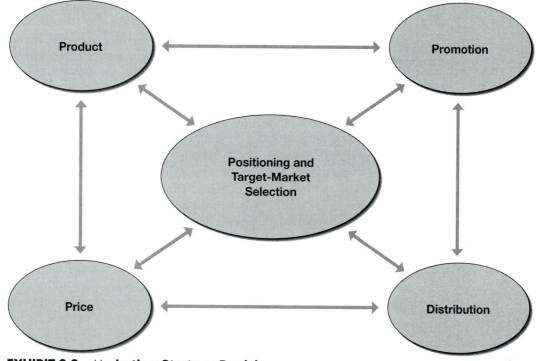

EXHIBIT 3.2 Marketing-Strategy Decisions

Drill-Down

Why Segmentation Matters on the Internet

One reason why segmentation is so important online is because of the changing demographics of Internet users. There are more than 80 million regular Internet users in the United States today. Very early Internet users might typically have been characterized either as students or as high-income, tech-savvy young males. Due to the Internet's increasing growth and accessibility, however, Internet users have become far more diverse. For instance, women now make up almost 50 percent of the online population, and usage among older Americans has also increased significantly. Seniors.com estimates there are between 3 million and 5 million seniors online, and expects that number to reach 20 million by 2006.[1] What was a small, self-selecting segment of the population in the mid-1990s is now becoming a better representation of larger, more diverse offline markets.

Segmentation, then, not only matters in the Internet—it has become more important. As the Internet eliminates boundaries in geography, firms can communicate and reach segments of customers previously difficult to access. And as the base of Internet users continues to grow, change, and become more heterogeneous, there will be an increasing number of marketing opportunities. Segmentation will be paramount in enabling new-economy firms to catch indications of new trends in a rapidly changing market, and consequently, help them take advantage of it.

Segmentation.   Most markets can be usefully divided into subunits of consumers who are similar in what they value within the product category, or in terms of their cost to serve, or characteristics that make them accessible to a particular marketing program. This process is known as **segmentation**, and these subunits are called market segments, and is typically the first step in the marketing strategy process. Two of the key factors involved with a market segmentation is ensuring that the analysis is both action-able and meaningful. Being actionable implies that once a segmentation study is complete, management can take clear actions to activate specific segments. Similarly, a meaningful segmentation implies that management is able to predict customers' behaviors, motivations, and barriers.

Target Market Selection.   The target market is the segment (or segments) of the market most attractive to the firm because of profitability, cost to serve, accessibility, growth potential, or a host of other criteria; the process of identifying and selecting these segments is known as **targeting.** This step follows the segmentation process.

Positioning.   According to advertising executives Al Ries and Jack Trout, **positioning** influences the mind of the prospect.[2] In other words, positioning is about affecting consumers' perceptions of the product. This usually means designing the marketing message so that the product is perceived to be both unique and valued by the target market. As the last step in the strategic decision-making process, positioning also requires a deep understanding of a product's position, or perception, in the minds of its target segment.

Marketing Mix.   Marketing strategy is also deeply integrated with the marketing program, or marketing mix. The **marketing mix** traditionally includes levers such as price, product, promotion, and distribution channels. For this reason, the marketing mix deals more with execution, and is not defined specifically as part of marketing strategy. Still, marketing mix is discussed here because it is often used in conjunction with strategy to help marketers promote the positioning message. While academics and practitioners alike have found that these levers are not as mutually exclusive or exhaustive as they were once thought to be, they still provide a useful framework for decision-making. However, a new set of levers exists in the online world that helps deliver the positioning message in innovative ways. This new online marketing mix is covered in later chapters.

Segmentation Prioritization, Resource Allocation, and Timing

Market segmentation analysis must be both actionable and meaningful. Being actionable implies that once a segmentation study is completed, management can take clear actions to activate specific segments. Similarly, a meaningful segmentation implies that management is able to predict customers' behaviors, motivations, and barriers.

In any segmentation analysis, senior management may find that there are several segments that are interested in the firm's products or services. Once these segments are identified, the firm must prioritize which segments it

should pursue. In general, firms prioritize segments based on selling potential and/or market size. Segmentation prioritization tends to be focused on two things:

1. **Buyer-readiness stage.** The goal is to target the segments that are ready to buy today.

2. **Attitude.** Similar to readiness, firms target the segments that are most receptive to a product.[3]

Oftentimes, firms initially target opinion/market leaders as a way to jumpstart their businesses. Trendy nightclubs tend to prioritize "A" list partygoers and attractive models as a strategy to bring in the masses. Similarly, when the Palm steakhouse opens up a new restaurant, it attempts to attract local leaders by drawing large caricatures of them on the restaurant's walls (see Exhibit 3.3). Once those leaders are drawn to the restaurant, the hope is that the masses will follow.

Firms may also prioritize segments in an attempt to maximize profits in the long term. Take, for instance, the rollout of cellphones or new PDA technology such as PalmPilots. When a new product is rolled out, many different segments may be interested in adopting the product. Instead of targeting the largest interested segment for mass adoption, a firm may instead target the segment(s) that have the highest willingness to pay. In the case of cellphones and PalmPilots, the segments that were willing to pay the most were initially targeted. As adoptions occurred, prices were gradually reduced and the marketing focus evolved to target more of the mass audience. By targeting segments according to their willingness to pay, firms are able to profit maximize.

Resource allocation and the timing of resource allocation are a function of segment prioritization. At an initial product rollout, firms allocate their marketing resources based on the prioritization of their target segments. Thus, it is likely that a firm will unevenly target its marketing resources to different

The evolution of Palm caricatures: A unique marketing strategy

The Palm caricatures serve as an effective local marketing tool as well as a signature element of the famous restaurant. Before each restaurant opens, 200-300 local notables are drawn on its walls and new caricatures are added monthly. Each Palm's walls become a "living mural" of thousands of regular and celebrity customers. A Palm regular who is asked permission to draw their caricature submits an 8x10 color and a few different facial shots to their local management. After a caricature is complete, the patron is asked to come in and sign his or her caricature. The number of caricatures added each year depends on the clientele. In the New York Palm, where space is limited, approximately five caricatures per year are added to the walls.

Many of the memorable moments at the Palm were made when celebrities visit to sign their caricature. Fred Astaire went so far as to tap dance on the bar at the Los Angeles Palm in celebration of his caricature unveiling.

Source: Palm Management Corporation. Used with permission.

EXHIBIT 3.3   Caricature Marketing at the Palm Restaurant

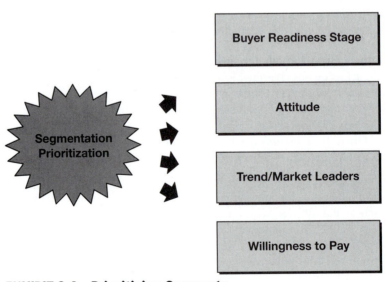

EXHIBIT 3.4   Prioritizing Segments

segments; it would not be unusual for a firm to allocate 70 percent of its marketing resources to its top target segment, 20 percent to its second highest priority segment, and 10 percent to its third highest priority segment.

It is important to emphasize that a firm's resource allocation evolves over time. Thus, while a firm may initially target 70 percent of its marketing resources to its priority target segment, over time, it will reallocate its budget toward other priority segments. This can occur once the firm is reaping solid results from its priority segment and feels that the marginal benefit of its marketing budget dollars would be better used for another segment. This reallocation could also occur once crossover is achieved. Thus, even if the saturation point has not been reached with the primary target segment, it may be profitable for a firm to reallocate its budget in favor of other segments. This often occurs when product adoption by the initial priority segment creates crossover adoption by other segments. For example, PalmPilots were initially targeted toward high-end, technically savvy business executives. Over time, Palm shifted its segmentation priorities toward more of the mass market.

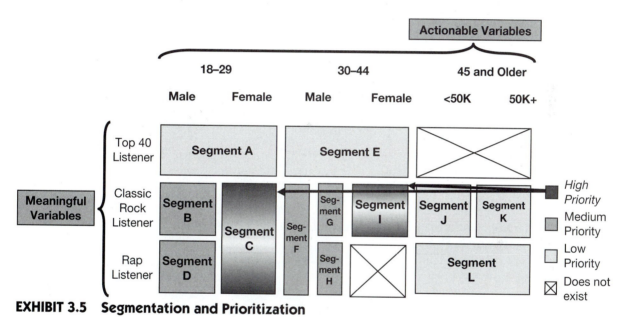

EXHIBIT 3.5   Segmentation and Prioritization

Crossover marketing often occurs in the marketing of movies. The movie *Pearl Harbor* initially focused its marketing campaign on attracting teenage boys by emphasizing the movie's action scenes. However, once the marketing campaign created awareness among this segment, the campaign shifted and began to emphasize the movie's love story in an effort to attract teenage girls.

Internet Marketing Scenarios: Pure Play Vs. Bricks-and-Mortar

So far, this chapter has outlined how segmentation, targeting, and positioning form the basis of traditional marketing strategy. While this strategy can effectively be used on the Internet by both a purely online (pure play) firm and a traditional BAM firm, the marketing decisions that these two players will face

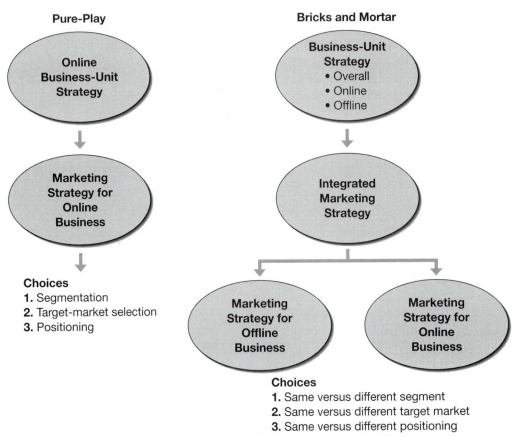

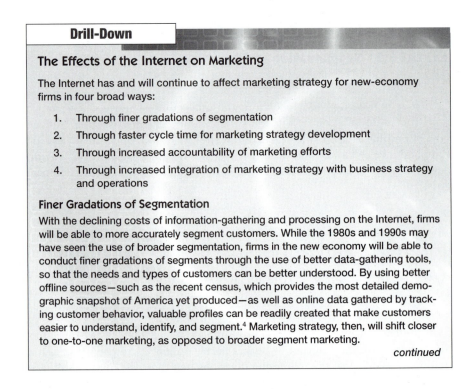

EXHIBIT 3.6   Marketing-Strategy Formulation for Pure-Play Vs. Bricks-and-Mortar Firms

---

Drill-Down

The Effects of the Internet on Marketing

The Internet has and will continue to affect marketing strategy for new-economy firms in four broad ways:

1. Through finer gradations of segmentation
2. Through faster cycle time for marketing strategy development
3. Through increased accountability of marketing efforts
4. Through increased integration of marketing strategy with business strategy and operations

Finer Gradations of Segmentation

With the declining costs of information-gathering and processing on the Internet, firms will be able to more accurately segment customers. While the 1980s and 1990s may have seen the use of broader segmentation, firms in the new economy will be able to conduct finer gradations of segments through the use of better data-gathering tools, so that the needs and types of customers can be better understood. By using better offline sources—such as the recent census, which provides the most detailed demographic snapshot of America yet produced—as well as online data gathered by tracking customer behavior, valuable profiles can be readily created that make customers easier to understand, identify, and segment.[4] Marketing strategy, then, will shift closer to one-to-one marketing, as opposed to broader segment marketing.

continued

Faster Cycle Time of Marketing Strategy Decisions

Marketing strategy will also be affected by the increased speed with which marketers can gather information through the Internet. For example, while customer and management interviews once took months for a given marketing project, now customer feedback and interviews can be gathered continuously and much faster online, so that up-to-date information is always available. As a result, marketing plans can change more quickly and flexibly—more "on the fly"—rather than in discrete projects.[5] In addition, marketers can understand—in real time—which marketing vehicles are most effective. If a marketing campaign includes several different types of banner ads, marketers can determine, by looking at click-through statistics, which banners draw the most attention. This real-time evaluation gives marketers the opportunity to replace less effective marketing vehicles with more effective ones.

Increased Accountability of Marketing Efforts

As information-gathering becomes quicker and easier, so too does tracking marketing efforts. As a result, accountability for good marketing strategy will increase, making marketing successes (or mistakes) more transparent. Accountability for past successes and failures will heighten the awareness and need for good Internet marketing strategy.

Increased Integration of Marketing Strategy with Business Strategy and Operations

Finally, and most importantly, marketing strategy will increasingly become integrated into the different functions of the organization, so that marketing strategy will necessarily become more aligned with business strategy and operations. As firms realize the benefits of alignment in this and other aspects, marketing will increasingly become integrated with various firm-wide goals and operations.

Ajay Kohli and Bernard Jaworski posit that the core of marketing is a focus on the customer through coordinated efforts in the pursuit of firm goals.[6] These authors define market orientation as organization-wide behaviors related to the generation of market intelligence and its dissemination and use across functional areas.[7] Importantly, they also find that this firm-wide, coordinated market orientation is positively related to overall business performance.[8]

This shift to a firm-level orientation has several important implications. First, marketing will not be confined to the marketing department. Rather, it will become a worldview that permeates the entire organization. Providing value to customers will require that a firm's R&D engineers incorporate ideas from a good understanding of what customers want; that finance ensures that customer billing and financing requirements are in place; and that the human resources department makes certain that the call-center staff is properly trained and motivated.

The ultimate focus of all these activities should be on the relative value delivered to the customer given coordinated company objectives. Simply put, winning in the marketplace requires a strong link between marketing strategy and business strategy.

---

can differ significantly. For instance, a pure play that is just beginning its marketing campaign will have more freedom in positioning a product than an offline company that is moving its 20-year-old brand online. Naturally, the options available to each player will not be the same. (Consider the process flow outlined in Exhibit 3.6.) The following sections briefly illustrate the two separate discussion processes that unfold for pure plays versus BAM businesses.

Pure-Play Scenario

The business and marketing strategy formulation process for Internet pure plays such as Yahoo! and eBay is depicted on the left side of Exhibit 3.6. First, the business-unit strategy is defined. Then, the marketing strategy is specified, following the traditional processes of segmentation, targeting, and positioning. It should also be noted that while Internet marketing strategy is employed for the online business, it is highly likely that both online and offline marketing levers (e.g., customer e-mails and print advertisements) are going to be used to build a customer relationship.

In this scenario, the processes of segmentation, targeting, and positioning remain largely the same as for a completely offline business.

Bricks-and-Mortar Scenario

Now consider the marketing strategy formulation process for the retail firm Gap. The first task is to define the scope of the business unit. Let us assume that the business unit has both an offline retail store (Gap) and an online store (*www.gap.com*).

Looking now at the right side of Exhibit 3.6, Gap must first consider its overall business-unit strategy—mission, goals, competitive advantage, and revenue model. Within this context, the firm must develop an integrative marketing

---

Drill-Down

Under What Conditions Should a Firm Incorporate Internet Marketing into Its Marketing Plan?

While the hype of the Internet becoming the holy grail of marketing has died down, it is clear that the Internet can be a highly effective component of a company's marketing strategy. Today, practitioners are struggling to understand whether Internet marketing is relevant, and, if it is relevant, what type of campaign they should undertake. The level of impact that the Internet will have on marketing will vary by industry type. But asking the following questions can help clarify the degree and type of Internet marketing effort that a firm might utilize.

- Are the product's target segments online, and do consumers have to physically inspect the product? If these conditions are true, the Internet can be a significant sales channel and an effective marketing vehicle. Industry examples include books, music, videos, catalog items, travel, software, and financial services.

- Are the product's target segments online, and do the products require significant purchase consideration? If these conditions are true, the Internet has the potential to materially affect offline sales. For these types of products, the Internet can be used both to create awareness and as an exploration/expansion to provide more information to interested customers. A well-designed Internet information campaign can be used to usher customers from the exploration to the commitment stage. Industry examples include automobiles, real estate, and prescription pharmaceuticals.

- Are the product's target segments online, and is the product a highly branded impulse good? If so, the Internet can be used to build and reinforce brand equity as well as marginally lift sales. In this case, marketers are generally limited to branding and reactive Internet marketing levers. Industry examples include beer, tobacco, fast food, and snack foods.

- For other types of products, such as highly commoditized products with minimal brand differentiation, planned purchase consumer packaged products, and products whose consumers are primarily offline, the Internet will likely have a small marketing impact. For these types of products, the role of the Internet is likely limited to promotions/coupons, product sampling, and liquidating excess inventory.

plan, one that reflects both the online and offline efforts. This integrative marketing planning effort combines the marketing effort for the retail stores (noted as marketing strategy for offline business) and the marketing effort for the online store (noted as marketing strategy for online business).

Given that Gap stores preceded the development of the website, it is clear that Gap.com must optimize its online marketing strategy within the context of Gap's broader strategy—its offline positioning, image, and asset base (manufacturing plants, vendor relationships, etc.). Thus, Gap.com strategy is not a "green field" exercise; there are certain contexts and parameters that the marketing strategy must take into account. Formulating the marketing strategy, then, requires choosing the degree of correspondence and consistency between the existing offline brand and assets.

Gap's online marketing strategists must make choices related to (1) segmentation approach, (2) target segment, and (3) subsequent positioning in light of the constraints and opportunities posed by the firm's offline operations and strategic focus. This makes the job of the online marketing strategist very complex. These choices are examined in more detail toward the end of this chapter.

Internet Marketing Strategy: Pure Plays

Pure-play Internet firms can still effectively use the basic building blocks of marketing strategy. In this section, the marketing strategy process for pure-play firms will be more clearly articulated, and it will be shown that the execution of this process remains generally the same online and offline. Throughout this section, several firms within the online automobile market will illustrate key concepts.

Segmentation for Pure Plays

The process of segmentation involves breaking up a market of customers into large, identifiable groups, or segments. This division is done on the basis of certain variables, which can range from age and address to lifestyle and loyalty to a certain product. The logic behind this is fairly simple: Within a large market of customers, it is likely that there will be several subgroups of customers, each with different needs, that one product alone cannot satisfy. Segmentation is the first step in allowing firms to create or market products for specific groups of customers. It reveals potential marketing opportunities and provides a firm with clearer guidance for product development and marketing strategy. Ideally, this strategy also serves customers' needs more appropriately. In return, firms might receive higher sales or higher prices for more effectively meeting a consumer group's needs.

For instance, within the market for automobiles, there may be customers who highly value negotiation-free purchasing and the convenience of buying cars through the Internet. Segmentation can reveal this and other characteristics that groups of customers value. Equally important, segmentation can show the sizes of these groups, or segments, to determine if they are large enough to be financially attractive. A firm might then differentiate and position a product or service so that it meets the needs of a specific segment not currently targeted by competitors.

For example, CarPoint found through segmentation that 17 percent of Internet users were intimidated by or dissatisfied with the car-buying process, and that another 10 percent sought greater information on cars.[9] These segments of users showed high levels of interest in the CarPoint concept of buying used and new cars online, providing CarPoint's founders direction for where to target their marketing efforts. In return, CarPoint received arguably greater financial success than if it had chosen to design and market its services to a broader range of automobile buyers.

Bases for Segmentation.   Though a more detailed approach to segmentation is presented in Chapter 2, it is useful, in discussing marketing strategy, to briefly review the different ways a market can be carved. Marketing literature often cites four broad segmentation categories.[10] Examples of variables within each category are included in the following list.

- Demographic: age, gender, occupation, ethnicity, income, family status, and life stage
- Geographic: ISP domain, country, region, city, and density (urban, suburban, rural)
- Psychographic: lifestyle (e.g., thrill-seekers), social class (e.g., white-collar workers), and personality (e.g., Type A)
- Cognitive and behavioral: benefits sought, usage rate, loyalty status, and attitude toward product

Consumers could be segmented according to one variable, such as benefits sought, or on several, such as gender, ISP domain, lifestyle, and benefits sought. The variables chosen for segmentation will depend on the particular marketing decision. For example, a study to broadly understand the market might include segmentation on the basis of benefits sought, usage patterns, needs, and brand loyalty. Studies on distribution decisions might include variables on store loyalty, benefits sought in store selection, and geography.[11]

Effective Segmentation.   Not all market segmentations make sense—a market might be segmented so minutely, into so many different groups, that the cost of serving each segment separately would be unfeasible. Designing different offerings for too many different groups would prove too costly and unprofitable. Segmentation would also not be useful if, for example, automobile buyers were segmented on an unrelated variable such as shoe size—an individual's shoe size does not factor into his or her automobile purchase decisions. In order for segmentation to be effective, it needs to follow three rules. Segmentation must be:

- Meaningful. It must help describe and explain why customers currently behave in a specific way.
- Actionable. It must allow for feasible execution, in terms of targeting and positioning to that segment.
- Financially attractive. Target segments must be economically worth going after.

Target Market Selection for Pure Plays

During the targeting process, firms choose among the opportunities that segmentation uncovers. For instance, segmentation might reveal groups of customers who have unmet needs—needs not currently being addressed by existing product offerings.[12] These unmet needs can mean potential opportunities for existing or new products to gain position. The next task is to more closely evaluate these segments and decide which is (or are) most attractive.

The marketing strategy now changes to targeting, or the process of evaluating market segments for overall attractiveness, and choosing segments that are consistent with the firm's marketing strategy and capabilities. In evaluating market segments for overall attractiveness, firms can look at three factors: (1) segment size and growth, (2) structural attractiveness, and (3) company resources.[13]

Segment Size and Growth. A primary factor in the targeting process is deciding if the segment would be worthwhile financially—not only now, but in the future as well. Appropriately, attractive segment size depends largely on the firm. For instance, small companies might avoid large segments if they require too many resources to serve. Segment growth is usually a natural attraction for choosing segments; ideally, a firm can hope to grow in line with the growth of the segment. Note, however, that growing segments often attract competitors, which is why other considerations, such as segment structural attractiveness, need to be taken into account.

CarPoint's target segment size is both significant and growing. According to research firm Gomez, Inc., the market potential for online car-buying remains huge. Gomez estimates that approximately 10 million consumers will initiate an automobile transaction online by 2004, with new vehicles representing more than half that number—an overall revenue opportunity approaching $200 billion.[14] As a result, however, the segment has attracted a number of serious online competitors such as Autobytel.com, CarsDirect.com, and cars.com.

Segment Structural Attractiveness. Analyzing a segment's structural attractiveness can provide insight into a segment's future profitability. A segment that may be large and growing may still have many characteristics that make it ultimately undesirable down the road. The most widely used framework for analyzing an industry's current and future structural attractiveness is Porter's five forces model.[15]

Company Objectives and Resources. Even if a segment is financially and structurally attractive, it may not be in a firm's best interest to pursue that segment if it is not consistent with the firm's own goals and resources. A firm's own business capabilities must be able to meet the requirements of the chosen target segments, and different segments necessitate different skills and resources. If a company cannot meet, build, or acquire those necessary competencies, it would be wise to avoid such a segment. Instead, firms would do better to pursue segments that offer them a sustainable competitive advantage.

Positioning for Pure Plays

Once markets have been segmented and targeted, positioning then becomes the next step in the marketing strategy. Positioning allows companies to stake claims about their products in the minds of their target segment, letting companies communicate distinct advantages over competing brands. Strategies for positioning combine strategies for the product, distribution channel, price, and promotion (or marketing mix). Ultimately, positioning will articulate what the brand will stand for in the consumer's mind.

Finally, there are the strategies to promote a particular differentiation. Note that some marketers advocate promoting only one difference—for the sake of a singular, consistent, and easily remembered message—while others say that double or even triple benefit positioning can be successful if a firm is targeting a particular niche. With any of these choices, however, firms should remember that positioning is essentially about sacrifice, and that focus and effectiveness come from choosing not to say too much.

A number of positioning strategies exist, including:[16]

- Positioning on features/service to be perceived as the best in a particular product or service attribute, like style or speed of delivery
- Positioning on benefits to be perceived as effectively providing benefits such as happiness or fun
- Positioning on specific usage occasions to be perceived as being practical and functional for a given purpose
- Positioning on user category to be perceived as the appropriate offering for a specific type of user
- Positioning against another product to be perceived as better than a particular competitor
- Product-class positioning to be perceived as offering a different type of product from what consumers expect (for example, to position a pen as an instrument, rather than a tool)
- Hybrid positioning, or a combination of two or more of the above categories

CarsDirect.com positions itself as "America's No. 1 way to buy cars online." This strategy is primarily a positioning on features/service, because the firm is saying, in effect, that it is unique in executing this particular service. By differentiating itself through its instant, guaranteed low prices along with its full-service financing capabilities, CarsDirect.com is able to create a position that helps it increase the perception that it is trying to build.

The Positioning Plan for Pure Plays

Once markets have been segmented and targeted and a positioning strategy has been chosen, a **positioning plan** can be put into place. Norton Paley outlines five steps that firms should follow when creating a positioning plan:

1. Identify actual product positioning.

2. Determine ideal product position.

3. Develop alternative strategies for achieving ideal product position.

Drill-Down

Target Marketing Strategies

Once the evaluation of attractive segments is complete, specific target segment(s) must be selected. Targeting strategies can mean choosing one, all, or a combination of segments to achieve different goals. Three common strategies for choosing target segments are mass market, niche market, and growth market.[17]

Mass-Market Strategy

As the name suggests, this strategy markets to all customers, attempting to fill the needs of every segment in a market. In big offline markets, larger firms such as Procter & Gamble or PepsiCo are usually the only ones with the resources to feasibly choose this strategy. Firms can cover entire markets through undifferentiated marketing or differentiated marketing. In undifferentiated marketing, a firm ignores segments' differences and offers the market one product. Firms using this strategy hope to appeal to the commonalities of all buyers in the segment and also to reap savings by producing high volume and, consequently, economies of scale.

With differentiated marketing, firms attempt to cover the entire market by offering each segment different products. This delivers a more tailored (and arguably more effective) offering, but also at a higher cost, such as in product design, manufacturing, inventory, and promotion. Most online auto-buying companies are currently practicing a mass-market, undifferentiated strategy. Given that the defined scope of the market is online auto buyers only, this strategy makes sense if other segments within the market might still be small or unprofitable. Hence, most online auto-buying firms offer consumers a similarly wide choice of cars and fairly similar services.

Niche-Market Strategy

Firms can employ a niche-market strategy by choosing to serve one or a few segments. These segments are not the largest segments, but consist of enough customers to make it worthwhile. One benefit of such a strategy is the possibility of avoiding larger firms that are competing in bigger segments. Another advantage is that through specialization, firms do not necessarily have to compete solely on price, and can differentiate their products more effectively than mass-marketed products.

Currently, few (if any) sites practice a niche-market strategy in the online auto-buying industry. This may be due, again, to the notion that niche markets still do not exist in this arena. The online auto-buying market is not fully developed yet, so smaller segments within the market might still be unprofitable to serve. Future niche-market strategies, however, might arise for the online sale of collectible cars or high-end performance sports cars.

Growth-Market Strategy

This strategy chooses one or more smaller but fast-growing segments that will hopefully turn into a niche or a larger segment. The goal here is not short-term profits or return on investment (ROI); rather, it is building volume and future market share. The requirements for choosing this strategy tend to be high: Resources must be adequate to finance growth, and R&D and marketing departments need to be able to quickly identify and develop products for emerging segments. Success with such a strategy almost always attracts competitors, so choosing structurally attractive segments (that have high barriers to entry, for instance) will be critical in avoiding intense rivalry in the future.

Some might argue that most online auto-buying firms are actually practicing a growth-market strategy. Given that the defined scope of the market is all automobile purchasers (offline buyers included), this argument makes sense—online auto purchases are small in comparison to the offline purchases. Furthermore, the focus of many auto-buying firms has generally not been short-term profits, but building volume and market share. How segments and markets are defined can affect how marketing strategy is defined.

4. Select and implement the most promising alternative.

5. Compare new actual position with ideal position.[18]

Step One: Identify Actual Product Positioning.   This step identifies, through consumer interviews or questionnaires, the variables important to consumers and the perceived position of a product according to these variables. This

---

Drill-Down

Alternative Positioning Strategies

Other common positioning strategies exist, but are broader in nature. They tend to focus less on the product and more on the target market and relevant competitors:[19]

Monosegment Positioning

This approach creates a positioning strategy for the preferences of a single market segment. Such a strategy can take advantage of other firms that are less focused but operate within the target segment. The drawbacks are that few sales come from other areas of the market, and that there is an increased susceptibility to downturns in that segment.

Multisegment Positioning

This strategy positions a product between two different segments, hoping to capture sales from both groups. This can be advantageous when segments are small, so that firms can capture economies of scale. Also, this requires a smaller investment than trying to position two separate brands to each segment.

Imitative Positioning

Used in developed markets, new brands sometimes use this strategy to position themselves similarly to an existing successful brand. The hope here is to draw customers away from the old brand. This strategy can work more successfully if other differentiation advantages are promoted, such as lower price or a specific feature improvement.

Defensive Positioning

This strategy can be employed when an existing brand is already in a strong position, but vulnerable to the imitative strategy. By introducing a second similar brand positioned to appeal to the same market segment, a firm might preempt such a competitive move. This strategy, however, cannibalizes customers, resulting in higher investments and lower economies of scale. The logic behind such a strategy is that it is better for a firm to compete with itself than to compete with other firms.

Anticipatory Positioning

Even when research shows no clear customer preference for a particular location in a perceptual map, firms may want to position their products there if they believe customers will eventually develop that preference. Many Internet companies, including Autobytel.com, pursued this strategy, taking big bets that when markets do develop, they would be the first to take advantage of them. When anticipatory strategies are right, firms can often take a leading position in the market and reap long-term benefits. However, as the spring 2000 Internet market downturn showed, when those bets are wrong, the price can be equally great.

Competitor Repositioning

Al Reis and Jack Trout offer another positioning alternative specifically designed to be used when a target market is already being served by a similar competitor. Its aim is to reposition the competition. This strategy can be effective when perceived ideas about competitors' products are revealed as false or misleading. However, repositioning the competition should not be confused with simply benchmarking the competition. Positioning a product as more effective than a competitor's does not reposition the competition. Rather, repositioning occurs when a competitor's offering is now perceived to be serving a different target segment.[20]

step also identifies competitors and their positions in the broader market, primarily through establishing appropriate perceptual maps. These maps visually show where different products serve different segments of the market. The dimensions chosen for these maps should be relevant to the target segment. Perceptual maps can be valuable in finding out views about products, and also for identifying insights on new product or promotion opportunities.

Exhibit 3.7 illustrates a hypothetical perceptual map of the online auto industry (not just purchasing sites, but also sites that offer automotive information) based on a benefits-sought segmentation of auto buyers. Two axes define this perceptual map: (1) pure information-focused sites (e.g., Kelley Blue Book) versus sites that focus on selling (e.g., CarsDirect.com); and (2) the extent to which a site is a manufacturer site (e.g., General Motors) or a site that aggregates all automotive information (an automotive destination site that includes all makes and models, such as Edmunds.com).

Through perceptual maps like this, it is easy to see where firms are competing and how their offerings differ. For example, the perceptual map reveals that the aggregated selling arena is becoming quite populated with competitors, while the manufacturer sites are largely information-oriented.

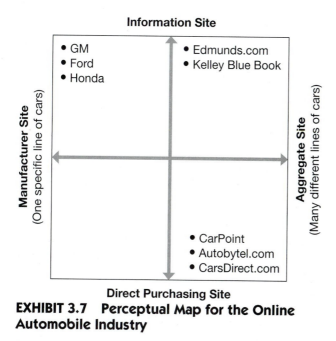

EXHIBIT 3.7   Perceptual Map for the Online Automobile Industry

Step Two: Determine Ideal Product Position.   This step determines how to position a product in a more favorable location on the perceptual map. Determining the ideal position depends largely on the positioning strategy chosen—for instance, if it is monosegment or multisegment positioning. Alternatively, a product's ideal positioning might be found by determining areas on the perceptual map not being served adequately by other products. By measuring customers' preferences for an ideal product and layering them on top of the perceptual map, a firm can see if customers' needs are being met by an existing product. Clusters of customer preferences might appear where there are currently no existing products. This might show potential opportunities for a new product or positioning plan.

Consider the example in Exhibit 3.8. Clearly, there are clusters of customers whose needs are not being met. This might indicate an opportunity to develop a unique offering for that segment, and cater more successfully to its needs. In this example, there is a customer segment in the lower left quadrant that would value the ability to buy a car directly from a manufacturer's website. Automobile manufacturers such as Ford or GM, then, might do well financially by catering to that segment in the future if the market environment is conducive to making such a move. (Today, manufacturers might tend to avoid such initiatives for fear of disrupting existing dealer relationships.)

Step Three: Develop Alternative Strategies for Achieving Ideal Product Position. To achieve a desired positioning, firms can either: (1) attempt to reposition an existing product to a new position, with or without a change in the product itself; or (2) introduce a separate a new product with the characteristics necessary for the ideal positioning.

With either decision, contingency plans should also be created. The plans should account for eventualities in which the market-environment conditions, such as customers' preferences, are different from what the original plan had assumed. Though it is difficult to forecast future events, it can be a useful and potentially critical step in avoiding big marketing blunders.

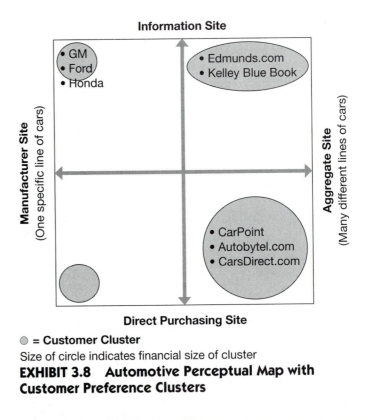

○ = **Customer Cluster**

Size of circle indicates financial size of cluster

EXHIBIT 3.8   **Automotive Perceptual Map with Customer Preference Clusters**

Step Four: Select and Implement the Most Promising Alternative. The success of this step depends on choosing a plan that is the most favorable and consistent with a company's objectives, resources, and strengths. Implementation of the plan should include specific guidelines concerning what activities to carry out, when they should be carried out, who should carry them out, and how they might ultimately be accomplished. A number of factors must be considered in order to ensure the effectiveness of implementation—namely, the skills of the people involved, incentives, and the effectiveness of the communication channels between parties.

Step Five: Compare New Actual Position with Ideal Position. The positioning process must also include measures to track the success of the positioning move. Marketing strategy is an ongoing process that involves decision making, implementation, and the equally important task of tracking. Tracking and evaluation might show that a strategy needs to be reviewed, and that a different positioning strategy may need to be chosen. Also, strategic evaluation of marketing performance should attempt to reveal new opportunities and threats. By serving as the link between the end of a particular strategy's execution and the beginning of a new strategy, evaluation helps ensure that marketing strategy is an ongoing process.

Internet Marketing Strategy: Bricks-and-Mortar

Internet pure plays use largely the same marketing strategy formulation processes as offline firms. Online marketing strategy, however, can still create a different set of choices within each step of the process. This is particularly true for offline companies.

Segmentation for BAMs Moving Online

The basis for segmenting markets will naturally change when offline companies begin looking at customers on the Internet; where variables such as geography were of primary importance in the past, ISP domain might now be considered. Alternatively, new variables such as Internet access speed or computing power might become important. While the methods for evaluating effective segmentation remain the same, the basis for segmentation commonly changes, as do the segments themselves.

Traditional firms new to the Internet will find that online segmentation can yield four different scenarios, characterized in Exhibit 3.9. The first dimension of this matrix focuses on whether the market segment size changes; the second dimension focuses on whether the actual criteria to segment markets change when the firm moves to the Internet. There are four possible results:

No Change. Firms might find that online segmentation does not reveal any significantly new segments, and that the relative compositions and sizes of the online customer segments might be generally the same as the offline segments. A good example would be a firm-specific business-to-business (B2B)

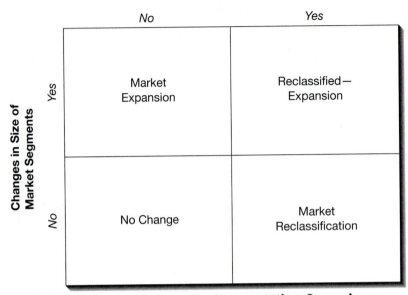

**Change in Segmentation Characteristics
Due to Internet**

EXHIBIT 3.9   Bricks-and-Mortar Segmentation Scenarios

site. Here, there may be few opportunities to significantly increase the size of the market, and the segmentation variables remain approximately the same. In a business-to-consumer (B2C) context, this situation might occur if all or most of a company's offline customers are regular Internet users and exhibit many of the same needs and buying behaviors when using the Internet. Moving online for the firm, then, becomes simple in the sense that online and offline marketing strategy remains largely the same.

Market Expansion.   Firms might find that the characteristics of the online segment are the same as the characteristics of the offline segment, but that the segment size changes. For example, a segment might actually get larger through the increased reach of the Internet. This might happen if a company's offering appeals to many consumers that were previously out of physical reach of the firm. For example, for those interested in French cheeses, there is a website (*www.fromages.com*) that enables users to directly order a wide variety of regional cheeses from France. As the Internet helps eliminate geographic limitations in selling products, firms can now reach more of the same types of consumers. Hence, customer segments might look similar in characteristics, but increase in size.

Alternatively, segment characteristics might stay the same while segment size shrinks. This can happen if only a small percentage of a firm's normal target segment uses the Internet.

Market Reclassification.   More interestingly, online segmentation could reveal that customer segments are different on the Internet, either slightly or significantly. This might be due to the Internet's ability to augment a company's offering (such as through increased service or customizability) and hence create online customers that are more demanding or discriminating.

This can work to the firm's advantage. An interesting example is Reflect.com, an interactive personalized beauty company that is majority-owned by Proctor & Gamble. Reflect.com designs truly personalized products for its customers based on their responses to a series of questions designed by top beauty experts and research scientists. Reflect.com claims to offer over 50,000 possible products and packaging options, and Proctor & Gamble's research labs are used to create the products (see Exhibit 3.10). Given that the Internet offered an opportunity to sell customized products by leveraging P&G's competitive advantages, it made sense that to avoid confusion, P&G opted not to include its brand name in the venture.

Reflect.com focuses on creating customized beauty products for its clients

Source: *www.reflect.com*. Used with permission.

EXHIBIT 3.10   Reflect.com

Reclassified Expansion.   Naturally, and more likely, firms might experience a combination of the previous two scenarios, so that segments might simultaneously change in both size and characteristics. This complicated scenario makes Internet marketing strategy all the more important because targeting and positioning play a crucial role in determining online success. These different scenarios have distinct implications for the targeting process, examined in the next section.

Targeting for BAMs Moving Online

Segments must still be carefully evaluated on the criteria mentioned earlier; chosen segments should be significant in size and structurally attractive, and segment needs should be consistent with firm resources. While the process remains the same, the online choices of segments may be very different from the offline choices.

The following scenarios show four possible strategies in which traditional firms can target online segments in relation to the traditional offline segment. Exhibit 3.11 highlights two important dimensions: (1) the focus of the marketing effort on an entire segment or a portion of a segment, and (2) customer similarity to the firm's offline market (similar or different customers). With this cross-tabulation in mind, four target market options for the BAM firm can be observed.

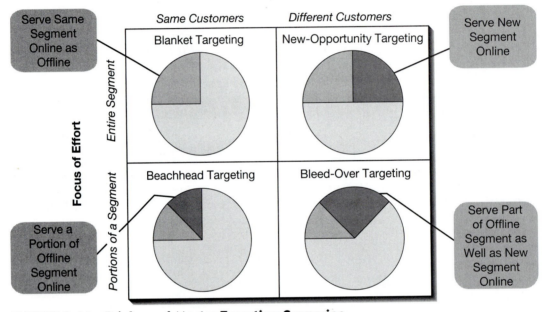

EXHIBIT 3.11   Bricks-and-Mortar Targeting Scenarios

Blanket Targeting. Firms might find that online segmentation does not reveal anything new—that, in effect, the general characteristics of the segments remain the same as those of the offline segments. Alternatively, they may find that segment characteristics stay the same, but that the segments get larger due to factors such as increased geographic reach. Earlier, it was mentioned that this situation might occur if many of an offline company's customers are typical Internet users, more customers are reached through the Internet, and all of them exhibit the same behavior and buying preferences online that they do offline.

In Exhibit 3.11, this is represented by the "entire segment–same customers" box, which shows that all members of the target segment display the same characteristics, online or offline. Hence, the targeting choice also remains the same. The firm's online offering blankets the segment in the same way that it blanketed the offline segment. While the online segment might also value the Internet's added capabilities, such as convenience and accessibility, the target segment's characteristics are generally similar to those of the offline segment. Perhaps the best example of a firm that has experienced this scenario is Schwab.com. The lion's share of Schwab customers visit the Web on a regular basis. Perhaps this is not surprising, because: (1) Schwab's offering is largely an information-based product that can be easily sold online or offline; (2) there is a need for real-time updates of stock quotes; (3) there is similar stock-buying behavior among online and offline customers; and (4) the Web may provide a more convenient environment to manage finances.

Beachhead Targeting.

Another possible scenario arises when the online segment of customers is found to be smaller than the offline segment, perhaps representing a more narrow band of tastes and preferences. This might be true if only part of a firm's consumer base uses the Internet to make purchases. These customers might show increasing preferences for using the Internet (to take advantage of the online offering) but still exhibit generally the same buying preferences as offline customers. Here, the firm's offering might be more targeted to a smaller customer segment, as it attempts to establish a beachhead so that it can attack its larger segment later down the road, when the rest of the segment moves online (see the "portion–same customers" box in Exhibit 3.11). This smaller segment is generally the same as the offline customer segment.

Electronic music companies such as pressplay and MusicNet face a situation where beachhead targeting may be a viable strategy. After all of the electronic music rights issues are clarified, the e-music market will virtually become a commodity. All of the major online players will be selling e-music. Thus, for pioneers such as pressplay and MusicNet to succeed, one strategy may be to focus on a key beachhead segment, such as high school or college students. By focusing on the needs of these key segments, they will be able to use this as a core base for their future expansion into additional segments.

Bleed-Over Targeting.

In this third scenario, the online target segment includes part, but not all, of the offline segment—but also targets part of a distinctly new customer segment. The new target segment might include different types of customers if the online offering is augmented from the offline offering. Here, the targeted segment can include individuals previously ignored in offline targeting choices because the online offering now has something enticing to attract these customers. To return to an earlier example, there may be new groups of online customers who seek increased customizability with their clothes. The Gap website might attract these customers, who would not normally shop at offline Gap stores because of limited choices in clothing measurements and color combinations. This targeting strategy attempts to bleed the online offering to make it attractive for new, slightly different customers. This scenario is depicted by the "portion–different customers" box in Exhibit 3.11, signifying that a portion of the new target segment is different from the offline target segment.

New Opportunity Targeting.

Finally, an online marketing strategy might choose an entirely different target segment. Here, the target customer segment represents distinctly different needs and preferences from the traditional offline segment. This scenario might occur when products take on a different, new meaning for customers in different geographic locations, or if previous marketing campaigns were not able to reach and influence product perception. Typically, this approach involves a new brand name and a new position. A recent example of a firm experiencing this scenario is Amway, which is attempting to revamp its image—and broaden its base—by focusing on online entrepreneurs with the new brand Quixtar.com.

Positioning for BAMs Moving Online

Each of these four scenarios requires a different positioning approach. As was the case in the targeting process, the criteria for effective positioning do not change; positioning strategy must emphasize differences that are meaningful, communicable, and financially attractive. However, the new positioning choices that arise online are still worth examining. Exhibit 3.12 outlines the appropriate positioning strategy and guidelines for each scenario.

Blanket Positioning. In the first scenario, the target segment does not change, and appropriate positioning is fairly simple. A good strategy would likely borrow heavily from existing offline positioning strategies, since the goal is to appeal to the same group of customers. Additionally, the offering would be positioned with the added advantages of the Internet, such as convenience and access.

Beachhead Positioning. In the second scenario, in which the target segment is a subsection of the larger offline segment, the positioning is similar—but might be more focused toward the smaller customer group. A positioning strategy here might stress more of the value-added advantages of the Internet. This positioning assumes that the smaller segment puts more value on the Internet's extended capabilities for convenience and access.

Customer Similarity

	Same Customers	*Different Customers*
Entire Segment	Blanket Targeting • Borrow heavily from existing offline positioning • Tout basic advantages of the Internet—convenience and accessibility	New Opportunity Targeting • Reposition entirely • Position differentiations which cater to the new segment
Portions of a Segment	Beachhead Targeting • Also borrow from offline positioning • Focus more, however, on needs of the smaller group • Stress value-added advantages of the Internet	Bleed-Over Targeting • Use dual positioning • Leverage existing positioning • Position added benefits, such as augmented offerings via the Internet (e.g., increased product customizability)

Focus of Effort

EXHIBIT 3.12 **Bricks-and-Mortar Positioning Scenarios and Guidelines**

Bleed-Over Positioning. The third scenario assumes that the target segment is composed of both old customers and a new type of customer. Here, the positioning would resemble the offline offering, but also make the online offering attractive to new types of customers. Such a positioning strategy will try to appeal to previously different segments. For example, Gap's online store might emphasize Gap's style (appealing to the traditional segment that values Gap's style) while simultaneously stressing the ability to tailor clothes through Gap's online store (appealing to newer segments that place equal value on customizability and fit).

New Opportunity Positioning. This last scenario repositions the offering entirely, attempting to capture the attention of a completely new target segment. Arguably, such a positioning strategy is more effective if previous offline positioning strategies have not yet affected the new segment's perception of the offering. This works, for instance, when increased geographic reach now allows a firm to communicate with new and different customers over the Internet, giving that firm a chance to build a new position.

As with marketing strategy as a whole, positioning becomes a new experience for offline firms moving online. As marketing strategy takes on new meaning on the Internet, clearly there will also be new implications for marketing strategy.

Drill-Down

Changing Marketing Strategy when Going Online

For most traditional firms, going online introduces distinct marketing challenges. Questions about who to target and how to position will inevitably arise. Often, many of these decisions are based largely on targeting and positioning decisions made offline. There are several examples, though, of traditional companies that have successfully chosen to position their image in ways less similar to their offline marketing message. Subsequently, a different target market and positioning message is chosen to transform the company's image.

Shoe manufacturer Hush Puppies is an example of a firm that has been able to transform itself successfully online. Hush Puppies used to be viewed as a maker of boring, comfortable footwear ideal for senior citizens. When the company decided to go online, it knew that it had to create an Internet strategy that would have significant implications both on its product and on its target audience. When the site launched, it featured a colorful, clean design and pictures of young models sporting funky styles. Products included slippers with college logos, and shoes with names such as Rhapsody, Utopia, and Orbit.

Hush Puppies played to the strengths of the Internet and created a remake that proved highly attractive to the company's new online target consumers. By remaking its image to appeal to the casual-is-in crowd, the company was able to position its brand in an entirely new way. Impressively, the firm has achieved this success without alienating its traditional core consumers. Other companies that have found success with e-makeovers include Avon, furniture retailer Ethan Allen, and muffler repair service Midas. These companies were able to achieve their objectives by researching the wants and needs of online consumers, as well as the emotional attributes linked to their products, and then incorporating that data into the brand's Web identity.[21]

---

eBay Example

---

eBay's Mission Statement

eBay's mission is to help practically anyone trade practically anything on earth.[22]

Corporate Strategy

Today, eBay users can bid on anything from office equipment to real estate to cars (see Exhibit 3.13). But when it launched, eBay users traded only collectibles. Because the company originally promoted the exchange of goods among individuals and small businesses, it naturally found itself in competition with classified advertisements, collectibles shows, garage sales, flea markets, and traditional auction houses. Fortunately, the personal trading market was perfectly poised to be transformed by the inherent interactivity of the fast-growing Internet phenomenon, and eBay's strategy took full advantage of this. In fact, consumers' eagerness for change and improvement partially explains the astounding pace at which the company, as well as its categories of products, expanded.

"We help people trade practically anything on Earth."

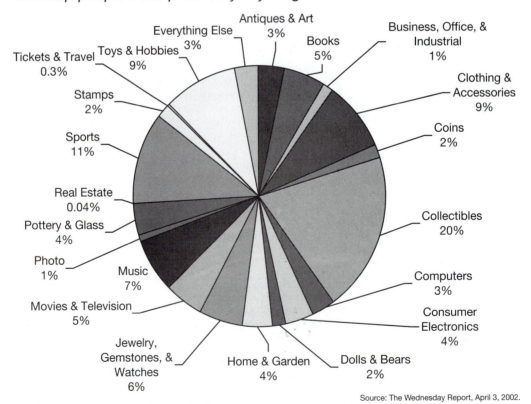

Source: The Wednesday Report, April 3, 2002.

EXHIBIT 3.13   Breakdown of eBay's Gross Merchandise Listed

Of all of eBay's key strategic decisions, three have proved perhaps most important in giving its business unprecedented scalability: (1) allowing anybody to sell anything, (2) adopting a hands-off approach to user transactions, and (3) taking a fanatically customer-focused approach to the business. These decisions allowed eBay to move in whatever direction had the most potential for growth. They also prevented the company from becoming particularly attached to any one product or category and made it possible to commercialize as many items as the current platform held and as many users as were willing to buy or sell.

eBay has embodied the strategic thinking process representative of the Internet era by adopting the flexibility to both change and act quickly. Doing so has proven the notion that successful strategies are often opportunistic and adaptive, rather than calculated and planned, and that the strategy formulation process is characterized by devising quick and reactive solutions to problems and opportunities as they occur.

Why has eBay prevailed where others have failed? Though many of its successes resulted from its adaptive approach, eBay's accomplishments can also be explained by the company's consistent focus on two long-term objectives: building upon its position as the world's leading community-commerce model and pursuing the following four strategic goals:

Strategic Goal No. 1: Broaden the eBay Trading Platform. By 1999, eBay's fourth year, a host of competitors had entered the online auction market. While eBay had the first-mover advantage, not all of its competitors were small startups. Some, including Yahoo! and Amazon, were significant Internet players with extensive, established user bases. eBay's response was to extend its core business into other attractive markets (see Goal No. 2) and categories to maintain its leadership position among the increased competition.

From its beginnings as a grassroots online trading platform, eBay has continually worked to expand its scale and scope to get to and maintain its market-leading role in the online auction world. In its earliest days, eBay had 10 categories in which users could list goods for sale. By the end of 2001, eBay was offering 18,000 categories—5,000 of which were added in 2000 alone.

eBay has expanded not only from internal initiatives but from external initiatives as well. For example, eBay broadened its offerings to include traditional offline auctions through a series of acquisitions. In May 1999, eBay acquired Kruse International, a notable name in the field of collector-quality automobiles and the largest collector-car auction company in the United States. This opened doors to another large market—used automobiles—and another acquisition, that of AutoTrader.com. Also in May 1999, eBay purchased Butterfield Auctioneers Corp., the largest auction house on the West Coast, which specialized in fine art, antiques, and collectibles.

Additionally, with its June 2000 purchase of Half.com, an online marketplace for used mass-market goods, eBay combined its traditional auction-house trading business with a fixed-price business (see Exhibit 3.14). eBay's fixed-price business grew further with its addition of its "Buy It Now" feature and the expansion of eBay Stores; by 2001, 19 percent of all sales revenue came from the fixed-price format.

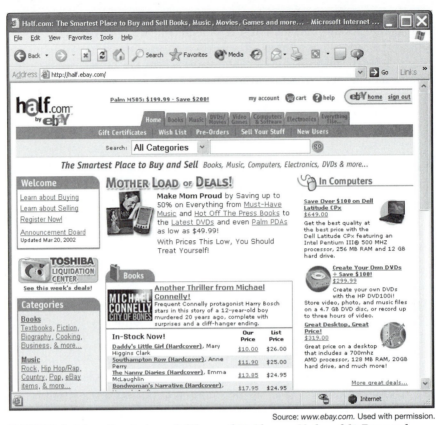

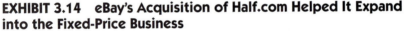

Source: *www.ebay.com*. Used with permission.

EXHIBIT 3.14   eBay's Acquisition of Half.com Helped It Expand into the Fixed-Price Business

Strategic Goal No. 2: Develop Global Markets.   eBay sees considerable opportunity to expand its trading platform to local, national, and international markets. eBay currently attracts users from 200 countries. With country-specific services for Australia, Austria, Belgium, Canada, France, Germany, Ireland, Italy, the Netherlands, New Zealand, Singapore, South Korea, Spain, Switzerland, and the United Kingdom already in place, there are still plenty of markets to expand into.

eBay uses several strategies to enter new international markets, including building a user community solely through internal efforts, acquiring a company already in the local trading market, and partnering with strong local companies. eBay has employed each of these strategies where appropriate, such as in the following instances:

- eBay built its platforms in the United Kingdom, Canada, France, and Italy with local management teams and a combination of grassroots and online marketing programs.

- Its Germany presence was built primarily through the June 1999 acquisition of an existing German trading service.

- In Australia, eBay entered into a joint venture with a subsidiary of one of the largest media companies in the country.

- In Japan, it joined with NEC in February 2000 and created eBay Japan, which was shut down in March 2002—a rare moment of defeat.

- In Korea, eBay acquired a majority ownership interest in Internet Auction Co. Ltd., South Korea's largest online trading service, in February 2001.
- In Europe, eBay announced an agreement to acquire 100 percent of iBazar S.A., Europe's largest online trading platform, in February 2001. IBazar has a leading presence in seven of its eight markets (France, Italy, Spain, Portugal, the Netherlands, Belgium, Brazil, and Sweden).
- In Taiwan, eBay acquired Internet auction site NeoCom Technology, Ltd.
- In China, one of the world's fastest-growing Internet markets, eBay invested $30 million in EachNet, the biggest online trading community in China, with 3.5 million registered users.

In addition to its global expansion, eBay has local sites in over 60 U.S. markets. These sites deliver a distinct regional flavor and give users the convenience of shopping locally for difficult-to-ship items such as automobiles or antique furniture.

Strategic Goal No. 3: Enhance Features and Functionality. By staying close to its customers, eBay is able to reinvent itself on a daily basis and offer new features that its customers want. For example, in January 2001, after an eBay user suggested speeding up auctions for impatient bidders, eBay debuted its Buy It Now feature that lets bidders end an auction at a set price. Now, 40 percent of all listings use it, attracting more mainstream buyers and helping close auctions nearly a day faster on average than a year earlier.[23]

Because eBay's strategy is to be as hands-off as possible when it comes to transactions, the company has to provide a reliable and straightforward way for users to manage the entire auction process on their own. Buying and selling on eBay are made easy for users of the site through the constant implementation of feature and functionality enhancements. eBay has been evolving from its earliest days into the user- and feature-friendly site of today (see Exhibit 3.16). Some of the notable enhancements to its features and functionality include:

- **Online Payments:** To enhance the payment process—an admitted difficulty for most buyers and sellers—eBay acquired Billpoint in May 1999. Billpoint's online bill payment service made it possible for buyers to e-mail their payments to sellers—a major improvement in both time and ease to paying by check or money order. In July 2002, eBay announced its intent to purchase PayPal, the leading online bill payment provider to eBay sellers, for $1.5 billion.
- **Live Auctions Technology:** Introduced in 2000 on eBay Premier, this feature provides real-time bidding via the Internet, enabling individuals to participate in live sales from auction house floors anywhere in the world.
- **eBay Stores:** This feature gives sellers a merchandising showcase for multiple listings and makes searching and shopping easier for potential buyers. Over 27,000 eBay stores have been created since they were introduced in September 2001.

Strategic Goal No. 4: Foster Community. As noted earlier, eBay has emphasized community-building since its founding. In order to further strengthen the connection that its users feel with the site and with each other, eBay introduced a variety of services, including chat rooms, bulletin

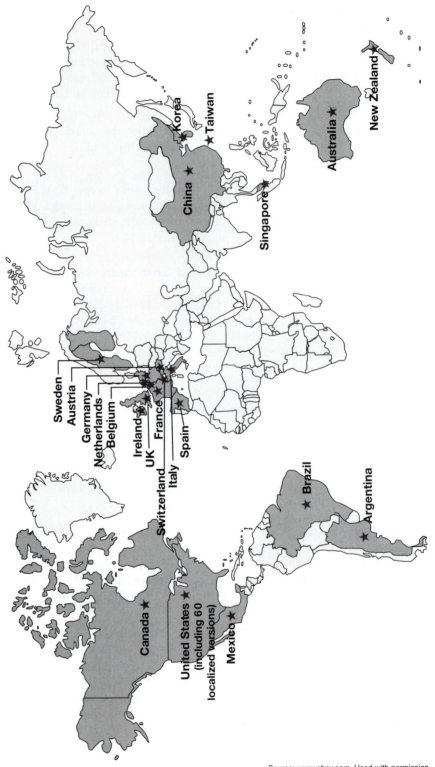

Source: *www.ebay.com*. Used with permission.

EXHIBIT 3.15   eBay's Global Expansion

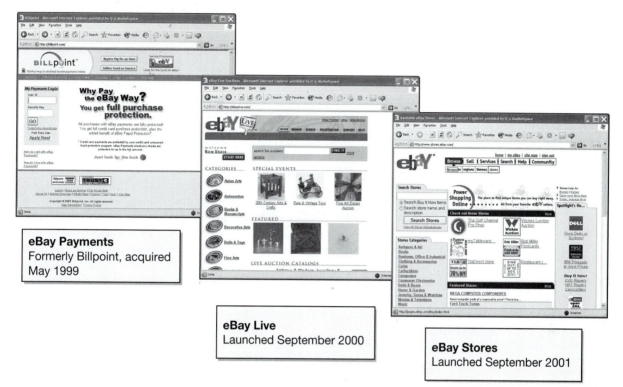

eBay Payments
Formerly Billpoint, acquired
May 1999

eBay Live
Launched September 2000

eBay Stores
Launched September 2001

Source: *www.ebay.com.* Used with permission.

EXHIBIT 3.16   eBay's Constant Evolution

boards, customer support assistance, feedback forums, site customization, and personal pages. Moreover, eBay's trust and safety initiatives—which include user verification, insurance, vehicle inspections, escrow, authentication, and appraisal—further positioned eBay as a user-centric site by promoting credibility and reliability. Some of the other customer-centric activities eBay has introduced over time include:

- **Message Boards (Fall 1995):** After being swamped by e-mails asking for help, eBay founder Pierre Omidyar created an online bulletin board for users to share tips. Since then, more than a dozen forums and chat rooms (with 100,000 posts a week) have been created, forming a community of eBay loyalists.

- **Buyer/Seller Ratings (February 1996):** After watching customers discuss ways to gauge the trustworthiness of other buyers and sellers, eBay created a ratings system.

- **Responding to User Feedback (Spring 1996):** Users constantly e-mail Pierre Omidyar with suggestions. During the day, he answers them. At night, he makes changes to the software to incorporate the suggestions. That makes users eager to offer advice, keeping support costs down.

- **Safe Harbor (February 1998):** Following complaints about fraudulent buyers and sellers, the company created its Safe Harbor program, offering services such as fraud reimbursement and identity verification. Today, less than 0.01 percent of auctions involve fraud, versus an average fraud rate of 0.09 percent for credit cards.

- **Voice of the Customer (April 1999):** Every few months, eBay flies 10 users from around the country to eBay's San Jose headquarters. The gatherings serve as ongoing focus groups to help eBay improve its service.

- **eBay University (August 2000):** After sellers clamored for training to improve their auctions, eBay began offering classes. Called eBay University, the program has attracted more than 20,000 people in 19 cities. It's a great marketing tool as well: Within a month, these users double their activity on eBay.[24]

Business-Unit Strategy

Fusing corporate and business-unit strategies can attract customers, but done poorly, it can also drive them away. One problem faced by online auction sites is achieving and maintaining a critical mass of sellers and buyers. While adding new business units, eBay has maintained constituents in both camps and achieved adequate numbers that keep each coming back. Still, eBay must be careful not to sacrifice corporate goals for those of individual business units. Such a lack of focus could cause significant problems with resource allocation and damage the company's valued sense of community.

From a business-unit standpoint, vertical segments can be clearly identified within eBay's business model. One could argue that each vertical falls under the "anything you can trade" umbrella, but the truth is that eBay had to develop a specific set of skills—including item handling, auction formatting, and customer support—to address the particular needs of each vertical. With this in mind, eBay can be split into four verticals, or specialty sites: eBay Premier, the offline high-end art and antiques market; eBay Motors, the car market; Half.com, the fixed-price market; and eBay Stores, the small-business market (see Exhibit 3.17).

How does each vertical's strategy stay in line with the company's overall strategy? How deep is each vertical, and what opportunities might eBay have to develop them further? To answer these questions, consider four aspects for each vertical: target audience, type of merchandise exchanged, business-unit goals, and competitive advantage.

eBay Premier.   Most buyers in this vertical are accustomed to the refined, high-priced world of traditional offline auction houses. Sellers tend to be reputable auction houses or recognized international dealers. Their merchandise comes from the consignment inventory of leading auction houses and dealers (including eBay-owned Butterfield & Butterfield). eBay Premier's goals include leveraging the eBay brand to a community that once regarded—or perhaps still regards—eBay as a flea market, while expanding the reach of its offer not only to a more select niche but also to the general community. It can achieve these goals by using its competitive advantages, namely providing any Internet user exposure to auction items that he or she might not otherwise have known about and offering a faster turnaround pace than that of traditional dealers.

Butterfield & Butterfield's offline operations remain untouchable, and its scope has remained practically unchanged since it was founded in 1865. It had a target audience very similar to the online auction world, though its sellers and buyers prefer to attend offline auctions. Essentially, the acquisition provided eBay with an influx of higher-priced inventory than its more

	eBay Premier	eBay Motors	Half.com	eBay Stores
Large User Base	Expands reach of offer to specific customer niche and general community	Offline car buyers, sellers, and collectors	Differentiated user base of customers averse to auction-like transactions	Targets profitable small-business segment
Local and International	Serves local and international users	Serves local and international users	Serves local and international users	Serves local and national interests
Strong Brand	Leverages eBay brand to traditional auction house community	Leverage eBay brand to collectible and used-car buyers and sellers	Sellers cost-effectively sell relatively inexpensive items previously prohibitively expensive to list	Provides sellers with a merchandising showcase for multiple listings and buyers with a single shopping destination
Broad Trading Platform	Expands core business	Expands core business	Expands core business	Expands core business
Community Affinity	High-end items appeal to a more affluent demographic	Replaces classified ads for sellers and used-car showrooms for buyers	Sellers can list items by entering the ISBN or UPC barcode number of their item, along with the item's condition and selling price	People can pick up or deliver items to others in their vicinity
Features and Functionality	Stable source of traditional auction house merchandise	Access to inventory and channels	Opportunity to roadtest fixed-price trading without risking core business	All of a seller's auctions are available in one place

EXHIBIT 3.17   eBay's Business-Unit Strategies

typical auction items. However, the company has yet to take advantage of the acquired client base.

eBay Motors.   From auto accessories to luxury sport cars, thousands of vehicles, parts, and accessories are sold on eBay Motors every day. Spurred by the phenomenal growth of the auto category on eBay, eBay Motors was officially launched as a separate site in March 2000. It proved an immediate success, landing in the list of largest categories for 2001, along with computers, consumer electronics, collectibles, books/movies/music, sports, and toys. The business unit's mission is to leverage the eBay brand to attract offline car buyers, sellers, and collectors by offering a fast and efficient one-stop shopping model.

Half.com.   Users of Half.com tend to be differentiated from the traditional eBay user. Auction lovers are excluded, because the used books, CDs, DVDs, and games offered in this vertical are traded at a fixed price. To become the No. 1 e-commerce site for used, mass-produced commodities goods, Half.com intends to expand its product categories by leveraging eBay's user base and infrastructure. It offers eBay users an alternative to the bidding format, attracting buyers who are averse to auction-like transactions and exposing eBay's dynamic-pricing model to Half.com's user base.

Half.com gives eBay the opportunity to road test fixed-priced trading without risking its core auction business. Also, the vertical's activity system is easily connected to that of the larger company, making it a transparent means of transaction for traditional eBay users. Half.com and eBay share a series of operations, such as customer service, database access, and maintenance and security features.

eBay Stores.   eBay Stores expands the marketplace for sellers by allowing them to create customized shopping destinations to merchandise their items on eBay. For buyers, eBay Stores represents a convenient way to access sellers' goods and services all in one place. For example, buyers are able to make immediate and multiple-item purchases for fixed-price and auction-style items. Buyers can also search for items and browse among stores across all categories from the eBay Stores Directory.

Many companies have expanded their businesses by opening eBay Stores; software and services giant IBM was one of the first sellers featured as part of the eBay Stores grand opening. eBay hopes to retain such sellers by providing them with all the tools they need to run their businesses online while ensuring them access to eBay's 42 million-plus user base. It is this combination of tools and potential customers that is eBay's competitive advantage over second- and third-tier online selling platforms.

After reviewing these four business segments, it is clear that eBay has been able to (a) maintain both an online and offline business focus, (b) efficiently operate individual business units under a single corporate umbrella, and (c) maintain a customer-centric operations mentality, offering buyers and sellers in each vertical a similar user experience.

Evaluating eBay Using Five External Market Tests

To expand the discussion of eBay's strategy beyond the classical strategic framework, it is important to evaluate the company using external market tests. The five key tests on firm strategy are evaluated below.

1. **Inimitability: Is the Resource Hard to Copy?** eBay's resources could easily be copied. Another Pierre Omidyar could create another eBay overnight and strike quick deals with a variety of other heavyweight players. However, the barriers to market entry are enormous because user reach, seller/buyer balance, and community loyalty—the cornerstones of eBay's success—are extremely hard to attain.

2. **Durability: How Quickly Does the Resource Depreciate?** eBay operates in a very dynamic environment, which means that the evolution and upgrade of its resources are crucial guards against depreciation. eBay has grown and built numerous resources that have proved robust, such as its community of users and its mutual promoting agreements.

3. **Appropriability: Who Captures the Value that the Resource Creates?** eBay certainly holds the most valuable resource for auction-like sites: critical mass. The company extracts significant profit from its community. Firms with similar business models—even

those that offer incentives such as free listings—have not achieved even a fraction of eBay's success.

4. **Substitutability: Can a Unique Resource Be Trumped by a Different Resource?** A different format of seller/buyer transaction could undermine eBay's successful model—if eBay is not able to adapt quickly to the changing environment, which is unlikely. Auction aggregators also pose a significant threat.

5. **Competitive Superiority: Whose Resource Is Really Better?** eBay has improved substantially in terms of committing internal resources to improving customer experience. Other sites such as Yahoo! or Amazon might still have better services along certain dimensions, but eBay has a near insurmountable lead, and one resource in particular that cannot be replaced: a large and fiercely loyal community.

Reflecting on eBay's strategic choices, the company's decisions determined how the company would compete in the marketplace. An argument could be made that eBay's mission to "help practically anyone trade practically anything on Earth" is too broad. However, examining how eBay has used its acquired business units illuminates the company's unique position in the marketplace. Furthermore, eBay has managed to adopt and adhere to a clear philosophy of community. It is a fundamental strategy that has drawn customers and linked corporate and business-unit goals.

eBay's Marketing Strategy

eBay's marketing strategy will be studied throughout this book; this section is intended to give a general overview of that strategy. eBay's broad marketing strategy can be characterized as targeting the mass market with a very broad positioning appeal. While eBay's fixed-price venue for selling goods is growing, the majority of its revenue originates from the auction segment.

Segmentation

Exhibit 3.18 shows an offering-based segmentation of the auction market. Two broad dimensions classify customers and the type of offering they seek: (1) type of offering and (2) breadth of business. With respect to type of offering, two options are specified: mass market (offering a wide range of market products) or niche (a narrow but deep range of a specific product category). Breadth of business includes traditional auctions, online auctions, and multitype retail (companies that include both auction and retail formats). When these two dimensions are cross-tabulated, five major segments emerge. eBay has developed products and platforms to address all of the sections—except the niche retail segment. However, eBay could enter this segment by creating product-specific versions of its Half.com brand.

Targeting

eBay as a whole is a mass-market service. Hence, it can lucratively target a mass audience. However, much like Procter & Gamble, eBay practices a differentiated, mass-market targeting strategy—meaning that it uses variations

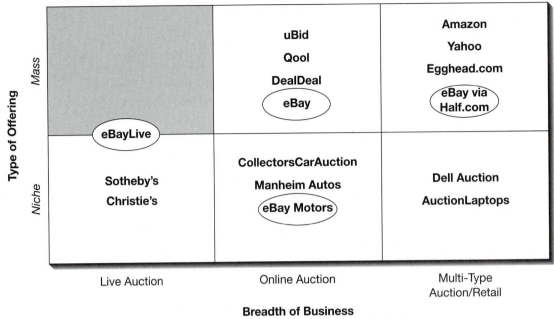

EXHIBIT 3.18   Offering-Based Segmentation of Auction Market

on its product to cater to different subsegments, effectively covering the mass market. eBay recognizes that while mass online and fixed-price formatted services are attractive to many, there are subsegments within the market that seek more specialized services and might shy away from a generic auction service—which is why eBay offers special services for smaller segments.

Positioning

How does eBay position itself? eBay's positioning message revolves around being "the world's online marketplace." This tagline expresses two of eBay's key benefits: (1) the size of its membership and product offerings, and (2) its sense of developed community. eBay has positioned itself as a global business with products so varied that they would attract consumers from around the world. By positioning itself as a marketplace rather than simply an auction site, eBay communicates its emphasis on community and the sense that there is more to the site than business transactions alone. The firm's positioning message consistently supports, and is in alignment with, the corporate strategy set out by eBay—selling nearly anything through a friendly, welcoming environment.

Summary

1. What is marketing strategy?

Marketing strategy has three main components: (1) segmentation, or identifying relevant market segments with specific needs; (2) targeting, or choosing an attractive segment consistent with a firm's resources and goals; and (3) positioning, or strategically communicating the product's benefits to the target segment.

2. **What is an effective segmentation? How does traditional segmentation change for BAMs moving online?**

For a segment to be effective, it must be: (1) meaningful (it must describe and explain why customers currently behave in a specific way); (2) actionable (segmentation must allow for feasible execution, in terms of targeting and positioning to that segment); and (3) financially attractive (segments must be describable and attractive in terms of their monetary growth, size, and profile, so that they are large and profitable enough to serve). Online segmentation can yield four different scenarios for BAMs moving online: (1) no change (segment characteristics and size stay the same); (2) change in size (segment size, financially or otherwise, changes); (3) change in characteristics (segment characteristics change, such that online consumer segments have distinctly different needs and tastes); and (4) change in both size and characteristics.

3. **What factors should be considered when evaluating segment attractiveness? How does traditional targeting change for BAMs moving online?**

Factors that a firm should consider when evaluating segment attractiveness include its size, growth, and structure, as well as the firm's objectives and resources. When applying traditional targeting to BAMs going online, the firm could (1) blanket target, or target all of the old offline segment; (2) beachhead target, or target part of the old offline segment; (3) bleed-over target, or target part of the offline segment and part of a new segment; or (4) new opportunity target, which means targeting an entirely different segment.

4. **What are the traditional positioning strategies? How does traditional positioning strategy change for BAMs moving online?**

Strategies for positioning combine strategies for product, distribution channel, price, and promotion. Such strategies entail differentiation as well as public awareness of such differentiation. For the positioning to cause significant impact in the market, the differentiation has to be meaningful—in other words, it must be valued by customers, communicable, clearly understood, and financially attractive. For BAMs moving online, positioning and targeting follow a similar scenario. When the target market does not change, positioning repeats the offline strategies with some additional pluses, such as convenience and access of the Internet (blanket positioning). When the target segment is a subsection, positioning should stress the value-added advantages of the Internet (beachhead positioning). If the target market consists of both old and new customers, another positioning strategy should be devised to attract this new group; the positioning could be a variation of the offline strategy (bleed-over positioning). Lastly, if the target market is entirely new, a completely new positioning strategy could potentially be used (new opportunity positioning).

5. **How does the Internet affect marketing strategy?**

The Internet affects new-economy firms through (1) finer segmentation; (2) faster development of marketing strategy through faster information-gathering; (3) increased tracking and accountability of marketing efforts; and (4) increased integration with business strategy and operations.

1. Select a well-known offline company that has entered the online market with a new opportunity strategy (e.g., the P&G/Reflect.com example in the chapter). Why did the offline company pursue this strategy? How was the company able to leverage its offline strengths in the online market? Should the company have pursued a new opportunity strategy or used a blanket, bleed-over or beachhead strategy?

2. Select a website that is clearly trying to target more than one segment. How does the site target different segments? Is the site's segmentation strategy effective or is the overall message blurred by targeting more than one segment?

3. Select an online company and describe how it created its five-step positioning plan (identify actual product positioning, determine ideal product position, develop alternative strategies for achieving ideal product position, select and implement the most promising alternative, and compare actual position with ideal position).

Activities for Students

Key Terms

marketing strategy	marketing mix	new opportunity targeting
alignment	positioning plan	blanket positioning
segmentation	blanket targeting	beachhead positioning
targeting	beachhead targeting	bleed-over positioning
positioning	bleed-over targeting	new opportunity positioning

Endnotes

[1] Statistics taken from Jupiter Media Metrix, November 2001. Figures also cited from Ferri, Lisa. 2001. To grandmother's house we go. TNBT.com, 30 January.

[2] Ries, Al, and Jack Trout. 1993. Positioning: The battle for your mind. New York: Warner Books.

[3] For more information, see Kotler, Phillip. 2000. *Marketing management*. Upper Saddle River, New Jersey. Prentice Hall.

[4] Merrier, Amy. 2001. Counting on the census. *Wall Street Journal*, 14 February, B1.

[5] Ellis, Michelle. 2001. Just-in-time marketing. *ClickZ*, 1 February.

[6] Kohli, Ajay K., and Bernard J. Jaworski. 1990. Market orientation: The construct, research propositions, and managerial implications. *Journal of Marketing* 54, April, 1–18.

[7] Kohli, Ajay K., Bernard J. Jaworski, and Ajith Kumar. 1993. MARKOR: A measure of market orientation: *Journal of Marketing Research* 30, November, 467–478.

[8] Jaworski, Bernard J., and Ajay K. Kohli. 1993. Market orientation: Antecedents and consequences. *Journal of Marketing* 57, July, 53–70.

[9] Rayport, Jeffrey F., Avnish Bajaj, Steffan Haithcox, and Michael Kadyan. 1998. *Microsoft CarPoint*, Boston: Harvard Business School Publishing.

[10] Donnelly, James, and Paul J. Peter. 1994. *A preface to marketing management*. Burr Ridge: Irwin, Chapter 5.

[11] For further discussions on segmentation bases for particular marketing decisions, see Wind, Yoram. 1978. Issues and advances in segmentation research. *Journal of Marketing Research* 15, August, 317–337.

[12] Aaker, David A. 1992. *Strategic market management*. New York: John Wiley & Sons, Chapter 3.

[13] Kotler, Philip. 2000. *Marketing management*. Upper Saddle River, NJ: Prentice-Hall, Chapter 9.

[14] Eisenmann, Thomas, and Gillian Morris. 2000. *Case update: MSN CarPoint*. Cambridge: MarketspaceU.

[15] Porter, Michael E. 1980. *Competitive strategy*. New York: Free Press.

[16] Kotler, Philip. 1994. *Marketing management*. Englewood Cliffs, NJ: Prentice Hall, 307.

[17] Boyd, Harper, and Orville Walker. 1990. *Marketing management*. Boston: Irwin, Chapter 10.

[18] Paley, Norton. 1989. *The manager's guide to competitive marketing strategies*. New York: AMACOM, Chapter 9.

[19] This positioning classification was created by Jean-Claude Larreche (Fontainbleau, France: INSEAD).

[20] See Ries, Al, and Trout, Jack. 1993. Positioning: The battle for your mind. New York: Warner Books.

[21] Williams, Claudine. 2000. Company e-makeovers: Starting over and over, established companies going online see the chance to reinvent themselves. TNBT.com, 8 December.

[22] *http://pages.ebay.com/community/aboutebay/overview/index.html*.

[23] The People's Company, *Business Week*, 3 December 2001.

[24] eBay: Of the People, by the People, for the People, *BusinessWeek*, December 3, 2001.

Designing the Customer
Experience

Once a firm has decided upon the positioning of its offering, it must clearly articulate the customer experience that it wants to create. The customer experience
articulation process can be considered a bridging exercise between the high-
level positioning strategy (Part II) and the tactics of the marketing program (Part
V). Part III focuses on the design of the customer experience. In this chapter we
define customer experience, describe a number of attributes, and provide a simple process that can guide firms in their design of a customer experience. We
also introduce the crucial notion of a customer experience hierarchy.

Customer Experience

The purpose of this chapter is to introduce and define the concept of customer experience. The chapter begins by discussing the seven elements of customer experience. It then proposes an experience hierarchy that outlines the three stages that customers go through as they become loyal to a site or product: functionality, intimacy, and evangelism. Next, we describe seven essential steps that website designers should take to optimize their sites from the user's perspective. The chapter concludes with a discussion of customer experience as it applies to eBay.

QUESTIONS

Please consider the following questions as you read this chapter:

1. What is customer experience?
2. What are the seven elements of customer experience?
3. What are the three stages of the customer-experience hierarchy?
4. What steps must a firm take when designing a desirable customer experience?

Introduction

Chapter 3 discussed marketing strategy—the process of segmentation, targeting, and positioning. Once a firm has decided how to position its offering, it must then clearly articulate the customer experience that it wants to create. This chapter focuses on the critical elements of this customer experience. The customer-experience articulation process can be considered a bridging exercise between the high-level positioning strategy (Part II of the book) and the tactics of the marketing program (Part V).

This chapter articulates a precise definition of customer experience. It introduces the experience hierarchy as a way to begin thinking about the concept, and also about the way customer experience evolves over time. Seven steps are advocated that will guide firms through the process of designing a desirable customer experience. Ultimately, these steps provide proper direction for the creation of the broader marketing program, to be discussed in the following chapters.

Co-authored by Kate Bernhardt. With substantive input from Javier Colayco, Ives Moraes, and Bruce Weinberg.

**Finding Hidden Customers;
Megan Smith, PlanetOut CEO**
"Gay and lesbian people are
among the most underserved
customers or community out
there, in terms of products that
really help people. You see
things like the couple in Des
Moines who have been paying
two auto policies for 12 years,
even though they've been a
couple, because they're too shy
to go in and talk to their insurance provider. These are called
pain points. They go through
commerce pain points all
throughout the day. You know,
trying to check into a hotel, and
they don't know if it's gay-
friendly, and the person's trying
to give them twin beds instead
of double beds. Or they're trying
to order flowers for their partner,
and hang up because they don't
want to say, 'Jim, I love you,
Bob.' And even in a more
extreme case, in the United
States you can be fired, in 39
states, for being gay. And you
can lose your housing. So people are really smart, and they
know, for their economic well-
being, they better not come out.

"But the Internet is a place
where they can be out. And so
PlanetOut is a destination
where they can find other people, find information, find entertainment, and find these kinds
of products that they can't find
in other places. So the business
is very much there. And there's
a customer who very much
needs this product. What's
interesting is that it's a $450 bil-
lion consumer buying power in
the U.S. alone, which is actually
a market larger than the Hispan-
ic market, and it's just shy of the
African-American market, and
yet completely untappable without an Internet, because of the
closet. Ninety-five percent of
the customers are hiding, and
won't identify in regular space."

*Get the full interview at
www.marketspaceu.com*

Definition of Customer Experience

The term **customer experience** is now commonplace in business periodicals. Many traditional publications as well as networked-economy publications tout the importance of building a unique, positive customer experience. What is not commonplace, however, is an accepted definition of the concept. In general, customer experience refers to a target customer's perception and interpretation of all the stimuli encountered while interacting with a firm. Hence, the customer experience at Starbucks includes reactions not only to the core product—the coffee itself—but also to the ambiance of the retail store, the merchandising, the cashier, and even the other customers. It includes all the desired or intended stimuli designed by Starbucks management, as well as nonintended and customer-initiated stimuli. The customer experience, then, is not solely based on the taste of that cup of coffee. Similarly, customer experience online includes the entire range of a visitor's perceptions of a website, from its ease of use to the emotional reactions to the site's content.

Consider the company NextCard (*www.nextcard.com*). The firm's tagline positions it as the "next-generation" credit card, and the firm's stated purpose is to make buying on the Web easy and hassle-free. Consistent with this message, its "concierge service" automatically fills in online merchant forms and remembers passwords when online transactions are completed. Account activities, such as paying bills online, reviewing checking balances, and transferring funds, are managed via the Web. Account information can be downloaded into Quicken or Microsoft Money. NextCard users also enjoy features such as live chat and account-balance alerts.

What is the customer experience for NextCard? Is it simply about the ease of using a credit card on the Web? Or is it much broader?

Let us also consider PlanetOut (*www.planetout.com*), the leading gay and lesbian website. Visitors expect more than basic functional elements such as message boards and community features. Underlying this feature functionality, PlanetOut exhibits a clear respect for privacy and other member concerns.

But when PlanetOut merged with another gay and lesbian site, Gay.com, PlanetOut's loyal membership base became concerned. Some members feared that the union could result in a more restrictive environment, less innovation, and more homogeneous information. The concern, in effect, was that a monopoly-like aggregation of competing sites would lead to less experimentation and responsiveness from members.

Is customer experience about how users react to the site and its associated community? Certainly. Yet, as in this example, it also mirrors the deeper interpretation of the encounter, moving much of the experience from the realm of site functionality to emotional, noneconomic considerations.

What do these two examples have in common? They both involve the development, nurturing, and harvesting of a customer base that has internalized and personalized the meaning of the experience on their own terms. The notion that customers can identify with a company—from prepurchase to purchase to postpurchase—is an old one. What is new is the idea that a rich, deeply personal customer experience can be created in a technology-enabled environment such as the Internet. How can a screen-to-face experience create as meaningful and trusting a relationship as face-to-face interaction?

At a minimum level, organizations need to deliver a consistent, clear, and dependable series of transactions (whether economic, as in the case of NextCard, or noneconomic, as in the case of PlanetOut). However, outstanding customer experiences deliver much more than traditional functional benefits such as the delivery of the right product at the right time at the right price. When customers initiate a relationship that expands beyond economic transactions—in other words, when they link themselves emotionally, symbolically, and experientially to the firm—the firm is able to realize much more than enviable profits or high levels of loyalty. In addition, the firm may find itself with a base of zealous customers who protect, market, evangelize, and defend the brand. Yet while the potential benefits to both customer and company are profound, the Internet-enabled experience, if handled poorly, can also significantly erode customer confidence—the last thing a company wants in today's online environment, where word-of-mouth spreads widely and uncontrollably.

An Example of Customer Experience

Consider the recent experience of a customer at Gap.com (*www.gap.com*). He found the website simple and straightforward, with plenty of white space, easy navigation, and clearly marked clothing categories. He searched the site for an everyday outfit for a 1-year-old and quickly found exactly what he was looking for, although it was obvious that the inventory was much more limited than in the Gap's physical stores.

Next, he proceeded to the checkout section, where two problems arose. First, he had trouble estimating shipping costs until the end of the transaction—no small consideration, since he was ordering just one item. He did, however, receive an e-mail at checkout with the exact amount of the total purchase, including shipping. While the number was a bit higher than he expected, he proceeded with the transaction. However, as he clicked on the final approval, he received an incorrect order summary. Rather than displaying his purchases, the site displayed the invoice for purchases that his wife had made the previous day. Because he did not know how to generate the correct invoice (nor did he care to e-mail the site for follow-up service questions, which he felt would be too cumbersome and time-consuming), he abandoned his shopping cart and moved on to a competitor's site.

If customer experience is defined as the user's interpretation of his or her complete encounter with the site—from the initial look at the homepage through the entire purchase experience, including the decision to abandon a shopping cart—what was this particular shopper's customer experience? It had some positive components: the site's ease of use, its functionality, and its intuitive placement of products. The incident with the incorrect invoice, however, resulted in a negative net result, and Gap.com lost the sale. The customer might return to the website someday, but that is by no means certain.

Seven Key Elements of the Customer Experience

There are seven key elements of the customer experience. These elements are related to the ways customers perceive their experiences, and they point to different methods by which users' interactions with a site can be evaluated. Collectively, these seven elements constitute the whole customer experience.

The Objective Element.   A basic level of functionality must exist in order for a site to be experienced as "working." If expected features are nonexistent, if links are broken, or if directions are impossible to interpret, it is easy to identify the problem. Other examples of **objective element** problems include complex checkout, poor site reliability or accessibility (e.g., the site is "down"), poorly designed or implemented search software, outdated information, and incorrect price listings. These are objective in the sense that almost all target consumers and third parties would agree that they are problems.

The Perception Element.   Each customer's experience is unique. While the objective aspect of customer experience focuses on the absence or disrepair of core functionality, the **perception element** relates to the individual's interpretation of each encounter with a firm. Some customers may not have noticed or cared about Gap.com's limited online inventory; others may have had quick and easy checkouts with clear invoices. Hence, their evaluations would have been much higher. The point is that every experience needs to be understood in terms of how each customer interprets his or her interactions with a site. The same site, with the same functionality, may be perceived differently by the same customer on different occasions, depending on how well the site fulfills the customer's needs at that time.

The Encounter Element.   Customer experience takes into account the entire customer encounter, not simply a single economic transaction. Thus, the **encounter element** includes both process and output measures of the shopping experience. The shopper who abandoned his Gap.com purchase noticed the inventory, the prices, and the delivery times, as well as contextual features of the website. But on another occasion his purpose may simply be to browse or to search the inventory for gift ideas. For that type of encounter, the customer experience may be defined largely by the ease of search, quality of the inventory, prices, and the contextual feel of the site—with no weight assigned to an economic transaction.

This is a critical point because many online retailers track output marketing measures—number of visitors, conversion rates, average order size, and frequency of purchase—and make inferences about customer experience from this data. There are two types of customer measures: those that capture outputs such as the direct measures just noted, and those that track the process of using the site. In order to fully track reactions, it is important to assess both process and output measures. Viewing site logs for customer traffic patterns can reveal areas of highest usage and give important functional clues for eliminating inefficiencies. Streamlining traffic flow can enhance the customer experience, increase conversion rates, and effectively delay dissolution. When output measures are off course, it can often be traced to customer process. Moreover, the objective measures often focus only on the transaction, not the comprehensive encounter. The lesson is perhaps obvious: The focus of data collection and assessment must be on both process and output measures throughout the encounter.

The Reactions-to-Stimuli Element. In a retail context, the **reactions-to-stimuli element** include a customer's response to the storefront, signage, store layout, merchandising, ambiance, and background music, as well as the traditional service encounter with the retail sales staff. It also includes reactions to higher-order stimuli, including brand presentation, other customers in the store, the retail location, and product assortment. Capturing the offline customer experience means measuring and assessing reactions to multiple variables, from the tactical layout of the store to high-level interpretations of the meaning of the brand.

The same is true for the online experience. Gap.com is consistent with Gap retail stores in terms of brand feel, presentation of merchandise, and types of merchandise, and this consistency is likely to prove reassuring for the online shopper. Hence, the user's online customer experience reflects his or her reactions to both tactical design decisions and the higher-order strategy choices of the firm.

The Sensory Element. Gap.com stimulates only one sense (sight) through text, photographs, and graphics. However, many sites now enrich the sensory experience by including audio files or the option of making direct contact with a service representative. Retail stores also include experiences related to touch, smell, and taste (for example, those that include cafeterias or

---

Drill-Down

Put Yourself in the Customer's Shoes

Offering customers a great overall experience can be a lot more difficult than one might think. This chapter offers several insights regarding what makes up the customer experience, and how firms can take steps to improve it. Unfortunately, even with a sound understanding of the key elements of the customer experience, many firms still fail in this area. The reason can usually be traced to one pitfall: looking at the offering from the firm's perspective rather than from the customer's perspective.

Companies often invest heavily in customer relationship management (CRM). But in order to make CRM effective, organizations first need to understand what their customers see and feel when using their sites. For example, online retailers should conduct extensive testing to find out what it is like to buy something from their websites. Testers need to go to the website, search for products, place orders, register complaints, and even call customer service. Customer interviews are another invaluable tool.

The results of such research will often show a breakdown at critical points of the customer experience. Slow or irrelevant responses from sales representatives, confusing navigation, disorganized content, and poorly executed postpurchase activities are typical examples of such breakdowns.

Once a firm understands the experiences that customers have on its site and where the breakdowns occur, it can start to create a more customer-friendly environment. Key to this process is the integration of all parts of the overall experience so that they work together seamlessly. When it comes to customer experience, the chain is only as strong as its weakest link. A weak link means lost sales and lost customers. When all the links are strong, the result is increased sales and happy repeat customers.

restaurants). To the extent that it is relevant, assessment of the customer experience needs to incorporate all five senses. This is not to say that all sites need to provide audio, video, etc. Our point is that a comprehensive assessment of the customer experience should take all sensory input into account, and careful evaluation of customer needs and expectations should drive the use of **sensory elements** online.

The Cognitive and Emotional Element.   Customer reactions can be both **cognitive** ("I think the site is easy to navigate") and **emotional** ("I feel good about this brand"). Cognitive responses are more thoughtful and evaluative in nature; emotional responses tend to capture the moods, attitudes, and feelings of the customer. While the author had a number of strong, positive cognitive reactions to the Gap.com site ("It is easy to use, and the colors are pleasant"), he also had strong negative, emotional reactions. ("Why can't this site track my order correctly? How did this mixup occur? Does this invoicing problem mean that my wife's purchase is also questionable?")

The Relative Element.   All consumers have prior shopping experiences, and most have experiences on other websites. This **relative element** affects a consumer's reaction to various stimuli during a website visit or a purchase. A consumer's prior experiences set up a number of expectations, and how well or poorly those expectations are met significantly influences the judgment of the current customer experience. To return to our recurring example, the Gap.com customer undoubtedly compared that experience to experiences he has had on other retail websites or at physical stores, when there were no confusing invoices or cumbersome customer service.

This scenario captures the essence of relative experience. All consumer experiences are compared with some other experience, whether online or offline or even tangentially related. The conclusion here is that rating customer experience on a 10-point scale—or on questions such as "How easy was the navigation?"—is not the best method. Rather, one needs to evaluate experiences relative to experiences with competitors or best-of-class experiences, whether online or offline. Hence, the experience of using Barnes & Noble.com is always judged relative to users' experiences at both Amazon.com and Barnes & Noble retail stores.

Stages of the Customer Experience: The Experience Hierarchy

This section further explores the concept of customer experience by introducing the **experience hierarchy**. This hierarchy includes three stages of customer experience, from a user's first click on a website to the point at which that user experiences site loyalty, or even site evangelism. It is clear that customer experience evolves over time, and that the process occurs in distinct, progressive stages. These stages also imply that certain customer experiences at one stage cannot be achieved without first meeting the prerequisites of the previous stage. For example, a customer who experiences intense loyalty must first pass through a stage that involves feelings of intimacy with the firm or website. In each of the following subsections, the focus is on the defining

Point–Counterpoint

Customer Experience Vs. Building Brand—What Is Mission-Critical for Startups?

Online startups face daunting challenges as they strive to become successful, profitable, well-known businesses. They must make important strategic decisions about where to focus their attention. One popular strategy is to concentrate on branding and building awareness; another is to make customer experience the focal point. While both elements are certainly vital and must be included in a company's overall strategy, which one should take precedence?

Those in the first camp argue that branding and awareness are the secrets of success in today's online business. Of course, customer experience is vital, but investors need to see site traffic and the likelihood of profitability. Hence, offering a great customer experience when nobody knows about the site is fruitless. Once the brand is established, awareness achieved, and traffic generated, then the customer-side details can be worked out. As long as the customer experience is meeting a baseline functional standard, honing it can be put off.

Others argue that focusing on customer experience is the single most profitable thing a business can do. Online businesses that design an optimal customer experience will find that consumers are more likely to visit and return. Positive customer experience leads to purchases at e-commerce sites, exploration of content sites, and involvement with community sites. Furthermore, when the customer experience is particularly effective or desirable, users tell their peers about it. Firms that don't focus on customer experience—opting instead for expensive advertising to build brand awareness—risk blowing their budgets on getting consumers to visit their sites once. Ultimately, the proponents of this viewpoint warn, failing to create an effective customer experience will fail to create repeat customers—a firm's most profitable source of revenue.

characteristics of each stage from the customer's perspective. To a lesser extent, we also discuss the broad goals that a firm can set to achieve these responses and move individuals through each customer-experience stage (see Exhibit 4.1).

Stage One: Experiencing Functionality— "The Site Works Well"

It is not an exaggeration to say that a positive customer experience can result from consistently delivering the basics. At a recent conference, the CEO of a large, well-known retail chain said that its profitability would increase by 50 percent if the company could simply implement the basics correctly—that is, deliver the right products to the right retail store in the right time period. He guessed that those three basic elements have a 50 percent impact on the bottom line. In the online world, understanding the basics can mean the difference between a satisfied customer and one who won't return. These core principles are outlined below.

Usability and Ease of Navigation.   Usability is measured by how well a website anticipates a user's needs and creates an intuitive path that allows the user to achieve his or her goals. If a customer wants to search inventory, check prices, or make a purchase, usability would describe the degree to which the site facilitates or hinders the achievement of those goals. Usability is affected by many elements, including load speed, page structure, and graphic design.

Stages	If a Firm Gets This Right . . .	This Is What the Customer Experiences
Stage One: Functionality	• Design and information architecture • Deep understanding of customer behavior • Platform independence • Efficient transactions	• Site is easy to use • Quick download • Intuitive navigation • Site reliability
Stage Two: Intimacy	• Warehousing and mining • Tailoring of pages and offerings • Overlay human interaction • Integrated data • Consistent performance over time • Constant innovation and upgrading (incremental or significant)	• Personalization • Increasing trust • Repeated experiences of exceptional value • A sense of "being in the know" • Consistent experiences • Significant benefits relative to other offerings
Stage Three: Evangelism	• Support of evangelists • Acknowledgment of evangelists	• Desire to take messages to the market • Community benefits

EXHIBIT 4.1   Stages of Customer Experience

Speed. Speed refers to the time required to display a webpage on the user's screen. Despite the increasing availability of high-speed Internet connections, many consumers still use slower dial-up modems, so every bit of information must count. Graphics-heavy pages may be pleasing to designers, but customers want to accomplish their goals, not wait for irrelevant images to download.

Reliability. Reliability describes the extent to which a website experiences periods of downtime, or times when users cannot access its pages because of planned maintenance or system crashes. Reliability also is affected by how often the website downloads correctly; though the site may be running, it may not appear properly on users' screens.

Security. "Is the site secure? Will my privacy be protected? Can I trust the site with my credit card number?" In asking these questions, consumers want to know if they can trust a particular website. If this basic trust is violated, it affects not only the individual company but the entire industry. But when security and convenience are combined, the customer experience is enhanced. For example, users of PayPal can complete online transactions securely and anonymously. This leads to consumer confidence, which gives competitive advantage to websites that offer the PayPal option for payment.

Media Accessibility. With the proliferation of Internet-enabled devices, media accessibility—a website's ability to download to various media platforms—is becoming increasingly important. Hence, websites may need to be simplified and specifically designed for multiple platforms until there are accepted standards across all platforms.

The five characteristics in this section represent the price of entry to play in the online world. However, firms often violate these basic tenets by designing graphics-heavy sites, overloading the customer with information, or creating complex navigation. Each holiday season, consumers tell horror stories about products that did not arrive or incorrect invoices. The end result is that customers are not likely to visit those sites again. See Chapter 5, Customer Interface, for further discussion of these five characteristics.

Stage Two: Experiencing Intimacy—"They Understand Me"

If a company is able to provide the basics of functionality, it is positioned to move its customers to the second stage of the experience hierarchy—an experience that invites intimacy with the firm.

Customization. Customization is a website's ability to change itself for each user. Customization initiated or managed by the firm is called tailoring; customization initiated or managed by the user is called personalization. For example, most portals, including Yahoo (*www.yahoo.com*), allow users to create personalized pages that reflect their needs and interests. Users modify the standard offering so that it suits their own purposes by specifying particular news categories and sources, creating individual stock tickers, tracking weather conditions in any city in the world, and viewing local television programming. In turn, Yahoo! can use the personal-profile data entered when users register to tailor e-mail messages, banner ads, and content to the individual—and even to post a happy-birthday message across the top of the My Yahoo! page on the user's birthday.

Once the functionality groundwork is laid, the user begins to assess the degree to which the website provides a rich, meaningful experience that is customized for him or her. Customization moves the customer from "Does the site work?" to "How effectively does it meet my individual needs?"

Communication. Communication refers to the dialogue that unfolds between the site and its users. This communication can take three forms: firm-to-user communication (such as e-mail notification), user-to-firm communication (such as a customer-service request), or two-way communication (such as instant messaging). The website of the clothing company Lands' End (*www.landsend.com*) has a communication feature called Lands' End Live that lets users communicate with a customer-service representative while shopping. Clicking the Lands' End Live button gives the visitor two options: connection by phone or connection by live text chat.

Clearly, good communication requires high performance on the part of the online vendor. This can be measured in terms of efficiency (i.e., time to respond) as well as effectiveness (i.e., accuracy of response). Again, because this second stage concerns the intimacy of the customer experience, key metrics become less relevant. Instead, the focus shifts to customization. Communication is discussed in more detail in Chapter 9.

Consistency. Consistency refers to the degree to which a customer's experience at a website or retail store is replicable over time. A customer may have one good experience purchasing from the Lands' End website. The consistent replication of that experience, however, is another matter.

This difference can be explained by the expectancy/discrepancy notion of customer satisfaction, which holds that customers establish a reference level of expectation. For example, a customer's first order with Landsend.com

---

Drill-Down

Nordstrom.com Provides Online Shoppers Better Search Capabilities

Perhaps the most important issue facing e-commerce websites is profitability. In order for them to become profitable, they need to attract customers, but they also must be able to sell merchandise to browsing online customers. To that end, upscale retailer Nordstrom redesigned and revamped its website, Nordstrom.com.[1]

In an effort to enhance its customer experience (and, in turn, its sales), Nordstrom.com first improved its search capability. It hired a full-time editor to analyze the online behaviors of its users, including the search terms they commonly used. Because fashions and fashion trends can be called virtually anything, using only a technical search methodology was likely to result in inaccurate searches, user frustration, and lost sales. With human intervention, esoteric terms were made meaningful and relevant, so that when customers conduct searches they are more likely to find the items they are looking for.

By developing a better search function, the company fulfilled several criteria of the first stage (experiencing functionality) of the experience hierarchy. The better search enabled users to find what they are looking for (usability), conduct faster site searches (speed), and search the site according to customer terms, not industry terminology (reliability).

This new browser also fulfills the customization criteria in the second stage (experiencing intimacy). By adding the human intervention component to the search technology, Nordstrom.com provided a behind-the-scenes mechanism that let users search the site with their own fashion terminology.

With the introduction of the new browser, the relaunched Nordstrom.com experienced a 32 percent increase in website sales. Nordstrom continues to serve its customers by taking additional action: At press time, Nordstrom's search was provided by AltaVista, providing even more relevant matches to their customers' search requests.

---

might arrive in three days. In this case, the three-day delivery becomes the expectation. If the customer places several orders and receives them all in three days, and then for some reason has to wait six days for an order to arrive, the customer will probably be unsatisfied. The point is that expectations are established during the user experience, and deviation from these expectations—not the objective experience itself—is what ultimately matters.

Trustworthiness.   Can the customer trust the website, the salesperson, and the firm? Trustworthiness is a trait that is established over time, after users have had several opportunities to evaluate a company's services. Trust does, however, imply a certain degree of intimacy, which is why its development begins in this second stage.

Exceptional Value.   At this stage, the user is convinced the firm offers exceptional value, and he or she cannot be easily persuaded otherwise. Every consumer has an attachment to brands, products, or experiences that cannot be explained using pure economic logic. If asked, "What products do you believe provide exceptional value that you cannot wait to share with other users?" nearly everyone can easily identify the products he or she values most. The products may vary widely, but they are usually well known. Customers can become convinced and unwavering in their belief that the products they identify are the best. These are loyal, committed users.

Drill-Down

Customer Experience at the Home Shopping Network

The Home Shopping Network (HSN) has been very successful at selling retail items. In 1999, the firm sold $1.2 billion worth of feel-good items such as clothing, jewelry, and dolls to its 5 million viewers through a 24-hour lineup of cable television shows. Mark Bozek, president and CEO of HSN, attributes the firm's success to the entertainment the show provides. According to Bozek, many people click to the channels simply to watch, yet end up buying.

The first two stages of the customer-experience hierarchy explain how HSN attracts and retains customers. HSN gives viewers a positive functional experience: They watch the show, purchase products via the phone, and then receive those products in the mail. The broadcasts provide viewers with an intimate experience because they can tune in to a regularly scheduled show that matches their interests. And through a two-way communication channel, customers develop a high level of trust in HSN because they can return items and ask questions about an already-transparent selling process.

When HSN began to sell online in September 1999, it attempted to create an entertaining experience for website visitors. HSN.com offers many of the items sold on HSN broadcasts (Stage One), and also provides chat rooms and discussion boards for second-stage users who are looking for a more intimate experience. Finally, to strengthen its emotional tie with the offline show, the site has streaming video of the television broadcast.

Other firms have different approaches to making their sites more entertaining. Polo.com, for example, provides the usual online catalog experience (Stage One), but supplements its offering with links to its own ad campaigns and Polo.com Magazine, described as "The Ralph Lauren Online Lifestyle Magazine." These features are intended to add to the Polo image and enhance the shopping atmosphere, providing the user with a more intimate online experience (Stage Two).

Some feel, however, that these efforts to entertain users have not been wholly successful, and that companies should first focus on improving website functionality (Stage One). For example, some feel that these sites could do better by offering more efficient search functionalities (in fact, Polo.com does not offer search) or faster download times (especially important for users who access streaming media). HSN.com and Polo.com have not quite been able to replicate their offline customer experience success in their online businesses. Although HSN.com and Polo.com intended to advance their customers toward Stage Two, it seems that many have yet to pass through Stage One.

Shift from Consumption to Leisure Activity. As people bring the customer experience from the point of consumption into the role-playing arena, a subtle shift occurs: Instead of thinking about a visit to the firm's website as a task, users begin to see such visits as a pleasure. Thus, use of the product or discussions about the firm are no longer purely economic. This is also evident in site usage. Consider eBay. While customers do visit eBay to receive a good price on the item they are looking for, the eBay experience goes beyond the simple exchange of products for money, and it becomes recreational. Customers ask themselves questions such as: "Can I get the product?" "How much should I bid?" "What is the reservation price?" "Can I get a better fixed-price alternative?" The experience becomes a real-time game. Remember that in the offline world, people often window-shop or browse for entertainment, and the same is true for online sites that offer compelling experiences.

At this stage, customers may find that visiting the website is actually preferable to other work or leisure activities. Great customer experiences at this stage often preoccupy users even when they are not actively engaged in the experience. By shifting the emphasis from utility to entertainment, the firm is engaging customers even when they are not directly involved in economic transactions.

In sum, there are several characteristics that reflect the intimacy of the customer experience: the degree of customization (both personalization and tailoring), deeper levels of personal communication, the consistency of the experience over time, the degree of trustworthiness earned over time, the perception that the customer is the beneficiary of exceptional value, and the shift from a purely economic relationship to one with emotional overtones. When customers' expectations are met, their thinking shifts from "This website works very well" to "This website delivers what I need better than any other website."

In Stage Two, the customer begins to internalize the experience and co-create the meaning of the brand. The brand becomes a part of who they are, and customers are happy to share this intimacy with the brand.

Stage Three: Experiencing Evangelism—"I Love to Share the Story"

The final stage assumes that the customer has passed through the first two stages—namely, that the site works, that it is interpreted as an individual experience, and that users integrate the brand into their lives. In this final stage, the customer becomes an evangelist, or what has been variously termed an apostle, market maven, or cult-like user. No matter what term is used, these kinds of customers feel compelled to spread the word about the product or brand. They have so internalized the experience and been rewarded with such exceptional value that they cannot wait to share the story with friends, relatives, and acquaintances.

Taking the Word to the Market.   People love to tell stories about products with which they have had wonderful experiences. In the offline world, people commonly share tips on restaurants, sports equipment, and other products they feel passionate about.

We know an athlete who is devoted to a particular brand of socks. She finds Thorlo socks to be exceptionally comfortable, well padded, and soft. They are priced accordingly, at about $9 a pair. However, not only does this athlete feel that she is still getting a good deal on the product, but she often shares her emotional commitment to the brand whenever conversation turns to running, hiking, skiing, or other outdoor activities. Interestingly, a high percentage of others who have been persuaded to try the brand have come to feel the same way, with at least a 9:1 ratio of positive to negative experiences. They also become converts, eager to share their own "Thorlo experiences." In the online world, evangelists have had a profound impact on the rapid adoption of products such as Napster, the ICQ instant-message system, eBay, and the search engine Google.

The point is that customers who have passed through the first two stages are poised to become evangelists for the brand. They already have a clear emotional connection with its products, and are likely to develop a passion for telling its story. Even if the price point is high, evangelists feel they are getting a good deal relative to competitors' products, and will put considerable energy into convincing others.

Active Community Membership. This stage is also characterized by the emergence of community participation. While not all customers will engage in community offerings, those who reach this stage often want to participate with like-minded folk who share the same passion. And "lurkers"—those who read message boards or other community postings without contributing directly—are still cementing emotional ties to the company.

"The Company Cares About My Opinions." A key characteristic at this stage is the perception that the firm is either incapable of managing the experience without the user, or that the user is welcome to pitch in to help. Mattel's senior managers experienced a good example of this perceived need to protect the brand meaning. In 1997, they ran into trouble with loyal Barbie collectors, many of them club members who purchased more than 30 Barbies per year at price points that frequently exceeded $50 a doll. These dedicated customers were aghast that a newly launched Barbie had a look that was inconsistent with Barbie's image as the girl next door. They demanded (and received) a meeting with the CEO to ask that the company withdraw the new Barbie from stores. Realizing that these customers were among the most valuable of Mattel's assets, the CEO relented.

Drill-Down

Utilizing Customer Experience to Create Loyalty

Customer experience has become a popular business term lately. Firms do all they can to create a positive, compelling experience: They focus on creating and maintaining a comfortable and friendly consumer environment; they strive to engineer websites that are consistent with their brands and easy and enjoyable for the customer to navigate; they try to ensure that their representatives are well trained and helpful. They also add finishing touches to make their websites especially memorable. A firm that takes the time to create effective, desirable customer experience distinguishes itself from the competition and creates loyal customers.

Ticketmaster is a good example of a firm that has discovered that good customer experience can create especially loyal customers. Ticketmaster's website (*www.ticketmaster.com*) enables users to find out about upcoming events and to purchase tickets for those events online. To take its service one step further, Ticketmaster teamed up with an e-mail marketing service provider, e-Dialog, to e-mail thank-you notes to consumers after they purchase tickets. When Bruce Springsteen reunited with the E Street Band and played a number of shows at the Meadowlands in New Jersey, Ticketmaster sent e-mail messages to customers to confirm the sale and to thank them for buying tickets from Ticketmaster. The messages also included links to relevant partner websites such as Citysearch's New York visitors guide. Then, a few days prior to the event, ticket buyers received a second e-mail with directions to the venue, a seating chart, and other perks—such as a link to a website selling Springsteen CDs. A final message sent after the concert featured a play list for the show that the ticket buyer attended and more links to related websites, including those selling tour merchandise.[2]

Most ticket buyers probably expected their experience with Ticketmaster to be solely transactional. But Ticketmaster was able to offer customers a deeper, broader, more useful experience—and ultimately created very satisfied customers.

These collectors were not only profitable, but also carried enormous word-of-mouth impact—not just with customers, but with the creators of the Barbie brand.

Defender of the Experience.   Much like staunch liberals or conservatives, customers who reach this stage are ardent defenders of their viewpoints—so much so that they can become visibly angry when others either disagree or (heaven forbid) buy competitor offerings. If multiple generations of a family living in a small-town farming community have always bought Ford trucks, you can be quite sure that the next generation will also buy Ford. The alternative is to face the wrath of Uncle Ernie.

To summarize, in this stage the customer shifts from an experience that is deeply personal to one in which there is a need to spread the word about a product or service. Such individuals take great pleasure in telling others about how they use the product, about how others use the product, and their future plans for using the product.

EXHIBIT 4.2   Stages of Customer Experience over Time

Summary: Hierarchy of Customer Experience

Exhibit 4.2 provides a simple illustration of how these three stages can be thought of in terms of a hierarchy of a customer experience. The two key axes are (1) the nature of the customer reactions (general versus personal versus other-oriented), and (2) relationship development time. As customers begin to use a website regularly, they shift from a general experience to a personal experience. Dedicated users become the voice of the experience in the marketplace.

This is not to say that one stage automatically leads to the next, but rather that each stage is a prerequisite for the next one. It is difficult, for example, to imagine that a customer could internalize and personalize an experience

Drill-Down

The Internet Shopping 24/7 Project

In his "Internet Shopping 24/7" research project, Professor Bruce D. Weinberg shopped exclusively online for one year (from September 1999 to September 2000) in order to better understand the online customer experience. An ethnographic and entertaining diary of his experiences is posted on the Web (*www.InternetShopping247.com*). His purchases included a broad range of goods and services, including groceries, clothing, toys, plumbing tools and materials, books, lawn fertilizer, presidential campaign buttons, airline tickets, car rentals, calculator batteries, computer devices, diamond earrings, a Honda Odyssey minivan, and lots of diapers (his third child was conceived and born during the project).

The "Netty Professor," as he was coined in an *Inc* magazine article, finished the project with four important findings. First, online consumer decisions follow a well-defined process that can be used to understand online consumer experiences and to explain and predict online consumer behavior. The consumer buying decision process defines precisely the buying stages that a consumer may experience: recognizing a problem or a need (problem recognition), searching for information pertaining to the problem or need (information search), comparing and evaluating alternatives (alternative evaluation), making a purchase (purchase), and participating in after-purchase events (postpurchase behavior), such as returning a product or telling others about the product or purchase experience.

Second, he finds that consumer value, more than technological capability, should drive decisions related to serving customers through online vehicles. He comments, "I have a degree in computer science and earned my Ph.D. at MIT, so I appreciate the technological coolness of things such as Macromedia Flash. However, if these technologies do not add customer value or do not help the customer get from point A to point B in a more effective or efficient manner, then they are driving the customer mad!" He adds with a slight laugh, "Sometimes humans still perform better than machines when it comes to serving customers."

Third, Weinberg discovered that until many aspects of an online experience are second nature, it is extremely important for employees at *all* levels to engage in the online consumer experience in order to understand what customers go through. When asked about creating a great online consumer experience, Weinberg says, "It is almost the year 2003, and I am amazed that so many established companies still haven't got a clue as to how to create a valuable online presence or valuable online service for existing or potential customers. The fact is that the Internet is an important and frequently used touchpoint for most consumers in a variety of buying situations. Companies that are not aware of this or cannot leverage off of this are frustrating the daylights out of consumers, and leaving, in the aggregate, tens of billions of dollars in potential profit on the table. A big step in realizing the shortcomings and potential in customer experience is for employees to simply get online and see and feel what the online customer experience is like. Analysis and understanding of, as well as solutions for, a particular customer experience, however, does require careful application of the consumer buying decision process framework and other related marketing theories and principles."

Fourth, he learned that customers are much more than click streams. He is quick to point out that Amazon's recommendations are often amusing. "Sure, they know which pages I have visited and which products I have purchased, but for nearly two years they have been recommending that I purchase the Leatherman tool, and I continue to have absolutely no interest in purchasing such an item," Weinberg says. "I'm not saying that click-stream data are not informative when used properly. I am suggesting, however, that managers need to look beyond the click stream in order to understand a consumer and when considering the online consumer experience."

if a website does not work properly. Furthermore, it is unlikely that customer evangelists do not consider the broader product experience a part of their identity. Thus, the customer moves through the stages much like one moves

- No search feature. Customers must navigate a company-specified path or consult a site map in order to find what they're looking for.
- No indication until checkout that an item is out of stock.
- Hard-to-find contact information. The absence of phone numbers is especially irritating to customers, even though the company may find it beneficial.
- No gift certificates or gift shipping options.
- No shipping information or costs until the end of checkout process. This is one of the top reasons that shopping carts are abandoned.
- So-called "opt-in" marketing buttons. When check boxes default to settings in the company's favor, customers have to uncheck them to avoid unwanted marketing messages.
- No printer-friendly feature. This results in hard-to-read printouts and wasted paper.

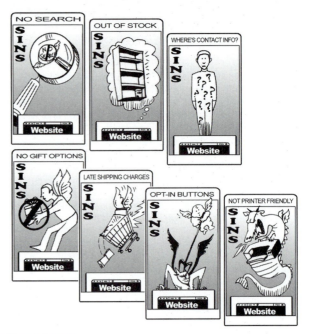

EXHIBIT 4.3   The Seven Deadly Sins of Customer Experience

through Maslow's hierarchy of needs—that is, one cannot progress to a higher stage unless the prior stage is satisfied.

Steps in the Process of Creating a Desirable Customer Experience

This section shifts from describing the stages of customer experience to describing appropriate steps for designing customer experience. These seven steps complement a firm's strategy for creating a desirable customer experience. Executing this strategy will depend largely on building an effective marketing program and customer interface (discussed in the following chapters), but the focus in this chapter is on planning rather than implementation. These seven steps, outlined below, should serve as guideposts for using the levers discussed later in the book.

Step One: Create a Rich Description of the Target Customer

The first step in designing a customer experience requires a deep understanding of the target customer. An especially effective way to bring the customer to life is to write a short story—even if it is only a few paragraphs—about the customer that can be widely understood by all constituents, including stakeholders inside the organization and partners such as distributors, vendors, and suppliers. The intent is to bring to life the market research, sales-force knowledge, customer-visit data, and collective insight from user tracking and profiling data.

Consider REI.com, the online channel of the outdoor clothing and equipment specialist REI.[3] Like most companies, REI must satisfy several customer segments in order to survive and thrive. Some REI customers are novice athletes, some are weekend outdoor enthusiasts, others are world-class climbers, kayakers, or mountain bikers, and still others are simply in the market for seasonal clothing. If REI.com is to provide a satisfying customer experience, each type of customer (and their stories) must be understood. For example, a description of a weekend warrior who also happens also to be a mother might go something like this:

> Many people love the outdoors, but find that there's just not enough time in their schedules to indulge this passion. A woman who spent vacations during college on extended backpacking trips may now be limited to infrequent day hikes with her children, generally within an hour's drive of home. Such customers still see themselves as highly motivated trekkers, and they are prime candidates for leading a new generation into the woods.
>
> In general, women with young children are budget-conscious, yet want the best gear they can afford. They will also search out age-appropriate events for their children, and may find themselves engaging in new outdoor sports when their kids try out activities. In addition, active mothers will seek weather-appropriate clothing and footwear for their children. They are likely to gravitate toward relevant gear, books, and gifts for their families and friends, and may be good candidates for all-inclusive travel packages that get the family outside yet don't require yet more work and organization by the mother.
>
> A good online customer experience for an outdoor-focused mother will take into consideration her budget and time constraints, and will therefore be both functionally efficient and offer a range of similar products at different price points. Special incentives (such as REI.com's participation in college savings plans, in which a percentage of each purchase is applied to a savings account) will encourage customers to return to the site. Content tailored to families, such as a message board area about family activities, should be offered. When events or trips are offered, difficulty levels should be clearly communicated, so that children are not brought along on outings that will end in meltdowns or other disasters. Easy-to-comprehend clothing size charts and product wizards that help parents choose the right gear for their kids would be welcome. Introductory events, held at family-friendly times, could entice families to try new sports.

This kind of story, which should be repeated for each class of important target customers, creates a deep, shared understanding of that kind of customer: what motivates them, what fears they might have, and which of their problems a firm can address. The key is to paint a clear picture of the people whom the organization is targeting.

Step Two: Develop Use-Case Scenarios for Each Target Segment

Once a rich description of each target segment has been written, the next step is to outline the scenarios that might bring a target customer to a website. In the case of REI.com, for example, a novice outdoor enthusiast might want to search for basic information about their sport of choice, find out if REI offers local workshops, explore the notion of buying (rather than renting) sport-specific gear, outfit themselves for the next trip, read message

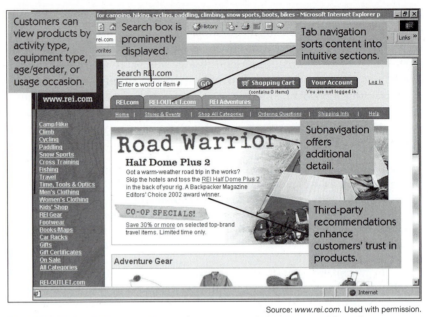

Source: *www.rei.com*. Used with permission.

EXHIBIT 4.4   REI.com Organizes around Customer Needs

boards, and so on. If a firm is to provide good customer experience, it must create an intuitive and comprehensive navigation path for each of the customers' possible needs. By putting itself in the customers' shoes and imagining such use-case scenarios, the company is better able to anticipate what the customer needs, and to design its website accordingly.

Step Three: Effectively Integrate the Online and Offline Experience

Because customer experience involves an entire encounter, and not simply a transaction, it is essential that online and offline customer experience be integrated.[4] There are two broad classes of variables to consider when creating an integrated experience: customer-facing and back-office forms of integration.

It is essential for the company to play to the strength of the online medium, and not to assume it is sufficient to provide merely a copy of its offline customer messaging. Toy stores give a good example of the potential for online/offline integration. In physical stores, toys are generally displayed by type (dolls, bicycles, electronic toys, or board games). Toy websites, however, often offer assorted views—by age range, gender, or activity—and let the shopper choose. The online experience should incorporate the uniqueness of the medium, and in fact may require a different call to action, which must be developed by analyzing the brand qualities and how consumers interact with the brand. Certain executions will close the loop and carry the customer through transaction, but it may be equally valid for a website to drive awareness for in-store business, which may yield increased sales because the layout of products on shelves and store aisles encourages additional purchases. Also, driving business to the offline environment may heighten customer loyalty and enhance brand impact because of the face-to-face interaction involved.

On the back-office side, there are two types of integration. The first involves the transfer of data between suppliers as well as the integration of supplier systems, distribution systems, and other data-centric systems. The second type of integration is database integration. If a customer can phone a catalog distributor and ask questions about the SKUs found on the website, it is clear that the databases of various channels are integrated. Ideally, such integration also incorporates data about the customer's history with the company, merging information on past purchases and preferences from each channel. Such integration supports the customer's sense of intimacy with the company.

In sum, integrating the online and offline customer experiences is critical for firms that target the same customers (or a subset of customers) with both operations. Any investigation into the whole customer experience must take into account both front-office issues and selected types of back-office integration that have customer-facing implications.

Step Four: Articulate Clear Stages of Desired Experience

REI.com is the most successful online retailer of outdoor gear, with $92 million in sales in 2000. Visitors to REI.com often move quickly through the three stages of desired experience, and an analysis of the website's offerings demonstrates why this is so. Exhibit 4.5 shows the stages of customer experience, with the generic desired customer experience in the center column. The right column shows the specific features and functionality delivered by REI.com. This exhibit also shows how each of the general measures can be tailored to a specific company, in this case REI.com. This level of detail not only communicates within an organization about what experiences are desired, but it also provides a very easy set of questions—a roadmap, if you will—to track the effectiveness of the website. After completing this step, an organization will have a specific set of delivery goals that map to the desired experience at each stage of the process.

Step Five: Effectively Assess Relative Levels of Hierarchy

The purpose of the fifth step is to see how customers are distributed across the hierarchy. This is perhaps best accomplished by allowing customers to self-classify themselves into one of the three stages: functional, intimate, or evangelist.

As noted earlier, each stage is a prerequisite for the next stage—that is, the evangelism stage will not be attained without a sufficient level of performance at the intimacy stage. It is possible to identify customers who are ready to move to the next level. Careful analysis of site logs and order history might indicate to an online retailer (such as REI.com) that a particular customer has moved from, say, the novice phase into a more expert ranking. An e-mail message (assuming, of course, that the customer has opted to receive messages from the company) about local workshops, product sales, relevant news stories, or upcoming television programs on outdoor sports would likely reinforce the customer's sense of his value to the company and could move the customer along the hierarchy.

The general point is that site-usage patterns can provide insight into a customer's commitment stage. In addition, it is also possible to design survey instruments that reveal the distribution of customers across the hierarchy.

Stages	Generic Desired Customer Experience	What REI.com Delivers
Functionality	• Site is usable • Easy navigation • Quick download • Speedy site • Reliable	• Content organized around user needs • Easy-to-find gear and activity information • Multiple views of products and services • Websites that rates high on efficiency and fulfillment • No crashes and limited downtime
Intimacy	• High trust • Consistent experience • Quick, effective communication • High personalization • Exceptional value • Consistent with brand message	• Authoritative content and information • Kiosks in store link to online channel • Easy access to customer service, including live online help • E-mail newsletter • Member discounts and rebates • Product returns to store or by mail • Adventure travel service
Evangelism	• Takes word to the market • Defends the experience	• Membership advantages • E-mail option for sharing information • Community message boards • In-store and local events

EXHIBIT 4.5 Stages of Customer Experience for REI.com

Similar instruments might query users about possible barriers that are preventing them from moving to the next stage.

Step Six: Highly Leverage the Evangelists

Evangelists are the most important group of customers. Their input and energy can help firms greatly improve the customer experience for all individuals. Not all evangelists, however, will be helpful in this regard.

It is possible (indeed, likely) that evangelists are evenly distributed across the profitability spectrum. That is, while the Barbie evangelists also happen to be among Mattel's most profitable customers, the same may not be true of the Harley-Davidson enthusiasts who show up in Sturgis, South Dakota, each year to share the Harley experience. Some of these buyers may be exceptionally profitable, while others may own only one Harley (or simply covet one), but all still have an unusually high level of association with the product and love to spread the word about it.

The question is, how can the firm enjoy the benefits of these die-hard loyalists and also allow them the freedom to coevolve the experience into new, innovative services? This section considers several actions that a firm can take to help leverage its evangelist community.

Freedom to Coevolve the Experience.   Evangelists will take the product into unknown and unpredictable areas. They will push the envelope on what is acceptable, as judged by other evangelists. Certainly, one might have predicted a clothing line for companies such as Harley-Davidson, whose aficionados share a culture along with the bike itself. But who would have expected the Marlboro brand to have its own clothing line? Some of the emergent areas may be acceptable to the firm; for example, an online community decides to stage a live event so community members can meet face to face. In other cases, the firm may strongly oppose the connections that customers are making. Untrained members in a computer-hardware community might (with the best of intentions) create forums that give out inaccurate repair information to new community members, for instance.

It is important for a firm to analyze what academics have termed "use innovativeness" by the evangelists. These are uses of the product that are atypical and were not conceived by the firm. Examples include the use of baking soda to deodorize a refrigerator, the use of nylons to shine shoes, the use of ginger ale to keep flowers fresh, or the use of eBay to sell cars. In each case, customers experimenting with the product introduced completely new uses.

Freedom to Confront and Challenge the Firm. The Barbie episode illustrates an important aspect of the evangelist group: the collective challenge of product introductions, feature functionality, acquisitions of other products in the category, or strategic direction of the firm. PlanetOut's loyal users were dismayed when the firm acquired Gay.com because they believed the purchase could stifle innovation and debate within the gay community. These confrontations and challenges should be closely monitored, because the activist subsegment is likely to be representative of the entire targeted segment. Their views can be early warnings of larger protests. However, engaging evangelists too deeply, or being perceived as allowing evangelists to have strategic influence, can result in negative backlash if evangelical concepts and actions are not implemented. Publicly divergent evangelical desires and corporate goals can have a negative economic impact on a brand.

Preferred Access to New Ideas Within the Firm. It is perhaps obvious that evangelist customers will want to be involved in the development and testing of new offerings. However, it may not be in a company's interest to give evangelists access to inside information. If it is determined that it makes sense to invite evangelists into the product development process, the company could issue invitations to unique events such as strategic sessions, tours of company facilities, or product introductions. These kinds of rewards give this group a level of access and sense of belonging that general customers do not receive.

Trickiness of Economic Incentives. One could argue that this group should be rewarded with economic incentives. However, the most motivated evangelists are usually not engaged with a firm or its product for economic reasons. Indeed, the economic incentives may fly in the face of the deep noneconomic commitment the individual has to the firm and its brands. Thus, Barbie collectors are higher in the experience hierarchy than NextCard affiliates because they are less motivated by economic incentives.

This does not mean that firms should ignore economic incentives. NextCard, for example, has 60,000 members in its affiliate network. Many are simply cardholders who promote the brand on their own websites. Similar to many Barbie evangelists, they have not only internalized the "NextCard experience" but have also reaped financial benefits: These individual cardholders can earn more than $100,000 a year as affiliate members. Hence, they have become profitable evangelists, much like the Barbie evangelists who profit by trading dolls and associated memorabilia.

Shrines, Clubs, Museums, and Other "Third Places."   Deeply committed customers often feel the need to develop shrines, clubs, or other "third places" that pay homage to the product, service, information, or individuals associated with the offering. This is particularly apparent in the entertainment industry, where fan club websites often emerge. It is appropriate and instructive for firms to monitor these sites. However, excessive micromanaging of homage sites may backfire. For example, sending "cease and desist" letters, using the rationale of copyright infringement, could alienate evangelists. These situations must be delicately handled.

Step Seven: Continuously Monitor and Adjust

Once the calibration has been set—that is, once customers have been classified and detailed tactics for transitioning them across levels have been specified—a firm must continually monitor performance and the barriers to movement across experience levels. This is necessary because competitors change, technology develops, and customers learn about feature-functionality considerations across a range of online and offline experiences. In addition, the online medium itself is maturing, which means that today's standard features may be clunky and obsolete tomorrow. A company must constantly monitor customer needs and expectations, identify gaps in the customer-experience process, and provide customer-centric adjustments that will effectively leverage the online channel.

Summary: Steps in the Process of Creating a Desirable Customer Experience

Exhibit 4.6 illustrates how each of the seven steps benefits both the company and the customer. Through a rich understanding of the elements of customer experience, the hierarchy of experience, and the steps required to deliver the experience, a firm has the opportunity to strengthen its relationship with customers, and to learn from them in order to serve them better. The customer-centric perspective presented in this chapter allows the company to move from a theoretical positioning of its offering to one that can bring mutual benefits to customer and company.

eBay Example

In this section, the stages of customer experience are applied to the online auction website eBay. Exhibit 4.7 shows the type of desired customer experience that maps onto the four-stage model. The final column of Exhibit 4.7 introduces customer metrics for eBay.

Stage One: Experiencing Functionality

As stated earlier, superior customer experience starts with understanding the basics. By understanding the basic needs of eBay customers (both buy-

Step	Benefit to Customer	Benefit to Company
Create Rich Description of Target Customers	• Company better able to imagine customer motivations	• Brings market research to life • Allows shared understanding of customer types
Develop Use-Case Scenarios for Each Target Segment	• Company better able to anticipate and meet customer needs and expectations	• Site designers put themselves in customers' shoes, which helps create intuitive navigation and ensures usability
Integrate Online and Offline Experience	• Customer experiences consistency across brand and channels	• Enhanced overall sales, lessening of perceived channel cannibalization
Articulate Stages of Desired Experience	• Customer experiences increased attachment to company, greater loyalty and potential for evangelism	• Company able to map desired outcomes to product and site deliverables
Assess Levels of Hierarchy	• Customers perceive that they are of value to the company	• Company able to consider strategies for moving customers along the experience hierarchy
Leverage the Evangelists	• Customer participation in brand and marketing is rewarded by feeling of belonging and community	• Company gains insight into product uses and product development; benefits from viral marketing
Monitor and Adjust	• Major and incremental changes to site diminish barriers to good experience	• Online channel's full potential is leveraged

EXHIBIT 4.6   Summary of Steps in Creating Good Customer Experience

ers and sellers), the company has created an experience that is simple and effective. Someone who wants to buy an item—anything from a Pez dispenser to a car—can locate it in a single click. Searches are easily narrowed by using the variables of category, geography, or special interest. For sellers, eBay provides a straightforward, step-by-step process and several helpful tools.

This seamless user experience did not happen by chance. In fact, eBay turned to its customers to create it. As former Chief Operating Officer Brian Swette said, "We start from the principle that if there's noise, you better listen."[5] Whether its managers are combing through hundreds of message board postings, holding Voice of the Customer focus groups, flying eBay users to its headquarters or reading user e-mails, eBay constantly reinvents itself based on customer suggestions. This method of building a customer experience has led to its position as the dominant online auction website. Exhibit 4.8 shows how eBay performs across the customer-experience basics outlined in this chapter.

Stage Two: Experiencing Intimacy

When users move to the second level of customer experience, they begin to invest emotionally in the site. Instead of simply browsing the auction notices, they begin to customize the site to suit their needs. eBay facilitates this process by having users create eBay user names. This not only enables buyers

Stages	Generic Desired Customer Experience for Auctions	What eBay Delivers
Functionality	• Direct message • Clean layout • Quick browsing, searching, and bidding • Straightforward selling • Good market segmentation (by category, region, special interests) • Reliable	• Easy-to-locate items • Easy-to-upload information about selling • Fast auction interactions • Easy-to-understand rules and auction interface • No crashes and limited downtime • Very efficient access
Intimacy	• Effective communication • Consistent experience • Trustworthy customer service • Only the necessary level of personalization • Exceptional value • Consumption for leisure • Channel for selling, especially B2C • Active community members • Assistance in brand building	• User constantly knows status of auction • Site is consistent across all areas • Quick, effective personalized e-mail responses • Users make "My eBay" their main interface with the site • Enabling transactions is regarded by eBay community as extremely valuable • Businesses use eBay as a distribution channel • Active users in personal and company's feedback forums • Feedback Forum becomes emotion driven: *"I wonder what people are saying about me"*
Evangelism	• Takes word to the market • Defends the experience • Look down on competitors	• Describes eBay as the ultimate experience in terms of great deals and trustworthiness • No need to visit other auction websites for better deals or more variety

EXHIBIT 4.7   Stages of Customer Experience for eBay

The Basics	eBay's Score
Usability and ease of navigation	• Intuitive interface guides both buying and selling process • Logical organizational structure reinforces where you are in the site at all times
Speed	• Site is light on graphics, making performance quick on dial-up connections • Item searches are extremely fast
Reliability	• Site can handle 800,000 transactions per minute • Outages, a problem in eBay's earlier days, have been reduced to a minimum
Media accessibility	• EBay Anywhere enables access from any wireless device
Security	• Security keys for payments separate from eBay passwords, adding extra level of protection • Encryption used on all transactions to ensure safe exchanges

EXHIBIT 4.8   eBay's Functionality

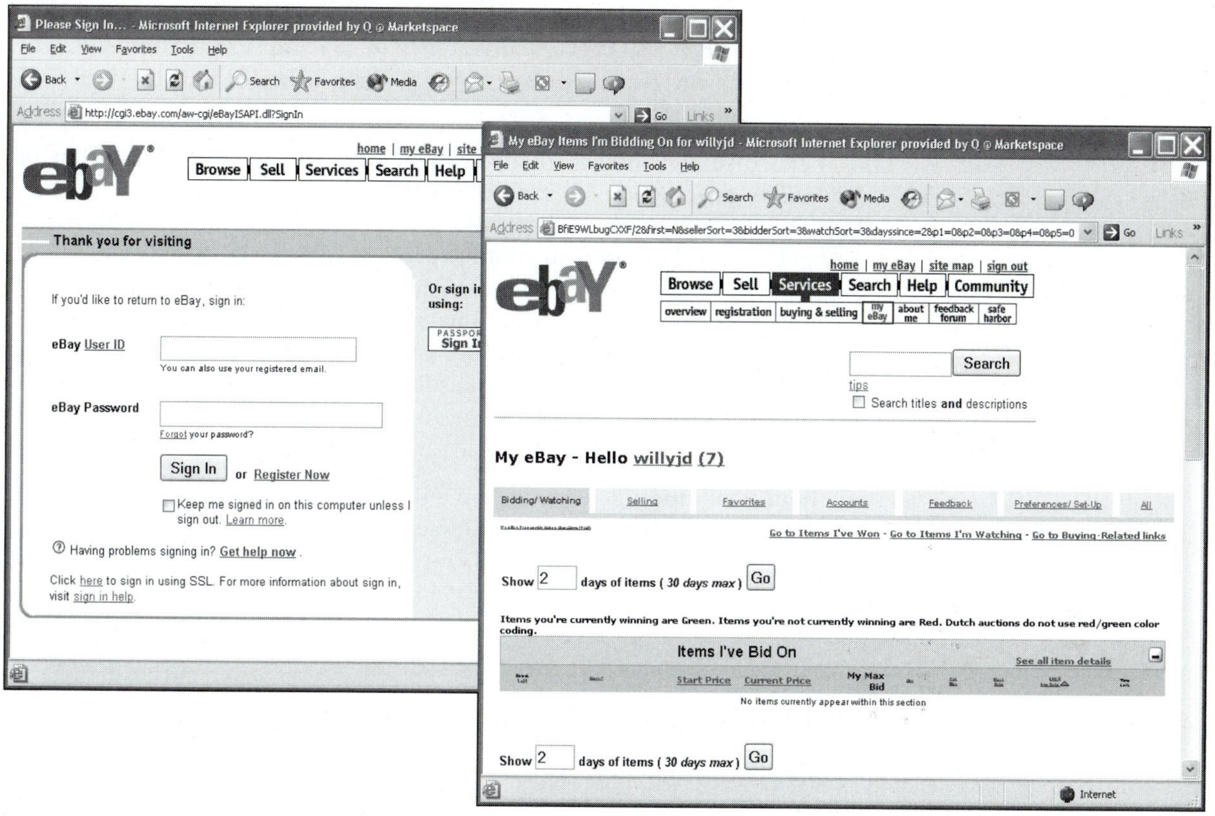

Source: *www.ebay.com.* Used with permission.

EXHIBIT 4.9   eBay Tailors the User Experience to the Individual User

and sellers to give and receive feedback on transactions, but it also enables eBay to provide them with a customized "dashboard" that shows what they are bidding on, what they are selling, their preferences, and several more options (see Exhibit 4.9).

In addition to providing this customized interface, eBay communicates well with its users. The eBay platform generates e-mails throughout the buying and selling process. For example, after bidding for an item, users receive an e-mail telling them that eBay has registered the bid. If someone outbids them, eBay e-mails again, giving them the chance to up the ante and stay in the running. When an auction finishes, eBay emails both the buyer and seller and provides each with an online template to complete the transaction. The form includes payment and shipping details and even links to a feedback page, thereby furthering each person's investment in the eBay community.

In the intimacy stage, users also begin to experience the consistency of the customer experience. eBay has ensured consistency by creating ground rules, or community norms, that are enforced both by eBay and the greater community. For instance, eBay explicitly defines the responsibilities of buyers and sellers and makes the rules accessible through a help button. Users maintain consistency and uphold trustworthiness by using a rating system. Such high value is placed on positive feedback ratings that both buyers and sellers are encouraged to be on their best behavior or risk being rejected by other users. eBay also creates consistency by making sure that offshoots of the original eBay (such as eBay Motors) have a similar look-and-feel and share the same tools.

eBay has instituted other initiatives to build trust, too. On the bottom of every eBay page is a small emblem that indicates the site is endorsed by TRUSTe, an independent, nonprofit initiative that sets privacy and disclosure guidelines that sites can voluntary follow. This seal assures visitors that they have full control over the use of their personal information. Similarly, eBay offers full purchase protection in case of fraud, and it posts a "Safe Harbor" page that gives its policies on payment disputes, use of discussion boards, trademark and copyright questions, and whether items can be legally offered for sale.

The intimacy stage of the customer-experience hierarchy yields a different kind of shopping behavior on eBay. At this stage, people think of reasons to go to eBay to buy or browse. They may even go just to fantasy-shop and get a vicarious thrill about items they probably will not ever purchase. EBay provides such great value that it becomes a top-of-mind destination.

Stage Three: Experiencing Evangelism

People who reach the evangelism stage feel a connection with eBay and want to spread the message. One eBay evangelist, Marsha Collier, has written two books about the website, *EBay for Dummies* (now in its third edition) and *Starting an eBay Business for Dummies*. Many more eBay evangelists have spread the gospel through word of mouth. In fact, people who told friends and coworkers about eBay's value in its early days were largely responsible for its quick growth.

Another sign of evangelism is community involvement. eBay recognizes the value of its community, even putting a link to its community area on every page of the website. It offers a host of community resources (see Exhibit 4.10), both online and offline. Through eBay University, it holds training classes for buyers and sellers, and even gives attendees an opportunity to meet CEO Meg Whitman—the eBay equivalent of introducing a kid to his favorite baseball player.

Increased community involvement may take on other forms. Someone who has crossed over to the evangelist stage may show community activism by participating in a category-specific message board. A stamp collector, for instance, may share news about recent stamp finds or tips on how to sell parts of a collection, or simply chat with fellow philatelists. Whatever the scenario, he is going to eBay to share experiences with like-minded people.

eBay pays great attention to its evangelists. After all, they serve as a kind of sales and marketing team. It shows it cares about evangelists in a number of ways: the creation of a "power seller" category, special benefits for top sellers, and occasionally flying them to its headquarters to listen to their concerns and suggestions.

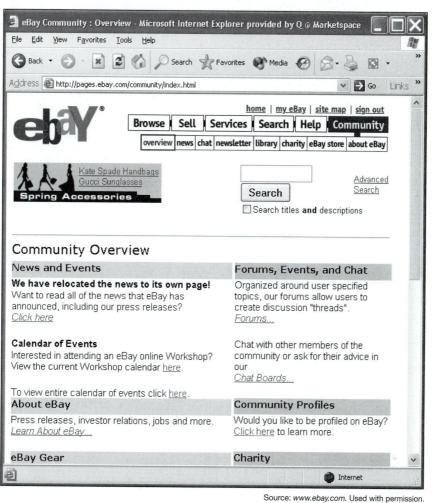

Source: *www.ebay.com*. Used with permission.

EXHIBIT 4.10   eBay Community Resources

1. What is customer experience?

Customer experience can be defined as the interpretation of a user's complete encounter with the site, from the initial look at the homepage through the purchase experience, including decisions such as whether to abandon a shopping cart.

2. What are the seven elements of customer experience?

The seven elements of customer experience are:

1. Objective
2. Perceived
3. Encounter
4. Reactions to stimuli
5. Sensory
6. Cognitive and emotional
7. Relative

3. What are the three stages of the customer-experience hierarchy?

The three stages in the customer-experience hierarchy are:

1. Functionality
2. Intimacy
3. Evangelism

4. What steps must a firm take when designing a desirable customer experience?

There are seven steps a firm should take to design a desirable customer experience:

1. Create a rich description of the target customer.
2. Develop use-case scenarios for each target segment.
3. Effectively integrate the online and offline experience.
4. Articulate clear stages of desired experience.
5. Effectively assess relative levels of hierarchy.
6. Highly leverage the evangelists.
7. Continuously monitor and adjust.

Activities for Students

1. Visit some of the websites mentioned in this chapter and determine how well they deliver the seven elements of customer experience.
2. Identify what steps eBay has taken to guide customers through the three stages of the customer-experience hierarchy.
3. Keeping in mind the seven steps for designing a desirable customer experience, visit your favorite and least favorite websites. Describe the changes you would make to improve the customer experience of each one.

Key Terms

customer experience	encounter elements	cognitive and emotional elements
objective element	reactions-to-stimuli elements	relative elements
perception elements	sensory elements	experience hierarchy

Endnotes

[1]Lieber, Ron. "She reads customers' minds." *Fast Company* www.fastcompany.com/online/43/kozuh.html.

[2]Anderson, Heidi. "Good CRM: The Ticket You're Looking For?" *Click Z.* www.clickz.com/article/cz.2855.html.

[3]Fisher, Lawrence M. "REI Climbs Online: A Clicks and Mortar Chronicle" *strategy+business.* www.strategy-business.com/casestudy/00111/page1.html (requires registration).

[4]As per our Chapter 3 discussion, a firm may choose to market to a different segment. Hence, this discussion is relevant only for firms that decide that the same group of customers is being targeted for both the online and offline efforts.

[5]Robert D. Hof, The People's Company, *BusinessWeek*, 3 December 2001.

Crafting the Customer
Interface

This section is a logical extension of the design of the customer experience and provides an overview of the design of a website. This section is analogous to the construction of the retail store. While Gap needs to build retail stores that bring to life its positioning as a fashion-forward store for professionals, Gap.com needs its website to convey particular look-and-feel and design considerations that bring to life its online brand. This section focuses on the 7Cs of customer interface design.

Customer Interface

Internet technology has caused a shift in the way consumers interact with firms. Today, the face-to-face encounters common in the traditional retail environment have been widely replaced by screen-to-face interactions. These interfaces can be accessed through a desktop PC, subnotebook, handheld device, cellphone, wireless application protocol device, or other Internet-enabled appliance. As this shift from people-mediated to technology-mediated interfaces unfolds, it is important to examine the interface design considerations that confront the senior management team, and how the resulting interface can affect the customer experience. This chapter explores the design principles for creating successful technology-mediated customer interfaces, with a particular focus on Web interfaces because they are such a critical part of a company's marketing program. As such, the chapter offers both a strategic framework for senior managers and tactical advice and recommendations for putting strategy into practice.

Before an interface is designed, a number of questions must be addressed. What is the look-and-feel, or context, of the site? Should the site include commerce activities? How important is community to the business model? To answer these and other important questions, the 7Cs Framework is introduced. The 7Cs are a rigorous way to identify the major interface design challenges that senior managers will encounter as they implement their business models.

QUESTIONS

Please consider the following questions as you read this chapter:

1. What are the seven design elements of the customer interface?

2. What determines the look-and-feel of the site?

3. What are the dimensions of content?

4. Why be concerned with community?

5. What are the levers used to customize a site?

6. What types of communication can a firm maintain with its customer base?

7. How does a firm connect with other businesses?

8. What are the main features of commerce that support the various aspects of trading transactions?

Co-authored by Kate Bernhardt. With substantive input from Leo Griffin, Yannis Dosios, Ives Moraes, and Melissa Pennings.

Introduction

The previous chapters have explored and discussed the marketing program and the need to address customer experience when translating the marketing program to the customers themselves. This chapter takes customer experience a step further by introducing the concept of interface design. As this chapter will show, a primary means for creating an effective marketing program and customer experience is through the effective use of several interface levers and design principles.

The chapter explores how strategy decisions significantly affect the type of customer interface choices that confront a senior management team. For example, consider the different approaches of two companies that target teenage girls: Alloy.com and Delias.com. Both offer catalog shopping, but their online presence is significantly different. Alloy's homepage stresses editorial content—trivia, gossip, quizzes, celebrity profiles, message boards, and contests. The site focuses on the experience of being a teenage girl, and at first glance it is not particularly obvious that you can shop there. Delias.com, on the other hand, presents shopping options boldly, on the homepage and throughout the site. There is lifestyle content on Delias.com as well, but it is given much less priority.

The challenge for managers is to match the strategic goals of the business with an interface that encourages customers to engage with the company in a way that achieves those goals. So for Alloy, whose business model includes several offline magazines girls can subscribe to, the site reflects its business strategy by doing more than simply selling clothes—it also drives subscriptions. Hence, the site's focus on editorial content. The goal of Delias.com, a catalog business with an online channel, is primarily to encourage buying—a fact clearly reflected in its interface choices. For both sites, of course, the success or failure of the online offering depends on delivering a positive customer experience, while aligning the customer interface with the company's business goals.

The purpose of this chapter is to introduce, describe, and provide a critical framework—the 7Cs—that act as a bridge between higher-order strategic considerations and the challenge of designing and implementing an effective customer interface. The first section offers a brief definition of each of the 7Cs. The sections that follow discuss the features or dimensions of each "C," how each C affects customer experience and the broader marketing program, and the implications of each "C" for interface design. Throughout the chapter, screen shots and exhibits illustrate the 7Cs at work. In addition, the chapter also examines two higher-order design principles to be considered when constructing a customer interface—fit and reinforcement—along with an exploration of best practices in Web design. The chapter concludes with a detailed analysis of how the 7Cs Framework can be applied to eBay.

What Are the Seven Design Elements of Customer Interface?

The 7Cs Framework

The interface is the virtual (and, to date, largely visual) representation of a firm's chosen value proposition. Similar to a retail storefront, a website provides significant information to current and prospective target market customers. If designed effectively, the site quickly answers a number of basic questions that confront users: Is this site worth visiting? What products or services does it sell? What messages does the site communicate? Consistent with a tightly constructed business model, well-designed sites should simultaneously attract target segment customers and deter nontargeted customers. Compelling sites communicate the core value proposition of the firm and provide a rationale for visiting and/or becoming a customer of a site.

Definitions of the 7Cs

Context.   The **context** of the site captures its aesthetics and functional look-and-feel. Some sites have chosen to focus heavily on interesting graphics, colors, and design features, while others have emphasized utilitarian goals such as ease of navigation.

Content.   **Content** is defined as all digital subject matter on a website. This includes the medium of the digital subject matter—text, video, audio, and graphics—as well as the message of the digital subject matter, including product, service, and information offerings. While context largely focuses on the "how" of site design, content centers on what is presented.

Community.   **Community** is defined as a set of interwoven relationships built upon shared interests. Community is useful from a number of standpoints. For example, community can create content or services that attract consumers to a website; it can also serve as a means to build closer relationships between consumer and firm, and between consumer and consumer. Standard community offerings include message boards and live chats.

Customization.   **Customization** is defined as a site's ability to modify itself to—or be modified by—each user. When the customization is initiated and managed by the firm, it is known as tailoring. When the customization is initiated and managed by the user, it is called personalization.

Communication.   **Communication** refers to the dialogue that unfolds between the website and its users. This communication can take three forms: firm-to-user (e.g., e-mail notification), user-to-firm (e.g., customer service request), or user-to-user (e.g., instant messaging).

Connection.   **Connection** is defined as the network of links between the site and other sites—in other words, clickable links that either take the visitor off

Sound Byte

The Importance of the User Interface; Heidi Roizen, Managing Director, Softbank Venture Capital
"I think that those who have spent some time on ergonomics and on a nice user interface and the aesthetics have seen some benefit from that. I think the more and more you get away from the desktop computer and toward the consumer devices, the more you'll have to pay attention to that. I think we're going to see it naturally evolve; the more you bring different demographics into the market—non-computer user, consumers, women, children, different age demographics, different economic demographics—you're going to see different types of machines become important."

a company's site or that exist on other sites to bring visitors to the company's site.

Commerce.   **Commerce** is defined as transactional capacity of a site—the sale of goods, products, or services on the site—along with shopping carts, shipping and payment options, checkout, and order-confirmation functionality.

How Do the 7Cs Influence Interface Design?

Context

Context is defined as the look-and-feel of a screen-to-face customer interface. This look-and-feel can be categorized by both aesthetic and functional criteria. A functionally oriented site focuses largely on the core offering, whether it is a product, service, or information. A good example of a functionally oriented site is CEOExpress (*www.ceoexpress.com*). CEOExpress (see Exhibit 5.1) is an information portal that aggregates magazine, newspaper,

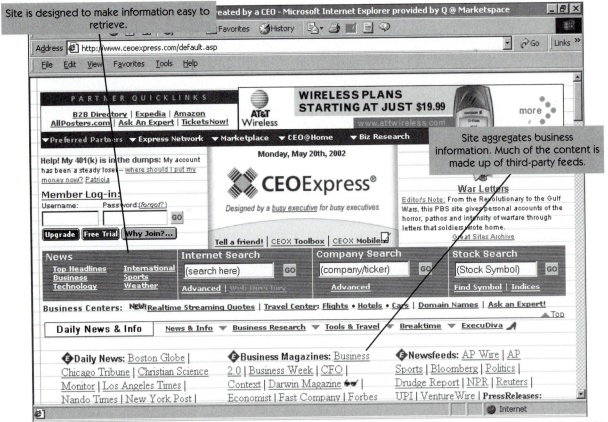

Source: *www.ceoexpress.com*. Used with permission.

Exhibit 5.1   Functional Design: CEOExpress

television, and other media sites into a single destination. The site allows for quick, no-nonsense access to information that would be relevant to business leaders, such as stock quotes and links to business periodicals, news magazines, and other content-oriented sites. Navigation on the site is simple, though the site itself is unlikely to win any design awards.

In contrast, Tiffany (*www.tiffany.com*) offers a more aesthetically oriented site. It has a very distinct look-and-feel that is artistic, visually appealing, and completely consistent in the use of color palette and graceful navigation, with the elegance associated with the Tiffany brand. The use of Macromedia Flash technology as a navigation tool is a bold aesthetic choice, since it demands more interaction from the visitor than simple HTML links. The design choices on the Tiffany site encourage visitors to slow down and contemplate each product, providing a customer experience sharply different than what would be encountered at CEOExpress or another functionally dominant site.

A striking example of an aesthetically conceived site is Apple.com, especially considering the vast amount of product, support, and technical information the site must convey (see Exhibit 5.2). Yet because of the use of white space and the limited amount of content presented per page, the customer experience at the site is one of spatial openness and intriguing navigation paths, encouraging extended browsing and exploration.

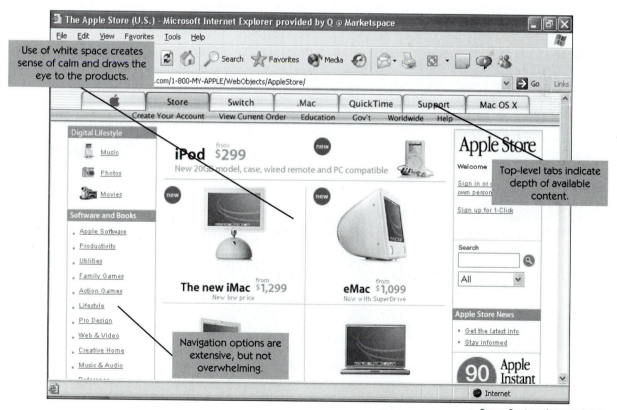

EXHIBIT 5.2   Aesthetic Design: Apple.com

Source: Courtesy of *www.apple.com.*

The Territory Ahead (*www.territoryahead.com*) is a hybrid site that combines both aesthetic and functional dimensions (see Exhibit 5.3). On the aesthetic side, The Territory Ahead, whose tagline is "Clothes for the Journey," is highly visual, with appealing images of products photographed in exotic settings. The company's site strategy not only communicates the product offering, but attracts the target customer through its identification with romance and adventure. Product descriptions are written in a style that matches the site's adventurous spirit, and a special feature section showcases the region where the clothing was photographed. Functionally, the site offers several options for accessing and viewing the clothing, detailed product displays, and all the checkout options that customers have come to expect, in a clean and simple design package.

Obviously, the look-and-feel of a site should reflect the sensibilities of the customers being targeted. Exhibit 5.4 shows a screenshot of the website of clothing retailers Lands' End and Diesel. Lands' End balances both aesthetic (e.g., pastel colors, simple warm visuals) and functional (e.g., crisp, uncluttered) design elements to communicate its core benefits—traditionally designed clothing, great service, and moderate prices. In sharp contrast,

Product descriptions reinforce sense of place and identification with exploration.

Exotic locales appeal to armchair adventurers.

Source: *www.territoryahead.com*. Used with permission.

EXHIBIT 5.3   Hybrid Design: The Territory Ahead

Diesel stresses "insider" content outside the mainstream.

Lands' End reassures with classic colors and designs.

Source: © 2002 Lands' End, Inc. Used with permission. Courtesy of *www.diesel.com*.

EXHIBIT 5.4   Lands' End and Diesel

jeans company Diesel is a more hip, nontraditional retailer; its website (*www.diesel.com*) is edgier, with bolder colors, product information presented as entertainment, and a more focused product line. Landsend.com customers might not find the Diesel site appealing, purely on its look-and-feel—and that makes sense, since Diesel.com is designed to attract a younger, more urban, and more fashion-forward segment.

Dimensions of Context

This section looks more closely at the two key dimensions of context: function and aesthetics. In particular, this section defines the subdimensions of function and aesthetics, then examines how they are put into practice on the website of retailer Bluefly.com (*www.bluefly.com*). Bluefly.com positions itself as "the outlet store for your home," and sells a wide variety of high-end, symbolically oriented retail goods including clothing, household items, and gifts (see Exhibit 5.5).

Function.   Most sites contain much more information than can be usefully presented on a single computer screen. However, this vast amount of information must be presented to the customer in a coherent fashion, and the customer must be able to move easily throughout the website. A well-designed site is built to organize all resident information into sets of pages

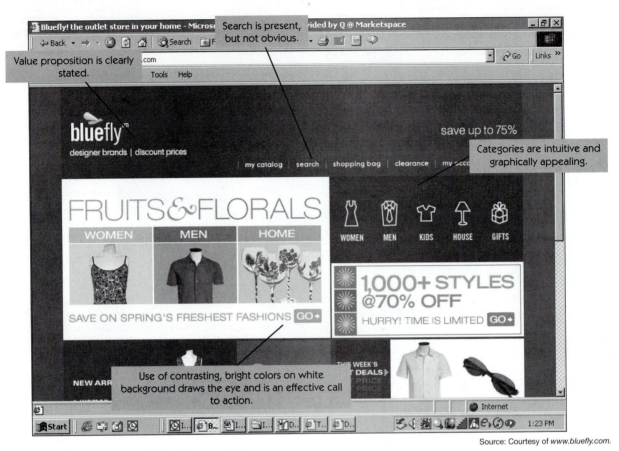

Source: Courtesy of *www.bluefly.com.*

EXHIBIT 5.5   Context: Bluefly.com Homepage

and to provide customers with effective navigation from page to page. Three factors are critical in the layout of the site:

1. *Section Breakdown.* This term describes the way that a site is organized into subcomponents. When this chapter was written, Bluefly organized its site with a top-level tab structure that included my catalog, search, shopping bag, clearance, my account, and help. Beneath this general tab structure were the categories of goods: men, women, kids, house, and gifts. The homepage also featured visually arresting promotional copy inviting visitors to the following sections: new arrivals, top designers, and sale items. Although the search feature is somewhat buried in the top-level navigation, the overall impact of the Bluefly homepage is one of clarity, with clear calls to action for its customers. (It is interesting to note that Bluefly.com has changed its site organization subtly over time, as all good sites will do in response to user behaviors gleaned from site log analysis and/or changes in business focus. Previously, for example, the link to "my catalog"—Bluefly's customer-tailored e-mail newsletter—resided only on the homepage, not as a tabbed choice on all pages.) Good underlying information architecture, which defines the way site content is structured and accessed, is

essential in providing customers with coherent, easy-to-understand navigation choices.

2. *Linking Structure.* Linking structure describes the way in which alternative sections of a site are linked, and is the way visitors experience a site's information architecture. Clicking on the Prada brand (see Exhibit 5.6) on the Bluefly homepage enables one to visit the Prada fashion section. At the same time, the Prada fashion section is framed by the top-level tab structure and general categories noted above. This linking structure enables the users to move easily back and forth between sections of the site. Again, the goal is to group content in ways that are easily understood by site visitors. Offering users the option of viewing by designer, as well as by clothing type and gender, ensures that people can quickly find what they want.

3. *Navigation Tools.* Navigation tools facilitate the movement of each user throughout the site. Navigation tools for Bluefly include two types of search: by price or by style number. Site maps are another common navigation tool.

Aesthetics. The other dimension of context is aesthetics. The aesthetic nature of a site is largely captured by visual characteristics such as colors, graphics, photographs, font choices, and other visually oriented features.

Sound Byte

Design with Customers and Goals in Mind, Marney Morris, Interface Designer, Stanford University
"The first thing is that the customer, or the user, is king. So if you start with the user and you know where they're sitting, what they're doing, what they want, what they need, everything else falls from that. When we start a project, we define who the user is, what the technology advantages and limitations are—because every project has them—and what the client's expectations are. And quite often we'll put in goals. Maybe customers increase 10 percent, sales increase 10 percent—actual quantifiable goals. A lot of websites are not goal-oriented, but that's where I would tell people to start."

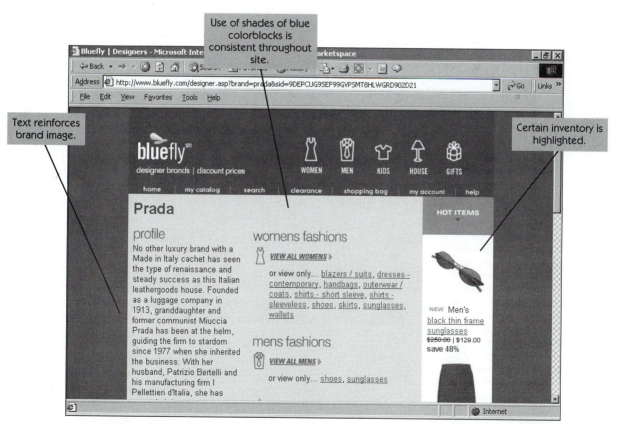

EXHIBIT 5.6   Context: Bluefly.com Designer Page

Source: Courtesy of *www.bluefly.com.*

As one might imagine, Bluefly has emphasized a blue color scheme for its site. Various blue tones are used to define content and navigation choices, and the default setting for links is also blue. In keeping with its name, Bluefly's use of color indicates its focus on creating a consistent online experience.

Impact on Performance and Usability.   Decisions about both functionality and aesthetics have implications for the performance of a site. (The key dimensions of performance, speed, reliability, platform independence, and media accessibility are described in detail in Chapter 4.) It should be a goal of all sites to load quickly and to experience as little "downtime" as possible. Currently, the limited speed of most commonly available connections to the Internet presents a constraint to website design. Sites with limited graphics or multimedia load more quickly than those that incorporate more graphics or multimedia, and thus present a more streamlined customer experience.

The combination of functionality and aesthetics is also experienced by the site visitor in terms of usability, defined as the ease with which a site can be navigated by users. Usability is an important component of Web design—in fact, its importance cannot be overstated, since sites that deliver a frustrating user experience risk losing customers to competitor sites. Designing highly usable websites is both an art and a science, and a new field has emerged to address usability. Practitioners such as Jakob Nielsen, Mark Hurst, and Steve Krug have become recognized as experts on designing for usability.[1]

What Are the Dimensions of Content?

Content refers to any digital information included on a website. Broadly, this includes audio, video, images, and text.

Dimensions of Content

This section considers the four dimensions of content: offering mix, appeal mix, multimedia mix, and content type. These dimensions are examined and then applied to a now-familiar example—REI.com.

Offering Mix.   The content of the site can include products, information, and services. Frequently, sites include a mix of these three elements. REI.com focuses primarily on product content, but also provides information and expert advice on outdoor sports and a message board area to encourage community. Product offerings include outdoor clothing, sport-specific equipment, and adventure travel packages.

Appeal Mix.   This refers to the promotional and communications messaging projected by the company. Naturally, one would expect that the appeal mix would be strongly linked to the value proposition. The academic literature has identified two broad types of appeals: cognitive and emotional. Cognitive appeals focus on the functional aspects of the offering, including such factors as low price, reliability, availability, customer support, and degree of

---

Drill-Down

Usability Tips and Tricks from the Experts

Here are six ways to create a good customer experience, provided by Mark Hurst, the founder and president of consulting firm Creative Good.

1. Make your site QUICK. Customers use slow modems, so make every bit count. Make graphics small, eliminate frames, and rely on text, not graphics. Customers want to accomplish their goals, not admire your developers' design talents.

2. Make your site EASY. Make your site serve the customer only. Don't design your site to look chic for your designers, or snazzy for your marketers, or gee-whiz for your VPs. Make your site the quickest, easiest way for customers to accomplish their goals. This means no browser plug-ins, no rude error messages, and for e-commerce sites, no complicated ordering processes.

3. Offer a good SEARCH. The search form should be simple and should make it easy for customers to find the products or basic info they want. Customers usually type one or two words that describe what they want—so make sure that the names of your most popular items bring up good search results. A poor search feature can end up hurting your site.

4. Get an OUTSIDE OPINION. Don't rely on your internal resources to get the objective eye you need to fix your site. By definition, resources inside the company are already biased by insider knowledge. Instead, get an experienced, professional third party to help.

5. Use clear CATEGORIES. When customers arrive on the homepage, most will click on the link that describes the category of the product they want. Prominently and clearly listing your product categories will help customers get to their desired product quickly and easily.

6. Use clear PRODUCT NAMES. E-commerce sites sometimes use product names that shoppers would only understand if they were already familiar with the product or the catalog. The website of Sharper Image, for example, lists strange product names such as "cordless personal wand." Don't assume customers understand your jargon.

---

personalization. Emotional appeals focus on emotionally resonant ties to the product or brand. These include humor, novelty, warmth, or stories. (Cognitive and emotional appeals are examined in more detail in Chapter 4.) For visitors to REI, cognitive appeal is conveyed by frequently changing front page promotions, which range from special sales to seasonal product groupings to gift suggestions (see Exhibit 5.7). Emotional connections are made via the site's communication of inclusivity, with content that targets novices and experts alike, as well as in the message board postings in the community section. In its "About REI" section, the company shares its operating values and encourages active participation by its customers, further reinforcing emotional ties.

Design Tip

Site designers should present a mix that will encourage the desired user action, while keeping in mind the requirements of the brand. Such vigilance should apply even as far as the types of advertising a site accepts, if any, with an eye on ensuring that the visitor does not experience brand confusion.

Multimedia Mix. This term refers simply to the variety of media—text, audio, image, video, graphics—incorporated into a website. REI.com's content is primarily product information and product photographs. There is no

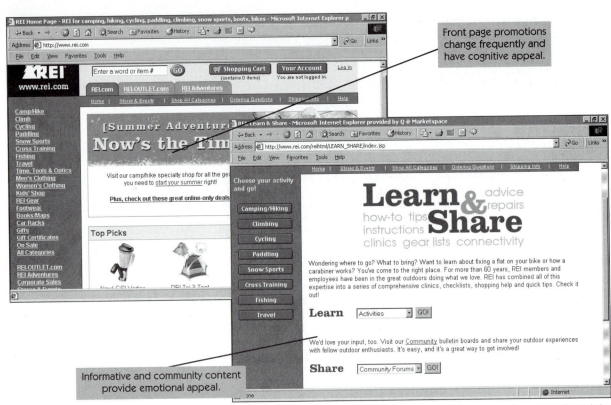

Front page promotions change frequently and have cognitive appeal.

Informative and community content provide emotional appeal.

Source: *www.rei.com.* Used with permission.

EXHIBIT 5.7   Content: REI.com

Design Tip

In planning for site design, managers should keep in mind that the appeal mix on the homepage can be considerably different from the mix on interior pages. Because the homepage is a company's key opportunity to express its value proposition, it is important to trim down its content to essential information and calls to action. More subtle or detailed messaging can occur elsewhere on the site.

Design Tip

In general, multimedia should be used carefully and sparingly on sites, and only in cases where the company has established from market research that its customers expect a variety of media types.

regular use of audio, video, and other complex graphics. Another sports-oriented site, the Burton Snowboards site (*www.burton.com*) takes a different approach, offering its visitors—snowboard aficionados—multimedia profiles of prominent boarders, along with information on the gear they use, as its main way of presenting products (see Exhibit 5.8).

Content Type. The information presented on a website has a degree of time sensitivity. Headline news, for example, is highly time-sensitive information with a very short shelf life. For some businesses, presenting time-sensitive content *is* their business—for example, Bloomberg and Reuters are proprietary sources of real-time financial market data. Week-old stock data have limited value, except for archival and research purposes, as compared with stock information that is instantaneous. On the other hand, reference content is less time-sensitive and has a longer shelf life. Often it is historical in nature and is used as supporting or related factual material. Most online newspapers, including NYTimes.com, the online version of *The New York Times,* offer an archive of past articles in addition to today's breaking news. Many commerce sites, including REI.com, will provide a great deal of current content, such as notices of special deals and discounts, as well as reference content, such as tips from the experts, that is designed to be "evergreen"—meaning that it does not require frequent updates.

Visitor can view video, read a bio, find out what gear this rider uses, and view stills.

Site is aimed at snowboarding enthusiasts, not beginners.

Commerce is secondary to brand reinforcement on the Burton site.

HUB ▸ WOMEN RIDERS ▸ NICOLA THOST

DEALERS | SEARCH | CONTACT | FAQ

RIDERS.WOMEN

Name: Nicola Thost
Date of Birth: May 3, 1977
Home Base: Munich, Germany
Stance: Regular: Front 27 / Back 3

This year was a tough one for Nicola, challenged with a knee injury early in the season. Before the injury, Nicola was able to get in a lot of riding, showing the world that she can boost with the same amplitude and style as always. Nicola set the

Check out Nicola's own site:
www.nicolathost.com

EXHIBIT 5.8   Content: Burton.com

Source: *www.burton.com*. Used with permission.

Why Community?

Why Community Can Attract Individuals to the Customer Interface

Community is a set of interwoven relationships built upon shared interests (see Chapter 10). A group of people can create strong, lasting relationships that may develop into a community through an engaged and extended exchange of ideas about members' common interests. This sense of community can encourage customers to return to a website, primarily because:

- *Community can create attractive content.* This content, either member-generated or administrator-generated, can serve as an attractive incentive for individuals to come to a site. Such content might take the form of member postings, community-exclusive research, or sponsored chats with special guests.

- *Community can make certain activities possible or easier, thus satisfying needs not attainable individually.* Chapter 10 discusses the various advantages to scale, and how online communities such as eBay can leverage their size to increase benefits for members. Large, well-run communities can have much to offer—they can make finding particular products, information, or even types of people possible or easier for members. By satisfying a need that could not have been satisfied otherwise, communities offer another attractive benefit for individuals to visit and return to a website.

Design Tip

Creating a site that combines fresh as well as evergreen content should be part of most companies' website strategy. Freshness brings customers back, and stable content provides a useful archive for the customer; it also limits a company's resource requirements.

Point–Counterpoint

Do Graphics Enhance or Encumber Website Usability?

A considerable number of articles have been written about the use of graphics on websites, their effectiveness for the online audience, and their impact on website usability. Over the past few years, particularly with the growth of the Internet, an increasing number of graphic designers from traditional print media companies have been employed to develop websites. These designers have incorporated proven print media techniques into their designs, creating sites that are not only familiar but also comfortable to the online user. This use of recognizable graphics can perpetuate an offline brand to the online marketplace. Brand-sensitive companies such as consumer products companies have an additional advantage in that their logos evoke brand loyalty and thus should draw users to their websites. Finally, customers like to be able to view products online. They want visual cues that the product described on a website is one that will meet their needs before they order or purchase.

On the other hand, such graphics-laden sites have their detractors, who say that users are looking for information, not distractions. According to a recent Poynter Institute study, users are far more attracted to text than they are to photographs, banner ads, and other graphics. This and other studies show that offline viewing preferences are for photographs first, then headlines, and finally text—the complete opposite order of the preferences of the online viewer. This study indicated that offline design rules might not always apply online. Other criticisms of the use of website graphics include increased site download time—which is especially the case for users with telephone modems. Also, depending on the user's browser, the image quality may be poor and render text unreadable.

In the end, it is important to weigh the purpose of placing graphics on a website. Once that function is determined, one must make careful choices that will heighten, not detract from, the site's appeal.

These incentives benefit both the community member and the parent firm—they give members a reason to visit the site, and give the parent firm increased traffic and a larger customer base. Parent firms also benefit from the community in several other ways; for example, communities can lower service costs, marketing costs, and customer-acquisition costs. The reader feedback and star-rating system at Amazon.com is a good example of how visitor interaction can both influence sales and allow the visitor to feel profoundly attached to the site, since they know that their opinions are welcomed by the company and other visitors.

A few sites have taken community a step beyond chat rooms and message boards. For example, the Lands' End website has an innovative feature that allows two users to shop simultaneously from their separate computers. This trademarked service, termed Shop with a Friend, enables two users to view the site at the same time, browse together, and trade impressions of a garment. It is a popular virtual shopping experience that serves to strengthen the shoppers' relationship. Amazon's "Share the Love" feature invites users to become viral marketers by making it possible for them to e-mail their own book recommendations to others in their real and virtual communities (and get a further discount for their efforts).

While the 7Cs can provide effective guidance in building community, firms must also be sensitive to other considerations—the types of individuals the community attracts, the community's stage of development, the level of involvement of its typical member, etc. All these considerations can affect

Design Tip

Active communities do not always have to be part of a company's own site for the company to experience their power. Opinion websites such as Epinions, Planetfeedback, and BizRate.com are gathering places for consumers seeking a forum to discuss their experiences with products, companies, and services. Managers are well advised to monitor the postings of such independent communities to learn what their customers are thinking. And whether the community content is hosted on the parent site or elsewhere, the emphasis should be on enhancing the customer experience.

optimal community functioning and site design. In general, community design implementation for parent sites should reinforce the brand and offer access through interface design and navigation to key actions to forward business goals. Yet not all sites should offer community functionality. Whether a company should add community to its site is a strategy decision. For further discussion of when community may or may not be applicable—and a holistic approach to building effective community—see Chapter 10.

What Are the Levers Used to Customize a Site?

To better address individual user needs, a site can be altered by the user or by the organization. Customization initiated by the user is called **personalization**; customization implemented by the film is called **tailoring**.

Dimensions of Customization

Personalization. Some websites allow users to specify their preferences in content selection, context selection, and personalization tools. Once personal preferences have been entered by the user and saved, the site uses a login registration (or cookies) to match each returning user to his or her respective personal setting, then configures itself accordingly. To attract users and keep them returning, the site provides a variety of features that include personalized e-mail accounts, virtual hard-disk storage, and software agents to perform simple tasks. Further descriptions of these features are provided below:

- *Login Registration.* Having previously registered on a site, the user returns and enters the requisite identification information through the site interface. The site recognizes the returning user and configures itself to the user's preset preferences.

- *Cookies.* Most website owners want to identify visitors and understand how they are using their sites. These sites attempt to track and gather data on returning users' behavior by quietly saving, identifying, and tracking information on the users' local disk storage in temporary files called cookies.

- *Personalized E-Mail Accounts.* Many sites provide e-mail accounts free of charge. Users may send and receive e-mail from the site, using a unique e-mail address.

- *Content and Layout Configuration.* Users can select screen layout and content sources based on their interests.

- *Storage.* Sites provide virtual hard-disk storage space. Users can store e-mail, URLs, and other content on these sites.

- *Agents.* Users can activate computer programs—also known as agents—that are designed to perform specific simple tasks (e.g., notify individuals via e-mail when a product is in stock).

Tailoring by Site. Many sites have the ability, through their interface software, to dynamically "publish" different versions of the site in order to better address specific users' interests, habits, and needs. For example, sites might present different content with different design layouts to different users depending on each user's responses and/or profile. A site can use a recommendation engine (e.g., collaborative filtering as developed by Firefly or Net Perceptions) to automatically adapt to each user's behavior; vary its mix of products, information, and service offerings; and recommend content or products that the user is likely to find of interest. Recommendations can be made based on past purchases by the user or based on purchases by other users with similar purchase profiles. A site can be automated to offer each user more suitable price and payment terms, and marketing messages can be developed for the individual user based on exhibited behavior or declared preferences.

- *Tailoring based on past user behavior.* Many sites adjust themselves dynamically based on a user's past behavior and preferences. Examples of automated adjustments include price, payment terms, and marketing messages.
- *Tailoring based on behavior of other users with similar preferences.* Sites make recommendations to the user based on preferences of other users with similar usage profiles (e.g., collaborative filtering).

Consider Amazon.com. In addition to greeting visitors by name (thanks to the use of cookies), Amazon provides recommendations based on past buying behavior, a user-defined "wish list" of desired products, and by querying the user directly about whether past recommendations matched his or her interests. Amazon also provides "My Store," where visitors see their favorite site sections, and a "Friends and Family" section where the user can define and interact with selected community members and "purchase circles" of people with similar interests or geographical location.

Lands' End has also implemented innovative personalization and customization tools (see Exhibit 5.9.) On the site, a user is able to personalize the site with the feature "My Model." Here, a visitor can enter basic size information, and in turn can see how particular items would look on them. An example of tailoring on Landsend.com comes in a unique customization feature. "My Personal Shopper," allows customers to describe their basic body type and style likes and dislikes, triggering a recommendation engine that matches appropriate items to the customer's preferences.

What Types of Communication Can a Firm Maintain with Its Customer Base?

Communication refers to dialogue between a firm and its customers. The dialogue may be unidirectional—that is, one-way from the organization to the user—or the dialogue may be more interactive.

Dimensions of Communication

The section below describes and provides examples of three dimensions of communication: broadcast, interactive, and hybrid.

Broadcast. Broadcast is a one-way information exchange from organization to user. With this unidirectional transmission of information, organizations provide no mechanism for the user to respond. In general, broadcast communication is a "one-to-many" relationship between the website and its users. Alternative forms of broadcast communication are described below. (Managers should note that current best practices for broadcast messaging assume that the customer has "opted in" and given permission for the company to contact them.)

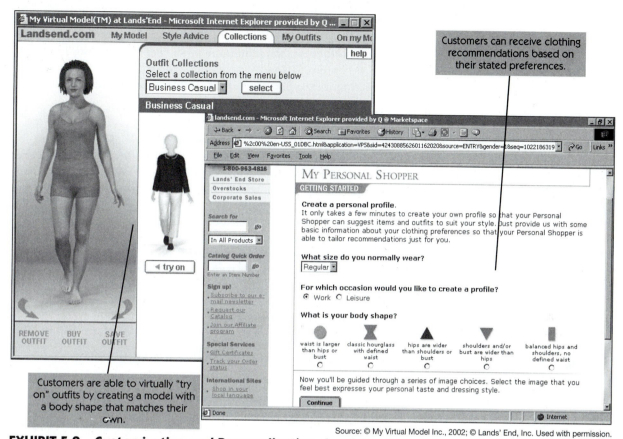

EXHIBIT 5.9   Customization and Personalization: Lands' End

Source: © My Virtual Model Inc., 2002; © Lands' End, Inc. Used with permission.

- *Mass Mailings.* Many times, broadcast communications are transmissions targeted at a relatively wide audience.

- *FAQs.* Organizations post webpages with clear answers to frequently asked questions about the site, goods, or services.

- *E-Mail Newsletters.* Regular newsletters are sent by e-mail to inform subscribers of new features or changes to a site, special offers, corporate news, etc.

- *Content Update Notifications.* E-mail messages can be further tailored to reflect each subscriber's interests and serve as notifications to users for relevant new content now available to them.

- *Broadcast Events.* Also, events can be broadcast from a website (for example, via a webcam) in a way that allows limited user control over variables such as camera view.

Interactive.   Interactive communication is two-way communication between the organization and a user. Below are alternative forms of interactive communication.

- *E-Commerce Dialogue.* Firms use two-way communication as part of their e-commerce dialogue. Firms and users regularly trade e-mail messages regarding order placement, tracking, and fulfillment.

- *Customer Service.* Firms can provide customer service through the swapping of e-mail or through live online dialogue.
- *User Input.* Another two-way communication occurs when user input is provided as content to a site—user-generated articles on topics of interest, user ratings of suppliers, and user feedback to the site.

Landsend.com is a pioneer in interactive communication with customers. Its tools include a communications feature called Lands' End Live that enables the user to interact directly with the customer service representative while shopping on the site. Clicking on the Lands' End Live button results in two options: (1) connection by phone (this assumes the user has two phone lines or high-speed Internet service), or (2) connection by live text chat.

Hybrid. As its name indicates, hybrid communication is a combination of broadcast and interactive communications. These sites offer software tools as "freeware" that users can download and use at no charge for their work or entertainment. Users often pass this free software to friends and, in essence, provide free marketing for the originating site. Companies use this technique of viral marketing with the hope of rapid, broad distribution and immediate creation of brand recognition.

How Does a Firm Connect with Other Businesses?

Connection is the degree to which a given site is able to link to other sites through a hypertext jump, or hyperlink, from one webpage to another. These links are embedded in a webpage and are most commonly presented to the user as underlined and highlighted words, a picture, or a graphic. Clicking on the link initiates the immediate delivery of a text, graphic, or sound file (or an actual webpage that can be a combination of all these types of files). Files might live on the local server, or on a server anywhere in the world.

Dimensions of Connection

Connections vary in type, magnitude, and direction. The five dimensions of connection are described below:

Links to Sites. These are links that take the user completely outside the homesite and into a third-party site. Users of NYTimes.com can access the book review section; in that section, a link to Barnes & Noble.com appears with an offer relating to its online retail bookstore. Users who click on the Barnes & Noble logo wind up at Barnes & Noble.com, where they can shop for the books they just read about.

Homesite Background. This refers to a situation in which the link takes the user to a third-party site, but the homesite is noticeable in the background. Upromise, for example, is an aggregator of affiliate shopping programs that applies a percentage of every purchase to a college saving account. When users click on a particular site, they are taken to that site—but with the Upromise top navigation framing the page. Such "framing" sites are less common than they used to be because linked sites often complain about brand confusion and possible copyright issues. If managers consider using this sort of frame, it is essential to clarify the relationship between homesite and third-party site.

Design Tip

Communication tools require careful planning and attention. While customers may agree, for instance, to receive notices about sales or special events, they quickly become irritated if they perceive that they are receiving too many company messages. In general, companies should understand that customers want to feel that they control the company/customer interaction. So designers should make it very easy for customers to "opt out" of the communications loop—for example, with a link in each e-mail taking the customer to a preferences page. Also, companies need to be explicit about customer privacy and the ways contact information will, or will not, be shared with others. Vague privacy policies are a deterrent for users, who will take their business elsewhere if they feel that they have been misled.

Drill-Down

Non-PC Interfaces

When marketers think "interface," they usually envision a consumer, sitting at a desk, viewing a website on a personal computer. The world of digital interfaces is much wider than that, however. And it is getting more diverse all the time.

In fact, the granddaddy of screen-to-face interfaces, the now-ubiquitous automatic teller machine, or ATM, has nothing to do with either the World Wide Web or the PC. (It predates both.) And a number of new mobile devices, from handheld computers to Web-enabled cellphones to e-books to multifunction portables with always-on connections, while still in their early stages, threaten eventually to untether the masses from their desktops and deliver the Internet in a whole new way, on wholly new media.

As a result, in addition to figuring out how to manage the Web, both marketers and content providers must plan for a future that will be, if not entirely "post-PC," at least far more diverse in terms of the platforms on which people consume digital data. What exactly does that mean? *The Wall Street Journal*, one of the earliest and most aggressive players in the mobile-devices marketplace, provides an instructive glimpse.

The *Journal*, which has offered its Web-based "Interactive Edition" since 1996, began its efforts to deliver handheld daily editions in early 1999, teaming up with AvantGo to prepare its articles for Palms and other handheld devices. AvantGo's system operates via a free "mini-browser" that users install on their handhelds to read articles provided by publishers and downloaded from AvantGo's servers.

The *Journal*'s conversion from big screen to small was aided by two factors: (1) it already stored its content in XML, the data-markup language used by many publishers to format content across a variety of platforms; and (2) its print edition already ran concise, two-sentence summaries of key articles—an ideal format for handhelds' tiny screens. (Other publishers have chosen to display an article's first line, which users can tap on to access the full text.)

AvantGo was only one of many mobile and wireless service providers with whom the *Journal* partnered to deliver its content across a wide variety of handheld devices, Web-enabled mobile phones, and e-books. Among the others: AT&T, Palm, Franklin Electronic Publishers, and Captivate, which beamed *Journal* headlines to office-building elevator passengers (via television screens).

The *Journal* also delved into a completely different and highly promising interface: not screen-to-face, but voice-to-ear. In 1999, the paper joined with Audible.com to deliver spoken-word digest summaries of articles that could be downloaded and played back on PCs, MP3 players, and some handheld devices. It also provided audio versions via OnStar, the General Motors-owned vehicle communication system, which allowed subscribers to "read" the paper while driving to work.

Whether the PC remains the primary Internet interface for many years to come or the future is entirely "post-PC," it is inevitable that mobile and wireless devices will constitute an increasingly large part of the media mix. That's something that *The Wall Street Journal* and a growing number of companies in nearly every industry understand.

Outsourced Content. Site content is often derived from third parties, but the user remains on the homesite while viewing or reading that content. Many sites use **outsourced content** such as stock quotes and news feeds to augment their appeal to users. These content "plug-ins" are usually identified by their sources (e.g., Associated Press, CNN.com, Weather.com).

Percentage of Homesite Content. Not all content on any given site is generated, owned, or controlled by that site. For example, newspapers publish wire stories that came from external sources. As a result, it is important to

Design Tip

Senior managers and their design teams must determine how important it is for them to keep visitors on their sites. Firms such as AOL and Amazon.com can be thought of as "walled gardens" that prevent visitors from straying because outside links are not offered. A portal such as Yahoo!, on the other hand, consists largely of links off the Yahoo! site. This leverages the strengths of the core functionality of the Internet, but makes it more difficult for Yahoo! to retain visitors for long. While it may seem intuitively smart to make it difficult for visitors to leave your site, many companies are discovering that links to third-party content create the positive impression that the company is providing objective information for the benefit of the customer, rather than simply marketing messages for the company.

understand how content is internally generated or outsourced with respect to a given site's content strategy.

Pathway of Connection.   The pathway of the connection can lead a user outside the environment of the site as a "pathway-out," or can lead to the retrieval of information from other sites without actually leaving the site as a "pathway-in." In other words, pathway-out links take a user off of a website and onto another website, while pathway-in links call up the desired information without forcing users to exit the website on which the link is located.

Few online retailers have connections to other sites. However, they sometimes offer an affiliate program that allows other sites to connect to the home site via banner ads or buttons. The affiliate partner earns a percentage of every sale that occurs on a click-through from the site. If a customer is a first-time buyer, the affiliate may also earn a finder's fee.

Drill-Down

Online and Offline Integration of the Customer Interface

While this chapter has applied the 7Cs Framework to the online customer interface, it is important to note that all the elements of the online interface can also be replicated offline. The design of mutually reinforcing online and offline interfaces provides a consistent offering and brand message to the customer. This section explores how each of the 7Cs might be implemented offline. The section also examines examples of the successful integration of online and offline interfaces.

Context in the offline world is the look-and-feel of the physical store. Context includes, among other things, the store architecture, the appearance and demeanor of the store's staff, the openness of the retail environment, the store's interior colors, and product style selection. J.Crew stores convey a sense of spaciousness and lightness by the use of open space and abundant natural and artificial light. Store colors match the colors of the clothing offered in the store, and the stylish and uncluttered look-and-feel of the physical store matches the look-and-feel of J.Crew's website. This look-and-feel reinforces the company positioning as a relaxed place to shop for stylish and casual clothes. On the other hand, Gap stores are designed to help shoppers navigate the store and to maximize sales. Customers know they can find new fashionable items at the front of the store, core lines (such as chinos and jeans) in the middle of the store, and sale items at the very back.

Content in the offline world includes all the products, services, and associated information about products and services offered at physical store locations. Barnes & Noble bookstores contain a very wide selection of books and magazines. Customers can get large discounts on some book categories, such as bestsellers, and find information on books by searching through catalogs or by using in-store computer terminals. Customer service is readily available through the many customer service representatives on staff at most stores. Barnes & Noble.com has nearly identical virtual offerings, providing the same easy access to information and prices through powerful search software.

Community in the offline world is communication between and among customers and staff. Community can be encouraged through store events or through store participation in and sponsoring of community activities. Borders bookstores often host author readings and book signings. At these events, readers can interact with each other and meet people with similar taste in books. Each year in Los Angeles, Revlon sponsors the Revlon Run/Walk for Women to increase breast cancer awareness, raise research funds, and bring together customers and noncustomers alike.

continued

Customization in the offline world takes a number of different forms. A store can personalize products and services that customers purchase. Credit card holders can have a photograph and a signature imprinted on the face of their credit cards, thus personalizing the card as well as reducing the risk of credit card fraud. Levi's customers can buy made-to-order jeans. To some degree, stores can also customize experience based on exhibited customer needs. Local restaurants recognize loyal customers by automatically seating them at their favorite tables. Airlines can automatically assign customers their preference of aisle or window seating each time they travel. Stores can also send targeted marketing messages to users based on their exhibited purchase behavior. Some catalog retailers send customized catalogs based on individual purchase history.

Communication in the offline world is either one-way (store-to-customer) or two-way (between store and customer). One-way communication can take the form of newsletters or catalogs that stores send to customers. Stores can also provide personalized alerts to customers. For example, investors using Merrill Lynch's full brokerage services can arrange for an alert from a broker by phone call whenever market conditions warrant it. Customers can participate in two-way communications with stores by filling out surveys generated by the store. Furthermore, customers can ask for live assistance either in person (when physically in the store) or via phone. Nordstrom is widely known for excellent customer service. Nordstrom customer service representatives have been known to deliver purchased products directly to customers' homes.

Connection in the offline world is the degree to which a store associates with other stores. Stores in large shopping malls are located near a number of other stores, which allows customers to move quickly from one store to another. A retailer can rent concession space in a large department store to provide an additional sales channel, to be associated with other nearby concessions, and to allow customers to easily move back and forth between concessions. Stores can also provide links to a large number of suppliers who offer products or services of interest to customers. Travel agencies provide links to a large number of travel providers that include airlines, hotels, and cruise-line operators. Furthermore, stores can increase their customer base through partnerships. For example, Coca-Cola increases its sales by partnering with McDonald's to make Coke products available at all McDonald's locations.

Commerce in the offline world is the transaction capabilities of a store. Stores provide transaction capabilities through means such as shopping carts, security verifications, custom gift-wrapping, and various delivery options. In addition, stores can offer a number of price-determination options. Most offline stores provide products and services at predetermined catalog prices. The auction house Sotheby's, on the other hand, offers members Dutch-style or English-style auctions to determine the prices of pieces of art, jewelry, or other items up for sale. Also, haggling remains a popular way of determining price in industries. Purchasing a car at a local dealership generally involves a lengthy negotiating process in which dealer and customer make offers and counteroffers and may or may not reach an agreed-upon price. Demand aggregation also occurs occasionally in the offline world. Travel agents sometimes prepurchase large blocks of airlines seats and pass along savings to buyers of package vacations.

What Are the Dimensions of Commerce?

Commerce capabilities are those features of the customer interface that support the various aspects of trading transactions. This section focuses on functional tools regarding commerce as a design element.

Dimensions of Commerce

Functional tools are any commerce-enabling features of a website. In order for a site to have e-commerce capabilities, a number of features must be present. These include, but are not limited to:

Registration.   User registration allows a site to store credit card information, shipping addresses, and preferences.

Shopping Cart.   Users can place items into their personal virtual shopping cart. Items can be purchased immediately or stored and purchased when the user returns on another visit to the site.

Security.   Sites attempt to guarantee security of transactions and related data through encryption (e.g., SSL) and authentication technologies (e.g., SET).

Credit Card Approval.   Sites can have the ability to receive instant credit approval for credit card purchases through electronic links to credit card clearance houses.

One-Click Shopping.   Amazon.com uses a patented feature that allows users to order products with a single click. Delivery default settings are applied automatically.

Orders Through Affiliates.   Sites with affiliate programs must be able to track orders that originate from affiliate sites, as well as determine affiliate fees for business generation.

Configuration Technology.   Users can put products and services together in a variety of permutations with the aid of configuration software, thus allowing analysis of performance/price tradeoffs, interoperability among complex components within a system, and substitution of generic for branded products.

Order Tracking.   Users are given the ability to check the delivery status of the products they ordered.

Delivery Options.   Users are presented with a choice of options to specify their desired speed and cost of delivery (next-day shipping, two-day shipping, etc.).

Drill-Down

Best Practices in Web Design

While the Internet is still a fairly new medium, several design and navigation conventions have become widely accepted. Firms whose offerings fail to adhere to these principles will encounter usability issues and will likely frustrate site visitors. In general, site designers should strive to understand customers' goals, anticipate them, and make it easy to accomplish them.

1. Put your most important content or links "above the fold" so that visitors do not have to scroll down the page, and remember that monitor sizes vary. It is currently safest to design for a screen size of 800 by 600 pixels. Avoid horizontal scrolling, which most users find extremely irritating.

2. Provide a search box that is easy to see, generally in the top left or right corner of the screen. This should be a box, not a link to search, and the box should be wide enough to accommodate a typical query. Make your search

continued

engine work the way your customers think. Analyze search logs to see what terms people are entering, and where they are getting no results or error pages. Search logs may also reveal problems with overall site navigation; for example, they may search for an entire category rather than an individual item if they do not understand your site's navigation structure.

3. Do not require users to register in order to browse product or information pages. Many visitors resent mandatory registration and will go to a competitor's site instead. Also, do not assume that registration should be required in order to buy; offer your visitors the option of purchasing as a guest.

4. Engage site visitors in the objective of the site as soon as possible. If your site is a shopping site, allow users to shop from the homepage or, at most, one click away from the homepage. In general, the homepage should clearly convey what visitors can do at a site. The average user spends less than six seconds on a homepage, and the homepage is the most frequent abandonment point. While you do not necessarily need to be able to shop from the homepage on a shopping site, you should be able to figure out that it *is* a shopping site.

5. In general, Web visitors do not read; they skim over content quickly, so text presentation should be qualitatively different from print media—more abbreviated, more use of bullets, highlighted keywords, more white space in between columns. The test should be: Is it easy to skim the text and still understand the point? Knowing and delivering for your particular audience is the key. *The New York Times* user expects something different than the *PC Gamer* user, even if he or she is the same person.

6. Allow users to easily access information about the full cost of products before buying (shipping cost, tax, etc.). Surprises at the end of checkout are a frequent cause of abandoned shopping carts.

7. Make your customer service telephone number easy to find on a global header or footer on your site. Also, provide alternate ways site visitors can contact you—via e-mail, or with a form to be completed and forwarded to your customer service department.

8. Site maps are an excellent way to let your visitors know what is where on your site, all in one convenient place. Many Web users will start there, preferring to bypass both screen navigation and search functionality.

9. Provide printer-friendly functionality for content-heavy pages, so that site visitors can read your materials offline in a familiar format.

10. Error pages should be written in plain English, not technospeak. They should offer the user exit options or alternative remedies, and, if possible, should contain an explanation of why the error occurred. It is acceptable to include technical explanations below the plain English version, since they give more technical users an idea of potential solutions and are also useful to site managers if the visitor is requested to report the error (and has been given explicit directions on how to do so).

11. If an item is out of stock, inform your customers of that fact as soon in the selection/buying process as possible. Customers who spend time searching for, locating, and selecting a product will become irritated if they find out the item is not available when they go to check out. A well-designed database will ensure that customers are only offered products that are currently in stock.

12. Any traveler who has attempted to drive in a foreign country can attest that the meaning of icons is not always obvious, and sometimes even indecipherable. Use only widely recognized icons (a shopping cart, for example) throughout your site, and label them so that users will immediately understand their meaning.

13. If you want visitors to become your evangelists, make it easy for them by providing "e-mail this page" functionality throughout your site.

Building Fit and Reinforcement

The previous section provided a basic overview of each of the 7Cs. However, the success of a particular business depends upon the extent to which all of the 7Cs work together to support the value proposition and business model. Two concepts—**fit and reinforcement**—are particularly helpful in explaining how it is possible to gain synergy among the 7Cs.[2] Fit refers to the extent to which each of the 7Cs individually supports the business model. Reinforcement refers to the degree of consistency between each of the Cs.

Consider, once again, the Lands' End website, which largely targets middle-class consumers. The content of the site "fits" this value proposition by providing mainstream and conservative fashions; its innovative live chat fits with great service; and the price points of regularly priced clothing fit the moderate pricing strategy. As for reinforcement, the aesthetic context of the Landsend.com site—with its pictures of happy, smiling customers, light-blue tones, and "soft sell" approach—works well with the focus on ease of product searches, ease of navigation, clean and clear visual displays of clothing, and detailed product descriptions. The elements of context, content, customization, and commerce all work well together to provide a clear, reinforcing statement of the value proposition. In designing for fit and reinforcement, the Lands' End team clearly took into consideration the tastes and values of its target customers.

The synergy generated by fit and reinforcement is a dynamic process, and companies may find that different target customers respond to each of the 7Cs differently. This does not imply that sites should be designed for a generic customer, only that managers should revisit the online offering regularly to assess how well the value proposition and business model are being expressed on the site.

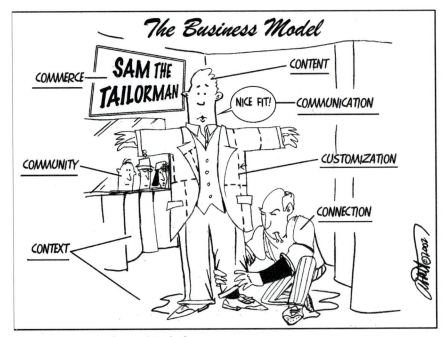

EXHIBIT 5.10   Fit and Reinforcement

Conclusion

The 7Cs Framework provides managers with a roadmap for designing a screen-to-face interface. Yet each of the 7Cs must be considered carefully during the design and prototyping process. For some companies the emphasis on commerce will be the most important; for others, it may be community or customization. Aligning business strategy with interface design is the goal, and underlying this endeavor is a key issue: usability. While creating a successful interface may appear to be a daunting challenge, a company has a valuable secret weapon—its own customers. To ensure that a design is actually meeting the needs of customers, it is essential to bring them into the process early in the development of the site—for example, to test out prototypes. Only by observing actual customers as they attempt to navigate a site can a design team transform the 7Cs Framework into an interface that works.

Every one of the companies cited as examples in this chapter offer thriving, successful interfaces. Yet they all have evolved, changed, and modified features based on customer feedback, gleaned either from of site log analysis or direct observation of customers using the sites. A benefit of digital technology is that rapid response is possible, and very few mistakes are fatal ones. If a company focuses on customer experience and customer feedback, keeps an eye on the competition, keeps current with best practices, and responds to customer needs, the chances of victory are considerably enhanced. Exhibit 5.11 summarizes each of the 7Cs and their associated design goals.

The 7Cs	Goals for Site Design
Context	Function: Site should load quickly, have good information architecture, and have an effective search. Aesthetics: Design should reflect brand and customer experience offline; use multimedia sparingly, if at all.
Content	Provide content to address both cognitive and emotional appeal. Keep the homepage simple, with effective calls to action. Make sure site content is regularly updated.
Community	Community is not applicable to every Internet venture. If site provides community activities, make sure that participants and their messages reinforce the brand.
Customization	Site visitors are drawn to customization and personalization. If possible, design an interface that individuals can interact with and modify.
Communication	Make sure customers have "opted in" to broadcast messaging. Place customer service information prominently throughout the site. Post a privacy policy and be vigilant about enforcing it.
Connection	Customers may be wary of sites that make it difficult to find appropriate information. Consider supplying links to third-party sites whose content complements your own.
Commerce	Provide secure checkout that asks only for necessary information, protects customer privacy, reveals shipping costs upfront, allows order tracking, and supplies customer service and order confirmation data.

EXHIBIT 5.11   The 7Cs and Design Strategies

eBay Example

This section examines eBay's customer interface in relation to the 7Cs, and discusses how eBay successfully meets each element of interface design.

Context

Recall that context, which focuses on how subject matter is presented, has two dimensions: function and aesthetics. Exhibit 5.12 shows the homepage for eBay.com. eBay's functional design is readily apparent to new and old visitors alike. It is designed, above all, to make it easy for users to find and sell items.

The site is divided into distinct sections. The center portion of the site highlights items that may be topically appropriate (e.g., spring fashions in springtime) or that may be hot items at any given point in time. The left-hand column is divided into three sections: specialty sites, individual item categories, and regional or global sites. Finally, the bottom portion of the middle part of the screen is reserved for featured auctions. Sellers pay a premium for these highly coveted slots.

eBay's design helps buyers locate desired objects within broad category ranges, as well as search for items by narrower geographic criteria. Sellers, on the other hand, can go directly to the "Sell" section of the homepage and learn about how to sell or how to add items to their current set of listings. Aesthetically, the site exudes an ease of use with a clean layout, making it easy to locate desired items. eBay reinforces its brand by using colors from its logo throughout the site. For instance, the blue from the "B" in eBay and the orange from the "Y" appear often. Visually, eBay maintains a consistent typeface, presenting users with a reliable and familiar interface. All in all, eBay's clean and predominantly textual site provides only the information relevant and necessary for buyers and sellers to make purchases and sales. The site design is direct, to the point, and transparent, and it is consistent with eBay's overall message and strategy.

Content

Content focuses on the types of material presented on the site and has four dimensions: offering mix, appeal mix, multimedia mix, and content type. In essence, eBay is a giant content company with two kinds of content: user-provided content and eBay-provided content. The combination of these two content types is part of what makes eBay a dynamic trading environment.

Offering Mix.   The eBay offering mix is predominantly focused on (1) product and information, on the buying/selling side, and (2) services. Exhibit 5.13 shows the combination of product and information on one page. In any individual listing on eBay, the item description and visuals are provided by the seller and serve as a way to merchandise the item to potential customers. eBay provides the framework in which sellers nest this content.

A different content mix is seen when one looks at eBay's services. By clicking on the "Services" button on the navigation bar, users are taken to a page that serves as a launching pad for eBay's entire range of services (see Exhibit 5.14).

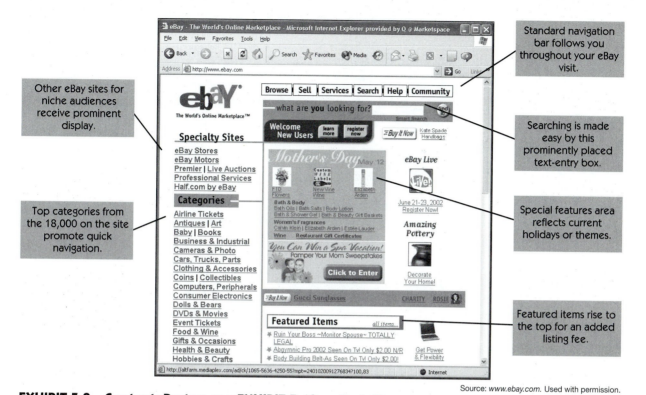

EXHIBIT 5.8   Content: Burton.comEXHIBIT 5.12   eBay's Homepage

Source: *www.ebay.com.* Used with permission.

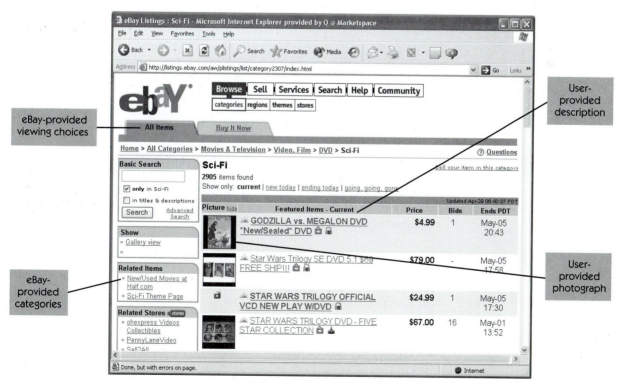

EXHIBIT 5.13   eBay Mix of Product and Information

Source: *www.ebay.com.* Used with permission.

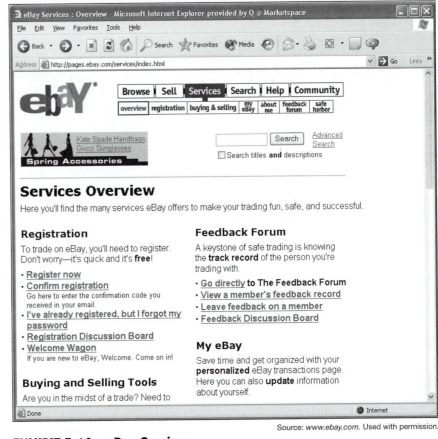

Source: *www.ebay.com*. Used with permission.

EXHIBIT 5.14   eBay Services

Appeal Mix.   eBay's appeal mix is primarily cognitive or functional. eBay's design is optimized to make searching for particular items as simple as possible. Users can find an item by typing its name into the search window, browsing by category or by region, or by accessing the "Live Help" feature. With millions of auctions underway at any one time, it is imperative that ease-of-use is conveyed to users from the outset.

Multimedia Mix.   For now, eBay's multimedia mix is limited to text and images, except for a small number of instructional slide shows. However, as broadband gains greater acceptance, one can envision a day when sellers could post videos of their products. For automobiles, a 360-degree view of a vehicle may make the difference between someone browsing for a car and bidding on it.

Content Type.   eBay places a priority on the timeliness of its information, and limits its auctions to a 10-day maximum. This adds an element of urgency to the traditional auction side of the business. With auctions compressed to 10 days or less, there is only so much browsing one can do before being compelled to join the bidding.

Community

Community is the cornerstone of eBay's stunning growth. As of the close of the first quarter of 2002, eBay boasted 45 million users—making it one of the largest online communities ever created. eBay has been extremely attentive to its users since its inception. Today, it offers a variety of services—such as chat rooms, community help boards, and newsletters—in order to attract and keep community members. In conjunction with its simple, easy-to-use interface, eBay's down-to-earth style of service has furthered its popularity and contributed to its continued growth as one of the most effective communities on the Internet (for more on this, see Chapter 10).

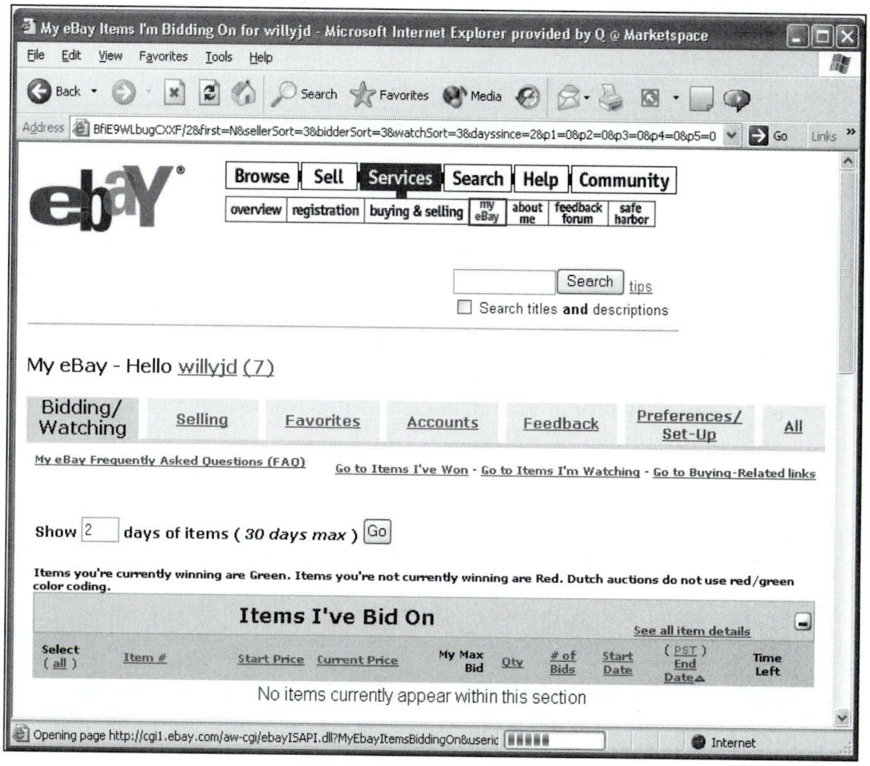

Source: *www.ebay.com*. Used with permission.

EXHIBIT 5.15   eBay Customization through "My eBay"

Customization

eBay gives users the ability to personalize the site to their preferences. After registering, users can customize eBay through the "My eBay" option on the site (see Exhibit 5.15). The major features on any personalized site are the default display, the user's account information, and other preferences and features selected or customized by the user. My eBay aggregates disparate information in one logical place and includes several features (see Exhibit 5.16).

Communication

eBay is a highly interactive site, hosting millions of auctions simultaneously. Communication on eBay occurs on both the broadcast and interactive dimensions. eBay broadcasts information through its FAQs, which are updated regularly to reflect both current policy and key user issues. eBay also broadcasts information through its "eBay Insider" newsletter. By far the most prevalent form of communication on eBay comes through the interactive

Type of User	Activity
Buyers	View items within a 30-day window that they have bid on, have won, or are currently watching
Sellers	View item within a 30-day window that they are selling or have already sold
All	Conduct favorite searches and view favorite categories
All	View account status
All	View all user feedback ever received
All	General site preferences can be set

EXHIBIT 5.16   eBay Personalization through "My eBay"

dimension. eBay facilitates two-way communication in numerous ways, whether it is between buyers and sellers, buyers and eBay, or sellers and eBay. One of the more original and important two-way communication devices created by eBay is its Feedback Forum, in which buyers and sellers rate each other (see Exhibit 5.17). A negative ranking can cause a seller to freeze out a buyer from his or her auction, or a prospective buyer to shun the auction of an unreliable seller.

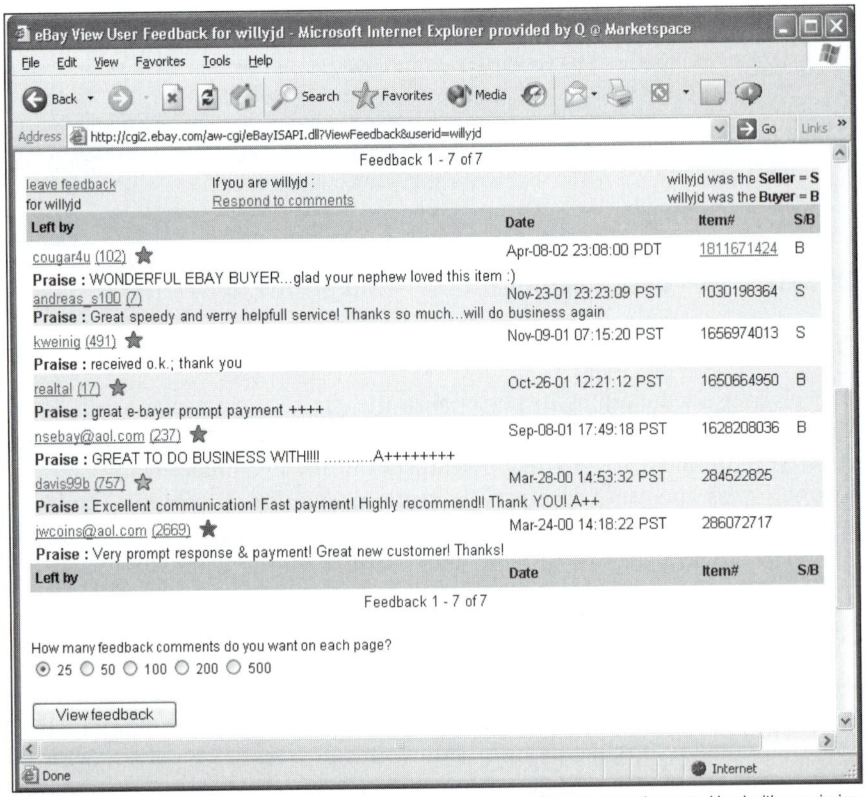

Source: *www.ebay.com.* Used with permission.

EXHIBIT 5.17   Feedback Forum—An Individual's Card

Connection

eBay is generally not connected to other sites. Unlike a portal, which encourages movement across a variety of different sites, eBay wants its members to browse and stay within its site. eBay positions itself as the ultimate destination for buying and selling wares on the Internet, offering a truly enormous range of products. The only visible links on the eBay site are to its suppliers, providers, and partners (see Exhibit 5.18). Noticeably absent from eBay are clickable ad banners that might take people away from the site.

To accomplish its mission of helping "practically anyone trade practically anything on earth," eBay must ensure that its entire customer interface is designed to facilitate the buying and selling of goods on its site. For this reason, it makes sense for eBay not to refer users to other e-commerce sites or to potential competitors. By intentionally minimizing its connection to other sites, eBay reinforces the notion that it is focused on serving everyone's buying and selling needs.

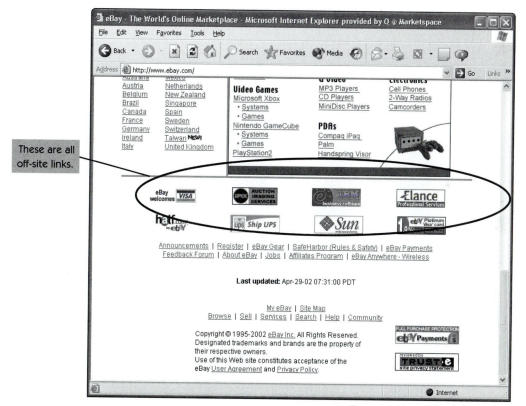

Source: *www.ebay.com*. Used with permission.

EXHIBIT 5.18   Linked Sites

Commerce

While most of eBay's commerce is conducted through an auction format, about one in five sales are now fixed-price (including those conducted through Half.com). Whether auction or fixed-price, eBay provides the same set of tools to facilitate transactions. Among these tools are:

- *User Registration.* Only registered users who have given their credit card information can purchase goods through eBay (unregistered users can browse but must register to bid).
- *Security.* Safe Harbor, eBay's comprehensive safety resource, is accessible from every page.
- *Auction Tracking.* Through My eBay, bidders can manage their auction process and use links to consummate successful transactions. Links include "send and receive shipping information" and "transmit payment from buyers to sellers."

Interestingly, commercial transactions made through eBay are handled primarily by community members—eBay itself acts as the interface/facilitator overseeing these activities, a role that fits well with the company's strategy and the content that it promotes.

Reinforcement among eBay's 7Cs

The two pillars of eBay's unique strategy are its hands-off approach and its "trade anything possible" policy. Such a value proposition is supported by the 7Cs and could be depicted as a web of reinforcement (Exhibit 5.19).

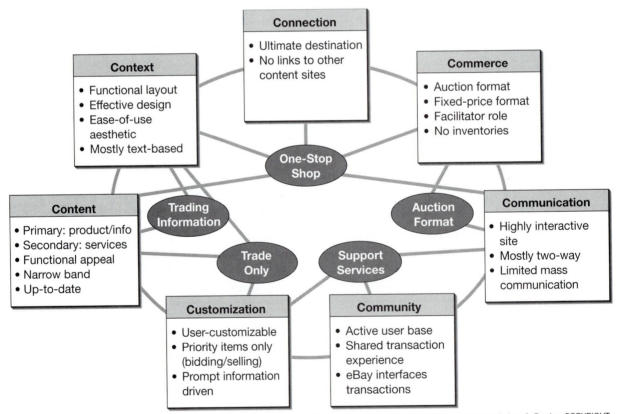

EXHIBIT 5.19   eBay's Reinforcement Web

An example might help further explain this web of reinforcement (see Exhibit 5.20). Suppose an individual wants to sell a car on eBay. The first thing the seller might do is visit My eBay (customization) to check feedback on how other users have rated their transaction experiences (community). From there, an individual might have further questions on how the feedback forum works and also some specific questions on how to proceed when selling a car. The prospective seller might then browse through the site's help services (communication).

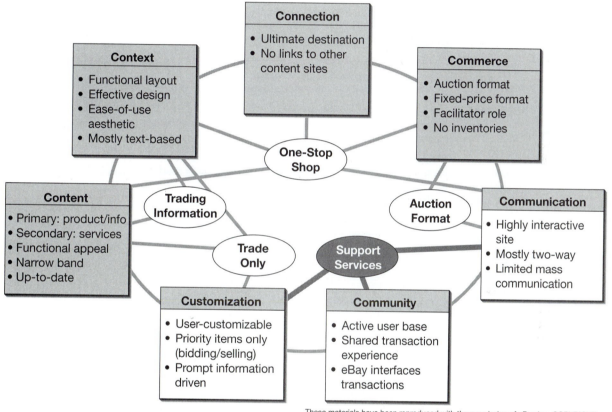

EXHIBIT 5.20   eBay's Reinforcement Web—Support Services

After becoming knowledgeable about the process, the individual moves on to the seller's homepage. Here, the seller can learn how to post a photograph of the car being sold and write a detailed text description (content) that can be posted on the car's selling page (see Exhibit 5.21). Once the individual has entered all of the required elements, the auction finally starts, and all of the pertinent item information provided by the seller is displayed on the selling page (content). The individual might then visit My eBay again to check the status of the process (customization). Here, individuals might track how many users have bid on the car and the value of each bid. This information is all presented in a largely text-based interface context (see Exhibit 5.22).

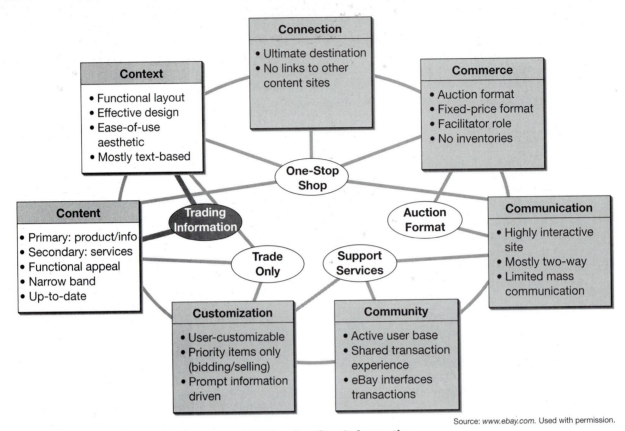

EXHIBIT 5.21   eBay's Reinforcement Web—Trading Information

Take a different example. Suppose that a different individual—a buyer—wants to bid on a car. There is no need for any immediate, direct interaction with the seller (communication). As the transaction falls under the laissez-faire style auction format (commerce), the potential buyer bids and executes the transaction without any outside influences (see Exhibit 5.23).

The potential buyer now searches for a car that he or she likes by browsing through the text and photographs (content). The buyer knows that visiting another website to shop for the same car may not be as successful, since there is a fair chance his or her highest bid (connection and commerce) would be lower than what he or she might pay elsewhere. The buyer also learns (communication) that eBay provides end-to-end online services such as financing, inspections, escrow, auto insurance, vehicle shipping, title and registration, and a lemon check (content).

Through repetitive fit and reinforcement of the 7Cs—experienced through use of the customer interface—eBay reinforces its image as a one-stop shop for individuals seeking to buy or sell new and used goods (see Exhibit 5.24).

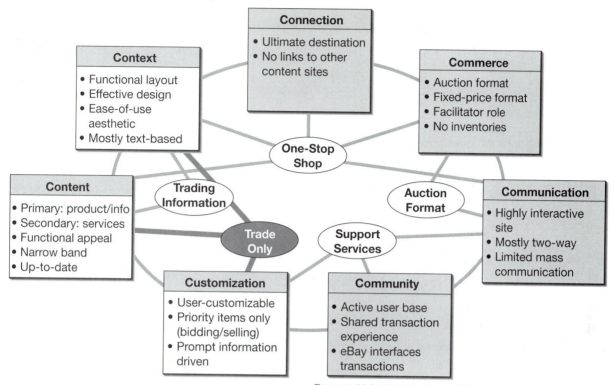

These materials have been reproduced with the permission of eBay Inc. COPYRIGHT EBAY INC. ALL RIGHTS RESERVED.

EXHIBIT 5.22   eBay's Reinforcement Web—Trade Only

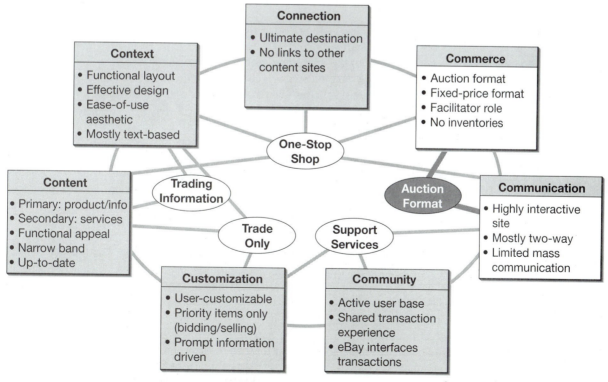

Source: *www.ebay.com.* Used with permission.

EXHIBIT 5.23   eBay's Reinforcement Web—Auction Format

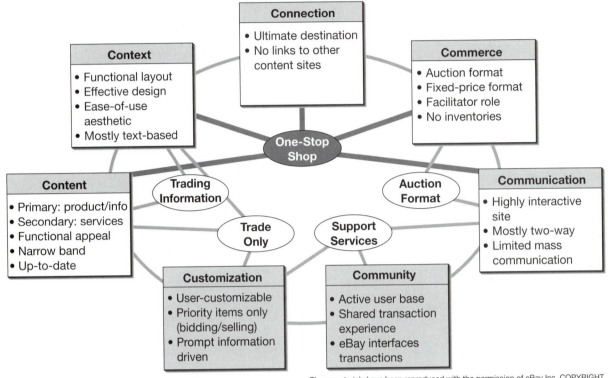

These materials have been reproduced with the permission of eBay Inc. COPYRIGHT EBAY INC. ALL RIGHTS RESERVED.

EXHIBIT 5.24   eBay's Reinforcement Web—One-Stop Shop

Summary

1. What are the seven design elements of the customer interface?

The seven design elements are content, context, community, communication, customization, connection, and commerce. Each of the 7Cs needs to "fit" and "reinforce" the others while satisfying the business model.

2. What determines the look-and-feel of a site?

A website's look-and-feel has two dimensions: form (or aesthetics) and function. Aesthetic design focuses on the artistic nature of the site. Function, on the other hand, involves the pragmatic usability of the site. Some argue that these are opposing design aspects, while others maintain that advancing technologies lead to new techniques and new aesthetics and therefore fewer tradeoff decisions between form and function, with the result that both aesthetic and functional dimensions continue to expand rather than compete.

3. What are the dimensions of content?

Content has four dimensions: offering mix, appeal mix, multimedia mix, and content type. The first two dimensions define the body of the content, in terms of product, services, promotion, and communication. Multimedia mix defines the frame within which this content is presented, namely the form and layout. Last, the content type adds the time component to the content exposure.

4. Why be concerned with community?

Communities foster feelings of group membership as well as a sense of involvement. A group of people can create strong, lasting relationships that may develop into a sense of community through an engaged and extended exchange of views about shared common interests. This sense of community—and the way that it is shared through member-generated content—can help encourage users and customers to return to a website.

5. What are the levers used to customize a site?

Users can personalize the site, or the site can tailor itself to users. The levers for personalization include login registration, personalized e-mail, content and layout configuration, storage, and agents. A firm can tailor its site to users based either on users' past behaviors or on the behaviors of other users with similar preferences.

6. What types of communication can a firm maintain with its customer base?

There are three forms of communication: broadcast, interactive, and a broadcast/interactive hybrid.

7. How does a firm connect with other businesses?

There are two generic approaches to forming such connections: pathways in and pathways out. The pathway of the connection can lead a user off the site (pathway-out) or can retrieve materials from other places without formally sending users away from the site (pathway-in).

8. What are the main features of commerce that support the various aspects of trading transactions?

There are nine main features that support commerce in interface design: registration, shopping cart, security, credit card approval, one-click shopping, orders through affiliates, configuration technology, order tracking, and delivery options.

Activities for Students

1. Compare Bluefly.com with eluxury.com. Both provide designer goods, but they have a distinctly different look-and-feel. In looking at each site, attempt to identify the business strategies of each parent company, and assess how well each site expresses those goals.

2. Amazon.com and Barnes & Noble.com are the top booksellers on the Web. Compare the customer experience on each site. How easy is it to find, evaluate, and buy a book from each? Does one offer a competitive advantage in site functionality?

3. Lands' End and Amazon have each been pioneers in customization. Are there sites you commonly visit that could increase your loyalty by providing such services? List the sites and the customization features that would benefit you.

4. Visit an opinions site such as BizRate.com and evaluate user feedback on several commerce sites. Is there a common theme in the praise or complaints? How would you advise a management or design team to address the complaints?

5. Go to a site you use often, and analyze it along the lines of the eBay application above. Can you identify instances of the 7Cs on the site? How effective is fit and reinforcement?

Key Terms

context	communication	tailoring
content	connection	outsourced content
community	commerce	fit and reinforcement
customization	personalization	

Endnotes

[1]Park, Choong Whan, and Gerald Zaltman. 1987. *Marketing management.* Chicago: Dryden Press. Park and Zaltman introduced the concepts of consistency and complementarity to refer to the degree to which various marketing management concepts resulted in synergy. Complementarity is equivalent to reinforcement, and fit is equivalent to consistency. Given the number of concepts that begin with the letter C in this chapter, the terms fit and reinforcement were chosen.

[2]For more on usability, consult Nielsen, Jakob. 2000. *Designing web usability.* Indianapolis, IN: New Riders Publishing. Also of interest are Krug, Steve, 2000. *Don't Make Me Think: A common-sense approach to Web usability.* Indianapolis, IN: New Riders Publishing, and Hurst, Mark, *www.creativegood.com.*

Designing the Marketing
Program

Once the customer experience has been articulated, the firm must now create that experience through the marketing levers at its disposal. Thus, if eBay is positioned as the "largest and most trusted marketplace on the Internet," the firm must deliver a customer experience that is consistent with that position. As discussed in the previous chapter, it is critical that the firm understands the various ways in which customers' interactions with the site can be evaluated. The next step is to design the marketing levers (i.e., product, price, communication, distribution, branding, and community), that support the positioning and deliver the desired customer experience. The marketing levers are tactics that are under the direct control of managers and that affect both the objective and perceived offering to consumers.

Students of marketing will notice that we have introduced two marketing levers beyond the traditional 4P model (i.e., price, product, promotion, and distribution or place) used in most marketing textbooks. We have included branding and community to the traditional list of marketing mix variables to reflect new thinking about the decisions that marketing managers must make, in part because of the advent of the Internet. In this section we also introduce two new concepts that reflect the incredible impact of the Internet on modern marketing practices —individualization and interactivity. Individualization refers to a firm's ability to target each consumer with personalized messages and programs. Interactivity signals the shift from broadcast forms of marketing to dialogue or conversational marketing. These elements—we call them the 2Is—greatly influence the Internet marketing mix's effects on customer behavior.

Finally, this section introduces the concept of buyer-seller relationships as a fundamental objective of marketing activities. Rather than adopt a supply-side view of marketing, or one that focuses on marketing activities, we propose a demand-side view that focuses on building and maintaining customer relationships. We argue that good marketing involves moving customers from the awareness stage to the exploration stage and, eventually, the commitment stage.

This section concludes with two chapters that are designed to integrate the material introduced in all of the previous chapters. The first chapter relates the six marketing levers (product, pricing, community, communication, distribution, branding) to the four stages of customer relationships, resulting in a two-dimensional matrix that we call the Marketspace Relationship Levers Matrix. It illustrates the activities that the marketing team must manage to create a successful marketing program. We conclude Chapter 13 by discussing the principles of matrix design.

The last chapter in Part V will look at how the Marketspace Matrix can be used to build a comprehensive marketing program. We demonstrate by applying the matrix to the marketing campaign for the motion picture *The Lord of the Rings: The Fellowship of the Rings*, the first film in New Line Cinema's trilogy based on J.R.R. Tolkien's classic novels.

Customer Relationships

In order to be profitable, firms must create profitable relationships with their customers. To achieve this, firms must first identify the levers they can use to strengthen the various stages of the customer relationship. This chapter sets forth a framework for how to do just that. The Internet is an important part of this process, and its role is discussed in detail.

This chapter takes a customer-centric approach to Internet marketing. The emphasis is on how firms are using the Internet to increase customer awareness, encourage customer interaction, and create customers who are committed to the firm and its products. Sometimes, firms want to dissolve relationships with certain customer segments, and this chapter also discusses those circumstances. Of particular importance to online firms is an understanding of how interactivity and individualization—the unique characteristics of the Internet that we call the 2Is— are fundamental to building close buyer–seller relationships. The chapter concludes with a discussion of how eBay develops relationships on the Internet.

QUESTIONS

Please consider the following questions as you read the chapter:

1. What is a relationship, and why is developing a buyer–seller relationship important?

2. What are the various types of relationships?

3. What is the relationship model?

4. How do the 2Is of the Internet contribute to the development of buyer–seller relationships?

5. When are customers likely to want a relationship with a firm or brand?

Introduction

This chapter describes the customer-relationship stages and explains the techniques that firms can use to move consumers through those stages, and toward a committed—and profitable—relationship. The Internet affects this process in unique ways, which are incorporated into the framework we introduce.

What is a relationship? This section defines what constitutes a relationship between firms and customers, and describes different types of relationships. The section also examines the degree of relationship involvement as a function of product characteristics, purchase situation, and the consumer's personal interests.

Why do firms want relationships with their customers? This section discusses how establishing relationships with customers increases profits. This claim is supported by two principles: Serving existing customers is less expensive than serving new customers, and existing customers are willing to pay higher prices. This section also provides guidance on how to measure a customer's value to the firm. Determining the net-present value of customers helps firms decide how much to invest in specific customer relationships.

The stages of a relationship. This section looks at the four key customer-relationship stages: awareness, exploration, commitment, and dissolution.

Interaction intensity. This section describes the general pattern of interaction that should develop as buyers and sellers move through the relationship stages. As the relationship deepens, the intensity and frequency of interactions should increase; if not, the customer is likely to find other exchange partners and dissolve the relationship.

The 2Is. This section explains how the interactivity and individualization characteristics of the Internet help to create customer relationships.

Creating customer relationships through the Web. This section presents an integrative framework for building relationships on the Web. The framework is organized around the levers that firms can use to establish and maintain close buyer–seller relationships.

Not everyone wants a relationship! This section highlights the fact that some customers are not interested in having a relationship. Some customers would rather maximize the value of each transaction than commit themselves to one firm. Attempts to create relationships with such customers could lead to consumer resentment and alienation.

Building relationships at eBay. This section examines the four stages of the customer relationship—awareness, exploration, commitment, and dissolution—and eBay's online auction business.

What Is a Relationship?

Simply put, a **relationship** is a bond or connection between a firm and its customers. This bond can be strong, weak, or nonexistent. It can be intellectual ("I know that I cannot get a better deal elsewhere"), emotional ("I feel good when I am wearing my Nikes"), or a combination ("I want to remain loyal to my alma mater"). Relationships can be categorized according to at least two dimensions: type and involvement.

Relationship Type

Relationships exist along a continuum, and range from communal to exchange based.[1] A purely **communal relationship** is altruistic; each person focuses on meeting the needs and wants of the other(s). They interact with no requirement or expectation that they will receive something in return. Parent–child relationships, or those between close family or friends, tend to be communal.

In contrast, parties in an **exchange relationship** give one thing in return for another. When one person helps the other, an obligation is created, and at some point it is expected that the debt will be repaid. In exchange relationships, each person tracks the other's contributions to ensure that there is equity. Researchers have found that the exchange-based relationships become stronger when payment for value is received quickly.[2] Buyer–seller relationships are perhaps the best examples of exchange relationships because their primary purpose is the trading of products or services for monetary compensation.

However, exchange relationships can involve emotional, social, and psychological benefits as well as financial ones. A person may help someone because he wants to feel good about himself, or perhaps to avoid guilt.[3] Helping might also be motivated by a desire for social approval, acceptance, or praise. Or a person might offer help simply because he realizes that he will likely require help in the future. These factors also relate to buyer–seller interactions. For example, customers often have face-to-face relationships with service providers, including mechanics, clerks, and customer-service representatives, not to mention doctors, dentists, and lawyers. The interpersonal aspects of buyer–seller exchange are important components of the shopping or consumption experience.

Can online firms build emotional, social, and psychological benefits into the exchange process? The low degree of interpersonal interaction in Web-based exchanges makes this difficult, but not impossible. There are strategies available to firms that want to enhance the noneconomic aspects of exchange. For example:

- Instilling confidence is critical in online buying situations. Allowing a long-term American Express cardholder to use that credit card to complete a Web-based purchase, for instance, may boost that consumer's confidence in that website.

- Sending customers the wrong message can inhibit the formation of a buyer–seller relationship. Remember the online retailer called 911gifts.com? It changed its name to RedEnvelope because potential consumers thought the original name implied that one would purchase gifts there in a last-minute, emergency situation—an impression that is inconsistent with a loving relationship.

- Firms can create emotional exchanges by supporting charities. For example, Ben & Jerry's and The Body Shop commit a percentage of their profits to social causes. Buyers feel a sense of pride and satisfaction that their purchases help others.

- Careful selection, training, and deployment of service personnel can impact the development of noneconomic aspects of a buyer–seller relationship. For example, a customer relationship manager who interacts well with both online and offline consumers humanizes a firm, and also leaves customers feeling that their needs are being personally addressed.

- Firms can create an online presence with entertainment or informational value. For example, the Cap'n Crunch website gives children the opportunity to interact with the cereal's cartoon mascot. The site provides fun games that increase user interaction with the brand in a positive way (see Exhibit 6.1).

The distinction between communal and exchange relationships is an important one. Businesses are economic institutions, with the goal of generating economic value through exchange. Although firms may take a long-term view and do not expect to maximize the economic return from each individual transaction, they ultimately require profits to survive and prosper. Firms provide products and services that are valued by customers, but also must attend to customers' social, emotional, and psychological needs.

EXHIBIT 6.1   Cap'n Crunch Website

Relationship Involvement

The development of an exchange relationship is a direct function of the level of customer involvement.[4] **Involvement** is defined as the degree to which a relationship is relevant to the consumer—the extent to which it relates to the consumer's values, interests, or needs.[5] Consumers who are highly involved in a relationship see it as an important part of their lives or their personality. They commit time and energy to the relationship, perhaps by visiting the firm's website, reading advertisements, requesting an electronic newsletter, or offering their opinions and ideas to the firm.[6]

It is useful to distinguish between two types of involvement: enduring and situational. Consumers who have a strong interest in a product or service category over an extended period of time are said to have **enduring involvement**. For example, a hockey enthusiast will probably exhibit a variety of behaviors that are related to the sport. He might play the game on a recreational or semi-competitive basis. He might participate in hockey fantasy pools and follow his favorite team on the radio, television, or through the newspaper. He probably checks websites such as NHL.com or ESPN.com for hockey scores and articles. He may also subscribe to *Hockey News* or similar publications. This person views hockey as an essential part of his life, and feels intense emotions when he is occupied by hockey-related activities.

In contrast, **situational involvement** is temporary and occurs only when a person is undertaking a purchase or consumption activity. For example, someone who is not a hockey fan might go to NHL.com to learn the rules of the game because he has been invited to a playoff game. The involvement in the sport is caused by the free ticket, and probably will not last. Firms do have the opportunity, however, to stimulate enduring involvement in these cases. NHL.com can promote the sport's speed, teamwork, and skill, which can spur interest in individual players. Over time, situational involvement can become enduring involvement.

Involvement is a function not only of product characteristics, but also of the purchase situation and the consumer's personal interests. These factors are considered in the following sections:

Product Category.   Customers form more emotional relationships with certain brands or products than with others. Most consumers do not feel strongly about, say, a particular brand of toilet paper, although they might be loyal customers. Emotional bonds are less likely for a variety of low-involvement products such as milk, shoe polish, film, chewing gum, paper towels, and hand soap. These products are relatively low-cost, there is little risk of making a bad decision, and there are a large number of brand and product category substitutes. Such brand and product choices are not highly relevant to the lives of most consumers, making them unwilling to invest in a relationship.

Purchase Situation.   Buying a bottle of wine as a gift is very different from buying a bottle of wine for home consumption. Purchase involvement is likely to be greater in gift-buying situations because of the social context and the buyer's concern with the recipient's reaction. In other words, a low-involvement purchase—buying a bottle of wine, in this case—can become a high-involvement purchase under certain circumstances.

Although most aspects of a financial services relationship are transactional and routine—ATM withdrawals, for example—the potential for high involvement always exists. Unexpected circumstances such as a lost credit card require special customer service. A need for online financial planning might arise because of a marriage or a new baby, and suddenly a low-involvement relationship with a bank becomes more intense (albeit temporarily). Similarly, a credit card might represent a low-involvement relationship until the bank begins to give a percentage of charges to a favorite charity. Notice that in these examples the relationship is not with the credit card or the website, but with the bank. The credit card or the Internet is the mechanism through which buyer–seller interactions take place, but customers have relationships with the firm and its brand.

On the other hand, in some situations the Internet creates value for customers by *decreasing* purchase involvement. Some customers value the anonymity of using a website to shop for certain products or to request customer service. Others use the Internet to arm themselves with product information before encountering high-pressure sales tactics, or to avoid salespeople altogether. Consider the following situations:

- Requesting additional credit or reporting an inability to meet a credit card's minimum balance
- Purchasing adult films or photographs
- Researching a complex or expensive product, such as a car[7]

In each of these instances, a firm's website can differentiate it from offline competitors by reducing buyer involvement. Many types of emotionally charged, stressful transactions become casual because of the Internet.

Consumer Type. Of course, not everyone has the same interests. Some people are highly involved in their choice of soft drink, while others could not care less. Some people are highly involved in the type of athletic shoe they wear, yet others will buy whatever brand is on sale. Although most people are somewhat involved in expensive purchases (automobiles, home appliances, etc.), some people are more involved than others.

Involvement levels are related to how people see themselves and how they would like others to see them. For example, consumers' life stages and lifestyles often determine the relevance of a product. Teenagers usually care a great deal about athletic shoes, clothes, music, and fast food. They tend to be heavy users in these categories, and therefore more interested than older consumers in forming a buyer–seller relationship. Avid cooks are more interested in and knowledgeable about differences among types of olive oil, flour, and cooking utensils. The Internet helps firms target consumers on the basis of their interests. Individuals who register at a cooking website are likely to be interested in this category, and therefore more likely to establish a relationship.

It seems clear, then, that involvement is not just a characteristic of product category. But whether it is the product category, the purchase situation, or personal interests that guide them, buyers must believe that a product, brand, or firm is relevant to their lives before a relationship is possible (see Exhibit 6.2).

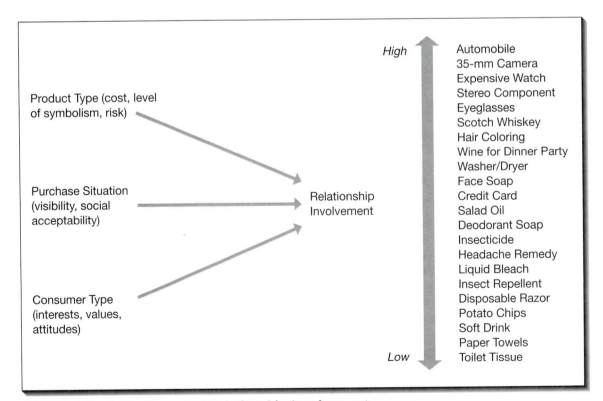

EXHIBIT 6.2   A Continuum of Relationship Involvement

Why Do Firms Want Relationships with Their Customers?

The opposite of a relationship is no relationship. This seems obvious, but it imparts the fact that without some sort of connection, customers view each transaction as an independent event. Firms do not have relationships with customers who do not place any value on previous transactions, or who do not expect to interact with the firm in the future. This type of customer has no loyalty to the firm and will go elsewhere if the firm does not provide acceptable value on each and every exchange.

Think of an electronic exchange for financial services in which the suppliers are unbranded. Buyers know the interest rates offered on automobile loans, investment certificates, mortgages, and so forth, but the firms are anonymous—no relationships get in the way of a purely objective decision. In this situation, the sellers must compete strictly on price because their products are unbranded commodities. Now consider the same situation, only the financial products are branded, and one of the prospective buyers has a solid, long-standing relationship with one of the sellers. That buyer now takes into consideration the noneconomic benefits of choosing the familiar seller. The long-standing buyer–seller relationship might lead the customer to:

- Anticipate the positive feelings from remaining loyal to the seller.
- Trust that the seller will provide good value. Even though the seller's interest rate on loans may be a little higher, the buyer expects the seller to compensate in other ways. Trust may also lead the customer to abandon plans to check competing websites.
- Feel that the brand represents who he or she is, because it has similar values. Feeling this way leads the customer to promote the seller to friends, family, and acquaintances.
- Seek out and actively read the seller's promotional material.

Exchanges that occur within the context of a relationship are viewed as part of an ongoing stream of transactions. Transactions are evaluated on the basis of noneconomic benefits as well as on price and functionality.

Some have likened the buyer-seller relationship to a marriage. As one writer put it, the sale "merely consummates the courtship."[8] This perspective is useful because it highlights the fact that all types of relationships have costs and benefits. A marriage decreases uncertainty, allows a sharing of household costs and tasks, and provides companionship and intimacy. However, marriage also increases personal responsibilities, requires care and nurturance, and can end with a costly dissolution. To some degree, these same costs and benefits also apply to buyer–seller relationships.

Consider the costs and benefits of a revenue-sharing alliance, a style of partnership pioneered by Amazon.com in 1997. In this arrangement, also called an associate or affiliate program, a seller pays a commission to an Internet partner for click-throughs, sales leads, or actual sales that originate from the partner's site. For example, clicking on one of the banner ads in Exhibit 6.3

Sources: Courtesy of *www.wine.com*; Clairol, a division of Procter & Gamble; *www.barnesandnoble.com*. Used with permission; *www.time.com*; *www.ediets.com*. Used with permission; Courtesy of SharperImage; *www.cdnow.com*. Used with permission; Courtesy of Telocity; Courtesy of *www.disney.com*.

EXHIBIT 6.3   Examples of Banner Ads

delivers a potential customer to the partner's site, where he has the opportunity to shop and buy. These revenue-sharing alliances require both parties to invest time and resources in several areas, including:[9]

- Technical capabilities. The seller must distribute HTML code, graphics, and logos to its partner. It must also provide technical help and support via e-mail or telephone.
- Reporting system. A reporting system for commissions and customer understanding. This system must provide online tracking capability with a reasonable level of security.
- Marketing. The buyer and seller will need to coordinate their advertising and promotions, pricing levels, and other marketing levers. For example, Joy Athletic sells equipment for a variety of sports, but it will want to highlight its hockey equipment for visitors who arrive from its link on NHL.com. It will also want to promote certain products or offers in its banner ad, and ensure that its prices are in line with what is expected by the NHL.com visitor.

Of course, these investments must be balanced against the revenues that are expected from clicks, leads, and sales. Also important is the potential for brand value to increase if customers see the alliance as a benefit, or if the association between the two brands is positive.

Drill-Down

Are Buyer Seller Relationships Really Necessary?

Some argue that not all successful firms need strong relationships with their customers. However, the question is not whether firms would like to have relationships with their customers, but to what degree customers see value in those relationships. Consider the following situations:

- An industrial firm purchases from a supplier only when its regular suppliers are experiencing shortages. Because the supplier is used as a backup on short notice, it cannot predict future purchases. A relationship does exist in this situation—it might be less than ideal, since the buyer's commitment is low or nonexistent, but the supplier does have both the awareness and trust of the purchaser. Would the supplier like to establish a closer relationship with the firm? The answer is probably yes. However, the low commitment of the firm may suit the supplier just fine because of low excess capacity (it couldn't become the primary supplier if it wanted to) and because it is able to charge a premium price for emergency shipments. In this way, the supplier may be highly committed to serving the industrial firm.

- Consumers may select a firm randomly, perhaps arriving at its website by accident—a mistyped URL, for example. Clearly, no relationship exists if the selection of the firm is completely random; indeed, no model or framework can predict random behavior. However, even random behavior can lead to awareness and exploration, which in turn can lead to commitment. Further, it seems unlikely that many selections are completely random. Seemingly inconsequential factors such as the position of the website in a listing created by a search engine or electronic phone book may affect awareness. More important, perhaps, is the potential for the brand name or symbol to affect firm or product image and influence choice. When the customer associates a brand with admired people, objects, emotions, or ideas, a connection to the brand is being formed.

- Customers may strongly dislike aspects of a firm or brand, but still receive overall value. For example, although users may dislike a website for a variety of reasons (slow to load, poor navigation, etc.), they continue to purchase loyally because they don't perceive any viable alternatives. In other words, customers are dependent on the site for something they value, but they have a less-than-ideal relationship with the firm. The firm will keep the customer only as long as no competitors spring up.

- An electronics firm sells an unbranded component via a third-party Internet exchange. Although the customers gained through this exchange provide a significant level of profitability to the electronics firm, there is no buyer–seller relationship because the manufacturer is anonymous. The long-term prospects for the firm are tenuous because customers will most likely build a relationship with the exchange rather than the electronics firm.

It seems clear that in each of these examples the firm would like to have a relationship with its customers—the benefits appear to exceed the costs. The examples clearly highlight the fact that having a relationship cannot be equated with buying the product or even with the level of interaction between buyers and sellers.

A recent study also reminds us that firms must constantly engage in transactional marketing, which emphasizes new customer acquisition and product promotions.[10] The study finds that transactional marketing forms a basis for building relationships. Transactional marketing is thought to provide feedback on marketing programs quickly and relatively inexpensively, and provides a basis for identifying customers who are likely to be profitable relationship partners.

Understanding the Value of Customer Relationships

One basic assumption of customer relationship management, also called CRM, is that maintaining long-term customer relationships increases a firm's profitability. True, CRM does cost something. Firms must spend money to understand customer preferences, purchase patterns, and values. Then they must use that information to design programs that create stronger customer bonds— perhaps by investing in a monthly online newsletter, enhancing customer service, or upgrading customer interface technologies. Still, the benefits are clear. Here are three reasons why customer relationships increase profitability:[11]

- It costs less to serve existing customers than new ones. The firm does not have to invest in strategies to identify these customers and persuade them that the firm is a reasonable exchange partner, assuming that they were serviced adequately in their previous transactions. This is particularly true of contractual relationships. When customers sign up for Internet service or subscribe to online publications, companies can reasonably forecast costs and revenues. Marketing costs are dramatically reduced, and cross-selling boosts revenues. Customers who sign contracts are more likely to trust the firm, and as a result are more willing to buy its products.

- Some evidence suggests that established customers will pay higher prices than new customers, even after introductory offers are considered.[12] It appears that long-term customers value the noneconomic benefits of the relationship. Some experts have argued that a reward program tied in with superior customer service helps take the consumer's eyes off price.[13] For example, members of a frequent flier (or frequent shopper) program will not be as price sensitive as nonmembers because of their economic investment in continuing the relationship.

- Strong buyer–seller relationships increase the likelihood that customers will disclose personal information. A study by Fulcrum Analytics (then called CyberDialogue) in July 2001 found that 90 percent of users will divulge their address to websites they visit, but only 18 percent will to third-party ad servers.[14] Detailed customer information enhances the firm's capacity for targeting, which lowers costs and increases customer value.

As a result of lower costs, higher margins, and perhaps higher volumes, the general association between customer–relationship tenure and profitability should be strong and positive (see Exhibit 6.4).

Measuring a Customer's Value

It is not enough, however, to keep existing customers. A second, critical requirement is to build strong relationships that increase the frequency and profitability of purchase behaviors.[15] Firms want relationships only with customers who are profitable, and that usually means customers who fall into the heavy-user segment. Otherwise, relationship-related investments such as electronic newsletters, customer relationship managers, and individualized advertising will be wasted. This perspective reinforces that firms must think of buyer–seller relationships as an investment that is profitable only under specific circumstances.

How do firms measure the lifetime value of customers? They must make some critical assumptions about the time horizon, marketing and services costs per customer, expected gross contributions, and interest rates. Consider the following simplified example. After developing a database of customer activity, a

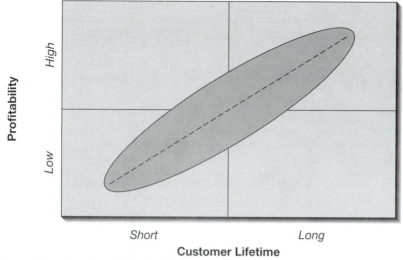

Sources: Adapted from Werner J. Reinartz and V. Kumar (2000), "On the Profitability of Long-Life Customers in a Noncontractual Setting: An Empirical Investigation and Implications for Marketing," Journal of Marketing, 64 (October), 17-35. Used with permission by American Marketing Association.

EXHIBIT 6.4   Expected Relationship between Length of Customer Tenure and Profitability

firm identifies two segments that differ in purchase frequency and in profitability (based on the types of products that are purchased and the levels of marketing support needed to achieve sales). See Exhibit 6.5 for a summary of revenues and costs associated with the typical customer in each segment. Segment A is characterized by sporadic purchases that are driven by price discounts. These customers buy low-margin items, but they require frequent contact via direct mail and catalogs. On the positive side, they require little ongoing customer service. In contrast, Segment B has a consistent purchase pattern, with higher margins and lower marketing costs. However, customers in this segment demand higher levels of customer service. A final difference is that the customers in Segment A are not as loyal as those in Segment B. Thirty-three percent of the customers in Segment A switch to a competitor each year, whereas the switching rate for Segment B is only 25 percent. Hence, the firm can expect that, on average, customers in Segment A have a three-year life with the firm, and those in Segment B have a five-year life with the firm. As a result of all of these factors, and a 10 percent cost-of-borrowing assumption, the net present value of an average customer in Segment A is $124.27. In Segment B, the average value is $261.91. (See Exhibit 6.5 for more detail.) This calculation can help determine how much to invest in each kind of customer to ensure that they have a profitable relationship with the firm.

In order to calculate the value of a customer or customer segment, the firm must develop and maintain a database of customer activity. Next, it must create a mathematical model that incorporates a series of assumptions about its customers and how they will behave over time. The above example is simplified; the process is often much more complex. (See Drill-Down titled "A Model for Measuring the Lifetime Value of Customers.")

Large commercial banks are the leading industry in the study of customer profitability.[16] When Gartner surveyed 241 banks, it found that three-quarters of those with more than $4 billion in deposits were calculating customer

Customer Segment A	Year 1	Year 2	Year 3
Purchases	$400.00	$ 0	$600.00
Less: Cost of Goods Sold (70%)	$280.00	$ 0	$420.00
Gross Contribution	$120.00	$ 0	$180.00
Less: Marketing Costs			
Catalog ($10.00 × 3 per year)	$30.00	$ 30.00	$ 30.00
Direct Mail ($5.00 per package × 3 per year)	$15.00	$ 15.00	$ 15.00
Customer Service (1% of sales)	$ 4.00	$ 0	$ 6.00
Total Marketing Costs	$49.00	$ 45.00	$ 51.00
Net Contribution Per Year	$71.00	$−45.00	$129.00
Net Present Value of Customer A at 10% discount rate per year*	$124.27		

Customer Segment B	Year 1	Year 2	Year 3	Year 4
Purchases	$200.00	$200.00	$200.00	$200.00
Less: Cost of Goods Sold (50%)	$100.00	$100.00	$100.00	$100.00
Gross Contribution	$100.00	$100.00	$100.00	$100.00
Less: Marketing Costs				
Catalog ($10.00 × 1 per year)	$10.00	$10.00	$10.00	$10.00
Direct Mail ($5.00 per package × 2 per year)	$10.00	$ 5.00	$10.00	$10.00
Customer Service (6% of sales)	$12.00	$12.00	$12.00	$12.00
Total Marketing Costs	$32.00	$27.00	$32.00	$32.00
Net Contribution Per Year	$68.00	$73.00	$68.00	$68.00
Net Present Value of Customer B at 10% discount rate per year*	$261.91			

*Note: Assumes that all sales and costs occur at the end of the year.

EXHIBIT 6.5   Calculating a Customer's Lifetime Value

profitability by the end of 1999, and that almost all planned to do so by the end of 2000. Banks reported that they used their findings to develop products, to determine prices, to identify customers to move to other products or delivery channels, and to target their marketing.

Although banks have traditionally analyzed customer profitability through allocated costs based on averages, this approach can be misleading. The use of activity-based costs associated with individual transactions reveals more about customer and product profitability because it distinguishes among ATM, mail, Web-based, and face-to-face interactions. Measuring customer profitability is critical, especially when firms have multiple ways of serving customers.

Point–Counterpoint

Customer Rewards Programs: Do They Create Loyalty or Not?

Customer rewards programs abound—just take a look in your wallet or on your key chain. There are loyalty cards for supermarkets, department stores, convenience stores, and automotive clubs, not to mention credit cards that earn points with each dollar charged.

In his book *Loyalty.com: Customer Relationship Management in the New Era of Internet Marketing*, Frederick Newell found that the average U.S. consumer participates in 3.2 loyalty programs. The market is becoming increasingly crowded, forcing marketers to design effective, low-cost programs.

In a 1995 article in the *Harvard Business Review*, Louise O'Brien and Charles Jones argue that "rewards can and do build customer loyalty," but that the real issue is how the program is implemented.[17] They offer the following "rules of reward" for companies hoping to develop an effective plan:

- Recognize that all customers are not created equal, and provide the best value to the best customers.
- Create meaningful incentives.
- Reward and therefore reinforce desirable behaviors (and discourage undesirable ones, such as switching).
- Take a long-term perspective—one-time promotions do not typically engender loyalty.
- Take a segmented approach so that the best customers self-select into the plan.

However, there are some concerns that loyalty programs, even if implemented properly, may not be effective. In their book *Marketing Services: Competing Through Quality*, Leonard L. Berry and A. Parasuraman argue that there are three levels to the buyer–seller relationship.[18] The first (and lowest) level is financial, and includes frequent-shopper programs such as those offered by CDNow or Barnes & Noble.com. The financial bond created by such incentives is not only easily imitated by competitors, but it is likely to have a negative effect on profits if not properly targeted. Moreover, once customers have cashed in their rewards, they may have little incentive to remain.

The second level of relationship is social, and produces a much stronger customer bond. Consider Yahoo! The company has a clear personality—youthful and fun—that it consistently strives to reinforce in both offline and online media. Also, Yahoo! has created a rich, functional service that is based on an interactive and individualized relationship with its millions of users. Free e-mail, chat rooms, and club software help establish and maintain connections between like-minded users, and ultimately with Yahoo! itself. Other websites, such as CommunityZero and the one operated by the American Center for Wine, Food, and the Arts, use similar mechanisms to create social bonds.[19]

The final, and strongest, level of relationship includes structural bonds. Here, the seller offers target customers value-added benefits that are difficult or impossible to find elsewhere. In a B2B setting, a structural bond is created investing in assets that are specific to the relationship. For example, Federal Express places dedicated computer terminals in the offices of its high-volume customers. The automated shipping and invoicing system, called Powership, increases the ease of using FedEx and effectively locks out competitors who do not have their own shipping system in place. Such investments create stronger relationship bonds and reduce customer switching behaviors.

Overall, rewards programs that focus only on financial incentives may not be effective. E-marketers must consider social and structural drivers as well. Fortunately, the interactivity and individualization afforded by the Internet make it possible to build relationships with millions of customers. Social bonds can be built with individualized websites that provide for personalized content and real-time interaction with the firm and with like-minded customers. Structural linkages are made possible by the improved communication capabilities, as well as the additional value that comes from collaboration.

Drill-Down

A Model for Measuring the Lifetime Value of Customers

Companies often try to estimate customer lifetime and profitability in order to segment their customer base and increase the effectiveness of their marketing expenditures. It is an imperfect science, however, because each customer's individual purchase activity is difficult to predict, and firms do not always know when a customer has defected to another firm. To illustrate this, consider the problems that clothing retailer Eddie Bauer might face when trying to determine which of its customers is "loyal." Although people might typically purchase clothing at predictable times of the year, individual patterns may vary significantly from year to year. Given that Eddie Bauer does not know whether a given customer has purchased from another firm or whether he or she simply has not bought anything this season, loyalty is hard to assess. Firms can use relatively sophisticated models such as the one developed by Werner J. Reinartz and V. Kumar to predict which customers are active and which are not.

Reinartz and Kumar developed a model for measuring customer lifetime value for noncontractual relationships.[20] The following formula can be used to develop a probability estimate that a customer is still active with the firm:

$$P[\text{Alive}|r,\alpha,s,\beta,x,t,T] = \left[1 + \frac{s}{r+x+s} \left\{ \left(\frac{\alpha+T}{\alpha+t} \right)^{r+x} \left(\frac{\beta+T}{\alpha+t} \right)^5 \right. \right.$$

$$\left. \left. F[a_1, b_1; c_1; z_1(t)] - \left(\frac{\beta+T}{\alpha+T} \right)^5 F[a_1, b_1; c; z_1(T)] \right\}^{-1} \right].$$

The probability of a customer being active is thought to be a function of x (the number of previous purchases), t (the time since trial at which the most recent transaction occurred), T (the time since trial), and a set of terms (i.e., r, x, s, alpha, beta, and y) that describe a probability function. Then, the continuous probability estimate (between 0 and 1) is translated into a dichotomous active or inactive measure.

In the equation below, Reinartz and Kumar calculate the net present value of profit on an individual customer (in this case, for 36 months):

$$LT\pi_i = \sum_{t=1}^{36} (GC_{ti} - C_{ti}) \left(\frac{1}{1+.0125} \right)^t$$

where $LT\pi_i$ = individual net-present lifetime profit, GC_{ti} = gross contribution in month t for customer i, C_{ti} = marketing cost in month t for customer I, and 0.125 = monthly discount rate (based on a 0.15% rate per year). GC_{ti} is the gross contribution calculated from the monthly revenue, which is expressed as the total household purchase amount for each month.

The Stages of a Relationship

A typical customer's relationship with a business is thought to have four stages: awareness, exploration/expansion, commitment, and dissolution.[21] It is important to note that customers do not necessarily pass through all four stages. Some customers stall at the awareness stage, never exploring the possibility of a relationship with the firm. Others jump directly from awareness to commitment—a commercial version of love at first sight. Exhibit 6.6 shows the possibilities of how customers can pass through the relationship stages.

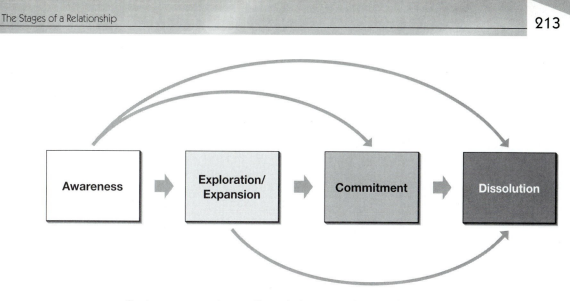

Customers can advance through the stages in several different ways

EXHIBIT 6.6   Moving through the Relationship Stages

It is also important to point out that many customers stay committed to the firm for an indefinite period, with no prospect of relationship dissolution. If committed customers are profitable to serve, the firm wants to keep them at this relationship stage. In some cases, however, firms may find committed customers to be unprofitable—the cost of serving them (through technical support, for example) might be higher than the revenue they generate. The firm would then want to advance these customers to the dissolution stage. Exhibit 6.7 shows the two possibilities for customers at the commitment stage.

The framework is useful because it encourages firms to think about what proportion of its customers are at each stage of the process, which types of consumers are most valued, and the activities or levers that can be used to move customers toward a committed relationship. We now examine each of the stages.

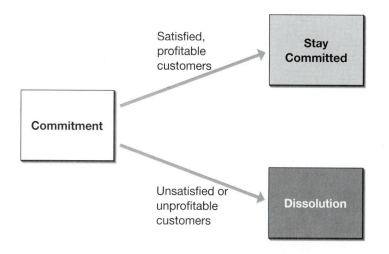

Customers can either stay committed or move to dissolution

EXHIBIT 6.7   Two Alternatives for Customers at the Commitment Stage

Awareness

At the **awareness** stage, the customer recognizes that the firm is a possible exchange partner but has not initiated any communication with the firm or purchased any of its products. Here, the critical levers are the traditional awareness-generating tactics that have been used by marketers for years, as well as some new approaches. In 2000, firms such as Monster.com and Pets.com invested an average of $2.2 million each on 30-second Super Bowl ads designed to generate awareness and drive website traffic.[22] One E*Trade commercial showed a monkey clapping to music, and joked that the sponsor had just blown its entire advertising budget on a 30-second ad. Was the investment worth it?

In many instances, a single exposure creates awareness but does not translate into traffic—or, ultimately, into revenue. Pets.com went out of business in November 2000 despite having one of the most popular ads of the Super Bowl broadcast.[23] Epidemic, a company that paid consumers to attach links to their e-mail messages as a way of stimulating viral marketing, closed its doors about six months after its Super Bowl ad debuted. The ad showed a man receiving a gratuity from a washroom attendant, underscoring the idea that Epidemic would pay people for doing things they do anyway.[24] Other dot-com businesses found that their Super Bowl commercials caused a spike in website traffic that lasted for approximately one week. After that, traffic dropped back to normal levels.[25] The ads created awareness, and even caused some consumers to visit the advertised websites, but ultimately those sites had to deliver value in order to be successful.

Other advertising that creates awareness may not send the right message to customers. For example, electronics retailer Outpost.com created an ad campaign that won the coveted Grand Clio Advertising Award in 1999. The three-ad campaign depicted gerbils being shot out of a cannon, preschool children getting Outpost.com tattooed on their bodies, and a high school band being attacked by ravenous wolves. Appropriately, the ad invites viewers to "Send complaints to Outpost.com."

Other strategies that are important in awareness generation:

- A simple website address is easier for customers to remember. Monster.com's URL (*www.monster.com*) is more likely to stay in someone's minds than *www.wefindyouajob.com*. Yet some consumers may have trouble remembering that Monster.com is a job-hunting website because there is no obvious connection between the service and name. According to Gordon Paddison, senior vice president of worldwide interactive marketing and business development for New Line Cinema, movies with website addresses that do not follow the typical formula of the movie name followed by .com (for example, *www.americanbeauty-thefilm.com* rather than *www.americanbeauty.com*) generate 20 percent to 30 percent fewer hits.
- Awareness is often enhanced by consistency between the mother brand and the Internet brand. BMW.com and Sears.com are likely to benefit from the clear connection between their offline and online brands. But consumers need special information in order to know that Kmart's online brand is BlueLight.com. Confusion can also exist with names that are controlled by cybersitters, or those who exploit a connection with a well-known institution or brand.

- A coordinated effort across online and offline media can drive awareness. Starting with only $15,000 and no venture-capital backing, Girlshop.com underwent consistent, sustainable growth, in part by investing its $100,000 advertising budget in local TV ads, a few national print executions, and postcard campaigns. Laura Eisman, founder of the New York-based firm, says that Girlshop.com posted sales of $900,000 in 1999 and has grown dramatically since then. In 2002, GirlShop is highly regarded by leading fashion magazines as a place that sells clothing and accessories usually found only in small, hip-and mostly urban-boutiques.

Of course, awareness is only the first step. In order to benefit from an online presence, awareness needs to lead to at least an exploration of the website, which in turn may lead to purchase behavior and perhaps commitment to the brand.

Exploration/Expansion

In the **exploration/expansion** stage, the customer considers the possibility of exchange and perhaps initiates trial purchases. If the commitment stage is analogous to a marriage, then the exploration stage is analogous to dating. The two parties, particularly the consumer, gather information that enables them to choose whether to establish a stronger bond with the other. There is minimal investment in the relationship for both parties, so termination is simple.

Exploration requires that the parties communicate. For B2B relationships, this is slightly different than with B2C relationships, because B2B companies tend to have fewer customers but more high-volume purchases. As a consequence, exploration in B2B settings tends to involve greater face-to-face bargaining on price, payment terms, volume discounts, trade support, and product design. This is particularly true of "new task" buying situations—that is, decisions that are new to the firm and involve significant purchase risk. The exploration stage in both B2B and B2C relationships focuses on attraction, the development of trust and norms, the establishment of power relations, and satisfaction.

Attraction. The customer is motivated to develop ties to the firm only to the extent that the firm is an attractive or desirable exchange partner. This usually means that, at a minimum, the customer perceives the firm to offer benefits that exceed the costs of buying from the firm. In most instances, however, customers will feel **attraction** when they perceive an offer of value that is superior to what can be obtained from competing firms. The firm can provide value through such things as functional performance, the social benefits associated with owning a prestigious brand, or the emotional pride of supporting a socially conscious organization. These benefits are weighed against the price of the product or service, and the difficulties in finding and interacting with the firm through the Web or other means.

Relationship Norms. Although **relationship norms** have been defined in a variety of ways, they are essentially expected patterns of behavior.[26] Norms are behavioral rules that guide individual actions and often specify precise sanctions for violations. If a certain situation occurs, a person or firm is required to either perform or abstain from specific behaviors. Failing to act in accordance with the norm results in sanctions.

Within B2C and B2C settings, some norms predate the first contact between the parties. Most customers and businesses subscribe to basic expectations about payment for services rendered, common courtesy, and equity. However, in other instances, particularly on the Internet, the establishment of norms is often explicit. For example, AOL's terms of service include rules concerning conduct and communication. These rules govern some obviously objectionable behaviors such as posting, transmitting, or promoting unlawful content, but also softer behaviors. For example, users are asked not to disrupt the normal flow of dialogue in a chat room or on a message board by "causing the screen to 'scroll' faster than other members or users are able to type to it or any action with a similar disruptive effect."[27] Yahoo! banned the sale of Nazi military objects and Ku Klux Klan memorabilia from its auction website in 2001.[28] Actions that are contrary to expectations are likely to be met with "flames"—hostile or derogatory e-mails—from other users, or a loss of access or privileges.

Trust.   **Trust** can be defined as "the belief that a party's word or promise is reliable and the party will fulfill its obligations."[29] Trust is an essential ingredient in any exchange relationship. If customers do not have faith that the firm will fulfill an order, deliver acceptable goods, or honor a warranty, exchange is unlikely.

The notion of trust is essential to online marketing; indeed, it has been called the "currency of the Web."[30] As eBay founder Pierre Omidyar states, "People won't conduct transactions with each other unless they have trusting relationships first."[31] Unlike transactions with traditional retailers, there is often no personal contact on the Web, and no visible physical presence to reassure the customer that the firm will be in business tomorrow. When making an online transaction, consumers must trust that a firm they may never have "met" will provide accurate product information, protect their financial information, stand behind product guarantees, and not sell their personal data to third parties.[32]

A recent study identified seven factors that lead to trust in online B2B transactions:[33]

- *Brand:* Recognition and reputation play a significant role in developing online trust. Strong brands have the advantage of high awareness levels and positive associations in the minds of consumers. New brands can create immediate trust by cobranding with successful brands to create a sense of stability and familiarity. River Run software conspicuously indicates on its website that it is an "IBM Business Partner" and "Microsoft Certified."
- *Third-party ratings:* Firms without a track record can enhance trust through certifications by third-party organizations. One popular certification approach for B2B markets is supplier performance ratings by firms such as D&B.
- *Security and privacy:* Visitors must be sure that transactions are secure. Firms need to employ the services of well-known firms such as VeriSign and TRUSTe that specialize in online security. Digital certificates and repudiation logs help ensure security, as do authentication and authorization protocols. While consumers worry most about protecting credit

card information, B2B firms are more concerned about their sales information being leaked to competitors.

- *Technology:* Trust is affected by the overall level and stability of a website's technology that is incorporated in a site. Unreliable websites and outdated technology will decrease trust; high levels of personalization, speed, and other aspects of performance will increase trust.

- *Order fulfillment:* Firms must be committed to fast, accurate, and reliable order fulfillment, and they must communicate that to website visitors. Websites will also benefit from functions that enable customers to check the status of their orders, or to specify deliver times. The firm should signal its desire to measure customer satisfaction and follow up on order problems.

- *Customer service and support:* The study found that poor customer service is holding back the growth of online B2B businesses. There is a real need to integrate service capabilities across face-to-face, Internet, telephone, and other interactions. Customer interactions should be coordinated across all points of contact, and the same high level of service should always be provided.

- *Management knowledge:* The final aspect that leads to trust is management knowledge. The study's authors recommend that B2B firms have a dedicated management team made up of experts not only in technology, but also in customer needs.

Seth Godin, former vice president of direct marketing for Yahoo!, argues that building trust requires firms to devote resources to customers who have not even spent their first dollar with the firm. He believes that firms need to teach customers, provide them with information, and engage them in a meaningful dialogue instead of a "narcissistic monologue." In other words, it is the firm that must make the first move to initiate trust and build a relationship.[34]

Power Relations.   **Power** can be defined as the ability to influence. One key question in a relationship is which party is the more dependent. Given the free-market nature of most Internet exchanges, buyers have multiple choices. The seller, ideally, wants to convince the buyer that substitutes do not exist, perhaps through the value of the brand, or the functional, symbolic, or experiential aspects of the product offering.[35]

Power enables one party to impose rules or conditions on the other. Firms that have strong brands or large resources can use their market clout to ensure that existing channel members live up to their agreements.[36] A detailed discussion of power within the personal-computing industry can be found in Chapter 11.

Amazon.com's Honor System, a payment method that allows websites to solicit small donations from visitors or charge for content on a pay-per-use basis, is an example of how power affects online relationships.[37] Third-party websites recognize Amazon.com customers and make it easy for them to donate as little as $1 for access to their content. The system capitalizes on the 29 million customers who have already shopped at Amazon.com. At least initially, payments made through the system are voluntary and fully refundable up to 30 days after the transaction. The success of the payment system depends upon the willingness of customers to make donations for the content they receive. Participating websites don't have the power to enforce payment, perhaps because users see a multitude of substitute websites that are willing to give them similar content for free (see Exhibit 6.8).

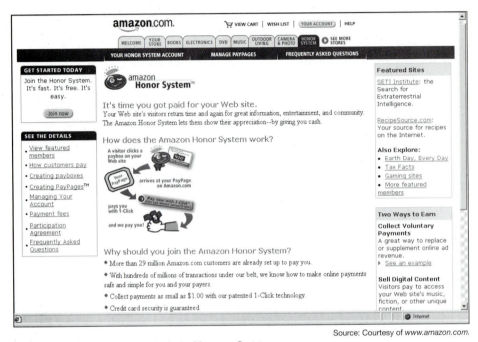

Source: Courtesy of *www.amazon.com*.

EXHIBIT 6.8   Amazon.com's Honor System

Satisfaction.   Ultimately, if customers are dissatisfied with their exploratory interactions with the firm, no amount of communication or trust will help. As noted by Richard L. Oliver, consumers want to be satisfied because it is a reinforcing, desirable experience; it means that the consumer avoids suffering the consequences of a bad decision, and it reaffirms the consumer's ability to make decisions. Although **satisfaction** can be defined in a variety of ways, Oliver defines it as a judgment that an offering "provides a pleasurable level of consumption-related fulfillment."[38] In order to provide satisfaction, and avoid dissatisfaction, firms must therefore meet or exceed customers' requirements. To do this, firms must understand and respond to customer needs.

The range and depth of relationship interactions will increase to the extent that the customer is satisfied with the interactions that have taken place and trusts the firm to act in his or her best interests. Consequently, the firm and customer become more interdependent as the economic aspects of the relationship expand. It is critical that firms also recognize the importance of the emotional and psychological aspects of building relationships.

Commitment

In the **commitment** stage, the parties in a relationship feel a sense of obligation or responsibility to each other. A very strong sense of obligation or responsibility is created, for example, when an individual goes on record about wanting a relationship. People tend to act in a way that is consistent

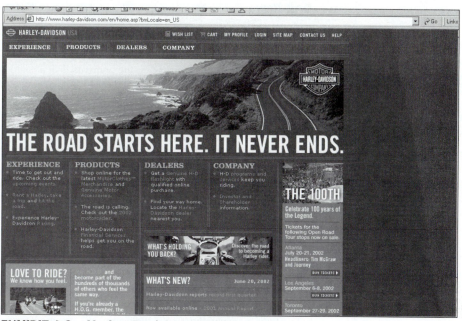

EXHIBIT 6.9   Harley-Davidson Website

with their stated intentions because a sense of commitment is created.[39] However, a commitment need not be signaled by an explicit statement of intention, or even a contractual agreement. Commitments also can be informal or implicit.

Some writers argue that commitment is best reflected by three types of behaviors exhibited by the parties in a relationship.[40] The first indicator of commitment is the extent to which the parties contribute to the relationship. From the customer's perspective, the contribution may be emotional, in the form of the product or brand becoming a part of his or her life. For example, owners of Harley-Davidson motorcycles who participate in the Harley Owners Group (HOG) are more likely to understand the heritage of the brand and to want to form an ongoing relationship with the firm. Harley-Davidson facilitates the creation and maintenance of this bond through its website (see Exhibit 6.9), where enthusiasts can find out about upcoming rides and events and learn about recommended maintenance procedures. In this instance, the buyer–seller dialogue goes far beyond the exchange of money for products or service.

Also important is the opportunity for dialogue between customers. Communication features on Yahoo!, for example, encourage commitment by providing e-mail service and chat rooms. Both features not only keep customers coming back frequently, but also establish social bonds between users that increase commitment to the service.

A second indicator of commitment is the extent to which each party invests in aspects of the relationship that are likely to encourage future interactions. Customers who purchase a Brita water purifier expect to purchase replacement filters from the firm over the useful life of the container. This commitment requires trust and an expectation of satisfaction. In the online world, customers who take the time and energy to customize a webpage for a portal

---

Drill-Down

The Confusing Thing About Loyalty

Customer loyalty can be thought about in at least two distinct ways. The first way is behavioral—that is, loyalty is determined by the percentage of a customer's purchases within a category that is captured by a specific firm. For example, someone who makes all of his or her online book purchases at Barnes & Noble.com is a loyal customer. In this sense, loyalty is measured or understood after the fact; a customer is loyal because of past behavior. The problem with measuring loyalty by behavior is that past behavior is not necessarily a sign of future behavior. That "loyal" customer of Barnes & Noble.com might switch to another firm if offered a better opportunity.

A second perspective on loyalty is psychological. *Webster's New Collegiate Dictionary* defines loyalty as "the tie binding a person to something to which he is loyal." The notion of a tie echoes our definition of a relationship as a "bond or connection."

Both the behavioral and psychological definitions of loyalty are useful. Marketers sometimes talk about loyalty in terms of how customers behave, and at other times discuss loyalty as a psychological bond. The important thing is to know which way is being used.

How do customers create loyal customers? Frederick F. Reichheld and Phil Schefter believe that the Web is actually a very sticky space for both the business-to-consumer and the business-to-business markets [41] The authors indicate that the first issue facing online firms is to earn the trust of the customers they are targeting. As you know from this chapter, trust is fundamental to the development of buyer–seller relationships. They suggest that the second critical issue is to identify and target those customer segments that are most closely aligned with the firm's ability to deliver a superior customer experience. Firms vary in their skills and resources, and therefore also in their capacity to provide something exceptional to customers. The trick is for a firm to know what it is good at, and to deliver it consistently. The authors argue that firms make a fundamental mistake when they focus on attracting rather than retaining customers.

We agree with Reichheld and Schefter that loyalty is a critical metric of online success. However, the bottom line is that it seems impossible for firms to have loyal customers without having a relationship with them—firms must develop customer relationships in order to create customer loyalty. Our relationship framework helps illuminate the factors that lead to loyalty behaviors and the process by which the firm can encourage customers to develop relationship bonds.

---

such as Yahoo! is making a commitment to the firm. Users who undertake this process are not only ensuring that Yahoo! meets their needs, but they are also signaling their desire for a long-term relationship with the firm. An even further commitment is made when the customer registers with the online firm. Registration is perhaps the single most important signal of customer commitment because customers willingly provide information about themselves in exchange for access to services. Both registration and customization are visible signs of commitment that increase the likelihood that customers will return to the site.

A final indicator of commitment is the consistency of the exchange. The notion here is that increasing the predictability of buyer–seller interactions increases the stability of the relationship. One of the benefits of going online for *USA Today* is that the online and offline versions of the paper reinforce each other. This reinforcement quality is critical for *USA Today* because it relies on customers who buy the paper daily (rather than subscribe), and so must convince approximately 2 million people each day to purchase a hard copy of the paper. A single-paper business model means that a high percentage of customers do not buy the paper every day. Therefore, the potential for customers to pick up another paper, or to get out of the habit of buying *USA Today* altogether, is high. The creation of the online version of *USA Today* helps maintain commitment by facilitating a higher level of buyer–seller interaction. Although executives had real concerns that USAToday.com might cannibalize the print version, especially because the online version was free, they found instead that the two versions reinforced each other. When a person in their target market does not have the opportunity to purchase the print version, he or she can go to USAToday.com to catch up on the top stories, view the sports page, or read the national classifieds. Many users bookmark the front page of the Money section and check their investments throughout the day. By increasing the frequency of customer interactions, USAToday.com has undoubtedly increased commitment.[42]

Dissolution

Dissolution occurs when one or both parties exit the relationship. One study suggests that, on average, U.S. firms lose half of their customers every five years.[43] As in personal relationships, the potential for buyer–seller relationships to fail or dissolve always exists. What causes the loss of commitment that ultimately leads to dissolution?

- A better alternative may come along, or the customer may just want something different.

- Relationships in the online world may dissolve as a direct consequence of neglect or apathy. For example, a recent report by NFO Worldwide found that when U.S. consumers change their e-mail address, only about one-third inform the websites that they regularly visit of the change. Consumers complain that there are just too many websites to notify.[44]

- Dissolution can be triggered by a core failure such as a poor service response, product or service failure, or an ethical issue with the firm or an employee.[45]

- Customers simply outgrow some product categories. For example, purchases of music, video games, and athletic shoes are likely to diminish after the teenage years.

Because creating new customers is generally more expensive than keeping existing ones, firms typically want to avoid dissolution. Yet in some instances, firms benefit from "firing" customers. For example:

- Some customers constantly switch to whichever firm offers the best price. These customers are often not profitable because of the high costs of attracting them (e.g., a lower price or promotional offer) and their lack of loyalty. Successful firms are more likely to focus their efforts on attracting and retaining high-margin, high-growth customers.[46] In order to achieve this goal, firms must have the capacity to audit customers on the basis of profitability and accurately predict their growth potential.

- As discussed in the section on exploration, some users violate the norms of the community. One extreme type of norm violation involves illegal activities such as fraud, theft, and counterfeiting. Yahoo! and eBay routinely cancel the accounts of users who break copyright laws.[47]

- Although some customers may be heavy purchasers, they may also be high maintenance. High costs for customer service, technical support, and product returns may overwhelm the firm's ability to achieve profitability.
- The company may change its target market or strategy so that some existing customers can no longer be served profitably.

The Internet facilitates the appropriate firing of customers because it provides a basis for tracking customer behavior and profitability. Measuring customer page views and conversion rates enables firms to predict the costs and benefits of serving each customer (as opposed to customer segments) in their portfolio. Chapter 15 contains detailed information about the types of customer information that can be generated online and their uses.

Interaction Intensity

As buyers and sellers move through the relationship stages, there should be a pattern of **interaction intensity**, defined as the frequency of interaction. In the awareness stage, there is a very limited degree of interaction. The customer may have only seen a single banner ad, or heard of the website through a friend. The number of interactions increases very quickly, however, during the exploration phase. Here, the user visits the website to assess the firm as an exchange partner. The user may check out sections related to the frequently asked questions (FAQs), go to the site map, pose a question by e-mail, read the company history or policy pages, or even buy something. The user may also seek out information from third-party providers, checking the Internet for discussion groups, editorials, or news stories that relate to the firm. As the user moves to the commitment stage, the frequency of interactions is likely to increase again. The user may sign up for the firm's newsletter, bookmark the site, join a frequent-shopper program, or post to a discussion group.

Committed users are also more likely to personalization a website and perhaps even choose it as their homepage. Buyer–seller and buyer–buyer social bonds develop as the parties make emotional and financial investments in the relationship. The frequency of interaction is consistently high in this stage. If the level of interaction declines as the customer finds other exchange partners or moves out of the life stage in which the product or service is purchased, commitment erodes and the relationship dissolves. The association between relationship stage and interaction intensity is represented in Exhibit 6.10.

The 2Is: Why the Web Is Unique in Creating Customer Relationships

The Internet does not change firms' fundamental need to establish strong customer relationships. Businesses must still attract consumers, engender trust, develop and enforce norms of behavior, use power appropriately, and

Four Key Stages of Customer Relationships

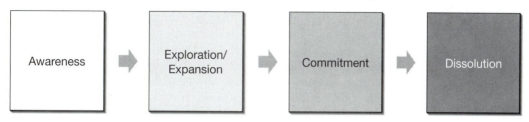

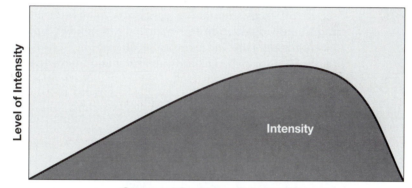

Level of Intensity

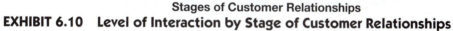

Stages of Customer Relationships

EXHIBIT 6.10   Level of Interaction by Stage of Customer Relationships

---

Drill-Down

Relationship Marketing by Any Other Name

Creating strong customer relationships via new information technologies and the Internet is a hot business topic. A variety of terms or buzzwords have been coined to describe the development of a bond between buyers and sellers. Perhaps the most ubiquitous term is customer relationship management, or CRM. Other names for this philosophy are listed below, along with the authors who have used them.

- **One-to-one marketing** (Don Peppers and Martha Rogers, *The One-to-One Manager: Real World Lessons in Customer Relationship Management*)

- **Permission marketing** (Seth Godin, *Permission Marketing: Turning Strangers Into Friends, and Friends Into Customers*)

- **Customer intimacy** (Michael E. Treacy and Frederik D. Wiersema, *Customer Intimacy and Other Value Disciplines*)

- **Communities of commerce** (Stacey E. Bressler and Charles E. Grantham Sr., *Communities of Commerce*)

Other writers such as Frederick Newell,[48] Frederick F. Reichheld, and Phil Schefter[49] have also emphasized the ability of the Internet to create customer loyalty. All of these writers agree on the need for close customer relationships. Although each author takes a slightly different approach, they all present strong arguments that firms must focus on understanding and responding to the customer. Information technologies such as database software and the Internet are simply means to this end.

create satisfaction. Thus, building a committed relationship requires that firms interact with their customers—meaning, listen to them and respond appropriately. It also means that firms must strive to treat customers as individuals by allowing them to control the timing and extent of buyer–seller interactions, and through the customization of the products and services they buy. It is difficult, if not impossible, to have a relationship where communication flows in only one direction instead of being interactive, with each party responsive to the other. It is also difficult to imagine a relationship in which the parties do not respect and accommodate the uniqueness of the other.[50]

With the advent of the Internet, businesses are able to both interact with large numbers of customers yet treat them as individuals.[51] Previously, firms could be interactive, such as in a face-to-face setting, but only with a small number of customers. Similarly, firms could individualize their product or service offerings, but not on a large scale. The Internet allows for interactivity and individualization to be carried out in a way never possible before. It has fundamentally and irrevocably altered the "economics of information" by allowing for rich (i.e., individualized and interactive) communication on a grand scale.[52]

Given that interactivity and individualization are both prerequisites and drivers of relationships, it is important to develop the concepts fully.

Interactivity

Interactivity is defined as a two-way flow of communication between the firm and customer. It is not enough that communication flows are frequent—interactivity requires a dialogue between firm and customer in which both parties listen to, respond to, and serve the needs of the other. Although the Internet may be the channel through which customers initiate a request for information or carry out transactions, firms must recognize the need to integrate Internet responses with more traditional interactions via the telephone, mail, or face-to-face meetings.

The most personalized two-way dialogues are, of course, between human beings. Although not fully developed, mechanisms that facilitate a marriage between the Internet and human involvement include:

- Retail selling systems in which store personnel are responsible for customer service over the Internet. Video cameras at both ends could aid interaction.
- Coordination between the Internet and retail service personnel. Indeed, it is critical that Internet inquiries, problems, and requests are tracked and responded to by the appropriate employees. The Internet presence may become a liability otherwise—for instance, if customers are told one thing on the Internet and another at a retail location, or if customers have to explain their problem to more than one employee.
- Chat rooms for product-related issues. These rooms might be organized by customer segment or product. Customers can share information with one another as well as with the firm.

Individualization

The level of **individualization** reflects the degree to which firm–customer interactions are tailored or customized to the individual user.[53] Low-individualization information is distributed to a set of users in much the same way that a newspaper is delivered. The information contained in an online newspaper may take a particular perspective (e.g., liberal or conservative), but it does not tailor itself to a specific audience member. The user must select what he or she finds interesting or relevant. Examples of low-individualization information include:

- Dow Jones and Nasdaq exchange data for online investors
- Automatic newsletters for seat sales or vacation packages to travelers
- The standard online versions of *Time, Newsweek, The Wall Street Journal,* or *USA Today*
- Internal company publications, newsletters, or advertisements that are broadcast to present or future customers

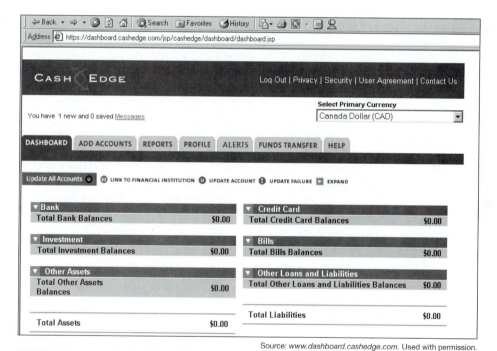

Source: *www.dashboard.cashedge.com.* Used with permission.

EXHIBIT 6.11   CashEdge Website

In contrast, high-individualization interactions transmit information that is customer specific. This type of information ranges from highly personal information (such as account information, transaction statements, or billing statements) to a customized selection of reports from the public domain (such as a Yahoo! search result). Individualized content can also be produced automatically by websites based on user behavior or registration information. Also, many websites allow the user to personalize the interface and the types of content that are routinely provided.

One of the Internet's most provocative examples of individualization is CashEdge (*www.cashedge.com*), a type of software that offers users a secure way to view all of their financial accounts from multiple financial institutions (see Exhibit 6.11). CashEdge enables financial advisers—with the consent of their clients, of course—to aggregate information from separate banking, brokerage, and credit card accounts into a single dashboard view. Clients can select the accounts they want their advisor to view, categorize transactions within their personal budget, and test "what if" scenarios based on their financial situation. Advisors and their clients have a consolidated, "real-time" view of the clients' financial situation. It also provides clients with access to their own personal financial management websites.[54]

Products such as CashEdge could radically change the financial services industry. By facilitating easy management of accounts from several financial institutions, the system may weaken traditional bank–client relationships. Customers have direct access to all their accounts, so adding or deleting a relationship involves only small changes to the user's financial services homepage.

Despite the advantages of individualization, one of the costs is consumer privacy. A PricewaterhouseCoopers study found that Americans are very concerned about online privacy.[55] (See Exhibit 6.12 for key findings.) Close to 60 percent of U.S. Internet users would shop online more often if they knew that retail websites would not do anything with their personal information. Furthermore, 40 percent would shop online more often if they knew how the websites were using the checkout information that consumers are required to supply. The situation is different, however, when the information is used for promotional deals. PricewaterhouseCoopers says that 67 percent of users are comfortable with retail websites using their purchase history to sign them up for frequent-shopper programs. Likewise, more than 50 percent are not troubled when websites use their information to send them information about store sales or specials, or to personalize their online shopping experience.

Other studies support the PricewaterhouseCoopers findings.[56] One survey found the 91 percent of online users consider it an invasion of privacy when unknown third parties gather information about their online behavior without notifying them. Eighty-two percent of users said they would be likely to stop visiting a particular website if a third party was collecting information about their behavior and consolidating it with information from other websites without their knowledge. Other disadvantages, or at least barriers, to high levels of individualization include:

- It require involvement, expertise, and motivation on the consumer's part.
- The approach will appeal only to consumers who feel that their preferences are not currently being met by the current service provider.
- Personalization increases costs and complexity of service, and may reduce service speed.

Overall, online marketers must recognize that individualization can have negative consequences and seek to minimize their effects.

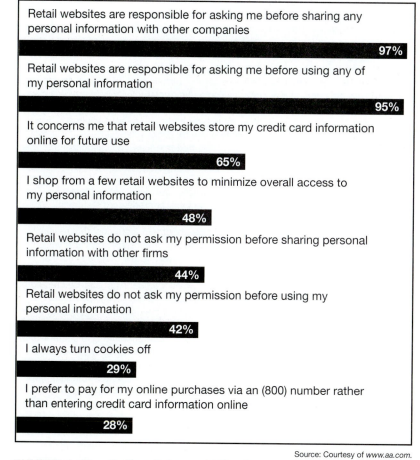

PWC: Online Privacy Attitudes, 2000
(% of Internet users in US who agree/strongly agree)

Retail websites are responsible for asking me before sharing any personal information with other companies — **97%**

Retail websites are responsible for asking me before using any of my personal information — **95%**

It concerns me that retail websites store my credit card information online for future use — **65%**

I shop from a few retail websites to minimize overall access to my personal information — **48%**

Retail websites do not ask my permission before sharing personal information with other firms — **44%**

Retail websites do not ask my permission before using my personal information — **42%**

I always turn cookies off — **29%**

I prefer to pay for my online purchases via an (800) number rather than entering credit card information online — **28%**

Source: Courtesy of *www.aa.com*.

EXHIBIT 6.12 Online Privacy Attitudes

Drill-Down

Are Interactivity and Individualization Always Necessary?

Although large-scale interactivity and individualization are considered advantages of doing business on the Internet, it is not clear that all customers want them all the time. Consider the following three alternative forms of communication and interaction via the Internet:

- **Low Individualization, Low Interactivity.** In these types of interactions, information is distributed to a mass audience, without being tailored for particular audience members. A user must search through it to determine what he or she finds interesting or relevant. Moreover, no response is expected from the user—he or she simply reads (or does not read) the information. The Internet is often used to communicate with customers in this fashion. For example, individuals who sign up for a news service receive regular mailings that are delivered automatically. Another form of low-individualization/low-interactivity communication is spam, or unsolicited promotional materials. Spam is rarely appreciated by its recipients, and many Internet service providers are working to eliminate this form of broadcast. The significant difference between spam and an online newsletter is that the former is unsolicited, while the latter is requested.

(continued)

- **Low Individualization, High Interactivity.** This type of Internet interaction can be compared to the activity at a library. The degree of individualization is low because the online customer selects from a menu of prepublished reports; however, interactivity is enhanced by access to a search engine or other software that acts as a librarian. This program is at the disposal of the consumer to support his or her search for information. For example, an investor might want to understand more about a mutual fund. The investor will have questions related to the strategies of the companies involved; the types of countries they are investing in, and their environmental records. To some degree, portals such as Yahoo!, Excite, and Lycos are providers of low-individualization/high-interactivity information. Users type in a search term and find websites that match their interests. They engage in an interactive, or at least iterative, search for information that has already been created at other websites and therefore can be accessed by anyone. Sites that provide access to such search capabilities become a user's collaborators or allies by providing convenient access to content created by third parties.

- **High Individualization, Low Interactivity.** These types of interactions are ones in which communications are highly personalized, but require little interaction. For example, the information listed on a typical bank or credit card statement includes numbers and details specific to one customer's account. However, it is unusual for the customer to have questions about that statement that require interaction with the bank or credit card company. The Internet provides value by increasing the frequency with which customers can obtain updated information. Updates can occur minute to minute on a 24-hour basis rather than daily or monthly during traditional banking hours. Superior value might also be created by implementing a "by exception" reporting of customer account information. For example, customers might receive a notification if their accounts dip below a certain point, or they might be automatically alerted to interest changes that may impact their banking decisions. Routine individualization might also occur as customers receive automatic updates of their net worth. These reports, though private and tailored to the individual customer, can be standardized through either customer or bank initiatives. For instance, the bank can create a standard package for each customer type or segment, or perhaps a baseline package for all Internet customers. In this situation, the bank can use customer behavior profiles to design messages that are specific to the user. For example, AdCritic.com has a relationship with Amazon.com. When a viewer watches an ad that incorporates music by the Rolling Stones, a small ad for Amazon.com pops up to suggest Rolling Stones books, videos, and CDs. This type of interaction doesn't require the user to request personalized information. It occurs automatically.

In each of these situations, what appears to be most important is the balance between customer needs and information or interaction characteristics. Sometimes customers simply want an online newspaper or newsletter, without the 2Is. Sometimes they want a highly interactive and individualized experience. Savvy online marketers are able to tell the difference.

Creating Customer Relationships through the Web

The remaining chapters in the book examine the levers that firms can use to establish and maintain close buyer–seller relationships. The chapters on product, price, promotion, and distribution each discuss tactics that enable firms to create customer awareness, encourage exploration of their sites, establish commitment, and, if necessary, dissolve or end dysfunctional relationships. Chapter 12, Branding, is designed differently because of branding's unique position in the relationship model. Unlike the other levers, which can operate independently, branding is conceptualized as a factor that is a part of every marketing effort. Consequently, branding can be thought of as a lubricant that enhances the effects of the other levers. When a firm has a strong brand, it increases the effectiveness of the pricing, promotion, distribution, and product levers. An integrative view of the relationship model and the marketing levers is developed in the following chapters. Exhibit 6.13 reflects the framework that guides the rest of the book.

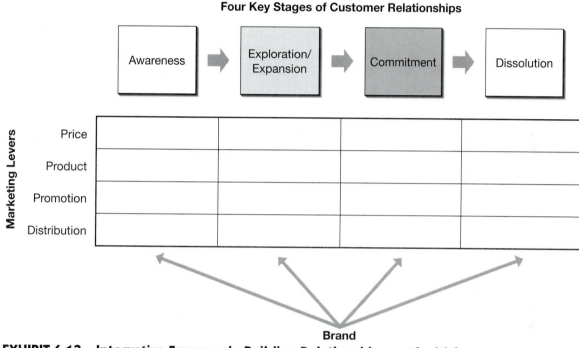

EXHIBIT 6.13   Integrative Framework: Building Relationships on the Web

Not Everyone Wants a Relationship!

It is important to note that, just as not everyone wants to be married, not all customers want to have a relationship. Some customers just want the transaction, and do not want a connection with every (or any) business they patronize. These customers seek to maximize the value of each transaction, or perhaps simply do not care enough about a firm or its products to become connected. Thus, it is critical to understand that not all customers seek an ongoing committed relationship with a firm. These customers often:

- Place little value on the brand and view products within the category as commodities
- Switch companies frequently, often because of price
- Purchase for functional reasons, and therefore read *Consumer Reports* and other independent rating sources

Although it may be in the firm's best interest to develop relationships with its customers, it is clear that not all customers are interested in having one. Attempts to create a relationship with an unwilling partner will not only be ignored, but also may lead to consumer resentment and alienation.

Building Relationships at eBay

This section explores how eBay develops strong customer relationships and examines the strategies that the company has used in each of the four stages of the relationship model.

Awareness

Because of eBay's position as the No. 1 general auction service on the Internet, buyers and sellers alike know that is where the action is. Individuals and businesses interested in selling their goods immediately recognize eBay as a possible exchange partner. To maintain high awareness levels, eBay also undertakes online and offline advertising and promotion.

Has eBay benefited from its brand name? One could argue that, at least initially, eBay benefited from a relatively simple name that customers could easily remember. The company name has only four letters, including the "e" prefix that was then ubiquitous in the online world. On the other hand, "Bay" is a relatively common name that has no strong connection to online auctions. Names such as Bid.com and uBid.com are more descriptive, and may even have been better names—at least, before eBay was able to create a strong market presence. Now, eBay is almost as generic as Kleenex or Scotch tape.

eBay has promoted its brand name predominantly through online means. For example, eBay's alliance with AOL gives it access to more than 60 million AOL customers. This is a very good fit in terms of awareness creation, not only because of the sheer size of the AOL customer base, but also because of its general demographics.

Exploration/Expansion

eBay encourages exploration of its website by not requiring visitors to register before they browse. They can look at the items for sale, watch the bidding process, and read about the sellers' reputations without having to buy or sell. Access to the chat rooms, however, requires registration.

Attraction.   As noted earlier, eBay's attractiveness is a direct function of the numbers of buyers and sellers it counts as users. It is also affected by system reliability, high-quality customer service, and support services.

Relationship Norms.   eBay is very clear about its relationship with buyers and sellers. For example, the website's letter of greeting from founder Pierre Omidyar outlines the firm's core values: honesty and the openness of the system. More specific rules govern appropriate behaviors and what products may be sold. They spell out what items are uniformly prohibited or questionable because of copyright and trademark law. By communicating these standards to new users and continually enforcing them, eBay sets the parameters for consumer-to-consumer relationships. These norms are fundamental to the development of a safe and enjoyable community.

Trust. eBay's business model is unusual in that users do not buy directly from the firm. Although customers may trust eBay implicitly, the real issue is whether they can trust the buyer or seller in the deal. eBay does not provide a warranty for the goods sold on its website.

It is critical that eBay provide a safe transaction environment for its users. One way eBay does this is through a feedback feature called Transaction Forum. Before bidding on an item, shoppers can evaluate a seller's transaction history and see how previous buyers have rated the experience of buying from him or her. After each transaction, users can add to the other party's profile, giving positive points for appropriate behaviors and negative points for inappropriate ones. Sellers who do not play by the rules are suspended from trading. eBay has also introduced a verified user program (through credit agency Equifax), an insurance program, an escrow service, and a customer-support resource called Safe Harbor.

Power Relations. At times, eBay has exercised its power to enforce the rules and regulations governing exchange. For instance, eBay cracks down on deals between buyers and sellers who meet through eBay and then conduct business offline. The firm is now enforcing a rule that prohibits sellers from contacting a losing eBay bidder and offering that person a similar product without going through the auction house. Initially, eBay ignored this behavior because users felt that it built a sense of community.[57] Now, however, fraud related to offline transactions has become the biggest source of complaints to the firm. Many members do not agree with the change and have complained in various chat rooms and on message boards, but it is too soon to tell whether the outcry will cause eBay to reverse the new policy.

Satisfaction. Overall, eBay has done an outstanding job creating customer satisfaction. This claim is supported by Satmetrix Systems, a leading provider of customer experience management products and services, which granted eBay its Best Customer Satisfaction award for the Internet category. Less than 0.1 percent of transactions on eBay are problematic, and customers are fiercely loyal. However, eBay has had its share of problems. Server crashes have plagued the site, and disgruntled customers are exploring Amazon.com and other competitors.[58] Further, SmartMoney claims that eBay is "the perfect venue for scams," and auction fraud was declared the No.1 problem on the Web by the National Consumers League in 1999.

Commitment

eBay encourages customer commitment in all three of the ways identified earlier in the chapter. First, eBay works hard to create a strong sense of community among its users; the site's community-based culture is reminiscent of the early days of traditional commerce, when face-to-face transactions were commonplace. Although eBay interactions are virtual, there is a sense that the organization is providing a forum that empowers individual buyers and sellers. Second, eBay encourages users to invest in their relationship with the

---

Drill-Down

Setting Norms at eBay: A Letter of Greeting from Founder Pierre Omidyar

I launched eBay on Labor Day, 1995. Since then, this site has become more popular than I ever expected, and I began to realize that this was indeed a grand experiment in Internet commerce.

By creating an open market that encourages honest dealings, I hope to make it easier to conduct business with strangers over the Net.

Most people are honest. And they mean well. Some people go out of their way to make things right. I've heard great stories about the honesty of people here. But some people are dishonest. Or deceptive. This is true here, in the newsgroups, in the classifieds, and right next door. It's a fact of life.

But here, those people can't hide. We'll drive them away. Protect others from them. This grand hope depends on your active participation. Become a registered user. Use our Feedback Forum. Give praise where it is due; make complaints where appropriate.

For the past three years, we have dealt with complaints among participants. But those complaints have amounted to only a handful. We've had over 12,000,000 items offered on eBay since opening. And only a few dozen complaints.

Now, we have an open forum. Use it. Make your complaints in the open. Better yet, give your praise in the open. Let everyone know what a joy it was to deal with someone.

Above all, conduct yourself in a professional manner. Deal with others the way you would have them deal with you. Remember that you are usually dealing with individuals, just like yourself. Subject to making mistakes. Well-meaning, but wrong on occasion. That's just human. We can live with that. We can deal with that. We can still make deals with that.

Thanks for participating. Good luck, and good business!

Regards,

Pierre

—Posted on eBay

---

firm. eBay offers individualization options for keeping track of transactions, and encourages users to evaluate other buyers and sellers through the Transaction Forum feature. The users hold the rights and responsibilities for the transactions, and user commitment is increased when they participate in community-related behaviors. Finally, eBay is a well-designed service that stimulates repeat interactions that sustain the buyer–seller relationship. Moreover, the site offers higher value because of its large market share and wide-ranging appeal. Customers can bid on everything from a $1 souvenir to a $100,000 piece of real estate. The high-priced items bring in large profits, while the low-priced items create volume and visits.

Dissolution

As in most online situations, the customer always has the option of terminating the relationship. Users can simply stop buying or selling when they no longer have the need, or they can simply seek a better option. Most customers use eBay to sell a few items that are sitting around the garage or basement, and they may not return for an extended period of time.

eBay is less likely to terminate a relationship, but it can if a seller violates a basic rule—attempts to sell counterfeit software, for example—or if it receives several complaints about that individual. Also, the firm utilizes its internal rating system, which is based on feedback from other members of the community. Members who have good reputations have a star symbol placed next to their name. The stars are color coded to show the net amount of positive feedback they have received. Members who receive negative feedback are shunned, and their relationships are essentially dissolved because of the lack of desire to do business with them.

1. What is a relationship, and why is developing a buyer–seller relationship important?

A relationship is a bond or connection between the firm and a customer. The bond can be intellectual, emotional, or a combination. The benefits of having a relationship are thought to be twofold. First, the costs of serving established customers are lower. Significant costs are associated with finding and attracting new customers, whereas established customers already have an awareness of the firm and have purchased from it at least once. As a result, the firm does not have to invest in strategies to identify these customers and persuade them that the firm is a reasonable exchange partner. Second, some evidence suggests that existing customers will pay higher prices than new customers will, even after introductory offers are considered. This suggests that long-term customers place some value on the noneconomic aspects of the relationship.

2. What are the various types of relationships?

Relationships can be described as either communal or exchange based. Communal relationships are altruistic—each person is focused on meeting the needs and wants of the other. Close interpersonal relationships, such as those between a parent and child, tend to be communal. In contrast, exchange relationships are based on the giving or taking of one thing in return for another. When one person helps the other, a specific obligation is created, and it is expected that the debt will be repaid. Buyer–seller relationships are exchange based.

3. What is the relationship model?

The relationship model comprises four stages that reflect an idealized representation of how buyers and sellers progress from awareness to exploration, commitment, and (perhaps) dissolution. A description of each of the four stages follows:

- *Awareness.* The customer recognizes that the firm is a possible exchange partner, but has not initiated any communication with the firm or purchased its products.
- *Exploration/Expansion.* The customer considers the possibility of exchange, gathers information, and perhaps makes some trial purchases.
- *Commitment.* The parties in a relationship feel a sense of obligation or responsibility toward each other.
- *Dissolution.* The relationship is severed by either the buyer or seller. A loss of connection results.

4. How do the 2Is of the Internet contribute to the development of buyer–seller relationships?

The 2Is, interactivity and individualization, are fundamental to relationships. To maintain a relationship, firms must interact with their customers by listening to them and responding appropriately. A firm that sends only broadcast (i.e., one-way) communications cannot create a relationship. Also, firms must strive to treat customers as individuals by allowing them to control the timing and extent of buyer–seller interactions, and by customizing the products and services they buy. It is difficult, if not impossible, to have a relationship without some degree of interactivity and individualization.

5. When are customers likely to want a relationship with a firm or brand?

Buyers are most likely to want a relationship with firms or brands with which they are highly involved. Involvement describes the degree to which a relationship is relevant to the consumer. Relationships that are more relevant relate more strongly to consumers' values, interests, or needs. Consumers who are highly involved in a relationship see it as an important part of their lives. Relationship involvement is a function of the product categories, the purchase situation, and consumers' personal interests. Customers are more likely to pursue relationships with firms offering products that pose higher risks in terms of the functional or social consequences of purchase. These categories include products that are expensive and visible, such as gifts, clothing, jewelry, and athletic shoes. Some low-involvement purchases become high-involvement purchases under the right circumstances, particularly when the buyer is concerned with the reactions of others. For example, buying a gift or shopping with a friend might increase the purchase involvement in some categories. Finally, some consumers are more interested in certain product categories than others. For these consumers, both involvement and the likelihood of forming a relationship are higher.

Activities for Students

1. Do you have a business relationship with an online brand? If so, visit the brand's website and identify characteristics that encourage you to explore and commit to the brand. Are there aspects of the website that, if changed, would increase or decrease your desire to maintain a relationship?

2. Keep a journal of your online use. Pay particular attention to websites you visit for the first time. How did you become aware of the firm's online presence? What was the purpose of your visit? How many times did you visit before you purchased anything? Did you move through the relationship stages identified in this book?

3. Visit a chat room and observe the conversations there. What are the norms that govern behavior in the room? What types of behaviors are rejected or sanctioned by the group? How do people treat newcomers? What purpose do these norms have in governing behavior?

Key Terms

relationship	awareness	satisfaction
communal relationship	exploration/expansion	commitment
exchange relationship	attraction	dissolution
involvement	relationship norms	interaction intensity
enduring involvement	trust	interactivity
situational involvement	power	individualization

Endnotes

[1]Mills, Judson, and Margaret S. Clark. 1994. *Communal and exchange relationships: Controversies and research. In Theoretical frameworks for personal relationships*, eds. Ralph Erber and Robin Gilmour. Hillsdale: Lawrence Erlbaum Associates, pp. 29–42.

[2]Clark, Margaret S., and Judson Mills. 1979. Interpersonal attraction in exchange and communal relationships. *Journal of Personality and Social Psychology* 27:12–24.

[3]For example, see, Cialdini, Robert B., Mark Schaller, Donald Houlihan, Kevin Arps, Jim Fultz, and Arthur L. Beaman. 1987. Empathy-based helping: Is it selflessly or selfishly motivated? *Journal of Personality and Social Psychology* 52:749–758.

[4]It seems likely that communal relationships are high involvement because they require both empathy and selflessness.

[5]Zaichkowsky, Judith Lynne. 1985. Measuring the involvement construct in marketing. *Journal of Consumer Research* 12:341–352.

[6]Zaichkowsky, Judith Lynne. 1986. Conceptualizing involvement. *Journal of Advertising* 15 (2):4–14.

[7]Greenman, Catherine. 2001. Women turn to Web to avoid sales pressure. *New York Times on the Web*, 2 January.

[8]Levitt, Theodore. 1981. After the sale is over. *Harvard Business Review* 61:87–93.

[9]Trask, Richard. 2000. Developing e-partnerships. *Association Management* 11:46–52.

[10]Coviello, Nicole E., Roderick J. Brodie, Peter J. Danaher, and Wesley J. Johnson (2002) "How firms relate to their markets: an empirical examination of contemporary marketing practices," *Journal of Marketing* 66, (July) 3, 33-46.

[11]Reinartz, Werner J., and V. Kumar. 2000. On the profitability of long-life customers in a noncontractual setting: An empirical investigation and implications for marketing. *Journal of Marketing* 64:17–35.

[12]Reichheld, Frederick F., and Thomas Teal. 2000. *The loyalty effect*. Boston: Harvard Business School Press.

[13]Mohs, Julia. 1999. Frequency marketing. *Retail Report* 12:3.

[14]Naples, Mark, April 2002, Target Marketing, volume 25 (4), pages 28-30.

[15]Reinartz, Werner J., and V. Kumar. 2000. On the profitability of long-life customers in a noncontractual setting: An empirical investigation and implications for marketing. *Journal of Marketing* 64:17–35.

[16]Halperin, Karin. 2001. The profit picture. *Bank Systems & Technology* 38:40.

[17]O'Brien, Louise, and Charles Jones. 1995. Do rewards really create loyalty? *Harvard Business School*, May–June: 75–82.

[18]Berry, Leonard L., and A. Parasuraman. 1991. *Marketing services—competing through quality*. New York: Free Press.

[19]Bressler, Stacey E., and Charles E. Grantham, Sr. 2000. *Communities of commerce*. New York: McGraw-Hill.

[20]Reinartz, Werner J., and V. Kumar 2000. On the profitability of long-life customers in a noncontractual setting: An empirical investigation and implications for marketing. *Journal of Marketing* 64 (October), 17–35.

[21]Dwyer, Robert F., Paul H. Schurr, and Sejo Oh. 1987. Developing buyer–seller relationships. *Journal of Marketing* 51:11–27.

[22]CBS: Super Bowl ads getting price hike. 2000. *USA Today Online* 7 December.

[23]USA TODAY Super Bowl ad meter results. 2000. *USA Today Online* 23 March.

[24]Start-up with pricey Super Bowl ad goes bust. 2000. *CNET* 11 June.

[25]Dot-commercials. 2000. *CNET* 21 February.

[26]Baron, Robert S., Norbert L. Kerr, and Norman Miller. 1992. *Group process, group decision, group action*. Pacific Grove: Brooks\Cole.

[27]AOL Terms of Service, Spring 1998.

[28]Wolverton, Troy, and Jell Pelline. 2001. Yahoo to charge auction fees, ban hate materials. *news.com* 2 January.

[29]Rotter, Julian B. 1967. A new scale for the measurement of interpersonal trust. Journal of Personality 35:651–655.

[30]Urban, Glen L., Fareena Sultan, and William J. Qualls. 2000. Placing trust at the center of your Internet strategy. *Sloan Management Review* Fall, 39–48.

[31]Tempest, Nicole. 1999. Meg Whitman at eBay Inc. (A). Case No. 9-400-35, 1 Oct. Boston: Harvard Business School Publishing.

[32]Crosby, Lawrence A., Kenneth R. Evans, and Deborah Cowles. 1990. Relationship quality in services selling: An interpersonal influence perspective. *Journal of Marketing* 54:68–81.

[33]Sultan, Fareena, Hussain A. Mooraj. Design a trust-based e-business strategy. 2001. *Marketing Management*: Nov/Dec.

[34]Godin, Seth. 1999. Permission marketing: Turning strangers into friends, and friends into customers. New York: Simon and Schuster.

[35]See the chapter on distribution for a discussion of the bases of power.

[36]Geyskens, Inge, Katrijn Gielens, and Marnik G. Dekimpe (2002), The Market Valuation of Internet Channel Additions," *Journal of Marketing*, 66 (April), 102-119.

[37]Wolverton, Troy. 2001. Amazon debuts honor system. *news.com* 6 February.

[38]Oliver, Richard L. 1997. *Satisfaction: A behavioral perspective on the consumer*. New York: McGraw-Hill.

[39]Cialdini, Robert B. 1993. *Influence: Science and practice*. New York: Harper Collins.

[40]Scanzoni, J. 1979. Social exchange and behavioral interdependence. In Social exchange in developing relationships. eds. R.L. Burgess and T.L. Huston. New York: Academic Press.

[41]Reichheld, Frederick F., and Phil Schefter (2000), E-Loyalty: Your Secret Weapon on the Web, *Harvard Business Review* (July –August), 105-113.

[42]Deighton, John, and Anthony St. George. 1998. USA Today Online. Case No. 9-598-1333. Boston: Harvard Business Publishing.

[43]Reichheld, Frederick F. 1996. Learning from customer defects. *Harvard Business Review* March-April, 56–69.

[44]No forwarding e-mail address. 2001. *e-Marketer* 1 February.

[45]Coulter, Robin A., and Mark Ligas. 2000. The long good-bye: The dissolution of customer-service provider relationships. *Psychology & Marketing* 17:669–695.

[46]Slywotzky, Adrian J., and Benson P. Shapiro. 1993. Leveraging to beat the odds: The new marketing mindset. *Harvard Business Review* September–October, 97–107.

[47]Konrad, Rachel. 2001. Hobby industry looks to sew up thieves' loose ends online. *news.com* 8 February.

[48]Newell, Frederick. 2000. *Loyalty.com: Customer relationship management in the new era of Internet marketing*. New York: McGraw-Hill.

[49]Reichheld, Frederick, and Phil Schefter. 2000. E-loyaly: Your secret weapon on the web. *Harvard Business Review* July–August.

[50]Duncan, Tom, and Sandra E. Moriarty. 1998. A communication-based marketing model for managing relationships. *Journal of Marketing* 62:1–13.

[51]Evans, Philip, and Thomas S. Wurster. 1997. Strategy and the new economics of information. *Harvard Business Review* September–October, 71–82.

[52]Ibid.

[53]The term individualization is used in this text to connote the degree to which a website accommodates user personalization in terms of the website interface and communication with the company.

[54]*Microbanker.com*, May 1, 2002 Monday, CashEdge and Ticoon to Deliver First Live "Web Based" Aggregated Wealth Management Platform.

[55]Consumers' Privacy Concerns Are a Barrier to Individualization—*eMarketer*, November 29, 2000).

[56]Naples, Mark, April 2002, *Target Marketing*, volume 25 (4), pages 28-30).

[57]eBay cracks down on members' offline deals. 2000. *news.com* 28 December.

[58]Roth, Daniel. 1999. Meg muscles eBay uptown. *Fortune* 5 July.

Product

Once a marketplace opportunity and value proposition have been identified, the next step is to develop a product. This chapter examines the impact of the Internet on products, product portfolios, and product development. It also considers the various ways in which companies can make their product development processes more customer-informed by taking advantage of the 2Is of the Internet—learning more about customers as individuals and interacting with customers on a broad scale. While the focus is clearly on the Internet and how it can be used to further an enterprise's business objectives, a completely integrated approach, with both online and offline marketing initiatives, is the formula most likely to yield success. This chapter will also consider how products enable customer relationships by examining how product development levers influence the four customer relationship stages. It thus sets the stage for a discussion of how the Internet has altered the product levers available to marketers.

QUESTIONS

Please consider the following questions as you read this chapter:

1. How is product defined?

2. What are the characteristics of Internet-based products and services?

3. What Internet product levers can marketers use?

4. How do interactivity and individualization (the 2Is) contribute to product offerings?

5. What factors do companies consider when managing their product portfolios?

6. In what ways has the product development process been affected by the Internet?

Introduction

The Internet has given rise to new forms of products and services. The Internet is also frequently used to provide additional features that enhance existing offline products and services. Even firms with no Internet products and services are turning to the Internet as part of their product development efforts. Thus while this chapter concentrates on Internet products specifically, its contents are highly relevant for offline marketers and online marketers alike. The chapter is divided into the following sections:

Co-authored by Katherine Jocz. With substantive input from Eric Paley, President, Abstract Edge Web Solutions.

What Is Product? This section introduces the basic building blocks of product, explores the differences between products and services, and positions product as part of the product portfolio.

How the Internet Affects Product. This section discusses the types of products, services, and augmented products made possible by the Internet, as well as implications for product assortments.

How the 2Is Affect Product. This section focuses on how the interactivity and individualization features of the Internet enable more personalized and customized products that can deepen customer relationships.

The Dynamic Nature of Product Portfolios. This section emphasizes the importance of actively managing the product portfolio strategy to create a sustainable strategic advantage for a firm.

Product Development. This section discusses the importance of a customer-informed approach to product development. It reviews the standard product development process and discusses the influences of the Internet on product development.

How Products Enable Customer Relationships. This section shows how product can be used to create relationships with customers across the four relationship stages.

eBay Example. The chapter concludes with a look at how the product principles discussed in this chapter apply to eBay.

What Is Product?

The Basic Building Blocks

Broadly defined, **product** is something created for the purpose of a transaction. The product satisfies buyers' specific wants or needs, and provides sellers with revenue or customer goodwill that will ideally provide revenue later down the road. A product offering comprises a basic product or service that provides a core benefit to customers, as well as the product packaging and labeling, and can also include other attributes or features that augment the basic product.

Core Benefit.   The **core benefit** is the most fundamental value offered by the product. Consider the products in Exhibit 7.1. The core benefit of a sports utility vehicle (SUV) product is transportation; the core benefit of eDiets.com, an interactive website, is dieting information. The buyer will nearly always assume that whatever product he or she purchases will deliver the core benefit. However, the core benefit is not a point of differentiation that the buyer uses to distinguish between products.

Basic Product.   The **basic product**[1] refers to the minimum product offering needed to deliver the core benefit a customer expects to obtain. It thus represents a customer's threshold for considering a purchase. For an SUV, the basic product might include a radio, engine, four tires, and other baseline items. The basic product for eDiets.com is accurate information, advice, and motivational support for individuals who want to lose weight. Basic products

EXHIBIT 7.1   Product Value Hierarchy

are differentiated from one another by how well they meet customer expectations, on their unique branding, and perhaps on price. However, the opportunity to differentiate increases by augmenting a product.

Augmented Product.   An **augmented product** delivers features that go beyond a customer or buyer's minimum expectations. For an SUV, augmented products might include an extended warranty, trade-ins, and financing. For eDiets.com, the augmented products might include an individual diet plan, a customized workout schedule, and online support groups and meetings. Augmenting a product allows a firm to further differentiate its offering from those of its competitors and establish a compelling basis of comparison for prospective buyers. The augmented product should be designed to deliver the benefits identified in the positioning and target-market selection stage of marketing strategy. In more mature markets, augmenting offerings is a means of circumventing price-based competition.

Interestingly, an augmented product in one market may be considered a basic product in another. For example, in one country a radio player in an automobile may be considered part of the basic product, but in another country it may be considered an augmentation of the product. The distinction between an augmented product and a basic product is based on the expectations of the customers in those particular markets. Adding to this complexity is the fact that customer expectations are not static. As marketers continue to make augmented products available, customers will incorporate what was once an augmented product into their baseline expectations. For instance, as CD players became standard features in luxury cars, within that product category customers began to expect them, and soon they were no longer considered a product augmentation. Such shifts in expectations require marketers to constantly redefine their basic and augmented product offerings.

Several factors should be taken into account when deciding whether to implement a product augmentation strategy. Depending on the pricing model, each augmentation can add cost; additional costs should only be added to the basic product when the augmentation offers a differentiation that buyers will value. Market research tools such as conjoint analysis can be used to determine the value customers put on product augmentation and the price that customers are willing to pay for the augmentation.

Physical Goods and Services

There are two general types of products: **physical goods** and **services**. While both product types exist in pure form, a competitively advantaged value proposition would likely incorporate elements of each product type in order to increase the probability of success in the marketplace.

Physical Goods. The word "product" usually conjures up the image of a tangible good. In market exchanges of physical goods, buyers are able to take possession of the good and consume or use it at their convenience. Elements of physical products include their features, design, and packaging, all of which buyers can readily comprehend. In general, since buyers can often see or even at times directly experience or test tangible goods before purchase, they can understand the product's benefits before acquiring it.

Services. Services can be defined as actions that companies offer to customers for the purpose of transaction (in order to achieve either revenue or increased customer goodwill). Types of services can range from artistic performances to the delivery of information. In market exchanges of services, buyers do not take possession of the service itself, although they may take possession of associated goods. Traditionally, this occurred for four reasons:

- *Intangibility.* The service itself is not a physical object that can be possessed.
- *Simultaneity.* The producer and customer need to come together at a single time for the exchange of services to take place. For example, getting a haircut requires the customer to go to the salon, the shop to be open, and the stylist to be available.
- *Heterogeneity.* Services provided by people are inherently subject to variability. For example, a doctor interacts directly with a patient and diagnoses and treats an ailment on an individual basis.
- *Perishability.* Excess service capacity cannot be stored. For example, unsold seats at a performance or on an airline flight are of no value after the performance or flight has taken place.

Services account for a large part of the economic activity in the United States: They represent approximately 22 percent of gross national product (GNP) and 30 percent of employment. In addition, retail services (businesses primarily engaged in selling merchandise to the general public) and wholesale services (businesses primarily engaged in selling goods to other businesses) respectively account for 9 percent and 7 percent of GNP and 18 percent and 6 percent of employment.[2]

The Product Portfolio

Product marketing involves making decisions about what mix of products the company will offer to implement, the firm's choice of positioning, and target market. The **product portfolio** may include a number of product lines, or groups of products belonging to the same basic product category. Among Hewlett-Packard's product lines, for example, are notebook personal computers, laser printers, and scanners. In order to target different market segments, companies often vary the features, quality, and price of the products belonging to a single product line. For example, Hewlett-Packard sells a wide variety of laser printers that differ in terms of speed, capacity, price, and suitability for individual versus business use. To stimulate demand, firms also introduce product variants, such as new colors, flavors, or sizes. The choice of number and type of product lines—as well as the balance struck between new and existing products—flows from corporate strategy, market opportunity analysis, and competitive activity, as well as the firm's resources and capabilities.

How the Internet Affects Product

A wealth of commercial activity exists on the Internet, some conducted purely online and some integrating online and offline transactions. To understand how marketers can take advantage of the Internet and how offline and online products and services differ, it is useful to classify products into four general categories based on whether they are a good or service and on their primary purpose. The first two categories are products or services whose purpose is to deliver core benefits directly on the Internet. The third is Internet services that exist primarily to sell or distribute products that are delivered offline. The fourth is Internet services that are used to augment product offerings.

In each of these categories, the Internet presents companies with unique opportunities to enhance their product offerings (see Exhibit 7.2). At the same time, it is blurring the lines that used to separate services from physical goods and is changing some of the age-old accepted limitations of service-based offerings such as intangibility, simultaneity, heterogeneity, and perishability.[3]

Digitized Goods

In order for a product to be delivered online, it must be digitizable. The Internet transfers digital data in the form of a series of discrete bits (represented by 0 or 1) across a network. This means that any product that can

Product Type	Primary Purpose	Internet Properties	Examples
Digitized Good	Provides core benefit in digitized form online	Is not used up in consumption; easily reproducible; transferable	Downloadable software or music, online newspapers
Service	Performs core service benefit online	Standardizes service; allows producer and consumer to be separated in space and time; adds vividness to intangibles	Schwab.com, eDiets.com, Yahoo! Sports Fantasy Baseball Plus
Retail or Distribution Service	Sells, brokers, or distributes products delivered offline	Helps dispose of perishable inventory; aggregates demand	Amazon.com, Priceline, FreeMarkets
Product Augmentation	Adds extra services or benefits to a service or product	Differentiates at low incremental cost	FedEx, Fidelity websites

EXHIBIT 7.2   Internet Product Types

be converted into digital information can be delivered directly to customers over the Internet. Software, music, video, and news are examples of information-based products that can be distributed to customers via the Internet. Virtually any product appearing in print, audio, or visual media as well as software and other sets of digital instructions qualify. Currently, the primary limitation on digitizable products is the amount of bandwidth going into customers' offices or homes.

Information products have some unique properties compared with those of a physical good or service. Like services, they are highly intangible, yet they can be readily converted into a more tangible good. For example, consumers have the option of printing out articles from NYTimes.com or burning music files onto CDs. Another property of digitized information is that it does not get used up or worn out like physical goods, and in fact can be easily duplicated. This ease of duplication and distribution often makes it difficult for companies to control their ownership and capture the value of information products once they are in digital form. The record labels' legal battles against online music-swapping service Napster and the succession of free music distribution services attest to the difficulty of preventing unauthorized copying and dissemination. Furthermore, the legal system draws a sharp distinction between physical property and intellectual property; producers of intellectual property retain ownership of that property only for a specified period of time, after which it enters the public domain.

Different types of products, whether physical goods or not, differ in the extent to which the benefits they offer can be directly experienced or tested prior to purchase.[4] When a customer cannot experience the product prior to buying it, marketers provide assurances through advertising and packaging; for example, cookies might be sold in clear wrapping so that buyers can see what they are getting. In the case of information products offered on the Internet, the visual presentation and description of the product are the equivalent of packaging. Internet marketers may also offer a sample product to customers or offer a mix of free and paid content. The website of *The Wall Street Journal* allows readers free access to articles for two weeks, after which it begins charging an annual subscription fee.

Services

Services that are highly dependent on stored information and can be broken down into routine or well-structured interactions with customers are the most well-suited for delivery over the Internet. Travel services are a good example. Consider the multiple inquiries and responses generated by a budget-conscious airline customer who wants to investigate a range of travel dates, a range of departure and arrival times, a range of fare options, a range of flight connections, and perhaps alternative arrival and departure airports. While many steps may be involved in the process, they can easily be broken down into routine inquiries and discrete responses. Furthermore, for this type of service, traditional travel agents provide limited or no added value. On the other hand, a customer who wants to book a once-in-a-lifetime African safari requires the assistance of an expert; here, the expertise required is more idiosyncratic and less capable of being provided by even the most sophisticated interactive system.

The Internet also eases the enormous constraints so often associated with offline service delivery and production. These constraints arise from the properties of intangibility, simultaneity, and heterogeneity.

Intangibility. Intangible services are often more difficult than physical goods for customers to comprehend simply because they cannot touch them or see them. In most cases the customer does not really know what he or she is getting until the actual service takes place. Given the intangibility of the service, marketers must regularly remind customers of its benefits so that the awareness or importance of the service does not diminish over time.

The Internet can help make intangible services or experiences seem more tangible through virtual tours, video clips, and other advanced technologies. Consider Outside Online (*www.outsidemag.com*), the website of Outside magazine. Through a collection of global travel resources, Outside Online makes traveling more tangible by bringing together people with similar travel interests and asking those who have visited a particular destination to share their experiences. Through discussion groups, posted photographs, and other forms of Internet communication, an intangible product becomes a tangible experience.

Simultaneity. One limiting factor of many traditional service products was the requirement for the seller of a service and the buyer of a service to be in the same place at the same time. On the Internet, however, this is not a requirement. Because websites are accessible 24 hours a day, seven days a week, the scale and cost of delivering highly customized services via the Internet would be close to impossible to match in the offline world.

Heterogeneity.   The variability of personal services has historically limited the ability to provide them on a mass production level. The Internet has removed this limitation by allowing scalable personalization. Websites such as InfoBeat, for example, allow users to receive personalized news or alerts. In such applications, customers generally specify their preferences with the company providing the service—and by doing so become coproducers of the service being offered to them. The time customers spend identifying their preferences reduces the company's efforts and also supports a closer customer/product relationship. Customers perceive the results as better meeting their needs, and companies recognize the potential cost savings of having the customer do most of the work associated with personalization. In this case, it is a win-win relationship.

Retail and Distribution Services

As will be discussed in more detail in Chapter 9 and Chapter 11, the Internet serves as a versatile marketing lever to spread information about products, as well as to facilitate their exchange through online retailing, wholesaling, or other forms of distribution such as auctions. In fact, much of the commercial activity on the Internet consists of retailers or business-to-business distributors selling online the same kinds of products they sell offline. For direct marketers and catalog retailers such as Lands' End, the transition to the Internet simply involves extending their offline business model to encompass their online operations. Other distribution services, such as the B2B exchanges that arose in the late 1990s, developed entirely new Internet-only business models.

In general, the most successful websites offer an augmented service through which to purchase a product. For example, Amazon.com offers customers the convenience of ordering from home, online literary and customer reviews, the ability to search a database of book titles, and price savings that are a result of a sales channel that does not require a physical presence.

Perishability.   Perishability is a particularly acute problem for companies whose business models are characterized by a high fixed cost, such as airlines. But the Internet can alleviate the perishability problem for many of these companies. Travel service firm Priceline.com is an example of how excess inventory can be liquidated online. Priceline.com acts as an agent for airlines and hotels, selling excess tickets and rooms at a discount once traditional sales mechanisms are exhausted. The Internet's direct access to customers and its ability to provide updates in real time makes this possible.

Product Augmentation

For offline firms, the Internet often opens the doors to new product augmentation possibilities. FedEx customers, for example, can easily monitor shipments by entering their packages' tracking numbers into the FedEx website. The Apple Computer website provides product documentation, software upgrades, and online support to registered buyers. The Internet is particularly effective in augmenting basic products or services with additional services such as presales support, postsales support, and customer care programs.

Presales Support.   Websites can offer a number of enhanced functionalities to facilitate the buying process. These functionalities include comparison shopping, product selection guides, or product demonstrations. In the future, when more customers have access to broadband connections, applications such as simulcasting, Web conferencing, and streaming video will offer greater opportunities to augment products.

Landsend.com offers several enhanced features to shoppers. For example, the website's Personal Shopper feature asks the customer a set of questions about his or her style preferences, then uses an algorithm to match the customer with the right clothes. Another feature is called My Virtual Model, which is depicted in Exhibit 7.3. Online shoppers are often reluctant to order clothing on the Internet because they are unable to try it on. Lands' End attempts to mitigate this limitation by letting the customers create a virtual version of themselves. A shopper can customize a virtual model to reflect his or her body proportions, and then use that model to "try on" clothes that they might want to purchase. CDNow, an online retailer of music and movies, provides recommendations, bestseller lists, e-mail notifications, and other services to inform customer choices.

Fulfillment Options.   Flexible fulfillment is another augmented offering that can add significant value for a customer and increase product differentiation. Giving customers the option of placing orders through a toll-free number, by mail, by e-mail, on the Internet, or through a dealer is one example of flexible fulfillment. Another is allowing customers to mail items to multiple addresses. In the case of digitized goods, flexible fulfillment might mean a choice of downloading a product from the company's website or receiving it through the mail. To effectively exercise this form of augmentation, a company must help customers buy when and where they please and

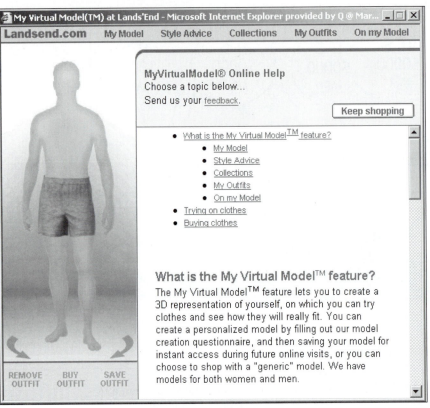

Source: © My Virtual Model Inc., 2002. © Lands End, Inc. Used with permission.

EXHIBIT 7.3   The Lands' End Virtual Model

must insulate customers from the tangled web of channel conflict. Successful and efficient fulfillment establishes reliability in customers' minds, thus increasing the likelihood that they will return.

1-800-Flowers.com offers its customers a range of fulfillment options. The gift site allows shoppers to send gifts from one shopping cart to an address book of recipients, making online gift ordering a painless process. Because many of its gifts are perishable, 1-800-Flowers.com uses a sophisticated regional fulfillment system to make sure orders arrive in proper condition. However, this regional system means that some gifts are not available in particular locations. To overcome this limitation, the site asks customers to enter a zip code as they select each product to be put in the shopping cart (see Exhibit 7.4). This way, when the shopper looks at the cart he or she knows immediately whether the product is available in that zip code. Additionally, if 1-800-Flowers.com anticipates a delay in the shipment of an order, customers are notified about the delay as they are ordering. After the purchase is complete, customers are kept informed of the progress of the order via e-mail and can easily log in to the site to get an immediate status update. All of these fulfillment capabilities augment 1-800-Flowers.com's core products and bolster customer confidence in the company.

Postsales Support.   Contracts for postsales service have two primary benefits. First, they can open an ongoing dialogue between company and customer, which can lead to a valuable relationship. Second, postsales support

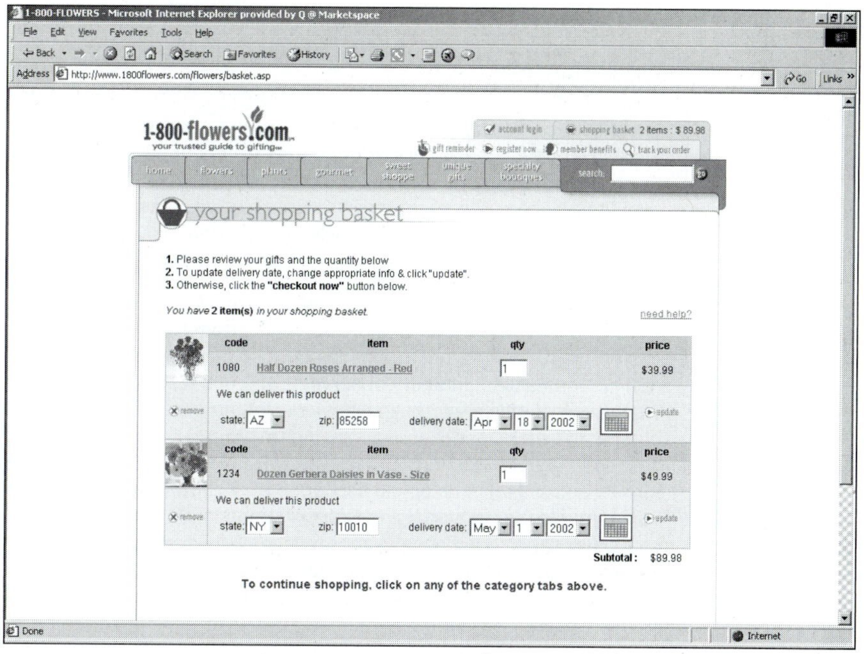

Source: *www.1800flowers.com*. Used with permission.

EXHIBIT 7.4   1-800-Flowers.com

can result in a considerable annuity stream. While augmented postsales services certainly exist in the offline world, the Internet has made it possible for companies to greatly enhance these offerings. For example, a company can increase the value it delivers to the customer by sending reminders of routine product maintenance requirements; electronically scheduling appointments; registering, filing, and making accessible warranty information online; or providing tips and troubleshooting advice via the Internet.

Gateway has recently introduced a postsales support program for customers that provides both an annuity stream and an ongoing dialogue. Based upon Gateway's interpretation of the needs of its customers—which include technical support, equipment repairs, and integration with previous equipment—the company has structured a monthly fixed-fee program specifically designed to address them. A customer can lease computer equipment and receive complete tech support for a fixed monthly fee; the equipment is replaced every three years with a comparable state-of-the-art system. In addition, Gateway migrates all of its customers' files from their old computers to their new ones. While Gateway's physical products are probably quite similar to those of its competitors, the company has clearly differentiated itself with its approach to postsales support.

Customer Care.   The Internet has enabled a radical shift from a company's traditional complaint management system to true customer care. Previously, packaged-goods companies might have placed the toll-free numbers for their call centers in extremely obscure places on a package and in small type because they viewed each customer call as an avoidable cost. While creating an excellent customer care system on the Internet requires significant upfront investments, once the system is in place, the incremental cost of an additional customer inquiry is negligible.

Drill-Down

Staying One Step Ahead

The banking industry is a natural fit for Internet services that augment the basic product. Banks already have information systems in place that manage routine customer account activity. With the success of ATMs they know firsthand the economic benefits of weaning customers away from expensive face-to-face encounters. Looking up account balances, paying bills, transferring money among accounts, and investigating interest rates are all services customers can easily accomplish online.

But not all banks are equal in how well they use the Internet to provide additional value to customers—and to improve their bottom lines. Wells Fargo excels in luring customers to the Internet and enticing those customers to do about half of their transactions online. Industry observers attribute Wells Fargo's success to superior integration of offline and online services, letting customers know about other products that fit their needs, and increasing retention.[5] Still, Wells Fargo cannot rest on its laurels. As one observer put it: "Wells' challenge is to keep snaring new customers and enhance its online service to stay ahead of the competition, which is constantly trying to overtake it. Bank of America plans to let online customers view images of canceled checks, a service that Wells doesn't offer."[6] As this example shows, product or service augmentation is a moving target. Excellent execution today does not guarantee success in the future.

Product Assortment

Historically, the number of products or product variants carried in a product line has been limited by manufacturing constraints, uncertainty about customer demand for specialized attributes and features, and inefficiencies in matching supply and demand in particular geographical areas. For products and services whose core benefit is delivered on the Internet, the ease of eliciting customer preferences, tweaking attributes and features, and delivering anywhere has led to an increase in the number of product variants offered. However, manufacturing constraints still apply to new Internet services and products, and customers may be overwhelmed if too many choices are presented.

Bundling. Sometimes firms offer different combinations or bundles of products to customers. Bundling is often a simple way to appeal to and serve different customer segments. For example, a personal computer sold with a choice of extra memory, a printer, or a scanner gives customers the ability to select the combination they like best. Bundles can also be used to "sell up" or "lock in" a customer. Season tickets to a baseball team's games, or series subscriptions to a theater's annual productions, encourage customers to commit to buying tickets for multiple events, rather than purchasing them singly. Product bundling often goes hand in hand with price bundling. *The Wall Street Journal* offers its print subscribers an additional subscription to its website at half the normal price. Online bundling is easier than bundling offline: It is difficult for manufacturers of physical goods to ensure the proper bundle components are in the right place at the right time; in contrast, Internet services can be produced on demand and have nearly unlimited capacity.

Complementary Products. Some products are of little or no use unless **complementary products** are available. (For example, what good is film without a camera?) Complementary products can offer basic functionality, additional functionality, tools, or other enhancements that improve the value of the focal product. For example, many analysts blamed the weak sales figures for the Apple Macintosh in the early 1990s on the lack of available complementary products such as software and peripherals. Modular product design and open-platform products, which allow third-party companies to easily develop complementary products, greatly improve the value that complementary products can add.

The Internet makes it easy for customers to learn about the availability of complementary products. For example, the website for the Handspring Visor personal digital assistant (PDA) showcases a range of complementary products that enhance the PDA's usefulness and value (see Exhibit 7.5). Intuit.com shows how complementary products offered can create value in the online information domain. Customers who use Intuit.com for online bill payment can automatically download the information directly into personal finance programs such as Quicken, eliminating the tedious task of entering the information twice. Competitors to Intuit.com such as PayMyBills might lose customers if they fail to provide a similar complementary product.

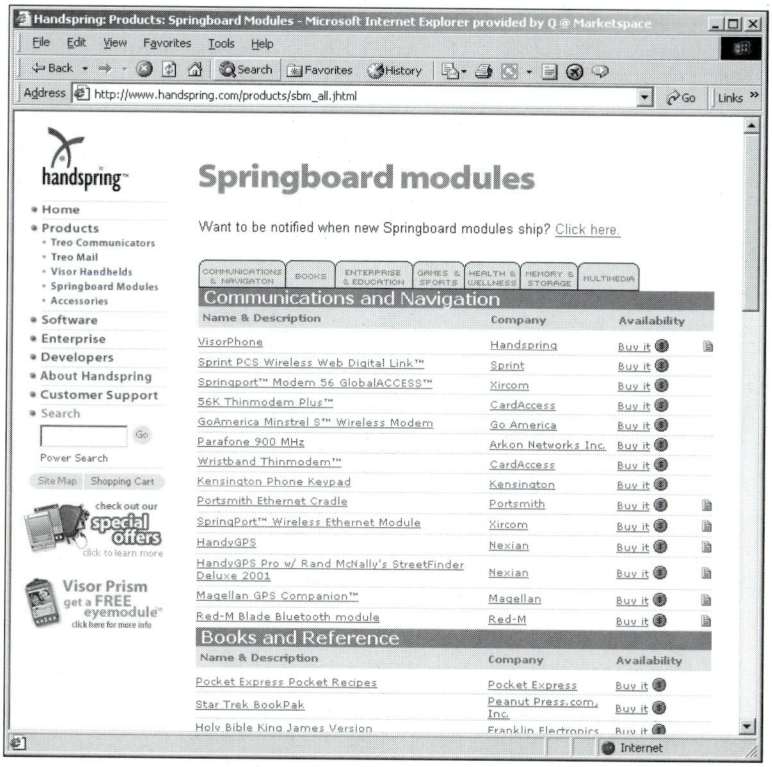

Complementary products for the Handspring Visor include:
- VisorPhone (cellphone)
- Wireless modems
- Radio
- Wireless messaging modules
- Pager
- Video games
- Electronic books
- MP3 player
- Digital camera
- Voice recorder
- Universal remote control
- Memory expansion modules
- Finance and graphing calculator
- Global positioning system

Source: *www.handspring.com*. Used with permission.

EXHIBIT 7.5   Handspring Product Availability

Aggregated Product Demand.   Because the Internet is global, many manufacturers are able to retain products in their product lines that would not be profitable if marketed to limited geographic areas or through distribution channels requiring greater volume. For example, Ann Taylor, a maker and retailer of women's clothing, no longer stocks its classic line of jeans in its stores, because they do not fit into the retailer's current, more upscale line. But Ann Taylor does sell the jeans on its website. Without the Internet, Ann Taylor might have had to discontinue a line that can still be profitable.

How the 2Is Affect Product

The Internet is a powerful tool through which marketers can learn more about individual customers. Interactivity and individualization have fundamentally changed a company's ability to respond to its customers, and are especially valuable in helping the company form a meaningful relationship with a customer. In particular, the 2Is allow a company to provide superior service and configure products to meet individual customer needs (see Exhibit 7.6).

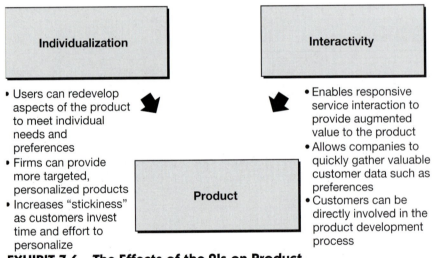

EXHIBIT 7.6   The Effects of the 2Is on Product

Highly Responsive Service Interactions

The 2Is of the Internet have brought about a significant shift in customer service. Good customer service requires an organization to listen to its customers' concerns and respond accordingly. Creating an institutional memory of individual customer needs, and giving employees access to this information, is what sets apart state-of-the art customer care from routine customer service. The Internet allows companies to interact with customers quickly, efficiently and cheaply. Customer care can be tiered, with higher levels of service delivered to a company's most profitable customers and less service delivered to those whose profit margins do not justify the investment.

Effective customer service requires completely integrated customer care centers established to support both online and offline interactions and operations. Websites should provide an easy-to-find e-mail address that customers can use to contact a customer service representative. Furthermore, customers have begun to expect companies to respond within 24 hours. Customer care represents an opportunity to solicit important feedback from customers, add value, and save both shopping carts and customer relationships from being abandoned.

Fidelity Investments offers a model of effective customer care. Customers have the option of interacting with the company's website or with the highly knowledgeable staff at its call centers. Customer service representatives (CSRs) have real-time access to Fidelity's website, individual customer accounts, and integrated computers and telephone systems. In this system, callers do not have to identify themselves nor explain the details of their last site session because the CSRs already have that information and are fully prepared to assist the customer. Customers do not get transferred around to different representatives when there are questions across multiple lines of business or products. Further, Fidelity's call centers distribute different support phone numbers to different tiers of customers whereby the highest skilled agents work with the most valuable tier of customers, who also benefit from shorter holding times.

Personalization

Firm-Initiated. Websites that require their customers to register to use the site can recognize those individual customers when they return and tailor the webpages presented to them accordingly. Using log files, a site can track a specific individual's click streams, following where he or she goes on a site, how long he or she spends on each page, and various other information. Tracking a click stream allows a company to gain a much deeper understanding of visitor behavior and to interact with the visitor by reactively individualizing the content of the site. Even if a visitor has not registered, the site can still track his or her click stream by setting cookies, which are electronic labels that uniquely identify individual computers. This deep insight into a customer's online behavior greatly increases a firm's ability to develop products based on its customers' interests and preferences. This is particularly useful information when it comes to developing product augmentations.

The more an individual interacts with a website, the more relevant the content presented to him or her becomes; the website simply has more nuanced information to input into its predictive behavior models. Amazon.com, for example, tracks the purchases of each of its individual users, as well as the aggregated purchase patterns of all of its customers. Amazon.com continually evolves its predictive behavior models based on that aggregated data, which makes it better able to recommend books and products that best fit each individual's preferences.

Customer-Specified. Another aspect of the 2Is is the advent of **personalization** tools that allow customers to specify features of a product to better meet their needs and preferences. A customer interacting with an organization can individualize services, billing options, personal preferences, and a host of other augmented offerings. Many sites are offering personalization features as a product augmentation to create "stickiness," or features that drive a visitor to return to a site for multiple visits. A personal homepage such as

My Yahoo! allows individuals to choose the color, layout, and even the font that they see on their pages. Calendars and address books are some of the more popular personalization tools that My Yahoo! offers. In order for these tools to be personalized, a visitor must invest in a relationship with a site by setting up these tools, which can be time-consuming. In order to reap the rewards of these efforts, the user must return to the site. The more often the user returns, the more value he or she receives and the more potential sales and customer loyalty Yahoo! acquires.

As discussed previously, information is a core product for many Internet service firms. In fact, firms that integrate, aggregate, and otherwise transform information into insights are referred to as infomediaries. Many of these infomediaries design customer-specified attributes and features into their offering. Customers can specify what types of news they want and how they would like to receive it, whether through e-mail, a customized personal page, a handheld device, or a wireless device. Additionally, users can control the frequency of delivery and the format, either text-based or HTML. MSN, AOL Time Warner, and Lexis-Nexis are all examples of infomediaries. The inherent value that these firms deliver is not just the information itself, but also the greatly improved usability of the content they offer.

Customer-Configured Products

An advantage of Internet marketing is the increased ability for **customization**, that is, allowing customers to specify the attributes and features they want for physical goods. The Internet offers tremendous efficiencies in gathering customer preferences and feeding them into the manufacturing process so that basic and augmented products can be modified in a short time cycle. The Internet also potentially makes customization possible on a much larger scale than ever before—often referred to as mass customization—thereby improving the value propositions of some manufacturers. However, for other companies, the benefits are slower in coming: Customization is hard to do well, many customers don't really want it, and few customers are willing to pay for it.[7]

The success of computer manufacturer Dell derives in large part from its ability to build computers to order. Dell enables its customers to select from myriad attributes and features; collectively, these attributes and features are referred to as the computer's personalized configuration. In corporate sales, a professional within the information technology (IT) department of a company usually sets the company's purchasing standards for computers. He or she works with Dell to predetermine the mandatory and the elective attributes of the configuration. Dell stores the configuration specifications for the customer so that anytime an employee of that company purchases a computer, it is 100 percent compatible with the company's IT infrastructure. At the same time, employees can individualize the elective elements based on the parameters set by the IT professional.

Lendingtree.com is a loan site that has mass-customized the application and approval processes of lending. Customers select the type of loan in which they are interested, the amount of the loan, whether they are applying alone or with a coapplicant, and their preferences regarding closing costs and loan duration. The application process becomes increasingly intelligent because each successive page of the loan information form is predicated on the answers to previous questions. Once the form is complete, the site sends the application to lending institutions that match the customer's criteria and relative risk profile. Customized publications are another emergent example of mass customization. For example, Primis has created an information repository containing textbooks, articles, and other publications in a number of subject areas. Professors can review, select and combine material to create a customized textbook specifically for their course.

Upgrades

As with postsales service contracts, product upgrades have become a common way for companies to develop long-term relationships with customers. This is

---

Drill-Down

Information: Custom-Made for Customizing

During the Internet's early go-go years, pundits giddily heralded the arrival of "mass customization"—a post-assembly-line future in which products would be custom-tailored (sometimes literally) for each individual consumer. And in fact, anyone with a computer, a modem, and a credit card could pull on a pair of hip-hugging, individually tailored jeans (from the Interactive Custom Clothes Company); apply custom-formulated moisturizer (from Reflect.com); shoulder a custom-built messenger bag (from eBags); and hit the ground running in a pair of custom-colored Air Pegasus sneakers (from Nike.com).

But before concluding that the Internet is well on its way toward fragmenting the mass market into millions of "markets of one," consider this:

- Customization is hardly a digital-age development. The rich have long had their clothing individually tailored, and anyone who has ever had their L.L.Bean backpack monogrammed, or ordered a new car in metallic green with a gray leather interior and premium sound package, knows you don't need a computer to customize. Microchip technology has certainly facilitated the *production* of custom-made products—pattern-making software and computer-controlled cutters have drastically reduced the cost of creating a personalized pair of jeans, for example. And some websites enhance the selection process by allowing consumers to view virtual products before placing their order. But overall, the Internet has hardly spawned a mass-customization revolution.

- Products that are essentially agglomerations of standardized components—cars and computers, for example—are already relatively easy to customize. Others, such as clothing and packaged foods, will always be more time-consuming and expensive to custom manufacture than they are to mass-produce. This makes it likely that they will remain niche products with limited consumer demand, with or without the Internet.

So is Internet-driven mass customization more myth than reality? When it comes to physical products, perhaps. When it comes to *information*, however, the Web may be every bit the powerful customization engine it is touted to be.

Anyone who has ever received a book suggestion from Amazon.com based on their own (and likeminded others') past purchases; configured their Yahoo! start page to display news from Canada, the weather in Alberta, and the Edmonton Oilers' schedule; signed up for e-mailed employment listings from Monster custom-tailored to their location and profession; or created their own personal compilation CD at an online-music site understands and has benefited from the Web's ability to dynamically rearrange mass quantities of information into a virtually infinite number of unique configurations.

The bottom line: Internet-based mass customization lives—not in knits, but in bits.

particularly the case for software companies and other firms selling digitizable products and services, because their upgrades are downloadable. Further, the interactivity of the Internet fosters quick and efficient customer feedback, which gives companies a steady stream of ideas about how they might improve and upgrade their products. Expert users who have extensive experience and understand the benefits and potential shortcomings of the previous version have put time and effort into learning the product and therefore have a vested interest in providing feedback. Not only can these customers help design product upgrades, but they can also participate in rigorous beta testing. In migrating customers to new versions, an important point to keep in mind is the investment customers have made in learning to use the old product and the need for a seamless transition to the newer version.

Turbo Tax is an example of a software product that adds value by augmenting via upgrades. When changes occur in the tax code, existing Turbo Tax customers receive e-mail notifications of updates that can then be downloaded from the Turbo Tax website. Another example is ProQuest, an information provider to schools and public libraries. Customers access the ProQuest services daily via a live Internet connection. Prior to the mass adoption of the Internet, ProQuest upgraded its services quarterly via a lengthy CD-ROM installation process. But because the site is accessed so frequently, can provide real-time information, and is an extremely familiar interface for customers, ProQuest now delivers its product upgrades over the Internet.

The Dynamic Nature of Product Portfolios

Product portfolios are not static. Even mature companies must renew and refresh their product lines. In competitive, fast-changing markets, particularly those propelled by emerging technologies, changing the product portfolio is an imperative.

An organization needs to consider the product portfolio in the context of the overall business strategy, organizational resources, and industry dynamics. A product portfolio should be managed much like an investment fund, striking a balance within the portfolio across dimensions such as risk profile, time horizon, potential payout, investment requirements, and revenue stream. In dynamic industries, changes in customer needs and competitive offerings limit the period of time during which a product generates strong revenues; a new generation of the product or a disruptive new product is always around the corner. A strong product portfolio generally includes (see Exhibit 7.7):

1. Innovative products

2. New versions and line extensions of current products and services

3. Existing products, including variants and augmentations[8]

The most innovative products in the portfolio are those that are new to the firm, new to the market, and based on a new technology. They generally require a long development period and a substantial commitment of

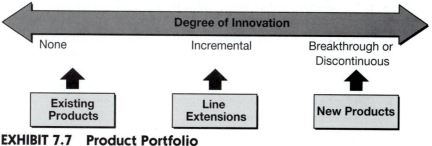

EXHIBIT 7.7 Product Portfolio

resources. The least innovative are products that are already in the market and use a technology the firm already possesses but are nevertheless new to the firm. In between are products that are new to the firm and either employ a technology the firm does not currently have or are new to the market.

In addition to balancing the mix of new and existing products in the portfolio, companies also have to time the introduction of new products and changes to current products. Factors that enter into timing include speed to market, the order of market entry for new products, and the life-cycle stage of existing products.

Innovations and New Products.

The rewards of a breakthrough innovation can be extraordinary. Innovations may compete with an existing product, change the basis of competition by creating a new position/niche in a market, or sometimes even create a new industry. According to studies by Booz Allen Hamilton and *Fortune*, as few as 10 percent of new products are truly "new-to-the-world" products.[9] This relatively small number of discontinuous products or breakthrough innovations is likely a result of the relatively high risk and cost associated with these undertakings, as well as the short-term time horizon of many U.S. firms. The Segway Human Transporter and the PalmPilot are examples of recent breakthrough products; pet daycare centers, eBay, and instant printing services are examples of recent breakthrough services.

Speed to Market and Early-Mover Advantages.

Generally speaking, the first product to be commercialized in a market and its early followers are believed to have enduring competitive advantage. This advantage derives from the ability to communicate something new and exciting to customers, to lock in distribution, and to set expectations for the product. Late followers with "me-too" products have nothing new to say to customers, have more difficulty gaining distribution, and must compete on the terms established by successful early entrants. First-to-market companies often have the benefit of high interest from alliance partners and other third-party suppliers seeking to do business with them. Such alliances can plug product or marketing gaps, help a company gain momentum, and accelerate its time to market.

Being a fast follower can also be a winning strategy for introducing a product to the marketplace (see Exhibit 7.8).[10] Indeed, companies such as Microsoft actually make a business out of being a fast follower. A fast-follower strategy can be effective only if the enterprise enters the market prior to the point of inflection in the market growth trend—a time when the product or service category is still very early in its development. This type of market adoption is colloquially referred to as a "hockey stick" because initial growth is slow and then catapults. At this point, intermarket competition has yet to develop and a substantial portion of development and marketing costs have already been absorbed by the first to market, so the opportunity to achieve high profit margins is optimal.

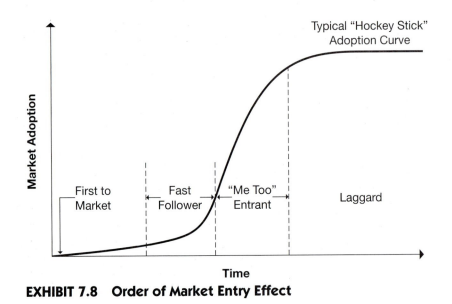

EXHIBIT 7.8   Order of Market Entry Effect

A successful strategy for later entrants is to introduce a new feature or quality level that is valued by a segment of the market. The objective can be to create a new market niche, or it can be to achieve production efficiencies in order to provide a good-quality product at a lower price.

Line Extensions.

A line extension is an incremental advance of an existing product, and therefore lies somewhere between existing and new products on the product development continuum. Specifically, a line extension is any effort that successfully leverages a brand name to launch product modifications or related products.[11] The strength of a line extension is that by capitalizing on an existing brand name, a company is saved the exceedingly high expense of introducing and promoting a new brand. If a company can identify and target customers of the parent brand, marketing the line extension to them via the Internet is extremely efficient from both a time and cost standpoint. The risks of this strategy are possible cannibalization of the parent brand and erosion of the current user base or brand equity if existing customers deem the line extension a failure. An Internet-based example of a line extension is Amazon's expansion from books into additional product categories.

Product Life Cycle.

The **product-life-cycle** concept holds that products naturally follow a life cycle that begins with an introductory stage and passes on through growth, maturity, and decline (see Exhibit 7.9). This progression is not immutable and, in fact, many marketers of mature or declining products see their task as reinvigorating the product and moving it back to the growth or early-maturity stage. While the life-cycle concept can apply to an individual product, a product category, or an industry, it is more often applied to the product category or product line. A typical life cycle would include the following stages:

- *Introductory*. The market consists of basic products offering a core benefit.
- *Growth*. A range of basic and augmented products, with additional features and varying quality levels, is introduced.
- *Maturity*. Product variants, brand extensions, and "new and improved" products begin to proliferate. Offerings tend to bifurcate into low-margin, low-cost products stripped down to the basics and high-margin, high-cost products that are highly augmented.
- *Decline*. As demand diminishes, firms prune down the product line to the most profitable items.

In highly competitive industries—and particularly when new technologies are introduced that enable different ways of providing the same core benefit—product categories will move through the life cycle at a faster rate. The Internet and e-commerce profoundly disrupted existing industries and product categories. As technology continues to evolve, Internet-based products and services themselves remain in a nearly constant state of evolution. To be successful, Internet marketers must continually gauge where they are in the life cycle and act accordingly. Even successful early entrants need to revise their product portfolio to avoid erosion of their market share.

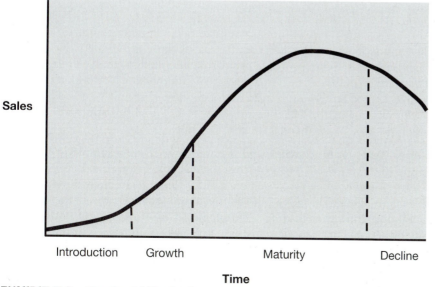

EXHIBIT 7.9   Product Life Cycle

Product Development

Without product development, companies risk being left behind in the marketplace. A fast, efficient product development process that results in high-quality products is an important source of competitive advantage. Because the product development process is of such strategic importance and spans virtually every functional area—often including R&D, manufacturing, purchasing, marketing, sales, and finance—it is typically directed by senior management. Product development requires firms to strike a balance between breakthrough innovations and incremental advances on existing products; it also requires making decisions that carry a high degree of uncertainty. Relative to many other activities undertaken by the firm, managers must tolerate an expanded time horizon for product development and return on investment.

There is no one formula or process to ensure the success of a new product. However, taking a customer-informed view of the market, its boundaries, potential substitutes, and the customer's buying process(es) helps a company to uncover opportunities that may lead to market success. While the type of formal, sequential stage-gate process used by companies such as 3M is not always possible or appropriate, a disciplined approach that incorporates many of the same check points used in a stage-gate process can be fashioned to suit a firm's unique circumstances.

A Customer-Informed Approach to Product Design

In the reality of day-to-day business there can be multiple drivers of product development. Manufacturing-driven product development is based upon gaining production efficiencies of some type. These approaches are generally focused internally on the manufacturing operations, with the goal of reducing costs or leveraging existing assets. While there may be some new product ideas generated from this process, the commercial viability of these products is more questionable, since neither the customer nor the marketplace drove the development effort.

Another product development driver can be an organization's research and development team. The R&D staff is particularly astute at understanding what is possible today, probable tomorrow, and likely to evolve in the future. This vantage point can be a catalyst for true innovation. However, if the R&D team is kept at arm's length from understanding customer needs, as they are in the vast majority of U.S. organizations today, then this approach may not meet with much commercial success.

Xerox PARC (Palo Alto Research Center) is a classic example of an R&D group that was too far removed from the customer. Composed of world-class scientists and engineers focused on breakthrough technology development, this talented team developed the compact disc, early versions of the computer mouse, and other leading technologies. Unfortunately, the PARC team was developing its products without fully taking into account customers' wants and needs; potential marketplace applications were not considered, and marketing teams were not consulted. These factors contributed to Xerox's inability to commercialize its technologies, leaving others to successfully bring these products to the marketplace.

A customer-informed design process has a much higher probability of success because it is based upon likely customer acceptance and a ready-made market. Beginning the development process with a detailed understanding of customer needs, supported by strong market research, will make product launches more efficient and effective over time. A clear statement of customer needs serves to align all the different functional areas involved in a new product development project, including manufacturing, R&D, finance and marketing, around a common understanding of the problem and the objective.[12]

Firms doing business on the Internet have the opportunity to learn about both individual and aggregate customer needs either through observation or through direct inquiry and market research; gaining insights into individual needs can begin at site registration and continue with each subsequent interaction. However, one potential shortfall of driving product development based solely on such information is that customers at times poorly predict their long-term needs—and the more innovative a product, the more acute the problem. Moreover, the length of the product development process can outlast a customer's ability to assess his or her own needs. As a result, customers can misdirect a company toward developing products that customers ultimately do not want.[13] For this reason, customer needs should be one among a number of factors considered when a company is developing a new product.

Product Development Process

Once the decision to develop a new product is made, the actual product development process begins. A prototypical product development process encompasses seven steps:

1. Idea generation
2. Idea screening
3. Concept development
4. Product design
5. Prototype development
6. Test marketing
7. Commercialization

At the end of each step, a decision is made about whether to continue to the next step, revert to a previous step, stall, or kill the project. In the classic application, these steps are pursued sequentially via a waterfall or **stage-gate process**, which requires both the completion of each step and an explicit management decision to move forward to the next step (see Exhibit 7.10). However, oftentimes several of these steps can be compressed or omitted, depending on such factors as the newness of the product.

Idea Generation.   The objective of the idea generation phase is to accumulate a host of ideas for new products or product improvements. Ideas may come from internal groups such as R&D, manufacturing, marketing or marketing research, and individual employees, or externally from customers. Applying a structured approach to encourage divergent thinking in a group is often successful in the idea generation phase. The objective of divergent thinking is to conjure up as many product ideas as possible without filtering

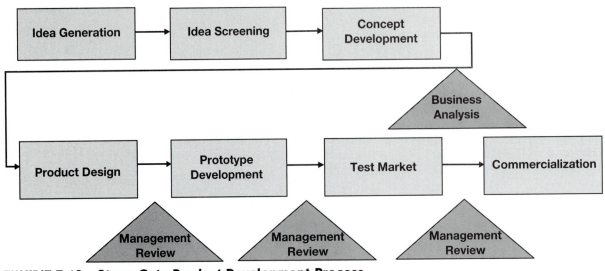

EXHIBIT 7.10   Stage-Gate Product Development Process

them in any way. A group typically generates more ideas than individuals do because of the synergies between participants; what one group member says or does can bring about a completely new idea from another participant. Most businesspeople are trained in convergent or critical thinking. An expert facilitator with proven exercises and stimulus materials can get people to stop filtering their ideas and encourage them to think far outside of their comfort zone or normal thought processes. In addition, the objectivity of an external facilitator can help the group stay true to the creative process and minimize the potential interference of corporate politics (see Exhibit 7.11).

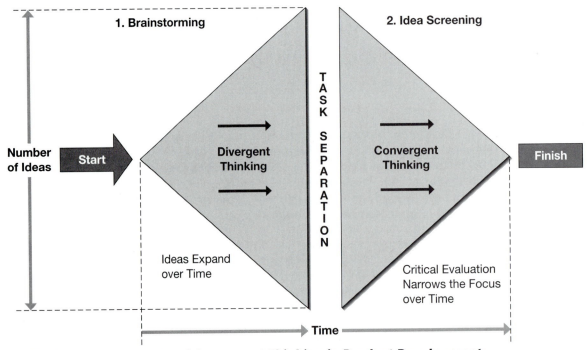

EXHIBIT 7.11   Divergent and Convergent Thinking in Product Development

Idea Screening.   Once brainstorming is complete, the next step is to begin grouping and screening ideas. This process, known as convergent or critical thinking, begins with the participants in the development process revisiting all the ideas that emerged from their divergent thinking and objectively identifying those that were most valuable. It is best to clearly delineate the divergent part of the process from the convergent portion so that ideas are not rejected too early. The team can begin screening by outlining a clear set of objectives and metrics for the new product. The ideas should then be put through a scoring system, which acts as a filter and allows only the best ideas to move forward. There are a multitude of decision-support software tools that may be useful in this process, depending upon how many ideas need to be screened.

Concept Development.   An idea that passes the screening stage is next developed into a concept that includes a statement of the customer needs being addressed, the form of the product solution, preliminary product specifications and design, product positioning, and economic feasibility. Many companies believe that spending more time and care at the front-end or "fuzzy development" stage of the product development process speeds up the process overall and ultimately leads to more successful products.

Once an idea passes the concept development stage, the risks and resource requirements of the process increase exponentially. Therefore, the development team must apply additional rigor to the gate at this stage to ensure that the due diligence of the business analysis is commensurate with the magnitude of the decision being make. Key considerations include initial market forecasts, manufacturing feasibility, supply chain availability, and financial benchmarks. Exhibit 7.12 provides some illustrative examples of these metrics; however, each project will require customized metrics that are appropriate for the specific circumstance.

Product Design.   Given the pace of competition and the advantages of beating competitors to market, businesses are under pressure to reduce the time it takes to design a product. The key to rapid cycle time is modularity. Process modularity is the cornerstone of a distributed innovation model—a model that allows parallel work streams to act independently and relatively nonsequentially. As long as the interdependencies between modules are clearly understood and managed at the outset of a project, modularity can greatly reduce development time and reduce the cost of new product development. Product modularity is the backbone of mass customization.

Ongoing communication among module teams is essential; without nearly seamless communications the modules are unlikely to line up upon completion. Breakthrough products in particular require tight integration between R&D and marketing.[14] The entire body of software tools that facilitate product teamwork is commonly referred to as groupware. One example of groupware is Silicon Graphics' InPerson desktop conferencing software, which, among other things, lets users in different locations see and hear one another as they discuss a 3D model on a whiteboard. CoCreate Software sells software tools that facilitate real-time design collaboration. Such advanced technologies can greatly facilitate many aspects of the product development process.

Prototype Development.   Prototypes are models or working versions of the product. During the course of a project, a whole series of prototypes might

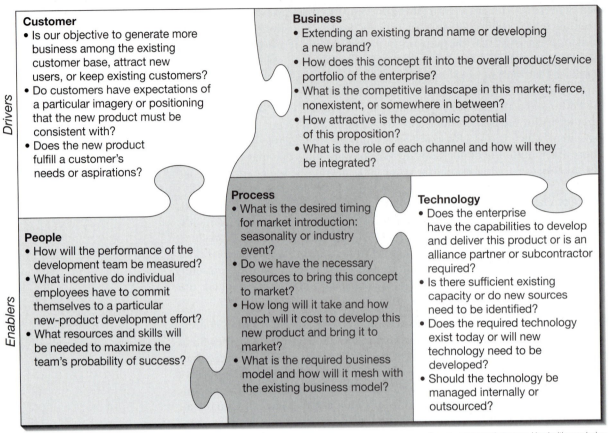

Customer
- Is our objective to generate more business among the existing customer base, attract new users, or keep existing customers?
- Do customers have expectations of a particular imagery or positioning that the new product must be consistent with?
- Does the new product fulfill a customer's needs or aspirations?

Business
- Extending an existing brand name or developing a new brand?
- How does this concept fit into the overall product/service portfolio of the enterprise?
- What is the competitive landscape in this market; fierce, nonexistent, or somewhere in between?
- How attractive is the economic potential of this proposition?
- What is the role of each channel and how will they be integrated?

People
- How will the performance of the development team be measured?
- What incentive do individual employees have to commit themselves to a particular new-product development effort?
- What resources and skills will be needed to maximize the team's probability of success?

Process
- What is the desired timing for market introduction: seasonality or industry event?
- Do we have the necessary resources to bring this concept to market?
- How long will it take and how much will it cost to develop this new product and bring it to market?
- What is the required business model and how will it mesh with the existing business model?

Technology
- Does the enterprise have the capabilities to develop and deliver this product or is an alliance partner or subcontractor required?
- Is there sufficient existing capacity or do new sources need to be identified?
- Does the required technology exist today or will new technology need to be developed?
- Should the technology be managed internally or outsourced?

Drivers

Enablers

Source: *www.emarketer.com*. Used with permission.

EXHIBIT 7.12   New Product Development Metrics

be created, from working drawings to full-size three-dimensional mockups. Alpha prototyping is a relatively new approach to prototype development that allows design engineers to create high-level and more conceptual prototypes without investing the usual time and resources to create an in-depth model. This shifts the resource-intensive in-depth prototyping to a later stage in the development cycle, when the idea is more stable and building a prototype can be done concurrently with other tasks. Over the next decade, it will become increasingly common for products to undergo virtual product development, a process in which a full and exact representation of each product and its associated data will be created, tested, detailed, and manufactured in completely digital form.[15] Prototypes are sometimes beta tested among a key user group in order to learn what customers think about the offering and then make the appropriate adjustments.

Test Marketing.   Test marketing is a small-scale experiment in which a new product is introduced and supported by a clearly defined marketing mix: advertising, distribution, packaging, pricing, and promotion. Numerous marketing variables are then closely monitored, measured, and manipulated in order to identify the appropriate marketing mix for broad-scale product introduction. The objective of a test market is to learn how the product is likely to perform once introduced on a larger scale and how various combinations of the marketing mix affect the product's performance.

Point–Counterpoint

Beta Testing

One perspective on beta testing was articulated by Ward Hanson in *Principles of Internet Marketing*: "Rapid product introduction is critical in new product categories. Speed to market leads to learning. By getting product to customers quickly, companies are able to learn what is desirable and what is just a frill. Early entrants in a product category can count on large amounts of customer interest, feedback, and free advice. Because they are pioneering an important solution, users take the time to provide in-depth information. A company that can use this feedback has an important advantage over later rivals. Software companies have refined this early release, in-depth customer feedback strategy. They release rough versions, with bugs, mistakes, and flaws, to a set of early users. These beta versions provide extremely valuable sources of feedback."[16]

The opposing point of view is that public beta testing of rough products is not a good idea. First, there is no consistent or reliable feedback mechanism, so in actuality a company is launching its product while it is still incomplete. The testers are not necessarily putting the product through its paces and will likely report only what they find by happenstance. Then there are the potential risks to consider. These risks can be quite large because a less than favorable experience with a beta product might permanently turn off prospective users and result in negative word-of-mouth. Another risk of broad-based public beta tests is the competitive threats they create. Any competitor of a firm can readily obtain a beta prototype and replicate, preempt or fast-follow the technology. For example, Yahoo! thought the risk of competitors emulating its beta technology was unacceptably high and deployed a modified beta testing approach, putting early versions of its new services online for internal use only. Given the technical prowess and vested interest of its staff, many of the major bugs were identified and corrected internally. Then a predefined panel of external users was solicited for its opinions. Once the initial testing was complete, Yahoo rolled out the test prototype to a broader self-selected group of advanced existing users without revealing it to less sophisticated users who might be frustrated by the early product version, which still had some bugs to be corrected before the actual product launch.

Commercialization. This is the final step of product development, and involves planning for the product's introduction and rollout. Commercialization requires a highly complex implementation plan in which timing, required resources, marketing, supply, and distribution—as well as the interdependencies between them—have to be carefully understood, planned, and orchestrated. Because there is only one chance to introduce a new product, it must be done right the first time. Even the best new product may not survive a faulty commercialization process.

How Has the Internet Affected the Product Development Process?

The Internet has introduced a new level of flexibility to the product development process. "Learn as you go" and "sense and respond" are common credos among many Internet firms. Flexible product development is predicated upon concurrent work and a modular approach, which delays commitment to a final design configuration until the last possible moment. In a dynamic product development process, a sequential approach to product design is not only inefficient but also carries the risk of creating obsolete products that do not leverage new technologies or reflect emerging customer needs.[17] The industries that are leading the development and application of these new development techniques include software (Netscape, Microsoft), high-tech (Motorola), and automotive (Toyota, Fiat).

A streamlined product development process enabled by the Internet includes five steps: ideation, concept development, development plan, iterative development and testing, and launch. The movement from one step to the next is less formal and structured than in the classic development process model.[18] The rigor with which the analyses are performed at each step should be commensurate with the level of risk the company faces, the risk tolerance of the management team, and the market requirements. In other words, an Internet firm without brand equity, an existing customer base, and a high need for revenues may introduce a very early beta version of its offering and pursue a sense-and-respond development effort. AOL, Amazon, or Yahoo!, on the other hand, have tremendous brand equity and would therefore pursue a more conservative or traditional development process.

The Internet has particularly affected the product development process in the following areas: continuous customer input, product design and communication tools, and experimentation and testing of products. Exhibit 7.13 shows a flexible model for the new product development process that uses these capabilities at each stage.

Continuous Customer Input.   In order for a flexible development approach to be successful, a company must be smart about the way it generates information about the marketplace and integrates that information into the development process. All products must be built upon a deep understanding of customers' current or future needs and continuous, reliable customer feedback. It is often beneficial for a company to develop a detailed plan for encouraging customer feedback early in the development process. The Internet is an ideal vehicle for enabling this type of communication because of its relative immediacy, low cost, and high degree of interactivity.

One process that companies are increasingly using to learn about customer needs is called customerization.[19] Customerization requires that products, the marketing of those products, and the overall customer experience be customized to each customer, albeit in a modular way. The process is customer-initiated and customer-controlled, the customer is involved throughout the entire design process, and the actual product can be manufactured after customers purchase it. However, putting customerization into practice generally requires highly sophisticated marketing IT systems.

FreeMarkets.com is an example of a website that is transforming channels and exchange relationships in B2B markets to reflect customerization concepts. FreeMarkets is a global online marketplace for industrial parts, raw materials, commodities, and services across 195 product and service categories. On the buying side, FreeMarkets worked very closely with an aerospace company to develop a comprehensive RFQ (request for quotation) for aerospace forgings. The aerospace company had experienced less than ideal market dynamics in the past due to a highly concentrated supply base in the United States and Europe. The RFQ resulted in 218 bids and approximately

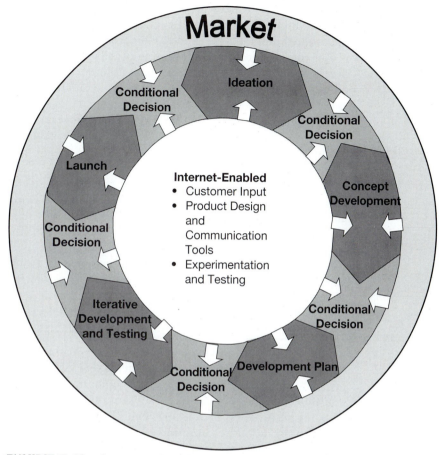

EXHIBIT 7.13   Internet-Enabled Product Development Process

$2 million of savings. On the supply side, Square D, an electrical compo-
nents supplier, won a 30-part contract worth $1 million of new business on
FreeMarkets.com. A design team leader at Square D said, "Instead of focusing simply on cost, we used the Internet-based bidding process as a new
product development tool." Its key account manager elaborated: "We supplied exactly what their engineers wanted. We weren't selling them our product; we were selling them theirs."[20]

The 2Is of Internet marketing give marketers ready access to customer ideas
flowing in through response mechanisms on websites and requests for personalization and customization. Internet marketers also have the ability to
observe behavior patterns at the individual level (as users move through a
website) and at the aggregate level (by analyzing patterns of behavior). Finally, marketers can monitor discussions on Internet bulletin boards and in
online community groups. For the most part, however, customer suggestions
will focus on existing products and upgrades, not entirely new products.

Product Design and Communication Tools.   Continued advances in Internet
technology are likely to increase the role that the Internet plays in rapid
product development. New Internet tools such as 3D representations and

videoconferencing have helped break down some of the traditional walls between R&D, marketing, and sales, and have enabled true collaboration in the product development process. One tremendous advantage of these tools is that they foster communication and collaboration among multicountry development teams. International time differences enable teams to work on product design around the clock. These cross-functional teams use intranets and extranets to integrate tasks, synchronize changes, and incorporate customer and market feedback into their design process. In fact, many organizations use these same tools and techniques for managing service-based products.

Experimentation and Testing of Products. Computer-aided design, computer simulations, and other advanced technologies allow companies to readily take advantage of real-time market data. Many attribute the success of Team New Zealand's 1995 America's Cup challenge and 1999 cup defense to this type of integrated rapid design and development process.[21] Such technologies lower development costs early in the design process by creating virtual products and virtual tours for prospective customers. Furthermore, the creation of a physical prototype can be postponed until a later stage of the process when the product is more complete and less subject to change, which lowers the product development costs even further.

In the online world, marketers can evaluate various product offerings by conducting online marketing experiments. For example, if three different products are under consideration, the company's server can randomly present different visitors with these different offerings, then gauge their reactions to the products by tracking their click stream. The objective is to be able to draw definitive cause-and-effect insights to determine the potential performance of a new product. These insights become more valuable through careful planning, control, and measurement throughout the testing process.

How Products Enable Customer Relationships

Marketers can use products to help enable a customer relationship in two primary ways: (1) by offering a product that is appropriate for the existing relationship, or (2) by using the 2Is and a well-balanced product portfolio to transition customers to a deeper relationship stage (see Exhibit 7.14).

Awareness

A company must make its target customers aware of its products and services, and have them understand the core benefits. When the product or service is complex, marketers need to work extra hard to ensure that the product or service's ancillary features do not obscure its core benefit. When direct experience of the product before purchase is not possible, presentation and packaging can help drive product awareness, communicate specific product benefits, and even differentiate the product from its competitors.

Four Key Stages of Customer Relationships

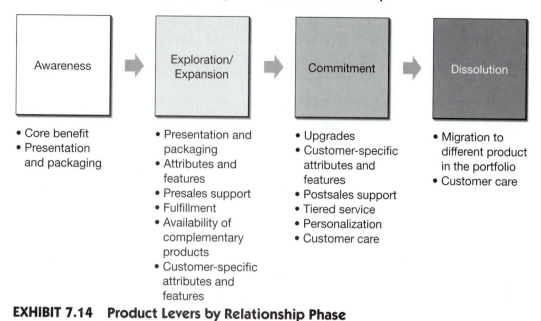

EXHIBIT 7.14   **Product Levers by Relationship Phase**

Exploration/Expansion

During the exploration phase, companies need to demonstrate the relevance of their offering to the prospective customer and induce trial. Packaging and presales support are both important in this phase because they help educate the customer about the product and also help differentiate the product from its competitors. Fulfillment capabilities such as efficient delivery help a company capitalize on the customer's interest. Providing the product while the customer is actively motivated increases the probability of purchase and creates a positive image of the company in the customer's mind.

The marketing objective for the expansion phase is to have customers become more deeply involved, loyal, and eventually commited to the product. Providing complementary products gives incremental value to the customer, which is particularly important for long-purchase-cycle items such as computers or cars. These complementary products can increase the number of positive experiences a customer has with an enterprise and create a rich platform for establishing an ongoing dialogue, thereby significantly reducing the time it might otherwise take to develop a committed relationship. In addition, many of these products represent an annuity stream, are purchased more frequently than the core product, and have relatively high margins, thus making them extremely profitable items within the product portfolio.

Customer-specified attributes and features allow customers to design products that fulfill their unique needs and desires. The ability to personalize a product often greatly increases the likelihood that a customer will want to buy it. As the customer takes the time to select different attributes and features, his relationship with the product grows deeper, and he becomes more likely to commit. Mars Inc. has a website for its popular M&M's product that lets visitors choose from 21 colors to create their own customized M&M's mix (see *www.m-ms.com*). Further, the site suggests picking mixes for special occasions, or picking team or school colors, as a way of deepening involvement.

Commitment

Once customers enter the commitment stage of a relationship, the company's objectives are (1) to keep them committed to a product or product line and (2) to expand the amount of business they do with the company. Loyal customers are typically very profitable, and buy a disproportionate amount of product; as the Pareto Principle states, 20 percent of customers can often account for 80 percent or more of a company's profits. The product levers that help win this loyalty are much the same as those used to grow a company's share of customers.

For example, upgrades can create an ongoing dialogue with customers after initial purchase. Once a company demonstrates that it is interested in designing products to better meet its customers' needs and in actively soliciting their insights, and once customers have invested time and energy in helping a company design the next version of its product, it is very likely that customers will move more deeply into the commitment stage and buy the product upgrade. Customer-specified attributes and features are also an effective lever in the commitment phase. When a company delivers on its promise to produce a customer-designed product, long-term customer commitment is deepened. Using customer insights throughout the design and development process greatly enhances the utility that the product delivers to the customer. Allowing individual customers to personalize a product to fit their unique needs is likely to extend and deepen the customer's relationship with the company.

Postsales support is a traditional lever for creating customer commitment and ongoing customer dialogue, and it is generally self-sustaining. Customer care is another lever that can be used to cement a relationship. Customer care departments are usually the first to know that the customer is experiencing some type of difficulty and are the first line of defense in resolving customer concerns. If the department staff is well trained, armed with customer information, and empowered to make decisions, it can turn a potentially negative situation into a pleasant customer experience. Because an organization's most profitable and committed customers are mostly responsible for the company's growth and reputation, highly skilled customer care specialists should be reserved for those customers.

Dissolution

If a company is unable to maintain a customer's commitment, the customer will proceed to the dissolution stage of the relationship. In the early phase of dissolution, a company can try to migrate the customer to another one of its products. For example, it might offer a stripped-down or lower-cost version of a product, or suggest a different product in its line that might meet the customer's changed needs.

Customer care is the key lever to professional dissolution. AOL is one company that handles dissolution extremely well. Its customer care representatives politely probe to understand why a customer is considering dissolution and immediately attempt to address the customer's issues. If the customer is at all interested, AOL provides attractive incentives for continuation of service. If a customer does decide to end the relationship, AOL has a number of effective win-back tactics such as keeping the customer's e-mail address reserved for a given period of time, providing upgrades to the latest version of the software, and offering extended free trial periods.

If salvaging the relationship is not possible, then the company should attempt to end the relationship on a positive note and hope for the opportunity to do business with the customer at some point in the future.

eBay Example

eBay's success is the result of offering a series of services and service innovations that appeal to a broad customer base. From the original offering to today's multiple eBay platforms and extensions, eBay has continually evolved. This example looks at how eBay used its core service as a launching pad for further innovations, which together are largely responsible for the company's multibillion dollar growth.

Core Benefit

As mentioned earlier in this chapter, the core benefit is the most fundamental value offered by a product or service. eBay's core benefit is summed up succinctly in its registered trademark: "The World's Largest Marketplace." As Bill Cobb, eBay's senior vice president of global marketing, said: "We want people to think of eBay first when they're in shopping mode."[22] eBay has built itself around this core benefit, beginning with its basic service and evolving it over time.

Basic Service

eBay's basic product closely resembles the website that Pierre Omidyar originally launched in 1995 to help sell collectibles. The original and current website service share many features and functionalities, including the abilities to:

- Register as a buyer or seller of physical goods
- Choose among an assortment of auction formats
- Send feedback to eBay regarding users and the site itself
- Easily browse through item listings

These primary features (as well as numerous others) form the baseline offering that delivers eBay's core benefit. However, to make the leap from a versatile commerce platform to the world's largest marketplace, eBay had to provide additional services and develop new and improved products.

Augmented Product

eBay's efforts to augment its core service to meet the needs and expectations of a greater spectrum of customers have largely been successful. In general, eBay's product augmentations fall into two categories: additional features and additional platforms (see Exhibit 7.15).

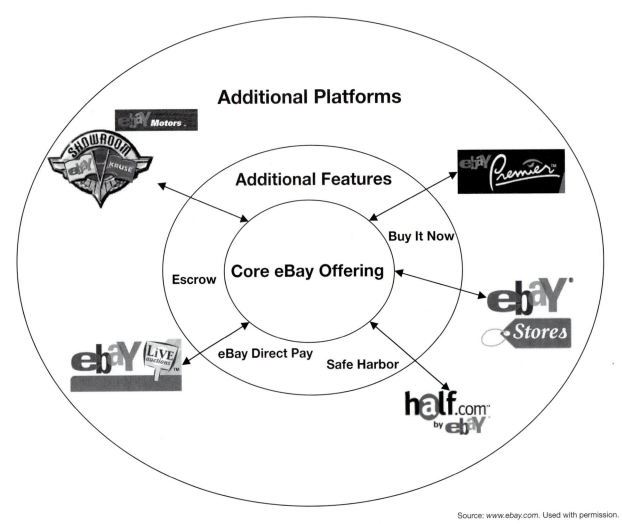

Source: *www.ebay.com*. Used with permission.

EXHIBIT 7.15   eBay Expansion through Features and Platforms

Additional Features.   From its earliest incarnation, eBay has introduced numerous features to enhance the buying and selling experience on its website and to differentiate itself from the competition. These include:

> *Buy It Now.* This feature appeals to those who do not want to bother with the uncertainty of an auction's outcome. For Power Sellers, the result of this feature is speedier auctions, which enable them to turn over inventory more quickly.

> *Safe Harbor.* This is actually a host of features developed to ensure a safe and protected environment for eBay commerce. Among Safe Harbor's features are fraud protection, item authentication, and dispute resolution.

Escrow. This feature enables buyers to place money in the custody of a trusted third party and pay it to the seller only once certain conditions are met. Escrow is a particularly useful feature for the sale and purchase of high-price items such as cars and antiques.

eBay Direct Pay. The ability to pay for an auction item without leaving the website adds a degree of efficiency not present in the original eBay. It also enables eBay to collect back-end fees on transactions.

Additional Platforms. Platform expansion has played a significant role in eBay's growth. Without the following platform extensions, eBay would not have been able to reach its current sales levels so quickly.

eBay Motors. eBay's formal expansion into cars has made it the country's largest car dealer; $1 billion worth of cars and car parts were auctioned on eBay in 2001.[23]

eBay Premier. This expansion enabled eBay to enter into the high-priced collectibles market. Some notable high-priced auctions include the July 2000 auction of a T206 Honus Wagner card, one of the rarest and most sought-after baseball cards; it sold for $1.27 million.[24] In May 2001, Levi Strauss & Co. paid $46,532 for one of the world's oldest pairs of Levi's jeans.

eBay Stores. Since eBay's launch, over 27,000 stores have been created, enabling thousands of entrepreneurs and businesses to conduct business online without having to build their own online infrastructures.

Half.com. This platform for fixed-price deals instantly broadened eBay's reach.

eBay Live Auctions. This proprietary technology allows online bidders to participate in traditional offline auctions. Since its launch in September 2002, auction houses using Live Auctions technology have seen 20 percent of their lots sell to Internet bidders.[25]

There is speculation among analysts regarding where eBay fits on the product/service life cycle. Certainly it is no longer in the introductory stage; less clear is whether it is still in the growth stage or if it has reached maturity. To ensure continued growth, however, one thing is clear: eBay must continue to listen to the market and provide new services and service augmentations to meet future customer needs.

Summary

1. **How is product defined?**
A product is defined as something that is created for the purpose of a transaction. The basic product delivers the core benefit; the augmented product differentiates the product through additional attributes and features. There are two general types of products: physical goods and services.

2. **What are the characteristics of Internet-based products and services?**
Internet-based products and services are those that can be converted into digitized information. Digitized goods are less tangible than physical products and their ownership is more difficult to control. Internet services have fewer constraints than offline services; for instance, they are more scalable and less perishable. Additionally, Internet services are frequently used as product augmentations for offline products and services.

3. What Internet product levers can marketers use?

Internet product levers include presales support to customers, flexible fulfillment options, postsales service, customer care, product bundles, complementary products, and increased product availability.

4. How do interactivity and individualization (the 2Is) contribute to product offerings?

The 2Is allow a company to learn about its customers, personalize a product to meet customer preferences, and offer higher levels of services to customers.

5. What factors do companies consider when managing their product portfolios?

Companies treat their product portfolio much like an investment portfolio. They balance the number of new products, line extensions, and existing products and services. They evaluate the advantages of developing breakthrough innovations and being a market leader, fast follower, or early follower. They also evaluate where their products are in the life cycle and whether to expand or prune the product line.

6. In what ways has the product development process been affected by the Internet?

The traditional product development process consists of seven stages: (1) idea generation, (2) idea screening, (3) concept development, (4) product design, (5) prototype development, (6) test marketing, and (7) commercialization. In the fast-paced Internet environment, this sequential process has been replaced by a more rapid and flexible process that is characterized by iterative development and testing and conditional decision-making. The Internet also provides tools for continuous customer input, improved product design and communication, and experimentation.

Activities for Students

1. Select three websites and analyze how the framework in Exhibit 7.2 applies to them. Which category or categories does the product offering fall into? What is the core benefit?
2. Consider the eBay example. At what stage of the life cycle would you place eBay? Be prepared to discuss the criteria you used to come up with your answer.
3. Choose a website that permits personalization and provides daily updated content, then personalize your own page. What kinds of information are you asked to give? How might giving this information benefit you?

Key Terms

product	physical goods	personalization
core benefit	services	customization
basic product	product portfolio	product life cycle
augmented product	complementary products	stage-gate process

Endnotes

[1] Includes Theodore Levitt's "generic product" and "expected product." See: Marketing success through differentiation—of anything. 1980. *Harvard Business Review* January–February, 83–91.

[2] U.S. Census Bureau, 2000. *Statistical Abstract of the United States: 2000* (120th Edition), Washington, DC, p. 544, 756

[3] Pitt, Leyland, Pierre Berthon, and Richard T. Watson. 1999. Cyberservice: Taming service marketing problems with the World Wide Web. *Business Horizons* 42(1), January–February 11–18.

[4]Levitt, Theodore. 1981. Marketing intangible products and product intangibles. *Harvard Business Review* May–June, 94–102.

[5]Lee, Louise. 2002. Wells Fargo: blazing a trail online, *BusinessWeek Online*, March 20.

[6]Lee, Louise. 2002. Wells Fargo: blazing a trail online, *BusinessWeek Online*, March 20.

[7]The failure of customization: or why people don't buy jeans online. Strategic Management at Wharton. *http://knowledge.wharton.upenn.edu/print_version.cfm?articleid=535&catid=7.* Accessed 3/27/02.

[8]Wind, Jerry, and Vijay Mahajan. 1997. Issues and opportunities in new product development. *Journal of Marketing Research*. XXXIV (Winter) 1–12.

[9]Booz, Allen & Hamilton. 1982. New product management for the 1980's. New York: Booz, Allen & Hamilton.

[10]Golder, Peter N., and Gerard J. Tellis. 1992. Do pioneers really have long-term advantages: A historical analysis. Marketing Science Institute Working Paper. Boston: Marketing Science Institute.

[11]Kotler, Phillip. 1988. Marketing management: Analysis, planning, and control. 6th ed. Englewood Cliffs, NJ: Prentice Hall.

[12]Dougherty, Deborah, 1992. Interpretive barriers to successful product innovation in large firms, *Organization Science*, 3:1, pp. 179-202.

[13]Christensen, Clayton M. 1997. The innovator's dilemma. *HarperBusiness*.

[14]Song, X. Michael, and JinHong Zie. 1996. The effect of R&D-manufacturing-marketing integration on new product performance in Japanese and U.S. firms: A contingency perspective. *Report Summary* 97–117. Cambridge, MA: Marketing Science Institute.

[15]Alberthal, Les. 1998. The once and future craftsmen culture. *Business 2.0* (Sept. 01).

[16]Hanson, Ward. 2000. Principles of internet marketing, Southwestern College Publishing, 226.

[17]Iansiti, Marco, and Alan MacCormack. 1997. Developing products in Internet time. *Harvard Business Review* (September–October) 108–117.

[18]Cooper, Robert G. 1994. Third-generation new product processes, *Journal of Product Innovation Management* 11, pp. 3-14.

[19]Wind, Jerry, and Arvind Rangaswamy. 2000. Customerization: The next revolution in mass customization. *Marketing Science Institute Working Paper Series*, Report No. 00-108.

[20]See: (http://www.freemarkets.com/benefits/).

[21]Iansiti, Marco, and Alan MacCormack. 1997. Developing products in Internet time. *Harvard Business Review* (September–October)108–117.

[22]Brown, Eryn. 2002. How can a dot-com be this hot? *Fortune* 21 January.

[23]Hof, Robert. 2001. The people's company. *BusinessWeek* 3 December.

[24]Olsen, Stefanie. 2000. Baseball card fetches $1.27 million on eBay. *CNet News.com* 17 July.

[25]eBay expands live auctions. April 24 2001 eBay Press Release

Pricing

Setting prices is a key challenge for firms, and the fact is that prices are often set in an unstructured manner. Firms often have a wide variety of potential pricing strategies and price points to consider when deciding how to best implement profit-maximizing strategies. In addition, the Internet has strongly influenced old-economy pricing strategies; moreover, it has created an entirely new category of pricing tools for new-economy firms to use: dynamic pricing strategies. Dynamic pricing has revolutionized business-to-business (B2B) and consumer-to-consumer (C2C) transactions, and has created new opportunities for business-to-consumer (B2C) firms.

This chapter discusses the wide assortment of old- and new-economy pricing tools available to firms. Also provided is a framework process for firms to use when deciding which pricing strategy is best suited for their products. The effects of the 2Is—interactivity and individualization—on traditional pricing levers, as well as the influence of the 2Is on dynamic pricing strategies, are also discussed. A key section of the chapter showcases ways that various pricing levers can be used to move consumers through each of the four consumer relationship stages. The chapter concludes with a discussion of the pricing levers used by eBay.

QUESTIONS

Please consider the following questions as you read this chapter:

1. What is the relationship between price and demand? Why is it important for a firm to price at the point at which marginal revenue is equal to marginal cost?

2. Why should a firm consider fairness when pricing its goods?

3. How has the Internet enhanced opportunities for dynamic pricing strategies?

4. Why would a firm want to implement a price-discrimination strategy?

5. What is the difference between static and dynamic markets? Why must a firm consider its pricing strategies within the context of a dynamic market?

Introduction

As firms strive to grow their profits, they often focus on decreasing production costs or increasing product demand. In doing so, firms tend to neglect one of the most important strategic areas involved with growing profits: pricing. This chapter provides a comprehensive overview of both traditional and

With substantive input from Patrick J. DeGraba, Daniel Kim, and David Ruben.

new-economy pricing levers, and also presents two new pricing process frameworks:

- A framework called the Pricing Pentagon for firms to use when selecting which pricing strategy best suits their product under the current market conditions.
- A framework that highlights which pricing levers are best suited to guide consumers through the four relationship stages.

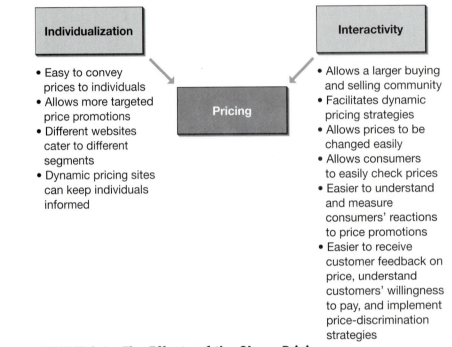

EXHIBIT 8.1   The Effects of the 2Is on Pricing

The chapter also focuses on how the 2Is have affected pricing strategy (see Exhibit 8.1). The *interactivity* force of the Internet has affected pricing by making it:

- Easier to reach wider audiences. New markets are created, or existing markets are made more efficient, by bringing together disparate groups of buyers and sellers in a low-cost manner. Sellers who offer their products over the Internet have the potential to reach buyers from around the world. By increasing the number of potential bidders, firms benefit in both the selling of product (more customers can translate into increased bidding for products) and procuring supplies (more potential bidders can result in lowering price bidding for supply contracts).
- Easier and cheaper to implement dynamic pricing strategies. Auctions, for instance, can be implemented in a less costly and more efficient manner. While auctioning is an effective selling process, it has often been difficult to implement auctions in a manner that encourages many buyers and sellers to participate. The Internet allows auctions to be implemented in a very cost-efficient manner.

- Easier and cheaper to adjust prices in accordance with demand conditions and to remain competitive with other firms. Prices can be changed instantly on websites.

- Cheaper for consumers to investigate prices. With an easy click, consumers can check prices instantly. Customers can also register with sites to receive e-mail notification of changes in product prices.

- Easier to understand and measure consumers' reactions to price promotions. Tracking consumers electronically makes it easier to understand what types of customers are stimulated by price promotions and then develop strategies to best design and implement pricing promotions.

- Easier to receive customer feedback on price, understand customer willingness to pay for a product, and implement price-discrimination strategies. By better understanding how customers navigate a website or by requiring information such as the consumer's zip code, firms can more easily customize prices for individuals.

The *individualization* force of the Internet has affected pricing in the following manner:

- By informing companies of their pricing and product desires, consumers make it easier for firms to convey prices of products in which they have an interest.

- Customers can register their preferences with firms, making it easier for those firms to offer targeted, individualized pricing promotions.

- Customers can more easily participate in dynamic pricing processes. Sites that practice dynamic pricing can notify customers via e-mail when their bids are no longer the highest.

- The Internet offers many different distribution outlets (i.e., websites) that cater to different segments, which allows firms the flexibility to set prices specifically for the segment(s) being served by the website.

This chapter is divided into the following sections:

The Economics of Pricing. This section provides an overview of the economic principles that are relevant to product pricing. It begins with a discussion of the attributes of demand curves, as well as the key variables that determine the composition of demand curves, then considers the general profit-maximizing rules associated with a basic demand-curve pricing analysis. The section concludes with the warning that most pricing decisions are made in a dynamic environment. Thus, a basic demand-curve analysis is a good starting point in thinking about pricing strategy, but often more sophisticated analyses are required to properly price a product.

Retail Price Decisions. This section discusses the three key positioning strategies that retailers can employ regarding price: cyclical promotional pricing (Hi-Lo), everyday low pricing (EDLP), and retail/outlet pricing.

Basic Pricing Strategies. This section discusses standard pricing strategies, including cost plus, brand pricing, and promotions. The role of fairness in pricing is also considered.

Dynamic Pricing Strategies. This section highlights the role of the Internet in dynamic pricing. Several variations of dynamic pricing strategies are outlined, including English auctions, reverse-price English auctions, Dutch auctions, first-price sealed-bid auctions, reverse first-price sealed-bid auctions, and exchanges.

Advanced Pricing Strategies. This section discusses more sophisticated pricing strategies that firms can employ to maximize product profits, including volume discount pricing, two-part pricing, bundling, price discrimination over time, and frenzy pricing. It also provides an overview of the three generic categories of price discrimination.

Strategic Responses to Competitor Price Cuts. This section discusses how a firm can respond to competitor price cuts, focusing on strategies that avoid competitive price-cutting that could lead to a price war.

The Pricing Pentagon Framework. This section offers a Pricing Pentagon framework for managers to use to set prices for their products.

Implementation Across The Four Relationship Stages. This section lays out a framework for the pricing levers used to move customers through each of the four customer relationship stages.

eBay Example. The chapter concludes with a discussion of the pricing strategies used by eBay.

Retail Price Decisions	**Basic Pricing Strategies**	**Dynamic Pricing Strategies**	**Advanced Pricing Strategies**
• Cyclical Promotional Pricing (Hi-Lo) • Everyday Low Pricing • Retail/Outlet Pricing	• Cost Plus • Brand Pricing • Promotions	• English Auctions • Reverse-Price English Auctions • Dutch Auctions • First-Price Sealed-Bid Auctions • Reverse First-Price Sealed-Bid Auctions • Exchanges	• Volume Discount Pricing • Two-Part Pricing • Bundling • Price Discrimination Over Time • Frenzy Pricing • Three Categories of Price Discrimination

EXHIBIT 8.2   Key Pricing Strategies

Point–Counterpoint

Will the Internet Commoditize Prices?

Commoditization is a natural process in a world of competition and technological advances. People learn to do things faster, cheaper, and better; essential differences between products vanish; quality becomes reliable; and competitive pricing drives prices down. Will the unique characteristics of the Internet accelerate this process across products or instead work to offset the commoditization process?

Three arguments can be made to support price commoditization on the Internet. First, the Internet makes vast amounts of information available to consumers. Before making purchase decisions, potential buyers can compare prices and features of competing products and can view rankings and reviews. As a result, markets will become more efficient, and differences in products and pricing will decrease. Second, the Internet is global—consumers are no longer restricted by geography when making their purchases. Hence, consumers will be free to choose among a wider range of providers and may switch more frequently. Finally, on the Internet, providers will have difficulty differentiating the product by putting it in a seductive surrounding or engaging in personal sell. Thus, they will find it hard to compete on anything but price.

continued

Consider a consumer who is shopping for a stereo sound system. In a store, sales associates will demonstrate different models to the potential buyer. They will explain features, change the volume, play different types of music—and typically speak warmly about one system in particular. A context like this may convince the consumer to pay a premium. On the Internet, however, consumers will compare sound systems with similar performance data and features and ultimately make a decision based on price.

A case could also be made for the opposite outcome: that the Internet will not commoditize prices but may even lead to further price differentiation. First, even if all else is equal, brand will still command a premium. Assume, for example, that the exact same PC is available at LarrysDirtCheapPC.com for $950 and at Dell.com for $1,000. Would everybody purchase from Larry? Some people would indeed buy a PC from Larry, but a majority of consumers will value the Dell brand and buy from Dell. Second, providers will be able to differentiate their offerings by bundling products and services. Few products are sold without being bundled with services such as one-click shopping, tailored suggestions for additional purchases, delivery or payment options, or access to customer support. Consumers will value these features differently and place a premium on them. Moreover, the Internet makes it possible for consumers to create their own products and bundles. On the automaker Saturn's website, for example, potential car buyers can build their own cars and make choices on a range of features such as alloy wheels, seat covers, floor mats, wood-trim kits, and insurance plans. Third, the Internet offers consumers a new purchasing experience, and they will be willing to pay for it. On the Saturn site, customers can see images of their own cars emerge on the screen. A hotel website can provide in-depth information about features and facilities, show photos of the rooms, display current weather, and enable a real-time view of the area via a webcam. Such a virtual visit may educate potential customers and differentiate the hotel.

The unique characteristics of the Internet will enable companies to continue to differentiate their offerings based on brand, features, or experience. This will build customer loyalty and create switching barriers that competitors will not be able to overcome with price alone.

Drill-Down

Going from Free to Paid Services

Pricing is one of the biggest strategic challenges facing Internet companies today. When competition for online customers first began, Internet companies focused on giving products away or selling them at a high discount in order to beat out rivals and capture a loyal customer base. The hope was that that customer base could then be monetized. For companies such as Amazon.com, this strategy worked; Amazon achieved pro forma profitability in its fourth quarter in 2001. For most companies, this strategy backfired. Most Internet companies that took this approach are still trying to figure out how to get their customers to pay for their services.

For most companies, the strategy has been to retain some level of free services and hope that some consumers will be inclined to pay for an upgraded package. For example, Yahoo! is well known for offering its free e-mail service, but has begun charging for enhanced e-mail services. Another strategy has been to use the notion of fairness in pricing to their advantage. While fairness is generally considered a constraint to charging high prices, fairness can be used as a way to justify certain charges; for example, companies can justify the need to begin charging for services by discussing what the company must spend to provide those services. Charging for services also brings clarity to a company's value proposition. However, not all customers will agree to pay for a service that used to be free. A consumer who likes to send free e-cards, for instance, might balk at the notion of paying $11.95 for the privilege. Another key lesson is that you cannot control your competitors. If competitors are offering services for free or at high discounts, there is not much that a firm can do. In the e-card dilemma, the consumer might simply turn to another e-card site that offers its services for free.

The Economics of Pricing

While it will be clear in this chapter that strategic pricing goes far beyond the foundation concepts presented in this section, it is important to begin with a review of a basic demand-curve pricing analysis.

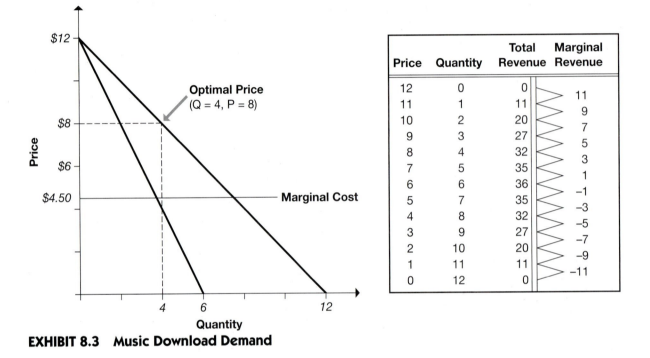

Typical Teenager's Semiannual Demand for Pop-Music Downloads

Price	Quantity	Total Revenue	Marginal Revenue
12	0	0	11
11	1	11	9
10	2	20	7
9	3	27	5
8	4	32	3
7	5	35	1
6	6	36	−1
5	7	35	−3
4	8	32	−5
3	9	27	−7
2	10	20	−9
1	11	11	−11
0	12	0	

EXHIBIT 8.3   Music Download Demand

Exhibit 8.3 shows a hypothetical demand curve for a firm selling online music downloads. While many will recognize the downward sloping demand curve, it is important to understand the key variable inputs into this demand curve, as well as the factors that affect its position, shape, and slope. These key variables include the following (see Exhibit 8.4):

Price. There is an inverse relationship between price and quantity. This relationship is intuitive. As a product price decreases, more units of the good will be demanded by the market. Likewise, as the product price increases, some consumers will not find it worthwhile to purchase the product, so total aggregate demand will decrease.

Substitute Offerings/Prices. Both the types of substitute goods and their prices affect a product's demand curve. If there are close substitutes for a product, the product has limited maneuverability in terms of pricing. Due to the availability of close substitutes, a product is not able to raise its prices significantly above the prices of close-substitute products.

EXHIBIT 8.4   Key Variables That Affect Demand Curve Slope and Position

Complementary Offerings/Prices. The prices of complementary goods affect a product's demand curve. If complementary product prices decrease, this will stimulate demand for a product. Likewise, if complementary product prices increase, this will negatively affect product demand. Consider a Caribbean island economy that is dependent on the tourist trade. If airlines significantly raise airfares to the island, this will negatively affect the island's economy. Since arriving by air is essential for the tourist trade, an increase in airfares will negatively affect complementary products such as hotels and restaurants. Likewise, if airlines decrease airfares, demand will be stimulated for island businesses.

Income. In general, income is positively correlated with demand. For most products, as income increases, so does product demand.

Market Size. As market size increases, so does demand for a product. For example, the baby-boomer generation is a significant and influential demographic group. As boomers age, their consumption patterns change, and those changes in turn have a substantial impact on demand for products. As boomers age and consider retirement, for instance, demand will increase for financial retirement services.

Taste. Consumer taste is a very important variable, regardless of market size, price, income, and the number of substitute and complementary products. In order for a product to achieve market success, consumers must have a desire to purchase it.

The latitude that a firm has to price its product is dependent on the slope of its demand curve. Exhibit 8.5 demonstrates the two extremes of demand curves and degree of flexibility in pricing. The demand-curve slope is often indicative of the degree of pricing flexibility for a firm. The steeper the demand curve, the more power firms have in terms of pricing.

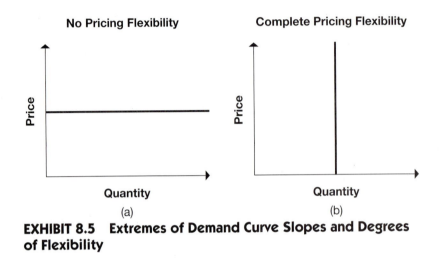

No Pricing Flexibility   **Complete Pricing Flexibility**

(a)   (b)

EXHIBIT 8.5   Extremes of Demand Curve Slopes and Degrees of Flexibility

Exhibit 8.5(a) shows a demand curve for a firm that has no pricing flexibility. Firms that produce commodity-type goods—goods that are homogeneous and easily purchased from other sellers, such as wheat—can sell all of their products at the prevailing price. As a result, such firms have no incentive to decrease price. Commodity firms are not able to increase their product price because buyers can readily purchase the same goods from rival sellers at a lower price.

Exhibit 8.5(b) shows a demand curve for a firm that has flexibility in pricing its products. While extremely rare, this type of demand curve shows a firm that can charge virtually any price for its product. There are few real-world examples of such a demand curve. Many eager fans are willing to pay higher prices to obtain a new electronic music download of a popular artist on the day of its release. This strong demand implies that there is a wide range of prices that record companies could charge for the download.

Exhibit 8.3 provides an example for demand-curve pricing analysis. Two key terms in demand-curve pricing are *marginal revenue* and *marginal cost*.

Marginal Revenue.   Marginal revenue is the additional (or negative) revenue achieved by lowering or increasing the product price by increments. In the example presented in Exhibit 8.3, nobody purchases the product at a price of $12. At a price of $11, one person purchases the product. Thus, the marginal revenue derived from decreasing the price from $12 to $11 is $11. Likewise, a decrease in the price of the product to $10 will lead to marginal revenue of $9 (total revenue increases from $11 to $20). However, marginal revenue is not always positive. Consider what happens when the product price drops from $5 to $4. At a price of $5, seven units are sold, and the total revenue is $35. At a price of $4, eight units are sold, and the total revenue is $32. In this case, the marginal revenue is −$3.

Marginal Cost. Marginal cost is the cost associated with producing an additional good. In many cases, marginal costs vary by how many units of the goods are produced. Often, a marginal cost curve is U-shaped—as more goods are produced, firms often experience increasing returns to scale. Consider the efficiency that a retail website experiences when it increases its daily sales from one sale a day to 100 sales a day. The entire process becomes more efficient with increased volume. At some point during production, inefficiency sets in, and the firm experiences decreasing returns to scale. Think of the increasing costs associated with that retail website further increasing daily sales from 100 to 1 million sales a day. For simplicity, the example in Exhibit 8.3 assumes that no matter how many goods are sold, the marginal cost of producing an additional good is $4.50.

**Key Takeaway: Firms Should Price at the Point at Which
Marginal Revenue = Marginal Cost**

To maximize profits, product price should be set at the point at which marginal revenue is equal to marginal cost. In the example set forth in Exhibit 8.3, this price is $8. If the firm lowered the price to $7, it would sell one additional good; the marginal revenue would be $3. However, by lowering the price to $7, the firm would incur an additional cost of $4.50, which would result in a net loss of $1.50. Thus, there is no economic justification for lowering the price to $7.

Similarly, if the firm increased the product price to $9, it would sell one less good, but all of the goods it sold would reap an additional $1 for each good sold. The marginal revenue derived from increasing the price to $9 is −$5. By increasing the price to $9, the firm loses $5 in revenue, but does not incur $4.50 in additional costs. The firm's overall loss would be $0.50. Thus, increasing price to $9 is not profitable either.

Pricing in a Dynamic Market

While it is important to conceptually understand how firms can set prices using a basic demand-curve analysis, it is critical to realize that most firms are not selling in a **static market**. A static analysis assumes that competitors will not react to how a firm prices its product—and this is an unrealistic assumption. Most firms are selling in a **dynamic market**. The assumption in a dynamic market is that competitors will react to changes in price.

When undertaking a basic demand-curve pricing analysis, it is essential to realize that once a firm sets a price, competitors will react to that price. This competitor reaction will have repercussions on the firm's business. Thus, a basic demand-curve analysis may reveal that a firm will be rewarded with increased sales from lowering its price because it will inevitably steal customers from its competitors. In a dynamic market, competitors will not allow their customers to defect to other firms. In most cases, they will react by either lowering their prices or enhancing value in order to retain customers and maintain market share.

Since most firms operate in a dynamic market, why is it necessary to understand a static market analysis? The answer is because a static analysis is a key pricing-analysis component that firms must understand before contemplating a dynamic market analysis. The theory and process behind dynamic pricing is discussed in the pricing process section of this chapter.

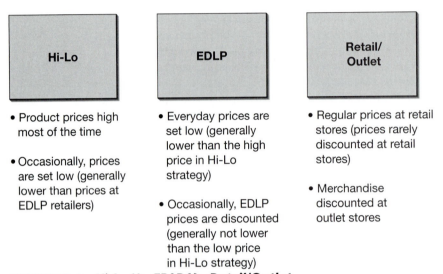

Hi-Lo

- Product prices high most of the time

- Occasionally, prices are set low (generally lower than prices at EDLP retailers)

EDLP

- Everyday prices are set low (generally lower than the high price in Hi-Lo strategy)

- Occasionally, EDLP prices are discounted (generally not lower than the low price in Hi-Lo strategy)

Retail/ Outlet

- Regular prices at retail stores (prices rarely discounted at retail stores)

- Merchandise discounted at outlet stores

EXHIBIT 8.6   Hi-Lo Vs. EDLP Vs. Retail/Outlet

Retail Price Decisions

Retailers must position themselves in terms of setting pricing expectations for their customers. There are three key brand positioning strategies with respect to price that retailers can adopt: cyclical promotional pricing (Hi-Lo), everyday low pricing (EDLP), and retail/outlet pricing. By selecting one of these three pricing branding positions, consumers can better understand the store's brand and how to maximize the value derived from shopping at the store. Each is examined in more detail below.

Cyclical Promotional Pricing (Hi-Lo)

Many retailers use a cyclical Hi-Lo retail pricing strategy. The strategy works as follows: For the majority of the selling time, retailers set a high price for products. However, on a regular cycle, these retailers offer deep discounts. Often considered promotional, deep discounts garner shoppers' attention and stimulate visits to the store. Stores adopting the Hi-Lo pricing strategy are often regular advertisers in the Sunday editions of local newspapers.

Hi-Lo retail pricing is a form of price discrimination (a concept discussed more fully later in this chapter). Put simply, price discrimination means charging different prices for the same good to different consumers. Suppose that a consumer needs a product immediately (e.g., needs to replace a toothbrush or buy a new suit for an upcoming party). Given the urgency, the customer is generally willing to pay more than he or she normally would for the product—and certainly more than a consumer who does not need the product immediately. The strategy relies on time-sensitive customers (as well as customers who are not price-sensitive) willing to purchase the product at the inflated price.

Quite frequently, Hi-Lo retailers will drastically reduce prices and then advertise the discounts. It is important to note that these low prices are not offered just on slow-selling merchandise but on popular products as well. The deeply discounted price is offered to attract price-sensitive customers (who are willing to wait for the price to decrease) as well as to stimulate product demand. The result of this strategy is that the seller is able to increase profits by charging different prices to different consumers for the same product. Time-sensitive and price-insensitive customers generally purchase when the price is high; price-sensitive customers purchase when the price is low.

An additional benefit of Hi-Lo pricing is that promotional items are often priced in a "loss leader" manner to draw consumers to the stores. Retailers that use the Hi-Lo pricing strategy run promotions often. Dayton Hudson, former parent of Marshall Field's, held 140 promotional sales at its department stores in 1995—which means that the stores featured sales on more than one out of every three shopping days.[1]

Everyday Low Pricing (EDLP)

Both manufacturers and retailers have adopted the EDLP strategy, which involves setting relatively low product prices—though not as low as the low prices in the Hi-Lo strategy. EDLP retailers also run sales less often than Hi-Lo retailers (see Exhibit 8.6 for comparisons). On most days, prices are lower at EDLP stores than they are at Hi-Lo stores. However, during discount cycles, Hi-Lo stores may offer the lower product prices. Safeway (in the supermarket category), Wal-Mart (in the general retailer category) and Saturn (in the auto category) are examples of firms that have adopted the EDLP strategy.

There are two key axioms to keep in mind when implementing an EDLP strategy:

1. Firms using an EDLP strategy must find a way to communicate the benefits of that strategy to consumers. A key goal is to associate EDLP with the firm's brand.

2. Firms must anticipate a lag time between the launch of an EDLP strategy and consumers figuring out how to incorporate EDLP into their shopping routine. While there are many EDLP success stories, well-known firms such as Sears and American Airlines have faltered when they tried to switch from a Hi-Lo to an EDLP strategy.[2]

Amazon.com has adopted an EDLP strategy, positioning itself as a low-pricing leader for the products that it sells on the Internet. In July 2001, Amazon announced that it was lowering the price of all books that cost less than $15. Six months later, it made another implicit price cut by offering free ground shipping on orders of more than $99. In April 2002, Amazon reinforced its EDLP image by offering a 30 percent discount on books that were priced at more than $15.[3]

Retail/Outlet Pricing

Some high-end retailers such as Coach have adopted this pricing strategy, in which a wide selection of non-discounted products is offered to customers at retail stores. Instead of discounting slow-moving or end-of-the-season merchandise at these stores, these retailers ship that merchandise to their outlet stores. Outlet stores are often located outside of metropolitan areas where there is low demand for a store's products at full retail price. In effect, the retail/outlet pricing strategy segments customers. Customers that are willing to pay for products will pay full price at retail stores, where discounts are rarely offered. More price-sensitive customers willing to drive to outlets pay discounted prices on a limited selection of products. Customers who live near the outlet stores (and are often unwilling to pay retail prices) are also enticed by the low prices.

Basic Pricing Strategies

This section provides an overview of the fundamental strategies that retailers and manufacturers use to price products. In particular, it focuses on cost-plus pricing and its derivatives, target profit growth and target return pricing; brand pricing; and promotions pricing. In addition, this section discusses the role of fairness in pricing and the ways that fairness affects short-term and long-term pricing strategy.

Cost Plus

This basic pricing strategy involves simply adding a fixed markup to the product cost. This markup is added to the firm's total or variable costs; for most consumer goods, the markup is added to the total cost of goods. Total cost includes both variable costs—the incremental costs of producing an additional good—and an *appropriate allocation* of fixed costs. Variable costs often include the raw material and labor necessary to produce an extra good. Fixed costs—factory, management, and general overhead costs—do not vary with the level of output. In general, manufacturers add a 15 percent markup to their total costs; wholesalers add a 20 percent markup; and retailers add a 40 percent markup.[4]

Professional-services firms such as law firms, accounting firms, and consulting firms often set their fees based on a markup of each individual's hourly wage. Firms calculate an individual's hourly wage by dividing his or her total yearly salary by the number of expected billable hours. Thus, if a professional's salary average is $50 an hour, his or her hourly billing rate will be a fixed multiple of this hourly wage; for example, a multiple of four for this individual translates into a $200 hourly billing rate. While such a multiple may appear high, the multiple often covers expenses such as overhead (office, phone), benefits (health and disability insurance, 401(k) plan), and some risk insurance to account for the possibility that the professional may not have enough work to bill for the entire year.

It's Often the Case . . . Pricing in the Real World

Drill-Down

Is Cost Plus a Realistic Pricing Strategy?

The key advantage of cost-plus pricing is that it is easy to compute. However, there are several disadvantages associated with this pricing method:

- *Demand conditions are not built into the price.* If demand for Sony PlayStation 2 is high, cost-plus sellers would have seen higher profits by increasing their price in accordance with demand conditions. Likewise, if ticket sales for a Broadway play are slow, the Broadway theater could increase revenue by decreasing prices below the cost-plus price. This decreased price would be profitable as long as the price was greater than the variable cost of accommodating an additional patron.

- *It is often difficult to accurately and fairly allocate fixed costs to product prices.* In the era before the Egg McMuffin, McDonald's was profitable just serving lunch and dinner. What percentage of fixed costs, then, should have been allocated to its breakfast products once it started serving breakfast? Should McDonald's have allocated zero fixed costs, since fixed costs were being covered by lunch and dinner, or perhaps one-third of its fixed costs? It would be ridiculous if, by pricing its breakfast items to cover one-third of the fixed costs, McDonald's lost business to competitors due to its relatively high prices. Realistically, because fixed costs are being covered by lunch and dinner, as long as a breakfast item price covered variable costs, profits would increase.

- *It is difficult to forecast sales.* Estimates of variable and fixed costs—the key costs involved in cost-plus pricing—may be based on an inaccurate sales forecast. If actual sales fall below the forecast, the fixed-cost allocation estimate may be too low. This will result in the firm losing money, because its reduced sales did not cover its fixed costs.

- *Cost-plus pricing does not take into account the slope and inverse relationship between price and quantity in a product-demand curve.* Thus, while cost-plus pricing may be profitable, by taking into account the slope of the demand curve, the firm may be able to increase profits by increasing or lowering product price.

Target Profit Growth

Target profit growth pricing is a close relative of cost-plus pricing and is most often used in mature industries. The sole focus of managers is to meet or exceed the growth target. If the target growth-rate goal is met, managers are considered successful.

To increase profits, managers have three levers to consider: reduce costs, grow sales, and change (increase or decrease) prices. In mature industries, costs are generally considered fixed. Thus, managers can either increase marketing efforts or experiment with price. Effective marketing will help to grow demand in current markets and create demand in new markets. From a pricing perspective, based on the shape/slope of the demand curve and competitor reaction, a manager can experiment with price in the following ways:

- Decrease price with the hope that the increase in units sold will more than cover the decrease in profit margin per unit.
- Increase price in hopes that the decrease in product sales (due to the increase in price) will be more than covered by the increased profit margin per product.

Target Return Pricing

Also a close relative of cost-plus pricing, target return pricing aims to maximize the return on capital for a company and its shareholders. Consider a firm that has a cost of capital of 15 percent. The firm is funded by a variety of types of investors and investing instruments that on average are charging (or demanding) a 15 percent return on their invested capital. Thus, managers are given the mandate to produce financial returns that exceed 15 percent. This financial return is computed by dividing total profit by total capital. If a company is targeting an 18 percent return on capital, managers must price products with the goal of meeting this target rate of return.

Brand Pricing

Pricing strategists have argued that buyers feel a sense of prestige when they purchase and consume a high-priced product. More realistically, the customer derives that sense of prestige from the implicit value and image that is conveyed by owning the good. This value is typically associated with the perceived value of the brand.

The brand value associated with prestige pricing is the result of the concerted efforts of the firm to create a high-end brand. The firm has often invested significantly in building its brand in hopes that there will be a customer market that values the brand and will pay for it. This brand-building work has influenced consumers to pay a premium for such items as a specially colored credit card, a meal at a trendy restaurant, or a standard cotton T-shirt with a brand name or logo displayed on it.

Under certain circumstances, sellers can use price to signal high quality to consumers. This strategy is most effective when consumers are not well informed about the product and its attributes, such as when they purchase the product infrequently or the product is insignificant in terms of price. Then consumers often use price as an indicator of product quality.

Is price a good indicator of quality? Sometimes—but it may depend on how a consumer measures quality. Hotels rated highly by Zagat, for example, are usually expensive. However, consumers evaluate the quality level of a hotel using many different criteria. Some customers might be most concerned with room quality; others might rate a hotel on the quality of its room service or whether or not it has a swimming pool. Thus, the fact that a hotel is expensive does not guarantee that the hotel represents high quality to each consumer.

The discount clothing chain Syms at one time used an "anti-price" as a signal of quality in its marketing strategy. For many years, Syms' tagline was "the educated customer is our best customer"—the implication being that knowledgeable clothing consumers would appreciate that Syms had the lowest prices on well-known brand-name clothes and therefore patronize the chain. This branding sent a powerful message to its cost-conscious customer segment.

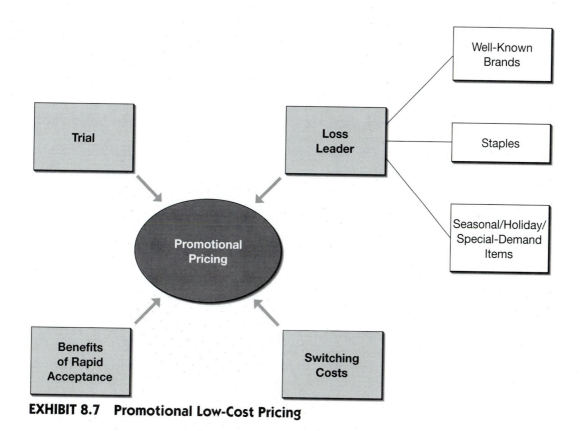

EXHIBIT 8.7   Promotional Low-Cost Pricing

Promotions Pricing

Stores and manufacturers often significantly decrease prices for the following reasons (see Exhibit 8.7):

Trial.   Marketers often offer low prices on new products in order to gain trial. The theory is that a low price will induce consumers to purchase a product, then realize its differentiating attributes. The hope is that in the future, consumers will pay the regular (higher) product price. While price lowering is a relatively easy strategy to implement, it does have significant long-term implications. Trial consumers, nurtured on a product's low introductory price, may use that introductory price to form a reference price and therefore may balk at paying the full price at a later date. Alternative trial pricing strategies to consider include free samples (with the consumer clearly knowing that "free" should not be used as a reference price) and manufacturer coupons (so consumers code the true price when they purchase the good).

Benefits of Rapid Acceptance. There are many benefits to being a first mover in a new product category. However, while being a first mover is important, gaining market acceptance is critical. The frenzy pricing associated with the less-than-market clearing price that Sony set for the PlayStation 2 will be discussed later in this chapter. One possible explanation for the low price is that Sony knew that Microsoft and Nintendo planned to release their own advanced game systems in the near future. Sony's long-term strategy may have been to set the below-market clearing price of $299 as a reference in consumers' minds so that as supply increases, consumers would not hesitate to purchase the product. If Sony had capitalized on the initial high demand by setting a high price, that price may have become coded as the reference price. As supply increased, Sony could have lowered its price, but it would be difficult to communicate the price change to consumers. This could have resulted in fewer consumers adopting the PlayStation 2 before Microsoft and Nintendo introduced their products.

Switching Costs. A firm may set a low cost to make its product part of the consumer's routine. Once that happens, switching products might prove costly to the consumer. Once a customer has signed up for an ISP service and circulated his or her e-mail address to friends (and permission marketers), there is a significant cost associated with changing services (e.g., a less-than-optimal user name and notifying friends of a new e-mail address). There are similar switching costs associated with stock brokerages. Once a consumer has created a portfolio, there is significant paperwork associated with moving that portfolio to a rival brokerage firm.

Loss Leaders. Retailers often discount prices with the hope that once customers come to the store to purchase these low-price loss-leader products, they will also purchase other high-margin products. The types of loss leaders that retail stores offer tend to fall into three product categories:

- *Well-known brand goods.* While consumers enjoy discounts on well-known brands, upscale-product producers often dislike it when their brands are used as loss leaders because discounting can damage their established brand.
- *Staples for price-sensitive customers.* Price-sensitive customers are often keenly aware of staple-good prices, and a lower price on staple goods is likely to draw customers to the store. Duncan Simester maintains that a store has two primary types of customers: regulars and price shoppers (customers who will purchase from the cheapest seller).[5] Given that regular shoppers will patronize a store regardless of promotions, the types of products selected to be loss leaders should be staples, because those are the discounts that attract price shoppers to the store.

- *Seasonal/holiday/special-demand items.* During a particular holiday or season, demand is often high for specific items—champagne on New Year's Eve, for example. Given their high demand, retailers often discount those items to induce customers to visit their stores. For similar reasons, retailers often discount prices for popular goods that are in immediate demand, such as the latest Harry Potter book or Britney Spears album.

Patrick DeGraba posits that loss leaders should have a demonstrated correlation to additional sales.[6] In each of the above loss-leader categories, retailers hope that by getting customers into the store, these customers will purchase additional goods. Instead of hoping for additional sales, retailers should select loss-leader goods that have a high probability of driving additional sales. By discounting turkeys at Thanksgiving, for example, retailers know that there is a high probability that shoppers will purchase additional, presumably higher-margin, products for their Thanksgiving dinners. Thus, by making a splash with consumers by offering a discounted price on turkeys, stores are implicitly offering these consumers a discount on the purchase of their entire Thanksgiving meal.

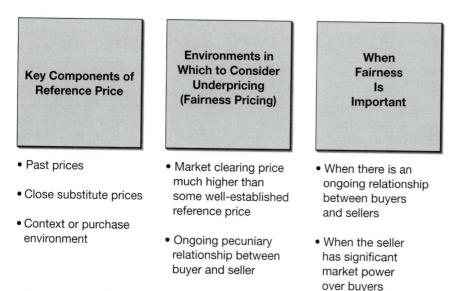

Key Components of Reference Price	Environments in Which to Consider Underpricing (Fairness Pricing)	When Fairness Is Important
• Past prices	• Market clearing price much higher than some well-established reference price	• When there is an ongoing relationship between buyers and sellers
• Close substitute prices		
• Context or purchase environment	• Ongoing pecuniary relationship between buyer and seller	• When the seller has significant market power over buyers

EXHIBIT 8.8   Fairness in Pricing

Fairness in Pricing

Consumers often think about pricing in terms of how fair the price is. To determine if a price is fair, consumers often compare an observed price with a price that they have constructed internally—a reference price. An observed price is judged fair, low, or high depending on where it lies within the customer's reference-price spectrum. Consumers generally form reference prices by considering three factors:

- *Past prices.* These are prices that consumers recall having paid (or seen advertised) for a product or specific brand.

- *Close-substitute prices*. Consumers often consider the price range of available close substitutes; the lowest price often plays a key role in determining an appropriate reference price.[7]
- *Context*. In judging fairness, consumers often factor in the purchase environment of the good. Consumers might be willing to pay more for an item at a convenience store than at a supermarket.

Economists and free-market crusaders often shudder at the notion of incorporating fairness into pricing (see Exhibit 8.8). These parties often advocate pricing according to market demand and supply conditions. If demand increases and supply is fixed, firms should increase product prices. Likewise, prices should decrease when demand decreases. Despite the rationale associated with pricing according to demand and supply, consumers often revolt when they observe companies adjusting their prices upward in response to increases in demand and limited supply.

These situations often lead to interesting pricing decisions. For example, summer comes on strong in the Boston area, and when summer hits, demand skyrockets for portable air conditioners, fans, and air conditioning services. In essence, consumers are at the mercy of their local retailers to bring some cool air into their lives. Under normal supply and demand conditions, one would expect retailers to increase the prices of air conditioners and fans during a demand onslaught. However, these price increases rarely occur. While this could be due in part to retail competition, it could also be argued that retailers do not want to jeopardize their ongoing relationship with their customers by increasing prices.

A similar example involves street vendors who sell umbrellas in big cities such as New York or Washington, D.C. When it begins to rain, these vendors unabashedly raise their prices in an attempt to capture profits from customers that forgot their umbrellas. The key difference is that these street vendors generally do not have an ongoing relationship with their customer base.

Coca-Cola considered the idea of adjusting soda prices at its vending machines according to the weather. The company figured that consumers would place a higher value on an ice-cold beverage on hot days than on colder days. To capitalize on weather-based shifts in consumer demand, Coca-Cola considered increasing its vending-machine soda prices on warm days and lowering prices on colder days. When it tested this concept, Coca-Cola found that customers strongly disliked the notion of being "gouged" on hot days. Coca-Cola abandoned the idea after marketers warned that its brand image could be damaged by implementing this demand-based pricing strategy.[8]

Richard Thaler posits that underpricing (below-market pricing) occurs when *both* of the following two conditions are present: (1) the market clearing price is much higher than some well-established reference price; and (2) there is an ongoing pecuniary relationship between the buyer and seller.[9] These conditions help to explain the below-market pricing of popular rock concerts, reservations for Saturday night dining at hot restaurants, and the overwhelming demand for sporting-event tickets (e.g., season tickets, Super Bowl tickets, and World Series tickets).

Pricing in a capitalist market is based upon the concept of adjusting prices according to market (demand and supply) conditions. On Wall Street, stock prices change by the second, based on market conditions. Participants in the stock market are generally sophisticated and understand pricing based on market conditions. Unfortunately for firms, the general population does not always understand the rationale behind market-based pricing. Thus, as much as Coca-Cola was concerned about damaging its brand if it implemented market-based pricing, so must other firms heed the same considerations. Firms that use a market-based pricing strategy risk a public outcry and being unfavorably labeled a price gouger—outcomes that are not beneficial for future business.

That said, firms that meet Thaler's two below-market pricing conditions are not doomed to leave potential profits on the table by keeping prices low. A gradual market education campaign can be implemented to sensitize consumers to market-based pricing. While the hotel industry is very attuned to hospitality and customer goodwill, it has effectively implemented market-based pricing. Room prices at popular Caribbean resorts swing drastically according to market demand. During popular in-season periods, it is not uncommon for room prices to be inflated 500 percent above off-season prices. Likewise, rock musicians used to underprice concert tickets (often resulting in instant sellouts) in an effort to maintain fan goodwill. In recent years, concert fans have become sensitized to market-based pricing, thus allowing popular acts such as the Rolling Stones to charge $350 for tickets to their concerts.

Customers' perceptions of price fairness are also strongly correlated with the market power that firms have over their customers. If substitutes are readily available, customers may become less angry than if there are few close substitutes. Many analysts have speculated that the anger expressed in the riots that occurred at the end of the 1999 Woodstock concert were due in part to the high prices that promoters charged for food and drinks. Fans went to the multiday event expecting to purchase meals on the concert grounds, and the unfair pricing almost certainly contributed to their widespread anger and rioting.

Other industries face similar dilemmas. For instance, the pharmaceuticals industry is well known for having high research and development costs that lead to both spectacular losses and spectacular successes. When they compare the variable cost of producing a popular drug with the retail price, critics often claim that pharmaceuticals companies are gouging customers. Even taking into account the substantial research costs that did not lead to a successful commercial drug, readers have to keep in mind that pharmaceuticals companies are private for-profit companies. Should the government regulate pharmaceuticals companies' rate of return? How will rate of return regulation affect the innovativeness of those pharmaceuticals companies?

Many business travelers are angry about skyrocketing airline fares. Roundtrip flights from Boston to Los Angeles in coach class range from a discounted fare of $208 to a full fare of over $2,500. Thus, if two people sitting next to each other in coach compared their ticket prices, they might find that one paid over 10 times more for a ticket than the other. The full fare ticket offers virtually no restrictions compared to the myriad restrictions (advance purchase, Saturday stay, limited opportunity to change ticket, etc.)

associated with a discounted ticket. Despite the significant value associated with no restrictions, business travelers still complain. The goal of the airlines is to charge different segments close to what they are willing to pay for the trip. Business travelers are willing to pay more than leisure travelers. Thus, business travelers implicitly subsidize leisure travelers. One question for readers to ponder is what will happen to travel if airlines begin to charge similar prices for leisure and business travelers. While business travel may certainly increase if prices are reduced to $1,000 for a roundtrip ticket from Boston to Los Angeles, what will happen to leisure travel? Leisure travelers have strongly benefited from the airlines' pricing structure.

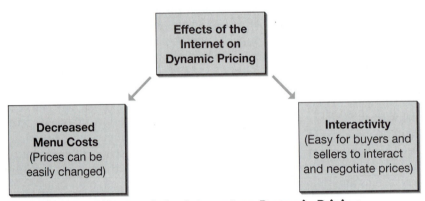

EXHIBIT 8.9   Effects of the Internet on Dynamic Pricing

Drill-Down

How the Eagles Started the Revolution in Market-Based Pricing for Rock Concerts

"Every couple of years, I'd run into Irving [Azoff, the Eagles' manager] and he'd go, 'You know, there is a bushel basket of $100 bills waiting for you if you guys could just do an album or do a tour.' But I'd go, 'Yes, but I have a nice life now, Irving. It's not that important to me.' "[10] —Glenn Frey, Eagles band member

After a 14-year hiatus, the Eagles re-formed in 1994 to record a new CD (a compilation of new songs and live tracks of top hits) and to embark on their "Hell Freezes Over" concert tour. The title of the tour referred to how unlikely it once seemed that the rock band would ever reunite.

It is widely acknowledged in the concert industry that this tour broke the glass ceiling of rock-concert ticket prices. Previously, rock bands deliberately maintained ticket prices below market clearing price because they feared alienating the fans with whom they were trying to establish a long-term relationship. Overall, however, fans were not alienated by the Eagles' top ticket prices (in the $100 to $125 range), and the reunion tour was a smashing success—despite the high prices, most concerts sold out. More than 3.5 million people paid more than $210 million to attend the reunion tour concerts. In addition, sales of the new album and tour memorabilia totaled between $200 million and $250 million.[11] The risk that the Eagles and their management took in setting concert prices brought tremendous financial success, and opened the door for other rock acts—the Rolling Stones, The Who, U2, even the working-class superstar Bruce Springsteen—to significantly increase the prices of their concert tickets.

Dynamic Pricing Strategies

Dynamic pricing is one of the most significant contributions the Internet and the 2Is have made to pricing strategy. Dynamic pricing is a pricing environment in which prices are not set but are fluid. The Internet has enhanced the attractiveness of dynamic pricing in two primary ways (see Exhibit 8.9):

- *Decreased menu costs.* Menu costs are the costs associated with changing the price of a good. When a retail store changes its product prices, there is a cost associated with physically changing all of the price tags. Likewise, when a mail-order catalog changes its prices, there are considerable costs associated with reprinting the catalog with the new prices. For goods advertised on the Internet, it is easy and virtually costless to change product prices. Given this environment, it is very attractive for firms to change their prices based on demand and supply conditions.

- *Interactivity.* The Internet makes it easy for sellers and buyers around the world to interact and negotiate prices. In the old economy, it was costly to create a dynamic pricing market due to the costs associated with bringing together sellers and buyers to negotiate. The fact that buyers and sellers can easily interact from their homes or workplaces via the Internet makes it easy to conduct dynamic pricing structures.

In the new economy, forecasters view **auctions** as a key pricing strategy. This section discusses the wide variety of auction types and how they are being implemented on the Internet (see Exhibit 8.10).

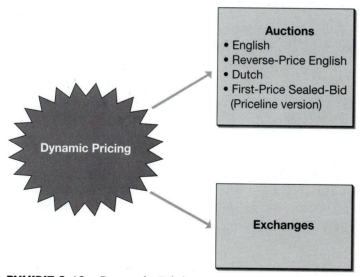

Auctions
- English
- Reverse-Price English
- Dutch
- First-Price Sealed-Bid (Priceline version)

Dynamic Pricing

Exchanges

EXHIBIT 8.10   Dynamic Pricing

English Auctions

English auctions are the most common auction type. Also known as ascending or oral auctions, English auctions are open auctions in which buyers successively raise their bids until only one buyer remains. The term open auction

eBay France: The Price (Increase) Is Right

If you don't think that pricing can be a powerful marketing tool, consider the case of eBay France. Launched by the online auction giant in late 2000 and bolstered by the quick purchase of its largest European rival, iBazar, eBay France was hosting a healthy 300,000 listings by early 2002.

Then the company announced a radical pricing change: Instead of paying only a transaction fee after a successful sale, sellers would also be charged an upfront listings fee. The fee was modest (ranging from about $0.13 to just over $2) but the impact was massive: Within days, the number of listings on the site dropped by nearly 50 percent. After three weeks, the site was hosting a mere 37,000 auctions—a precipitous 90 percent plunge. Meanwhile, eBay's main rivals in Europe, Yahoo! France and QXL France, were enjoying a listings boom as sellers fled eBay.

Disaster, right? Not necessarily. It turns out that with no upfront fees to worry about, many sellers had been clogging the site with items that had little chance of selling. With those sellers gone, eBay France was a leaner site, but a more attractive one for serious buyers and sellers. And in fact, slowly but surely, the number of listings began to rebound. As Deutsche Banc Alex Brown analyst Jeetil Patel told CNet News, the imposition of listing fees functioned "as a self-policing mechanism to encourage sellers to clean up poor inventory and poorly merchandised product on the site." In other words, eBay's pricing policy led to less. And oftentimes less, as we all know, is actually more.

indicates that all of the bidders know the amount of the highest bid at all times. English auctions can occur in person (for example, the in-person bidding at Sotheby's and Christie's art auctions) or via the Internet, proprietary data network, or phone. In many instances, the product seller can maintain a reserve price; if the final bid does not equal or exceed the reserve price, the item is not sold. Depending on the auction structure, this reserve price is either known or unknown to bidders.

Reverse-Price English Auctions

Many auction sites—B2B sites, in particular—use reverse-price auctions to help firms save on supply costs. On these sites, firms often submit a request for proposal (RFP) or request for quotation (RFQ) to initiate a supply auction. The auction winner is the firm that provides the lowest bid to supply the requested goods or services. FreeMarkets has become well known in the B2B space as a site that helps firms significantly lower their supply costs by implementing reverse auctions. One analysis of B2B auctions estimated that from November 1995 to January 1998, firms saved between 1 percent and 43 percent (with an average of 17 percent) on their supply costs by using FreeMarkets' reverse auction to procure supplies.[12] Imandi.com is a B2C site that facilitates reverse-price English auctions in which potential suppliers bid to serve customers. Registered imandi.com customers can post what goods they are searching for and select which suppliers they would like to have bid on their requests (imandi.com lists customer ratings and references for each affiliated retailer). The customer-selected retailers then proceed to bid for the customer's business. At the end of the process, the customer can review the bids and decide which retailer to use.

Drill-Down

How Auction Rules Affect Bidding Strategies

Auction strategists have grown increasingly interested in how the framework of an English auction affects both bidding strategies and the final amount of the winning auction bid. As it so happens, the difference between how Amazon.com and eBay handle last-minute bids offers some insight.

While there is a final bid deadline for auctions held on Amazon, the site has a rule that if a bid is placed within the last 10 minutes of an auction, the auction is automatically extended for an additional 10 minutes. The auction finally closes when no one has bid within 10 minutes of the last bid. On eBay, however, an auction ends at the stated deadline regardless of whether there is a flurry of last-minute bidding. Interested buyers who bid seconds too late see their bids rejected.

Research on the difference between the last-minute bidding rules of Amazon and eBay has yielded some interesting results. In a representative sample of eBay and Amazon auctions, researchers found that 37 percent of eBay auctions received bids within the last minute, and 12 percent received bids within the last 10 seconds. In contrast, researchers found that only 1 percent of Amazon's auctions received bids in the last minute. Furthermore, in eBay auctions, experienced bidders tended to bid at the last minute; in Amazon auctions, experienced buyers tended to submit their bids early.

Some interesting hypotheses have been offered to explain this difference in bidding behavior:

- Stanford researchers Patrick Bajari and Ali Hortacsu posit that recognized experts do not want to bid early because doing so would reveal that the auction item is valuable. While this a viable explanation for auctions in which significant information is necessary to determine the value of the offered item (e.g., art or antiques), it does not convincingly explain the difference in bidding behavior for relatively common products whose value is generally easy to ascertain.

- Harvard researchers Al Roth and Axel Ockenfels posit that late bidding in eBay auctions offers shrewd bidders the opportunity to avoid bidding wars—thus allowing them to purchase goods at a cheaper price than if they had started bidding earlier. If serious eBay buyers wait until the last minute to bid, the bidding community has less time to digest the information revealed by the bid, such as what other bidders are willing to pay. By bidding at the last minute, rival bidders have little time to analyze the bid, decide if they want to raise their bid, and submit their bid. Conversely, during an Amazon auction in which bidding is extended by 10 minutes after each bid, buyers have significant time to analyze the bid and decide what their next action should be.

Thus, at least in theory, it appears that bidders participating in eBay auctions get the better deal.[13]

Dutch Auctions

There is a difference between how economists and eBay define a Dutch auction, which gets its name from the process by which flowers have been sold in the Netherlands for the last century. Typically, at Dutch flower auctions, an auctioneer will start by announcing a high price for the product and then begin to slowly decrease the product price until a bidder accepts the price. This auction is the exact opposite of an English auction. Dutch auctions have two key drawbacks:

- The process does not allow the price to be increased when buyers reveal their interest in goods. In English auctions, when a buyer reveals interest in a product by bidding, other parties may reevaluate the worth of the good and increase their bids.

- It is important for Dutch auctions to start at a price that is higher than the market clearing price, or else profit has been left on the table.

On eBay, Dutch auction refers to a special auction format in which a seller sells multiple identical items. The seller specifies the minimum price (the starting bid) and the number of items available. Buyers bid at or above that minimum price for the quantity they are interested in purchasing. At the close of the auction, the highest bidders purchase the items at the price offered by the lowest winning bidder.[14] This derivative of Dutch auctions is called a *new-economy Dutch auction*.

Suppose a seller has two pens, and the seller is demanding a minimum bid of $20 for each pen. In the simplest case, two buyers will bid $20 for one pen—thus each bidder will end up purchasing one pen for $20. Now consider a more difficult case. Suppose Buyer A bids $20 for one pen, Buyer B bids $20 for one pen, and Buyer C bids $21 for one pen. At the end of the auction, Buyer C will get to purchase the pen for $20, Buyer A will get to purchase the pen for $20 (because Buyer A was the first to bid $20), and Buyer B will not be able to purchase the pen.

WR Hambrecht & Co. is using the new-economy Dutch auction format to change the way that initial public offerings (IPOs) are conducted, in an effort to be financially equitable to its IPO clients. Most investment banks (I-banks) handle IPOs in the following manner. The I-bank sets a share price for the stock and personally guarantees to the IPO firm that it will receive this premarket determined price for each IPO share. It would be unprofitable if the I-bank set the share price too high and investors did not buy the full amount of available shares. In this case, the I-bank would be stuck owning shares that it bought at a higher-than-market clearing price. Thus, I-banks tend to be conservative in setting the initial stock price. As a result, most IPOs end their first trading day at a market price that is significantly higher than the initial stock price.

Typically, I-banks and the IPO companies offer blocks of stock priced at the initial stock price to favored clients (i.e., institutional buyers) and friends and family of the IPO company. These (generally) lucky IPO stock recipients often instantly make money by selling their shares on the first day or holding shares that they received at an initially below-market cost. During the glory days of Internet IPOs, the initial price of the stock was often significantly underpriced relative to the first-day ending price of the stock. One classic example of this type of under-market pricing is the initial public offering for theglobe.com. At the end of the first day of trading shares of theglobe.com, the final trading price was 606 percent above the initial stock price set by the I-bank. While such sensational IPO trading was cited by the press as an example of how high the market valued a new company, the owners of the company could have garnered more investment capital had the initial stock price been priced higher.

WR Hambrecht's Dutch auctions work this way: Any person that has an account with WR Hambrecht or any members of the company's OpenIPO network are allowed to bid online for shares. Prior to the first day of trading, WR Hambrecht allocates all of the available shares by starting with the buyers who bid the highest price for each share and then allocating shares in descending order by bidder price until all of the shares have been distributed. Each buyer is charged the price bid by the lowest buyer who was allocated a share.

WR Hambrecht used a new-economy Dutch auction for the IPO of online magazine Salon.com. Prior to the first day of open market trading, all of the Salon IPO shares were allocated at the lowest accepted share price, $10.50 per share. The share price dropped slightly at the end of the first trading day and increased slightly the next day.[15] The relative stability of the initial stock price indicated that the new-economy Dutch auction offered the IPO firm a good financial approximation of how the market valued the company.

First-Price Sealed-Bid Auctions

This is a very straightforward type of auction. Sellers offer a good for buyers to evaluate and consider bidding on. Potential buyers have the option to submit one sealed bid for the product by a specified time. One implication of this auction is that since the bidding is sealed, buyers do not know the amount of competing bids. After the deadline, the product is sold to the highest bidder. The seller also has the right to specify a minimum reserve price. If the bidding does not reach this reserve price, the seller does not have to sell the good. Sellers have the option of making the minimum reserve price either known or unknown to potential bidders.

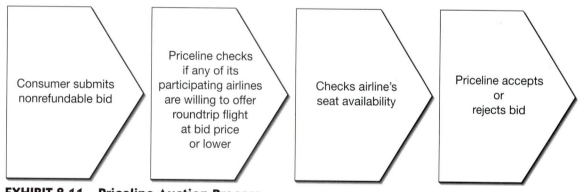

EXHIBIT 8.11   Priceline Auction Process

Priceline has created a new-economy variant of the first-price sealed-bid auction. In Priceline's auction model, bidders might submit a price (guaranteed by a credit card) for a roundtrip airline ticket on specified days (see Exhibit 8.11). Once they submit their bids, bidders agree that Priceline can place them on any airline flight (the bidder has some control over the number of connecting flights) departing anytime between 6 AM and 10 PM, and that the tickets are nonrefundable. Once a bid has been submitted, Priceline automatically checks if the bid price is in line with the fares and restrictions that participating airlines have offered to Priceline for its customers. After Priceline checks if an airline is willing to sell a ticket at or below the customer's bid price, the airline then checks to see if it has available seat inventory for the specified travel dates. If the airline does, it charges the bidder's credit card and notifies him or her of the itinerary. Priceline derives revenues from this process in two primary ways:

- Based on availability, participating airlines have agreed to supply tickets on selected routes for a set price. Priceline makes money on the spread—the difference between the airline's ticket price and the bid price.
- Priceline charges a nominal ticketing fee.

The Priceline auction is a unique variant of the standard auction. The interactivity offered by the Internet affords Priceline the opportunity to offer these types of auctions efficiently. Priceline was able to capitalize on its first-mover advantage in this space by patenting this unique-to-the-Internet "name your own price" auction process.

Priceline's service appealed to travel companies not only because it proved an easy way for them to discretely sell of excess capacity, but also because the pricing process did not seriously affect a company's brand; bidders did not know exactly what products were being offered until after they successfully won a bid. If a bidder knew that Priceline always used the same airline and flight, this *would* affect the airline's brand. The bidder would generally use Priceline over paying retail.

However, Priceline has not fared as well with hotel reservations as it has with airline reservations, in part because it is more difficult to commoditize hotels than air travel. Travel website biddingfortravel.com has become a huge thorn in Priceline's hotel business. Biddingfortravel.com encourages its devotees to post the results of their Priceline bids, therefore revealing patterns in the hotels to which Priceline sends bidders. For example, by looking at the four-star Upper East Side section of New York City, users can see that Priceline really only deals with one major hotel: the Stanhope (Park Hyatt). Due to the active posting on bidding for travel.com, readers have strong confidence that when they bid for a four-star hotel on the Upper East Side, they are bidding on the Stanhope. Recent postings have the Stanhope accepting Priceline bids as low as $75 a night, while the hotel is offering official rates for the same room type at $299. The information offered on this website, recently highlighted by *The Wall Street Journal*, is a detriment to Priceline's business model—and the hotels with which it does business. If bidders know what hotels they are bidding for, the hotel's brand could be damaged, thus decreasing the incentives for hotels to participate in Priceline's program.

Reverse First-Price Sealed-Bid Auctions

In a similar fashion, firms can use reverse first-price sealed-bid auctions to purchase goods. The U.S. government often uses this auction method to procure supplies. A federal agency will post an RFP or RFQ on which potential suppliers can bid. Suppliers can submit only one sealed bid to fulfill the supply request; they do not know the prices that other bidders have submitted. At the end of the auction, the federal agency awards the contract to the lowest bidder.

Drill-Down

The Winner's Curse

Many academics have commented on the phenomenon of the winner's curse that seems to appear in auctions: Winners often end up paying more than the true value of the product.[16] Similarly, if a firm has put out a contract for bid, the auction winner often ends up bidding too low for the project. Economists posit that the winner's curse occurs because of uncertainty about the product's true value. While bidders do not have any preconceived biases in their bid, economists assume that the mean bid will be the true value of the good. However, due to uncertainty, some bids will be higher or lower than the good's true value. Since the highest bid wins the auction, the winner's curse theory holds that the winning bid is actually higher than the value of the product.

Similarly, if a firm creates an auction in which the lowest bidder wins a contract to supply a product or service, the winner's curse often negatively affects the winning bidder. Given the uncertainty about the actual costs associated with fulfilling the contract, economists assume that the mean bid is the actual cost of fulfilling the contract. However, given uncertainty, some bids will be above or below the true cost of fulfilling the contract. Since the lowest bid wins the auction and, due to uncertainty, the lowest bid is below the real cost of fulfilling the contract, the winner's curse posits that the winning bidder ends up losing money on the contract.

Exchanges

Electronic exchanges are marketplaces that have arisen to bring buyers and sellers together. Typically, an electronic exchange acts as the middleman for a sale, and collects a percentage of the total sale price. Exchanges serve as a meeting ground where sellers can post goods that they have for sale for a set time period. During this time period, prospective buyers can submit product bids. In a similar fashion, prospective buyers can post a request for a specific product. During a fixed time period, potential suppliers can post bids to supply the product. A key advantage for buyers using the exchange is the exposure to a large number of sellers. Given the increased number of sellers, economic theory posits that the average buying price should be lower than it would be if fewer sellers bid for the project. Similarly, a seller's products are exposed to more potential buyers through such an exchange. Given that there are more buyers when a seller uses an exchange, sellers will theoretically receive higher prices for their products.

FastParts.com is an example of an electronic exchange designed to give its members access to a global marketplace in which to more efficiently buy and sell electronic components. FastParts.com prequalifies all buyers and sellers to ensure integrity within its trading community, and buyers and sellers negotiate anonymously online to arrive at a mutually agreeable price. Because buyers and sellers are anonymous, FastParts.com acts as an intermediary, providing a one-year warranty on all parts bought and sold and guaranteeing payment before the seller ships the product.

While there was a great deal of hope behind the concept of exchanges, the reality is that most exchanges have failed; a thriving online community of buyers and sellers proved too difficult to sustain. Many companies have turned instead to private exchanges. In addition to offering ordering and invoicing services, private exchanges are being used to share supply chain information with suppliers and for collaborative product development. IBM

Drill-Down

Sometimes You Just Have to Ask

A popular business travel route is Boston to Los Angeles. Oftentimes, firms have a policy that their employees fly that and other domestic routes in coach. To get around this policy, some business travelers would book their tickets on US Airways. The airline does not offer a nonstop Boston-to-Los Angeles service, but it does have an ongoing promotion that if you fly to the West Coast from the East Coast and agree to connecting flights, you can fly first class for the price of coach. While it takes longer to connect planes, passengers experience the luxury of first class.

Then Delta began aggressively promoting its nonstop Boston-to-LA route, which offered both coach class and BusinessElite class service. Intrigued, we called Delta to price its BusinessElite class service. The reservationist quoted a price that was about 33 percent above the airline's standard coach price. After a bit of grumbling, we asked the reservationist if there was a cheaper price for BusinessElite. After searching her computer, the reservationist inquired if the traveler was in Delta's frequent-flier program. When she heard "yes," the reservationist quoted a Business-Elite ticket price that was actually $40 less than the coach price. Then, on Delta's website, we noticed a link offering a Boston-to-LA BusinessElite special. If booked on the site, a Boston-to-LA BusinessElite ticket was being offered for $649 one way.

Thus, for exactly the same one-way ticket—same class of service, same refund and change restrictions, etc.—Delta's reservations line quoted $1,757. Once the customer was identified as a frequent flier, that price dropped to $1,220. Booked on the Internet, that price further dropped to $649.

Sometimes, all you have to do is ask.

currently has a private exchange with 28,000 suppliers, General Electric has one with 36,000 suppliers, and Wal-Mart has a private exchange with 30,000 suppliers.[17]

Advanced Pricing Strategies

Price Discrimination

Pricing strategists loathe using the word discrimination because of its negative connotations. When applied to pricing, the word discrimination refers to the practice of charging different prices to different people for the same product, based on their willingness to pay. **Price discrimination** raises interesting questions about whether such tactics are appropriate or beneficial to society. Pricing strategists often classify discriminatory pricing into three categories: (1) first-degree price discrimination, (2) second-degree price discrimination, and (3) third-degree price discrimination (see Exhibit 8.12).

First-Degree Price Discrimination. First-degree price discrimination gets consumers to pay exactly what they are willing to pay for an item. This implies that in order to charge each consumer exactly what he or she is willing to pay for a product, firms must know each consumer's demand curve—

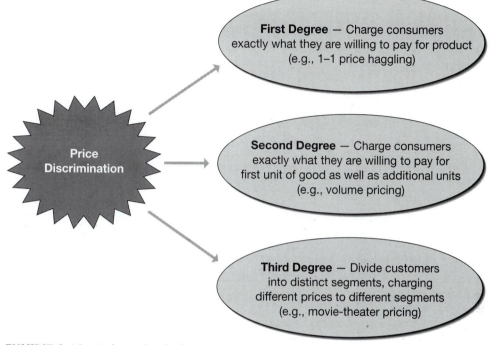

First Degree — Charge consumers exactly what they are willing to pay for product (e.g., 1–1 price haggling)

Second Degree — Charge consumers exactly what they are willing to pay for first unit of good as well as additional units (e.g., volume pricing)

Third Degree — Divide customers into distinct segments, charging different prices to different segments (e.g., movie-theater pricing)

Price Discrimination

EXHIBIT 8.12   Price Discrimination

which is unrealistic. In addition, while a consumer may be willing to pay a high price for a good, even if a firm tries to implement first-degree price discrimination, other sellers may be offering lower prices. Consumers will flock to these other sellers to avoid being charged higher prices. What is more realistic is for the merchant to elicit more information from consumers in order to gauge what they are willing to pay for a product. This often occurs when merchants haggle with prospective buyers. After a few minutes of haggling, skilled merchants can get a good idea of what a consumer is willing to pay for a good. Similarly, when salespeople ask, "What's your budget?" they are trying to understand a consumer's willingness to pay.

Second-Degree Price Discrimination.   Second-degree price discrimination is a close cousin of first-degree price discrimination. When a firm implements first-degree price discrimination, it is striving to find the maximum price that each consumer is willing to pay for the good. In second-degree price discrimination, the firm tries to ascertain how much consumers are willing to pay not only for the first unit of a good but for each additional good. The upcoming discussion in this chapter on volume pricing in the CD singles market shows how firms can implement the principles of second-degree price discrimination.

Third-Degree Price Discrimination.   This is by far the most common type of price discrimination. It involves classifying customers by category, according to their willingness to pay. Price discrimination by age is often used in the movie-theater business: Theaters charge children and seniors less than they charge regular customers. Likewise, media companies such as *The Wall Street Journal* often offer significantly discounted prices to students under the theory that the optimal price for students is lower than that for the general public. Firms offer different prices to different customers for the same product because these different customer segments have a different willingness to pay for the good. As long as it is easy to discern the characteristics of consumers (such as age or student status) and it is not easy to resell goods (buy the goods at a low price and resell the goods to segments that are paying a higher price for the goods), third-degree price discrimination makes good business sense. In economic terms, it is necessary for the lowest price offered in a price discrimination strategy to be greater than the variable cost of producing the good.

Hotels engage in price discrimination by offering a wide array of prices for the same type of hotel room. For example, hotels offer AARP rates for the elderly, AAA rates for auto club members, government rates for government employees, a generic corporate rate if you mention that you are traveling on business, special corporate rates negotiated directly with businesses, Internet rates, special rates if you call the hotel directly, discount rates sold through wholesalers, and specially negotiated rates if you book through certain offline (e.g., American Express) and online (e.g., Travelocity) travel agents. The list goes on.

Simple Volume-Discount Pricing Plan

- Buy the first three singles at $4 per single.
- After three singles have been purchased, buy two additional singles for $2 each.
- $4 is "left on the table" (consumer was willing to pay $20 for five songs).
  - Revenue: $16
  - Profit: $8.50

Consumer's Demand for Electronic Music

Value of …	
First Single:	$6.00
Second Single:	$5.00
Third Single:	$4.00
Fourth Single:	$3.00
Fifth Single:	$2.00
Sixth Single:	$1.00
Seventh Single:	$0.50
Production cost of a single:	$1.50

Two-Part Pricing

- A flat subscription fee of $12.50 can be charged.
- In addition to the flat subscription fee, a fee of $1.50 per single can be charged.
- Given its demand schedule, the consumer is willing to pay the subscription fee and purchase five singles at $1.50 per single. Recall that the consumer values the five singles at $20.
  - Total Revenue: $20
  - Total Profit: $12.50

EXHIBIT 8.13   Volume Discounts and Two-Part Pricing

Volume Discount Pricing

Theoretically, if a music company could estimate the exact individual demand for CD singles, it could design a volume pricing plan that would charge customers exactly what they are willing to pay for the first CD single and each additional one (see Exhibit 8.13). Pricing strategies that decrease price as the quantity purchased increases are designed to try to capture the inverse price/quantity relationship that consumers have for products. Pizza restaurants are notorious for offering specials such as a "buy one, get the second one for half price" promotion. In this example, the music company could offer a consumer the opportunity to purchase CD singles at the following price schedule:

- First single @ $6
- Second single @ $5
- Third single @ $4
- Fourth single @ $3
- Fifth single @ $2
- Total revenue = $20; total profit = $12.50

While this pricing schedule fully extracts from the consumer exactly what he is willing to pay for each CD single, this pricing structure is difficult to understand, and this difficulty could adversely affect sales. A more simplified schedule could be structured as follows: Buy the first three singles for $4 each, and the next two singles for $2 each. While this pricing structure is clearly easier to understand, the tradeoff is that this simplicity costs the music company profits. Total profit under this simplified volume discount pricing plan is $8.50 (total revenue is $16).

Two-Part Pricing

In an effort to better capture what consumers are willing to pay for an increased number of goods, firms often use a two-part pricing strategy. This strategy is composed of a fixed fee and an associated variable charge for each purchased item. In the CD-single pricing example, the optimal two-part pricing structure is for the music company to charge a flat fee of $12.50 and a price-per-single fee of $1.50. After paying the flat fee of $12.50, consumers can buy as many CD singles as they want for $1.50 each. From an economic standpoint, it is important that the variable price in a two-part pricing strategy equal the variable cost of producing the good. In this case, the cost of producing a CD single is $1.50, thus the variable fee should be $1.50. To maximize profits, it is necessary to structure two-part pricing in a way that restricts consumers from buying a product at a variable price that is less than the cost of producing that product.

In the above music example, pricing has been structured so that the consumer will buy five singles. Had the pricing structure been set in a manner that encourages the consumer to buy six or seven singles, the company would sacrifice profits. If the music company has a pricing structure that encourages the consumer to buy the sixth single, and he is only willing to pay $1 for it, the most the firm can charge for the additional single is $1. This is not profit-maximizing because it costs the firm $1.50 to produce the single. Thus, the two-part pricing strategy should be set up in a manner that will encourage the consumer to buy five singles and *not* purchase the sixth single. Given that two-part pricing is structured as a flat fee and a variable fee for each good consumed, by setting the variable price at a price equal to (or, in this case, slightly higher than) the cost of producing the CD single ($1.50), the consumer will not be induced to purchase a single that costs more to produce than he is willing to pay.

The key to understanding a two-part pricing strategy is realizing that the firm would like to sell its goods to consumers at the exact price they are willing to pay. If the firm knows exactly what a consumer will pay for each quantity level of good, it is in the firm's best interest to sell each good at that price—up to the point at which the price is equal to the variable cost associated with producing the good. The following steps describe how a firm might implement a two-part pricing plan:

- Gain an understanding/estimate of the individual's demand curve. In the CD example, this means trying to understand how much the consumer is willing to pay for the first CD single and then each subsequent CD single.

- Determine the optimal number of CD singles that should be sold to each consumer. This optimal number occurs at the point at which the price that the consumer is willing to pay for the single is equal to the cost of producing the single. In this example, the music company should try to sell five singles to each consumer. At this point, the consumer is willing to pay $2 for a single, while the cost of producing the single is $1.50. If the music company tries to sell six singles, it will lose money because the consumer is willing to pay $1 for a single, while the cost of producing the single is $1.50.

- Calculate how much the consumer is willing to pay for five singles. Structure a fixed price and variable price that will encourage the consumer to purchase five singles. In this example, the consumer is willing to pay $20 for five singles. If the variable price is set at $1.50, the firm should set the fixed price at $12.50 [$20 − (5 × $1.50)].

From a practical standpoint, it is difficult to construct a market demand curve for a product. To create a market demand curve, a firm has to sum up the individual demand curves of everyone who is interested in purchasing the product. This is a very difficult task. Once a firm creates an estimate for a demand curve (which can result from an educated guess, past experience, market research, or creating econometric forecasts), firms can use the theories discussed in this chapter to create a demand curve.

This section has explained why the variable price in a two-part pricing strategy should equal the cost of producing the product. However, while economically sound, this strategy may not be appropriate from a marketing perspective. For example, many parents like the idea of paying one price for admission to Disneyland and not having to worry about paying per ride. Since many consumer segments value paying one price for unlimited services, there is a strong marketing value associated with a one-price-covers-all value proposition. In addition, it may prove costly for firms to collect a per-use fee. Disneyland visitors may actually try out more rides on an unlimited pass than they would had they paid for each individual ride. Also, paying for

Drill-Down

The Chicken Delight Bundling Strategy

Beginning in the 1960s, Chicken Delight sold retail fried-chicken businesses with an innovative twist on the traditional franchising model. Chicken Delight allowed entrepreneurs to enter the fast-food market with fewer barriers by bundling the franchise into a single package with no upfront licensing cost. Unlike traditional franchises, which charge a licensing fee and ongoing advertising and royalty costs, Chicken Delight did not charge any fees as part of its franchise arrangements, which included the rights to its recipes, brand names, and trademarks. Instead, it gave away franchises in exchange for an agreement from franchisees to purchase paper goods, equipment, and prepared foods on an ongoing basis from Chicken Delight.

The low initial cost of starting a Chicken Delight franchise contributed to its tremendous growth. Prospective franchisees were overwhelmed by the opportunity to start their own business without fees or royalties. Hence, Chicken Delight successfully built more than 800 operations nationally. What the franchisees did not fully grasp was Chicken Delight's powerful revenue model. Chicken Delight's core pricing structure was to require that packaging bearing the franchise trademark, cooking equipment, and prepared foods be purchased directly from Chicken Delight. This arrangement allowed Chicken Delight to collect revenues from the sale of the items on an ongoing basis, producing enormous revenues. By removing capital barriers to entry, Chicken Delight was able to quickly capture a large number of franchisees and continually collect revenues.

An integral part of Chicken Delight's strategy was to place a higher upcharge on the paper products associated with dinners versus those associated with buckets. As a percentage of gross sales, dinner meals were more profitable to retailers than buckets of chicken; hence, Chicken Delight charged more for paper dinner boxes than for paper buckets. Essentially, this allowed Chicken Delight to collect differential royalty revenues from franchisees based on profitability rather than sales.[18] Franchisees initially accepted this as an efficient and fair pricing model. Using price discrimination, Chicken Delight was able to do extremely well by being the sole direct provider of paper products.

Chicken Delight planned to assure future revenue growth by tying in the purchase of differentially priced paper products. Despite this well-devised pricing strategy, Chicken Delight's franchisees filed suit in 1967, charging violations of Sherman Act antitrust provisions. The court favored the franchisees; it ruled that Chicken Delight's franchise model was illegal and declared it illegal for the once-leading West Coast franchise system to continue its pricing strategy.[19] Consequently, Chicken Delight's innovative pricing strategy led to its demise.

each ride individually might result in longer lines and congestion costs. All things considered, an "all you can ride" policy may prove more efficient than a pay-per-ride policy.

Bundling

If there is one pricing strategy best suited for true Internet products, it is bundling. Indeed, bundling can be thought of both as a product strategy and a pricing strategy (see Drill-Down). There are two primary types of **bundling** (or packaging) strategies: pure bundling and mixed bundling. Pure bundling occurs when a firm offers its products only as part of a bundle. For instance, Michael Ovitz pioneered the use of pure bundling in the motion picture industry. At the talent agency that he co-founded, Creative Artists Agency, if a studio wants a hot actor, director, or writer, the studio

---

Drill-Down

It Isn't All About Pricing—Bundling Should Also Be Thought of as Creating Products

The Internet has made bundling a more attractive pricing/product proposition for the following reasons:

- *Internet content is easier to package.* Most products being revolutionized by the Internet involve content delivered in the form of bits. This content can be music, news, research reports, software, and, with the adoption of broadband, movies and television shows.

- *There is low friction between consumers and firms on the Internet.* For both consumers and firms, it is often far easier to interact online than offline. The interactivity of the Internet makes it easier for customers to create their own bundles and convey their preferences to firms.

- *Online content is a fungible product, and the costs associated with adding new customers are low.* Given the relative ease of creating new product bundles and the low marginal costs often associated with selling content, firms have an incentive to create many different bundles to serve as many segments as possible.

- *The cost of metering usage is decreasing.* Many subscription series involve the metering of content usage. The Internet allows many low cost metering options.

Given the ease of creating bundles, it is important for firms to view bundles as products that can be designed for key target segments. In the digital music market firms will, at minimum, have to create bundles that are attractive to different genres and different usage occasions. The type of bundles that a classical music fan demands will differ from the bundles desired by rap or country music fans. Similarly, bundles should be tailored to usage occasions. Some fans may only want to download an occasional new music release, while others may be willing to pay a significant monthly subscription fee for unlimited usage at home, at the office, and in their car. Digital music retailers need to create bundles that are attractive to both type of segments and also offer a path of bundles designed to turn low-margin light users into high-margin heavy users.

---

has to accept a package that, along with the person that it wants, also includes other talent that Ovitz represents—for example, other directors, writers, scripts, and actors.[20] This pure bundling strategy leverages Ovitz's high-powered clients and helps his up-and-coming clients by providing them with an opportunity to display their talents and establish reputations. Similarly, bundling can be used as a promotional vehicle for new products. To target new customers, a firm can bundle new products with established products. For example, a toothpaste company could bundle its newest complementary product, a toothbrush, with its most popular toothpaste brand. This bundle is attractive to customers because they are getting an additional product for free or at a discounted price.

Firms might bundle complementary products simply for convenience reasons. The In-N-Out burger chain, based in California, offers bundles of its products without a price discount. Thus, the chain's No. 1 bundle simply includes its double-double hamburger, fries, and a soda. There is no cost advantage to buying the bundle. However, ordering a bundle is convenient, and the notion of purchasing a No. 1 puts customers in the frame of mind to purchase all items in bundles. The same is true for complementary con-

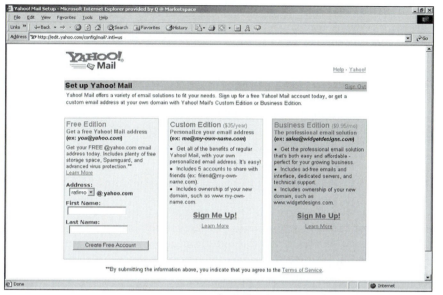

Source: Reproduced with permission of Yahoo! Inc. © 2000.
by Yahoo! And the YAHOO! logo are trademarks of Yahoo! Inc.

EXHIBIT 8.14   Yahoo!'s E-Mail Bundle Pricing

	Financial News	Legal News	Current News	Value Bundle
e-information's Price	$3,000	$1,500	$1,250	$5,000
Company A's Valuation	$3,000	$1,500	$500	
Company B's Valuation	$3,000	$750	$1,250	
Company C's Valuation	$3,250	$1,000	$500	
Strategy Net Result				
Company A:	Purchases value bundle. Implicitly pays $1,500 for legal news, $500 for current news.			
Company B:	Purchases value bundle. Implicitly pays $750 for legal news, $1,250 for current news.			
Company C:	Purchases financial news. Pays more ($3,250 vs. $3,000) for financial news relative to Companies A and B.			

EXHIBIT 8.15   e-Information's Mixed-Bundling Strategy

sumer products: Offering a bundle is convenient and stimulates customer demand.

Mixed bundling is a popular marketing strategy that involves selling goods both individually and in bundles. The bundle price is generally less than the sum of the individual component prices. Mixed bundling is a particularly easy and profitable pricing strategy to implement for Internet electronic service products. Consider an electronic-research company that offers financial, legal, and current-news research products. Exhibit 8.15 displays the demand and price structure for a hypothetical company, e-Information. In this example:

- Company A purchases the value bundle. By purchasing the bundle, Company A implicitly pays $1,500 for legal information and $500 for current news.
- Company B purchases the value bundle. B implicitly pays $750 for legal information and $1,250 for current news.
- Company C purchases the financial news package only.

A key benefit of using price discrimination is that the firm can sell more goods by implicitly selling the same products to different consumers at different prices. In this example, the bundle induced Company A to buy the legal information product by implicitly charging a lower price than others paid, and induced Company B to purchase the current news product by implicitly charging a lower price relative to others.

Price Discrimination over Time

A common strategy to induce consumers to pay different prices for the same product is to implement price discrimination over time. Given the low menu costs associated with the Internet, this strategy can be easily implemented by Internet retailers. When a new product is released, the price can be set high and slowly lowered over time. This is often the case with clothing and new technology: Despite knowing that the price will be lowered over time, consumers who are willing to pay significantly for the product will often make the purchase immediately instead of waiting for a lower price (and risking that the product will no longer be available). Similarly, consumers who are willing to pay less will often wait until the price is lowered before purchasing the product. By embarking on a strategy of price discrimination over time, consumers self-select by paying different prices (delineated by time) for the same product.

In industries such as publishing and music, price discrimination over time is often implemented in reverse order. For popular music, it is not uncommon to have fans line up at stores at 12:01 AM on the release date of a much-anticipated CD in order to be among the first to purchase it. If these fans reveal their diehard consumer status by going to such measures, music retailers could probably charge a higher price during the first week of sales. Instead, retailers often significantly discount new releases during the first few weeks that they are on the shelves, after which they generally increase the price. This pricing is in direct contrast to the principles of the strategy of price discrimination over time. The reverse pricing strategy evolved because retailers view new CD and book releases as a promotion to bring customers into their stores. Thus, knowing that there will be strong demand for the new CD or book, retailers will heavily advertise it (often with financial assistance from the music or publishing companies) at a discounted price. Music and publishing companies do not discourage this practice because sales figures from the first few weeks have become a major market-

Drill-Down

How Profitable Are Mixed Bundling Strategies? Empirical Evidence from the Rock Concert Industry

At many rock concert amphitheaters in the United States, promoters use an interesting variant of mixed bundling called *intertemporal mixed bundling* to sell concert tickets. Promoters divide the summer concert season into two distinct ticket-selling periods. In the first period, promoters only sell subscription series (bundles of four to five concert tickets targeted toward the same demographic group). During this period, promoters do not sell individual tickets. In the second period, promoters sell any remaining tickets individually. In an interesting twist on typical mixed bundling, the bundle price is generally greater than the sum of the individual ticket prices.

Using subscription series to sell concert tickets creates incentives for diehard fans (consumers willing to pay significantly for concert tickets) to purchase the bundle. Diehard concert fans may be induced to purchase the series simply to secure good seats for their favorite show(s). This, in turn, creates uncertainty for diehard fans of less-popular concerts in the series. Prior to the subscription model, diehard fans of less-popular bands could obtain good seats with relative ease. Now, because their favorite band is included in the series, diehard fans of less-popular bands become concerned about obtaining good seats. Because diehard fans of popular concerts in the series are buying tickets for the entire series, this will extract from the available supply of tickets for less-popular bands in the series. This new uncertainty often induces fans of less-popular bands in the series to purchase the series, which creates an endless cycle characterized by more market uncertainty. Since diehard fans of less-popular bands will purchase the series, this further decreases the chances that diehard fans of popular acts will get good seats to their favorite popular band(s), which provides further incentive to purchase the subscription series.

The result is that every band in the series benefits from additional concert ticket sales—sales that would not have been realized had the band not been included in the subscription series. In a study of the effects of using subscription series to sell rock concert tickets during the 1991 summer concert season, Rafi Mohammed found that highly popular bands in a series benefited from the sale of an additional 724 tickets and less-popular bands benefited from the sale of an additional 3,187 tickets. This study controlled for many demand factors (e.g., a band's popularity in one region relative to another) and attempted to isolate how many additional ticket sales were directly attributable to subscription series.

Subscription series are profitable for promoters, venues, and the bands included in the series. A typical subscription series features two popular and two less-popular concerts. Thus, a typical subscription series sells an additional 7,822 tickets (extra tickets for two popular bands: 1,448; extra tickets for two less-popular bands: 6,374). At an average ticket price of $30, this is additional revenue of $234,660 per subscription series. Amphitheaters that use subscription series generally feature two to three of them during the summer season. Thus, on average, using subscription series can increase revenues by $469,320 to $703,980. Given that the concert is going to be held and there is excess capacity, the costs associated with accommodating extra concertgoers derived from the subscription series strategy are negligible. In addition to gaining extra ticket sales, bands in a subscription series benefit because new potential fans—fans that otherwise would not have attended their concerts—are exposed to their music. Additional revenues directly derived from using the subscription series strategy include series premium charges, parking fees, facility surcharges, and merchandise revenues.

ing vehicle for new releases. Being highly ranked on *The New York Times* bestseller list or *Billboard*'s music charts is a significant marketing vehicle and a signal to the industry and consumers.

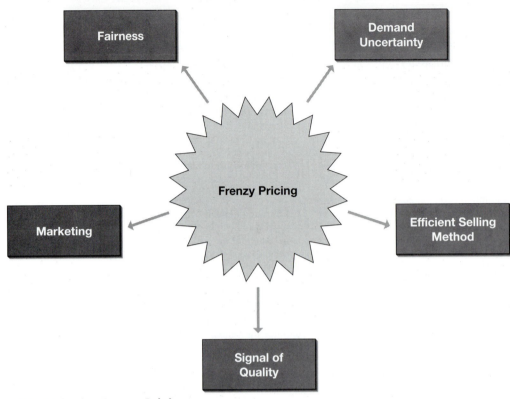

EXHIBIT 8.16   Frenzy Pricing

Frenzy Pricing

Firms often implement pricing schemes that result in significant excess demand due to low prices. This can occur for a variety of reasons (see Exhibit 8.16):

- *Fairness pricing.* As previously discussed, firms faced with excess demand may opt to keep prices below the market clearing price in an effort to maintain goodwill. This can create a buying frenzy.

- *Demand uncertainty.* When a firm brings a new product to market, there may be uncertainty about whether the market will accept the product. If demand is unexpectedly high, retailers and manufacturers are often risk-averse in terms of increasing prices once some products have been sold at a lower price. As discussed in the fairness section, consumers often accuse firms of price gouging when they raise prices during periods in which demand exceeds supply. While it may be more profitable to increase prices, the potential for adverse publicity may dissuade firms from doing so.

- *Marketing.* A key derivative of frenzy pricing is the frenzied nature of the consumers who are trying to obtain a good. This frenzy often leads hopeful consumers to sleep outside of stores, bid on auction sites, or frantically drive from store to store to find the product. This consumer frenzy often creates media coverage. During the 2000 holiday shopping season, one of the "must have" gifts was the Sony PlayStation 2. The buying frenzy began in late October 2000, when Sony announced that, due to production problems, it was only going to ship half of the 1 million units that it had promised to release in the United States. This announcement created a frenzy among consumers eager to purchase the machines.

Despite the significant demand and low supply, Sony maintained its suggested retail price of $299. After the late October release of half a million units, Sony added an additional 100,000 units per month. Many consumers capitalized on the shortage and took to reselling brand new PlayStation 2s on Internet auction sites such as eBay. AuctionWatch.com reported that when the PlayStation 2 was released, its average selling price on auction sites was $950. By mid-December, after initial demand had been satisfied and supply had increased, the average auction selling price dropped to $445.[21] The result of the tremendous consumer frenzy surrounding the PlayStation 2 was an unprecedented amount of free publicity. With the media playing up the PlayStation 2 as the must-have product of the season, consumers became aware of the product and demand significantly increased.

- *Signal of quality.* If prices are set so that there is excess demand, many may view this as a signal or verification of high quality. For consumers, there are often high search costs involved in determining product quality.

- *Efficient selling method.* Disney has created buying frenzies with the release of several of its classic animated movies (e.g., *Fantasia, Pinocchio*) by announcing that the films would be sold for a limited time; after that time period, the company said, the video would not be available at retail outlets for several years. This type of strategy creates hype in the media and encourages consumers to purchase the item immediately. It also allows Disney to concentrate its marketing in a very finite phase and efficiently sell as many or more videos than it would if it made the videos constantly available.

Strategic Responses to Competitor Price Cuts

Competitors often attempt to decrease price in an effort to gain market share. As a general rule, competing solely on price is not a wise long-term strategy for any company. When a firm embarks on a major competitive price cut, Wall Street often punishes all of the companies in the industry by lowering stock prices. Wall Street's intuition is that when a firm initiates a price cut, competitive companies will be forced to match. Price wars lower profit margins. These lower prices are not generally made up for by increased sales, thus they negatively affect profits (see Exhibit 8.17).

When a competitive firm initiates a price decrease, a firm's first response should be to understand why its competitor is decreasing prices. Understanding a competitor's motives can help a firm decide how to respond to the price cut. Typical motives for price-cutting include:

- *Financial trouble.* Decreasing prices may be a desperate attempt to raise cash, or signal to competitors an interest in being acquired.

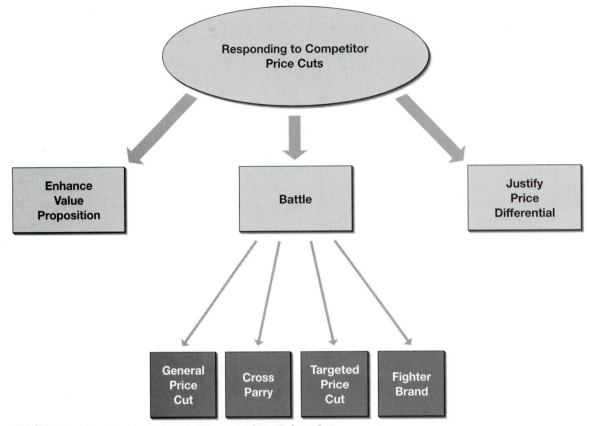

EXHIBIT 8.17   Responding to Competitor Price Cuts

- *Attempting to become an industry leader.* Decreasing prices is sometimes a show of strength. Slashing prices may indicate that a firm is doing well enough to withstand the lower costs, or is willing to endure hardship to become an industry leader. This action may intimidate competitors into allowing the firm to become an industry leader.

- *Signaling displeasure over a competitor's strategy.* A firm can use a price cut to punish a competitor for a change in its strategy.

As a general rule, firms should avoid competitive price-cutting that could lead to a price war. Discounting price lowers margins, often damages the brand, and conditions customers to pay less. While price wars are beneficial to consumers, they are detrimental to firms' balance sheets. In general, firms have three responses to competitors' price cuts: (1) enhance the value proposition, (2) battle, and (3) justify the price differential.

Enhance the Value Proposition

One price-cut reaction is to boost the product value proposition by maintaining the price level and offering product enhancements. Typical product enhancements include additional services, extended warranties, and the inclusion of ancillary products. While arguably similar to decreasing price, offering enhancements does not condition consumers to expect lower prices or potentially disrupt the image of the brand. Hotels often use enhanced packages to entice travelers. Weekend packages often maintain price levels but include such extras as complementary wine, free parking, late checkout, and dining discounts. These enhancements increase the attractiveness of staying at the hotel without lowering the price.

Battle

In addition to the often costly general price-cutting attack, there are three potentially less costly surgical attacks that a firm might launch: (1) a cross-parry attack, (2) a targeted response, and (3) fighter brands.

General Price-Cutting Attack.   Responding to a price cut with a matching or lower price cut sends a clear signal to competitors. In the delicate chess game played in many industries, responding with a price cut indicates to competitors a willingness to fight strongly—and puts the industry in a position in which all the market players will lose money. It also conveys resistance to letting the initial price cutter become the industry leader. Battling may prove costly, but in the long run it may be the most profit-protecting strategy to employ because it establishes an aggressive reputation that may inhibit similar future actions by current competitors and/or potential entrants.

Cross-Parry Attack.   In order to grow profits, an established firm might branch out into a new product line or extend its geographical presence. As a company like Amazon.com tries to monetize its large customer base, it will undoubtedly enter new product markets and harm market incumbents. Instead of engaging in a price war, incumbent firms can enter into marketing agreements with Amazon's strategic competitors (e.g., Tower Records) that would hurt Amazon's core business—selling books and music. As a result, Amazon may have to pull resources from its effort to enter the new market in order to protect its core business. Moreover, the incumbents have sent a strong message to Amazon and other potential entrants not to enter their market.

A similar response can be employed when a firm expands into a new geographic territory. Instead of fighting on price in the new territory, established firms may opt to fight on the new entrant's primary turf. The effects and intent of geographic cross-parry are similar to the effects of a core product cross-parry. A geographic cross-parry attack may force the price-discount aggressor to retreat in order to concentrate on protecting its geographic territory. This action also sends a signal to future potential entrants/price aggressors.

Targeted Response.   Localized response is a form of price discrimination. A competitor may heavily advertise a discounted product price in certain markets and media formats. Instead of simply lowering the product price to match the competitor's price, a firm may opt to heavily advertise in the same markets and media. This strategy involves requiring consumers to mention a special promotion code when ordering the product. By structuring a matching price decrease in this fashion, the firm only discounts prices to consumers who may otherwise defect to the competing product simply because of a lower price.

Fighter Brands.   One method of responding to a price decrease is to create a fighter brand. Fighter brand products are noticeably different from the firm's regular product and are used to retain the firm's price-sensitive customers. The hope is that the firm's price-insensitive customers will continue to purchase the primary product and that price-sensitive customers will purchase the fighter brand. Fighter brand products are frequently seen in the fast-food industry. For example, Burger King often significantly discounts its signature Whopper. In response to this price promotion, McDonald's created a fighter brand by offering a non-regular menu item—a double cheeseburger—at a discounted price. McDonald's hoped that its price-insensitive customers would continue to purchase the Big Mac; it also hoped that instead of defecting to Burger King, its price-sensitive customers would stay with McDonald's and purchase the double cheeseburger. In a response similar to McDonald's price promotions on its signature brand sandwich, the Big Mac, Burger King often offers a discounted sandwich that is suspiciously similar to a Big Mac. Burger King's fighter brand, the Big King, has two beef patties and three bread pieces.

Justify Price Differential

In many industries, firms could do a better job informing consumers about how their products are differentiated from competing products. Price wars often occur when new low-cost airlines enter a market currently being served by well-established airlines. Incumbent airlines are often quick to match a new entrant's price when they may have other options. Instead of matching prices, incumbent airlines could inform consumers of the benefits of flying with them. These benefits may include:

- Excellent frequent-flier program
- Spare aircraft in case one is grounded due to mechanical problems
- Routing options (due to an established airline's large network, it has a wide range of options for routing passengers experiencing flight problems such as cancellations and delays)
- Better statistics in terms of customer service, on-time arrivals, service personnel-to-passenger ratios, maintenance excellence, etc.

Instead of matching low prices by new entrants, a winning strategy for incumbent airlines may be to highlight why their services are significantly better, thereby justifying the higher price.

The Pricing Pentagon Framework

The Pricing Pentagon is a framework designed to help managers price products. It consists of a series of integrated steps that use both hard data and managerial insight to determine ideal pricing. When completed, the Pentagon yields two results: a coherent pricing strategy for managers to follow, and a set of price points that achieve the firm's pricing goals.

—Leaving money on the table. Don't discount unless you have to.

—Having a one-size-fits-all mentality. Offer options! Some people will want basic functionality while others will want super-functionality.

—Thinking that every segment is the same. It's not true! Some segments will value your product more than others. Try to price accordingly.

—Implementing price experiments on the Internet. Customers do not like companies to charge different prices for the same product without proper justification.

—Underestimating your competitors' reactions. Many companies have been burned by innocently changing prices only to be met by a full-fledged price war by outraged competitors.

—Discounting because everyone else is doing it. Brand strength or adding extra features (e.g., free upgrades) may temper the need to discount price.

—Misjudging the value of goodwill. Sure, goodwill is important in maintaining relationships, but think about whether you are giving up too much in terms of price. Customers may remain loyal even if you don't offer them the 10 percent discount.

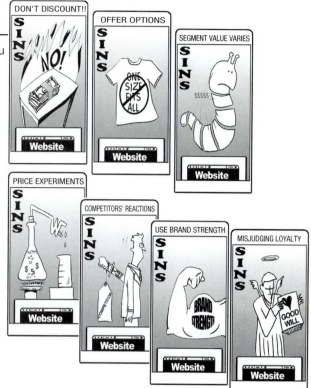

EXHIBIT 8.18   The Seven Deadly Sins of Pricing

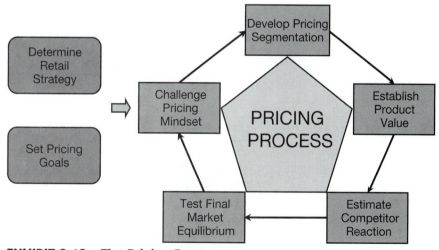

EXHIBIT 8.19   The Pricing Pentagon

Pre-Pentagon Decisions

The firm must make several important decisions before beginning the Pricing Pentagon process. Entering the process without adequate preparation will not yield optimal results.

Determine Retail Strategy

Firms must decide if they plan to pursue an everyday low pricing, Hi-Lo, or retail/outlet strategy.

Set Pricing Goals

Firms can use pricing to achieve a wide array of objectives; for example, fairness in pricing can serve as a tool to promote a brand in the same way that setting an artificially high price can convey a sense of superior quality. These goals represent marketing objectives, not strategic ones, but setting pricing goals must also map onto a firm's overall strategy. Achieving a substantial market share is a strategic pricing goal; using price to reach a particular segment of customers is a lever to achieve the goal.

Strategic pricing goals have widely varying implications, but in general can be divided into two categories: long-term value maximization and target pricing. Both provide the two critical components of any strategic pricing goal: a measurable determinant of success or failure, and objectives that are aligned with the firm's overall strategy.

Long-Term Value Maximization. This strategy requires managers to select price points that maximize discounted cash flow over a specified period of time. That is, a product should be priced to deliver the maximum revenue that can be realized (adjusted to consider the cost of capital used to finance the product's development). Few companies would claim that they strive to accomplish something other than long-term value maximization. However, managers often adjust their pricing tactics to achieve shorter-term objectives. This tension between long- and short-term goals can lead firms to set prices that do not necessarily lead to optimal value maximization over the long term, but that still may be the right decision from the overall strategic perspective of the firm.

Target Pricing. When firms choose an objective other than maximizing value, they usually do so because they want to use price to meet a particular short-term objective. Companies might use price to meet goals such as market share, revenue or profit growth, number of customers, or return on investment.

Pricing Pentagon Steps

Challenge the Mindset

Before identifying and testing any price points, managers must first challenge their assumptions about pricing. This is the most effective way for managers to establish if the company's mindset prevents the firm from meeting its pricing goals. Identifying those assumptions is perhaps the most difficult part of this process. Managers should start by looking at how they set prices in the past, and how those past decisions may have affected or limited current pricing strategies. What assumptions were made? What research formed the basis for the decision? If the answer is, "We've always done it this way," managers need to ask why. In order to best test their pricing mindset, managers should do the following:

Examine Artificial Constraints. Artificially imposed pricing boundaries limit a firm's creativity and flexibility, especially when they are unexamined. For example, deregulated companies often maintain a regulated mindset, and regulated companies often fail to shed the regulatory baggage when pricing products that are not regulated. Internal bureaucratic constraints, dated market research, risk averseness due to a past blunder, and goodwill constraints can all conspire to prevent firms from optimal pricing. Managers need to assess the effects of these factors on their pricing, and work to overcome incorrect or invalid assumptions.

Rethink the Value Proposition.   Does a firm's value proposition enable or prevent it from reaching its pricing goals? Managers need to understand what the market values, and what the firm's resources allow it to deliver. Manufacturers of rental bowling shoes, for example, are reluctant to sell shoes to the public. Bowling shoe rentals are a key revenue stream for bowling alleys; manufacturers fear that bowling alleys, their core customers, will lose revenues if too many people own bowling shoes. However, there is a segment of customers that wants to wear bowling shoes purely as a fashion statement segment, and has no intention of bowling in them. Understanding that segments may use a product for entirely different reasons could lead the rental shoe manufacturers to find a new outlet for their shoes—perhaps even at a premium price. Managers also need to understand the significance of switching costs, especially in the context of how they affect pricing power. Amazon.com has millions of loyal users. How many would stop buying if prices rose a mere 2 percent? Firms need to understand their market power and leverage it in their pricing.

Rethink the Competition.   Managers who price the same way their competitors do should reexamine their tactics; as the old adage goes, just because everyone is doing it does not make it right. Managers also need to reexamine their assumptions regarding who their competitors are. Perceived competitors are not always real. Also, responses to price cuts and competitive moves should be rethought. Historically, airlines have tended to overreact to competition. Why should American and United, which control the nonstop Boston-to-Los Angeles route, respond to a low-price competitor by slashing all their fares, especially if the new carrier flies only once per day? More recently, airlines have limited their responses to compete only with flights that depart at similar times. Last, managers should consider versioning to meet the competition, instead of fighting head-on by slashing prices. Health clubs offer versioned products; for example, a membership that does not allow prime-time usage of the facilities is often priced lower than one that does.

Challenge the Pricing Strategy.   Firms can rethink their overall pricing strategy by focusing on two primary issues: bundling and an often overly cautious attitude on reference prices.

There are three points on the price bundling continuum: single product pricing, mixed bundles, and pure bundles. Each pricing strategy offers different profit opportunities for firms to explore. Managers need to establish where they are on the bundling continuum and examine whether their position is unnecessarily limiting their options in a way that detracts from their goals. In some situations, firms will only need to play at one point to reach their goals; in others, they can play profitably at different points on the continuum. In some instances, firms that have traditionally bundled their offering might benefit from unbundling it. CNN, for example, which is traditionally bundled with a cable package, could broadcast over regular airwaves to customers who buy a descrambler and pay a monthly fee. The point here is not that CNN *should* do this, but that they ought to consider all options for improving their pricing strategy.

Finally, managers need to ask if reference prices matter in their business. Many have argued that once a firm cuts its price, it is very difficult to turn around and increase it later. While this may hold true in some industries, it is not universally applicable. For example, hotels often vary prices by a multiple of three or more, depending on demand; this is especially true at resort properties with high and low seasons. If reference prices are indeed less important, firms can use pricing levers to capture additional revenue without fear of alienating their current customer base.

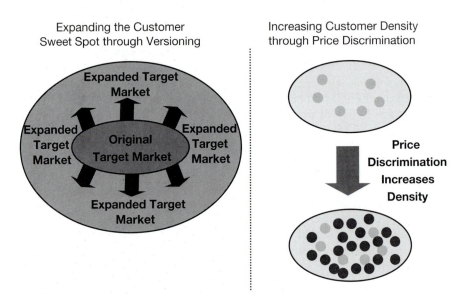

EXHIBIT 8.20   Strategic Segmentation: Expanding and Increasing the Density of the Target Customer Sweet Spot

Price Maximizing Segmentation

Once detrimental mindsets have been eliminated, the next step of the Pricing Pentagon requires firms to implement a price segmentation. Two such segmentations designed to help firms price-maximize are (1) versioning segmentation, and (2) price discrimination segmentation.

Versioning Segmentation.   Versioning segmentation helps firms increase the size of their target market's sweet spot by creating new versions of the core product that appeal to additional segments (see Exhibit 8.20). By giving an existing product new attributes that appeal to new segments, firms can amortize their core development and service costs over a larger customer base. The result is both increased margins and more potential customers. The level of profit per product may vary by versioning segment because some segments offer more profit potential than others. But as long as each versioning price is greater than the product's average variable cost and cannibalization is minimized, versioning is a profitable strategy.

Consider the credit card versioning strategy of American Express (Amex). The company offers more than 20 different credit card versions, each of which has attributes specifically designed to be attractive to its target segment. The range of Amex cards includes affinity cards, hip Blue cards, and prestige cards such as the Centurion card (annual fee: $1,000). The benefits on various credit cards range from music-related perks for Blue card members to elite frequent-flier status on several major U.S. airlines for Centurion card members. In addition to creating new products and profits at a relatively low cost, versioning has also enabled Amex to increase profits by amortizing its credit card fixed costs over a larger customer base as well as achieving economies of scale.

Bundling as a form of versioning can also be used to increase a firm's customer base. An airline, for example, can expand its sweet spot by selling travel packages (plane tickets, hotel accommodations, rental car, etc.) to customers interested in such packages—often an entirely different segment than customers interested in air travel exclusively.

Price Discrimination Segmentation. A price discrimination segmentation enables firms to serve more customers within a target segment—thus allowing firms to increase the density of customers served in their target customer segment. Within any firm's target segment, some potential customers may be interested in purchasing the product but unwilling to pay the full product price. A price discrimination segmentation allows a firm to serve more customers in its target segments by creating pricing strategies that are more sensitive to customers' willingness to pay (see Exhibit 8.20). Successful price discrimination requires that: (1) each price in a price discrimination strategy exceeds the variable cost of producing the product, (2) firms can readily identify price-sensitive customers, and (3) customers willing to pay the regular price can be isolated and prevented from buying the product at the lower price.

Oftentimes, a readily distinguishable characteristic is used to identify different customer segments. In an effort to increase sales to all film genre segments, movie theaters offer discount tickets for segments that they have identified as price-sensitive: students and senior citizens. Both segments can be easily identified by student ID or driver's license. Price discrimination can also involve segments that are implicitly identifiable; for example, retail stores may offer significant discounts during special sales that run from 6 AM to 8 AM on Saturday mornings. Staging a sale so early in the morning creates a price discrimination hurdle that distinguishes price-sensitive customers from less price-sensitive customers. Less price-sensitive consumers will not find it worthwhile to show so early. Similarly, price-sensitive customers will go through the hassle of clipping coupons while less price-sensitive customers will not.

Establish Product Value Relative to Substitutes

While company employees and market experts often have strong opinions about the value of a product relative to competing products, it is often helpful to gain quantitative insights about how *consumers* value a product relative to its potential substitutes. This data helps pricing managers not only set a product price, but also justify that pricing decision to senior management. Below is a brief overview of three general market research methodologies that provide quantitative insights into a product's value. The three methodologies that we focus on are: (1) traditional market research methodology, (2) conjoint analysis, and (3) discrete choice theory.

Traditional Market Research. Market research surveys cannot simply describe the product and ask customers how much they are willing to pay for it. The price that customers say they are willing to pay is invariably lower than what they are really willing to pay. However, by using multiple samples and designing the right series of survey questions, managers can derive data-driven insights that help establish how customers assign value to products. For instance, a survey might include various product and marketing related questions and end by asking if the respondent would purchase at a specific price. If three different surveys are distributed—one offering a relatively high price, one offering a medium price, and one offering a low price—overall demand can be estimated at each price level. Hence, price can be optimized. This data can then help managers sketch a demand curve to better understand how price affects consumer demand.

Conjoint Analysis. Conjoint analyses ask consumers to rank or rate products with differing attributes. By understanding how a group of customers ranks or rates these products, marketers can gain a clearer understanding of how customers value different product attributes and therefore what they might be willing to pay for them.

Discrete Choice Modeling. Discrete choice modeling is similar to conjoint analysis in that they both measure how consumers decide between competing products. The key difference between conjoint analysis and discrete choice modeling is that in the latter, consumers choose one preferred product rather than rank and rate different product versions. Discrete choice modeling tends to be more reliable because it closely mimics the product purchase process, asking consumers to select a preferred product from a set of competing products. Conjoint analysis is also more susceptible to imprecise data results because consumers have difficulty accurately ranking lower choices (for example, their seventh versus eighth choice), thereby introducing imprecise data to the analysis. Finally, discrete choice modeling allows firms to estimate induced demand. Simulators that estimate how consumers will react to increases or decreases in price can easily be constructed.

Estimate Competitor Reaction
While often informally done, it is essential for managers to formally incorporate anticipated competitor reactions into the pricing process. This is because no matter how meticulous managers are in setting price, their process becomes moot if competitors opt to respond to a new product price with a vigorous price war. Price wars often result in firms one-upping their competitors by repeatedly decreasing prices.

Avoid Setting a Price That Leads to a Price War

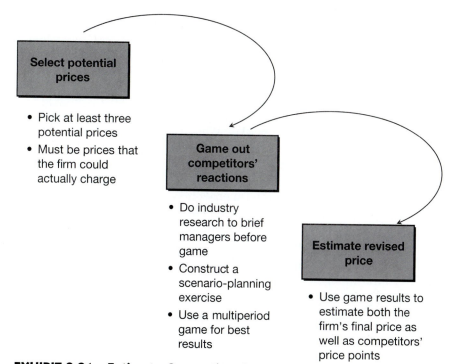

Select potential prices

- Pick at least three potential prices
- Must be prices that the firm could actually charge

Game out competitors' reactions

- Do industry research to brief managers before game
- Construct a scenario-planning exercise
- Use a multiperiod game for best results

Estimate revised price

- Use game results to estimate both the firm's final price as well as competitors' price points

EXHIBIT 8.21   Estimate Competitor Response

There is no question that competitors will react to a new product's entry and price. Thus, it is beneficial for firms to anticipate how competitors will react before they set a price—not after. Two strategies that firms might consider when deciding their pricing strategy are judo economics[22] and limit pricing.

Judo Economics.   One way to challenge large market share competitors is to be content being a small player in the market. Consider a new airline entrant that aggressively tries to take on established airlines by offering several new flights at prices lower than current prices in the New York-to-London market. This entry strategy leaves established airlines no alternative but to react strongly by matching or lowering airfares. If this occurs, the new entrant generally will lose; it is virtually impossible for a new entrant to match the quality and service level of established airlines or offer the same type of frequent-flier incentives. By entering the market in a way that gives competitors no choice but to lower or match prices, new entrants have little chance of surviving.

By being willing to be a small player in the market, a new entrant has a significantly better chance of surviving in the long run. Instead of entering the market with many flights at a low price, the new entrant could enter with a small number of flights at a low price. Established entrants must then decide how to react to the new entrant. It may not make economic sense to react strongly; decreasing prices may prove too costly. Established airlines would have to slash prices on all of their flights to fight a new entrant with low capacity. While established entrants may lose some business to the new entrant, it may be profit-maximizing to accept the entrant and the loss of business instead of embarking on a costly fare war.

Limit Pricing. When a firm produces a new product that consumers truly embrace, the firm is often faced with a difficult pricing decision: Should it maximize short-term profits or price in such a manner that discourages new market entrants? For popular new products, firms often charge high prices and earn significant profits. New entrants and fringe competitors will note the profit and try to enter the market. While it may take time to enter the market, once competitors enter, price competition is inevitable. This results in decreased profits. However, the firm does have an alternative. Instead of pricing high and making significant profits, the firm can strategically set a price that is lower than the short-term profit-maximizing price in an effort to deter new market entrants or fringe competitors. The firm sets a limit price that, because the firm is making profits (though they are not as high as they would be under short-term profit maximization), deters entry into the market. Whether a firm should profit-maximize in the short term or practice limit pricing depends on several variables:

- How long will it take for new entrants to enter the market?
- Once new entrants enter the market, how will profit be affected?
- How much profit will be made if the firm implements limit pricing (and how low will the price be)?
- If the firm implements limit pricing, how long does the firm realistically expect to reap profits?
- At what rate does the firm discount future profits?

Based on the above limit-pricing criteria, firms can determine whether it is realistic and profitable to price in a way that deters competitors from entering the market.

While there is no way for firms to unambiguously know how their competitors will react to a new price, some quantitative methods at least help narrow the range of possible reactions. The Pricing Pentagon draws upon basic game-theory principles to predict competitor reactions to pricing.

Select Potential Prices. From the information derived in the previous Pentagon steps, select a small set of potential prices. These prices should represent a range of high to low prices that a firm thinks it could realistically charge. This spectrum incorporates the price variance represented in a typical demand curve. The selected price levels should include high, medium, and low prices.

Game Out Competitive Reactions. "Gaming out" means estimating competitors' reactions to a new price through scenario planning. For each potential price, a potential competitive response is determined. Exhibit 8.22 illustrates a simple one-period analysis. A richer picture can be drawn from a multiperiod analysis. Consider a two-period analysis. In period one, the firm sets a new product price and then estimates how competitors will react to the new price. In period two, the firm may change its price in response to how its competitors reacted in period one. After deciding on a new price, the firm then estimates how competitors might react to the revised period-two price. At the end of this analysis, pricing managers will

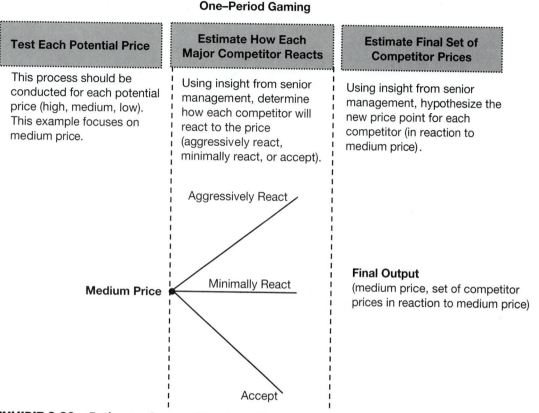

One–Period Gaming

Test Each Potential Price	Estimate How Each Major Competitor Reacts	Estimate Final Set of Competitor Prices
This process should be conducted for each potential price (high, medium, low). This example focuses on medium price.	Using insight from senior management, determine how each competitor will react to the price (aggressively react, minimally react, or accept).	Using insight from senior management, hypothesize the new price point for each competitor (in reaction to medium price).

Aggressively React

Medium Price — Minimally React

Final Output
(medium price, set of competitor prices in reaction to medium price)

Accept

EXHIBIT 8.22   Estimate Competitor Reaction

have an informed estimate of their revised product price as well as the reactive prices of their competitors.

Test Final Market Equilibrium

This final step of the Pricing Pentagon focuses on testing various prices with customers. At the conclusion of this step, a firm will have an estimate of the final market share and volume for each equilibrium set of its price and competing firms' final prices (see Exhibit 8.23). The firm can then select the price that best achieves its pricing goals. A wide variety of methods can be used to test how consumers will react to an equilibrium set of product prices. These methods include:

- *Market research.* This can be conducted by telephone, in person, by mail, or on the Internet.
- *Test markets.* By using a test market, a firm can observe how both rivals and consumers react to a new set of product prices. Information derived from test markets can help the firm decide what its final product price should be.
- *Senior management judgment.* In some cases, it may not be feasible to undertake market research or use a test market. In these cases, management judgment can serve as a substitute.

One clear output of the Pricing Pentagon is the ability for managers to estimate a product demand curve (see Exhibit 8.23). Once this demand curve is

Final Price and Volume Points Yield Estimated Demand Curve

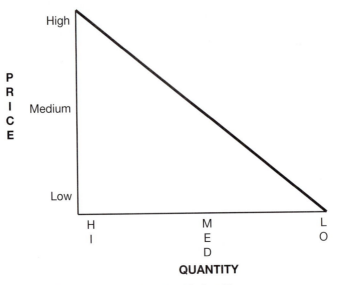

Note: Quantity Derived from Estimated Market Shares

EXHIBIT 8.23   Test Final Market Equilibrium

built, pricing managers can better understand and estimate demand at each price level, derive price elasticities, and select the price point that best achieves their pricing goals.

Implementation Across the Four Relationship Stages

So far, this chapter has discussed the variety of pricing levers and processes that firms can employ in their pricing strategies. This section describes which pricing levers should be used to bring customers through the four key stages of customer relationships (see Exhibit 8.25).

Awareness

Promotions.   These include:

- *Click-through promotions.* By clicking a banner ad, customers can receive price savings for purchases on the Internet.
- *Web referral promotions.* Promotional advertisements in print, mail, television, or radio point customers to a website by offering a price-discount promotional code.
- *Bricks-and-clicks promotions.* A firm can encourage consumers to start using its website to print out promotional coupons that are valid at retail outlets.
- *Web price discounts.* A firm can encourage consumers to use and become familiar with its website by offering discounts on products offered on the site. For example, many airline sites offer customers a 5 percent discount or additional frequent-flier miles for bookings made on the Internet.

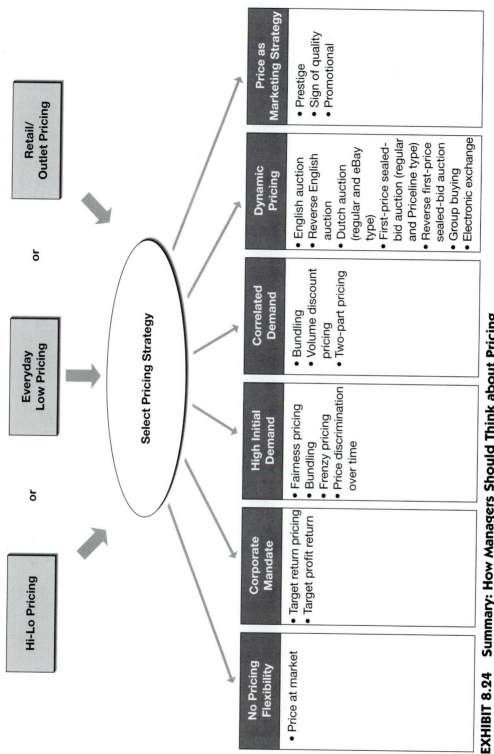

EXHIBIT 8.24   Summary: How Managers Should Think about Pricing

Four Key Stages of Customer Relationships

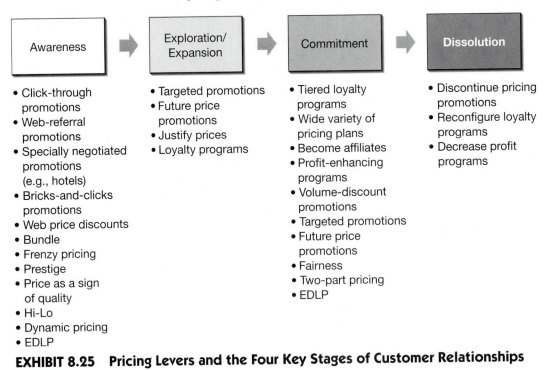

EXHIBIT 8.25   Pricing Levers and the Four Key Stages of Customer Relationships

Bundling.   To promote a product and gain awareness, a firm can create a bundled package of goods. By including a product in a bundle, the firm introduces new products to consumers.

Frenzy Pricing.   Consumer buying frenzies often occur when demand significantly exceeds supply. These frenzies often stimulate awareness because of media reports and frenzied consumers discussing their dilemma with others.

Prestige Pricing.   Prestige pricing creates an awareness signal to consumers.

Price as a Sign of Quality.   Again, price can be used in the awareness phase to signal quality to consumers.

Hi-Lo Pricing.   The low price associated with the Hi-Lo pricing strategy is often so low that it creates customer awareness.

Dynamic Pricing.   In some B2C cases, the novelty of the selling mechanism (e.g., auctions) creates customer awareness.

Everyday Low Pricing.   Consumers gain awareness and brand the EDLP retailer as offering value in the form of low prices.

Exploration/Expansion

Promotions.   These include:

- *Targeted price promotions.* As firms better understand their customers' needs, targeted price promotions can be used to guide customers to particular products.
- *Future price promotions.* Offering coupons (either for the firm's goods or specific goods that may be of interest to the consumer) that can be used in the future encourages consumers to learn more about the product and its related offerings.

Justify Prices.   While not a clear pricing tool, it is important to justify prices to consumers because it is easy for them to search for and understand competitive price offerings. Thus, it is important to convey to consumers a firm's product value and justify prices relative to competitive offerings. Websites offer firms the opportunity to comprehensively describe their products and justify their prices.

Loyalty Programs.   Loyalty programs encourage consumers to further develop a product relationship. In essence, loyalty programs are financial kickbacks. By receiving rebates for increased use, consumers are drawn into a deeper product relationship.

Commitment

Promotions.   These include:

- *Volume discount promotions.* Consumers are generally willing to purchase additional quantities of a good at a lower price. Given that online firms can easily track consumer purchases, they can encourage commitment by offering volume discounts to customers.
- *Targeted promotions.* Targeted promotions can be designed in a manner that compels customers to remain committed.
- *Future price promotions.* By being offered promotions that provide discounts on future purchases, customers are encouraged to maintain commitment.
- *Fairness.* By offering fair, nonopportunistic pricing, firms can maintain goodwill and commitment from their customers.
- *Two-part pricing.* By using a high fixed fee and a low variable fee pricing structure, firms induce consumers to remain committed. After paying the high fixed fee, consumers are likely to remain customers because they are charged a low variable payment for additional goods.
- *EDLP.* The branding derived from an EDLP strategy promotes commitment; EDLP promotes customer trust, and this trust in pricing promotes commitment.

Tiered Loyalty Programs.   Tiered loyalty programs encourage loyalty among a firm's most committed customers by creating high switching costs. Frequent-flier programs are often tiered according to the frequency with which customers travel; for example, travelers who fly occasionally are offered different rewards than travelers who fly more than 100,000 miles per year. Travelers who fly occasionally generally receive one frequent-flier mile for every mile flown. Meanwhile, most airlines award travelers who fly more than 100,000 miles per year two frequent-flier miles for every mile flown, and also provide them with first-class upgrades. These rewards make it difficult to switch airlines.

However, such programs can become excessively expensive if not targeted well. A colleague of ours used to regularly commute between the East and West coasts, and was in a major airline's 100K frequent-flier tier. He watched airfares carefully, and many times ended up paying under $250 for a roundtrip flight. Thus, for $250, he flew roundtrip in first class (he received unlimited first-class upgrades because he was in the airline's 100K tier) and also earned over 15,000 frequent-flier miles on each roundtrip due to the special promotions targeted toward him. Given that it generally takes 20,000 to 25,000 miles to earn a free roundtrip, he was being rebated more than 50 percent of a free flight each time he flew across the country.

Wide Variety of Pricing Programs.   For most products, there is a wide spectrum of consumers who have different product needs. By offering a variety of pricing plans, firms give consumers the opportunity to select the pricing program that best suits their needs. For example, cellular phone companies offer a wide range of pricing plans, which allows customers to select the plan that best suits them based on their usage patterns.

Affiliates.   In the commitment stage, a firm can use prices to turn committed customers into product evangelists. By becoming affiliates (e.g., Amazon's affiliate program), committed customers can financially benefit from advocating the product to others. Likewise, many firms offer "refer a friend" programs that provide financial incentives to current customers who refer friends.

Profit-Enhancing Opportunities.   Dynamic pricing websites such as eBay can help sellers increase their profits. By offering community feedback, eBay gives buyers the opportunity to comment on the quality of their interactions with sellers. Positive feedback can build a seller's brand. On average, buyers are willing to pay more for products offered by sellers with good reputations than for products offered by sellers with poor reputations.

Dissolution

Discontinue Pricing Promotions.   By tracking consumer purchases, a firm can identify unprofitable customers and discontinue targeted price promotions.

Reconfigure Loyalty Programs.   Firms can reconfigure programs to discourage relationships with unprofitable customers. In the case of our colleague who made the most of an airline's tiered frequent-flier program, the airline could have imposed a minimum airline ticket price as a criterion for being a full-fledged 100K member.

Adversely Affect Profit Programs.   Much like the profit-enhancing opportunities discussed in the previous section, offering critical feedback about sellers can be used to negatively affect their brand. Poor community feedback will dissuade buyers and adversely affect sales.

eBay Example

Pricing at eBay can be viewed from three different perspectives: the buyer's, the seller's, and eBay's. Buyers on eBay are exposed to two kinds of pricing: fixed-price auctions and dynamically priced auctions. Fixed-price auctions appeal to buyers who do not want to experience the stress and uncertainty of the traditional auction format; they also provide a way for eBay to compete with major online and offline retailers on a range of commodity and easy-to-find items. Both strategically and financially, the fixed-price format (which was not a feature of the original business launched in 1995) has become important to eBay. In 2001, 19 percent of eBay's sales revenue came from fixed-price auctions on eBay Stores, Half.com, and Buy It Now, with the bulk of the revenue coming from Buy It Now.[23]

The majority of eBay auctions are dynamically priced auctions, whether of the English or new-economy Dutch variety. In these auctions, it is the seller, not eBay itself, who determines the pricing strategy. Some individuals, such as those using eBay to rid themselves of items gathering dust in the attic, may not spend much effort determining their pricing strategies; others, including small-business owners, increasingly rely on eBay auctions for some or most of their revenue. For them, pricing decisions can mean the difference between the success and failure of their business enterprises.

EBay does not charge individuals for browsing, bidding, or buying items. Instead, the company generates revenue by charging listings fees and, increasingly, for final payment collection.

Listings Fees

The eBay model is a simple one: Sellers register items they want to sell, either on the eBay platform (dynamic auctions or fixed-price Buy It Now auctions) or the fixed-price Half.com platform. Half.com charges a flat 15 percent commission based on the final sale price, but no insertion fee. However, all items on eBay are charged a small insertion fee, which varies according to the minimum bid sellers are asking for, the type of item being auctioned, and the length and format of the auction. Insertion fees for standard auction items range from $0.30 to $3.30. These fees can reach as high as $300 for certain real estate auctions. eBay provides sellers with basic templates to use to list their auction items, but charges a premium for special treatments, placement, and other frills. The insertion fees are nonrefundable, and they vary by the type of listing chosen. There are three types of listings:

- Vehicle listings cost $25 for motorcycles and $40 for passenger and other vehicles.
- Real estate listings vary depending on whether they are timeshares, land, residential houses, commercial buildings, etc. (see Exhibit 8.26).
- All other listings, including eBay Dutch auction listings, are charged insertion fees based on the minimum bid for an item; reserve auction listings carry an additional fee ranging from $0.50 to $2 depending on the amount of the reserve price.

Real Estate Timeshare and Land	
Listing Type/Duration	**Insertion Fee**
Auction Format	
3-, 5-, 7-, or 10-day Listing	$50
30-day Listing	$75
Ad Format	
30-day Listing	$100
90-day Listing	$200

Residential, Commercial, and Other	
Listing Type/Duration	**Insertion Fee**
Auction Format	
3-, 5-, 7-, or 10-day Listing	$100
30-day Listing	$150
Ad Format	
30-day Listing	$150
90-day Listing	$300

All Other Real Estate Categories	
Listing Type/Duration	**Insertion Fee**
Auction Format	
3-, 5-, 7-, or 10-day Listing	$100
30-day Listing	$150
Ad Format	
30-day Listing	$150
90-day Listing	$300

Source: *http://pages.ebay.com/help/sellerguide/selling-fees.html.* Used with permission.

EXHIBIT 8.26   eBay Real Estate Insertion Fees

Exhibit 8.27 offers a more detailed look at eBay's insertion fee scale. For additional fees, sellers can promote their items with more visibility, more detail, longer duration, or in different categories. Exhibit 8.28 provides a list of these options and their costs.

Final-Value Fees

Final-value fees are charged only when an item on eBay is sold. For successful vehicle auctions, this is fixed at $25 for motorcycles and $40 for passenger and other vehicles. For real estate, there is no final-value fee even for successful sales. For other regular and reserve-price auctions, this fee is based on the closing bid. In Dutch auctions, the final value upon which the fee is

Minimum Bid, Opening Value or Reserve Price	Insertion Fee
$0.01–$9.99	$0.30
$10.00–$24.99	$0.55
$25.00–$49.99	$1.10
$50.00–$199.99	$2.20
$200 and up	$3.30

Reserve price auctions carry an additional fee, fully refunded if the item sells:

Reserve Price	Reserve Price Auction Fee
$0.01–$24.99	$0.50
$25.00–$199.99	$1.00
$200 and up	$2.00

EXHIBIT 8.27 eBay's Insertion Fee Scale for Regular, Reserve Price, and Dutch Auction Listings

Listing Option	Description	Fee
Homepage Featured	Item appears in a special featured section and will most likely be rotated for display on the eBay homepage	$99.95
Featured Plus!	Item appears in the featured-item section and in bidder's search results	$19.95
Highlight	Item listing is highlighted with lavender-colored band	$5.00
Bold	Item listing is displayed in bold	$2.00
Gallery	Item listing includes a small picture in the Gallery (eBay's miniature picture showcase)	$0.25
Gallery Featured	Item listed in the Gallery will also be featured at the top of the Gallery in a larger size	$19.95
List in Two Categories	Item listing appears in two categories, increasing visibility	Double the insertion and optional features fee
Ten-Day Auction Duration	Item listed for the longest listing duration available	$0.10
Buy It Now	Item available for sale instantly to the first buyer meeting a specified price	$0.05

Source: *http://pages.ebay.com/help/sellerguide/selling-fees.html*. Used with permission.

EXHIBIT 8.28 eBay's Listing Option Fees

Final Value	Final Value Fee
$0–$25	5.25% of the final value
$25–$1,000	5.25% of the initial $25 ($1.25) plus 2.75% of the amount above $25
Over $1,000	5.25% of the initial $25 ($1.25) plus 2.75% of the initial $25–$1,000 ($24.38) plus 1.5% of the amount above $1,000

EXHIBIT 8.29   eBay's Final-Value Fee Schedule

based equals the lowest successful bid multiplied by the quantity of items sold. The final-value fee for regular, reserve price, and Dutch auctions is determined as follows (see Exhibit 8.29):

1. Take 5.25 percent of the first $25 of an item's final value. If the item sold for less than $25, that is the final-value fee.

2. If the final value is between $25 and $1,000, calculate 2.75 percent of that number.

3. If the final value is more than $1,000, take the amount above the $1,000 and calculate 1.5 percent of that number.

4. Add the amounts together for the total final-value fee.

Sometimes, final-value fees are partially or fully credited back to individuals, such as when the highest bidder's check bounces.

Fairness

To ensure fair auctions, eBay has implemented the following procedures:

- It insures its auctions with fraud protection if an item is not received or is less than advertised, and will refund bidders up to $200 (with a $25 deductible).
- It investigates allegations of abuse of the online auction process.
- It offers an escrow service in which the buyer pays the escrow service, the seller ships the item to the buyer, the buyer inspects and approves the merchandise, and then the escrow service pays the seller.
- It offers an online dispute-resolution service. Disgruntled buyers and sellers can try to solve their disputes on their own or with the assistance of a professional mediator.[24]

Payment Fees

eBay realized that there was more value to be captured from its auctions than listings and placement fees. In 1999, eBay acquired BillPoint, a Silicon Valley startup that provided technology for person-to-person payments through the Internet, and rebranded the service eBay Payments. In July 2002, eBay announced its intent to acquire PayPal, the largest automatic payment provider on eBay. With these acquisitions, eBay is able to capture back-end transaction fees on an increasingly large percentage of its auctions. Transaction fees range from $0.35 for items under $35 to 2.5 percent of the auction's final value, capped at $200 per transaction (see Exhibit 8.30).

Payment Type		Account Type	
		Merchant Account	Standard Account
Credit Card			
Transaction Fee	Transaction of $15 or less	35¢	35¢
	Transaction over $15	35¢ + 1.75%	35¢ + 2.5%
Auto Deposit Fee (for transactions over $15)		0.50%	0.50%
Per Transaction Limit		$2,000	$500
Electronic Check			
Transaction Fee	Transaction of $15 or less	35¢	35¢
	Transaction over $15	35¢ + 0.75%	35¢ + 1.5%
Auto Deposit Fee (for transactions over $15)		0.50%	0.50%
Per Transaction Limit		$200	$200

EXHIBIT 8.30   eBay Payments Fee Schedule

1. **What is the relationship between price and demand? Why is it important for a firm to price at the point at which marginal revenue is equal to marginal cost?**

Most goods exhibit an inverse relationship between price and demand. Consumers set internal reservation prices for products, and they will purchase a product as long as the price is less than or equal to their reservation price. Within a limited price range for any good, there will be a set number of product units demanded at a price point. As price increases, demand will decrease because fewer consumers will have a reservation price that is greater than or equal to that price. For instance, fewer consumers will purchase a product if it is priced at $100 than if it is priced at $1.

At the point at which marginal cost equals marginal revenue, it is not profit-maximizing for the firm to change its price. If marginal cost is less than marginal revenue, it would make sense for the firm to sell an extra good because the additional revenue would be greater than the good cost. Similarly, if marginal cost is greater than marginal revenue, the cost of selling the good (in terms of the cost of an additional good) is greater than the revenue derived from selling the additional good.

2. **Why should a firm consider fairness when pricing its goods?**

Consumers often develop a relationship with a brand; they also label firms that raise prices when demand exceeds supply as opportunistic. By being labeled opportunistic, the firm risks aggravating consumers and losing profits in the long run. To avoid this backlash, firms often opt to price in a manner that consumers deem fair. By maintaining fair pricing, firms sacrifice short-term profits to maintain a long-term relationship with consumers.

As discussed in the Drill-Down on pricing in the rock concert industry, firms have latitude when considering price points. By gradually educating/exposing consumers to market-based pricing, consumers will be more accepting of market pricing.

3. **How has the Internet enhanced opportunities for dynamic pricing strategies?**

While various forms of dynamic pricing have been in existence for centuries, the Internet has made dynamic pricing more viable because it has enabled a larger community of buyers and sellers to participate in dynamic pricing. This enhanced community of buyers and sellers has made auctions more efficient. Additionally, the 2Is have fostered dynamic pricing. Buyers and sellers utilize the interactivity component of the Internet to easily post new products, new information, and new bids. The interactivity component of eBay's community creates a forum for users to provide input on the reputations of buyers and sellers. This feedback is important in establishing trust in the auction process. From an individual perspective, the Internet allows sellers to post products or RFPs to bid on. In a similar matter, bidders can individualize their product bids.

4. Why would a firm want to implement a price-discrimination strategy?

Price discrimination involves a firm selling the same (or similar) product to different customer segments at different prices. Many different customer segments are interested in purchasing most products. Given that each segment has a different demand structure, it is often profit-maximizing to set different prices for each segment. For instance, the optimal price for *The Wall Street Journal* is higher for the Wall Street investment-banking segment than it is for the business-student market. By setting different prices, firms can profit-maximize in each segment. The two important characteristics of a price discrimination strategy are as follows:

- It must be difficult, or not worth it, for customers who receive the product at the lower price to resell the product to customers who are paying higher prices.
- It should be easy to distinguish members of one segment from members of another. If it is difficult to identify customers in different segments, it will be difficult to charge them different prices.

5. What is the difference between static and dynamic markets? Why must a firm consider its pricing strategies within the context of a dynamic market?

Static markets assume that markets are fixed—in other words, that they do not change or react due to the actions of a firm or outside forces. Dynamic markets assume a changing market. The market will shift and react to any movements by competitors or outside forces.

It is important for firms to assume that the markets that they are operating in are dynamic. The implication of operating in a dynamic market is that firms should assume and anticipate that competitors will react to a firm's actions. Thus, if a firm decides to embark on an aggressive pricing strategy, it should anticipate a response from its competitors. The final market equilibrium that results after a firm sets a new price is dependent on how competitors act—and then how consumers react to the final set of market prices.

Activities for Students

1. Select three consumer-to-consumer (C2C) auction sites, including eBay. Create a chart that compares and contrasts the attributes of each auction site. Under what conditions or circumstances would a seller use an auction site other than eBay?
2. Hotels often sell the same room to different customers at different prices. Use the Internet to search for sites that allow consumers to reserve hotel rooms (e.g., Expedia, Travelocity, Hyatt's website). For the hotel of your choice, find at least three different prices for the same room type for the same day. Why would these different sites offer different rates for the same hotel room? Often the savviest customers get the best prices—is that fair to the less savvy?
3. Amazon.com is currently positioning itself as an everyday low price leader. Select five different products offered on Amazon, then use the Internet to compare Amazon's prices with competitor prices. Does Amazon always offer the lowest price? After conducting this research, do you believe that Amazon is truly an everyday low price leader?

Key Terms

static market
dynamic market
dynamic pricing
auctions
price discrimination
bundling

[1]Bird, Laura. 1996. Back to full price? Apparel stores seek to cure shoppers addicted to discounts—A switch to 'value pricing' may help boost profits; outlet malls are chic—Avoiding a 'sale du jour.' *Wall Street Journal*, 29 May, A1.

[2]For more information, please see Hoch, Stephen J, Xavier Dreze, and Mary E. Purk. 1994. EDLP, hi-lo, and margin arithmetic. *Journal of Marketing*, October, 16-27.

[3]For more information, please see the Amazon press release site: http://www.corporate-ir.net/ireye/ir_site. zhtml?ticker=AMZN&script=410&layout=8&item_id=282755.

[4]Wilson, Ralph F. 2000. P4: Pricing strategy as part of your internet marketing plan. *Web Marketing Today*, May 9, 2000.

[5]Simester, Duncan. Note: Optimal promotion strategies: A demand side characterization. *Management Science*. Vol. 43 (2), 251-256.

[6]DeGraba, Patrick. 2001. The loss leader is a turkey: Volume discounts in competition. Federal Communications Commission Working Paper, 2 January.

[7]For more information, please see Rajendram, K.N. and Gerald J. Tellis. 1994. Contextual and temporal components of reference price. *Journal of Marketing*, Winter, 22.

[8]Coy, Peter. 2000. The power of smart pricing. *Business Week*, 10 April, 160.

[9]For more information, please see Thaler, Richard. 1995. Mental accounting and consumer choice. *Marketing Science*, Summer, 199–214.

[10]Hilburn, Robert. 1994. They can tell you why; welcome back to the Hotel California: After split-up that left anything but peaceful, easy feelings, the Eagles are together again, Don Henley and Glenn Frey are writing songs—and they promise it's not a money thing. *Los Angeles Times* 22 May, Calendar, 6.

[11]Hilburn, Robert and Jerry Crowe. 1996. Return of the dinosaurs; Long-gone bands from the 70's are reuniting with alarming frequency. Why?Because they can. Even the Sex Pistols realized that going on tour would make sense. Or at least dollars. *Los Angeles Times* 23 June, Calendar, 8.

[12]Rangan, Kasturi. 1999. *FreeMarkets online*. Case no. 9-598-109, 26 February. Boston: Harvard Business School Publishing, 19.

[13]Varian, Hal. 2000. Economic scene:Online auctions as a laboratory for economists to test their theories. *The New York Times* 16 November, Business/Financial.

[14]For more information, please see the eBay.co.uk site. http://pages.ebay.co.uk/help/basics/f-format.html#dutch.

[15]Fox, Justin. 1999. The Salon.com IPO and other paragons of reason rational exuberance. *Fortune*, 19 July.

[16]Milgrom, Paul. 1989. Auctions and bidding:Aprimer. *Journal of Economic Perspectives Summer*, 3–22.

[17]Moran, Nuala. 2002. Fallout is far from over in electronic marketplaces: Although many public online B2B exchanges have failed, there is optimism concerning private exchanges. *Financial Times*, 13 March 2002.

[18]Klein, B. and L. Saft. 1985. The law and economics of franchise tying contracts. *Journal of Law and Economics* 28:345–361.

[19]Siegal v. Chicken Delight, Inc., No. 46271-GBH, United States District Court for the Northern District of California, 311 F. Supp. 847; 1970.

[20]See the following two cites: Grover, Ronald. 2000. Doing what he does best Mike Ovitz is packaging his clients all over town. *Business Week*, 24 July, 42. Grover, Ronald, Mark Landler and Michael Oneal. 1993. Ovitz—How Many Fields Can the King of Hollywood Conquer. *Business Week*, 9 August, 50.

[21]Barnes, Julian F. Sony toy is less costly, but still scarce. 2000. *New York Times*, 17 December, 39.

[22]Gelman, Judith R., and Steven C. Salop. 1983. Judo economics: Capacity limitation and coupon competition. *Rand Journal of Economics*, 14, no. 2:315–325.

[23]Rick Gagliano, *The Wednesday Report*, 16 January 2002.

[24]For more information, please refer to the "Why is eBay safe" section of eBay.com. http://pages.ebay.com/help/basics/n-is-ebay-safe.html.

Communication

Communication, at its simplest, is about delivering a message. While companies have traditionally had options for delivering both personalized and interactive messages to customers, the Internet now enables a business not only to target its advertisements and to personalize its communications but also to engage in nearly constant two-way dialogue with its customers. With this powerful new set of tools, firms can interactively and personally communicate with users in order to move them from awareness to commitment, and in some cases, to dissolution.

This chapter will review the levers that firms can use to communicate with customers. It will also cover the major steps of the communication process, from identifying the target audience to executing and evaluating the campaign. The effect of the 2Is (interactivity and individualization) on the levers will be discussed, and examples of implementation of the marketing levers across the four consumer-relationship stages will be developed. The chapter concludes with an examination of eBay's approach to marketing communications.

QUESTIONS

Please consider the following questions as you read this chapter:

1. Why is marketing communication important?

2. What is the role of the Internet in a marketing communications campaign?

3. What are the main categories of communication types? Within each category, what are the tools, or marketing levers, that marketers use to communicate with consumers?

4. What are the six steps in the communication process?

5. How do the 2Is of the Internet affect marketing communications?

6. What levers are used in each of the four customer relationship stages?

Introduction

The Internet was designed to foster connectivity and allow efficient exchange of information. It has the potential to be more versatile than any other mass media channel, and is superior at targeting individual prospective buyers.[1] From its early days as a repository of free information, group discussions, and noncommercial linkages, the Internet has

---

Co-authored by David Bennion, George Eliades, and Katherine Jocz. With substantive input from Felice Kincannon.

evolved into a highly commercial medium replete with advertising and targeting opportunities. While the downside of this evolution is intrusive advertising that irritates many users,[2] the Internet is also unrivaled for providing customers with richly informative and entertaining marketing communications.

Communication in the form of mass advertising is often perceived as a one-way, one-to-many message from the firm to consumers. This fails to take into account the more personal forms of offline communication, such as direct mail and telemarketing, as well as the broad communication capabilities of the Internet. The possibility of two-way, real-time communication, and other characteristics, such as the 2Is, make the Internet a unique tool that has profound effects on the marketing process.

While the Internet introduces new possibilities, it does not change the fundamental principles of marketing communication. Companies must still move customers from awareness to commitment and, in some cases, to dissolution. Marketers must still choose specific communication objectives, plan and execute the communications campaign, and measure results.

The Internet does, however, change the game in crucial ways. Already, it has created a new communications context for all companies. Consumers' expectations are higher because of the capabilities they have experienced on the Internet, and that intensifies the need for firms to concentrate on managing communications with users. Internet customers expect easy interactions with a high degree of customization—and they expect them in Internet time. Firms that do not meet these expectations will become second-tier players.

This chapter is divided into the following sections:

- *Consumer-Centric Marketing Communications.* This section addresses the importance of effective communication in customer relationship management.
- *Importance of Integrated Communication.* This section discusses the importance of integrating online and offline communication levers in any marketing campaign.
- *The 2Is: Interactivity and Individualization.* This section highlights how the 2Is affect the communication levers.
- *Communication Types—The Marketing Levers.* This section explains and analyzes the communication levers available to marketing managers. It divides the levers into four categories: mass offline, mass online, personal offline and personal online.
- *Communications Process.* This section describes the process for communicating with users, from identifying a target audience and choosing a message, to developing a media plan and measuring its effectiveness.
- *Implementation Across the Four Relationship Stages.* This section integrates the levers into the marketing framework by demonstrating which levers should be used to advance customers through the four relationship stages.
- *eBay Example.* eBay's communication strategy is analyzed to show which communication levers it uses to move customers through the four relationship stages.

Customer-Centric Marketing Communications

Every interaction with customers involves communication. One trend in marketing communications is that the firm–customer relationship is becoming much more **customer-centric.** In other words, the balance of power is shifting toward the customer's side. For one thing, media options are proliferating, giving consumers more choices about how to spend their time. For another, the sheer amount of competitive communications forces companies to differentiate themselves by the overall experience that they offer to consumers. This is perhaps the main driver behind the emergence of **relationship marketing.** Relationship marketing strives to establish positive, comfortable relationships with customers—relationships in which firms anticipate individual customers' needs or wants and then present the relevant solution at the appropriate time. Establishing such relationships at the individual level raises consumers' switching costs, encouraging them to remain long-term customers of the firm.

As a communication medium, the Internet offers users tremendous power over how they interact with its content. A television viewer can use the remote control to avoid unwanted advertisements, but if he is interested in a commercial, he has no power to lengthen the ad or to further explore the offering. On the Internet, on the other hand, if an ad attracts attention, the consumer can elaborate on the message, go to a related website, and even make a purchase.[3]

The two-way dialogue that the Internet enables, and which Internet users have come to expect, transforms communications that have not traditionally

been considered marketing communications into advertisements. Customer service becomes a critical marketing component because users expect prompt, fast responses to messages during the exploration and commitment phases. Firms that fail to conduct a dialogue with their users will have less success than others.

The Internet, therefore, increases the power of both the customer and the firm. Customers have more control over what information they view, and the firm has more opportunities to move the customer through the relationship stages.

Importance of Integrated Communication

The goal of marketing—and thus communication—is to convey the right message to the right customers at the right time. Sometimes the right message is a billboard that creates awareness; sometimes it is a targeted e-mail offering a great deal or a personalized recommendation; sometimes it is a trade-show exhibit. Choosing relevant messages for particular customers takes a lot of work. It means not using the wrong medium and not giving a customer a message that is irrelevant based on previous behavior. It means that there must be synergy among all the messages sent to the consumer. All of this is part of what is called **integrated marketing communications** (IMC).[4]

Although this book concentrates on Internet marketing, any discussion about marketing communications must also include traditional marketing communication vehicles. The Internet does not replace existing channels; rather, it is a powerful addition that should be utilized in an integrated approach to marketing communications. Traditional and interactive marketing methods (and agencies) are converging as it becomes apparent that an integrated approach is crucial in today's world. Effective campaigns will mix online ads with traditional communications options, and will integrate strategies across the various Internet tools. Today's marketers must foster customer relationships, integrate media messages, and build and use consumer-information databases in tandem to communicate effectively.

The Internet wears many hats. It can be a distribution channel, an advertising vehicle, or a customer service vehicle, each of which plays a part in marketing communications.[5] The Internet also marries traditionally separate communication modes: Data, voice, and video media converge on the Web. (For example, the Internet can act as a radio, a DVD player for movies, and, to some extent, a television.) As this trend continues, there will be significant implications for marketing communications within these media. Wireless devices and broadband access are two vehicles that facilitate such convergence, and already they are gaining widespread acceptance. Marketers will have to discover how to best take advantage of these tools, and most agree that integrated communications is the best solution.

Unfortunately, integrating and coordinating marketing messages in a way that fluidly moves customers through the customer relationship stages remains one of the biggest pitfalls in the marketing communications field.

Problems can arise not only between the online and offline branches of campaigns, but also among internal company departments such as advertising and promotions.[6] Back in the late 1990s many Saturn automobile owners suffered from a blunder of this sort. GM is Saturn's parent company, and unfortunately for Saturn car owners, GM, GMAC, and Saturn all ran targeted postpurchase e-mail campaigns without coordinating their efforts. As a result, Saturn customers complained of e-mail boxes filled with special offers and other marketing messages, many of which had essentially the same content, from all three companies.

To be effective, an IMC approach requires support at the highest corporate level. Only then can a business avoid conflicts or confusion between different functional areas. High-level coordination is also imperative to ensure that marketing communications adhere to the marketing strategy and positioning objectives that define the target audience and value proposition for the firm's offering. These should guide the implementation of communications objectives over time and across multiple message platforms.

The 2Is: Interactivity and Individualization

The 2Is help firms to move users through the relationship stages efficiently and smoothly. By utilizing the online marketing communications levers in an interactive and individual way, firms can streamline the progression of the customer relationship in ways never before possible. For example, a banner ad can generate awareness and exploration due to the interactivity that a click-through provides. A user sitting at a browser can see an ad, click through to a website, explore it, and make a purchase. It is a seamless, interactive process that television, radio, and print cannot match, even if they provide a toll-free telephone number. This easy progression seems very promising for Web firms, but it can also be dangerous: The same characteristics allow Internet users to dissolve a relationship easily, too. An inaccessible site, poor navigation and controls, or a cumbersome registration process can lead users to point their browsers elsewhere.

The opportunity to communicate to users via the Internet in a more personalized and interactive manner is itself a significant boon to marketing communications (see Exhibit 9.1). The fact that the Internet also allows marketing communications campaigns to be executed and evaluated in real time makes Internet marketing even more attractive.

Interactivity

Interactive marketing communications are those that incorporate a mechanism allowing a recipient to respond. In other words, they facilitate two-way communication. Direct-response marketing, which includes direct mail, television ads with (800) numbers, and telemarketing, is a form of interactive marketing communications. However, the Internet excels at enabling dynamic marketing by providing multiple, near real-time interactions.

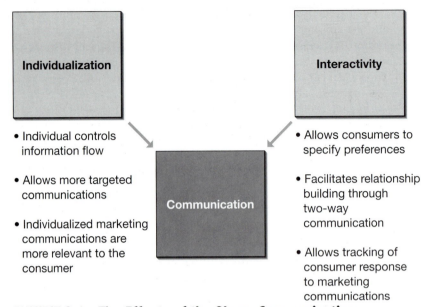

EXHIBIT 9.1   The Effects of the 2Is on Communication

Internet interactivity can create a closer relationship with customers through a number of mechanisms. For individuals looking for information, speedy provision of relevant details in response to an inquiry or a click of a button will encourage loyalty to the website. Some websites offer incentives such as giveaways or sweepstakes to promote trial or repeat purchases. Websites with games and entertainment create stickiness via fun activities. Other websites involve individuals on an emotional level by engaging them in a rich-media experience. John Hancock's famous banner ad—"I'm _ years old and I make $_ a year. What will I need to retire?"—followed a curiosity-based, or partial-information, strategy to create involvement with the communication and, ultimately, the product. Giving customers an opportunity to interact with a company through the Internet has been shown to increase commitment.[7] Interaction on the Web helps drive customers through the exploration stage and into the commitment stage, where the firm–customer relationship continues to deepen.

The more sophisticated forms of interactive marketing, both online and offline, employ **database marketing.** Here, all customer interactions are tracked, and the captured information is gathered, stored, and interpreted to help firms create a smooth, progressive relationship with their customers. Based on knowledge of an individual customer's behaviors and preferences, a firm can more effectively tailor messages and cross-market products. USAA, a company that provides insurance and other financial services to individuals and families with a military connection, is renowned for capturing such data and using it to select the form and timing of the next communication sent to the customer. USAA is also recognized for its ability to use individual and aggregate customer data to model a customer's needs during different life stages, including young adulthood, parenthood, and retirement. Effective database marketing gives businesses a way to avoid or manage premature dissolution of a relationship.

Thus, one of the main goals of Internet marketing is to use websites as a vehicle to drive consumers into the firm's marketing databases. These databases, full of consumer information, can help develop targets for future campaigns and provide ideas for new products or product improvements.[8] It is because of the Internet's ability to make messaging interactive that companies can do so much with database marketing. Sites like Amazon.com and My Yahoo! utilize the interactive nature of the Internet in order to offer customers individualized and customized online experiences. Indeed, either of the 2Is can be leveraged to enhance the other one, thus giving consumers more involved, intense marketing communications experiences online.

Individualization

Individualization of Internet marketing communications can be initiated by the user or the marketer. The power of the user to navigate a site in a unique pattern according to personal preference makes the Web medium an individual one. A user can also submit personal information and preferences in order to sign up for communications about specific items, on a specific schedule, and perhaps in a specific format (for instance, a daily digest version of an e-mail newsletter about country and western bands). The interactive characteristic of the Internet is what enables this kind of individual experience—users can generally state their preferences by clicking on a link.

Marketers can customize communications based on information stored in a database or according to information gleaned from tracking either a user's point of origination into a site or the user's navigation path on the site. Clearly, the more information the firm has about behavior and preferences, the more personalized an experience it can offer. When individualization is not possible or not warranted, marketers can still tailor communications to a narrow segment of consumers by choosing media placements apt to be seen by individuals in that segment. On the Internet, finer gradations of targeting are easier to achieve than with offline marketing tools. Furthermore, it costs much less to create and deliver individualized messages online.

One of the easiest and most common forms of personalization on the Internet reflects an understanding of the fact that people like to be recognized. Whether they are visiting the barber shop, buying something from the local grocer, attending church, or logging on to a familiar website, people feel good when they are greeted by name. Many sites use registration information to make their customers feel valued in this way. For example, once users register at *The New York Times* website (*www.nytimes.com*), each time they return they are greeted by a message that reads, "Welcome, <first name>."

Applying the 2Is

When marketers take full advantage of the interactive and individualization possibilities of the Internet, they can achieve much faster progression through the customer stages than with traditional media. To illustrate this point, imagine a father perusing the Internet. From a portal site, he sees a banner ad for the Crayola website, which specializes in creative activities for kids. If this were a magazine ad or a television commercial, it might create awareness, but these media do not offer any opportunity for further exploration, although they may refer consumers to a phone number, address, or

Point–Counterpoint

Personalization and Predicting Behavior

How can firms best reach customers? By targeting them with advertisements that they will find interesting and, therefore, be more likely to respond to. Of course, one of the most effective means of doing this is through personalization.

The major Internet-based marketers, such as Amazon.com, rely on the premise that they can determine which consumers will respond to certain banner ads or products based on their past behavior—that is, they depend on the notion that past behavior is predictive of preferences and current behavior.

But does behavior translate easily into preferences? Net Perceptions, an Internet firm that develops targeted marketing, claims that it can understand "what makes people tick." Certainly, its predictions are more accurate than random guesses, especially in product categories where people have strong preexisting loyalties or are purchasing out of habit.

On the other hand, Allen Weiss, a professor of marketing at University of Southern California, argues that prediction based on past behavior isn't reliable because purchase behavior is driven by goals, not past behavior. Moreover, personal goals constantly change. People make purchases to meet goals: to feel good, to make others feel good, to be fashionable, among others. Behavior doesn't provide much insight into these goals.

For example, how does past behavior really predict the likelihood of someone buying an infrequently purchased product like a television set, especially since both the product category and the consumer have changed substantially since the user's last purchase? Can Amazon.com really predict what kind of TV I will want in five years? What if I'm buying a TV for my bedroom instead of my living room? When a user buys gifts, what happens to his or her personalization profile?

So while predictions based on behavior can provide some value and are easier than guessing, they will not consistently meet the needs of users. Weiss suggests being sure that a website has an outstanding search engine to "accommodate the vagaries of human behavior."

---

website. Interested to see what the website is like, the dad clicks on the banner ad and immediately arrives at the Crayola homepage. After checking out the pictures and exploring a few of the links, he sees that it has sections specifically for kids, parents, and educators, with lots of fun children's activities. A pop-up window asks if he would like to register and obtain access to activity pages, contests, discounts, and a personalized newsletter. The father likes these features and immediately fills in his name and e-mail address and answers questions about his family.

A few minutes earlier, the father did not know such a site existed. Yet because of the unique characteristics of the Internet, especially its interactive nature and the individual's control of information flow, he quickly moved from the awareness stage, through the exploration/expansion stage, and started to cross the line into the commitment stage (see Exhibit 9.2). The Internet becomes a versatile marketing tool, as shown by its capability to deliver a seamless experience from the time it creates awareness until the user becomes a registered customer and perhaps even makes a purchase.

Ad targeting based on individual variables and click-stream data should increase conversion and engage customers. In practice, however, marketers are far from realizing the Internet's potential for delivering targeted com-

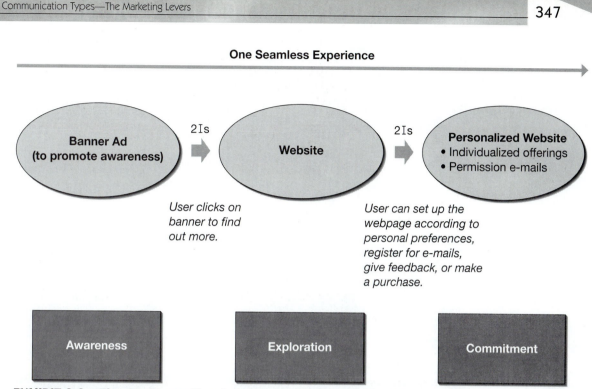

One Seamless Experience

Banner Ad (to promote awareness) → 2Is → **Website** → 2Is → **Personalized Website**
- Individualized offerings
- Permission e-mails

User clicks on banner to find out more.

User can set up the webpage according to personal preferences, register for e-mails, give feedback, or make a purchase.

Awareness   Exploration   Commitment

EXHIBIT 9.2   The 2Is Streamline Advancement through the Stages

munications with relevant content. There is still not enough integration between click-stream consumer data and the mechanisms that serve up individualized ads. Further, poor targeting and inappropriate frequency or sequencing in online advertising leads to consumer malaise. While the Internet provides unparalleled opportunities to communicate often, effectively, and personally, it also offers unlimited potential to communicate offensively and ineffectively. Now that consumers can choose to opt in or out of the communications they receive, companies have to make marketing communications, interactive or not, more direct and relevant on an individual level. One of the most interesting findings regarding marketing on the Internet is that giving consumers more control over information flow helps them better understand what they are examining, better match their preferences, and have more confidence in their decisions.[9]

Communication Types—The Marketing Levers

Moving customers from the awareness stage, through exploration and expansion, and ultimately to commitment or dissolution is a complex process that requires the interaction of multiple forces, including marketing communications. In the realm of communication, companies have a wide array of levers to move consumers through the stages. Marketing communications, which includes all the points of contact that the firm has with its customers,[10] can be grouped into four categories: (1) mass offline, (2) personal offline, (3) mass online, and (4) personal online. Exhibit 9.3 shows where

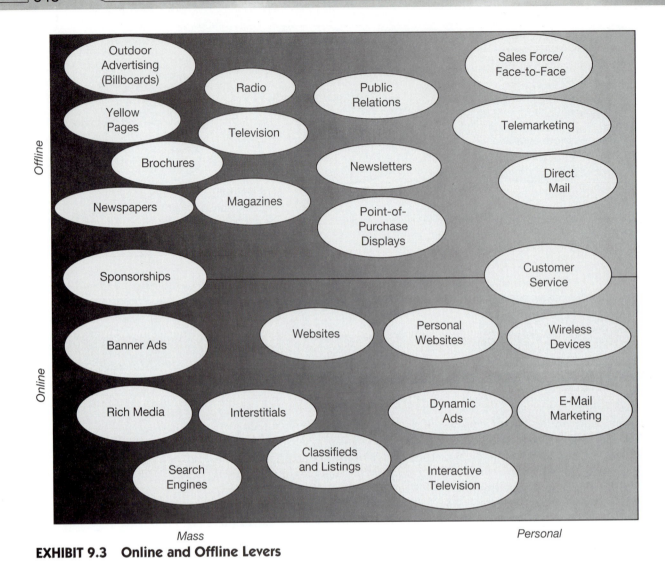

EXHIBIT 9.3   Online and Offline Levers

the available levers fall on the axes of mass to personal, as well as online and offline.

Categorizing each marketing lever can be difficult, not only because there are so many levers (and new ones are developed continually), but also because many can be used in multiple ways. E-mail, for example, fits best in the personal-online category, but "spam," or junk e-mail, might be better defined as a mass online marketing lever. Although gray areas do exist and not every lever fits perfectly into one category, understanding them in terms of the role they are best suited to is helpful.

Mass Offline Marketing Levers

Broadcast Media
Television.   Television advertisements come in two primary forms: the spot, which typically runs for 15, 30, or 60 seconds, and the infomercial, which can run for a half-hour or longer. Television's combination of visual, audible,

and moving images makes it the most persuasive and the most attention-getting medium. TV ads offer high reach, high frequency, and high believability. However, the trade-offs are substantial: high clutter, high absolute costs, fleeting exposure, and limited potential for targeting. Network television does not allow for easy viewer segmentation, although cable channels such as the History Channel and VH-1 do offer a less expensive way to reach a more targeted audience.

Consequently, television advertising is best suited for products that appeal to broad customer segments. Studies have also shown that television advertising is effective for new products. Apart from new-product promotion, however, substantial empirical evidence shows that TV advertising is generally not effective at increasing sales volume.[11] Despite such evidence, and despite its high clutter and lack of targeting potential, television remains the most popular medium among national advertisers, and many large firms allocate the bulk of their marketing budgets to TV ads. Two arguments for doing so are that TV ads help build brands over time, and that some level of advertising is needed to protect against competitive incursions.

Surprisingly, TV networks' advertising rates steadily increased through the 1980s and 1990s, even as their viewership numbers were shrinking. From 1980 to 2000, the networks' prime-time share of viewers fell from 92 percent to 56 percent, while the cost of a 30-second spot increased by more than 100 percent, and the cost to reach 1,000 homes increased by a factor of nearly four.[12] The trend did change in 2001, when broadcast advertising revenues declined by 12 percent from the previous year.[13]

Radio. Radio advertisements offer excellent selectivity by geographic region, demographics, and listener interests for a low cost in absolute terms. Radio also offers excellent reach and frequency, along with good impact. It can reach listeners at the same time they are consuming other media, such as reading print or using a computer, and in many places, including cars and shopping malls as well as workplaces and homes. More than 94 percent of Americans listen to radio each week, tuning in an average of more than 20 hours per week as of summer 2001.[14]

Disadvantages to radio advertising include radio's lower capacity to generate attention and its fleeting exposure, as well as the limitations of being an audio-only medium.

Outdoor. Outdoor advertising consists primarily of billboards, which can be either static or dynamic. A dynamic billboard may have moving parts or an electronically displayed text message that varies (for example, a lottery billboard that display this week's jackpot). These billboards come in various sizes and shapes, and are sometimes attached to mass transit vehicles, railroad cars, blimps, and planes.

Billboards offer excellent frequency, lower costs, and low clutter, but targeting is very difficult and reach is limited. They are best applied for image and branding. It is difficult to measure their effectiveness, because measuring impressions is extremely difficult and is typically limited to traffic counts, which bear little similarity to impressions. In the Unites States, spending on outdoor advertising grew less than 1 percent between 1999 and 2000 and accounted for only about 1 percent of advertising expenditures.[15]

Public Relations.   Public relations is an important part of a firm's marketing plan, and a firm's PR department can be used in various ways as an effective marketing lever. Most efforts would apply to the awareness and the exploration stages of the customer relationship spectrum, and would most likely be offline, though there are online PR applications.

For example, the duties of a large software company's PR department would include providing press releases to news sources such as industry magazines. Another important role would be to collect articles written about the company and the company's products and to extract highlights for use in promotional material. Often, third-party news and information providers such as Hoover's, Gartner, and CNet, which offer industry and company reviews, use releases from a PR department when writing their reviews. Effective public relations can clearly help to advance consumers through the early customer stages.

Print Media

Newspapers.   Newspaper advertising comes in several forms: traditional print advertisements, inserts, and classified advertisements. Newspapers offer excellent local market coverage. Over half of adults read a newspaper each day, and 64 percent read a Sunday paper.[16] Newspapers enjoy broad acceptance and trust as well as immediacy. Because of their immediacy, local retailers frequently run ads designed to trigger immediate action by consumers.

Consumers often look for ads in newspapers, and are predisposed to a firm's message. The various sections of newspapers, such as a living or arts section, can create additional context for advertisements. The regular publication schedule allows firms to tailor their messages to holidays or other events. Readers are actively involved in reading the paper; even needing to perform the simple act of turning the pages increases the level of attention.

Newspaper ads have a short life, however, and extending the range and frequency of a newspaper campaign can prove costly. Targeting is difficult, as the firm must pay to reach the paper's entire audience instead of a particular segment. (One exception is newspapers with local editions.) Image quality is generally poor. Also, newspapers have suffered significant declines in readership, especially younger readers. In the last 50 years, newspaper circulation has risen 4 percent while the population has grown over 80 percent.[17]

Magazines.   Magazines offer excellent selectivity on geographic and demographic terms. While general-interest magazines such as *Life* have declined in popularity, niche publications that focus on hobbies, professional interests, sports, business, and travel continue to attract readers and advertisers. Focused publications offer outstanding targeting opportunities, and because they often imply credibility and prestige, are ideal for advertising new products to enthusiasts and early adopters. Moreover, advertisers reap the benefits of high-quality reproduction and pass-along readership. Finally, magazines have a long life span, as many people save and reread them.

One drawback of magazines is the long lead time between an issue's preparation and publication. Also, while hundreds of new magazines appear each year, almost all of them special-interest magazines, failure rates are high.

Yellow Pages. The yellow pages offer credibility, local coverage, strong reach, and low cost. They offer an attractive value proposition: People who use yellow pages are ready to buy. Disadvantages include poor print quality and outdated information due to annual publishing schedules.

The use of printed yellow pages is declining, in large part because of competition from easy-to-use Web directories.

Brochures. Brochures offer low reach and low frequency in exchange for high flexibility in describing a product.

Newsletters. Newsletters allow for high selectivity and targeted messages at a very low cost. However, increasing reach and frequency can be extremely expensive.

Point-of-Purchase Displays

Point-of-purchase displays work on the premise that 60 percent of buying decisions are made at the store. Signs, displays, interactive computer terminals, and candy stands at checkout lines can all be used to influence consumer spending. Reach is limited to customers who enter and browse a store. (Only 20 percent of supermarket shoppers, for example, browse the aisles and notice promotions.) Of course, point-of-purchase displays work only for products available in that store. Last, the opportunities for targeting consumers are quite limited.

Personal Offline Marketing Levers

Personal offline marketing communications differ from mass offline communications in that the firm directs its message to particular individuals about whom the firm has some level of understanding. In the offline world this understanding could come through demographic information, previous purchases, or direct communication with consumers (through the mail or a telephone call, for example). A firm that has such information has the valuable ability to target individuals with relevant marketing messages. A firm selling retirement getaway packages, for instance, can achieve significant savings and gain much higher response rates if, rather than sweeping the general population, it targets its marketing by using accurate demographic information regarding age and income.

Sales Force / Face-to-Face. Face-to-face marketing communications includes visits from sales representatives, trade shows, and manned kiosks. It is the most expensive form of communication for marketers but the one best suited to selling complex products in a business-to-business situation. In addition to being expensive, face-to-face marketing has limited reach, and companies are looking for ways to shift lower-level activities to other media, including the Internet.

Telemarketing. Telemarketers call people at their house, ask for them by name, and then attempt to sell something. The practice has wide reach, because almost all households have a telephone. But because of the intrusiveness, high-pressure tactics, and a frequent failure to target consumers effectively, telemarketing is widely disliked by consumers. Predictive dialing techniques that call numbers at random often leave consumers getting dead air when they answer their phones. In the United States, 20 states have enacted laws establishing do-not-call lists, and as of early 2002 similar bills were pending in another 20 and the District of Columbia.[18]

Direct Mail.   Another example of personal offline communication is direct mail. A company mails announcements, advertisements, and special offers based on the information it has on a given household or person. Generally this information is demographic in nature, such as age, gender, income, and so forth. Catalogs, which are basically enhanced, full-size, glossy-cover pieces of direct mail, would also fall into this category. Leading distribution companies that do direct mailing have redefined themselves by offering integrated marketing services including direct mail, call centers, websites, and e-mail. Such companies utilize sophisticated technology to store consumer data and target appropriate consumers with relevant marketing messages. Direct-mail advertising was projected to generate $582 billion in sales in the United States in 2001, and international growth is also strong.[19]

Customer Service.   Customer service can also be a form of personal offline communication. While customer service is primarily a product lever, it is also a communications lever because it typically involves interactive communication with customers. Customer service includes all of the activities involved in making it easy for customers to receive help, answers, or service from the firm. Some firms' customer service department is little more than an employee who answers the phone and transfers calls, while others see customer service as a core strength and even an opportunity for cross-selling their offerings. The message that consumers receive through a positive or negative experience with customer service representatives can be the difference between establishing a long-term, potentially profitable relationship and losing a customer—not to mention the effects that a positive or negative experience with customer service can have on word-of-mouth publicity.

Capital One Financial Corp., which was founded as a credit card company in 1994, has seen large sales increases thanks largely to its innovative use of telephone customer service. In-house tests showed that people are more likely to purchase something when they call Capital One than when the company calls them. By using powerful databases full of background information, the company is able to predict the reason for incoming calls and route them accordingly. The databases also predict what the caller might be interested in buying so that once the reason for the call has been taken care of, the customer service representative can try to make a sale. The company is able to target its customers very efficiently, offer them relevant products and services —anything from a vacation package to life insurance—and create selling opportunities wrapped around a positive customer service experience. Within one year, half of all new Capital One customers purchase something.[20]

Mass Online Marketing Levers

In the virtual world, the masses cruise by banners rather than billboards, and see pop-up and pop-under windows rather than television commercials or print ads. Online audiences and online advertising are growing: In 2001, 50 percent of Americans (141 million) were online. It is projected that by 2006, 71 percent of Americans (211 million) will be online.[21] Worldwide, the number of Internet users was estimated to be somewhere in the range of 500 million in 2002, increasing to over 700 million in 2004.[22] Statistics for Internet advertising spending in the United States vary, but it is believed to be in the range of $4 billion to $8 billion in 2000, or between 2 percent and 4 percent of total ad spending. While Internet ad spending declined by about 9 percent in 2001, it held steady relative to overall ad spending.[23] Despite the growth and potential of online advertising, questions abound regarding which types of Internet advertising are most effective and most worth significant monetary investment. Below, we review the main marketing levers for reaching the masses online (see Exhibit 9.4).

Basic Online Tools

Websites.   Many websites exist to advertise and promote the owner's corporation or product. These are called brochure sites. Like brochures, one of their advantages is that the marketer controls the way the company or product is communicated and differentiated to customers. E-commerce websites also offer purchasing capabilities. Although the reach of corporate and

EXHIBIT 9.4   Profiles of Online Media Types

Medium	Advantages	Disadvantages
Websites/ personalized websites	Communicate rich, detailed information that users can navigate at will; can track users and customize site accordingly	Narrow reach
Banner ads	Link directly to buying opportunity; easy to measure effectiveness; wide reach; potential for effective targeting	Low attention and click-through rates; short life; limited "pass-along" audience; very high clutter; fleeting exposure
Interstitials	Catch users' attention; link to buying opportunity	Can annoy users; limited "pass-along" audience
Rich media	Attention-getting; link to buying opportunity	Can annoy users without broadband access
Dynamic ad placement	Serves up customized ads to users in real time	Difficult to execute well; can annoy users, other advertisers
Search engines	Good credibility; high believability; guarantee of position available; significant audience at major sites	High competition; information overload; limited "pass-along"
Classifieds and listings	Relatively inexpensive; potential for wide exposure; qualified audience	Clutter
Opt-in e-mail	High demographic selectivity; high credibility; significant flexibility; proven high click-through rates; absolutely inexpensive; some pass-along	Requires substantial user base before effective; high clutter
Mass e-mail	High reach; inexpensive; flexible	Low attention and significant resentment (spam image)
Customer service	Interested parties asking for help, thus high targeting value; generates loyal customers	Very expensive to provide comprehensive telephone, e-mail, and online support

product websites is potentially large, firms generally rely on other forms of advertising to drive traffic to their websites.

Banners.   **Banner advertisements** exemplify the conversion of old offline advertising techniques to the Internet. They are essentially electronic billboards. They come in a variety of types and sizes, and standard formats have been developed by the Interactive Advertising Bureau (*www.iab.net*). These ads usually display a simple message that is designed to entice viewers to click the ad. In general, this click-through leads to a company's website. Buttons and hypertext links have similar capabilities. The fact that such ads can serve as gateways to the advertiser's own website is one great advantage to advertising on the Web.[24]

A single webpage will often simultaneously display multiple banners. A page could display one across the top, for example, and one or two smaller ones running vertically down each side. Ad space is often sold on the basis of what is called cost per thousand impressions (CPMs). Depending on the popularity and reach of the website, CPM rates can vary from less than a dollar to well into double figures. On high-traffic sites like Yahoo!, which may be seen by more than a million people in a day, advertising may be charged by a flat weekly or monthly fee. Another pricing structure is based on the click-through rate, or the number of times viewers go to the advertiser's website by clicking on the banner ad (see Exhibit 9.5). By paying additional slotting fees to the owner of a popular site, an advertiser can buy premium positioning on the website, exclusivity in that product category, or some other advantageous treatment. Internet advertising spending is heavily concentrated, with the top 10 and top 50 advertising sellers accounting for 50 percent and 95 percent of advertising revenues, respectively.[25]

Several different methods exist—and others are being developed—to measure success rates for banner ads. While banners have received a lot of negative hype, due mainly to low click-through rates and static appearance, they are the most common type of online advertising and have proven effective in promoting brand recognition.

E-commerce players continually try to improve upon the banner ad. There is a trend toward using larger formats for banner ads, including the vertical skyscraper ad.[26] Larger banners that allow interaction within the banner box without leaving the original site are another example.

Interstitials.   **Interstitial** is the broad term for an ad that runs between pages on a website (see Exhibit 9.6). Interstitials, superstitials, pop-up windows, and pop-under windows are all part of the same family. Several types of interstitials have been tried: Some play in the main browser window, some play in new, smaller windows, and some use streaming and rich media, while others use less enhanced, faster-loading content. However, some experts believe that such interruptive, noninteractive commercials placed in the participatory environment of the Web will be little more than a passing fad until the presentations involve users in an interactive manner.[27] Despite complaints that interstitials are interruptive and that they slow access to the destination webpage, interstitials are quite popular with advertisers because they perform very well in terms of brand recall and they have higher click-through rates than traditional banner ads.

Ad Clicks	• Aggregate number of user clicks on a banner ad.
Ad Views (Impressions)	• Number of times a banner ad is downloaded to a user's browser and presumably looked at.
Click-Through	• Percentage of ad views that are clicked upon; also called "Ad Click Rate."
CPC (Cost-per-click)	• Formula used to calculate what an advertiser will pay to an Internet publisher based on number of click-throughs that a banner generates.
CPM	• Cost per thousand impressions of a banner ad. A publisher that charges $100,000 per banner and guarantees 500,000 impressions has a CPM of $20 ($10,000 divided by 500).
Hit	• Measurement recorded in server log files that represents each file downloaded to a browser. Since page design can include multiple files, hits are not a good guide for measuring traffic at a website.
Unique Users	• Number of individuals who visit a website in a specified period of time. Requires the use of registration or cookies to verify and identify unique users.
Visits	• A series of requests made by an individual at one site. If no information is requested for a certain period of time, a "time-out" occurs and the next request made counts as a new visit. A 30-minute time-out is now standard.

EXHIBIT 9.5   Internet Ad Terms

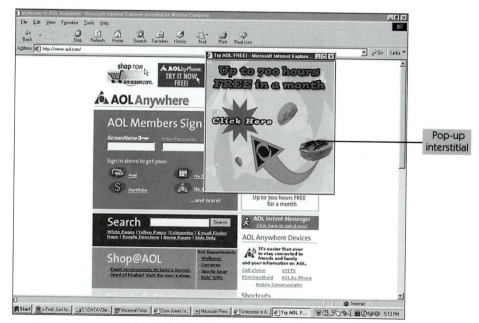

Pop-up interstitial

Courtesy of *www.aol.com*

EXHIBIT 9.6   Interstitial Example

Pop-up ads are the most common type of interstitial ad. Pop-ups appear in the form of a smaller browser window that pops up when a new page begins loading. They tend to be smaller and less rich than other types of interstitials, but they can be easily targeted and are not as intrusive as their counterparts. Many publication sites, such as *Time* magazine's website, Time.com, use pop-up interstitials to entice visitors with free trial issues or other special offers. Pop-under ads are similar but are concealed in a separate window below the open window until the top window is closed, moved, or resized.

Rich Media.

Rich media is defined as a communication method that incorporates animation, sound, video, or interactivity and is deployed through Web and wireless applications such as e-mail, Web design, banners, buttons, and interstitials.[28] It can work alone or with languages and technologies such as DHTML, Java, streaming media, sound, and Flash. One application is "webmercials," which are generally run four to seven seconds in the form of an interstitial. Some marketers believe that the ultimate goal is to create ads with the expressiveness of a TV commercial and the interactivity of the Internet.[29]

Rich media is more expensive to produce and deploy than other online advertising, and is currently hampered by bandwidth issues and a lack of technological standards, which leads to problems with cross-site compatibility. However, the Internet advertising industry is working to establish standards, and as more customers gain broadband access, bandwidth issues should be alleviated.[30]

Search Engines.

Entering keywords into search engines is the most common method for finding websites and searching for products.[31,32] With well over billions of documents on the Web and millions of new pages added each day, it is no wonder that search engines are an important part of Internet marketing strategy.[33]

Advertisers can buy rankings and keywords on search engines. When someone searches for a purchased keyword, the purchaser's website will be one of the first to appear in the search results. Also, that search may trigger targeted banner advertisements (see Exhibit 9.7). Overture.com operates on a pay-per-click model that allows companies to bid for a ranking based on the price they are willing to pay per click-through. A search on software at Overture.com might list 40 links, and next to each URL is listed how much the advertiser pays for a click-through. The first site listed may pay 62 cents, the next about 61 cents, and on down to the fortieth, which might pay about a dime per click-through. A number of large Internet search websites have adopted similar models.

Because a search query often turns up hundreds or thousands of matches, the top 10 spots are hot commodities. A company can do certain things to enhance its chances of being a top match. Of course, buying rankings and keywords is the surest step, but there are other methods that do not cost anything, such as positioning strategic keywords in crucial locations on the webpage, adding meta tags, having HTML links, and having relevant content on the pages of the website. The way that pages must be coded in order to be picked up by particular engines changes constantly, so coding should be checked and modified often, preferably monthly.

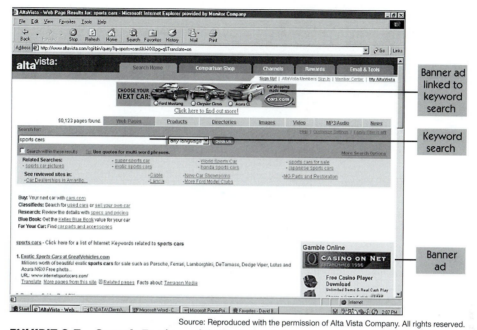

EXHIBIT 9.7   Search Engine with Targeted Ad

Classifieds and Listings.   Portals such as MSN, Yahoo!, and AOL are among the most heavily trafficked websites.[34] At one time, directory listings on such sites were free, but now it is more likely that companies must pay annual listing fees, and sometimes fees for each click-through. Classified listings, particularly job listings on sites such as Monster.com, account for an increasingly large share of Internet advertising revenues. With their greater reach, online classifieds are taking a heavy toll on newspapers' classified advertising revenues.[35]

Sponsorships.   According to the Internet Advertising Bureau, website sponsorships account for more than 25 percent of the online ad market. Although studies suggest that sponsorships have less impact on brand perception than other advertising methods, sponsoring a highly trafficked site can be a good way to build brand awareness (see Exhibit 9.8). Also, studies have found that viewers of a sponsored site become more likely to consider purchasing the sponsor's product.[36] Sponsorships are generally displayed as a banner or a link, usually toward the top or bottom of a webpage. A firm can sponsor a website, a targeted chat room, an electronic newsletter, or even specific content such as an article or series. MaMaMedia (*www.mamamedia.com*), a website that enables children to interact with each other online, play learning games, and design their own multimedia stories, has invested heavily in sponsorships of high-traffic children's zones. It also provides content for children on AOL and EarthLink.

Personal Online Marketing Levers

The Internet is an ideal tool for personal communications, as evidenced by the popularity of e-mail. Firms are taking advantage of this opportunity to engage in marketing communications in a more personal, individualized

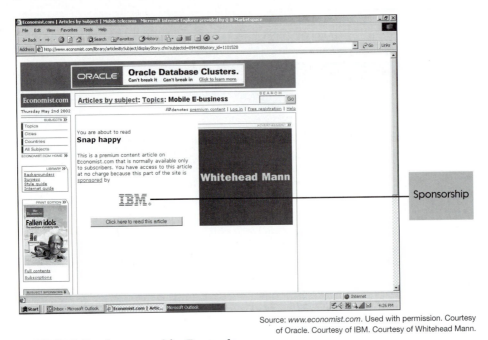

Sponsorship

Source: *www.economist.com*. Used with permission. Courtesy of Oracle. Courtesy of IBM. Courtesy of Whitehead Mann.

EXHIBIT 9.8   Sponsorship Example

manner. One important point to note is that some of these levers, as well as some of the mass online levers, can be effective even if a firm does not have its own website.

Personalized Websites.   Many commercial websites strive to give users personalized experiences. Some firms figure out visitors' preferences by tracking online interaction and purchase behavior and then customizing their websites accordingly. This popular technique is used by many e-commerce sites. Outpost.com, a computer hardware and electronics site, for example, uses registration information and online tracking to offer customers an individualized storefront that reflects their preferences.

Other online firms allow users to personalize the website themselves. Yahoo!'s personalized My Yahoo! pages are an example. Users can choose the news, links, and other content that is displayed on their homepages. Because users have what they want on the page, their switching costs are raised, they visit the page more often, and they spend more time there. This translates to increased advertising exposure time—and because the user must register to set up the page, and reveal detailed personal information by doing so, advertisers are able to target these consumers with relevant ads. Of course, these enticing advertising conditions translate into an opportunity for a site like Yahoo! to charge higher ad rates as well.

Dynamic Ad Placement.   Dynamic ad placement is the process of inserting an ad into a webpage depending on instructions given by the advertiser. It allows alteration of ads based on usage data such as what site the current user came from, the last page viewed by the user, or demographic data. Gator.com, one supplier of these ads, attracts consumers to its database by providing software that automatically fills in a person's name and address in forms on websites in exchange for delivering pop-up ads tied to their Web usage patterns. These ads can be intrusive: Gator has been heavily criticized for delivering pop-up ads that obscure editorial content and other ads.[37]

E-Mail Marketing.   E-mail marketing is seen by many as the most effective online marketing communications tool for retaining customers and increasing sales, although less effective for attracting new customers.[38] A survey of direct marketers, advertising agencies, and corporate media directors recently showed that three-quarters of respondents believe that "e-mail is the most responsive form of marketing available, garnering better results than television, radio, print and direct mail."[39] With competitors a simple click away, companies see e-mail as a key to building loyal relationships with their customers so that switching costs are raised.

One of the advantages of sending marketing messages via e-mail is that the messages can be targeted to individuals. **Permission marketing** takes targeting one step further: In exchange for some offered benefit, consumers give marketers permission to e-mail them on relevant topics and may also volunteer information about themselves. By e-mailing customers who have "opted in"—granted permission to be contacted—the marketing relationship becomes more personal. Opt-in permission and personal information such as e-mail addresses can be obtained in a variety of ways: when a customer makes an online or an offline purchase, requests information, registers to use a site, or enters a sweepstakes. Some companies specialize in creating lists of people who agree to receive e-mail in exchange for points that can be redeemed for rewards including gift certificates and frequent flyer miles.

Both business-to-business (B2B) and business-to-consumer (B2C) marketers find e-mail to be effective. B2C marketers primarily use audience interest to target their mailings, with geography and demographics as secondary information. B2B marketers, on the other hand, rely primarily on demographic and geographic information for targeting purposes.[40] E-mail is a very cost-effective medium in terms of campaign costs and response rates and one that is especially attractive to smaller companies.

The increasing volume of commercial e-mail may require marketers to come up with more creative strategies to break through the clutter. Jupiter Research predicts that by 2005 promotional e-mails sent to consumers in the United States will grow to 22 times the levels in 2000, reaching a volume of 268 billion messages. The average online consumer in the United States received about 12.8 permission e-mails per week in 2000, a number that is projected to grow to 31 per week by 2003.[41] With such an increase in volume, the high consumer response rates will likely fall.

Of course, spam (unsolicited or junk e-mail), which would fall into the mass online category, has received a tremendous amount of negative response from the public. Perpetrators of this method of marketing are frowned upon, and so most agencies refrain from activities that might be interpreted as spam. As a precaution, most advertisers will include in their e-mails a simple way to opt out so that no more messages will be sent.

Interactive Television. Interactive digital television (iDTV) enables two-way communication between the television viewer and service provider. It also allows the user to tailor content to individual preferences. For advertisers, it combines the richness and immediacy of television commercials with the targeting and individualization of e-mail. Advertisers can customize ads according to demographic information or based on input from the viewer. Europe, particularly the United Kingdom, is the leader in adopting iDTV. By 2007, iDTV is expected to reach 44 percent of European households, up from 11 percent in 2002.[42]

Wireless Devices. Cellular phones, personal digital assistants, and other wireless devices can access the Internet through the Wireless Application Protocol (WAP). The screen on a WAP device can also be used to deliver ads directly to the device. In mobile commerce (sometimes called "m-commerce") applications, WAP devices are used to conduct monetary transactions. The geographic location of devices equipped with global positioning systems (GPS) can be identified with great precision. Consequently, marketers envision the ability to target ads according to location (e.g., when the consumer is passing a vending machine), as well as according to stored data on demographics, behaviors, and preferences. However, wireless service providers have a vested interest in protecting their customers from unwanted messages and intrusions on their privacy, and will want to limit the ads that are passed along. Responsible marketers agree that wireless communications should be governed by opt-in provisions, especially when users pay for incoming messages.

Customer Service. Customer service is a vital part of online firm-to-consumer communication. This personal-level communication can be a highly profitable marketing contact because of the potential to turn an apprehensive customer into a firmly committed one. Personalized and interactive online customer service can make the difference between an abandoned shopping cart and a completed sale. Unfortunately, one of the most common complaints of online consumers is the failure to get the customer service they need.

Online customer support is improving, though. Aside from e-mail centers and telephone representatives, websites are discovering the value of searchable FAQs (frequently asked questions), live representatives who push webpages to individual shoppers' browsers, and live chat capabilities. Also, powerful customer-support technology is used by larger companies to boost their call center and Web-hosted customer-support services.[43] Lands' End provides a service for online users who desire help while shopping. They can request and immediately receive a phone call from a company representative who will answer any questions or even talk the user through navigating the site. BestBuy.com allows customers to pick up and return items purchased online at its offline stores. By taking such measures to boost customer service, these companies are addressing one of the top two criteria upon which consumers base their choice of online retailer. (The other leading decision factor is cost.)[44]

Customer service is primarily a product lever, but its interactive communication component renders it a significant communications lever as well.

Communications Process

In order to successfully build and execute a marketing communications campaign, a firm needs to establish the best way to use the appropriate levers. The starting point for any communications campaign should be the segmentation, targeting, and positioning choices made as part of the marketing strategy. The process of planning a communications campaign in accordance with marketing strategy has six stages:

1. Identify the target audience.

2. Determine the communication objective.

3. Develop the media plan.

4. Create the message.

5. Execute the campaign.

6. Evaluate the effectiveness of the campaign.

While each step will be guided by the segmentation, targeting, and positioning choices, the communications process will typically be at a greater level of specificity. Of course, the process is an iterative one, and the lines between the steps are not always distinct.

Because of the integrated online/offline nature of the process, each of the four categories of tools discussed in the previous section needs to be considered. The process should not be looked at in absolute terms of which category is best, but rather in terms of the most effective mix for each particular case. The Internet is not taking over marketing communications, but it has become an integral component. As we cover the six steps in the marketing communications process, the role of the Internet in each step should be carefully considered.

Identify the Target Audience

Who is the potential customer? Whose need is being met by the product? Who is willing to pay for it? Questions such as these drive the customer research that determines the audience that is best to target. Generally this information is obtained in one of three ways: from experience (an established firm is likely to know who its consumers are and can target like consumers), from demographics, or from tracking previous behavior.

Demographic information can be obtained through original customer research or through customer-research firms. It is the major source of consumer targeting data in the offline world. The information focuses on age, gender, income level, ethnicity, location, and other similar categories.

The Internet has made tracking consumer behavior easier and less expensive, and developing target audiences based on Internet tracking is becoming a promising reality. By keeping track of the webpages that users visit, time spent on specific webpages, ads and links clicked on, and purchases made, marketers can develop an extremely valuable database.

Many websites, even those that offer free access, require users to register and give personal information. Retail websites also require personal information before allowing a customer to make a purchase. In this way, critical demographic information, including e-mail addresses, is obtained, and the user's behavior can be linked with a personal profile. The combination is very valuable to marketers. Some argue that the behavior-tracking capability of the Internet is a more effective targeting method than demographic-based targeting, because all the demographic information available on an individual amounts to little if that individual is not interested in purchasing the offering.

Particularly for new products, marketers will want to identify the most likely adopters and the most influential adopters, those whose opinions will guide other potential customers. An extreme form of word-of-mouth adoption is **viral marketing,** which can be described as the buzz that develops when a product or offering suddenly takes off because of user-to-user recommendation.[45] The likelihood of trusting and trying a new offering rises significantly when trusted friends and acquaintances are the messengers. With such subtle endorsement, the product stealthily spreads at a steeply increasing rate, much like an actual virus. ICQ had great success with viral marketing. Before being acquired by AOL for close to $300 million, the company signed 12 million subscribers to its instant messaging service. For a subscriber to use the service to communicate with someone, both parties needed to download the ICQ software. Therefore, people solicited their friends to download the software. Once these new users experienced the product, they recruited other friends, and so on.[46]

Drill-Down

Dynamic Trio: Marketing, Databases, and Internet Technology

While some companies, such as Capital One, have been able to take advantage of the powerful potential of database marketing, many large companies are not in a position to do so. There are two reasons for this: First, they are not structured for setting up such powerful databases, and second, even if they were, most don't yet have the magnitude of customer data to put such a system to full use. Most large manufacturers of consumer package goods, for instance, sell through retailers and have little interaction with consumers.

For this reason, third-party companies that bring together marketing expertise, huge databases of consumer data, and Internet technology are emerging to fill this need. By capitalizing on digital and Internet-based technology, they can help corporations generate highly targeted, consistent direct-marketing campaigns practically in real time. Such a system can be applied not only to online e-mail campaigns but also to automatically distributed direct-mail campaigns.

New marketing software adapted to take advantage of databases and Internet technology offers firms a variety of options as well. Tools are available to automate campaign planning, execute targeted customer acquisition and retention strategies, determine campaign channels based on historical performance and forecasting, and integrate customer touchpoints in real time so that a sales representative who picks up the phone can know that the caller has been at the firm's website for an hour looking at a particular product. Other functions of such software include campaign tracking and analysis, and the creation of Web-based customer files that can be used to push real-time marketing messages based on the objects that a user clicks on while online.

Once the target audience is identified, the issue of how to reach that audience arises. A baby-food company should have no difficulty concluding that its target audience is parents, especially mothers of infants. But how will it get its message to that audience? Determining the best way to reach the audience will help resolve questions further along in the process, such as which media to use, which selling points to stress, and what sort of personality to give to the message.

Determine the Communication Objective

Before creating the communication, its intent must be clear. The message should focus on developing one of the four customer relationship stages. If the firm or the offering is new to the target audience, the message should build awareness. A new Internet bank, for example, might want to achieve a high degree of name recognition within a specific time frame. If the target audience is aware of the offering but not completely familiar with it, the message should aim to foster the exploration/expansion stage. The bank's objectives in this case are to increase the target audience's knowledge of specific products and services, and to attract new customers. Eventually, a follow-up campaign would have the objective of deepening customer commitment. Each campaign will make use of a different combination of levers.

Once overall objectives are set for an integrated marketing campaign, individual goals should be set for each of the media elements in the campaign. Traditionally, communications have been classified according to whether they are intended to (1) build brand awareness, knowledge, and preference, or (2) provide an immediate stimulus to purchase. Advertising that focuses on the emotional and functional benefits of the product belongs to the first category. Its success is measured by the communications' impact in increasing awareness, recall, and liking, and only indirectly to sales, due to difficulties in tying a person's exposure to a commercial to a subsequent purchase. Advertising that focuses on prices and promotions such as coupons, sweepstakes, and giveaways falls into the second category. Its success is measured by direct sales impact. Many communications, such as telemarketing, half-hour infomercials, and direct mail, will try to achieve both objectives, but will be primarily measured on sales. With interactive communications, there is a third goal: to stimulate customer interaction. Success is measured by metrics such as the number of resulting click-throughs, registrations, or requests for information.

No matter what the desired outcome, a corresponding objective should be explicitly articulated for each marketing message. A clear strategy, with a clear communications objective, is key to executing a successful integrated marketing communications campaign. The necessity of determining the communications objective may seem self-evident, yet marketing teams often fail to establish and adhere to one. They get caught up in the creative process of making the message, only to realize too late that they have strayed from the intended objective. The result is usually a muddled campaign that does little to help the consumer progress through the relationship stages.

Some experts argue that one main reason so many Internet companies have failed is that they overspent on expensive advertising and neglected to outline a communication strategy or establish a clear objective. Many dot-com companies launched ads intended to build name recognition, but failed to go one important step further and tell consumers what the offering was. As a result, consumers never even made it all the way through the awareness stage: They may have recognized the company name, but still had no idea what the company offered.

The objective of the campaign should reflect the customer stage that the firm desires to encourage. Furthermore, the firm should look ahead and fit into its plans the future campaigns that will be necessary for a continual progression—for example, beware of shortsightedly blowing the entire marketing budget on a Super Bowl commercial that does little more than mention the company's name.

Develop the Media Plan

Developing a media plan involves choosing the right media for the message and deciding how to use them (see Exhibit 9.9). The media plan must meet the following criteria:

1. It must be consistent with the target audience. To reach people at the beach, use beach towels or skywriting. If women with arthritis are the target audience, an electronic newsletter or an ad in a women's health magazine is more appropriate. To target business travelers, Premier Lodge, a British hotel chain, uses outdoor advertising and the Web as part of its direct marketing mix.

2. It must be consistent with the communication objective. If the objective is to promote the exploration/expansion stage by increasing knowledge about a specific offering among the target group, then key chains printed with only the company name are not the most effective medium.

3. The different parts of the plan must fit together well. In other words, the online and offline levers that the firm chooses must have synergy so that consumers are given a well-integrated campaign. The media should contribute to creating a pleasing experience for the consumer so that a positive, progressive relationship can be established and nourished.

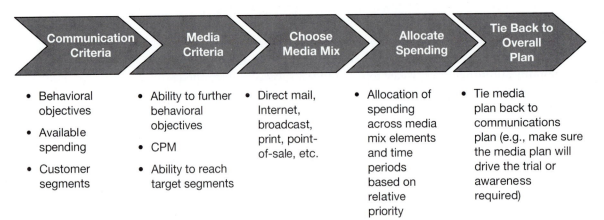

EXHIBIT 9.9   A Process for Defining Media Choice and Mix

Media Choice

The media mix can be very diverse. For example, given the target audience and the communication objective, an effective arsenal of media might include the Internet, radio, posters, T-shirts, and key chains. How much importance should be allocated to each medium? To make this decision, determine the relative weight of each medium, as well as other factors such as cost restraints. One advantage to marketing on the Internet is that, in many cases, it is more cost efficient than traditional media.

Another issue to consider is which vehicles within each medium should carry the message. To reach a particular audience through television, advertisers often take advantage of shows that attract their target group— commercials aired during *Friends*, for example, would reach a much different audience than commercials aired during *Larry King Live*. An upscale winemaker would probably advertise in a gourmet foods magazine. On the Internet, there are many vehicles to choose from, including broad-reach portals like Yahoo!, retail and publisher sites, focused directories, community chat rooms, and special-interest sites. Consider the communication objective along with behavioral and demographic data on the target group to help guide the decision.[47]

Drill-Down

Reach, Frequency, and Impact: Gross Rating Points

Media selection hinges upon how many exposures of an advertisement are necessary to create the desired level of awareness in the target audience. Then, a marketing team can select media that will generate that awareness.

The effect of an advertisement's exposures is measured by three factors:

- **Reach (R):** The number of unique people or households that are exposed to a media schedule once during a given time period.

- **Frequency (F):** The number of occasions during the given time period that the average person or household is exposed to the advertisement.

- **Impact (I):** The perceived value of an individual exposure via a specified medium. For example, an advertisement for a teen star's new pop music CD would have more impact in *Teen People* than in *Gramophone*.

- **Total Number of Exposures (E):** Reach multiplied by average frequency. This is also referred to as gross rating points (GRPs). If a planned buy of media reaches 70 percent of homes with an average frequency of 5, it has 350 GRPs (R of 70 multiplied by F of 5).

Advertising prices are typically evaluated in terms of cost per thousand persons reached, also referred to as CPMs. If *The Wall Street Journal* charges $150,000 for a full-page advertisement that reaches 8 million people, then the cost of exposing the ad to 1,000 people is about $19.

Marketing teams need to factor audience quality—or impact—into considerations of CPMs. For example, an advertisement for a book about adjusting to retired life that appeared in a magazine read by 500,000 retirees would have an exposure value of near 500,000. If it were in a magazine read mostly by teenagers, it would have an exposure value of near zero.

Scheduling

There is a tendency to think of advertising as a constant activity. However, factors such as seasonality of demand, new-product introductions, and competitive activity will affect the timing of a campaign. For instance, sales in many product categories peak in the fourth quarter due to holiday buying, so advertisers concentrate their advertising then. If a campaign is tied to introduction of a new or significantly improved product, the advertiser must decide how far in advance to start building awareness and when the advertising should peak. It may start with advertising directed at potential early adopters first, and then advertise to other target audiences as word of mouth spreads and the product becomes more available.

Timing the deployment of the various media is another issue. For example, a firm should consider whether to begin the campaign on a modest scale, via one or two channels, and then build from there, or whether a simultaneous deployment of all media would be more effective than a staggered deployment.

More specific scheduling issues include whether to deploy advertising continuously or intermittently and whether to vary the level of intensity. Relevant factors include the number of consumers that can be reached by any one media placement, the number of repetitions needed to achieve the communication objective, and consumers' retention of the message (see Exhibit 9.10).

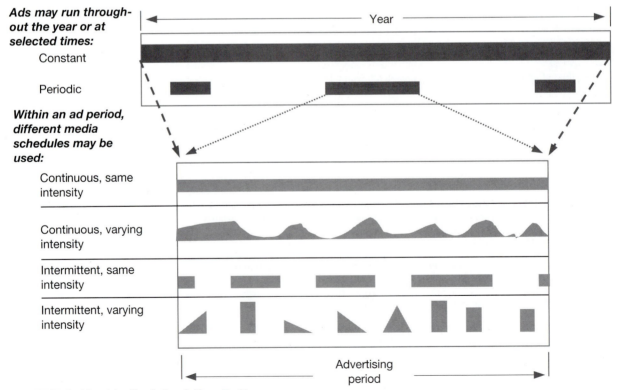

EXHIBIT 9.10   Media Scheduling Patterns

Create the Message

Creating the message requires significant planning and analysis. If it has not done so already, the firm will probably hire an agency at this point to create the messages and help coordinate the rest of the campaign. One of the first things to consider is the communication theme. It must be one that the target audience will be receptive to, and it must be consistent with the objective that has been determined. The theme of a message designed to promote awareness may need to be adjusted when it comes time to focus on the later stages of the customer relationship. The theme should also be consistent with the offering's function and with the brand personality. Is the brand intent to be serious? Frivolous? Warm and friendly? Finally, the theme must be appropriate for the marketing levers that will be used in the campaign.

Within the guidelines established in the communications process so far, the creative team (including at least an art director and a writer) usually has a great deal of leeway in devising fresh approaches to keep audiences receptive to the advertising and to build interest in the product. Often the creative approach will be to build a story over time, providing new information or new executions in a series of messages. For the third Austin Powers movie, *Austin Powers in Goldmember*, New Line Cinema devised an online campaign that called for the "Austin-ization" of the Web through "groovy" enhancements, including a 3-D virtual Austin to guide visitors through the movie's website. Subsequent elements of the campaign happened in stages over the next few months. Among these were 360-degree iPix images of the set, including Dr. Evil's million-dollar lair and Austin's shag pad; AOL instant-messenger icons for each of the film's characters; desktop patterns, wallpapers, screensavers, and pictures of each character; and a splashy Super Bowl television commercial.

There will most likely be particular messages tailored for particular media. For example, messages in print, such as a magazine ad, no matter how colorful or exciting, are static and therefore put together differently than a message that is broadcast on television, which essentially allows the creation of a 30-second film. Each channel and vehicle—whether it is the Internet, radio, a brochure, or a billboard—has its own characteristics, advantages, and limitations that affect how the message is put together.

Companies that are Internet based or rely heavily on their websites must be especially careful to ensure that their websites, their online marketing messages, and their offline marketing messages are coordinated. Genuity launched a well-integrated campaign starting in fall 2000 for an offering called Black Rocket, a network services platform for e-business. The marketing campaign was designed to create a mystique around the Black Rocket and the ways it can help executives achieve their e-business visions. Genuity was careful to apply a consistent look and theme across various media (see Exhibits 9.11 and 9.12). When consumers go to the Genuity website after seeing an advertisement, they can easily find information about the Black Rocket product, or click on a link to go directly to the ad campaign. By working its marketing messages into the site, Genuity builds a smooth transition from the awareness stage to the exploration/expansion stage. The offline ads create awareness and invite customers to check out Genuity's website to find out, on a much deeper level, how they could benefit from the offering.

EXHIBIT 9.11   Genuity Ads

Once the message has been created for the desired medium, it can be tested against the communications objectives with a sample of the target audience. If there are multiple messages or multiple media being used in the campaign, different combinations should be tested to determine what works best. One of the more common mistakes that turns up during testing is a message that has been created from the firm's perspective rather than the consumer's perspective. One example comes from the American Cancer Society. In the early 1990s it launched a campaign to promote the use of SPF 15 sunblock in order to prevent skin cancer. The target group was young men and women who spend a lot of time in the sun. The American Cancer Society's communication objective was to encourage this group to use the product so that they would not die of skin cancer. Its initial selling line was, "Save your life!" After some testing, it found there was a problem with this message. The target group was not concerned about dying of skin cancer; they were concerned about getting tan so that they could look attractive to the opposite sex. After shifting to the consumer's perspective, the society decided to try creating another message, one that the target group would be more likely to heed. It enlisted models from the annual *Sports Illustrated*

Courtesy of *www.Genuity.com*

EXHIBIT 9.12   Genuity Website

swimsuit issue to endorse the sunblock and created messages about safely enjoying more time in the sun.[48]

If an online advertisement such as a banner is being created, taking advantage of the interactivity of the Internet is critical. Electronics manufacturer Samsung launched an integrated ad campaign in 2002 designed to drive consumers and business customers to Samsung's website, where they could find more product information and connect with selected retailers. The campaign included ads running 24 hours a day on 50 prime websites, magazines, TV, outdoor and radio. The online component will help Samsung measure the demand for products and manage promotions in real time.[49]

After the messages pass tests on all counts, the marketer is finally ready to move on to the next stage, the execution of the campaign.

Execute the Campaign

Once the content for the integrated marketing communications campaign is ready for distribution, the firm can take the final steps to execute the campaign. It will need to buy media placements and consider whether to participate in a partnership with other marketers. It will also need to distribute the execution materials to the media. Thanks to the Internet and advancing digital technology, the distribution process has been greatly simplified and streamlined for both online and offline content. Print ads, sound bytes, and video, for example, can all be distributed digitally over the Internet.

Buying Media

In marketing circles, one often hears the phrase "making the buy." It refers to buying the media space for the message, whether it is space on the Internet, radio, television, print, or some other medium. For online advertising, an agency that specializes in managing online marketing campaigns will likely be hired. Relevant capabilities include databases that profile target categories, technology that instantly tracks online behavior, as well as media-buying and distribution services.

The most basic measure of a media buy is the number of impressions purchased, or in other words, the number of times the ad is seen by any consumer. **Reach** and **frequency** are also measured. Reach refers to the number of individuals who see an ad, and frequency is the average number of times they see it.

With traditional print media, such as magazines, the selling of impressions (sold on a basis of **cost per thousand impressions,** or CPM) is based on circulation and readership figures. Readership figures take into account the pass-along rate, so if each copy of a magazine is seen by about six people, the readership would be the circulation figure multiplied by six. In broadcast media such as television and radio, CPMs are based on ratings that are somewhat more complex, but still stem from how many pairs of eyeballs or ears are reached. Television ratings, for example, are determined in the following manner: If 50 percent of households with a television were watching television, and 50 percent of those households were watching *Sesame Street*, that show's rating would be 0.25 ($0.50 \times 0.50 = 0.25$).

Making the buy on the Internet is usually based on CPMs as well. However, because of the ability to measure user behavior online, the buy can also be based on other measurements. For example, buyers can pay according to the number of times users click on their ads, called **cost per click-through.** It is also possible to track users from the webpage where the ad appears to the intended website. This has led to media sales based on how many people make a purchase after clicking through an ad, a method called **cost per transaction.**

Beyond price, other considerations are important in media placement. A panel of industry experts recently assessed the top three Internet portals according to seven categories important to media buyers: understanding of the ad business, ability to customize ads, flexibility, willingness to negotiate, responsiveness, improvement, and overall average score. It found substantial differences among the three portals, with Yahoo! scoring highest.[50]

In the end, regardless of publicized CPM rates, the media buy is made only after extensive negotiation. Negotiations can vary depending on the relationship between the buyer and the seller, but often a deal is reached that includes some leeway so that post-purchase analysis can be taken into account. The purchase price is often significantly lower than the publicized price tag. After the buy has been made and the message is consumer-ready, the message may finally be distributed.

Partnering

Setting up partnerships can be an effective means for executing a campaign. In the Internet space, partnerships are generally formed between complementary sites so that they can offer the consumer a more complete bundle of services. The terms and extent of a partnership can vary widely. A simplified model would be a relationship where partners post each other's banners or

---

Point–Counterpoint

Which Online Ad Pricing Model Is Best?

The capability of the Internet to track and measure user behavior is one of its greatest marketing strengths. Yet, despite the promise of the Internet to be the most accountable medium ever, there is a fierce debate regarding which performance measurement model is best for pricing Internet advertising: the traditional CPM model (based on cost per thousand impressions), or an action model such as cost per click-through or cost per transaction. The fact is, firms are unsure how to measure the return on their online advertising dollars.

Argument for CPM: The CPM model is consistent with the way traditional media, such as television, radio, and most print media, are structured. This model makes firms pay for putting marketing messages in front of consumers. There is no question that online ads, including banner ads, increase brand awareness and can have positive results even when there is no click-through. To base the cost of advertising solely on click-throughs or transactions gives firms that advertise online a free ride, in the sense that they are paying nothing for the branding and exposure that they receive. Their free ride, of course, comes at the expense of websites that ought to be paid for giving up that media space.

Argument for performance-based pricing: The CPM model does not fit in an environment like the Internet, where consumers have so much control over information flow. They do not go to the Internet to flip through pages and look at ads as they would with a magazine, or to passively watch their screen as on television, but to achieve some end such as using their e-mail or checking the news. On the Internet, users can go right where they want to go, do what they want to do, and log off. Most consumers have trained themselves to ignore the static banner ads. Finally, considering the low click-through rates and high customer acquisition cost of online ads, CPMs are egregiously overpriced.

---

refer users to each other's websites. Of course, partnerships can involve traditional media as well.

In one strategic alliance, America Online (AOL) and the National Basketball Association (NBA) partnered to promote NBA.com and WNBA.com (a website for the Women's National Basketball Association) and to promote AOL's Internet service provider and AOL websites. The deal included Internet and television marketing agreements, including extensive promotion of AOL on the TNT and TBS Superstation cable channels (both owned by Time Warner, soon to merge with AOL) during NBA games, as well as commercials plugging AOL on NBC, ESPN, and Lifetime during WNBA games. Part of the deal allowed AOL access to NBA trademarks, logos, player names, video highlight packages, and real-time game statistics to use on its site. In addition, AOL members were allowed to sign up for an Audio Pass on NBA.com or WNBA.com and get live radio broadcasts of every game of the season. In return, the NBA and WNBA could leverage AOL technologies, including AOL's Instant Messenger and AOL Search, on their websites. Also, they could promote their content on AOL sites, including CompuServe, Netscape, and the ICQ live chat network. The result was exposure to tens of millions of AOL members and visitors.[51]

Affiliate marketing programs, sometimes called associate or referral programs, are a popular means of partnering to attract online attention. In Amazon.com's associates program, an associate website can independently advertise any book that Amazon.com sells. When a customer enters

Amazon.com from the associate's site and purchases the advertised book, the associate receives a commission. There is no media buyer in this model—the process is controlled independently by the Web publishers. Also, the associate in this model gains nothing when a user is attracted by an advertisement, chooses not to click-through at the time, and later goes directly to Amazon's site to make a purchase. So, in this example, Amazon pays only for performance, the associate has some opportunity for gain, and the advertising company is out of the picture.

Evaluate the Effectiveness of the Campaign

The evaluation process begins as soon as the message is distributed. Each element of the campaign should be evaluated against its objectives. In addition, the synergy of the integrated messages in the campaign should be evaluated to determine whether the messages and the media are integrated optimally. In the case of messages that are targeted to individual consumers, the evaluation should include a look at whether the communication method and content are consistent with the customer's history. For example, referring back to the Saturn example at the beginning of the chapter, if the GM, GMAC, and Saturn marketing departments had coordinated their evaluations of the post-purchase e-mail campaign, they might have avoided some unhappy customers by making sure that each e-mail was appropriate and relevant to the receiving individual.

One thing that makes the Internet such a powerful medium for evaluation is its capability for tracking and measuring online behavior. Through technology used by agencies like DoubleClick, online behavior is tracked so that firms can know each time a consumer is exposed to their marketing messages.[52] They can also know each time a consumer clicks on their banners or links, which tells the company the ad has been seen, though not necessarily noticed. Thus, while the ability to capture such data enables firms to bring in the principle of accountability more than ever before, it is also useful to look at measures of communications effectiveness.

For instance, DoubleClick cooperated with Information Resources Inc., a firm that tracks sales through retail scanner data, to measure the impact of online advertising on eight major brands of consumer goods. Overall, they were able to show online advertising increased offline sales by an average of 6.6 percent. More precisely, they found "growth in brand awareness, message recall and sales that was incremental to the base level achieved through TV, radio, and print advertising." Their report went on to say, "The sales lift resulting from online advertising ranged from flat for two brands up to a remarkable 22.5 percent for a brand with a new line extension."[53] One value of this type of analysis is that it shows how advertising affects customer perceptions as well as sales.

Evaluative data obtained by tracking user interactivity online is very valuable because it gives firms results in close to real time. The closest parallels for marketing communications are the tracking methods employed in direct-response marketing efforts such as direct mail, infomercials, and, of course, telemarketing. In the case of infomercials, by posting a unique (800) number to each version of an infomercial, marketers can tell which version is most successful. And with caller ID, they can track consumer response information by region. In the case of direct mail, it is easy to track response rates at the individual level. However, once the mailing is sent out, no changes can be made, and evaluative information cannot be retrieved faster than the speed of the postal service allows.

Not only is it faster and easier to track behavioral data online, but it is also much faster, much easier, and much less expensive to make adjustments to the message if the evaluation indicates the need to do so. New software can make real-time changes to online marketing messages even after they have been distributed. This real-time versus lag-time difference is one of the starkest contrasts between online and offline marketing communications. Through real-time data collection and analysis, advertisers can make quick adjustments, drop certain websites from later media buys, and use high-performing, well-placed ads that lead to significant cost savings.

The Internet's great potential for tracking campaigns and measuring behavior has alleviated much of the initial trepidation regarding online advertising. Although evaluating the performance of marketing messages in offline media is certainly a slower process than it is online, many companies are still more comfortable with the traditional offline process. The main reason for this is that they have more knowledge of the various measurement pitfalls, more experience in interpreting results, and more baselines for comparison. Another consideration is understanding the relative dynamics across the traditional media. A manager of Internet branding and advertising at General Mills put it like this: "A couple of years ago it was all about click-throughs and banners, then impressions, then brand awareness. The next step in this whole evolution is to connect the Internet much more effectively to the overall media mix."[54] As the large, traditional companies that control the lion's share of marketing dollars gain more confidence with online measures and results, they are highly likely to make a more significant investment in advertising on the Internet.

Implementation Across the Four Relationship Stages

Firms have a tremendous array of communication strategies and levers available to deliver their message. Yet this wide variety of choices also increases the difficulty of firm-to-user communication, precisely because the overflow of advertising information makes it difficult to reach a consumer directly. People are hit with hundreds, if not thousands, of commercial messages per day. A fraction of these are consciously noticed, and only a few provoke some reaction. Faced with these odds, firms need to focus on customers who are likely to respond to their messages.

Traditional offline marketing has solved these problems in two ways. First, through media as diverse as television advertising and the yellow pages, mass media allows blanket communication to millions of people at one time. These forms of communication allow a firm to increase the reach and frequency of its messages in hopes that a sufficient number will reach the appropriate people. Second, telemarketing, direct mail, and some radio advertising allow for high demographic and geographic selectivity. In other words, the offline world of marketing communications has developed some effective targeting techniques to increase the impact of advertising. In B2B contexts, the sales force can target narrow segments and interact one on one with customers.

Drill-Down

BMW, an Interactive Communications Case Study

The Ultimate Driving Experience Online

In 2000, BMW followed the time-honored practice of launching a new product—in this case, its new X5 sports utility model—with Super Bowl TV commercials and a print advertising campaign. But to capture the interest of its Net-savvy target audience, it also kicked off a high-tech online campaign. Consumers signed up on the company's website to receive four interactive episodes delivered via e-mail every two or three weeks. In each episode, by clicking on photo-quality images on their computer screens, viewers could take a virtual test drive of the X5. They could see close-ups of the interior, hear the engine, open and shut doors, and brake the car as it went downhill. BMW promoted the episodes via banner ads on portals and car enthusiast websites. The result: The campaign succeeded in enlarging BMW's database, because viewers needed to register to see the episodes.[55]

Following up on this success, in April 2001 BMW debuted a series of five short films commissioned for its website. These featured acclaimed directors and actors (including Ang Lee, John Frankenheimer, Guy Ritchie, Forest Whitaker, Mickey Rourke, and Madonna) and, of course, the "ultimate driving machine." The objective was to build the brand among high-income, middle-aged males who usually buy high-performance autos and younger "BMW buyers-in training." BMW estimated that 85 percent of its target segment was online. To send consumers to the website, the integrated campaign included extensive print, Web, and broadcast ads. When people went to the website, they could register to download a special film player and files containing the films and product information. The website also featured still images, animations, audio, and video drawn from the films, and the ability to send a postcard about the films to a friend. As of June 2001, more than 3 million visitors had watched at least one film.

BMW says it received more traffic in six weeks than it expected in six months, and ended with a 500 percent spike in unique visitors over a three-week period, a preponderance of visitors who fit the desired demographics, and a sizable opt-in e-mail list. Meanwhile, BMW recorded its best May and June ever in terms of car sales. According to an article in *Business 2.0,* BMW's marketing vice president, Jim McDowell "won't give the BMW Films campaign direct credit for the sales record, nor will he disclose the campaign's undoubtedly enormous budget, but he says he's ecstatic about the results."[56]

Ryan Jones' BMW Experience

One of the first things I did when looking for a car was visit BMW's website (*www.BMWUSA.com*) and other car manufacturers' websites to do some preliminary research. I thoroughly enjoyed using the shopping tools I easily found on their website. I priced different new-car packages, looked at different colors and configurations, and studied down payments and interest rates. I immediately saw the results of those choices in terms of overall cost and monthly payments. I was also able to research older models and do searches on certified pre-owned inventory all over New England that matched my specifications. I could immediately tell in what geographic locations I was going to get the most car for my money. I stored my configured BMW on their website for later retrieval, and it stayed there for nearly a year as I considered different

continued

makes and models of other vehicles. As I researched those models, I always came back to BMWUSA.com to look again and again at the vehicle I had specified online.

But I didn't buy new, nor online. As it turned out, I bought my BMW from a private dealer located two hours from my home. One of my concerns in doing so was, of course, whether or not BMW "disowns" owners who buy from a dealer that is not BMW-certified. But that hasn't turned out to be the case. Because my car is still under the manufacturer's warranty, the local BMW service center always treats me like a customer of their own when I bring the vehicle in for service. I do have to be careful, though, because they assume that being a BMW customer also means having more money than sense. I have to be on my toes when dealing with their service representatives in order to avoid incurring astronomical costs for relatively simple service, and that leaves me feeling anxious. But I have never been anything but pleasantly surprised upon picking up my vehicle, finding it not only serviced to my specifications and finished on time, but also washed, waxed, and vacuumed.

Like clockwork, two days after my service I receive a customer-feedback phone call from BMW. While I sometimes find this type of phone call intrusive, I am always happy to share with BMW my experience with the service center. It's always a quick phone call, and never an attempt to sell anything to me, which I find refreshing. It gives me a chance to tell them that I don't like being treated as if I have money flowing out of my ears, but also compliment them on the speed and attention to detail of their work. That phone call really does make me feel like I have input into how I will be treated next time I show up for service.

Since buying my BMW, I have registered on their website's "Owners' Circle." While I don't find the Owners' Circle to be entirely useful (I have never used several sections, including priority e-mail, owners' comments, my BMW center, owners' survey, owners' news, accessories, lifestyle, publications, online banking, credit card account access), it has given me opportunity to access owner rewards such as discounted lift tickets at ski areas. Last year BMW released a series of short films (*www.bmwfilms.com*) directed by leading directors, including John Frankenheimer and Ang Lee, and featuring BMW vehicles. I always thought the films were really fun to watch, and they also had me dying for the latest and greatest BMW vehicles. I even forwarded the link to the movies to my friends, who also really enjoyed them. At some point I got a phone call from BMW asking if, as a BMW owner, I would like a courtesy DVD copy of all of the films. I thought that was really great. It's not as if I watch the films every night, but it was a small gesture that left me feeling as if BMW thought I was a valuable customer.

Ryan Jones is in his 20s and has owned his BMW for a year.

Because of the role of the 2Is in online marketing communications, firms that use the Internet can increase the impact of their advertising by using personalization and interactivity. On the Internet, mass advertisements can be targeted to a degree that was previously unfeasible.

Each of the four stages—awareness, exploration/expansion, commitment, and dissolution—requires unique consideration for reach, frequency, and impact. Thus, the choice of levers to bring a user from awareness to commitment, and in some cases to dissolution, will vary throughout the marketing cycle. The firm needs to develop a precise understanding of where various groups of customers are placed in the cycle to maximize its success. Well planned Internet marketing will give companies a much better sense of where they stand with their users throughout the relationship. Each stage will require a different set of levers to bring users to the next step (see Exhibit 9.13).

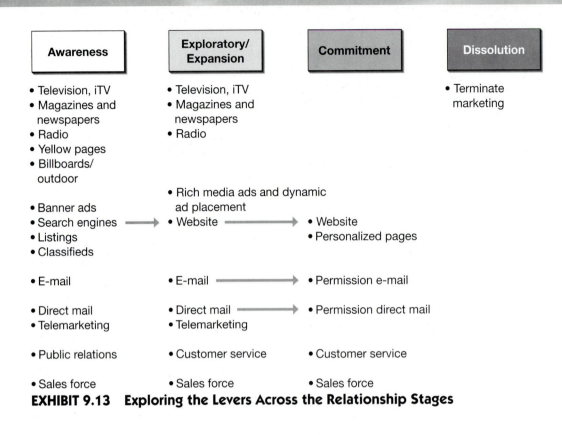

EXHIBIT 9.13   Exploring the Levers Across the Relationship Stages

Awareness

A firm can tap multiple levers in order to generate awareness.

Online Levers

Banner Ads.   Banner ads can provoke curiosity and develop awareness. Unfortunately, many users ignore them because of clutter and because their standard placement at the margins of a page allows for easy skipping. Banner ads have a notoriously low click-through rate (less than 1 percent) but can be cost-effective. Placing banner ads on websites and in contexts relevant to the product and user segment is an important factor in generating a response. Creativity can also increase response. John Hancock's banner ads, which ask users if they will have saved enough for retirement, are a good example. Banner ads cannot typically generate awareness, exploration, and commitment in one single swoop, although they are often expected to do so.

Search Engines, Classifieds, Listings, and Sponsorships.   Portals and search engines are the gateway to the Internet for most users. Paying for key words and listings generates qualified leads because searchers have already indicated they are looking for something. Therefore, buying ad space in a search result or on a portal is an outstanding way to generate awareness.

Public Relations.   Firms can gain free publicity and awareness through PR efforts. The trade-off is that they cannot control how the message will appear in the press.

E-Mail. Firms can purchase lists of e-mail addresses and send out a bulk mailing. The best lists consist of people who have given permission to receive targeted mailings. Users typically resent unsolicited e-mail, and therefore it is a problematic lever at best. Nevertheless, an e-mail that is opened and read does lead the user into the awareness stage.

Interactive Television. While iTV is in its infancy, it promises to combine the characteristics of traditional television (see below) with the interactivity of the Internet. It remains to be seen whether viewers will prefer to remain in a passive mode or engage in a more active mode when using this medium.

Offline Levers

Television. Television advertising is polished and engaging and has broad reach but is a very expensive way to develop awareness. It is most used by big companies with deep pockets and large numbers of customers. Creative execution is paramount to stand out from the clutter of television ads. Television advertisements can also offer some interactivity, by promoting a telephone number to call or a website to visit for more information. Victoria's Secret ran a Super Bowl advertisement that generated one million hits for its website in just one hour after the ad aired. While TV does offer limited interactivity, it can offer almost no personalization.

Magazines and Newspapers. Specialized magazines are an excellent way to generate awareness among users likely to be interested in a product. For example, eBay generated enormous awareness among stamp collectors by frequent advertising in *Linn's Stamp News*. Magazines are an effective lever for reaching early adopters of products. Newspapers are an excellent way to reach adults or to generate awareness within a particular geography.

Radio. Radio offers advertisers good geographic and demographic selectivity, as well as solid potential for impact. Reach is narrow, but can be expanded by purchasing advertisements on multiple stations regionally and nationally. Frequency can also be easily expanded by purchasing more ads. Radio can be used to reach consumers when media such as television and advertising are out of reach (e.g., during commuting time).

Yellow Pages. The yellow pages reach consumers who are ready to buy, which makes it an attractive medium for advertising. One principle applies: Have the largest ad. Thirty percent of yellow pages shoppers call the firm with the largest ad. Prominent placement generates a high level of awareness that often leads directly to exploration in the form of a phone call.

Billboards/Outdoor. Billboards offer excellent frequency, lower costs, and low clutter, but targeting an audience is very difficult. Reach is also limited. Their format, of course, excludes almost any opportunity for individualization or interactivity, though there is plenty of room for creativity. Billboards are best applied for image and branding, as they can generate awareness, but do little to facilitate the transfer to the exploration/expansion phase.

Exploration/Expansion

Online Levers

Many of the tools used as awareness levers double as levers for exploration and expansion. Once a user has clicked on a banner ad, for example, the exploration stage begins.

Rich Media and Dynamic Ad Placement. Clicking on a rich-media ad exposes consumers to a multimedia message akin to television commercials. It has the potential of conveying rich imagery and detailed information that users can access at will. When dynamic ad placement is used, the message should have a better chance of reaching a receptive audience. However, the use of rich media depends on viewers having broadband Internet access.

E-Mail. In addition to generating awareness, an e-mail message can describe product benefits and give reasons to consider a purchase. A well-crafted, targeted e-mail is likely to encourage a click-through to the website and further exploration. Once the user has interacted with the firm, the firm can use the data gathered from the exchange to make useful offers. Targeted e-mail can help develop expectations. It can also increase the interaction between the firm and the user, helping drive a user to expand the relationship.

Website. Once the user is aware of the website and has visited it, the firm's best leverage is at the website itself. A clear, easy-to-navigate site will help a user to understand the value proposition of a company and develop a clear understanding of the terms of interaction. Websites can help move customers to the expansion stage with informative articles or videos containing product information or general information.

Offline Levers

Television, Magazines. In addition to using television and magazines to create awareness, a marketing team can exploit these levers to foster exploration and expansion of the relationship. The levers can build brand image and remind customers that the product exists.

Sales Force. Traditionally the sales force was used for all stages of the communications and relationship-building process with B2B customers. However, its extremely high cost and the availability of new online resources mean that firms now use salespeople much more selectively. Thus, a firm may use the sales force to establish a personal relationship with a large account and to walk buyers through a complex product offering, but use its website to provide detailed product specifications and to take orders.

Online/Offline Levers

Newspapers, Radio, Banner Ads. Sales promotions featured in newspapers, radio, and Web ads give customers an immediate reason to purchase the product. They are very effective at driving immediate sales. Yahoo!, in partnership with 1,000 Web merchants, promoted a 72-hour "sale days" event through radio, newspapers, outdoor advertising, banner ads, and homepages. It achieved a 25 percent surge in gross merchandise sales over the three days, with some merchandisers reporting sales increases of nearly

500 percent over the previous week.[57] But many marketers believe sales promotions should be used judiciously because they do not differentiate products and attract mostly bargain seekers, who do not offer the greatest long-term value.

Customer Service. Customer service can, of course, be both Web-based and offline. Quality customer service contributes substantially to the development of commitment. A customer who is in the process of exploring or expanding a relationship with the firm may quickly dissolve the relationship at little personal cost if he or she cannot get important questions answered. This is confirmed by the fact that more than half of all online shopping carts are abandoned. Some e-commerce websites have added live chat help to answer shoppers' questions immediately. Martha Stewart Living's website (*www.marthastewart.com*), for instance, offers multiple ways for people to interact with the company or with other shoppers.

Commitment

The following communication levers are best applied to generate commitment.

Online Levers

Fostering commitment in an Internet marketing campaign relies extensively on the 2Is: individualization and interactivity. Because of their inherently high level of personalization and interactivity, the online levers offer a greater ability to generate and sustain commitment than most of the offline levers do.

Permission E-Mail. Permission e-mail is one of the most powerful levers for keeping consumers in the commitment stage. As the relationship grows, so too must the level of personalization—the firm needs to make good use of its customer data in order to justify the continued collection of such information. Permission marketing requires interactivity in order to make the user feel that he or she is in a two-way conversation with the firm, learning about products that he or she wants and needs. A firm can mine substantial information from user profiles and purchase patterns. By utilizing this information, the firm can continue to provide value to the user. Moreover, e-mail can be used to promote both the durability and the consistency of the relationship. A firm can encourage regular buying with well-targeted e-mails that offer consumers goods or services that they want.

Personalized Webpages. Personalized pages are webpages that are, to some extent, custom built for each registered user. Such pages generate expansion and exploration of the firm–customer relationship by making the site more relevant to the individual, and thereby easier to navigate. Yahoo!'s personalized My Yahoo! pages let the user choose the type of content they see. The payoff for Yahoo! is the ability to use that information to build ad-targeting databases. Moreover, the pages promote consistency and durability. As users can get more and more information that they want from Yahoo!, they spend more time on Yahoo! properties and generate increased page views. After users build a personal homepage with one company, they are unlikely to invest the effort to do so elsewhere.

Drill-Down

Permission Marketing

"Opt-in," "opt-out," and "do not contact" lists are hotly debated in the interactive marketing industry. While reputable marketers adhere to voluntary industry guidelines allowing consumers to opt out of receiving marketing communications, many fear that requiring consumers to opt in to receiving messages will be a great handicap. To their dismay, various countries and states have enacted laws regulating direct marketing to consumers. But permission marketing—giving consumers the choice of what communications they receive—makes sense in any case.

Permission marketing is based on a simple premise. The bulk of marketing is, in the words of Seth Godin, interruptive—that is, in order to attract the attention of a potential customer, an advertiser must interrupt and capture a customer's most precious commodity: time. Permission marketers, on the other hand, seek to reach only those users who have signaled an interest in a firm's products. Permission marketing, therefore, is based on offering consumers incentives to voluntarily accept advertising.

The value proposition of permission marketing lies in its ability to build a long-term relationship with customers. Instead of focusing on grabbing new customers, permission marketers concentrate on expanding their relationship with current customers, who do not have to be reached through the clutter of mass-media advertising.

Permission marketing campaigns have several steps, but each one has the same goal: The next step is always to expand the level of permission. Typically, the first step will require some interruptive techniques, because the firm must get users to volunteer to begin the information exchange. The focus of the interruptive ad is to get permission, not to make a sale—an interrupted consumer is typically less willing to buy something than to ask for more information. When the firm makes its initial offer in the attempt to gain volunteered permission, the offer should have no downside to the consumer.

Once the firm has volunteers, it needs to patiently and frequently teach the consumer about its products and services. This is an input from the firm to the relationship that goes beyond providing goods and services. The firm is providing information that the consumer trusts. As long as the firm provides useful information, the consumer will continue to read the messages and interact with them. Thus, the relationship is durable and consistent.

The success of this system derives from a simple marketing concept: Frequency works. Permission empowers frequency. Therefore, permission marketing allows firms to be in constant contact with their customers. This, in turn, fosters commitment.

Online/Offline Levers

Customer Service.   In the commitment phase, customer service plays an important role in ensuring durability of the relationship. Users who are in a committed relationship with the firm should receive excellent customer service. Firms should implement multiple levels of customer service for their best customers, including toll-free telephone numbers to ensure faster, better support. Firms should also quickly answer e-mails from their best customers. Customer service can be a make-or-break consideration for customers in the commitment phase.

Offline Levers

Sales Force.   A sales force call helps cement commitment on the part of the consumer. It signals that the customer is valued, and when salespeople have good communication skills, it is the most interactive and individualized form of communication possible.

Direct Mail with Permission. Targeted mail sent to customers who state they want to receive it allows the firm to ensure a durable and consistent relationship with its customers. While direct mail lacks the powerful interactivity of permission e-mail, targeted, personalized offers will certainly raise the effectiveness of a direct-mail campaign. Catalog retailers such as L.L.Bean effectively use customer data to determine which version of the catalog should be mailed and when it should be mailed.

Dissolution

The Internet's dynamic nature makes it easier for firms to dissolve their relations with unprofitable customers. There is software that enables firms to identify customers who frequently return goods so the firm can charge them more money per transaction. However, discriminatory pricing has proven unpopular and can generate an unwelcome backlash, as Amazon.com found when it tested the process in spring 2000. This is compounded because the Internet's community nature allows disgruntled customers to voice their frustration and be heard by a large group of people.

Personalized Pages. Firms wishing to dissolve a relationship can personalize pages to make the relationship less attractive to the user, or they can charge a premium price to certain users who are not profitable.

Termination. Firms can terminate permission marketing, telemarketing, and direct mail to customers who are not providing enough business to sustain a mutually profitable relationship.

eBay Example

Few firms communicate as successfully as eBay. The leading auction website focuses its marketing strategy on brand promotion and attracting new buyers and sellers. In the time right after its 1995 launch, eBay relied almost exclusively on word-of-mouth advertising to attract customers. Since those humble beginnings, eBay's communications efforts have resulted in phenomenal growth in both users and items being auctioned.

eBay's extraordinary success in attracting buyers and sellers provides an example of how highly successful and targeted communications throughout the four stages can increase the intensity of the consumer's relationship with the website.

Awareness

Offline Levers

In its early years, faced with the need to rapidly expand its user base to reap the benefits of the network effect—as more users join, the value of a community increases geometrically rather than arithmetically—and to stave off competitors, eBay used offline levers to reach potential customers. The firm sent representatives armed with laptops to trade shows to demonstrate the eBay service. By 1999, eBay ambassadors were at more than 120 shows each year and two recreational vehicles were dedicated to traveling the country to spread the eBay experience.

Trade show appearances and word of mouth dominated eBay's marketing efforts until late 1998, when the company added traditional media levers. One way of promoting awareness was targeting collectors where they congregated. For example, eBay reached stamp collectors through the publication *Linn's Stamp News*.

eBay launched its first major marketing campaign in 1998 with three components:

- Strategic alliances with online partners: eBay bought substantial advertising space on AOL and partnered with Go.com.
- Public relations: eBay sponsored bidding on Mark McGwire's and Sammy Sosa's homerun baseballs, and a charity auction with television personality Rosie O'Donnell garnered lots of free press.
- Print and radio campaigns: The slogan "You just might find it on eBay" aired on more than 12,000 radio stations across the country.

Online Levers

eBay's Internet marketing campaign was very adaptive to current trends. For example, during the Furby toy craze of 1998, when Furbys became the hottest and most elusive Christmas toy, eBay created a special Furby homepage on its website. eBay used its own site to promote the Furby page, as well as buying Furby keywords from Yahoo!, Infoseek, and Lycos. Finally, eBay sought out vertical websites created by Furby fans to promote its Furby auctions. One of the best-known sites was run by a 14-year-old Canadian boy— and eBay bought banner ads from him, too. The niche placements proved to be cost effective and positioned eBay as the ultimate source for buying and selling Furbys.

eBay also leveraged its power as an advertiser to negotiate a test period for all advertisements it placed. This proved especially powerful in the Furby campaign, because eBay estimated that it could tell within two days whether a placement worked and could therefore curtail underperforming placements.

eBay maintained this strategy of increasing awareness with great success. During a time when the average cost of acquiring a customer on the Internet was $82, eBay spent approximately $13 per new customer. Interestingly, eBay's decision to start using television advertisements in late 2000 coincided with a sharp downturn in the use of television ads by Internet companies. eBay entered the arena to control its image; it wanted to shake its reputation as the world's largest garage sale.

Exploration/Expansion

Offline Levers

In late 2000, eBay unveiled its first television campaign with two thirty-second spots. The ads ran on the three major U.S. networks during popular prime-time shows, including *Who Wants to Be a Millionaire?* and *The West Wing*. Other spots ran on the weekend, including during National Football League playoff games. In one spot, a dog buries several expensive items in the back-yard. In the other ad, a couple watches as their appliances explode, their fix-tures break, and their car gets crushed. Both end with the tagline "If you broke it, lost it, need it cheap, or just can't find it anywhere else, eBay."

"We want to show that buyers can buy a wide range of products in areas not typically associated with eBay," explained eBay spokesman Kevin Pursglove. "The goal is for us to reach people who are familiar with eBay but not mak-ing much of an effort to buy or sell with us."[58] These ads not only prompted people to explore eBay, but it helped them to think about going to eBay for other categories besides collectibles.

In addition to its television campaign, eBay utilized radio and print adver-tisements, and kept up its frequent advertisements in specialized journals.

Online Levers

eBay is most effective using online levers in the expansion stage. Until early 2000, eBay used banner ads placed at high-traffic sites to promote explo-ration and expansion. When the effectiveness of banner ads began to be questioned, eBay bought keywords on prominent search engines. For exam-ple, someone looking for an Olympus digital camera may go to Google and type "digital camera" and "Olympus" in the search box. Along with numer-ous results, a sponsored link titled "OLYMPUS DIGITAL" would appear in the right-hand column (see Exhibit 9.14). This would prompt someone aware of eBay to visit the site to fulfill his or her camera purchase.

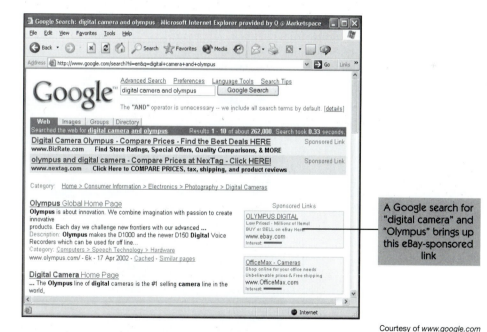

A Google search for "digital camera" and "Olympus" brings up this eBay-sponsored link

Courtesy of *www.google.com*

EXHIBIT 9.14   eBay-Sponsored Link

Additionally, eBay leverages its message boards to promote expansion. In fact, it has a message board dedicated to marketing services, features, and policy updates. One message announced a promotion where bidders on a day preselected by eBay could win one of hundreds of prizes, including free airline travel for a year (see Exhibit 9.15).

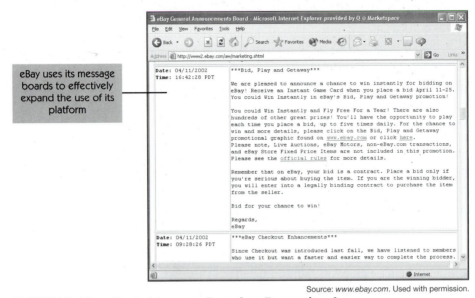

eBay uses its message boards to effectively expand the use of its platform

Source: *www.ebay.com*. Used with permission.

EXHIBIT 9.15   eBay's Message Board as Expansion Lever

Online/Offline Levers

Some of eBay's exploration and expansion efforts span the online and offline arenas. For example, in February 2000, eBay entered into a four-year marketing agreement with the Walt Disney Company to provide it with online and offline advertising and promotions and to develop a cobranded version of its service (see Exhibit 9.16). Deals like this give eBay prominent placement on its partners' sites and lead to a broader audience reach. For eBay, as with any Internet-based firm, driving users to the website is crucial for moving users from awareness to commitment.

Clicking on "Disney Auctions" from Disney.com takes visitors to this cobranded site, which combines eBay's look-and-feel with Disney's well-known brand.

Source: *www.pages.ebay.disney.com/* Used with permission.

EXHIBIT 9.16   eBay/Disney Cobranded Site

Commitment

One online lever eBay uses effectively to generate commitment is personalization. An example is the creation of eBay Stores, which give sellers the ability to create and personalize their eBay businesses and leverages both eBay's community and infrastructure. A seller of vintage cameras could create an online store to sell his wares and brand himself by creating an eBay user name that reflects the name of his eBay business. The success of this eBay store would preclude the owner from moving his business to another location or from investing in building his own online store. Similarly, a personalization lever for buyers is called My eBay. A buyer's ability to personalize her My eBay view enables her to program her favorite searches. Star Wars figurine collectors could set up My eBay to show only auctions containing Star Wars figurines, saving them the step of manually conducting a search each time they visited.

These personalization features increase customers' switching costs and build commitment. The more personalized and effective the eBay experience becomes, the harder it is for users to re-create it elsewhere. A switch from eBay to a second-tier online auction house makes it harder for buyers to find what they want in one place and harder for sellers to attract as many customers. Additionally, sellers leaving eBay would have to pay the costs of building their own site and attracting people to it.

Dissolution

Through its website eBay communicates to all users the clear way it manages dissolution. The anonymity afforded to people online removes some of the barriers that in the real world keep people honest. For example, it is much easier for a short, overweight person to describe himself as tall, dark, and handsome in a chat room than it is in real life. While this example is rather harmless, fraudulent online behavior could have a terribly detrimental effect on eBay if left unchecked. If buyers were unsure that auction items are authentic, or that they will receive the items they pay for, commerce on eBay would slowly grind to a halt as people flee for safer, more reliable shopping options.

eBay employs several levers to promote good behavior and to remove dishonest customers. For instance, eBay constantly patrols its listings for fraudulent activity with the assistance of members of its community. Those caught violating eBay's rules can be banned from buying and selling on the website. In some instances they can even be prosecuted for wire fraud, as one eBay user was for fraudulently selling rare, valuable and collectable baseball and basketball card sets.

eBay's feedback system serves as another lever to promote dissolution of unwanted users. When a seller is unable to achieve a market clearing price due to the negative feedback, or when a buyer is frozen from bidding due to a low rating, he becomes less likely to use the service (or more likely to improve his behavior). eBay needs to manage this process carefully because users who have bad experiences with eBay are unlikely to continue using the service.

Summary

1. **Why is marketing communication important?**

Marketing communication is important because it is through communication with consumers that firms establish marketing relationships. By creating positive, comfortable relationships with consumers, an environment is created in which consumers are more likely to advance through the earlier relationship stages and settle into the commitment stage.

2. **What is the role of the Internet in a marketing communications campaign?**

The Internet can play a role in virtually every stage of the campaign, from identifying the target audience to evaluating the performance of the campaign. The Internet's most important strengths as a powerful marketing tool include the characteristics of being interactive and individual, and its measuring and tracking capabilities.

3. **What are the main categories of communication types? Within each category, what are the tools, or marketing levers that marketers use to communicate with consumers?**

- *Offline mass:* Marketing levers include television, radio, outdoor ads, point-of-purchase displays, public relations, and print media including newspapers, magazines, brochures, newsletters, and yellow pages.
- *Offline personal:* Marketing levers include telemarketing, direct mail, sales force, and customer service.
- *Online mass:* Marketing levers include websites, banners, interstitials, rich media, search engines, listings, classifieds, and sponsorships.
- *Online personal:* Marketing levers include personalized websites, dynamic ad placement, interactive television, wireless devices, e-mail, and customer service.

4. **What are the six steps in the communication process?**

- Identify the target audience.
- Determine the communication objective.
- Develop a media plan.
- Create the message.
- Execute the campaign.
- Evaluate the effectiveness of the campaign.

5. **How do the 2Is of the Internet affect marketing communications?**

The fact that marketers can offer individualized messages to consumers in a medium that allows lively interaction and instant communication makes the Internet a unique and powerful tool for marketing communication. Most importantly, it allows for the creation of high-intensity relationships between the firm and consumer, and it streamlines the progression from awareness to commitment.

6. **What levers are used in each of the four customer relationship stages?**

- *Awareness:* Levers include online ad placements such as banners, keywords, classifieds and listings, e-mail, television, magazines and newspapers, radio, pubic relations, yellow pages, and outdoor ads such as billboards.
- *Exploration/Expansion:* Levers include rich media, websites, e-mail, television, radio, newspapers, sales force, and customer service.
- *Commitment:* Levers include targeted e-mail, personalized webpages, targeted direct mail, sales force, and customer service.
- *Dissolution:* Levers include personalized pages geared toward dissolution, and termination of permission marketing.

1. Go to the homepage of MSN, Yahoo!, or AOL. Then explore at least two sections of the website. Keep a log of every advertisement you see and classify them according to type of tool. Click on each ad and track what happens. Which ads were most and least effective? Why?
2. Pick one B2C product (one that is sold to consumers) and one B2B product (one that is sold to businesses). For each product, describe what media types and media schedule you would select to move customers through the relationship stages. Describe the decision-making process you use to make these selections.
3. Refer to the Drill-Down titled "BMW, an Interactive Communications Case Study." Why do you think BMW was pleased with the results of the two campaigns? What metrics would you use to assess the effectiveness of the campaign? Why would you use those metrics?

customer-centric marketing communications

relationship marketing

integrated marketing communications

interactive marketing communications

database marketing

banner advertisements

interstitial

permission marketing

viral marketing

reach

frequency

cost per thousand impressions (CPM)

cost per click-through

cost per transaction

affiliate marketing

[1]Balasubramanian, Sridhar, Bart J. Bronnenberg, and Robert Peterson. 1997. Exploring the implications of the Internet for consumer marketing. *Journal of the Academy of Marketing Science* 25 (4):329–346.

[2]The Internet sells its soul. 2002. *The Economist*, April 18.

[3]Chatterjee, Patrali, Donna L. Hoffman, and Thomas P. Novak. 1998. Modeling the clickstream: Implications for web-based advertising efforts. Project 2000, Owen Graduate School of Management, May.

[4]The American Association of Advertising Agencies defines IMC as a concept of marketing communications planning that recognizes the added value of a comprehensive plan that evaluates the strategic roles of a variety of communications disciplines—for example, general advertising, direct response, sales promotion, and public relations—and combines these disciplines to provide clarity, consistency, and maximum communications impact through the seamless integration of discrete messages.

[5]Gaeta, Julie. June 2000. Multichannel marketing. *eCRM*. (*www.destinationcrm.com/ec/dcrm/ec/article.asp?id541&ed56%2F1%2F00*).

[6]Zollman, Peter M. May 29, 1999. Confusion reigns. *MediaINFO.com*.

[7]Bauer, Hans H., Mark Grether, and Mark Leach. June 1999. Customer relations through the Internet. Working Paper, Mannheim University, Department of Marketing.

[8]Grover, Ronald. 2000. Lights, camera, web site: Interview with Jeffrey Gozsick. *Business Week* 18 September, EB 54.

[9]Ariely, Dan. 2000. Controlling the information flow: Effects on consumers' decision making and preferences. *Journal of Consumer Research* 27.

[10]Rayport, Jeffrey F. and Jaworski, Bernard J. 2001. *e-Commerce*. New York: McGraw Hill/Irwin.

[11]Lodish, Leonard M., et al., How TV advertising works: A meta-analysis of 389 real world split cable TV advertising experiments, *Journal of Marketing Research* 23 (May 1995):125–139.

[12]Network television cost and CPM trends, (*http://www.tvb.org/tvfacts/trends/media/1b.html*).

[13]Television Bureau of Advertising, 2002. Latest TV ad revenue figures. *www.tvb.org/tvfacts/2001revenue/index.html.* Webpage accessed May 6, 2002.

[14]Arbitron. 2002. Radio's leading indicator: audience ratings and their impact on revenue.

[15]AdAge.com. 2002. Domestic spending by medium (URL: *http://www.adage.com/page.cms?pageId*=681).

[16]Strupp, Joe. 2002. Rechecked ABC numbers are in the mail. *Editor&Publisher.* May 6.

[17]International Newspaper Marketing Association. 2000. The state of newspaper circulation. 23 March, *http://www.inma.org/reports_circsummitopen.html.*

[18]Direct 2001: Tradition driving the future—part 1. 2001. *www.the-dma.org/cgi/dispnewsstand?article*=524. Accessed May 6, 2002.

[19]Ibid.

[20]Fishman, Charles. 1999. This is a marketing revolution. *Fast Company* May, 204. (*http://www.fastcompany.com/online/24/capone.html*).

[21]Jupiter Media Metrix. 2002. US online users, 2000-2006. *www.jmm.com/xp/jmm/press/industryProjections.xml.* Accessed May 7, 2002.

[22]CyberAtlas Staff. 2002. The world's online population. *CyberAtlas.* March 21. *http://cyberatlas.internet.com/big_picture/geographics/print/0,,5911_151151,00.html.* Accessed May 14, 2002.

[23]PricewaterhouseCoopers. 2001. IAB Internet advertising revenue report. December, page 3.

[24]Briggs, Rex, and Nigel Hollis. 1997. Advertising on the Web: Is there response before click-through? *Journal of Advertising Research* 37 (2): 33.

[25]PricewaterhouseCoopers. 2001. IAB Internet advertising revenue report. December, page 7.

[26]Pastore, Michael and Christopher Saunders. 2002. Ad spending down, use of larger ads increases. *CyberAtlas.* March 8. *http://cyberatlas.internet.com/markets/advertising/article/0,5941_987871,00.html.* Accessed May 8, 2002.

[27]Pastore, Michael. 2001. Rich media Internet ads. *Internet.com* (*http://adres.Internet.com/stories/print/0,,7561_183431,00.html*).

[28]Interactive Advertising Bureau. 2002. IAB glossary of interactive advertising terms.

[29]Olsen, Stefanie. 2000. Image is everything as dot-coms cozy up to advertisers. *news.com.* 14 November (*http://news.cnet.com/news/0-1005-200-3682174.html*).

[30]Riedman, Patricia. 2001. Poor rich media. *AdAge.com.* February 5. *http://www.adage.com/new.cms?newsId*=1396. Accessed April 30, 2002.

[31]Pastore, Michael, 2001. Paid search engines endure advertising slowdown. *CyberAtlas.* July 30. *http://cyberatlas.internet.com/markets/advertising/print/0,,5941_856381,00.html.* Accessed May 8, 2002.

[32]CyberAtlas staff, 2001. Search engines fail to draw marketing dollars. *CyberAtlas.* August 22. *http://cyberatlas.internet.com/markets/advertising/print/0,,5941_870711,00.html.* Accessed May 8, 2002.

[33]Gikandi, David. 2000. Search engine marketing update. *Internet.com.* 6 September (*http://adres.Internet.com/feature/article/0,,8961_453571,00.html*).

[34]CyberAtlas staff, 2001. Search engines fail to draw marketing dollars. *Cyberatlas.* August 22. *http://cyberatlas.internet.com/big_picture/traffic_patterns/print/0,,5931_991681,00.html.* Accessed May 8, 2002.

[35]Fine, Jon. 2002. Newspapers mauled by Monster.com. *AdAge.com.* April 30. *http://www.adage.com/news.cms?newsId*=34591. Accessed May 2, 2002.

[36]Lawrence, Stacy. 2000. Making online ads click. *The Standard.* 11 December (*www.thestandard.com/research/metrics/display/0,2799,20696,00.htm*).

[37]Teinowitz, Ira. 2001. Software maker to suspend use of pop-up ads. *AdAge.com.* November 30. *http://www.adage.com/news.cms?newsId*=33538. Accessed April 30, 2002.

[38]Direct Marketing Association. 2002. New DMA report finds e-mail marketing coming of age. Press Release. April 3.

[39]Greenspan, Robyn. 2002. Media buyers prefer quality over quantity. *CyberAtlas*. May 8. *http://cyberatlas.internet. com/markets/advertising/print/0,,5941_1041891,00.html*. Accessed May 8, 2002.

[40]Greenspan, Robyn. 2002. Media buyers prefer quality over quantity. *CyberAtlas*. May 8. *http://cyberatlas.internet. com/markets/advertising/print/0,,5941_1041891,00.html*. Accessed May 8, 2002.

[41]Pastore, Michael. 2001. Increase in e-mail marketing could mean opportunity for providers. *CyberAtlas*, January 25. *http://cyberatlas.internet.com/markets/advertising/print/0,,5941_571001,00.html*. Accessed May 9, 2002.

[42]Forrester Research. 2002. Europe's iDTV penetration will reach 44 percent of households in 2007, Forrester calculates. Press Release. May 1.

[43]Rafter, Michelle V. 1999. At your service. *The Standard*. 10 May (*www.thestandard.com/article/display/0,1151,4532,00. html*).

[44]Hallford, Joshua. 2000. The customer (service) is always right. *The Standard*. 18 September (*www.thestandard. com/article/display/0,1151,18623,00.html*).

[45]Rayport, Jeffrey F. and Jaworski, Bernard J. 2001. *e-Commerce*. New York: McGraw-Hill/Irwin.

[46]Draper, Tim, and Steve Jurvetson. 1998. Viral marketing. *Business 2.0*. November.

[47]Most sites have an "advertisers" link that lays out ad opportunities that may be helpful in determining the media plan. Information can be found on sponsorships, contextual banners on content channels, banner impressions, or text links on front doors (e.g., a welcome screen), keyword banner impressions on a search page, contextual banners on a community page (e.g., a chat room), or contextual banners on a vertical directory (a directory specializing in a certain category such as auto manufacturers or computer software publishers).

[48]Schultz, Don E., Stanley I. Tannenbaum, and Robert F. Lauterborn. 1994. *The new marketing paradigm: Integrated marketing communications*. Chicago: NTC Business Books.

[49]Elkin, Tobi. 2002. Samsung massively boosts online advertising. *AdAge.com*. April 29. *http://www.adage.com/ news.cms?newsId=34575*. Accessed April 30, 2002.

[50]Taylor, Catharine P. 2001. Yahoo! lauded, MSN damned in ad panel portal assessment. *AdAge.com*. December 17. *http://www.adage.com/news.cms?nesId=33655*. Accessed April 30, 2002.

[51]Hillebrand, Mary. 2000. AOL slam dunks NBA marketing deal. *E-Commerce Times*. 5 June.

[52]Firms know when users are exposed to an ad by tracking when Web pages are fully loaded on a consumer's screen.

[53]Information Resources, Inc. 2002. IRI and DoubleClick study shows online advertising drives sales of consumer packaged goods. Press Release. April 10.

[54]Elkin, Tobi and Jack Neff. 2002. Package goods marketing continues online migration. *AdAge.com*. May 8. *http://www.adage.com/news.cms?newsId=34679*. Accessed May 10, 2002.

[55]Summer 2000: BMW drives brand experience online [no date]. *http:/www.leavcom.com/digi_bmw.htm*. Accessed May 9, 2002.

[56]Gaffney, John. 2001. Forget the new M3. BMW's hottest product is streaming online. *Business 2.0*. August. *http://www.business2.com/articles/mag/print/0,1643,16730,FF.html*. Accessed May 9, 2002.

[57]Elkin, Tobi. 2002. Online marketing experiment boosts sales nearly 500%. *AdAge.com*. March 28. *http://www. adage.com/news.cms?newsId=34317*. Accessed April 30, 2002.

[58]Regan, Keith. 2000. eBay Unveils First U.S. TV Campaign. *E-Commerce Times*. 28 December.

Community

This chapter examines online community—its definition, criteria, and the characteristics that successful communities share—with the aim of arriving at an archetype. This chapter looks at the evolution of communities—how and why they originated—and discusses how value is created and transferred within them. Ultimately, this chapter will reveal how community is linked to our four-stage framework. In addition to exploring the meaning and evolution of community, this chapter also explains when and how community should be used, as well as the specific ways in which it creates value.

QUESTIONS

Please consider the following questions as you read this chapter:

1. What is community?

2. What criteria define true communities?

3. What types of interests form the foundation of community?

4. What are the different ways in which communities function?

5. What are the three primary ways in which value is created within a community?

6. What benefits can community generate for a parent firm?

7. When is community development appropriate?

8. What are the different levels of community?

Introduction

This chapter is divided into the following eight sections:

What Is Community? This section defines community, providing clarity to an often loosely used term. The section also provides 10 criteria for assessing a successful community.

Co-authored by Javier Colayco and Jon Davis. With substantive input from David Ruben.

Why and How Do Communities Form and How Do They Function? This section explores the origins and formation of the various types of community. It also examines how communities function at a broad operational level, such as through real-time formats or asynchronous formats.

The Creation and Transfer of Value Within Communities. This section introduces three types of value created within communities through the Transfer of Value Triangle.

The Creation and Transfer of Value Outside of Communities. This section takes a more macro view of value creation by focusing on the benefits accruing to firms that sponsor community development.

How Do Individuals Become Part of a Community? This section discusses the stages of community membership, and how individuals progress as members in a community. A model for community membership stages, the Membership Life Cycle, is then examined, followed by a discussion of the role that intensity plays in community.

When to Develop Community. This section introduces guidelines that help determine when building community is a smart choice. The section also examines commonly found community types.

How to Create Successful Community. This section introduces two frameworks for building community. The first outlines three stages of community from a macro perspective; the second looks at community from the micro perspective, and shows how individuals can be moved through the membership stages and our four-stage framework.

eBay Example. The chapter concludes with a discussion of eBay's community. It looks in detail at how eBay satisfies the criteria of community outlined in the beginning of the chapter.

What Is Community?

Defining Community

Community is a set of interwoven relationships, built upon shared interests, that satisfies individual needs that would otherwise be unattainable.

Community consists of sets of **relationships.** This is different from sets of **interactions.** Relationships imply a higher degree of commitment and intensity between individuals, whereas interactions can involve communication at a very basic, noncommittal level. Relationships imply trust—a key ingredient of successful community—whereas interactions do not.

For example, a business partnership consisting of a photography store in San Francisco and a film vendor in New York is considered a relationship—trust drives its existence. In contrast, a tourist from San Francisco buying a newspaper from a street vendor in New York is merely an interaction. The latter is also a transaction, but lacks the commitment or intensity that characterizes relationships. Interactions, such as that between a tourist and a local vendor, amount to little. Relationships, such as those between business partners, are the building blocks of community.

Community, however, is not just a set of relationships—it is a set of *interwoven* relationships. A room can be full of couples involved in intense, committed relationships. But if the couples do not speak to one another and share interests and experiences, true community does not form. What results is a mere collection of relationships rather than any kind of community. In true communities, relationships between individuals need to be expansive and interwoven. True community, then, satisfies members' needs that are otherwise unattainable individually. This speaks to some of the unique benefits of community: There are advantages to large numbers and expansive relationships.

One last distinction: Community is a set of interwoven relationships *built upon* a shared interest, not simply *held together* by a shared interest. The words "built upon" imply that community rests upon the foundation of a shared interest. From this foundation, community rises to levels where members become more invested and active and provide more value. Hence, there are different levels of community. Community is often thought of as a discrete entity—you either have it or you don't. Rather, communities should be examined in terms of level of development. Communities typically start low, but, with proper guidance, build and evolve to achieve higher levels of functionality and meaning for their members.

Ten Criteria That Define Successful Community

The definition of community can be further clarified by identifying common denominators among successful communities—those that have reached the highest level of development. Examples of such communities are eBay, Microsoft Gaming Zone, and iVillage. These communities have developed interwoven relationships among members and have built upon a focused interest in order to satisfy member needs. Successful communities like these share the following 10 characteristics, which can be grouped into four categories (see Exhibit 10.1):

People criteria
1. Membership is a conscious choice.
2. Member base has achieved critical mass and sustainability.
3. Members feel a great sense of trust.

Process criteria
4. Members achieve benefits in scale.
5. Roles are not hierarchical or imposed.
6. Effective facilitation and site structure keep community activities on track.

Culture criteria
7. A spirit of participation and feedback is clearly cultivated.
8. A sense of affiliation is achieved through ownership of equity in the community.

Technology criteria
9. Efficiency in interaction is maximized.
10. The community is easily navigable.

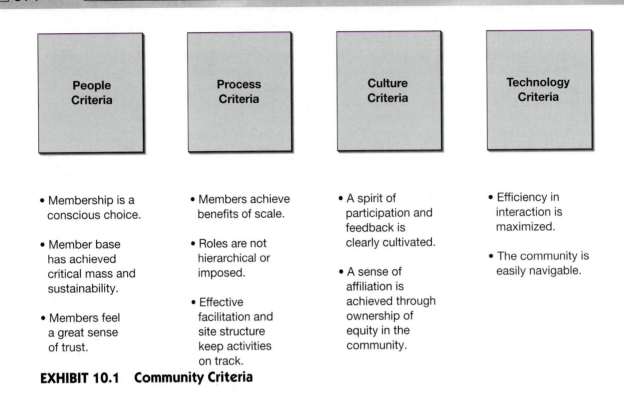

EXHIBIT 10.1   Community Criteria

People Criteria

Membership Is a Conscious Choice.   The purchase of a product, even if it occurs within community space, does not mean that a consumer can automatically be considered part of that community. Although a purchase indicates interest in a product, it does not necessarily indicate interest in joining a community. Many companies attempt to ignore this. For example, this can happen when buying products online. Companies will sometimes check a box that subscribes visitors to their mailing list, automatically considering them as part of their community. Such communities tend to be artificial, have inflated numbers of membership, and are not really communities at all. Companies forget that communities are built upon relationships, which implies a certain degree of commitment and intensity consciously volunteered by the individual. Being automatically subscribed to a mailing list does not involve any commitment or intensity on the individual's part, so what results are not relationships but a stagnant collection of e-mail addresses that happen to receive the same mailing every week. This is hardly a community.

Member Base Has Achieved Critical Mass and Sustainability.   Successful communities are fueled by a sufficiently large membership base that consistently gathers, participates, and adds value in community meeting areas. Achieving such critical mass is crucial for sustainability; attracting and retaining members can be difficult when individuals find chat rooms empty and message boards littered with old posts. Achieving critical mass is also paramount in generating two highly valued characteristics sought in communities: user-generated content (e.g., ratings, opinions, advice) and the ability to branch off into subgroups (i.e., the option for individuals to discuss a subtopic related to the community's main topic).[1] As membership grows and critical mass is achieved, user-to-user activity increases. Typically, both the quality and quantity of the user-generated content also increases. By achieving critical mass, more subgroups can more realistically branch off and sustain themselves. This makes the community diverse, attractive, and most important, sustainable.

Members Feel a Great Sense of Trust.   Communities cannot exist without relationships, and relationships cannot exist without trust. Successful communities earn and develop great trust from their members, allowing relationships to deepen and flourish within the community. Depending on the community, this trust can take many forms:

- It could be a feeling of safety when making a transaction.
- It could be a sense that an individual's personal information will not be misused (such as for e-mail spamming).
- It could be the knowledge that members generally respect and self-enforce community etiquette.

Trust is not engendered when websites automatically subscribe visitors to mailing lists and consider them part of their community. This lack of trust of their so-called community members to freely choose to join their community is another reason why this example does not meet the criteria of community.

Members who feel trust become increasingly likely to participate, give information, and add value. Also, high levels of trust allow community administrators to effectively leverage user-generated value like targeted product sales or subscription fees. Trust is a key ingredient in making a successful community—without it, communities such as eBay would never have succeeded, given the somewhat risky nature of peer-to-peer (P2P) online transactions.

Process Criteria

Members Achieve Benefits in Scale.   This criterion refers to the definition of community that says communities satisfy needs not attainable individually. Communities primarily satisfy these needs through benefits of scale. Tasks ranging from gathering information to forming a buyer consortium become possible or easier when large numbers of people gather in a community. Thus scale is a member-benefit enabler. Member benefits are achieved through increased levels of participation. An individual community member's benefits are directly proportional to the degree to which that member invests himself in the community—the more a member invests himself in the community, the greater the potential benefits. Examples of benefits could be tips on stock trading or for a video-game competition. The degree to which communities utilize benefits of scale and the network effect, or **Metcalfe's Law** (which states that the value of a network grows by the square of its number of users), often predicts a community's success. Successful communities effectively leverage their size to satisfy member needs.

Roles Are Not Hierarchical or Imposed.

This criterion clarifies the distinction between communities and organizations. Communities and organizations both build upon shared interests, create relationships among people, and satisfy member needs not attainable individually. Their structures, however, tend to be greatly different. Organizations usually impose distinct roles for all individuals, while communities tend to be less hierarchical and rarely assign members responsibility. Roles for community members, such as those for policing discussions, are often undertaken voluntarily and suggest an element of natural selection based on commitment level of the most active community members. Thus highly committed community members, identified by their active message posting, would be more likely to take a leadership role than a newcomer or less committed members. Naturally, there are exceptions to the volunteer rule. For instance, online communities like those in the video-game world can assign individuals certain roles for each game.

Still, communities can generally be differentiated from organizations by their less numerous and less defined roles. Also, communities encourage participation from all members. Community members volunteer for roles, and the consequences of not fulfilling those roles are limited. As such, goals of communities and organizations tend to be vastly different.

Effective Facilitation and Site Structure Keep Activities on Track.

Successful communities share a high degree of focus within their operations. Discussion topics are well organized, threads are easy to follow, inappropriate postings are weeded out, and **flame wars**—mean-spirited exchanges between members—are well controlled. Content is kept relevant and on track. Moderators (also called systems operators, or sysops) harness the energy of the group into useful discussion or activity.

Formal moderators are not always necessary; more developed communities are sometimes self-policed. For instance, committed members of eBay and iVillage tend to be well aware of community etiquette and behavior, and are encouraged to keep newer members in line. Effective site design and structure can also play a large role in keeping activities on track. For example, to prevent flame wars, site design could allow members to mute the messages of annoying individuals—thus diffusing and even curtailing arguments. Additionally, effective site structure could provide community areas where arguments can be played out privately.

Culture Criteria

A Spirit of Participation and Feedback Is Clearly Cultivated.

Communities are fueled by the participation of core members. However, communities that are *dominated* rather than *sustained* by this minority of individuals are not healthy communities. Activity clearly dominated by a minority of individuals can inadvertently discourage participation and feedback from newer members. If perceptions exist that activity is dominated by only a few, this can weaken the sense of open participation and feedback. New members will fail to join and new ideas will fail to circulate because of the lack of broad-based participation, ultimately causing the community to collapse.

The most successful communities cultivate not just intensity from core members, but an increased sense of openness. Successful communities *encourage* community-wide feedback (e.g., through feedback message boards) and also *seek* it through establishing feedback loops—community leaders should establish periodic checkpoints for giving and receiving feedback, such as through polls or surveys. This element of community culture is essential to making the community attractive to new members, helping them feel that their participation is welcome. Community-wide participation and feedback—from novices to elders (see the Membership Life Cycle)—keep the community fresh and relevant. It allows community administrators to appropriately refine community goals and operations as members' needs change.

A Sense of Affiliation Is Achieved Through Ownership of Equity Within the Community.

The most zealous online community members tend to be those whose sense of affiliation is driven by their ownership of equity within their community. A distinction needs to be made, however, between incentive-based and organic equity-creating vehicles. The former awards points for desired behavior. For example, AsianAvenue, a leading community for young Asian Americans, offers "member points" for every login and member referral. These points, which can be redeemed for weekly prizes such as sweaters or CDs, can create artificial value and possibly stimulate unwanted behavior. Members end up strip-mining the community for prizes instead of participating in the community for more intangible benefits. For example, members may log on multiple times a day to register their use but not participate in the community in any of their sessions. An organic equity-creation vehicle, on the other hand, is one where increased participation is its own reward with its own set of benefits. On eBay, members build equity through methods such as garnering a more credible online reputation—through a cumulative member ratings system, individuals can build better online reputations that can help them sell more goods. These subtle kinds of equity—created and owned within the community—are often more powerful than giveaways and can act as hooks that communities use to make members more committed.

Technology Criteria

Efficiency in Interaction Is Maximized.

In any well-developed community, it is a given that communication has become highly efficient. Whether through mailing lists, bulletin boards, or live chat, successful communities choose formats that maximize the efficiency of a typical community interaction. The most efficient communication tool, however, depends upon the type of community and topic of interest. For example, while a chat tool may be the most efficient tool for an online dating community—because chat allows for more natural conversation—chat may be less efficient in exchanging information on Java programming. A bulletin board might be more useful in conveying large amounts of text and complex information needed for later reference.

The Community Is Easily Navigable.

The simplicity of this statement should not be taken lightly; many communities could more successfully attract visitors by making it easier for them to explore. This can be accomplished by establishing a good taxonomy—the creation of meaningful subdivisions can make the difference between making exploring intuitive or a chore. Other methods can include providing an effective site map, topic directory, or comprehensive search engine. Some visitors may first want to find a visitor's center; others may want to look for a particular discussion. In any case, making a community site more navigable is an important step in making a more user-friendly and successful community.

The Role of the 2Is in Community

Individualization and interactivity are at the core of relationships, and hence community. Being aware of these forces and how they play out is important in creating effective online communities. This chapter will address the ways these two forces can affect how an online community forms, functions, and creates value. First, however, their main online community-related attributes will be described (see Exhibit 10.2).

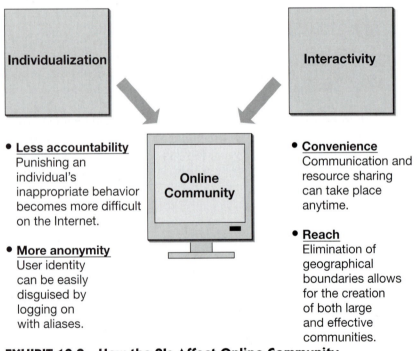

EXHIBIT 10.2   How the 2Is Affect Online Community

Individualization.   Two closely related features of individualization and online community are accountability and anonymity. Unlike offline community, where most of the interaction takes place in person among people who know each other in the context of their environment, online behavior is shrouded behind keystrokes and monitors. This poses challenges to managing individuals in the online community.

One consequence of the veiled nature of the online environment is reduced accountability of individual community members. The end result is that it is more difficult for community managers to punish inappropriate behavior. While societal norms and fears of acting inappropriately among members of a traditional offline community help prevent inappropriate behavior and keep people in line, these forces are much weaker online. Thus, it becomes important for online community managers to develop tools and methods to keep individual members behaving appropriately. Most established online communities have community rules or terms of service, usually containing a list of behaviors not allowed by their members. Individuals must agree to abide by these rules before gaining entry into the community. First infractions of the rules may solicit warnings, while subsequent ones may result in members being booted from the community. For example, on AOL's community message boards, members may report members who use vulgar language in message board postings to the message board managers. Repeated infractions could result in the community manager revoking the individual's message board rights.

Online communities also afford greater anonymity to individual members. In most online communities, the only identifier linking one member to another is a screen name or alias (some communities, such as Yahoo! Games, let individuals assign icons to the aliases for increased personalization). These can be personalized so that one can determine the sex or age or likes of the community member (e.g., "katesmith1957") or they can be a random set of numbers and letters (e.g., qrt38889). Even if someone's screen name is "katesmith1957," there is no guarantee that this is a woman; a man seeking to deceive others can just as easily choose that name. Community managers can exert some control over naming conventions. However, the ease of anonymity will always pose a challenge to keeping members honest.

Interactivity. Perhaps the greatest distinguishing attribute of online community from traditional forms of community is the freedom it affords members, both temporal and spatial. The benefits conveyed by this freedom—the twin features of convenience and reach—have fueled online community size and diversity.

The convenience factor opens the door for more people to join the community. Instead of having to commit to a set meeting place at a set time, community members can join a discussion at any time from virtually any location. Not being tied to a set time has been one of the key drivers for online higher education. Individual classes, each their own community, are composed of busy professionals, stay-at-home parents, and others who for job or lifestyle reasons cannot make time during traditional classroom hours to continue their education. With the freedom to participate in classroom discussions at nontraditional hours, these students can share in the learning process with their fellow classmates any time of day or night.

Similarly, the Internet releases community from the chains of proximity. With an Internet connection, it suddenly becomes possible to extend a community's reach beyond a tight geographical circle. Again, consider higher education. The University of Phoenix, one of the largest (in terms of number of students) providers of adult higher education online has spread its reach far beyond its school's Arizona roots. Students from across the

Sidebar

Instant Messaging Systems
Generally, instant messaging can be described as a service that lets individuals create private areas for instant communication with other individuals. Many instant messaging systems let you know when someone on your private list (chosen by you) is online. Messages can then be sent instantaneously between individuals or a true chat can be initiated. Unfortunately, there are several competing instant messaging systems, and there is no uniform programming standard for creating and processing instant messages. AOL, the leading instant messenger provider, has fought several battles with third-party programmers who have tried to gain access to its closed system of users. Until there is a universally applied instant messaging standard and instant messaging interoperability, users need to be using the same system in order to communicate with each other. To circumvent this problem, some users simply list their instant messaging address in a bulletin board or public chat room so that they can continue conversations privately with other members if they both have the same instant messaging systems.

Despite this challenge, some companies have begun to use instant messaging in conjunction with smart bots to build community. ActiveBuddy launched a smart bot with New Line Cinema to build community around the first *Lord of the Rings* film. People using AOL Instant Messenger could communicate with a bot under the username "RingMessenger" and ask it questions regarding the movie. Entire conversations could be had between movie fans and this intelligent bot. While an interesting tool, it suffers from several limitations, not the least of which is the manpower needed to program
continued

the bot to recognize people's questions and give appropriate answers. Partly because of such limitations and inconveniences noted above, the use of instant messaging systems in communities has been less prevalent than chat or a simple bulletin board system. Subsequently, this chapter does not heavily focus on the use of instant messaging as a tool for community administrators in developing communities.

Drill-Down

How Online Communities Function

Online communities function, from a broad operational level, in one of two primary ways. They communicate through either **real-time formats** (instant communication, where messages are sent, read, and replied to immediately) or **asynchronous formats** (delayed communication, where the time between a message being sent, read, and replied to can vary greatly).[2] Online communities can use real-time systems, asynchronous systems, or a combination of the two.

Real-Time Systems

- *Internet relay chat (IRC).* Chat functionality that operates through programs such as Microsoft Chat or mIRC. Chat functionality allows people to communicate in real time; messages are sent, read, and replied to immediately. Communities can use IRC by arranging for specific channels on IRC where their members can discuss certain topics.

- *Real-time chat.* Chat functionality that operates through a website and a browser or proprietary online service provider environment (e.g., AOL), creating an environment where multiple people can share text-based dialogue with others in real time.

- *Virtual worlds and MUDs/MOOs (multi-user dimensions/MUDs object oriented).* Programs that allow individuals to communicate through a computer-generated world, typically one that individuals can move around in and manipulate.

Asynchronous Systems

- *Mailing lists.* E-mail communication, where an e-mail message is sent to a special address and then forwarded to all other list subscribers. Mailing lists are often monitored to filter list content.

- *Newsgroups (Usenet groups).* Communication by message posting on a global system of virtual bulletin boards called Usenet, where boards can be read and replied to via a newsreader program. Newsreader programs are normally bundled with browsers, such as Netscape Communicator or Microsoft Internet Explorer.

- *Web-based message boards (bulletin board systems [BBS]).* Communication on a bulletin board through a specific website, rather than through a newsreader program.

country and beyond U.S. borders can participate in the learning community as easily as their Arizona-based classmates.

The forces of individualization and interactivity create exciting new scenarios for developing online communities, and can uniquely affect how online community forms, functions, and creates value.

Why and How Do Communities Form and How Do They Function?

The Origins of Community

Community has been with us since the dawn of man. Throughout time, individuals have formed and joined communities. How did this tendency evolve?

In short, community arose because it increased the chances of human survival—in the days of the wooly mammoth, benefits of scale emerged in a community of hunters. In time, however, communities began to satisfy different needs. As technology and society advanced—and survival became less daunting—communities attempted to fill higher-level needs such as psychological needs (e.g., the need for self-actualization and the need to develop oneself through honing a skill).[3] For instance, professional needs arose from individuals seeking vocational instruction and job security. Trade guilds subsequently emerged to bring together individuals in the same profession who shared the interest of honing skills and forming selling consortiums for their services. Social needs arose from individuals seeking to belong to a particular group. Religious groups served as one type of community that filled this need.

Over the centuries, communities were built upon an increasing range of shared traits and interests, from ethnic background to interest in video games to a common alma mater. More recently, online communities have emerged in order to satisfy other needs. The Internet's predecessor, the ARPANET, was originally used in the 1970s by a group of scientists seeking to communicate and share resources electronically. In the early 1990s, academic communities hastened the Internet's growth when the National Science Foundation linked universities around North America.[4] People found that online communities could satisfy many of the same needs as offline communities, only without the limitations of time or geographical distance. The Internet's interactivity had allowed individuals to transcend the traditional limitations of offline community.

The Foundations of Community: Three Types of Shared Interests

Community is defined as a set of interwoven relationships built upon the foundation of shared interests. What exactly are those shared interests? As one can imagine, shared interests can refer to an infinite number of topics, activities, or other commonalities. However, by dividing these interests into groups, the different foundations of communities can more easily be identified.

There are three broad types of communities, differing by their foundation of shared interests. The three different types of communities are (see Exhibit 10.3):

- Information-driven communities (built upon shared interests in information)
- Activity-driven communities (built upon shared interests in activity)
- Commonality-driven communities (built upon shared interests arising out of commonality)

Information-Driven Communities

Communities founded for this purpose seek mainly to exchange facts and opinions. One example of an information-driven community is Motley Fool. Here, members regularly exchange trading tips, voice opinions on the market, and discuss various companies. Information, rather than an interest

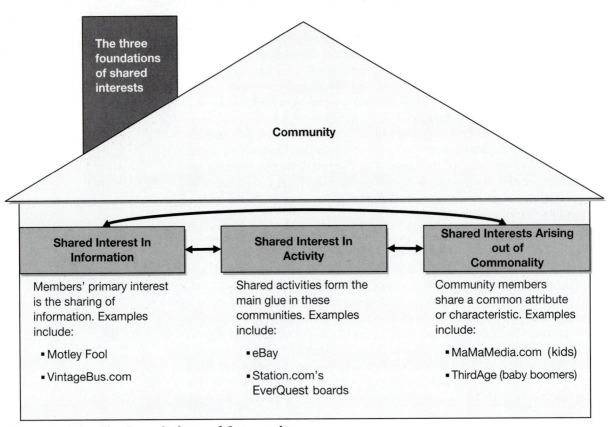

EXHIBIT 10.3   The Foundations of Community

to engage in activity, is the central focus of the community. Another example of a community built on information exchange is Buffettnews.com, a website for fans of the musician Jimmy Buffett. People share set lists, exchange tickets, and talk about the musician on a multitude of message boards. Without a shared interest in information—financial in the first example and concert-related in the latter—these communities would lose their appeal.

Activity-Driven Communities

Shared interests can also mean interests in an activity—specifically, engaging in an activity. Naturally, these activities vary greatly; interests in activity can range from buying antiques to meeting new friends to playing a role in an online game. When these activities occur within the larger context of a community—and drive the existence of that community—that community's foundation is a shared interest in activity. eBay is an excellent example of an activity-driven community. Individuals in the eBay community share an interest in buying and selling goods. While information is also exchanged in the community—through discussion groups about antiques, for example—the driving force behind the community is a shared interest in transacting rather than a shared interest in information. Another excellent example is the message boards Sony built for players of the virtual-world video game EverQuest. The boards are very active. New players can

Drill-Down

The [Ever]Quest for Community

Anyone who doubts that virtual worlds can breed real communities—with real consequences—ought to visit Norrath.

Norrath is the rich-media realm of wizards, dragons, and elves that is the second home to the legions who play EverQuest, one of the most popular multiplayer role-playing games ever created. EverQuest players choose and customize a character (noble paladins, greedy dwarfs, and a wide assortment of other creatures), then guide him through a series of quests, adventures, and interactions with other players, of whom there is never a shortage: As of 2002, there were nearly half a million EverQuest users (the overwhelming majority of them males)[5] paying a monthly fee to play. As many as 80,000 of them have been known to play simultaneously.[6] And EverQuest is just part of a booming online-gaming market that is projected to woo more than 40 million participants and generate nearly $2 billion in annual revenue by 2004.[7]

As anyone familiar with the 1970s Dungeons & Dragons craze can attest, fantasy, or "persistent world," games are hardly an Internet-era phenomenon. But online gamers are uniquely unconstrained by the bonds of time, space, and physical reality. In EverQuest, an adolescent boy can be a muscle-bound giant—or, for that matter, a seductive maiden. Sitting in his room at midnight, this boy/man/maiden is just a click away from dramatic interactions with tens of thousands of other players sitting in *their* rooms—on any continent, in any time zone—which is why the game is so seductive.

Or addictive. As of 2002, more than 40 percent of EverQuest users were playing the game at least 20 hours a week,[8] with many of them logging twice that many hours. Though some fret about the social consequences of such intense online gaming (among EverQuest's nicknames are "Neverrest" and "Evercrack") many players insist that in bringing together likeminded people from across the globe, the game has created its own virtual community—one built not around physical proximity, but around shared interests. In EverQuest, players interact with each other in real time; they form alliances, band together to hunt, and make arrangements to gather, chat, and explore online. Sometimes the bonds they form are strong enough to be transferred to the "real world." EverQuest has spawned a growing number of offline conventions where players meet each other in the flesh. People who met as avatars pursuing quests in Norrath have forged real-life friendships, love affairs, and even marriages.

"[EverQuest] is not a substitute for face-to-face communication; it actually reinforces it," MIT's director of comparative media studies Henry Jenkins told the *Los Angeles Times*. "Once you're in the game and have established a community, the impulse is to gather."[9]

post questions to more experienced players and others can share game tips. However, the main engine of the community is the shared interest in *playing* EverQuest, not in sharing information about it.

Commonality-Driven Communities

Finally, shared interests also arise out of commonality. For instance, individuals might share the same profession or ethnicity, or be members of the same age group. One example of a commonality-driven community is ThirdAge, which acts as a community for baby boomers interested in health and wellness. Arguably, such communities are also shaped by interests in information—members of ThirdAge might use the site for information and opinions on wellness trends, for example. However, the driving force behind the community can be attributed to the commonality of being in a certain age group. The shared interests then *arise* out of being in a community of other baby boomers. Since commonality often forms the foundation of such communities—even before interests in information or activity—this category needs to be made distinct.

Shared interests and shared commonalities, however, should not be confused—shared commonalities alone are not the basis of communities. Rather, communities can only be built upon shared interests arising out of commonality. For example, shared commonalities between two individuals can exist (e.g., they both might be working in a technology startup) but that in no way implies a desire to form a relationship or community unless they share an interest arising out of this commonality (e.g., they want to find out about the latest dot-com gossip and news, giving energy behind discussion sites like f**kedcompany.com).

Communities can and often do form out of combinations of the three types of interests. ThirdAge shows how communities sharing interests arising out of commonality also typically share interest in information. Similarly, communities driven by interests in activity can also be shaped by interests in information. eBay exemplifies this type of blending. In addition to buying and selling wares, members can gather buying and selling tips and other useful information through numerous discussion boards.

Multiple interests can also develop when a community evolves. For instance, information-driven communities can evolve to include interests in activity, such as forming relationships, once members become familiar with one another. One example is VintageBus.com, a site for owners and fans of the VW bus, built between 1949 and 1967. Bus owners who share wiring diagrams and buy and sell parts to fix their vehicles may end up meeting other bus owners at car rallies or other vintage VW events.

Despite the complications of blended interests, classifying community can still be accomplished. A particular community can be defined by determining the *primary shared interest* behind it, whether it is information, activity, or commonality generated.

In classifying community, it becomes evident that communities are often shaped by more than one type of interest. While this classification focuses on the primary driving interest in determining community type, communities built on foundations of more than one shared interest—such as activity *and* information—can be effective if that is what members seek, and the focus of the community can be maintained.

Commercial Vs. Noncommercial Community Building

Two communities can originate from the same shared interest, but can still look and feel very different. Traditionally, noncommercial communities have been created from the ground up by a group of individuals who share a particular interest and create a place where their relationships could be developed and interwoven. An example of this is a group of individuals with an interest in playing bridge, who later find a place where their community

---

Drill-Down

Classifying Community: Existing Frameworks

There are several notable frameworks that one can use to identify different types of community. Arthur Armstrong and John Hagel make their own distinctions for four types of communities: communities of transaction, communities of interest (e.g., specific topics like Byzantine history), communities of fantasy (e.g., online role-playing video games), and communities of relationship.[10] Robert Kozinets also delineates his own classification for communities; he describes the four kinds of communities as dungeons (i.e., virtual environments where players can interact, such as for online video games), rooms (i.e., computer-mediated environments where people socially gather, interacting in real time), circles (i.e., interest-structured collections of interests), and boards (i.e., online communities organized around interest-specific bulletin boards).[11]

These frameworks are useful in distinguishing communities at a more specific level. This chapter uses a different framework, however, because it is more broadly based on distinguishing among the foundations of communities—the different types of shared interests and where those interests originate.

---

of bridge players can regularly meet. More recently, with the advent of online commercial communities, the creation of community has started from the top down. Places where relationships can be formed are created first, with the hope that individuals with common interests will then come together.

EverQuest is an example of this. The multiple-player game built by Verant Interactive and then purchased by Sony was created to host thousands of paying players who would populate the virtual world and create multiple communities within the larger context of the playing environment. Its success has led to offline community extensions and inspired a host of competitors hoping to capitalize on its successful formula (see the Drill-Down titled "The [Ever]Quest for Community").

Commercial communities differ in other ways—most significantly, commercial communities typically offer goods to make revenue that in turn fuels community operations. These goods—defined as either products, services, or information—can range from auctioned wares to online video-game competitions to software technical help. In return, commercial communities usually expect revenue, either directly from the consumer (e.g., commission fees) or indirectly (e.g., advertising revenue).

Commercial communities, however, do not always expect significant revenue; many types of commercial communities are sponsored by a parent firm and serve primarily to *supplement* an existing business. For example, NYTimes.com creates mini-communities and forums through Abuzz, a community tool that allows readers to easily start Web and e-mail discussions. These small communities help like-minded readers meet and talk about issues that pertain to them. Though it is not critical to their online business, NYTimes.com values these communities as an effective supplement to their business. Such communities, though not tangibly profitable, can still offer many benefits to a parent firm. These specific benefits are discussed later in the chapter.

Drill-Down

Open Vs. Closed Communities

Communities can be described as either open or closed in regard to their membership policies, and it can be useful to know the distinction between the two. Open or closed refers to a community's policy toward accepting new members. On one extreme, completely open communities allow and encourage anyone—regardless of their qualifications or individual profile—to enter the community and participate. Open models for community (or at least *almost* completely open models) are common and can be quite successful if the community has a general focus. A community based on lifestyle interests, such as Epicurious.com, is a good example. People sharing an interest in food and wine can swap recipes on the site and share their thoughts in all things culinary. The only prerequisite for posting to Epicurious.com's message boards is to read and agree to the terms of the user agreement. No other qualifications or individual characteristics are required to join the community.

On the other extreme is a completely closed community, such as an extranet between a very limited number of buyers and sellers, created to communicate about business and to execute transactions. Outsiders are generally not allowed into the community, or membership is extremely difficult since the community has been designed and structured for only a certain number of individuals. For instance, corporations such as Ford commonly set up closed communities by using extranets with their communities of suppliers. Entrance into this community is impossible without a long process of applications, a certain degree of qualifications, and personal contacts.

Then there are communities that lie somewhere in between. Communities such as WebMD encourage different types of users to explore the site, though only physicians can log on to certain areas; application forms must be completed and approved for acceptance into this part of the community. This model works particularly well for this community—for example, it would not be appropriate to allow consumers to indiscriminately request prescription renewals. Other parts of the community, however, such as areas for discussing health issues and providing personal support, are generally open to anyone with that particular interest.

The most effective membership policy for your community—open, closed, or somewhere in between—will depend on its needs and objectives. Open communities tend to capitalize on large numbers, on making use of the network effect and Metcalfe's Law. On the other hand, depth might be sacrificed for breadth if a wide base of users is improperly segmented—discussions can be less rich and dynamic if members of a community are at different levels of experience, knowledge, and passion. More closed communities, in making membership more selective, will naturally attract fewer individuals but will also tend to attract more passionate and knowledgeable members. As such, discussions might be more lively and interesting, and tend to digress less than in a more open community.

Building community from either commercial or noncommercial perspectives can offer many rewards for its members, administrators, and the parent firm that sponsors the community. The type of value created in communities, and how that value is transferred, depends greatly on how a community functions. In cases where the community is not the firm's core business, community can still create significant benefits for the parent firm that sponsors it. The methods for creating this value vary between communities, as does the amount of value created. How online communities function can be better understood by first knowing how communities create value.

The Creation and Transfer of Value Within Communities

The value created within community is often defined by the benefits delivered to its members. While this is a large part of the value, the administrators of the community also benefit. This section aims to further clarify the value that community creates, who creates it, and how it is transferred within communities.

Communities satisfy needs not available individually, and hence, create unique value. This value can be created between users, through user-generated content such as member-posted opinions, or through administrator-created content such as proprietary research. Within a community, value can also be created for administrators by users. This particularly applies in commercial communities where users supply administrators with revenue such as subscription fees. Additionally, users can indirectly generate revenue for administrators through advertising revenue.

Three patterns emerge for creating and transferring value within communities (see Exhibit 10.4):

- *User-to-user:* User-generated content such as member-written articles, opinions, and advice.
- *Administrator-to-user:* Administrator-created content such as exclusive research and reports, and activities such as scheduled chats with special guests.
- *User-to-administrator:* User-generated value such as revenue from product sales, content fees, usage fees, commissions, and advertising sales.

User-to-User Value

User-to-user value is magnified through the effects of Metcalfe's Law. Through the benefits of scale, users more readily derive value from a number of processes ranging from gathering information and sharing insights (e.g., picking up stock tips on Motley Fool) to obtaining resources and goods (e.g., buying Beanie Babies on eBay). User-to-user value takes many forms, whether it is through sharing information, giving advice, creating shareware, or simply having a pleasant conversation.

Administrator-to-User Value

Members satisfy needs not just through one another, but also through community administrators. Administrators do more than facilitate user-to-user communication; they can create content that attracts individuals to the community and provides value for existing members. For example, Motley Fool not only encourages general member participation in its discussion rooms, but also arranges for more professional advice to be dispensed from seasoned analysts affiliated with the site. It creates proprietary content—separate from member-generated content—that provides unique value for potential and existing members.

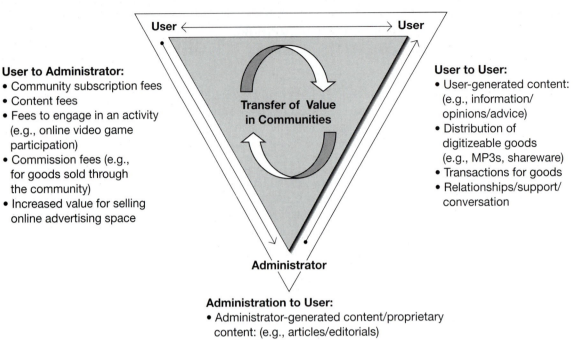

User to Administrator:
- Community subscription fees
- Content fees
- Fees to engage in an activity (e.g., online video game participation)
- Commission fees (e.g., for goods sold through the community)
- Increased value for selling online advertising space

Transfer of Value in Communities

User to User:
- User-generated content: (e.g., information/opinions/advice)
- Distribution of digitizeable goods (e.g., MP3s, shareware)
- Transactions for goods
- Relationships/support/conversation

Administration to User:
- Administrator-generated content/proprietary content: (e.g., articles/editorials)
- Mailing lists
- Newsletters
- Webcasts (e.g., of guest speakers)
- Supervised chats (e.g., chats featuring guest Q&A)
- Offline events (e.g., parties for members within geographic proximity)
- Rewards points (e.g., to use on goods or services traded within the community)

EXHIBIT 10.4   Transfer of Value Triangle

Administrators can also create value for users by keeping members updated with mailing lists and newsletters. Other methods for creating value include organizing special online events such as chats with special guests, a tool frequently used by online newspapers. For example, *The Washington Post*'s website provides administrator-to-user value by frequently arranging scheduled chats with diverse guests. Typical guests include columnists, authors, and movie stars.

Administrator-to-user value can also take the form of offline events, such as parties in major cities. For example, TheSquare, an online community for graduates of the nation's top undergraduate schools, frequently arranges parties in major cities for its members.

User-to-Administrator Value

Value is also created in the other direction, from user to administrator. Users do this in a number of ways, most of which take the form of revenue. Users, for instance, can create value for administrators by paying admission to the community. This can take the form of a monthly subscription, or a one-time entrance free. Alternatively, users might also create value by paying for the community's content, such as exclusive reports.

Users could also pay administrators a commission on transactions, as they do on eBay. Communities might gain additional revenue through products sold to the community. Along with charging members for online gaming services, video-game communities also typically raise revenue by selling newly released video games. What results from these three types of value creation is a Transfer of Value Triangle (see Exhibit 10.4), which graphically illustrates the creation and transfer of value in communities.

The Role of Functionality in Creating and Capturing Value

Certain types of value can be created only if a community functions in a specific way. The value created from a chat discussion, for instance, would not be possible if a community did not function in a real-time format. Still, many communities choose to function in asynchronous formats, where members communicate through discussion boards. For example, while Motley Fool members communicate through a discussion board, value is still effectively created and captured given the nature of the community. The main aim is to exchange bits of information, rather than to form deep personal relationships through conversation, where the use of a chat tool may be more appropriate. Communities that function in real time, then, are not necessarily more desirable—what makes one functionality better than the other depends highly on the nature of your community. The way in which a community functions—whether it be in real-time formats, asynchronous formats, or a combination—is a choice that should be based on the types of value sought in the community, the community's main objectives, and the website's technological limitations.

The Creation and Transfer of Value Outside of Communities

The previous sections have examined how a community functions, and how value can be created and transferred within a community. We have shown how value is typically created and contained within the community, especially in commercial enterprises where communities form the core of the business, such as eBay.

This section discusses, from a more macro perspective, the benefits a community can create that transcend community boundaries and benefit the parent firm that sponsors a community. Such benefits could include deepened customer relationships, and increasing trust and commitment between customers and the parent firm. Benefits like these move customers toward the commitment stage of our marketing framework. These benefits accumulate for the parent firm even if its community does not sell any goods, or if the community is not the main focus of its business. One example of such a community is Dell's DellTalk forum. Here, a small community of Dell customers and technicians can ask and discuss technical questions. Although the community does not sell any products or directly contribute revenue to the operations of Dell, this community provides

Drill-Down

Role of Trust in Creating and Capturing Value

As pointed out earlier, trust is crucial for the success of an online community—especially given individuals' increased anonymity and decreased accountability on the Internet. Without trust, members become reluctant to associate with each other or the firm (the community administrators). Subsequently, relationships do not form, and very little value can be created and captured.

In avoiding this, it is useful to point out that trust can be created and shared in two ways: between user and administrator and between user and user. For instance, a new user on eBay might feel user-and-administrator trust—because of eBay's reputation in the media and its financial success—and hence trust the services that eBay offers. Users trust that eBay administrators make an effort to protect their members, policing for fraud and offering a degree of reimbursement in case someone gets swindled.

Alternatively, users can trust each other more than administrators or the firm. For example, in less developed communities without such protective measures or safety nets, any trust would lie mainly between the members themselves. Such communities necessitate more self-policing and membership awareness of community etiquette.

Trust between user and user and between user and administrator should ideally coexist in any community. In some instances, however, they do not. New communities that have experienced little user-to-user interaction may lack user-to-user trust, and may need to rely on building user-and-administrator trust first, such as through associating the community with an established brand or company. Partnering with respectable firms can help create a sense of trustworthiness.

New communities, however, may not have the resources for partnerships or safety nets. Here, community builders should find ways to encourage the community members themselves to promote and diffuse a clear sense of trust for visitors and new members. Members should be induced to take it upon themselves to make one another feel safe and welcome, rather than leave the task solely to the firm.

By building great trust between both user and user and user and administrator, a firm can most effectively create and capture value within a community.

Dell several key benefits. These benefits fall into two categories: cost and revenue.[12]

Cost Benefits

Reduced Customer Service Costs.   Communities that do not generate revenue, such as the DellTalk forum described above, can still be indirectly lucrative for firms. Such communities have the ability to reduce customer service costs for parent firms. For instance, where customers once needed an expensive call-center network to answer questions about a problem, customers within a firm's technical community can get answers from each other via discussion boards. Not only is this method cheaper, it can also be more convenient for the customer; Web communities can answer questions 24 hours a day without making customers wait on hold. Another way communities can reduce customer service costs is through the use of professional technicians as chat moderators. This can still be significantly less expensive than using technicians in call centers. Dell uses this technique in its support forum.

Reduced Customer Acquisition Costs. Communities that reach critical mass also typically act as effective marketing vehicles. A large membership base increases a firm's presence and can be effective for word-of-mouth promotion—one of the cheapest ways to acquire customers. Getting the attention of new customers can become significantly cheaper for a firm that creates a large community known for its trustworthiness and ability to serve members' needs, such as eBay. More than 50 percent of eBay's customers come from referrals, which has helped eBay achieve one of the lowest customer acquisition costs in the online auction field.

Reduced Costs from Decreased Product Flaws and Marketing Mistakes. Communities can be a great source of market intelligence. Parent firms can benefit from communities by using them as test sites for new products and marketing plans. Committed community members can make for effective focus groups; they can give educated input regarding beneficial or harmful product changes, and provide product benchmarking against competitors' offerings. New marketing plans can also be tested for effectiveness among groups of community members prior to launch. The use of communities in this manner can save significant costs by identifying product weaknesses and potential marketing blunders.

Reduced Marketing Costs. General marketing costs, such as for the promotion of new products, can also be reduced using developed communities. For instance, it is much less expensive to advertise a new product once on a community webpage than to launch a direct e-mail marketing campaign that requires sending thousands of e-mails. Once community members consistently pass through community space, marketing to existing customers becomes more cost efficient. For example, a mutual fund company might decide to place ads for its no-load funds on ThirdAge's Money section, trying to appeal to baby boomer's interest in appropriate savings vehicles.

Revenue Benefits

Increased Customer Segmentation and Customization. Established communities typically possess profiles of their members, which can be used to sort out an individual's buying preferences. Parent firms, then, will be better able to segment customers and understand an individual's particular needs. Using knowledge gained through the community, parent firms can segment buyers and cater to individuals more specifically. If community members' needs are understood well enough, this tailoring can increase their commitment to the parent firm, increasing their intensity and moving them toward the commitment stage of our marketing framework. Firms might then push more targeted advertising and customized goods, ultimately increasing customer sales, all the while making sure that they honor the trust that community members place in them by not using this sensitive customer data irresponsibly and by honoring opt-in/opt-out preferences.

Increased Branding. A community can also act as the "face" of the parent firm. It can subtly relay to the customer a firm's values, its dedication to its customers, and the emphasis it places on building trust. To the extent that a community reaches critical mass and satisfies members' needs, a community will also tend to reflect positively on the branding of the parent firm. This can strengthen brand, increase product marketability, and grow sales. Saturn car owners are an example of this. The establishment and growth of this unusual car-owner community have increased and reinforced the notion that Saturn is "a different kind of company," inevitably strengthening Saturn's brand and increasing its attractiveness to customers.

Deepened Customer Relationships. Creating value within an online community builds trust and ultimately deepens customer relationships between the firm and the consumer. Community can help in bringing customers to the commitment stage. It does this by allowing the firm a new medium not just for providing information or selling products, but for increasing communication and building trust. Investments in online community do not pay off just in immediate gains. Rather, online community can deepen customer relationships that result in more loyal customers who create steady sales over time, helping offset customer acquisition costs. Past studies have shown that increasing customer retention rates by 5 percent can increase profits by 25 to 95 percent.[13] In this sense, online community can be a very profitable investment.

How Do Individuals Become Part of a Community?

The chapter has already looked, from a macro perspective, at how communities form and function. The following section examines, from a micro perspective, how individuals interact with and become part of a community. It explores how individuals progress to become community members and ultimately add value to the community. The section also looks at the role of intensity in this progression and its relationship to the four-stage framework.

Drill-Down

Legal and Liability Issues

When it comes to community, legal and liability issues are important to consider. In particular, different sets of issues arise when creating moderated versus unmoderated community forums. A firm trying to control the content and dialogue in specific communities, particularly in closed communities, can raise issues of liability. Businesses assume responsibility for these moderated environments and may be held responsible for threatening posts, for example.

Unmoderated environments pose different issues. Unmoderated message boards can be problematic from a brand management standpoint if, for example, competitors or disgruntled customers post damaging messages about that brand. They also might contain more abusive language and other undesirable messages due to their unrestricted posting rules. On the plus side, they are less resource-intensive than moderated boards and do not necessarily incur liability for the business housing them. Determining which type of community to develop will require a review of the hosting company's corporate objectives and an understanding of management's liability tolerance.

The Stages of Community Membership

The four stages—awareness, exploration/expansion, commitment, and dissolution—correspond well to the stages of an individual's membership in a community. Individuals first become aware of the community (awareness), explore the community, participate in the community (exploration/expansion), then become a member of it (commitment). In certain cases, individuals also leave the community (dissolution). While these four stages aptly describe the stages of community membership, there is an additional framework that takes community to the individual level and can be tied to the four membership stages. The value of this framework is that it creates a language for describing community members at different points in the membership process.

This individual-level framework is outlined by Amy Jo Kim in her book *Community Building on the Web*.[14] Kim's Membership Life Cycle breaks down individual community involvement into five progressive stages:

1. **Visitors:** People without persistent identity in the community. Visitors browse discussions and public elements of a community but generally do not participate in them. They are sometimes referred to as "lurkers" for their tendency to watch what is going on from the shadows without revealing themselves to others.

2. **Novices:** New members who need to learn the ropes and be introduced into community life. Novices are somewhat passive community members. They are learning the rules and culture of the virtual community and are therefore not that actively engaged in it. They are commonly referred to as "newbies" and can be identified by their line of questioning or behavior.

3. *Regulars:* Established members who are comfortably participating in community life. They tend to participate in activities and topics created by others instead of initiating new discussions or threads. Regulars make up the largest portion of mature communities.

4. *Leaders:* Volunteers, contractors, and staff who keep the community running. In nascent communities (see Three Levels of Community discussion), they are often the ones who create topics and plan activities that are of interest to other community members. They may also serve as intermediaries between community members, fulfilling a regulatory role in communities without a formal oversight body.

5. *Elders:* Long-time regulars and leaders who share their knowledge and pass along culture. Like their counterparts in offline communities, elders are respected members of the community and are oftentimes identified through signaling mechanisms. For example, Amazon distinguishes its elders, which in Amazon's case are its top reviewers, by giving them bio pages and distinguishing their reviews with icons (see Exhibit 10.5).

Top product reviewers are able to create bio pages with optional pictures.

Special icons accompany their reviews, lending more credibility to their opinions.

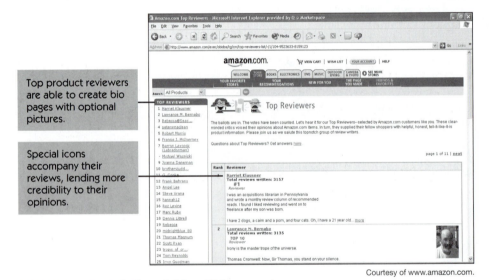

Courtesy of www.amazon.com.

EXHIBIT 10.5   Distinguishing Elders on Amazon.com

Clearly, individuals go through several stages of membership while in a community. Kim's framework will now be related to the concept of intensity and our own four relationship stages.

The Role of Intensity in Community Membership

In community, an individual's intensity directly reflects his or her degree of participation and commitment. This section further examines the role of intensity and its progression throughout the Membership Life Cycle. This progression is displayed through the perspective of our four relationship stages: awareness, exploration/expansion, commitment, and dissolution (see Exhibit 10.6).

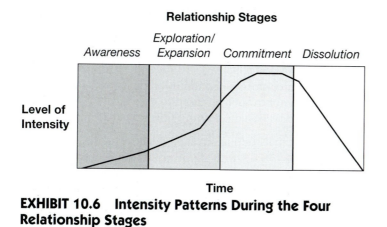

Relationship Stages

Awareness | *Exploration/ Expansion* | *Commitment* | *Dissolution*

Level of Intensity

Time

EXHIBIT 10.6 Intensity Patterns During the Four Relationship Stages

Individuals' intensity patterns during the four relationship stages tend to follow the diagram in Exhibit 10.6. While the exhibit does not explain intensity patterns of all members, it does provide insight into the process of member commitment.

In the awareness stage, individuals know about the community site and perhaps have even looked at it. These individuals have the lowest intensity levels, and would be considered visitors up until the exploration stage. In Kim's model, these individuals would not be considered part of the community yet. If individuals choose to formally join the community, such as through a sign-up process, they become novices. Now in the exploration stage, these novices commit to getting to know the site and determining which discussions they might like to read. They participate little, however, and are still generally unwilling to contribute resources such as money, opinions, or advice.

As a novice's intensity grows in the expansion stage, so does his commitment—partly as a function of the equity he begins to build within the community. As mentioned earlier, examples of **equity building** can include the formation of friendships or the development of a more respected online reputation. This equity makes the community worth more to an individual, and increases his commitment. Equity building begins to occur in the expansion stage and continues into the commitment stage. The equity-building process is integral in pushing novices to become regulars and later leaders or elders. Sometimes community members reach the dissolution stage. Even the most committed members can find that they outgrow a community, or a community has changed from its original mission. These individuals might be called "departing friends."

Exceptions to Normal Intensity Progressions Within Community
It is important to note that intensity patterns do differ between members and communities. In particular, medical communities—such as medical support communities for people recently diagnosed with a particular illness—can lead to quicker patterns of intensity building. A typical member of this community might begin with a much higher intensity level given time pressures to gather information about an illness and to find supportive community members. As such, intensity patterns may start out very high in these cases. Similarly, movie communities tend to have rapid development cycles. As blockbuster films become a more prevalent phenomenon, communities built around them build quickly and drop off precipitously once the movie cycles out of theaters.

When to Develop Community

This chapter has already looked at how value is created in communities and how individuals interact with and become part of a community. This section asks "When is it appropriate to develop online community?" and provides a framework to guide the community-building process. It also illustrates some common community types to put the discussion into perspective.

The Community Applicability Model

Businesses need to properly plan levels of community that will provide value to consumers while fulfilling internal business needs. To do this, a company must determine the reason why the creation and maintenance of community is a justified use of resources. Community for its own sake, even if it is a robust community, is not in itself a reason to create it. Any community development effort should be based on sound business strategy.

There are few things that send as strong a negative signal as a publicly inactive online community. Sites with empty chat rooms and message boards with small numbers of out-of-date posts are not welcoming signs to visitors or novices. Instead, they signal a failing community. What makes some communities work and others fail? Well-functioning communities are successful because they address an intersecting set of product and consumer attributes. The Community Applicability Model depicted in Exhibit 10.7 asks two sets of questions to help determine when to pursue community building. The model's premise is that marketers should consider developing online community if it is determined that their product or service addresses an intersection of the two sets of attributes.

Consumer Attributes — Pursue Community Creation — **Product Attributes**

Consumer attributes are behavioral
- Is the target group of your product or service composed of *active online* users?
- Are members of your target group likely or *willing to share* information with others?
- Are members of your target group involved in the *process of discovery?*
- Do members of your target group *value interaction* with like-minded people?
- Can the community *grow organically?*

Product attributes are emotional
- Can the product generate critical mass?
- Does the product elicit passion?
- Does the product address or revolve around a certain lifestyle?
- Do benefits of information aggregation arise from product complexity?

EXHIBIT 10.7   The Community Applicability Model

Consumer Attributes

The first set of questions the Community Applicability Model looks at is consumer attributes. These look at the people who would populate a community under consideration for development. These attributes are behavioral in nature.

1. *Is the target group of your product or service composed of active online users?* This is the most fundamental question—and yet the most

overlooked. Its importance cannot be overstated. The list of failed dot-coms is littered with websites that built first and looked for an audience second. An answer of "No" to this question should put a hard stop to any in-progress community development plans.

2. *Are members of your target group likely or willing to share information with others?* Community without sharing is an oxymoron. A willingness to share is critical for a healthy community. Willingness to share is evident at Raging Bull, a successful community site for financial investors. Its numerous stock-trading message boards thrive because members share company information with others in the community. Without this sharing quid pro quo the boards would turn from sources of valued information to boards filled with company propaganda.

3. *Do members of your target group value interaction with like-minded people?* This question also ties back to our definition of community, specifically the part that talks about shared interests. Potential community members should exhibit signs of valuing interaction with others. A community of people without this predilection would be one full of lurkers. A community full of people looking to take, not give, would inevitably collapse.

4. *Can the community grow organically?* This speaks to the community administrator's resource base. If you create community, you have to consider what its ongoing maintenance costs will be. If it is a high-maintenance community, costs could escalate beyond the administrator's means to absorb them. On the other hand, a low-maintenance community can thrive with greatly reduced resource demands. The more likely it is that community can grow organically (for example, by leveraging a preexisting offline community), the greater the likelihood that ongoing resource demands will be lower. This will give the site owner a greater likelihood for success if resources are limited.

5. *Are members of your target group involved in the process of discovery?* A final behavioral consideration revolves around the discovery process. Consider an individual who is diagnosed with diabetes. She would feel a need to learn about the condition and how to cope with it, and find others to share her experience. She may turn to WebMD's message boards. She could choose from a number of them, including one focused on diabetes support groups, another on diabetes nutrition, and a third moderated by a diabetes health specialist.

Product Attributes

The second set of attributes in the Community Applicability Model revolves around the product or service around which a community would be developed. These are emotional triggers.

1. *Can the product generate critical mass?* Unlike the line from *Field of Dreams*, "If you build it, they will come," just because a site with community aspirations is built does not mean people will flock to it. Successful online communities draw a critical number of people

to them, oftentimes with seeding from moderators or regulars, making them viable over the long term. Community does not take place in a vacuum. If critical mass is not attainable, a halt should be put to community-building plans.

2. *Does the product elicit passion?* Community builders need to think about whether their product incites passion. Product passion is a major driver leading people to the commitment stage. The stronger the emotional connection to a product, the greater the chance community can play a role in its promotion. For example, while it may be difficult to justify building community around mosquito repellant, building one around the love of the outdoors and then promoting your product to that community is a better approach to leveraging community.

3. *Does the product address or revolve around a certain lifestyle?* Lifestyle is one of the ties that bind groups of people sharing certain attributes. Creating a place for these groups to congregate online is often easier, and certainly more private, than doing so offline. For example, Gay.com serves gays, lesbians, bisexuals, and the transgender community by providing this community with articles, personals, chat rooms, and other resources. Members of this community can congregate free of any social stigma in the offline world. Another example is iVillage.com. The site offers women everything from pregnancy and health forums to relationship advice and career resources drawing women of all ages into its site.

4. *Do benefits of information aggregation arise from product complexity?* Digital cameras and automobiles are two examples where product complexity and information aggregation combine to make the Internet a perfect setting for online community to thrive. Both products require detailed prepurchase research and postpurchase support. The Internet's ability to store and make searchable large amounts of data and to promote the sharing of information with others serves both user segments. The website CarTalk@Cars.com provides places for automobile communities to share information and conduct research on these highly complex products. The site is useful for consumers (who can choose which product to buy) and product manufacturers (who can advertise their products to potential customers) alike.

Exhibit 10.8 illustrates how these criteria apply to a sampling of community sites. Not all of the criteria need to be met, but a cross-section must apply.

Types of Successful Communities

Successful communities come in many forms, and can be segmented into countless subcategories. While not exhaustive, the following list highlights some of the most common and successful categories of online community today.

- *Search Communities.* People in these communities are in the process of discovery and are willing to share with others. They come in search of something (an old friend, family genealogy, former classmates) and in

Applicability Questions	Lord of the Rings*	eBay	Match.com	RootsWeb
Consumer Attributes				
Active Online	very high	very high	very high	high
Willing to Share	very high	very high	high	very high
Process of Discovery	very high	high	very high	very high
Value Interaction	very high	high	very high	moderate
Organic Growth	very high	very high	high	high
Product Attributes				
Critical Mass	very high	very high	high	high
Elicit Passion	very high	high	low	moderate
Certain Type of Lifestyle	moderate	moderate	high	low
Information Aggregation / Product Complexity	very high	very high	moderate	high

○ = very low ◔ = low ◑ = moderate ◕ = high ● = very high

* (www.lordoftherings.net)

EXHIBIT 10.8 Mapping Online Community

some cases are willing to pay for these services. Network effects play a strong role in these communities—the larger the community, the more likely they will find what they are looking for. Thus, the ability to reach critical mass plays an important role. Examples include Match.com and Classmates.com.

- *Trading Communities.* These communities involve the exchange of goods or services. eBay is the best-documented trading community. However, many other examples abound. One example is Keen.com, a site providing a marketplace for live advice on numerous topics. Advisors, oftentimes community elders, charge for advice in their particular area of expertise.

- *Education Communities.* Education is one of the oldest forms of community. People in these communities are in the process of discovery, and value interaction with like-minded people. The University of Phoenix, one of the largest online education providers, has successfully leveraged the time and spatial distinguishing characteristics of online community to provide classes for thousands of people around the world.

- *Event-Based Communities.* These communities combine event information (schedules, locations, logistics) with forums where people can share comments with others who will be attending or have attended the event.

- *Subscriber-Based Communities.* These communities rely on critical mass. Without it, there is no way for community owners to leverage the membership base. One site that has achieved critical mass is EZBoard, which facilitates community by creating forums (over 1 million to date) where like-minded individuals can share lifestyle and other interests. EZBoard generates revenue through advertising to its large user base and by providing other services.

- *Advocacy-Based Communities.* These are generally extensions of offline communities and are composed of like-minded individuals with a passion for their cause. The World Wildlife Fund complements its offline efforts with its online Conservation Action Network, where members can receive e-mail updates and join campaigns to protect wildlife.

How to Create Successful Community

Creating successful community is not an easy task. Of the hundreds and thousands of so-called communities online, only a minority have reached the highest level of functionality and development. This section examines two approaches to creating successful community. The first approach introduces three broad levels of community. The framework examines how to affect your community more broadly and helps you determine appropriate strategy and marketing plans at each level, allowing your community to reach successively higher levels of development. The second approach ties community to the four relationship stages and examines how to push individuals through the membership cycle and through the four stages. The aim of this approach is to build community by focusing on the individual.

Guiding Principles: The Three Levels of Community

Why are there different levels of community? Communities do not launch in full bloom with a huge member base. Instead, they go through a progression from inception to full maturity. Along the way, they exhibit certain characteristics at each level of development. We group the various stages of community into the following three levels:

- *Nascent level:* Communities at their inception, typically marked and driven by community founders and a small number of core participants.
- *Formative level:* Communities that are growing and developing, typically marked by growing membership and evolving goals and functionality.
- *Mature level:* Communities that are near, or at, critical mass and sustainability. Community survival no longer depends on the community founders and original core participants. Structures exist to ensure feedback, maintenance, and change (as called for by the feedback of community members).

Communities at each level exhibit certain characteristics that can be tied back to the community criteria identified at the outset of the chapter (people, processes, culture, and technology). The characteristics that communities exhibit at each level of development are detailed in Exhibit 10.9.

The following section provides greater detail on and strategic guidance to the three levels of community. The strategic guidance aims to broadly affect community so that it reaches higher levels of development and stays there. Community administrators can broadly affect community in three ways:

1. Setting a general strategy for how the community operates and functions

Level of Community	Nascent	Formative	Mature
People Characteristics	• Small number of core members, small number of participants	• Small number of core members, higher number of participants • Users begin to build equity	• Increased number of core members, high number of participants • Users become operationally entangled
Process Characteristics	• Somewhat less defined and focused processes of communication • Lack of segmentation of users/little segmentation of discussion topics	• Small number of core members, higher number of participants • Users begin to build equity	• Efficient processes of communication established • Clear segmentation of topics and users
Culture Characteristics	• Momentum is kickstarted and driven by core group of founders • High on energy, low on focus • Community's brand is evolving	• Gains more momentum • Refinement of missions/goals (as defined by members) • Community is building a solidified brand	• Achieves critical mass • Mission close to fully defined according to members • Membership alignment in shaping of the community • Leadership positions within the community are established • Community establishes brand
Technological Characteristics	• Fewer technological options for communications	• More options for communication technology explored	• Preferred technology used for communication is established

EXHIBIT 10.9   The Three Levels of Community

2.   Defining marketing objectives

3.   Choosing marketing tools

Nascent Communities

Communities at their inception are by definition nascent communities. They are just beginning to grow and evolve, and can typically be identified by the characteristics in Exhibit 10.9. There are a small number of core members and perhaps a small number of participants. Communication is primarily done in one mode, most likely through e-mail or message boards. The community generally will not have enough critical mass to support synchronous communication such as chat rooms. Similarly, topics of discussion are limited, and appropriately so. It is clearly better to have a few lively discussion boards than many dead ones. Topics are broad and not very well segmented. The community is driven by the energy and passion of the core founding members. Examples of nascent communities abound. Many of these exist as a function of the ease with which groups can be created. For example, Yahoo! provides a set of tools through Yahoo! Groups that makes it possible for motivated individuals to create discussion groups. While creating the communities is simple, promoting them is not. Often these discussion boards are buried among the vast content offerings of the Yahoo! site. Typically, these nascent communities are informal ones formed between small groups of friends. Nascent communities are not near the point of sustainability, where the community can exist long after the core members have left.

Nascent-Level Strategy.   Communities at the nascent level should generally aim for growth in membership, because critical mass is necessary for long-term survival. To this end, users are often attracted to the community through administrator-generated content, promoted through techniques such as viral and guerrilla marketing. While other types of marketing work for nascent communities, leveraging these relatively cheap but effective tools can be particularly appropriate and beneficial. Given that nascent communities are not generally short on manpower and/or cash, use of these marketing tools can be a good choice for creating impact at a relatively low cost. eBay successfully employed viral marketing techniques in its early development, generating many of its customers through referrals. This allowed eBay to keep customer acquisition costs low and maintain profitability. In addition to these marketing tools, partnerships and affiliations can also be used to attract potential members.

Member profiles at this level might be heavily skewed. In nascent communities founded by a core group of individuals, profiles will be dominated by members already in the commitment stage. New members, those in the awareness and exploration/expansion stages, are just beginning to join, so leaving room to change and grow is essential to success. Nascent communities should also focus on using both behavioral and subjective feedback to determine where the community should be going. It is important to recognize that the community can change greatly between levels, both in purpose and in functionality.

Operationally, nascent communities tend to do better by finding and building upon one or a few well-used methods of communication. Many communities make the mistake of offering too much too soon (e.g., offering chat services, bulletin boards, and many subtopics all at the nascent level). As a result, many chat rooms are found empty, discussions are only four or five threads deep, and postings are outdated. This can be fatal for nascent communities—the perception of an empty community discourages both existing and prospective members alike.

> *Main objective for the nascent community:*
> - Aim for growth in membership.
>
> *Steps to take:*
> - *Create content.* Administrator-generated value can be effective for attracting new members.
> - *Promote with resource-effective marketing.* Nascent communities should be wise in how they spend their marketing resources. Partnerships and viral and word-of-mouth marketing can be low-cost marketing solutions.

- *Use feedback as a map.* Behavioral and subjective feedback can show you where your community ought to be headed.
- *Focus on quality, not quantity.* Do not offer chat rooms if they will not be used. Too much, too soon, is a common mistake for communities.
- *Be prepared for change.* The greatest changes for the community—both in mission and in function—are yet to come.

Formative Communities

Communities that have evolved and reached the formative level exhibit their own characteristics. Membership has grown, though primarily in total number of participants (such as visitors, novices) rather than core members (regulars, leaders, elders). Different communication options become possible as membership increases and individuals seek more ways to communicate. With increased membership, more subtopics are generated and sustained, providing richer community dialogue. At the formative level of community, equity begins to be built by various members of the community. The community's brand is becoming solidified as the community's functionality and membership grows. Goals are also being refined at this stage. The community is reaching the point where its survival is sustainable. The direction of the community is orchestrated less by the founders and more by the community members.

Formative-Level Strategy.   Communities in the formative level should aim for change in both their goals and functionality. Communities at this level typically experience growing pains that need to be handled appropriately. Member profiles will vary more greatly as the member mix shifts. As the community grows, there will generally be an increasing number of individuals in the awareness or exploration/expansion stage. A growing community will also have changing needs, such as for more discussion topics. Being responsive to these changing needs will be critical to success. At this level, it becomes more important to seek feedback to further refine a community's goals according to community members, so that it can accommodate the changing membership base. Increasingly, control and vision of the community should become more dependent on the members rather than the founders or site administrators.

Formative communities should also be exploring different processes of communication—either asynchronous, real-time, or both. Formative communities now have the sufficient membership base to keep those channels active. Also, formative communities can now effectively promote the branching of subtopics. This responds to member needs for more topic diversity while satisfying the needs for equity building (since this allows members to start and maintain their own discussion groups). Given increased members in the exploration/expansion stage, further initiatives for member equity building can be executed by establishing volunteer roles such as watchpeople and guides. This builds equity and develops members while refining the processes of community facilitation.

In refining member interaction, CRM (customer relationship management) marketing tools can also be used. The use of CRM tools in your community interface—such as the ability to recognize and respond to user preferences—

can provide a more customized experience for your members. For instance, as your online community becomes aware of a particular member's needs and preferences to view certain message boards first, it can more readily tailor to those needs by displaying those message boards when the member logs in. This kind of marketing also subtly builds equity in members by continuously providing them with a customized experience they would likely not get at other community sites.

Finally, formative communities should begin leveraging their increasing membership base to create user-to-user value—member-written articles, member-led information sessions, and opinions on products. Such user-generated content can also effectively be promoted to prospective members.

Main objectives for the formative community:

- Aim for change.
- Be responsive to new needs.
- Increase and leverage user-to-user value.

Steps to take:

- *Use feedback as a pulse.* Use it to monitor health and changes in your community. Recognize that growth does not always equal health, and that changing communities means changing needs. Use feedback to find out where you need to change functionality and tweak community goals.
- *Explore communication processes.* Find out—through feedback and trial and error—the most effective means for your community to communicate.
- *As they get older, give them more freedom.* Older, formative communities tend to demand more freedom and responsibility than younger, nascent ones. If you think the community is "old" enough, make it easier for members to form more subgroups and assume additional roles in the community.
- *Make the community special for each member.* The use of CRM in tailoring site functionality can do much for making an individual feel part of a community.
- *Users have value too.* Do not forget to leverage your greatest asset—your members. Give them freedom and encouragement in creating their own value.

Mature Communities

Mature communities have achieved sustainability and critical mass; they can exist long after the original core members have left the community. Core members are continuously recruited, and new participants keep the community fresh. Leadership and community roles have typically been established within the community to provide facilitation and timely feedback through the use of member-leaders, moderators, and guides. Increased membership, through participants and core members, has allowed for even finer segmentation of users and topics for discussion. Equity has been built among many members, helping to build loyalty and to ensure continued commitment to the community. Preferred methods of member communication have been found through trial and error. Finally, the community's mission and brand have become more firmly established (though not permanent) through the input and feedback of the community members.

Mature-Level Strategy. Mature communities should aim for sustainability in creating a membership base that continuously refreshes core members and attracts new participants. Member profiles will likely be a stable mix of individuals at all relationship stages. A community's brand should become solidified—as defined by feedback and the growth process in the formative level—and ultimately establish a presence for the community that lends the perception of increased stability. This can be achieved partly through the increased combination of offline and online marketing. With increased resources, the mature community can realistically engage in more expensive offline marketing efforts, such as television and print, to solidify brand and reach greater audiences. Offline efforts could also include member gatherings, like conventions in major cities, to deepen online relationships and further establish presence.

At the mature level, feedback loops between administrators and community leaders should be firmly established to ensure the continuous circulation of ideas. The most appropriate methods of communication, whether it be real-time or asynchronous systems, should also be chosen and developed. The options for equity-building should be increased as well. For instance, given the increased resources of the mature community, leaders might be given more tangible rewards, such as gift certificates to affiliate sites.

Finally, mature communities can now leverage their size to increase user-to-administrator value (e.g., charging for special content) and community-to-firm benefits (e.g., lower marketing costs).

Main objectives for the mature community:
- Aim for sustainability.
- Solidify brand and establish presence.
- Make feedback processes efficient.
- Leverage user-to-administrator value and community-to-firm benefits.

Steps to take:
- *Create stability.* Stability includes achieving the perception of being ever-present, of always being there for members. This makes people comfortable and willing to build equity in the community. Establishing presence and solidifying brand, as defined by feedback and the growth process in the formative level, will help lead to stability.

- *Keep listening.* Creating stability, however, does not mean turning a deaf ear to your constituents. Seeking and listening to feedback should remain priorities in maintaining proper community health. Establishing positive feedback loops can help this.

- *It is your turn.* After traveling a long road, communities that reach maturity now have much more to offer to administrators and the parent firm that sponsors a community. Find ways to leverage membership base, commitment, and intensity to reap user-to-administrator value and community benefits to the firm.

Strategic Objective at All Levels.   At any level of online community, administrators should keep in mind the foundations and strengths of *offline* community. As Amy Jo Kim points out, two of those strengths are traditions and rituals. Many communities, from religious groups to college campuses, rely on traditions and rituals to bring people together and provide a sense of context or history. Where applicable, online communities might try to incorporate these traditions into their daily activities. For instance, special events such as chats with the community founder can be scheduled to commemorate a community's founding. Another strength of community is creating social settings, through games and contests. The use of such activities not only helps members have fun, but might also help build equity if games help members get to know other members. Such games can range from simple puzzles and card games to more elaborate online team tournaments. eBay, for instance, helps members interact by creating an area called The Park where members can play word games, ask riddles, and just have fun.

Finally, communities are built on relationships and trust. As such, it is important to stress again one of the original criteria of community: At any level, recruiting and marketing to potential members should not be invasive or forced. Permission marketing, double-opt in, and other similar types of practices are consistent with this idea.

Exhibit 10.10 summarizes the framework and serves as a community-building reference guide. Rather than provide a step-by-step method, this framework is intended primarily to stimulate thinking for advancing community as a whole and, consequently, to stimulate the building of better communities.

Guiding Principles: The Community Growth Path

This approach is conducted from the perspective of the individual and the four relationship stages: awareness, exploration/expansion, commitment, and dissolution. This section details the appropriate steps to take at each relationship stage. The ultimate goal here is to outline ways for shepherding the customer from the awareness stage to the commitment stage, and keep him or her there (see Exhibit 10.11). This framework begins with the individual at the awareness stage. For simplicity's sake, community members are labeled according to the Membership Life Cycle.

Awareness Stage
In this stage, the individual first becomes aware of a community—what it is about and what it offers—and might arrive at the community site out of curiosity. Intensity and commitment are low, however, so efforts to learn about the site are superficial, without the intensity and commitment to call it exploration. In this stage of the relationship, visitors tend to be cautious and guarded, willing to give little in terms of time, personal information, or money. This point cannot be overemphasized. Given the individual's low level of intensity and commitment, solicitations for money or personal information will not likely be fruitful. Communities often make the mistake of overwhelming individuals when they first meet, bombarding them with offers and requests for registration. This approach, while well intentioned, might turn them off. A community's efforts would be better focused in getting the individual to the next relationship stage: exploration/expansion.

	Nascent	Formative	Mature
General Strategy and Operational Objectives	• Aim for growth (in membership) • Attract users by creating administrator-to-user value; promote administrator-generated content • Seek feedback to determine where the community is going • Find and build upon one or a few well-used methods of communication • Foment relationships and vibrant discussion within only a small number of community groups	• Aim for change (in functionality and mission) • Leverage increasing size to create user-to-user value and promote user-generated content • Seek feedback to further refine community goals and mission according to members • Explore different processes of communication (asynchronous vs. real-time, or both) • Refine community-facilitation processes; establish roles for which members are chosen and can volunteer (e.g., watchpeople, guides) • Leverage CRM to tailor site and functionality to the member • Allow for further segmentation of discussion topics	• Aim for sustainability (in solidifying branding and presence) • Leverage size to increase user-to-administrator value (e.g., advertising) • Establish reliable feedback loops to ensure the recognition of member needs • Determine most appropriate methods of community communication • Further develop community leaders/caretakers of the community to create sustainability • Incorporate offline events/marketing to further solidify community relationships, activities and community presence
	• Leverage processes of offline community (e.g., rituals and tradition)		
Marketing Objectives	• Increase member base • Get the word out • Use good content to attract members	• Refine community vision (as defined by members) • Generate equity for members within community	• Establish solid mission and brand • Establish community presence • Expand possibilities for equity generation

EXHIBIT 10.10   Community Building Strategy

Methods for pushing this transition forward could include simply outlining the benefits of joining the community, while not asking for any resources. At the same time, a call to action could be made to persuade the individual to explore the community free of charge and to learn more about the community and what it can offer. The main objective in this stage is to inform.

Main objective of the awareness stage:
• Inform and invite.

Steps to take:
• *Make it enticing.* Quickly outline clear, attractive benefits to joining. Individuals should be told, or quickly feel, why they should join. This should be done clearly in the marketing efforts or prominently on the community homepage.

Stages of the Relationship	Objectives	Do:	Don't:
Awareness	• Inform and invite	• Make it enticing; clearly define the benefits • Anticipate questions and concerns; let individuals find answers easily and quickly • Provide a call to action; find methods that encourage exploration	• Ask them for the world; individuals will be reluctant to give information, much less money
Exploration/ Expansion	• Encourage thorough exploration • Build a sense of trust • Begin the process of equity creation	• Provide an easily navigable interface • Show support to members, and a desire for them to participate • Format equity creation (both tangible and intangible)	• Make the membership process involuntary • Carelessly attempt a hard sell for products or contributions to the community
Commitment	• Heighten equity building • Develop existing members	• Harness individual momentum and passion • Allow the individual to build non-transferable equity (tangible or intangible) within the community (sink "hooks" into the individual)	• Take commitment for granted
Dissolution	• Keep an eye out for departing friends • Make the process easy • Leave the door open	• Identify departing friends early through both behavioral and subjective metrics • Make an effort to reverse the process and provide solutions (if they are feasible) • Define the dissolution process and make it fair and efficient • Treat the departing friend with respect • Ask and listen closely to feedback • Leave the door open and encourage the possibility of returning to the community	• Fail to make an effort to retain members • Make the dissolution process vague and difficult • Make the process cold and impersonal • Fail to ask for feedback

EXHIBIT 10.11   The Community Growth Path

- *Anticipate questions and concerns.* Allay fears of exploration through methods such as an effective FAQ section.
- *Establish a call to action.* Encourage the move to exploration through features such as a prominent visitor's center.

Exploration/Expansion Stage

In this stage, novices explore the community to determine whether its content and activity are worth their time. For community administrators, the foremost task in this stage is to provide an easily navigable interface so that exploration is easy. This should be achieved in a way that makes navigation intuitive. Methods for achieving this could include site maps, which clearly show where individuals can access certain topics, or a comprehensive site search engine. Different topics of interest should be readily accessible, so that individuals can quickly determine where they might fit and participate in the community.

A sense of trust, openness, and welcome participation should also be cultivated at this stage. This can be done through simple measures such as e-mails to welcome new members. These e-mails can help novices learn how to use the community interface and direct them to personally relevant subtopics within the community. Participation should be highly encouraged at this and every relationship stage. Some discussions with newcomers might be arranged and structured so that they are permeable. This helps newcomers feel comfortable and participate unobtrusively.

After the novice has had sufficient time to explore the community, administrators can ask for feedback. However, administrators should keep in mind that exploration does not always imply willingness to join, and membership should not simply be handed out to those doing the exploring. Seeking permission and making membership a conscious choice is particularly important for building trust. Making a hard sell for products or subscription fees at this stage is difficult. Given their relatively low level of commitment, potential members can be scared off by impressions of overt commercialism, or ulterior motives that do not concern the individual. If the product is relevant to the community, however, then this may be more feasible.

Keep in mind that conversions will vary at different levels within a community and that this is a function of intensity and commitment. Community members who have a high level of intensity and commitment do not require a hard sell and may provide the highest value to a business, whereas high-intensity community members that do not respond to sales messages may require targeting with a secondary sales strategy. This suggests segmenting sales offers by relationship stage. If consumers do not respond to any conversion attempts (while in exploration/expansion or commitment stages), the business can determine if their presence in the community alone justifies their ongoing efforts or if it is best to target that consumer for planned dissolution.

Individuals in the expansion part of this stage become regulars—they come to the community more regularly and participate more than novices. These individuals exhibit growing intensity and commitment, partly because they have already invested time in exploring the site, using its interface, and meeting a few members. Individuals at this stage have now begun the process of equity building within the community; they begin creating equity through processes like creating new friendships or simply learning a community's interface. This nontransferable equity acts like a hook that predicates the individual to invest further time and resources in the community. While this is not an indication of full commitment, it is the first step the individual takes just before moving to the commitment stage.

The main goals in this stage of the relationship, then, are to make for easy exploration, build trust, and begin the process of equity building.

Main objectives of the exploration/expansion stage:

- Encourage thorough exploration.
- Build a sense of trust.
- Begin the process of equity creation.

Steps to take:

- *Make exploring easy.* Provide an intuitive and navigable interface through features such as a site map and comprehensive search engine.
- *Show caring toward your members.* Show individual attention and the desire for them to participate. This might be achieved by sending welcoming e-mails, arranging guides for novices, and scheduling chat conversations for new members.
- *Make the community worth something.* Intangible equity can be built through facilitating relationships—for example, via meeting rooms for novices only. Tangible ways to build equity can include reward systems such as "community points," which are earned through activity in the community and can later be redeemed for services or goods. It is important to determine what provides value to your business while determining what is valuable to the community. This value exchange should be equal but noninvasive to consumers while also being transparent to community members. Never profiteer off of your community—the resulting backlash could break the trust that helps bind it together.

Commitment Stage

The commitment stage can be the most dynamic and interesting relationship stage—this is where individuals create the most value. Individuals at this stage are driven by higher levels of commitment and intensity. In this stage, the firm harnesses member passion to create newer types of value in the community, such as member-led discussions. Members at the beginnings of the commitment stage can be encouraged to further increase their stake and intensity in the community, leading them to provide even more value.

Equity building, which started in the expansion stage, is heightened in the commitment stage. For instance, members who display sufficient commitment might be given the option to form subgroups, or be given special meeting places for their groups. Committed members can be given awards to recognize their participation and contribution to the community. Members who display a certain level of commitment could also be asked to become leaders in the community. This further increases equity for individuals, but also supports community efforts of member development. As previously mentioned, certain members could be asked to become group leaders and create subgroups. Individuals could also be found to act as advisers to community administrators, providing regular feedback and serving as mediators when members have minor complaints. In return for their commitment, community administrators develop members by providing training programs and the opportunity to build leadership through online experiences.

The efforts of member development, however, do not need to focus on building leaders. Members who choose not to be leaders of the community can still be developed in other ways. Members at this stage could be trained

---

Drill-Down

Measuring Intensity and Commitment

What are the metrics that track an individual's commitment or intensity, and how will you know when an individual has reached the commitment stage in the first place? Naturally, measuring an individual's commitment and intensity—and then defining cut-off points for a particular relationship stage—will be highly subjective. Still, there are ways and proxies to measure the intensity and commitment in individuals.

The first way is through behavioral metrics, such as tracking an individual's site visitations, time spent on the site, number of chat discussions attended, and number of comments posted. Motley Fool, for instance, implicitly tracks and shows member participation by affixing stars next to individuals' names, depending on the number of postings they make. (Note: Similar to eBay's method for building an online reputation, this tracking and recognition of participation also serves as an equity-building tool.)

The second way of measuring intensity and commitment is through more subjective metrics such as surveys and questionnaires. For instance, questionnaires could be sent to small subgroups looking to recognize valuable contributors to the community. Direct questionnaires could also be sent to specific individuals asking them how much time and commitment they would be willing to give to the community, if they would be willing to help newcomers, or if they would be interested in becoming a leader of the community. All such questions attempt to gauge intensity and commitment. Benchmarks for defining high intensity can also be very different from site to site. For instance, a community on WebMD for supporting individuals through illness typically has members who display high emotion and intensity, as shown by lengthy visitations and frequent postings. Members in a bead-collecting community on eBay, however, might exhibit less lengthy visits and postings, but are also committed.

The usefulness of these metrics, then, is for intrasite use in judging, among members, who is exhibiting more intensity and defining the level of intensity that you aim to achieve from your members. Relative measures, rather than absolute measures, will be the most appropriate benchmarks.

---

to become guides or mentors for novices, or asked to become watchpeople over discussions and flame wars, reminding members of the broader community mission. Such individuals could also become elders.

The goal of the commitment stage, then, is equity building and member development. These processes effectively build hooks into the individual, preventing him or her from moving toward the dissolution stage, even in the face of negative events like flame wars.

Main objectives of the commitment stage:
- Heighten equity building.
- Develop members.

Steps to take:
- *Give credit where it is due.* Increase equity by recognizing an individual's heightened participation and commitment to the community. This can be done through participation awards or milestones for membership anniversaries. In gaming communities, individuals are given recognition, which boosts their commitment level, through high-score postings. Such "bragging rights" mechanisms can sustain entire communities. One example is Microsoft's Gaming Zone, which creates communities around its most popular gaming titles.

- *Let them grow if they want to.* Allow members the opportunity to take more responsibility and learn new skills. Provide the option to become a leader, guide, watchperson, or adviser.

Dissolution Stage

Although equity creation makes dissolution less likely, even the most committed individuals still reach the dissolution stage. Events like severe flame wars could turn off members, or more likely, members might feel that the community's goals have changed (or failed to change) and no longer satisfy their needs.

Community administrators cannot take commitment for granted from individuals at any membership stage. The transition from commitment to dissolution can be swift, especially on the Internet. Given the number of online communities attempting to fill similar needs and the ease of joining new communities, simply walking out the door is always a realistic option for members. Dissolution is a relationship stage for which communities must be ready.

Causes of dissolution can include flame wars or hurtful comments exchanged among members. Flame wars can lead to the deterioration of focus and, ultimately, trust in the community. Committed members may become disgusted and potential members might be turned away. More often, members can also reach dissolution if they or the community have changed, so that their needs are no longer satisfied. A growing community can find itself redefining its mission several times. During this process, members who valued the older mission will likely be left behind. Alternatively, a member who has become more experienced and informed might outgrow a community that is more suited for beginners. Or in some instances dissolution is planned. For example, matchmaking service Match.com's main goal is to find suitable partners for its members, who then leave the community having achieved their goal. Dissolution, then, is not an entirely bad thing. A community might even find dissolution beneficial if it seeks a more focused group of members.

Identifying individuals in the dissolution stage is not always easy. Individuals may just quietly stop showing up in the community. If behavioral metrics are not closely tracked, community administrators may lose a particular member long before knowing it. Under other circumstances, individuals in this stage are more noticeable if they unsubscribe to mailing lists or, naturally, if they stop paying subscription fees to the community. Identifying such members, or departing friends, is the first step in the dissolution-prevention process.

Once individuals have been identified as nearing or having reached this stage, the community can attempt to find ways to change the individual's desire to leave. Through direct feedback or conversations with group leaders, community administrators might be able to identify the causes for a committed member's drop in intensity. If personal conflicts are the cause, mediation might be the necessary action. If no realistic remedy can be found, dissolution will be inevitable. If the community has consciously changed so that it no longer satisfies some members' needs, little can be done to retain those members other than radical community change.

Still, the community has a duty to such individuals. Trust and integrity are values that successful communities should exhibit at every relationship stage, even dissolution. Community administrators should define the process for leaving the group, making it clear, fair, and efficient. Ideally, the process should retain a human feel, treating the departing friends with the same respect as visitors. In return, community administrators can ask them for feedback about the ways in which the community had failed them. Last, the door should be left open for individuals who change their minds and want to return.

The goal of the dissolution stage, then, is that of identifying departing friends, using fairness and respect in the dissolution process, and leaving the door open for individuals who might want to return.

Main objectives of the dissolution stage:
- Scan for departing community members. Departing friends can leave quietly and with little notice.
- Focus on the dissolution process. Listen closely to any complaints and let members leave efficiently, fairly, and with respect. Remember, departing community members may return one day or recommend others to join the community. What you do when they are leaving will influence both of these potential outcomes.
- Allow and encourage the option for returning. Dissolution is not a one-way street. Keep the door open for departing friends to come back again.

Steps to take:
- *Spot departing friends early and find possible solutions.* Personal conflicts—which can often be mediated—occasionally cause dissolution. Finding out why members are leaving can sometimes prevent them from doing so. The use of group leaders and watchpeople can be useful in this process.
- *Treat the leaving process with the same care as the joining process.* Maintain trust and integrity by making the dissolution process clean and efficient. Do not be careless in sending ex-members e-mails and newsletters that they asked to no longer receive.
- *Let them vent and listen closely.* Feedback is one of the major benefits community administrators can gain in this process. Ex-members who leave on a bad note can badmouth communities, return under aliases, start flame wars, or do any number of unpleasant things. Use feedback for all it is worth.
- *Leave the door open.* One step in preventing bad breakups is leaving open—and encouraging—the possibility of getting back together. This might alleviate any sense of bitterness or ill will created during the dissolution process.

Exhibit 10.12 summarizes the levers that can be used throughout the relationship life cycle.

eBay Example

"'Community' is an overworked term, too often applied artificially to any motley of people who share a skin color, an income level or a set of political bugaboos. But from the limitless ether of cyberspace, eBay has managed to conjure up the real thing."
—Time, December 1999

Four Key Stages of Customer Relationships

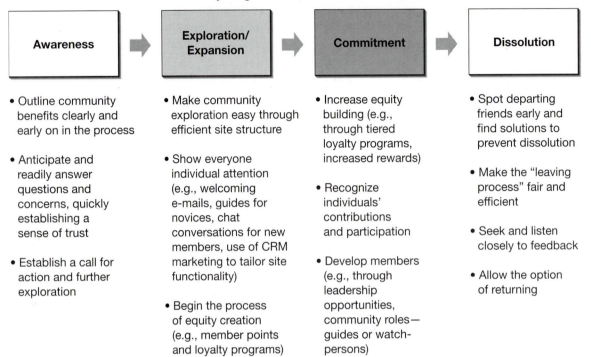

Awareness	Exploration/ Expansion	Commitment	Dissolution
• Outline community benefits clearly and early on in the process • Anticipate and readily answer questions and concerns, quickly establishing a sense of trust • Establish a call for action and further exploration	• Make community exploration easy through efficient site structure • Show everyone individual attention (e.g., welcoming e-mails, guides for novices, chat conversations for new members, use of CRM marketing to tailor site functionality) • Begin the process of equity creation (e.g., member points and loyalty programs)	• Increase equity building (e.g., through tiered loyalty programs, increased rewards) • Recognize individuals' contributions and participation • Develop members (e.g., through leadership opportunities, community roles—guides or watch-persons)	• Spot departing friends early and find solutions to prevent dissolution • Make the "leaving process" fair and efficient • Seek and listen closely to feedback • Allow the option of returning

EXHIBIT 10.12   Community Levers

> **"**EBay has created the largest and most successful online community that brings individual buyers and sellers . . . together to buy and sell goods.**"**
> —Journal of Business Strategy, January 2000

> **"**EBay's community is far and away the most valuable asset that any Internet company has created.**"**
> —Patrick Byrne, CEO of Overstock.com, May 2001[15]

What is it about eBay? Why and how did it become the hugely successful community it is today? The eBay community—which boasted over 46 million users in the beginning of 2002, making it the No. 1 auction market in the U.S. (as well as in Australia, the U.K., Canada, and Germany, among others)—originated, as all communities do, from the foundation of shared interests. This section will look at the ways in which eBay satisfies the definition of community and at some of the levers it employs in the four categories—people, processes, culture and technology—responsible for its tremendously successful community.

Exhibit 10.13 is a depiction of how eBay satisfies our definition of community as a set of interwoven relationships built upon shared interests that satisfy needs that are otherwise unattainable. First of all, there is an unmistakable set of interwoven relationships among the three main constituencies that make up eBay: buyers, sellers, and eBay itself. The interactions of these three groups are what create the eBay experience; without the active participation of all of them in unison, eBay's community would quickly disintegrate. The

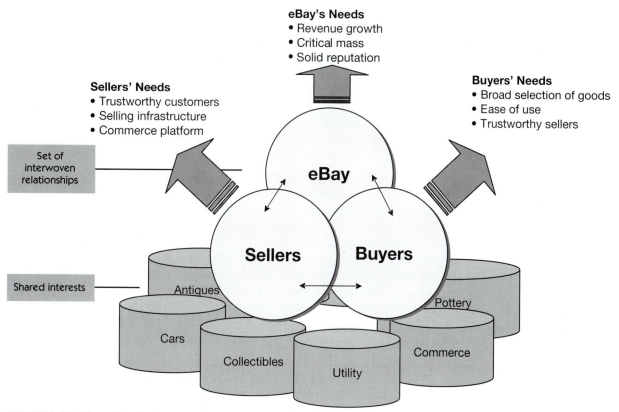

eBay's Needs
• Revenue growth
• Critical mass
• Solid reputation

Sellers' Needs
• Trustworthy customers
• Selling infrastructure
• Commerce platform

Buyers' Needs
• Broad selection of goods
• Ease of use
• Trustworthy sellers

Set of interwoven relationships

eBay

Sellers   Buyers

Shared interests

Antiques   Pottery

Cars   Commerce

Collectibles   Utility

EXHIBIT 10.13   eBay's Community

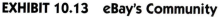

shared interests upon which their relationships are built are the pillars of commerce and utility, and the numerous individual interests that eBay divides into its 18,000 selling categories. Finally, each of the three groups has multiple needs fulfilled by their participation in the eBay community, whether it is profits for eBay, customers for sellers, or hard-to-find goods and great bargains for buyers.

Much has been written about eBay's community—mainly because it is seen as one of eBay's greatest assets and accomplishments. In addition to the great fit of its business model to the Internet, the secret ingredient to eBay's success has been the social capital that flows from social relationships. It is what enables eBay to harness the creativity of millions of entrepreneurs who use the site to meet the demands and needs of the even more numerous buyers who congregate there. Below are just some of the levers eBay has employed to create the community largely responsible for its success.

People Criteria

Member Base Has Achieved Critical Mass. In eBay's early days, it was not uncommon for early adopters to feel like they knew everyone on the site, particularly those who spent time in one of the site's vertical categories. One eBay user remembered when "me and my old friend the 'claw' were the only two users and all we did was trade Pez dispensers back and forth."[16] eBay has come a long way from its early days. As of the first quarter of 2002, eBay's registered membership base reached 46.1 million. This dwarfs the competition.

Members Feel a Great Sense of Trust.   eBay has implemented a number of measures to create a sense of trust. Unlike buying an item from a nationally known retailer with a well-established reputation, buyers on eBay may be dealing with unsophisticated sellers looking to part with items lying around the house. In such an instance, the buyer needs some sort of assurance that when they send payment they'll receive the item as described in a timely fashion.

The earliest innovation implemented by eBay to address this issue was the creation of the user rating system captured in registered users' eBay ID cards. With this system implemented, buyers could look at how many items the seller had sold, as well as the number of positive, neutral, and negative comments they received. They could also peruse individual comments from past customers. "Great speedy helpful service! Great eBayer. A+" is the type of remark commonly left by buyers. Similarly, sellers could see buyers' eBay history. This enabled a sense of security among both parties that the people they were engaging with were trustworthy and reliable.

For bigger-ticket items such as cars, eBay partnered with third-party providers to provide a number of services that help build trust in the transaction. These include the Secure Pay escrow service provided by Escrow.com. This benefits sellers by verifying a buyer's funds before the seller ships the vehicle. It benefits buyers by letting them inspect vehicles before Secure Pay releases payment to the seller, during an inspection period agreed to by both buyer and seller. Another trust-building service is the Fast Deposit option supplied through eBay Payments. In the offline world, a car buyer typically makes a deposit or down payment on a vehicle before the purchase is finalized. With Fast Deposit, eBay Payments collects an immediate $200 deposit from the winning bidder at checkout. This deposit serves two purposes: A seller knows he has a serious buyer committed to completing the vehicle purchase, and the buyer knows the vehicle will not be sold to another individual. Essentially, it solidifies the commitment between buyer and seller. Finally, eBay has built an entire section of the site, called Safe Harbor, that serves as a comprehensive safety resource and protective arm. Safe Harbor provides numerous resources and information that help create a sense of trust for the entire eBay community.

Process Criteria

Members Achieve Benefits of Scale.   Closely related to achieving critical mass are the network-effect benefits that eBay has gained from its market-leading size. The network effect is a feedback phenomenon that says that if it is in a person's best interests to be where everyone else is, then that is where they will be. eBay's size is a magnet that draws both buyers and sellers like moths to a flame (see Exhibits 10.14 and 10.15).

Effective Facilitation and Site Structure Keep Community Activities on Track. eBay has effectively managed the community experience at the individual shopping level. eBay provides a complete set of tools to control the experience of a given auction or fixed-price transaction. It was vital for eBay to cre-

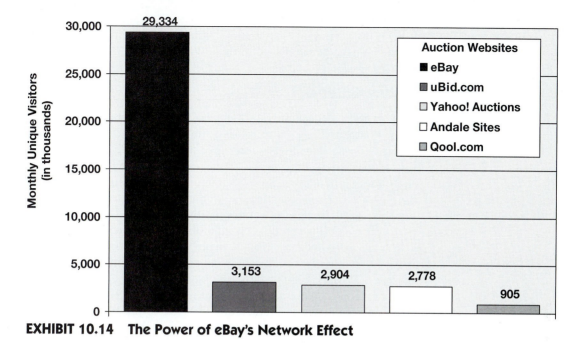

EXHIBIT 10.14   The Power of eBay's Network Effect

ate a common user experience because, unlike in traditional commerce exchanges (either online or offline), buyers are not interacting with a single corporate entity for transaction fulfillment but instead with thousands of individuals who act as their own fulfillment agents. To ensure that one buyer's experience is similar to another's, eBay wraps tools around the entire transaction, including links for winning bidders to send payment, ask sellers questions, and give feedback at the end of the transaction. The only

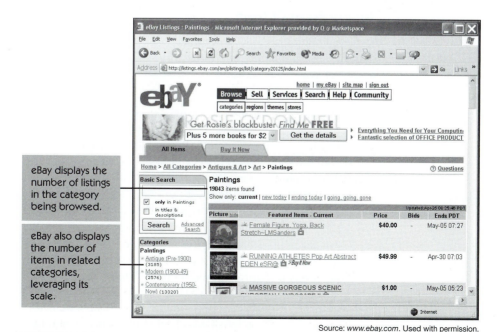

eBay displays the number of listings in the category being browsed.

eBay also displays the number of items in related categories, leveraging its scale.

Source: *www.ebay.com.* Used with permission.

EXHIBIT 10.15   Leveraging eBay's Scale

communication that may vary from auction to auction is the manner in which winning bidders share shipping information with sellers, but even this can be managed entirely within the eBay framework.

Culture Criteria

Spirit of Participation and Feedback Is Clearly Cultivated.   Feedback plays a big role in eBay's community, and buyers and sellers are well aware of its power. Whether a seller wishes to boost his credibility through a feedback rating that is devoid of any negative remarks or a buyer wishes to demonstrate that he understands how to conduct business the eBay way, participation in the feedback system is encouraged by all. In fact, it is common for both buyers and sellers to request that at the end of the auction the other person leave positive feedback so that the transaction can be viewed by others as successful and boost their credibility in others' eyes.

Affiliation Through Ownership of Equity Within the Community.   As noted above, eBay has turned its ratings system into a community-building vehicle. With its Power Seller program, it takes this to a whole new level. This program gives sellers a way to strengthen their affiliation through ownership of equity by turning the seller's feedback metric into the coin of the realm. Sellers who maintain a minimum feedback rating of 98 percent, have a minimum of 100 pieces of feedback from users, and sell a minimum of $2,000 a month through eBay are recognized as Bronze Power Sellers and get a special icon next to their name in all of their auctions. If they sell a minimum of $25,000 a month, they become Gold Power Sellers. In addition to getting 24-hour e-mail customer support, they also get 24-hour phone support and their own dedicated account manager, as well as other Power Seller benefits. eBay goes out of its way to ensure that they remain content and that their needs are served.

Technology Criteria

The Community Is Easily Navigable.   eBay is like a smartly designed supermarket with wide, well-lighted, clearly labeled aisles—the interface is intuitive and the navigation is clear. The features that create this user-friendliness on eBay include:

- *Simple browsing:* At the top of eBay's main page are the words, "What are you looking for?" followed by a text entry box and a button that says, "Find It." This interface, similar to that of Google and other top-tier search engines, makes it clear to first-time visitors what they need to do to find what they are looking for. For those who like to search by category, it puts some of the most popular ones in the left column, enabling category-level browsing with one click.

- *Easy taxonomy:* When listing an item—a Star Wars DVD, for example—eBay walks the seller through its taxonomy. In this example, first the seller would pick "Movies and Television," then "Video, Film," then "DVD," and finally "Sci-Fi." A buyer would then see "Home>All Categories>Movies and Television>Video, Film>DVD>Sci-Fi" when they get to the seller's auction page. Buyers could then navigate up one level by clicking on "Sci-Fi" to look at a broader video selection of science fiction films. This system was pioneered by Yahoo!, but eBay has put it to good use on its site.

- *Site Map:* For those who do not know where to go to find what they are looking for, the Site Map link—one of only four links that appear on the top of every eBay page—serves as a beacon in the dark. By clicking on this link, one is given a host of choices alphabetically organized under eBay's main content areas, including Browse, Sell, Services, Search, Help, and Community.

Obviously, eBay has used technology to help it build community. However, it is important to note that none of these examples alone is sufficient to build a strong community. It is when all of these mechanisms (and others not noted) are run concurrently that eBay is able to fully leverage community.

1. What is community?

Community is a set of interwoven relationships, built upon shared interests, that satisfies members' needs otherwise unattainable individually.

2. What criteria define true communities?

There are 10 criteria for true communities:

People criteria
- Membership is a conscious choice.
- Membership base has achieved critical mass and sustainability.
- Members feel a great sense of trust.

Process criteria
- Members achieve benefits of scale.
- Roles are not hierarchical or imposed.
- Effective facilitation and site structure keep community activities on track.

Culture criteria
- A spirit of participation and feedback is clearly cultivated.
- A sense of affiliation is achieved through ownership of equity within the community.

Technology criteria
- Efficiency in interaction is maximized.
- The community is easily navigable.

3. What types of interests form the foundation of community?

The shared interests that form the foundations of community can be grouped into three categories:
- Shared interests in information (e.g., stock trading tips)
- Shared interests in activity (e.g., buying and selling antiques)
- Shared interests arising out of commonality (e.g., being a doctor)

These different interests and foundations then form three different kinds of communities:
- Information-driven communities
- Activity-driven communities
- Commonality-driven communities

4. What are the different ways in which communities function?

Communities function, from a broad operational level, primarily in one of two ways. Communities can communicate through:
- Real-time formats: Immediate communication, where messages are sent, read, and replied to immediately

- Asynchronous formats: Delayed communication, where the time between a message being sent, read, and replied to can vary greatly

5. **What are the three primary ways in which value is created in a community?**

Value is primarily created in three ways:
- User-to-user: User-generated content such as member-written articles, opinions, and advice
- Administrator-to-user: Administrator-created content such as exclusive research and reports, and activities such as scheduled chats with special guests
- User-to-administrator: User-generated value such as revenue from product sales, content fees, usage fees, commissions, and advertising sales

6. **What benefits can community generate for a parent firm?**

Cost benefits can include:
- Reduced customer service costs
- Reduced customer acquisition costs
- Reduced costs from decreased product flaws and marketing mistakes
- Reduced marketing costs

Revenue benefits can stem from:
- Increased customer segmentation and customization
- Increased branding
- Deepened customer relationships

7. **When is community development appropriate?**

There needs to be a combination of both consumer and product attributes for community to be justified. Meeting one set is not enough. For example, on the consumer side, you need to be sure that your target audience has a record of online use. On the product side, the product needs to resonate with the target audience. There are many combinations of these two sets of attributes that in the end justify community development.

8. **What are the different levels of community?**

The three different levels of community are:

- Nascent level: Communities at their inception, typically marked and driven by community founders and a small number of core participants
- Formative level: Communities that are growing and developing, typically marked by growing membership and evolving goals and functionality
- Mature level: Communities that are near or at critical mass and sustainability, in which community survival no longer depends on original community founders and original core participants

Activities for Students

1. Choose a community site and discuss how it meets the four types of community criteria (people, process, culture, and technology).
2. Pick a community site and map it to the consumer and product attributes of the Community Applicability Model. Justify your scores across the nine dimensions.
3. Find a community site that has an established mechanism to reward equity building by members (e.g., a member ranking system) and discuss its effectiveness in promoting movement from awareness to exploration to commitment.

community	asynchronous formats	regulars
relationships	user-to-user value	leaders
interactions	administrator-to-user	elders
Metcalfe's Law	user-to-administrator	equity building
flame wars	visitors	
real-time formats	novices	

[1]Nobles, Robin. 1998. Can We Talk? *Marketing Tools*, June.

[2]Interested persons should refer to the following reference for more detailed discussions on community functionality: Young, Margaret Levine, and John Levine. 2000. *Poor Richard's building online communities*. New York: Top Floor Publishing.

[3]For deeper examinations on levels of human needs, refer to literature and descriptions of Maslow's Hierarchy of Needs. See: *http://web.utk.edu/~gwynne/maslow.htm*.

[4]Aboba, Bernard. 1993. *How the Internet came to be: The online user's encyclopedia*. Reading, MA: Addison-Wesley.

[5]Becker, David. 2002. When games stop being fun. *news.com* 12 April.

[6]Gladstone, Brooke. 2001. Internet game of EverQuest. *All Things Considered* 16 February.

[7]Kharif, Olga. 2001. Let the games begin — online. *Business Week* 13 December.

[8]*Ibid.*

[9]Pham, Alex. 2001. When 2 worlds meet. *LA Times* 26 April.

[10]Armstrong, Arthur, and John Hagel III. 1996. The real value of on-line communities. *Harvard Business Review* May–June.

[11]Kozinets, Robert. 1998. How online communities are growing in power. *Financial Times* 9 November.

[12]This section benefited from the following sources: Armstrong, Arthur, and John Hagel III. 1997. *Net gain*. Boston: Harvard Business School Press and also from Young, Margaret Levine, and Levine, John. 2000. *Poor Richard's building online communities*. New York: Top Floor Publishing.

[13]Reichheld, Frederick, and Phil Schefter. 2000. E-Loyalty: Your secret weapon on the Web. *Harvard Business Review* July–August, 105–113.

[14]Kim, Amy Jo. 2000. *Community building on the Web*. Berkeley: Peachpit Press, 117.

[15]Dennehy, Michelle. 2001. The Changing Face of eBay. *Auctionwatch*. 18 May. See: *http://www.auctionwatch.com/awdaily/features/face/*.

[16]Ibid.

Distribution

Is the Internet simply another channel of distribution, or does it represent a business revolution? On one hand, it seems unlikely that all consumers will someday buy personal computers, clothing, books, and groceries over the Internet. Some consumers will always want to touch, feel, hear, smell, or taste the merchandise before they buy it. Others will not want to wait for next-day delivery, and some will want the personal touch of a retail salesperson and a physical shopping environment.

On the other hand, it is impossible to overstate the Internet's impact on distribution. The Internet has transformed the industry structure for personal computers, books, CDs, clothing, travel, health services, and a host of other products. The Internet provides much more than low cost and convenience to customers—it enables firms to interact with millions of customers on an individual and real-time basis. Never before have organizations been so closely linked with their suppliers and customers. The result is a blurring of the boundaries between firms and their environments. Michael Dell, CEO of Dell Computer Corp., has termed this blurring "virtual integration."

QUESTIONS

Please consider the following questions as you read this chapter:

1. Is the Internet a distribution channel?

2. What are the objectives of distribution channels and their intermediaries?

3. What is disintermediation and what are its implications for channel intermediaries and customers?

4. What are the distribution levers and how do they affect relationships between intermediaries and buyers and sellers?

Introduction

A distribution channel is the system of organizations involved in the process of making a product or service available for consumption or use.[7] In other words, marketing channels facilitate the exchange of goods and services between buyers and sellers. The Internet, as any other marketing channel, has emerged as a way to better serve the needs of one or more customer segments.[8]

It is safe to say that all firms have been affected by the advent of this new **distribution channel,** no matter the industry or competitive circumstances. Some direct-marketing firms have naturally evolved from using mail orders or telephone sales to using the Internet. Dell Computer originally focused on selling customized personal computers to business customers via mail order, and now dominates the Internet marketspace for personal computers. Currently, more than one-third of Dell's business is conducted over the Internet. Similarly, Lands' End was a traditional direct marketer that joined the Internet revolution in 1995. It now sells more clothing online than any other company, generating approximately 10 percent of its total business on the Web ($138 million in fiscal 2000).[1]

The Internet has also affected traditional firms that have only reluctantly developed an online presence. The strategies of offline retailers such as Sears and Wal-Mart have been defensive. Their huge investments in traditional business models and their offline success have made them reluctant to embrace the Internet. Other traditional businesses, particularly manufacturers such as Levi Strauss & Co., Rubbermaid Home Products, and IBM, have found the transition to the Internet a difficult one, largely because of channel conflict.

The Internet has also driven the creation of new business models. Firms such as Amazon.com, E*Trade, and eBay originated on the Internet and compete strongly within their respective categories. These new competitors have often created or redefined entire industries. An excellent example of this is the market for long-distance telephone services (see the Drill-Down titled "The Internet Is Changing the Face of the Long-Distance Telephone Industry"). Many pure-play competitors have sprung up because it is far less costly to achieve national or even international coverage on the Internet than with traditional distribution systems. The Internet is now populated by thousands of small businesses that never would have survived in the offline world. Further, the Internet has reduced marketing costs related to customer identification, access, and interaction. The Internet enables a firm to automatically capture information about users who arrive at its site, and to encourage the user to interact further with the site.

Overall, the Internet is a direct substitute for the distribution systems of both online and offline firms. Many types of financial services, for example, are information- and communications-based. Making a payment, transferring money to another account, or checking a balance can all be done over the Internet. Online banks such as NetBank offer a full range of banking services and compete head to head with traditional banks. Similarly, buying an airline ticket or booking a hotel room are transactions that can be handled online. The Internet also can substitute for physical distribution systems. Consider the following three case studies.

SoftwareToGo. U.S. retailers and software publishers have begun experimenting with a new way of distributing software. SoftwareToGo developed an in-store kiosk that lets shoppers choose from a huge selection of software in "virtual inventory."[2] Once a customer selects and pays for the software, the system produces a receipt that can be scanned by a store employee. The system is then cleared to burn a CD-ROM to the customer's order within minutes. As of June 2002, Protocall Technologies was conducting trials of the SoftwareToGo system at three CompUSA stores (two in Dallas and one in New York). Based on the results at these trial sites, CompUSA and Protocall will determine a strategy for installing the system across CompUSA's chain of 225 U.S. stores.

The advantages of the system to retailers include the elimination of inventory ordering, storing, receiving, and tracking. Also, the retailer does not need to be concerned with shoplifting, lost sales because of product shortages, or adequate shelf space. Consumers benefit because selection will be great, even in smaller stores. Also, they will be able to quickly and efficiently find the products they want in one easy (electronic) location, without worrying about their being out of stock.

However, some key issues must be addressed before the system gains wide acceptance. Retailers must be willing to make the investment in store space and the cost of the system. Perhaps more important, manufacturers have very real concerns about software piracy. SoftwareToGo must convince software publishers that reproduction can be restricted electronically. Finally, there is the issue of who gets the profits. A joint venture between IBM and Blockbuster in the mid-1990s developed in-store technologies to offer virtual libraries of music and video games on CDs. The venture failed because publishers were reluctant to cede control of content and could not agree on how to divide the profits.

Digital Film. Some industry experts argue that the move to digital film will be the biggest revolution in movies since the introduction of sound in the 1920s.[3] One of the major barriers to adoption of the technology is that many major theater chains are not in strong financial shape, and the per-screen cost of a digital projector is about $150,000. A second barrier is image quality. Although you will never see dust, lint, or hair tracking across the screen, digital film does not have the same high definition and contrast that the traditional medium does. However, the technology offers some significant advantages. Directors can view scenes minutes after they are shot rather than waiting hours to develop celluloid film. The biggest advantage by far is the economics of the business for the distributor. For celluloid film, the first step is to create a master copy and send it to a film house, where prints are made. Each print costs about $1,800; if the film opens on 4,000 screens across the U.S., that adds up to $7.2 million. Then, there are the storage, shipping, and marketing costs, which might add another $700 per screen, or another $2.8 million. In contrast, a digital image can be beamed by satellites from the studio to a cinema for about $500, putting the per-movie savings in the neighborhood of $8 million.

Health Services. Although there are an estimated 20,000 health-related websites, providing healthcare services means more than just providing information. Business-to-consumer healthcare providers want to use the Internet to increase patient involvement, streamline operations, and complement the care that patients receive from doctors.

Experts see the Internet affecting healthcare services in two basic ways.[4] The first is by enhancing patient–doctor communication. Appointments, prescriptions, and referrals can be shifted, at least in some aspects, to the Internet. Further, some consultation can take place over the Internet, and advances in video communications may move doctors toward remote examinations for some ailments. A second contribution of the Internet is in disease management. Although chronically ill patients make up a small portion of the population, they require the vast majority of healthcare. Instead of treating patients in a healthcare facility staffed with expensive doctors, nurses, and equipment, healthcare organizations can cut costs by using the Internet. The Internet provides the basis for real-time monitoring and disease management of thousands of patients simultaneously. This decentralized approach to healthcare is not possible via traditional communications methods.

The purpose of this chapter is to examine the role of distribution in Internet marketing, beginning with a discussion of the Internet as a channel of distribution. The chapter also analyzes how individualization and interactivity (the 2Is) have revolutionized distribution channels, as well as what the objectives of distribution channels are. The chapter then focuses on disintermediation (the removal of one or more layers of channel intermediaries), using the Dell Direct model as a case study. The chapter traces the development of channels in the personal-computer industry from the mid-1970s until now, and examines the role of distribution channels in market segmentation. Direct and indirect distribution systems are contrasted to illustrate the trade-offs in channel design that result from each approach. With the Dell Direct model as a backdrop, the chapter discusses distribution levers, offers a process for designing channel systems, and addresses some of the key issues in channel management. The chapter then examines how the distribution levers can be used to develop strong buyer–seller relationships, and finishes with a discussion of eBay's distribution strategy.

This chapter is divided into the following sections:

> *How Have the 2Is Revolutionized Distribution Channels?* This section discusses the effects of interactivity and individualization on distribution channels. The Internet has changed the buyer–seller relationship and the customer shopping experience and has shifted the power toward consumers.
>
> *The Objectives of Channel Intermediaries.* This section illustrates the two primary objectives of channel intermediaries: efficiency and effectiveness. It then discusses the elements of channel member elimination and why it is not possible to eliminate the function(s) it performs. The section concludes with a discussion of how the Internet has played a major role in the disintermediation of the distribution channel.
>
> *A Case Study in Disintermediation: Dell Direct.* This section analyzes the evolution of the "build to order" concept. The analysis discusses the effects of disintermediation and how Dell has successfully implemented a disintermediation strategy and exploited the full potential of the 2Is.
>
> *Designing Channel Systems: The Distribution Levers.* This section discusses the primary distribution levers and how they affect the building of buyer–seller relationships.

Process: Designing Distribution Channels. This section discusses the five-step process to develop a distribution channel or redesign an existing system to accommodate changes in customer needs or the competitive environment. The five-step process involves:

1. Identifying and evaluating consumer preferences by segment
2. Designing a customer-based channel system
3. Modifying channel strategy based on firm objectives and constraints
4. Selecting channel intermediaries or partners
5. Developing a channel feedback system

Managing Distribution Channels. This section provides insight into how to manage channel conflicts, which often occur when firms change their distribution strategies. The section highlights how channel conflict can be resolved by appropriately using the channel power—that is, the reward power, the expert power, the coercive power, the legitimate power, and the referent power. The section concludes by presenting an alternative to using channel power, emphasizing the collaboration between channel members.

Distribution Levers and the Four Key Stages of Customer Relationships. This section examines how each of the distribution levers can be used to raise awareness and encourage exploration and commitment, and also to help dissolve the buyer–seller relationship.

eBay as a Distribution Channel. This section explains eBay's distribution position and examines alternate distribution channels that may threaten eBay's model.

<aside>

Sound Byte

Traditional Distribution Channels Are Changing

The marketing of CDs; Reese Jones, Chairman of Netopia
"Most of the money goes to the channel of distribution that is controlled or regulated by the distribution of a physical item, the CD. And that's a huge infrastructure that's built and constructed to [facilitate] payments going to all of the pieces that need to receive payment. That infrastructure has to collapse. Because it's very inefficient relative to Metallica playing their guitars right into a server and debiting your credit card every time you copy it from their server to your computer. It needs no employees. It needs no infrastructure. It needs no Tower Records store. It needs no music studios or music companies in the traditional sense. The same thing with television. This is very disruptive, of course, to the way things are done today. But it's an irreversible change. It cannot be stopped in a sense."

</aside>

<aside>

Drill-Down

The Internet Is Changing the Face of the Long-Distance Telephone Industry

The Internet is drastically affecting the distribution of long-distance telephone service. As the telecom industry tries to sign up customers for bundles of communications services such as local and long-distance calls, Internet access, and cable television, the long-distance component is being thrown in for free. Qwest Communications International is one such new entrant, offering 250 minutes of free long-distance calls to customers who sign up for its $24.95 monthly Internet service.[5]

Perhaps an even more significant development is the transition to Internet-based long-distance access. Internet firms are circumventing the traditional phone-delivery system and using a variety of revenue sources to subsidize free long-distance service. Consider the following examples:

- Some providers, including the now defunct HotTelephone.com, give users the ability to make free PC-to-phone calls from the websites of their partner organizations. HotTelephone.com offered a "Hot Button," which displayed a dialing pad through which visitors can call. The goal was to keep users at the website longer and to provide a reason to visit. Also, it hoped that the pleasure that the user got from the free calls would be attributed, at least in part, to the website providing the Hot Button.

continued

</aside>

- PhoneHog.com has a slightly different business model. It gives free long-distance calls in exchange for visiting designated websites. PhoneHog.com e-mails members with links to websites that offer discounts on music, books, clothing, travel, etc. It then rewards members with free calling time on the basis of the number and duration of visits.

- Net2Phone uses a revenue-sharing model. Manufacturers of computers, laptops, and Internet telephony-related products can become agents of Net2Phone at no cost by bundling Net2Phone software with their products. Each month, Net2Phone sends the manufacturer a share of the revenue from any purchases made by users with its source-coded version of the software.[6]

- Websites such as PhoneFree.com (see Exhibit 11.1) make money by selling members communications products from their sites, and through tailored banner advertising. Users can make free PC-to-phone calls within the United States and free PC-to-PC calls all over the world. Users also receive free services such as voicemail and video mail, video calls, and chat-room capability.

What will happen in this industry? As more and more people use the Internet, and as they are encouraged to take advantage of free telephone services and other benefits, consumer expectations of long-distance service are likely to change. Perhaps at some point consumers will expect to talk online for free as part of their ISP service. If this is true, it suggests a further shakeout in not only the pure plays that are competing in the Internet-based long-distance market, but also in the legacy firms. A list of free long-distance services can be found at the Free eCommunications Guide website (*www.fecg.net/phone.asp*).

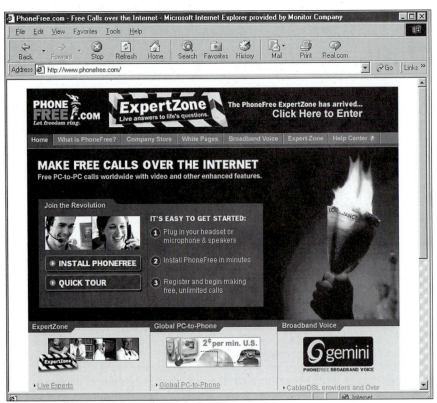

Courtesy of *www.phonefree.com*

EXHIBIT 11.1   PhoneFree.Com

How Have the 2Is Revolutionized Distribution Channels?

The 2Is have had a monumental effect on distribution channels. At a very basic level, the Internet is a substitute for other forms of communication between channel intermediaries. Instead of visiting, phoning, or sending a letter to customers or suppliers, firms can now contact them via the Internet. Yet, as this chapter will illustrate, the Internet is much more than a new communication channel. The interactivity and individualization of the Internet have changed distribution relationships in a variety of ways.

The Internet has radically changed buyer–seller relationships by facilitating real-time communication between channel members. As a result, companies such as Dell can create much closer links with both their suppliers and their customers. The links formed by the Internet have resulted in complex, dynamic, real-time relationships that lower inventory costs and improve market responsiveness. The Internet enables firms to individualize multiple customer and supplier relationships on a real-time basis. Interactions can be tailored to the interests of customers and suppliers, rather than forcing the firm to interpret their desires and then design systems to serve them.

The Internet has changed the customer shopping experience. Customers now have complete control over the nature, timing, and depth of interactions. Customer access and service are now 24/7. Customers can log off or terminate a transaction at any time without breaking any of the social norms that govern polite interactions. (As a comparison, imagine deciding *not* to purchase an item after bringing it to a checkout counter and giving the sales clerk your credit card.) The Internet enhances the shopping experience by making it easier to find product information, make comparisons, and order products. Further, customers do not have to travel to one or more stores, consider the various alternatives, find a salesperson, stand in line to check out, and so on. The Internet increases customer convenience and reduces the time spent on shopping. One of the most important issues facing Internet firms is the integration of all the activities involved in servicing customers across multiple distribution channels.

The Internet has increased the power of consumers. Searching for information is less expensive, in terms of both time and money, on the Internet. A basic search engine can give customers immediate access to third-party websites, chat rooms, and electronic bulletin boards that provide independent product ratings. Consumers can not only easily compare prices and secure product information, but they can also locate objective information sources. Increased access to this information creates more knowledgeable and capable consumers and helps insulate them from market pressures. Moreover, consumers avoid face-to-face sales pressure. Shopping at home or at the office rather than in a store might enable some consumers to avoid the impulse to buy.

Overall, the challenge to both traditional and pure-play firms is to recognize and adapt to the effects of the 2Is on distribution systems. Buyer–seller relationships have been irrevocably changed, the shopping experience has been transformed, customers have more power than ever before, and physical distribution systems have been displaced. Online marketing success requires firms to understand and take advantage of the Internet as a channel of distribution. The effects of the 2Is on distribution channels are summarized in Exhibit 11.2.

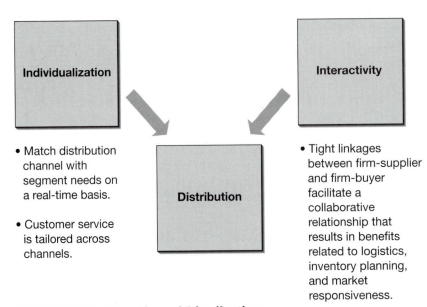

EXHIBIT 11.2   The 2Is and Distribution

The Objectives of Channel Intermediaries

There are essentially two objectives of channel intermediaries: efficiency and effectiveness. In order to illustrate these concepts, consider three manufacturers, each serving three customers directly. Assume that each customer requires one interaction, for a total of nine interactions. By adding an intermediary (i.e., a retailer), each manufacturer now has a single point of contact for all three customers. If this does not seem dramatic enough, think about a B2C Internet firm with a choice between interacting via a single electronic exchange or directly with 1 million online customers per month.

Channel efficiency can be defined as the amount of resources required by a distribution system to make a product or service available for consumption or use. The addition of the channel intermediary reduces the number of interactions that the manufacturer must undertake, although it is important to note that the total number of interactions has actually increased. In this example, distribution costs are reduced only if the retailers can perform the required functions more efficiently than the manufacturers could in the direct channel. In any distribution systems with more than two manufacturers serving two customers, the addition of a single intermediary reduces the number of transactions and therefore has the potential to reduce total distribution costs (see Exhibit 11.3).

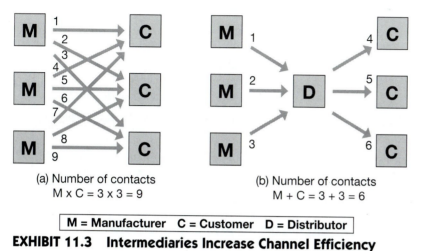

| (a) Number of contacts | (b) Number of contacts |
| M x C = 3 x 3 = 9 | M + C = 3 + 3 = 6 |

M = Manufacturer   C = Customer   D = Distributor

EXHIBIT 11.3   Intermediaries Increase Channel Efficiency

The intermediary plays an even more important role in terms of **channel effectiveness,** or the ability of the channel to perform functions that create value for customers. For example, a retailer might provide a personal sales staff that disseminates product knowledge to the customer, increases the convenience of purchasing the product by geographic proximity, offers complementary product lines (e.g., laptops and software), and offers easy returns, credit, and delivery service. A summary of distribution-channel functions is provided in Exhibit 11.4.

One or more of these functions are carried out by each channel member—manufacturers, wholesalers, retailers, etc.—within a channel system. Often a channel member will specialize in a particular function. For example, retailers in many traditional channels are completely responsible for personal selling and customer service. The retailer attracts the consumer to the store, provides relevant product and brand information, keeps track of the consumer's purchase behavior, and provides technical support. In these cases, the manufacturer never has a direct interaction or relationship with the customer.

In other situations, the same functions are carried out by multiple channel members. For example, both the manufacturer and the retailer hold inventory. Although this increases costs, it also provides for faster and more reliable delivery in some circumstances. Thus, the higher costs are offset by higher-quality customer service. Similarly, the manufacturer is likely to share with retailers the responsibility for marketing its brand. The manufacturer has the knowledge, skills, and resources to market nationally; the retailer has a better understanding of the regional market. The sharing of marketing expenditures and functions helps to increase channel effectiveness.

Market Information:	Monitoring sales trends, inventory levels, competitive behavior
Promotional Effort:	Banner ads, sales promotions, traditional advertising support, personal selling
Transactional Activities:	Bargaining on price and terms Order processing Credit Inventory and assortments
Storage and Transportation:	Warehousing Transportation to buyer Sorting and packaging into desired forms
Facilitation Activities:	Credit card processing, invoicing, shipping confirmations
Installation and Service:	Technical support, customer service lines, warranty work, repair, spare parts, etc.

Adapted from: Boyd, Harper W., Jr., Orville C. Walker, Jr., and Jean-Claude Larreche. 1995. *Marketing management*, 2nd ed., Burr Ridge, Il: Irwin, and George S. Day. 1990. *Market driven strategy: Processes for creating value*, New York: The Free Press, 220–221

EXHIBIT 11.4   Intermediaries Add Customer Value

Although it is possible to eliminate a channel member, it is not possible to eliminate the function(s) it performs. Specifically, Stern and El-Ansary argue that:

- Channel intermediaries can be eliminated within the channel system.
- However, the functions that are carried out by an intermediary cannot be eliminated.
- When a channel member is eliminated, its functions must be assumed by one or more other channel members.[9]

Disintermediation is a strategy that involves the elimination of a channel intermediary. For example, one hallmark of the new economy is a move from traditional manufacturer–retailer–consumer channels to direct online channels that eliminate the retailer. However, the functions that were carried out by the retailer are not eradicated, only shifted to the manufacturer. Traditional retailer functions such as monitoring competitive brands, attracting customers to the website (instead of a retail location), merchandising, order fulfillment, credit checks, and so forth become the responsibility of the manufacturer.

The Internet has become a driving force for disintermediation because it enables firms to interact at a much lower cost and higher speed than ever before. Although disintermediation increases the frequency and complexity of communication between buyers and sellers, the Internet creates much tighter links between channel members, which facilitates lower inventory and shipping costs. The overall result is positive, because the channel works more closely to create value for customers. In the next section, Dell is used to illustrate the principles of disintermediation in the PC industry.

A Case Study in Disintermediation: Dell Direct

Firms in the PC industry use a large variety of distribution channels (see Exhibit 11.5). The relative emphasis on each type of channel has systematically shifted from indirect channels to direct, Internet-based channels in both the business and consumer markets (see Exhibit 11.6). However, many buyers continue to purchase from retailers and other intermediaries, apparently because they value the functions performed in indirect channels. A look at how distribution strategies in the PC industry have evolved provides insight into the role of distribution channels in creating value, the specific role of the Internet, and the dramatic success of Dell.

From 1980 to 2000, the distribution strategies of the major players in the PC industry changed dramatically, as did consumers and the competitive environment (see Exhibit 11.7). In the industry's early stages, almost all sales were directly from manufacturers to consumers through mail order. The Mark-8 and Altair computer kits were advertised in the electronics magazines *Radio-Electronics* and *Popular Electronics*. Readers who ordered directly from the manufacturer tended to be technically proficient and understood how to assemble the computers and how to program them using complex instructional languages. By 1977, distribution had mostly shifted to retail channels. Small specialty retailers such as Radio Shack and ComputerLand sold mostly to consumers who viewed computers as a hobby and were interested in their technical aspects.

Although the late 1970s showed significant growth in the PC market with the entry of Apple, Radio Shack, Commodore, Texas Instruments, and Zenith, it was the entry of IBM in 1981 that legitimized the category. IBM created mass-market acceptance for the personal computer, and its market share grew from 5 percent in 1981 to 42 percent in 1983. IBM's focus with its large corporate customers was on direct sales via a large and well-trained salesforce. For the small- to medium-size businesses, IBM used retail dealers and increased its advertising budget to pull customers into these stores. Compaq, which entered the market in 1982, achieved a leadership position by 1987 by relying on independent retailers.

In the late 1980s, businesses began to demand specific and customized applications for banking, engineering, and manufacturing—services that were beyond the capabilities of traditional personal-computer retailers. Value-added resellers and independent software vendors entered the picture to address these needs.

Another major shift in distribution strategy occurred in 1984, when Dell entered the PC market by upgrading IBM compatibles. Dell developed a direct-distribution model in which business customers could buy "build to order" computing products through the mail. When selling to large companies and education and government accounts, Dell used field and telephone representatives who were responsible for understanding customers within a geographic area. The representative would market customized information products and services. Dell's information system allowed inside and outside field representatives to coordinate their interactions with customers.

Category	Distribution channels	Comments/Examples
Dealer Channels: 4 Segments	Computer Dealers or Corporate Resellers	Focus on selling PCs. Most focus on large companies: CompuCom, ComputerLand, MicroAge
	Value-Added Resellers and Systems Integrators (VAR/SI)	VARs are local/regional dealers focused on vertical/niche markets. Systems Integrators are large companies that build complex systems
	Local Assemblers	Local/regional dealers selling own brands assembled from subsystems
	Other Dealers	Office product dealers, educational dealers, distributors, etc.
Retail Channels: 6 Segments	Computer Superstores (CSS)	Focus on sellintg PCs and related products to consumers and businesses: CompUSA, Fry's, Micro Center
	Office Superstores (OSS)	Sell office equipment and supplies, SOHO focus: Office Depot, OfficeMax, Staples
	Consumer Electronics Superstores (CESS)	Sell electronics products and home office equipment: Best Buy, Circuit City, Good Guys, PC Richard
	Consumer Electronics Stores (CES)	Sell electronics products and home office equipment: Radio Shack, regional chains
	Warehouse/Wholesale Clubs	Sell a wide variety of products: Costco, Sam's, BJ's Wholesale
	Mass Merchants/Other Retailers	Dept. and discount stores, furniture stores, military stores, etc.
Direct Channels: 3 Segments	Manufacturer Direct, Direct Salesforce	Direct from manufacturer to customer via direct marketing (Dell, Gateway) or direct from salesforce (IBM, HP, Unisys)
	Mail Order, Catalog Sales	Any reseller using telemarketing, mail order, and catalog sales: PC Connection, Micro Warehouse, Multiple Zones
	Internet/Electronic Commerce	Manufacturers and resellers' sales via Internet/websites consist of Web sales from the 12 channels above plus Internet-only resellers and Web sales by indirect PC manufacturers

EXHIBIT 11.5   Distribution Channels in the PC Industry

In the late 1990s and early 2000s, we are seeing continued growth of direct and online distribution, but at a decreased rate relative to the mid 1990s. When and at what level will the mix of direct to indirect channels finally stabilize? It seems unlikely that all PCs will be purchased online, so at some point direct channels will stop growing. A related issue is how the PC firms will distribute their products and the effect this will have on their market shares (see Exhibit 11.8).

	1984	1987	1990	1995	2000	2001
Computer Dealers	60%	57%	41%	24%	7%	4%
VARs/Systems Integrators	10%	12%	10%	7%	5%	5%
Local Assemblers	3%	7%	9%	11%	11%	11%
Other Dealers	5%	5%	6%	4%	4%	4%
Computer Superstores	0%	0%	2%	8%	5%	4%
Office Product Superstores	0%	0%	1%	3%	2%	2%
Consumer Electronics Superstores	0%	0%	1%	7%	7%	6%
Consumer Electronics Stores	3%	4%	7%	5%	3%	2%
Mass Merchants/Other Retailers	2%	3%	3%	8%	5%	5%
Direct Mfgs/Direct Sales	15%	10%	17%	17%	23%	25%
Mail Order/Catalog	2%	2%	3%	4%	5%	5%
Internet/E-Commerce	0%	0%	0%	0%	23%	26%
Total U.S. PC Shipment 100%	100%	100%	100%	100%	100%	100%
All Dealer Channels	78%	81%	65%	47%	27%	24%
All Retail Channels	5%	7%	14%	32%	22%	21%
All Direct Channels	17%	12%	20%	21%	51%	55%
Total U.S. PC Shipment	100%	100%	100%	100%	100%	100%

Source: 1990-2001 data provided by Computer Industry Almanac, Inc. (*http://www.c-i-a.com*). Other data is estimated from various sources.

EXHIBIT 11.6   Estimates U.S. PC Industry Sales Volumes by Channel (Percent of Units Shipped) (1984-2001)

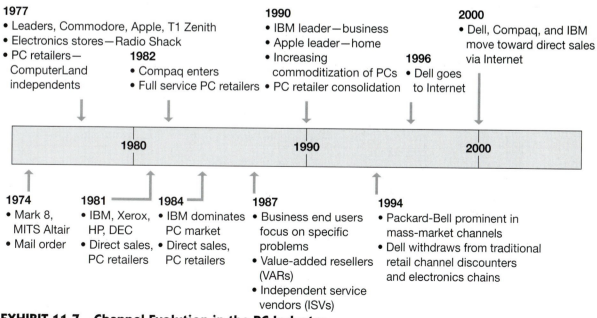

1977
- Leaders, Commodore, Apple, T1 Zenith
- Electronics stores—Radio Shack
- PC retailers— ComputerLand independents

1982
- Compaq enters
- Full service PC retailers

1990
- IBM leader—business
- Apple leader—home
- Increasing commoditization of PCs
- PC retailer consolidation

1996
- Dell goes to Internet

2000
- Dell, Compaq, and IBM move toward direct sales via Internet

1980   1990   2000

1974
- Mark 8, MITS Altair
- Mail order

1981
- IBM, Xerox, HP, DEC
- Direct sales, PC retailers

1984
- IBM dominates PC market
- Direct sales, PC retailers

1987
- Business end users focus on specific problems
- Value-added resellers (VARs)
- Independent service vendors (ISVs)

1994
- Packard-Bell prominent in mass-market channels
- Dell withdraws from traditional retail channel discounters and electronics chains

EXHIBIT 11.7   Channel Evolution in the PC Industry

Company		1980	1985	1990	1995	2000	2001
Apple	%	29.3	18.0	11.0	11.4	5.3	4.1
Compaq	%	0.0	4.0	4.1	13.3	16.7	13.6
Dell	%	0.0	0.0	1.5	5.4	22.2	26.5
Gateway	%	0.0	0.0	1.2	5.6	9.2	7.6
HP	%	5.3	2.7	0.9	4.8	12.2	10.3
IBM	%	0.0	37.0	12.6	8.8	5.8	5.8
PB NEC	%	0.0	0.0	4.8	15.5	0.6	0.5
Toshiba	%	0.0	0.0	1.4	3.5	2.7	2.4
Subtotal	%	34.6	61.7	37.5	68.3	74.7	70.8
Other Vendors	%	65.4	38.3	62.5	31.7	25.3	29.2

Source: 1990–2001 data provided by Computer Industry Almanac, Inc. (*http://www.c-i-a.com*). Other data are estimated from various sources.

EXHIBIT 11.8   Estimated North American PC Market Shares (1980–2001) in Units

What Happens When Firms Disintermediate, Go Direct, or Eliminate the Middleman?

Dell's advertising has often claimed that because Dell eliminated the middleman, consumers could expect the lowest possible prices. However, while eliminating a channel intermediary may lower a firm's costs, it may also eradicate channel functions that add value, or shift responsibility for these functions to another firm in the distribution system. Exhibit 11.9 compares the functions carried out when customers buy from Dell via the Internet versus at a traditional retail location.

It is clear from Exhibit 11.9 that Dell has reassigned some of the functions that have traditionally been assigned to PC retailers to create new value. In some instances, such as the need to invest promotional funds to attract customers, Dell has taken over the function from the retailer. In other instances, the function has been eliminated altogether. For example, customers can no longer see, touch, feel, hear, or smell the product. Consequently, some customers may expect a lower price when shopping on the Internet.

There appear to be two basic reasons why firms do not disintermediate existing channels: the desire to provide channel functions that are valued by customers and a lack of channel power. Although firms may find disintermediation beneficial because some market segments do not value the functions performed by a channel intermediary, they may be unable to implement this change because they do not have sufficient market power. New entrants, in contrast, do not have the same concerns about disintermediation because they do not have preexisting relationships with channel members or customers. Entering with a direct channel allows them to target specific customers without fear of retaliation from existing channel intermediaries.

Channel Function	Dell Direct via the Internet	Traditional PC Retailer
Market Information	Dell must predict demand for its products and understand the competitive landscape—manufacturer is competing with both manufacturers and retailers. As a result, Dell needs to be tightly integrated with both suppliers and customers to ensure coordination and cooperation.	Retailer provides information to the manufacturer.
Promotional Efforts	Dell is responsible for directing customers to its website through advertising, promotions, and Internet alliances. Customers navigate the site on their own and access information on Dell's products and competitive products as needed. Prices are posted, so no negotiation is possible.	Retailer advertises directly to customers and participates in cooperative advertising with the manufacturer. Sales people direct customer through various models and price ranges, answer questions, and may negotiate on the price and terms.
Transactions	Customer places order with Dell, which provides credit or leasing. Dell absorbs any inventory risk, but this can be minimized through the production process.	Retailer holds inventory and so assumes some risk of price reduction.
Storing and Transferring	Dell holds inventory and delivers to customer for an additional charge. Dell offers complementary products (e.g., software, peripherals) by holding assortment itself or via alliances.	Retailer stores product to provide immediate deliver. Retailer also stocks complementary products. Customer can examine the merchandise before sale.
Facilitation	Dell processes paperwork and provides information on product setup and maintenance.	Retailer processes paperwork and provides information on product setup and maintenance.
Installation and Service	Dell provides setup, warranty administration, repair, and parts through a third party or directly through a toll-free number, videos, etc.	Retailer provides setup, warranty administration, repair, and part through a third party or directly through a toll-free number, videos, etc.

EXHIBIT 11.9   Comparison: Buying from Dell via Internet or from Traditional Retailer

The Evolution Toward Direct Channels in the PC Industry

One of the most interesting aspects of the PC market is the evolution from a direct (mail-order) channel to the use of retailers, and, since the Dell Direct model was introduced in the mid-1980s, a major shift back toward direct channels. Why have PC manufacturers increasingly gone direct? Consider the following factors:

- All customers, particularly those in the home segment, have become more educated about personal computing, and therefore do not need as much face-to-face help in setup and operation. They also see less risk in making a bad purchase decision.
- Windows and Intel (i.e., Wintel) became industry standards, so there is less uncertainty about which platform to buy.

- Software has become much more intuitive with the use of graphical user interfaces, so computers are less difficult to learn how to use. Consumers do not need the after-sales service that they once did.
- Differences between the products sold by PC manufacturers have lessened, making brand selection less important.
- The average price for a personal computer has fallen dramatically. By 1997, the PC market was becoming saturated (approximately 40 percent of U.S. households owned a PC). Consequently, several manufacturers developed sub-$1,000 models for entry-level consumers. During the first nine months of 1997, the average retail price of a personal computer fell from $2,400 to $1,500.[10]

Overall, personal computers are increasingly thought of as just another household appliance. As a result, a significant percentage of the market is comfortable purchasing from low-service mass merchandisers or directly from manufacturers that ship the product from hundreds of miles away. In 2001, Compaq sold approximately 60 percent of the firm's volume directly (85 percent of its volume was through dealers in 2000).[11] IBM sold 50 percent of its volume directly in 2001, compared with 14 percent in 1999. IBM spent $20 million to promote its Internet presence in the first quarter of 2000.[12]

A second major factor leading to the popularity of the direct model is the technology that underlies it. As noted in Chapter 6, this technology has created the opportunity for interactive and individualized interactions with a large number of customers. For the first time, manufacturers effectively serve large numbers of customers at a very low cost.

Dell's Exploitation of the 2Is

Dell is a good example of a firm that has exploited the full potential of the Internet's 2Is (see Exhibit 11.10 for a screenshot of Dell's website). Dell's focus has been on Internet and information-systems technologies that help create and maintain collaborative relationships with suppliers and customers. Michael Dell states that his company "blurs the traditional boundaries in the value chain among suppliers, manufacturers, and end users."[13] More than just a way to outsource, Dell's "virtual integration" model enables it to treat other players in the value chain as partners. Consider some of the key aspects of this communications strategy:

- Dell routinely shares real-time production information with suppliers so that they can plan their production and delivery schedules.
- Products are built to order. In many ways, customers are treated as partners, as Dell salespeople work closely with large clients to forecast demand. They keep close track of customer software and hardware configurations, load customer software at the factory, and have customer-dedicated salespeople who work on location.
- Dell has created customized intranet sites called Premier Pages for its large global customers to give them direct access to purchasing and technical information. It provides tools that enable customers to set up their own versions of Dell.com.
- Dell holds regional meetings with large customers to facilitate buyer–seller understanding.

It is important to note that the Internet is only one component of Dell's strategy. But it is clear that Dell has used the Internet effectively, and in a fashion that is integrated with its business philosophy. The end results have been lower costs, increased customer loyalty, growing market share, and strong profitability. Dell sold $18 million of products per day via the Internet (about 30 percent of its sales) in the United States in 1999, with that number estimated at $25 million per day in 2000. Overall U.S. growth for 2000 was 45 percent higher than in 1999 (and 29 percent higher in Europe and 48 percent higher in the Asian–Pacific region).

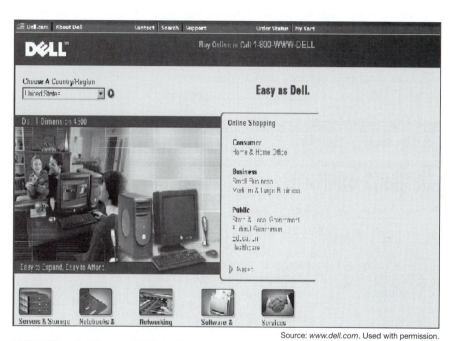

Source: *www.dell.com*. Used with permission.

EXHIBIT 11.10   Dell Website

Designing Channel Systems: The Distribution Levers

Firms have several key distribution levers available to them to serve customers and build buyer–seller relationships. The primary distribution levers are intermediary type, number of intermediaries, number of channels, degree of channel integration, and the functions and responsibilities of intermediaries.

Intermediary Type

The selection of **intermediary type** is important because different channel members carry out different combinations of functions that affect the value configuration provided to customers. Internet firms have a variety of choices for online channel intermediaries. Some of the key options are explained below.

Seller Direct.   Firms can go direct via the Internet, or perhaps via telephone or mail. Some firms, such as Columbia House, use both the Internet and mail to solicit orders and interact with customers. One recent trend in online direct channels is the use of "behind the scenes" e-commerce firms such as Cisco Systems (see Exhibit 11.11). Cisco Systems can provide integrated supply-side and sell-side IT solutions including inventory systems, order processing, shipping, payment collection, and Web marketing applications. For example, Cisco has developed an inventory management system that includes an array of supply chain management components, including shipping and invoicing, shipment tracking, service failure identification, and customized reports. Such services are particularly valuable to smaller firms who want highly integrated solutions but do not have the in-house IT capabilities or resources to create and manage them.

Courtesy of: *www.cisco.com.*

EXHIBIT 11.11   Cisco Business Solutions Website

Infomediaries.   Infomediaries are firms that bring together buyers and sellers to facilitate purchasing decisions.[14] Unlike the seller-direct method, the **infomediary** is a third-party agent or broker of customer information. This form of channel intermediary provides businesses access to customer information, while protecting the privacy of individuals who use their service. An infomediary such as Yahoo! collects personal information when you register, when you use Yahoo! products or services, when you visit Yahoo! or its partners, and when you enter promotions or sweepstakes. Once you register and sign in to Yahoo!'s services, you are no longer anonymous, and Yahoo! can then combine the information it gathers with information collected from other business partners.

Infomediaries provide benefits to sellers by helping them acquire new customers, develop customer profiles based on marketing research, and be more precise in target marketing. Infomediaries are uniquely positioned to develop rich customer profiles because they gather information beyond a specific product category. The information is also used to make the customer's Internet experience more effective and pleasant because it is used to tailor the user's online environment.

Infomediaries can take a variety of forms, including **portals** (e.g., Yahoo!, AOL), **virtual communities** (e.g., iVillage, communityzero.com), and **transaction aggregators** (e.g., CarsDirect.com, Travelocity).

Portals. A portal is a Web navigation hub such as Yahoo! and Lycos. Portals are often used as the homepage for many Internet users, and as a result provide a starting point for millions of Internet journeys. As a result, the top six websites on the basis of unique visitors are portals.[15] The ability to deliver a broad profile of potential customers is very attractive to marketers. These sites are able to track customer Web usage and purchase behavior and provide this information to marketers.

Virtual Communities. These infomediaries facilitate interactions between online users who have a common interest, and are therefore customer-focused rather than seller-focused. They develop strong relationships with their users based on a shared set of values (for detailed coverage of this topic, see Chapter 10). As a result, they tend to be trusted by community members, and hence marketing alliances with virtual communities can be very effective in creating or maintaining brand image, and ultimately sales. Although they do not create the same breadth of customer profile, a narrowly defined audience is very attractive to niche marketers. For example, marketers of products designed for women will probably find iVillage, Women.com, and Oxygen.com excellent places to advertise their product.

Transaction Aggregators. Infomediaries in this category facilitate buying and selling by creating links between interested parties. Autobytel, for example, matches consumers and dealers based on price, product availability, location, and other factors. Information is available from a variety of vendors and so aggregators often have credibility as independent providers of information. Other transaction aggregators such as Travelocity enable consumers to search for and book airlines, car rentals, or vacation packages online. **Virtual shopping malls** such as InternetMall.com are also aggregators that provide links to multiple online retailers. Virtual shopping malls provide much the same convenience online as they do in traditional retailing. This is especially important for brands with low awareness, product categories where customers want to comparison shop, or products that are often purchased on impulse. One growing form of virtual shopping malls is the charity mall. Sites such as GreaterGood.com and iGive.com donate a percentage of purchases from mall merchants to charitable causes.

In the B2B space, Internet exchanges are a form of transaction aggregator. For example, ChipCenter.com is a joint venture of Arrow Electronics, Avnet, and CMP Media, four of the world's largest suppliers of information and product services. The site provides electronics original-equipment manufacturers (OEMs) with information about products such as semiconductors and transistors made by Intel, Motorola, and other manufacturers. The site serves over 1 million electronics engineers and purchasing managers.

Number of Intermediaries

A second strategic decision is the amount of intermediaries the firm desires at each level of the channel. The three basic choices are exclusive, selective, or intensive distribution.

Exclusive Distribution. With this strategy, the firm uses a very limited number of intermediaries. Firms such as John Deere, Acura, and Kenneth Cole use **exclusive distribution** strategies because they want to retain direct control over the marketing of their products and limit the extent to which their retailers compete directly with one another. By reducing competition, the manufacturer increases the likelihood that the retailer will invest time and energy in the brand through salesperson training, advertising and promotion, and inventory. Retailers are willing to invest only to the extent that they are able to capture higher profits. Exclusive distribution arrangements are often characterized by large investments by the manufacturer in order to support the brand and pull customers into their stores.

Intensive Distribution. This is the opposite of exclusive distribution in that the firm places the product in as many outlets as possible. **Intensive distribution** is appropriate for low-involvement products that consumers select on the basis of convenience or impulse. Consumers are typically unwilling to delay buying products such as snack foods, toiletries, tissue, and magazines if a particular brand is unavailable at the location where they are shopping. Therefore, brands in these categories are placed in as many distribution outlets as possible.

Selective Distribution. This is a middle-of-the-road strategy in which the firm seeks a balance between making the product as widely available as possible and controlling availability. A **selective distribution** provides some protection for retailers against competitive pressures and encourages them to support the firm's brand. At the same time, it ensures that the product is readily available at a price that is subject to competition.

In the offline world, the decision about the number of intermediaries is often driven by cost considerations. The costs of intensive distribution can be higher because of the number of outlets that must be served. A manufacturer that uses its own salesforce with an intensive distribution system will have to hire a large number of sales reps, provide advertising and promotional support, and develop sophisticated informational and physical distribution systems. On the other hand, manufacturers can avoid many of these costs by using an additional intermediary such as a distributor or wholesaler that can carry out these functions more efficiently.

In the online world, nearly all distribution is extensive because of the massive reach of the Internet. Even the smallest manufacturer can advertise and sell worldwide and deliver its products via the same well-known courier services that major online firms use. However, online retailers do have some control over the number of Internet locations where their products are sold, as defined by their participation in alliances or affiliate programs. Issues of marketing control, customer access, and competition are just as important online as offline. Consider the very different approaches taken by the following two companies:

> *BT indirect channels* (www.bt.com). BT sells a portfolio of telecommunications products via 200 partners that resell to more than 1,000 firms. The firm has a product line that includes about 30 voice and data products, including narrowband, broadband, and business products. BT announced an affiliate program in January 2001 that will enable partners to select BT products for promotion on their websites. However, unlike many competing firms, BT has carefully selected less than 1,000 partners.[16]
>
> *Amazon.com.* Amazon.com has more than 400,000 affiliate sites. By clicking on a hot link, customers of one site gain direct access to Amazon.com. The cost of such an intensive distribution presence is low, given that partners are paid on a commission basis (between 5 and 15 percent of Amazon sales). This means that all of Amazon.com's costs are variable—they occur only when a sale is made.

The BT and Amazon.com strategies both seem appropriate because of their different products and customers. BT has a portfolio of technically complex products that are purchased by a limited number of engineers and technical personnel who compare specifications and price. They know BT.com and will seek out the firm's website as needed because telecommunications products are not typically a "reminder" purchase. These buyers will expect to see BT products in a limited number of outlets, and would find it inappropriate for BT to have a presence on a nontechnical site.

In contrast, Amazon.com's products are very much reminder, or impulse, purchases. It makes sense to co-market with as many related sites as possible. Interested in a Rolling Stones CD? Then it is reasonable that you might also want to buy a Rolling Stones book from Amazon. Similarly, a person's interest in South America or soccer or technology is revealed by his or her visit to a website with information on these topics.

An interesting variation of the strategy is the evolution of distribution over time. Just as a firm might use a market-skimming price strategy, so might it introduce a product with an exclusive-distribution strategy and then expand toward intensive distribution as the product matures. Indeed, this strategy is used by many technology-based marketers. The technology is introduced in a limited number of high-end retailers that provide superior service and sales support. As the price of the technology falls with larger production runs, mass-market acceptance is gained with more intensive distribution.

Number of Channels: Single-Mode Vs. Mixed-Mode

Firms can use several types of intermediaries simultaneously. In the B2B space, Arrow Electronics markets through three types of direct channels. The first is through its joint venture ChipCenter.com, mentioned in the previous section. A second direct channel is also online, but via its proprietary website (*www.arrow.com*). Finally, the company distributes through its approximately 300 sales and marketing representatives (SMRs) and 400 field sales representatives (FSRs). The SMRs handle telephone orders from customers related to pricing, parts availability, delivery times, and product questions. The FSRs work with customers to understand their needs and to explain and promote products carried by Arrow. The FSRs are supported by application engineers who provide technical information and solve specific design problems.

Nike is a prime example of a company that uses a multichannel strategy in the B2C space (see Exhibit 11.12). Nike has traditionally placed its newest and most expensive products in specialty sporting goods and shoe retailers such as Foot Locker. Mid-range products appear in department stores. Older, less expensive products go to mass merchandisers including JCPenney, Target, and regional discount department stores such as Mervyn's and Kohl's. In this way, Nike has been able to segment the market by providing the appropriate product through distribution intermediaries that serve very different market segments. Specialty retailers are best at serving the serious athlete, "weekend warrior," or style-conscious teenager who is willing to spend more than $100 on a pair of athletic shoes. In contrast, mass merchandisers and department stores attract Nike buyers who are less performance- and style-conscious and not willing to spend as much. At the same time, Nike has established Nike-Town stores in major metropolitan areas to provide the ultimate in fresh styles and technology, merchandised at its best and usually sold at list price.

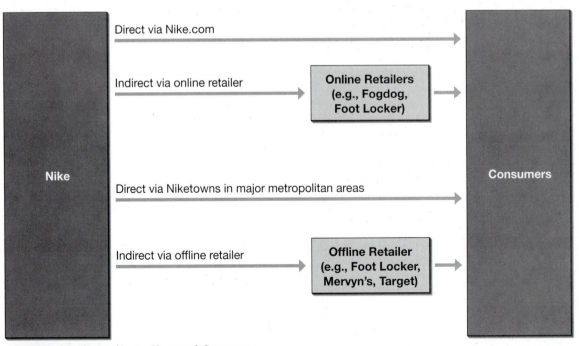

EXHIBIT 11.12   Nike's Channel Strategy

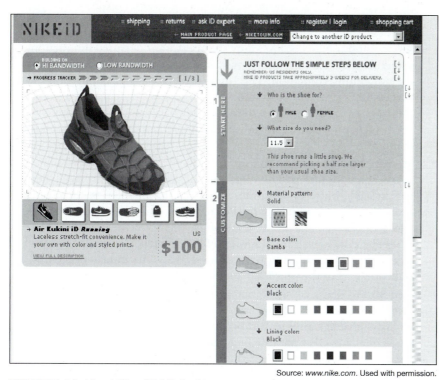

Source: *www.nike.com*. Used with permission.

EXHIBIT 11.13   Nike iD Website

The Internet has added significantly to Nike's distribution presence. Now customers can go to Nike iD, a website where users design their own shoes for a premium over "off the shelf" designs (see Exhibit 11.13). The site offers a variety of color schemes and textures, and the shoes can be personalized with up to eight characters of text. The process is easy, requiring a few steps, and the shoes are delivered in two to three weeks.

As implied by both the Arrow Electronics and Nike examples, mixed-mode channels have strong advantages and disadvantages. On the plus side, mixed-mode channels increase market coverage and allow the firm to gain access to customers or market segments that would not normally be served. For example, the office supply company Staples markets through its traditional retail channel, a direct-response Internet site, and virtual malls such as those found on Yahoo!, and it has approximately 30,000 links on affiliated sites.[17] A second positive trait of multiple channels is that each segment can be served in the way that best suits its needs. For example, customers who value immediate delivery can go to a bricks-and-mortar store to buy a new printer. Customers who value the convenience of ordering online and do not need the product right away can shop on a website. Consider the following examples of multiple channels, and how customers are served differently in online and offline channels:

• Many pundits predicted the demise of retail car sales after Internet auto sellers came along. Gary Lapidus, a Goldman Sachs analyst, likened them to the big comet that pushed the dinosaurs to extinction.[18] However, despite billions of dollars invested in various online sales approaches, car dealers are in a very competitive position because of the functions they perform. Selling cars is a very complex business that includes financing and insurance, warranties, parts and service, and used-car sales. Many shoppers want personal interaction, someone who takes them through the buying process and ensures they are not getting ripped off. The Internet, on the other hand, is highly successful as a way for consumers to comparison shop and as a selling mechanism for dealers who develop their own websites. In many ways, the two channels have evolved to be complementary rather than direct competitors.

- Many B2B exchanges sprang up in 1998–99 and were awarded huge market capitalizations. The valuations of these exchanges have fallen dramatically, however, because purchasing managers in many industries are not interested in taking dozens of bids from suppliers who are each trying to get business on the basis of price.[19] Many firms would rather develop deeper relationships with a few suppliers who provide a good price, but also quality, response time, services, etc. Internet access is only one part of the purchase decision.

- Levi Strauss & Co. began selling jeans from its own website in 1998 and told 3,000 retailers that they would not be able to sell various Levi's and Dockers products online. But because of pressure from its largest retail customers, Levi's stopped selling over the Internet. Consumers can now buy Levi's online, but only through retailers such as JCPenney and Macy's. These retailers have the power to "deliver" to customers who are not on the Internet, and most customers still want to see, touch, and try on the jeans and take them home right away.

In each of these examples, traditional channels continue to dominate within one or more market segments. The ability of the channel to serve target customers better than alternative channels is the most important reason for implementing a mixed-mode strategy. On the negative side, mixed channels provide significant management challenges.

- *Fear of cannibalization*: Adding a channel often means cannibalization. Traditional offline businesses are likely to fear that the Internet will not create growth, but rather will siphon off business from existing channels. These businesses fear lower profits because of the tremendous costs of establishing and maintaining an e-commerce site, as well as possibly lower prices through the Internet channel.

- *Channel conflict*: Manufacturers such as Rubbermaid Home Products have experienced a backlash from retailers that want to protect margins and sales. Rubbermaid sold a wide array of products online until 1999, when it removed e-commerce capabilities from its website. Now, the website only displays the products.

- *Channel management issues*: The addition of an online channel adds complexity to payment systems, marketing support, policies related to competitive products, training systems, and so forth.

- *Logistics*: Traditional offline manufacturers have inventory and logistical systems that are geared to large lot sizes rather than individual packages to be shipped to a single household. Their huge investments in physical distribution do not translate into an advantage.

- *First-mover advantages online*: The ability to rapidly scale up Internet-based businesses may create an advantage for online pioneers—those companies that are lucky or smart enough to create the right combination of market positioning, targeting, pricing, etc. Unlike old-economy situations where a firm might require an ongoing series of investments in distribution, contractual agreements, product partnerships, etc., the new-economy firm can grow much more rapidly. This effectively creates significant barriers to entry, as the attractiveness of market entry is diminished by the first entrant.

- *Product category*: It simply does not make sense for some firms to use some channels. For example, consumers will not go to the Web to purchase a tube of toothpaste, a pack of razor blades, or a can of tuna. To some degree, product-category issue can be addressed by channel strategies that direct a manufacturer's products through intermediaries that consolidate assortments that consumers demand. For example, although consumers are not likely to buy a single tube of toothpaste, they might purchase a large portion of their shopping list, including the toothpaste, from Netgrocer.com.

Degree of Channel Integration

Channel integration occurs when there is a high degree of coordination across all channels within a mixed-mode system. When customers interact with an online firm through more than one channel, the degree of integration can become a competitive advantage. For example, customers are likely to value integration because of the following benefits:

- The ability to order a product online and pick it up at a convenient retail location
- Having order history integrated across online and offline transactions
- Having online customer preferences updated based on offline transactions
- Receiving discounts on the basis of total purchases rather than just online or offline purchases.

Clearly, firms that can treat their customers in an integrated fashion reduce interactions that are unnecessary and potentially damaging to customer relationships. Customers who are penalized for shopping via more than one channel are unlikely to repeat the experience.

Even when a firm has contractual or ownership control across multiple channels (e.g., an Internet retailer that also has a traditional store), it is very difficult to properly manage channel integration. For example, the withdrawal of Internet-only initiatives by Citibank (which discontinued Citi f/I) in the United States, and Bank of Montreal (mBanx) in Canada points to the need for online and offline channel integration for financial services. In an article in *eMarketer*, Paul Mulligan emphasized the need for financial-services firms to integrate rather than isolate e-commerce initiatives.[20] He cited several pieces of evidence related to how consumers use online banks:

- Heavy users of online channels tend to be heavy users of ATMs, phone services, tellers, and supermarkets.
- The birth of a new channel does not necessarily diminish usage of older channels.

- The number of transactions across all distribution channels is increasing.

Overall, if banks (or other online firms) want to understand the entire customer, they must coordinate their information across all points of contact. Understanding customers' online behavior only gives a view that is insufficient at best and misleading at worst. Mulligan's perspective reinforces the call for integrated channel systems.

How should firms integrate online channels? One approach is to make the customer relationship manager (CRM) responsible for both types of channels. That way, the focus is on customer needs and the core value proposition of the firm rather than a particular channel. When the customer wants service, it is up to the CRM to develop and deliver it through the most effective channel. It is also important to present an integrated view to the customer at the tactical level, while still exploiting the unique aspects of the online channel. Some strategies include providing Web addresses on traditional advertising, providing online access in bricks-and-mortar locations, and allowing returns of online merchandise at traditional locations.[21] At the same time, it may be appropriate to develop offers and merchandising that are unique to a particular channel in order to exploit specific channel characteristics. For example, the graphic capabilities of the Web might enable customers to view a new golf club design being tested in the lab or being used by a professional golfer.

Intermediary Functions and Responsibilities

A final major issue in channel design is determining the functions and responsibilities of the selected channel members. These aspects of the distribution strategy are critical because they specify the "who does what" of the channel relationship. For example, the following are important considerations when developing a relationship with an affiliate program:

- *Commission*: Should the commission be based on clicks, sales leads, or actual sales? What should the commission rate be? Should the commission rate differ by product? Should all products be commissioned?

- *Promotional support*: What is the nature and level of promotional support? What proportion should be offline?

- *Inventory*: Should the partner be required to purchase the seller's product and carry it in inventory? What level and type of inventory is appropriate?

- *Training*: How much training should be required for affiliates? What level of customer service should be required?

- *Reporting system*: How often does the affiliate have access to the reporting system? How should clicks, sales leads, and sales be tracked and reported?

- *Coverage*: Are all channel partners allowed to sell in all geographic areas or to all types of customers?

Determining the responsibilities of each channel member is fundamental. Without a clear understanding, the potential for conflict and dissolution is high.

Process: Designing Distribution Channels

It is critical to remember that distribution channels are one component of the firm's entire marketing strategy. As a consequence, basic decisions about target marketing and positioning need to be made before designing the distribution-channel strategy. The balance of this section discusses the process a firm might use to develop a distribution channel or redesign an existing system because of changes in customer needs or the competitive environment. These five steps are summarized in Exhibit 11.14.

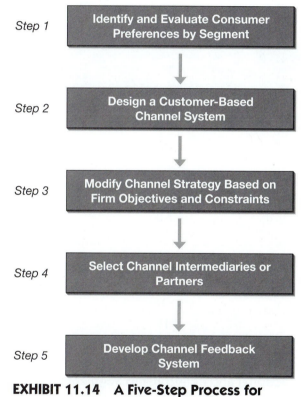

Step 1 — **Identify and Evaluate Consumer Preferences by Segment**

Step 2 — **Design a Customer-Based Channel System**

Step 3 — **Modify Channel Strategy Based on Firm Objectives and Constraints**

Step 4 — **Select Channel Intermediaries or Partners**

Step 5 — **Develop Channel Feedback System**

EXHIBIT 11.14   A Five-Step Process for Designing Distribution Channels

1. Identify and Evaluate Consumer Preferences by Segment

The starting point for the design of any channel system is the consumer—channel systems are designed to facilitate the flow of products and services to one or more customer segments. The first question should be, "What combinations of functions (or value configurations) do consumers want?" Although the Internet enables marketers to provide highly personalized service configurations (i.e., a unique product for "segments of one"), the essential process is the same for offline and online channel design.

Exhibit 11.15 shows a hypothetical segmentation of the market for online banking services. Segmentation can be achieved using either a priori or post hoc methods.[22] An a priori method begins with the selection of a variable of interest, such as age, sex, current brand choice, etc., whereas a post hoc approach clusters consumers who are similar in various attitudinal or preference-related characteristics. The goal of post hoc segmentation is to create groups of consumers who are maximally similar, and where the differences between groups are maximally large. Post hoc methods are highly appropriate on the Internet because of the relative ease of capturing online customer behaviors.

In Exhibit 11.15, a post hoc method found two customer segments, which have been labeled "transactional" and "relationship." The labels are based on the judgment of the analyst, whose goal is to describe the segments based on the characteristics that are most different between segments, and therefore lead customers to be a part of one segment rather than the other.

Characteristics	Transactional Segment (62% of customer base)	Relationship Segment (38% of customer base)
Agree with the statement, "I want the bank to help me create an integrated financial plan."*	4.5	5.5
Agree with the statement, "I would like a dedicated customer service representative."*	2.5	5.8
Agree with the statement, "I consult independent information sources for major financial decisions."*	6.3	3.2
Agree with the statement, "I would switch banks to gain a 1% higher interest rate on my certificate of deposit."*	5.9	4.5
Average number of years as a bank customer.	3.7	6.9
Average number of financial services purchased.	1.2	4.5
Modal number of branch visits per month.	1	4
Modal number of Internet visits per month.	11	1
Total	100	100

*Note: The numbers are based on the average agreement score using a scale of 1 (strongly disagree) to 7 (strongly agree).

EXHIBIT 11.15 **Average Scores for Transactional and Relationship Segments**

The characteristics described in Exhibit 11.15 originated from a survey. The bank asked a cross-section of customers to answer a series of questions related to their preferences, behaviors, and demographic information. The data were analyzed using a statistical technique called "cluster analysis" to identify market segments.[23] As seen in the table, transactional customers tend to be relatively self-sufficient people who seek out independent information on financial services. They are also price-sensitive. Their focus on the transaction leads them to buy fewer services from the bank, and they tend to have stayed with the bank for a shorter duration than relationship customers. In contrast, relationship customers want more face-to-face service, are less price sensitive, and tend to purchase more products from the bank. They usually have been with the bank for a longer period than transactional customers.

As seen in the exhibit, the transactional segment includes the larger percentage of the bank's customers. What is not known is the relative profitability of the segments, although the greater price sensitivity and fewer number of products purchased by the transactional customers would suggest that they are less profitable than relationship customers on a per-customer basis. The bank should examine the overall profitability of each segment to assess how much money should be invested in attracting and keeping each type of customer.

2. Design a Customer-Based Channel System

This stage asks the firm to design a channel system based entirely on the needs and wants of the targeted customer segments. The goal is to develop the optimum combination of services to appeal to each segment, regardless of any company or competitive constraints. This step helps the firm to think outside the box to try to meet or exceed customer expectations. Without this step, the firm might overlook important opportunities or competitive threats related to meeting customer needs through its distribution strategy.

The marketing research used in the first step helps the firm design distribution strategies that best meet the needs of each customer segment. For example, transactional customers are more likely to use the Internet than relationship customers. Therefore, aspects of this channel can be designed for the price-sensitive, self-directed transactional customers. Indeed, the bank will serve (and please) the majority of online customers by designing its homepage with the transactional customer in mind. Characteristics of the website that seem important to the transactional customer include:

- Real-time stock and interest rate information, and links to third-party content providers that have the objectivity demanded by this segment
- Automatic updates on interest rates
- Online financial tools that enable transactional customers to integrate across financial institutions
- Online newspaper that provides the level of detailed information needed to self-direct finances

In comparison, relationship customers place a greater value on the offline service aspects associated with the website. These customers are likely to value a customer relationship manager who can oversee their financial services portfolios. Relationship customers are less price-sensitive, and so up-to-the-minute stock and interest rate quotes are not as important and might even be viewed as a distraction. Instead, these customers need a channel system that is based on personal interaction and a rich understanding of their individual needs. The firm should attempt to direct these customers to the offline channels to ensure that they are not frustrated or confused by the online systems. Every attempt should be made to include ways for these customers to gain help or find offline support while they navigate the website.

Now for some thinking outside the box. The firm might ask the question, "How can we serve transactional customers better through nontraditional channels?" These customers might value information and, to a large degree, are not loyal to a particular bank. The bank might respond to this type of customer proactively by developing an electronic exchange that enables them to access all of their financial services on a single homepage; the exchange would be designed so that users could locate their checking, savings, mortgage, investment, and credit card accounts on a single page. The site would not only integrate the activities across multiple accounts so that users could immediately see the effect of a mortgage pay-down, for example, but would also include third-party information about competitive offerings. The bank could also partner with firms involved in tax, insurance, and financial planning to provide a financial services menu individualized to each customer. Although the bank might lose some business by making it easier for transactional customers to purchase and manage competitive products, it may benefit from gathering integrated information about the customer's financial situation, and by having the first opportunity to monitor and respond to customer demands.

3. Modify Channel Strategy Based on Firm Objectives and Constraints

After designing an ideal channel system based on customer needs, the firm must now assess what is possible and desirable from the company's perspective. Many highly desirable channel systems will not be possible because of financial or human resources constraints, or perhaps because of potential conflicts with current channel intermediaries. In terms of what is desirable, the firm should consider three types of objectives that can be achieved through channel strategies: economic, adaptive, and control.[24]

To illustrate the effects of these factors in channel design, consider a PC manufacturer that has determined that the ideal channel system is composed of both direct and indirect channels. In the direct channel, the firm wants to develop an online presence with both Internet and telephone ordering. In the indirect channel, the focus is on placement in traditional retail stores.

The online and offline channels will have different economic implications, in both costs and revenues. For example, placing products in traditional retail stores usually requires a strong brand name, consumer advertising, and trade promotional dollars. It also might require a salesforce to provide technical and marketing support to retailers. The direct channels also require financial support, in the form of website design and maintenance, customer service, and integration between the production, logistical, and sales systems. The respective costs of each system must, of course, be related to the revenue streams from each channel.

The second consideration, the adaptability of the system, is particularly important in fast-moving industries such as personal computing. How adaptable will the online versus offline systems be as customers and competitors change? In this example, there are two useful perspectives on change. First, by using a channel system that has multiple channels, the PC manufacturer does not have all its eggs in one basket. If there are dramatic changes in the importance of online and offline customers, the firm can shift its resources from one to the other and perhaps remain profitable. The second perspective, however, is that online channels may be more adaptable. The firm has direct control over the size and direction of the channel system without consulting independent retailers.

The final consideration is control, and it is inextricably linked to adaptability. With direct channels, the firm has complete control over all aspects of the marketing function. Training for salespeople, the sales approach, compensation, the timing of advertising and promotional expenditures, product emphasis, etc., are all managed by the manufacturer. In contrast, independent retailers usually do not have the same interest in the manufacturer's brand. The retailer is an independent business entity that does not always benefit from the same strategies as the manufacturer. For this reason, direct channels are best if control is desired.

4. Select Channel Intermediaries or Partners

Once the firm has designed the basic channel system, the next step is to select specific channel intermediaries or partners. There is no single approach to finding the right partners; the firm is looking for a match between itself and the channel partner, customers, and competitors. For example, selecting a channel partner for a revenue-sharing alliance requires an assessment of the partner's technical capabilities, reporting systems, marketing capabilities, and potential compensation type and rates.[25] More generally, firms use the following criteria to select a channel intermediary:

- *Brand/reputation:* How will the partnership affect perceptions of the firm's brand?
- *Financial strength:* Will the firm survive and prosper?
- *Sales performance:* How has the intermediary performed with related product lines? Has it been successful in reaching the desired target market?
- *Compensation:* What compensation plans are in place? What is the incentive system?
- *Marketing support:* Does the intermediary have the capacity to support our brand and product line adequately? What marketing levers are being used (for example, viral marketing, permission marketing, and online versus offline integration)?
- *Pricing:* What is the intermediary's current pricing strategy, and is it compatible with our strategy?
- *Customer service:* What level and type of customer service is currently offered?

One of the most challenging aspects of selecting online B2B channel partners is the rapid consolidation of firms. Large numbers of channel intermediaries (i.e., exchanges) are going out of business, often leaving gaps in the distribution strategies of manufacturers. The authors of a recent study suggest that there are four types of "winners," or intermediaries that are likely to survive consolidation.[26] They recommend that manufacturers seek out:

- Distributors that have highly specialized routines and capabilities in both markets and technologies
- Large, general-line distributors that stress viability over efficiency
- Specialized niche distributors that enter the market near the end of the consolidation period
- Distributors that have been consolidation "triggers" through rapid acquisition and growth

In rapidly changing or consolidating markets, they recommend that manufacturers select a portfolio of distributors that is balanced across the four types. Unfortunately, there is no magic formula for identifying the best channel partner.

5. Develop a Channel Feedback System

All marketing strategies need to be monitored on an ongoing basis, and distribution channel strategies are no exception. Once the firm has selected its channel partners and implemented its strategy, channel performance should be assessed on the two broad factors outlined at the beginning of the chapter: efficiency and effectiveness. As noted earlier in the chapter, efficiency is simply the degree to which the distribution channel lowers the costs of getting the product or service from the manufacturer to the consumer. Of course, efficiency should also take into account the effects of the channel on the margins and volumes demanded of the channel member's products.

Measuring efficiency requires that the channel member monitor multiple financial indicators, including profit margins (net profits/new sales), asset turnover (new sales/total assets), return on assets (ROA = net profits/total assets), and return on investment (ROI = net profits/net worth). These financial ratios help the firm to monitor the financial health of other channel members, as well as their return on distribution investments.

In terms of performance, the firm is interested in measuring the extent to which the channel system has delivered the functions, and ultimately the value, demanded by customers. As discussed earlier in the chapter, customers receive a different value configuration depending on the type and level of service received from each channel type. Firms must therefore understand the level of service quality provided to customers. Firms might use the measures of service quality designed by Parasuraman, Zeithaml, and Berry.[27] This approach involves understanding customers on a wide range of service outputs. Exhibit 11.16 presents a brief overview of this approach.

By understanding the degree to which customers are served, firms can better evaluate how well the channel meets customer needs. This is a requirement for ongoing success, especially in rapidly changing markets. Although it might sound easy to do, providing good customer service online is a real challenge for many firms when they go online (see the Drill-Down titled "The Challenge of Customer Service on the Web").

Managing Distribution Channels

Whenever firms change their distribution strategy, conflict typically ensues. Again, the PC industry in general, and Dell in particular, provide insight into the difficulties of managing channel systems.

Dell has never relied greatly on traditional retailers. (Though it did sell through traditional channels for a brief period, the vast majority of its sales have been direct.) Dell's target market values several characteristics: Dell's reputation for quality; its ability to provide configurations that are cus-

Reliability:	Is the service quality consistent, and is it delivered correctly the first time?
Responsiveness:	Are employees willing and able to provide good service?
Access:	Is service assessible in terms of hours of operation, convenience of location, waiting time, etc.?
Courtesy:	Are customers treated with respect, consideration, and friendliness?
Communication:	Does the firm keep customers informed and listen to them?
Credibility:	Does the firm have the customer's trust?
Security:	Do customers feel free from risk or doubt?
Customer Knowledge:	Are the needs of customers understood?
Tangibles:	Is the physical evidence of service quality appropriate?

Source: Parasuraman, Zeithaml, and Berry, 1985.

EXHIBIT 11.16   Assessing Service Quality, by Parasuraman, Zeithaml, and Berry

---

Drill-Down

The Challenge of Customer Service on the Web

A significant challenge to Internet retailers is providing adequate customer service on the Web.

- An informal telephone survey by CNet found that customers who called online retailers could expect average hold times of 10 minutes or longer, if they were able to get through at all.[28] One call to Amazon.com resulted in 30 minutes on hold and then a disconnection.

- A second study by CNet found e-mail response times ranging from 33 minutes by CDNow to a high of approximately four days for eToys and the J. Crew group.[29]

- An Andersen Consulting study found that 92 percent of online holiday purchase attempts were successful during the 2000 holiday season. Although impressive in some respects, an 8 percent failure rate still leaves money on the table and a high percentage of unhappy customers. Andersen reports that orders are unsuccessful when sites are under construction, when a site crashes, or when an order is somehow blocked.[30]

- Another important aspect is how responsive the firm is to customer complaints. When an order is incorrectly filled, shipped too late, or damaged en route, the customer needs a way to complain or achieve satisfaction. This is a particular challenge to online retailers because they lack physical locations. Also, because many consumers buy on the Web for convenience, they are particularly sensitive to hassles related to returning an unsatisfactory product or complaining about a billing problem.

Online retailers fail to recognize that many consumers want the reassurance of personal contact. Also, because offline businesses have the experience, resources, and skills necessary to provide topnotch customer service, online firms face stiff competition in this area. Traditional retailers such as Federal Express and Lands' End have

continued

set the standard for customer service, and customers expect online retailers to meet that standard.

However, online retailers are improving customer service. Lands' End, a pioneer in online retailing since 1995, has introduced several innovative features to enhance its online customer service. Here is a sample:[31]

- Shop With a Friend: This feature allows two consumers to shop together online. The two shoppers agree to log on to the website at a particular time with a shared password. Once they log on, their presence is confirmed by the system, and they begin their shopping spree. They can converse using a chat feature or by (their own) telephone. When one shopper goes to a specific page, that page automatically appears on the friend's screen.

- Your Personal Model: This service, for men and women, creates a virtual model (Exhibit 11.17) that reflects the customer's body shape, skin color, hair style, height, weight, and other attributes. The model then "tries on" outfits identified by the customer. It can also make recommendations about flattering outfits based on the customer's profile.

- Lands' End Live: The company offers a personal shopper who provides information about anything from order processing to style selection.

These features provide a level of customer service that rivals that of traditional retailers. They also have some advantages over offline stores. For instance, shy customers can shop in virtual anonymity.

http://www.landsend.com/

Source: © My Virtual Model Inc., 2002. © 2002 Land's End, Inc. Used with permission.

EXHIBIT 11.17 Lands' End Virtual Model

tomized, yet guaranteed to be consistent (and therefore compatible) with other Dell PCs; the provision of specific services such as software loading; and, of course, low prices.

The shift toward direct channels has not been as easy for the major PC manufacturers who traditionally used indirect channels. IBM and Compaq, for example, have developed manufacturing and sales programs to generate some of the cost advantages of going direct without alienating their dealer networks.[32] These plans have not been successful thus far, because dealers have retaliated against the companies. Because of their experiments with direct selling, IBM's revenues were down 24 percent in the first half of 1998 while Compaq's were flat. Hewlett-Packard, which did not try to go direct, experienced a 26 percent sales gain.[33]

What happened? Channel conflict arose because disintermediation brings IBM, Compaq, and other manufacturers in direct competition with traditional retailers. When IBM and Compaq limited their distribution to traditional retail channels, there was a cooperative relationship between the manufacturers and their retailers. If IBM made a superior computer, invested more in advertising, or cut prices, its retailers benefited. In contrast, if IBM is successful through a direct channel, retailers will probably lose sales and profits. By instituting a direct channel, the manufacturer is a competitor rather than a partner. Collaboration becomes a thing of the past.

Channel conflict tends to arise from incompatible goals. Channel members such as manufacturers and retailers are independent businesses, each striving for profitability, growth, market share, etc. Invariably, this independence leads to conflicts over what to achieve and how to achieve it. The goals of one channel member are frequently incompatible with those of another. Examples of areas where channel members often disagree include product availability, manufacturer support in terms of cooperative advertising and training, required inventory levels, product lines that overlap across retail outlets, and margins.[34]

Managing channel conflict is not easy. Manufacturers can try to use diplomacy or some other means to placate retailers, but, by definition, disintermediation means the elimination of the middleman. Consequently, there is very little room for discussion or compromise as wholesalers and retailers go into "survival" mode. Again, consider the transition toward direct channels in the PC industry. Major PC manufacturers who have traditionally marketed through indirect channels have tried to avoid retailer backlash and gain new customers through several innovative and dramatic strategies:

- Instead of going "manufacturer direct," IBM and Compaq have tried to go "distributor direct." In this model, they buy components from Intel and others and resell to distributors. In turn, the distributors assemble components based on customer orders and ship to dealers. One downside to this strategy is that distributors such as MicroAge, Tech Data Corp., and Ingram Micro Inc. may ultimately become PC competitors.

- IBM has shifted its strategy to become a components supplier. Dell recently promised to purchase $16 billion in storage systems, chips, networking equipment, and displays over a three-year period.[35]

- In 1996, Gateway, then the largest direct seller of PCs, opened two factory-direct showrooms to showcase its products. By July 2000, it had 270 U.S.

stores. In December 2000, Gateway began stocking inventory to boost sagging sales.[36]

- In November 2000, Apple gained approval to build its first retail store in Palo Alto, California. As of July 2002, Apple had 27 stores across the United States.[37]

- Compaq purchased Digital Equipment Co. in July 1996 to increase margins and overall profitability. Digital's $6 billion a year services business has 34 percent gross margins, compared to the overall PC industry's 25 percent.

As the above points indicate, major players in the PC industry continue to adjust their distribution strategies to gain competitive advantage. This is a necessity given the cutthroat competition—margins are razor thin, and technology is advancing rapidly. The industry will continue to evolve in response to customers, competition, technological advances, and other environmental changes.

The Use of Channel Power

Managing channel systems requires an understanding that other members of the system are independent businesses driven by economic outcomes such as profits, sales growth, and ROI. The challenge is that the strategies that lead to the highest returns are not the same for each member of the channel. For example, although Levi Strauss would benefit most from a retailer such as Sears promoting only Dockers casual clothing on its website, Sears will achieve more sales and profits by also selling competing brands such as Haggar. Further, Sears benefits from playing off Haggar and Levi Strauss to secure promotional funds, price deals, and favorable terms. Similarly, from the retailer's perspective, Sears is hurt when Levi Strauss sells Dockers products to JCPenney or Target, or when it ships the latest fashions to competing retailers before it ships to Sears. Consequently, channel members do not always see eye to eye.

Channel members use their power to maximize the likelihood that they will achieve the outcomes that are important to them. **Channel power**, very simply, is the ability of one channel member to influence another.[38] If one channel member has a dominant power position, other channel members must comply, and cooperation is achieved. Channel members can use five types of channel power to achieve their objectives.[39]

Reward Power.   **Reward power** is used when one channel member has the ability to offer another a benefit for complying with a request. For example, a request that a channel partner carry a larger inventory might include the promise of a higher commission rate on all sales. The firm making the request might also reward the partner by providing access to the firm's employee base or additional sales leads.

Coercive Power.   **Coercive power** is the channel member's ability to withhold resources if the partner does not act in accordance with its wishes. In this way, coercive and reward power are both based on the control of resources within the channel. The only difference is whether the resources are promised for good behavior (reward power), or withheld for bad behavior (coercive power). Missing a sales target or failing to undertake specific promotional investments could be met with specific financial penalties.

Expert Power.

Expert power is the ability to influence based on a channel member's expertise or skills. Past success in revenue-sharing alliances may influence the partner to agree to provisions they would not normally accept. Firms such as Amazon.com and CDNow have greater leverage when they negotiate contracts with prospective affiliates because they are thought to have special skills and knowledge that lead to success. By following the expert's direction, the affiliate expects to benefit.

Legitimate Power.

Legitimate power is derived from contractual agreements that specify the terms and responsibilities of a channel relationship. Patent and trademark laws also define the extent to which one party can use the assets of the other. Often, the penalties for noncompliance are specifically defined in the contract.

Referent Power.

Referent power is the ability to influence because of the firm's reputation or brand equity. Firms such as Microsoft, Intel, Nike, Procter & Gamble, and Lands' End have powerful online and offline brands. Most other firms benefit from being associated with such brands, and so they are willing to cooperate, and perhaps settle for less, because they value the association.

The five types of power are based on the firm's ability to control resources that are valued within the channel. Ultimately, the firms that create value for customers are the ones that have the most power. These resources include brand equity, technologies, knowledge, and processing capabilities that lead to product or service superiority.

The Potential for Collaboration

An alternative to using power is an emphasis on collaboration. When organizations collaborate, they function cooperatively and pool their skills and resources. Underneath **collaboration** is the desire to maximize the joint outcomes achieved by the parties, that is, to strive for a common good. Collaborative approaches are characterized by a bidirectional exchange of information and ideas wherein each participant listens to and responds to the other. The objective is to reach a final decision that synergistically represents the views and interests of each participant.

A collaborative approach attempts to create outcomes that are beneficial to all channel members, rather than exclusively serving the interests of one firm. For example, although Amazon may have the power to dictate unfavorable terms for a book supplier, it may seek a more collaborative solution in order to ensure that its prospective supplier can survive and prosper. Amazon is taking a collaborative approach to the extent that it tries to understand its supplier and to emphasize business goals that are compatible between the firms. This approach enables Amazon to incorporate aspects of the deal that will help the supplier be successful but also will benefit Amazon's business in the long run. A collaborative approach helps Amazon reduce its supplier turnover, increase supplier loyalty, and enhance the likelihood that it will be treated preferentially by the supplier in future dealings.

Researchers in a variety of areas have found that collaboration leads to improved business outcomes. For example, distribution channel research indicates that collaboration can improve manufacturer–retailer coordination, satisfaction, and commitment under some conditions.[40] Collaboration also has the potential to create more useful information exchanges and enhance new product development.[41] Other research has found that collaborative negotiations create better decisions.[42]

What strategies are associated with collaboration? Not surprisingly, perhaps, they are many of the same strategies that lead to stronger relationships (see Chapter 6). Researchers generally agree that collaboration requires interactive and individualized communications. Firms must communicate cooperatively and in both directions. This means that each party must recognize and be responsive to the needs and wants of the other—it is not enough to broadcast information and hope that it is received and understood. Thus, both interactivity and individualization are critical to collaborative relationships between channel intermediaries.

Distribution Levers and the Four Key Stages of Customer Relationships

Each of the distribution levers has a differential effect on establishing and maintaining customer relationships. This section examines not only how each of the distribution levers can be used to raise awareness and encourage exploration and commitment, but also how to help dissolve the buyer–seller relationship. Distribution channels are fundamental to building strong buyer–seller relationships because they are designed to facilitate buyer–seller exchanges. The levers associated with each relationship stage are discussed below.

Awareness

Distribution levers facilitate awareness primarily through strategies that increase the number of access points for consumers. Any strategy that makes it more likely that consumers will be directed to or find a way to contact the firm is likely to enhance awareness. As a result, the primary distribution levers that increase the level of consumer awareness are the number of intermediaries and the number of channels.

Number of Intermediaries.   An intensive distribution strategy should lead to greater awareness because the firm is accessible via more outlets. As noted earlier in the chapter, nearly all distribution in the online world is intensive because of the Internet's massive reach. However, participation in affiliate programs is one tactic that increases distribution intensity. Banner ads in multiple locations can provide access to the firm's website through a single mouse click. Affiliate programs create a high level of distribution intensity that is analogous to an offline firm that adds retail outlets.

Number of Channels/Intermediary Type.   Given that different customers are likely to shop at different channel types, a greater variety of distribution channels increases market coverage and, therefore, awareness. The number of channels can be increased by using a combination of offline and online channels, as in the case of many traditional retailers who have gone online (e.g., Target, Foot Locker, Circuit City). As discussed previously, retailers such as Nike offer multiple online and offline channels. The number of channels is also increased when a direct-sales online firm joins a virtual shopping mall or electronic exchange.

Exploration/Expansion

Here, the focus is on increasing the value of the channel to customers. Channels that create more value for customers increase consumer interest and exploration.

Degree of Channel Integration. As integration increases, the willingness to explore the potential for a relationship should increase. Very simply, integration increases the level of customer service, which increases the attractiveness of the firm as a relationship partner. Also important is the effect of channel integration on the reliability of customer service. Reliability is a necessary component of trust, satisfaction, and the development of relationship norms. Relationship quality comes not only from the level of the customer service, but also from whether the customer can count on the service from interaction to interaction.

Number of Channels/Intermediary Type. The likelihood of exploration increases as the number of channels increases. Each intermediary type has a different profile of functions and responsibilities that provides a different value configuration for consumers. Firms increase exploration and expansion of the relationship by ensuring that they target their customers correctly. By understanding the needs of each target segment, the product or service can be delivered through the most appropriate distribution channel. As the perceived value of the product is enhanced, the willingness to explore increases.

Commitment

Customers are more likely to commit to firms that provide exceptional value, making it easy and attractive to establish a relationship. In many ways, rather than being sufficient to create commitment, the levers are necessary aspects of the distribution function. In other words, customers will be unwilling to commit if these distribution levers are not implemented properly.

Degree of Channel Integration. The channel environment must be integrated for customers to commit. Customers expect to be treated in a holistic sense, rather than on a per-transaction basis. They expect that their previous interactions with the firm will be tracked and used to serve them in the offline world, and vice versa.

Intermediary Type. Making a commitment to the firm requires trust, and so the selection of a channel should be affected by the degree of trust that is associated with the alternatives. To illustrate, all else being equal, direct channels are more likely to create trust than indirect ones. If a customer buys a stereo from Sony directly, he knows that Sony is highly motivated to ensure that he is satisfied. In contrast, if he buys his Sony stereo from an independent retailer, he is not quite as sure who is responsible for his satisfaction.

A related issue is the ability to form a buyer–seller relationship in an indirect channel. Purchasing the same stereo from an online electronics retailer increases the likelihood that the customer will form a bond with the retailer rather than Sony. The retailer handles customer service, warranty problems, credit, and promotion. Manufacturers that go direct have greater control over the brand's marketing strategy and are more likely to generate commitment.

Number of Channels.   Although a major advantage of employing multiple channels is the ability to appropriately serve multiple market segments, this strategy can also increase customer commitment within a segment. Customers often have different buying requirements based on the purchase situation, and their requirements can evolve over time as they grow older or their life situation changes. Imagine that a customer who is loyal to Nordstrom is faced with an unexpected business trip and does not have time to shop at her local store. An online alternative is critical to maintaining the connection to the brand. Or, the connection to a brand could be maintained if a loyal online shopper does not feel comfortable buying an expensive new technology over the Internet. The ability to go to a local showroom for face-to-face advice and the ability to see and hear the product is necessary to keep her business.

Intermediary Functions and Responsibilities.   The firm can enhance customer value and strengthen commitment by using marketing research to understand customer perceptions of service quality. For example, a U.S. firm might find that its Canadian customers are often lost at checkout because of uncertainty about exchange rates, import duties, and shipping charges. The percentage of Canadian customers who complete the purchase process might increase dramatically if products are priced in Canadian currency, and shipping and duty costs are reduced or eliminated by a partnership with a Canadian-based channel member that holds inventory. Other channel functions and responsibilities that can lead to greater commitment include customer representative training, sales incentives that focus on customer satisfaction, and increased margins.

Dissolution

Restricting or eliminating customer access reduces the attractiveness of a website. Similarly, dissolution is encouraged by using channel types that provide services that are not well matched to consumer needs.

Elimination of Channel Types.   Some customers, particularly those who find value in the functions carried out by the channel type that has been eliminated, will complain; others will leave.

Reduction in Number of Intermediaries.   Customers will find it more difficult to purchase the firm's products and will complain or exit.

Reduction In Channel Integration.   By customers being treated based only on part of their transactions, they are much less likely to feel connected to the firm or brand. Dissolution is more likely to follow.

The distribution levers that affect customer relationships are summarized in Exhibit 11.18.

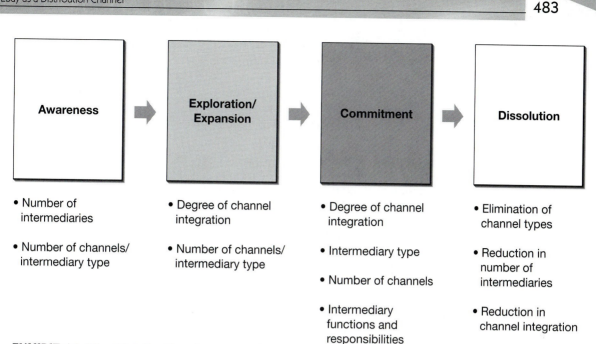

EXHIBIT 11.18   Distribution Levers and Four Key Stages of Customer Relationships

eBay as a Distribution Channel

eBay neither produces nor sells anything; rather, it connects buyers and sellers. In distribution terms, eBay is classified as a broker—that is, a channel intermediary that brings together buyers and sellers but does not carry inventory, participate in financing, or assume risk. As such, eBay does not have responsibility for the goods offered at auction, for collecting payments, or for shipping. Its role is to create the infrastructure necessary for buyers and sellers to find each other, and to maintain the integrity of the process.[43]

eBay enables anyone from individuals to small businesses to large corporations to distribute their products in a cost-effective way. Those selling antiques, collectibles, cars, computers, and a variety of other items have access to customers like never before.

Beyond maintaining a secure and reliable electronic exchange, eBay provides value through a number of services to facilitate an easy and smooth distribution process between sellers and buyers. All of these options encourage new users and stimulate continued business from existing ones by providing security and ease.

> *Shipping Center:* Through eBay's Shipping Center, eBay users can sign up with UPS to create a UPS Daily Pickup account, print their own postage, or order Priority Mail packs, envelopes, and other domestic service supplies from the U.S. Postal Service.
>
> *eBay Payments:* After acquiring Billpoint and PayPal, eBay began to provide secure online credit card transactions. Unlike purchases paid for with money orders or personal checks, credit card purchases can be shipped immediately.

What does the future hold for eBay? The firm faces competition from a variety of sources. While it does not face major competition from online auction houses, it has begun to compete with large online and offline retailers as more of its business is conducted through fixed-priced formats including Buy It Now and Half.com. For example, Amazon.com and Wal-Mart are two of eBay's closest competitors. While all three offer a huge assortment of products, Amazon and Wal-Mart, unlike eBay, operate on a different model. Instead of eBay's inventory-free distribution model, both Amazon and Wal-Mart have large amounts of capital tied up in warehouses and inventory. Whereas Wal-Mart's margins approach 5 percent, eBay's are in the 30 percent range, largely due to this significant distinction.

Other threats to eBay are new distribution channels that allow users to aggregate their buying and selling activities across more than one online auction house. In a typical aggregation approach, companies pool their listings so that any item listed on one auction website will appear in all allied websites. This type of distribution system introduces an online intermediary (i.e., the exchange) that aggregates across websites using an independent brand. eBay has pressed this issue in the courtroom, citing that aggregators infringe on its intellectual property and slow service for existing eBay customers. One aggregator, Bidder's Edge, paid eBay an undisclosed sum to end its legal dispute and is out of business. Another, AuctionWatch, does not link to eBay but does provide one-stop-shopping from multiple smaller auction sites.

Summary

1. Is the Internet a distribution channel?

Yes, the Internet is a distribution channel, because it is part of the process of making a product or service available for consumption or use. The Internet facilitates the exchange of goods and services between buyers and sellers. It has emerged as a way of serving needs that exist in the market.

2. What are the objectives of distribution channels and their intermediaries?

Channel intermediaries have two objectives: efficiency and effectiveness. Adding a channel intermediary increases channel efficiency by reducing the number of interactions that a channel member must undertake. Also, efficiency is increased to the extent that one intermediary can carry out a series of functions at a lower cost than other intermediaries.

Channels play an even more important role in increasing effectiveness, defined as the ability of the channel to perform functions that create value for customers. For example, a retailer might provide salespeople who have product knowledge, increase convenience with a nearby retail location, sell complementary product lines (e.g., laptops and software), and offer easy returns, credit, and delivery service.

3. What is disintermediation and what are its implications for channel intermediaries and customers?

Disintermediation is the elimination of a channel intermediary. In the new economy, disintermediation often means the elimination of the retailer through a move from a traditional manufacturer–retailer–consumer channel to a direct online channel. However, the retailer's functions—including monitoring competitive brands, attracting customers, merchandising, order fulfillment, credit checks, and so forth—are not eradicated, only shifted to the manufacturer.

The Internet has become a driving force for disintermediation because it enables firms to interact with customers at a much lower cost and higher speed than ever before. Although disintermediation increases the frequency and complexity of communication between buyers and sellers, the Internet creates much tighter links between channel members, which facilitates lower inventory and shipping costs. The overall result is positive, as the channel works together more closely to create value for customers. Dell's case study is a good example of how disintermediation causes certain functions to transfer from the retailer to the manufacturer, and how disintermediation affects the value received by customers.

4. **What are the distribution levers and how do they affect relationships between intermediaries and buyers and sellers?**

The distribution levers are activities that affect buyer–seller relationships through the type of intermediary, number of intermediaries, intermediary functions and responsibilities, number of channels, and degree of channel integration. The levers affect buyer–seller relationships by stimulating customers to become aware of, explore, or commit to the firm. The levers can also be used to weaken or dissolve relationships.

1. Evaluate your Web-buying behavior. What types of products do you buy most often? What types of products do you avoid buying online? Why? Try to relate your answers to the distribution functions that are carried out by online and offline providers.
2. The next time you need to buy something, compare your online and offline shopping experiences. How many online and offline stores did you visit? Why did you visit them? How did you feel about the interactions you had with the firms? Did you have any problems? What were the functions carried out by each of the distribution channels?
3. Evaluate the customer service from three online retailers. Ask the same product-related question and evaluate the responses. How long did it take to respond? Was the response personalized? Was the response complete? Did the retailers have different policies? On the basis of their responses, where would you shop?

distribution channel	transaction aggregators	reward power
channel efficiency	virtual shopping malls	coercive power
channel effectiveness	exclusive distribution	expert power
intermediary type	intensive distribution	legitimate power
infomediary	selective distribution	referent power
portals	channel integration	collaboration
virtual communities	channel power	

[1]Prior, Molly. 2000. Lands' End crosses threshold of internet retailing excellence. *DSN Retailing Today* 39 (21):6.

[2]See *http://www.softwaretogo.com*, and Lorek, Laura. 2000. Protocall introduces software kiosk. Interactive Week 24 July.

[3]Wahl, Andrew 2001, *Canadian Business*, Toronto: CB Media Ltd., Sept 3.

[4]Brick, Collin. 2001. Surfing for health: It's more than information: Part 3. *eMarketer.com* 12 January.

[5]Brull, Steven V., Amy Barrett, and Roger Crockett. 1999. Why talk is so cheap. *Business Week* 13 September, 34–36.

[6]Net2Phone to offer free phone calls, voice mail. 2000. *News.com* 20 November.

[7]Stern, Louis W., and Adel I. El-Ansary. 1996. *Marketing channels*. 5th ed. Upper Saddle River, NJ: Prentice Hall.

[8]Pelton, Lou, David Strutton, and James R. Lumpkin. 1997. *Marketing channels, a relationship management approach*. Chicago: Irwin.

[9]Stern, Louis, and Adel I. El-Ansary. 1992. Marketing channels. 4th ed. Englewood Cliffs, NJ: Prentice-Hall.

[10]Rangan, Kasturi, and Marie Bell. 1999. Dell online, Case No. 598-116. Boston: Harvard Business School Publishing.

[11]Wilcox, Joe. 2000. Compaq details its direct sales hopes. *News.com* 28 January.

[12]Wilcox, Joe. 2000. IBM plans a direct-sales assault. *News.com* 24 February.

[13]Rangan, Kasturi, and Marie Bell. 1999. Dell online, Case No. 598-116. Boston: Harvard Business School Publishing.

[14]John Hagel III and Marc Singer, Net Worth: Shaping Markets When Customers Make the Rules, *Harvard Business School Press*, January 1999

[15]US Top Web and Digital Media Properties, *Jupiter Media Metrix*, May 2002, *http://www.jmm.com/xp/jmm/press/mediaMetrixTop50.xml*

[16]Lewell, John. 2001. BT launches affiliate program. *Internet News* 3 January.

[17]Boman, Steve. 2000. Staples.com draws links with sales incentives. *B to B* 31 July, 26–28.

[18]McLean, Bethany. 2000. Revenge of the car salesmen: The Internet is a lemon. *Fortune* 27 November, 146–156.

[19]Useem, Jerry. 2000. Dot-coms: What have we learned? *Fortune* 30 October, 82–104.

[20]Mulligan, Paul. 2000. Banks need to integrate the Internet, not isolate it. *E-Marketer.com* 7 August.

[21]Girard, Dierdre. 2000. Paper, Bricks & Clicks: 10 steps to channel integration. Catalog Age 1 March.

[22]Green, Paul E., and Abba M. Krieger. 1991. Segmenting markets with conjoint analysis. *Journal of Marketing* 55:20–31.

[23]Cluster analysis is a statistical technique for grouping customers (or other objects) based on their characteristics. The technique is designed to find groups of customers that are highly similar on the selected characteristics, and where the differences between the members of each group are as large as possible. A very practical overview of cluster analysis in marketing can be found in Meyers, James H. 1996. *Segmentation and positioning for strategic marketing decisions*. Chicago: American Marketing Association.

[24]Kotler, Philip, Peggy H. Cunningham, and Ronald E. Turner. 2001. *Marketing management*, Canadian 10th Ed. Toronto: Prentice-Hall.

[25]Trask, Richard. Developing e-partnerships. *Association Management* 52 (11):46–52.

[26]Fein, Adam J., and Sandy D. Jap. 1999. Manage consolidation in the distribution channel. Sloan Management Review 41:61–72.

[27]Parasuraman, A., Valarie A. Zeithaml, and Leonard L. Berry. 1985. A conceptual model of service quality and its implications for future research. *Journal of Marketing* 49:41–50.

[28]Wolverton, Troy. 1999. E-tailers confront customer service challenges. News.com 10 December.

[29]Leaverton, Michael. 2000. CNET Buys online and tells all. CNET 8 December.

[30]eRetail improves customer service this holiday. 2000. *EMarketer.com* 18 December.

[31]Cross, Richard, and Molly Neal. 2000. Internet retailers are creating their own brand of service. Direct Marketing 1 June.

[32]Wilcox, Joe. 2000. IBM plans a direct-sales assault. *News.com* 24 February.

[33]Lyons, Daniel. 1998. Games dealers play. *Forbes* 19 October.

[34]Webster, Frederick E. Jr. 1984. *Industrial marketing strategy*, 2nd ed. New York: John Wiley & Sons, 205–207.

[35]Crothers, Brooke. 1999. IBM's Dell deal signals shift in strategy. *News.com* 9 March.

[36]Hachman, Mark. 2000. Gateway adds retail sales to spur PC demand. Techweb News 15 December.

[37]Anonymous, "Scenes from the Great Indoors," *Business Week Online,* July 8, 2002.

[38]Gaski, John. 1984. The theory of power and conflict in channels of distribution. *Journal of Marketing* 48:9–29.

[39]French, John R., and Bertram Raven. 1959. *The bases of social power. In Studies in Social Power*, ed. Darwin Cartwright. Ann Arbor: University of Michigan Press, 150–167

[40]Mohr, Jakki, Robert J. Fisher, and John R. Nevin. 1996. Collaborative communication in interfirm relationships: Moderating effects of integration and control. *Journal of Marketing* 60:103–115.

[41]Fisher, Robert J., Elliot Maltz, and Bernard J. Jaworski. 1997. Enhancing communication between marketing and engineering: The moderating role of relative functional identification. *Journal of Marketing* 61:54–70.

[42]Alper, Steve, Dean Tjosvold, and Kenneth S. Law. 1998. Interdependence and controversy in group decision making: Antecedents to effective self-managing teams. *Organizational Behavior and Human Decision Processes* 74:33–52.

[43]Bunnell, David. 2000. *The eBay phenomenon*. New York: John Wiley & Sons.

Branding

Chapter 12 examines the role of branding in the networked economy. Branding is fundamentally different from a firm's product design, pricing, communication, community, and distribution activities in three significant ways. First, brands are reflections or outcomes of the firm's marketing activities. As firms design, price, communicate, create community, and distribute their products, they affect how consumers perceive the brand, and hence its value or equity. Second, unlike the other activities, branding is a part of every marketing strategy. Firms always want to link marketing activities back to their brands to identify and differentiate their products. Whereas a firm might undertake a price cut without changing its product design, advertising, or distribution system, the brand is an integral part of every marketing activity. Finally, strong brands can be used to enhance the effectiveness of all other marketing activities. Consumers are more likely to respond favorably to marketing activities or even unforeseen competitive or environmental changes for strong brands than for weak brands.

QUESTIONS

Please consider the following questions as you read this chapter:

1. What is a brand? What is brand equity?

2. What are the consumer responses that make up brand equity?

3. What are some of the most significant ways to measure brand equity?

4. How are marketing programs used to create brand equity?

5. What is the seven-step branding process?

6. How do brands interact with other marketing levers to affect buyer–seller relationships?

Introduction

The chapter begins with a definition of brand and an introduction to the types of brands that exist in the online world. The chapter then examines the dramatic effects of individualization and interactivity on branding. The subsequent sections examine the concept of brand equity, discuss how it is measured, and examine ways to create it through marketing activities. Then, a seven-step process is introduced to guide firms in the development of strong brands. The principles and processes covered thus far in the chapter are then applied to the branding strategies of Citibank Online versus Chase

Online Banking, and CBS MarketWatch.com versus Bloomberg.com. The next section examines the effect of branding on the marketing levers used to move customers through the relationship stages. The emphasis here is on how brands interact to enhance the effects of the levers on buyer–seller relationships. The chapter concludes with an analysis of eBay's branding strategy.

What Is a Brand?

According to the American Marketing Association, a **brand** is a "name, term, sign, symbol, or design, or a combination of them intended to identify the goods and services of one seller or group of sellers and to differentiate them from those of the competition." The brand refers to all aspects that relate to identity. The Internet brands in Exhibit 12.1 are differentiated not just by their names, but by color, font size and style, and symbols such as the Monster.com "eye" and the Lands' End tag. Each element of the brand has the potential to influence consumers' perceptions, and so each should be carefully evaluated for its impact.

Selecting a good brand name is critical to competitive advantage. One study suggests that good brand names reflect the characteristics of the target market and create a product image that is unique and memorable.[1] It is also important that brand names are easy to understand, pronounce, and spell.[2] Firms should generate prospective brand names with writers aided by linguistics analysts who search for appropriate word roots and stems to suggest the brand's attributes. Then, consumer testing is required to ensure that the brand choice is appropriate. A brand name is a long-term investment, and so the evaluation process for selecting one must be appropriately rigorous.

The visual aspects of brands (that is, the logo) also contribute a great deal to corporate image and therefore brand equity. A study of 195 logos found that what constitutes a "good" logo depends upon the firm's objectives. However, the study's authors argue that the best logos are those that are recognizable and meaningful and produce positive feelings.[3] High-recognition logos tend to be memorable because they are distinctive in some way. This distinctiveness leads consumers not only to correctly identify the logo, but also to associate the logo with the brand or firm. Meaningful logos are those that clearly evoke the message the firm wants to communicate. Finally, it is critical that logos create positive feelings because of the expected transfer of emotion from the logo to the brand or firm. If a brand logo evokes positive, warm emotions, they will transfer to the brand and affect the customer's brand experience. The logo is only one aspect of the brand, but it is an important one.

Types of Brands

There are many different types of brands. One simple way to distinguish between brands is in terms of where they originated—that is, online or offline. Classic offline brands include Gap, UPS, OfficeMax, and Disney.

EXHIBIT 12.1   Examples of Internet Brands

Fogdog Sports is a registered trademark of Fogdog, Inc. E*TRADE is a registered trademark of E*TRADE Securities, Inc. These materials have been reproduced with the permission of eBay Inc. Copyright eBay Inc. All Rights Reserved.

Online brands include Amazon, Yahoo!, GeoCities, and Priceline. However, as the Internet expanded, offline brands began to cross over into the online world, and online brands shifted to the offline world (e.g., *Yahoo! Internet Life* magazine). The result is a blurring of the distinction between pure offline and pure online brands. Consider the following developments:

- Brands such as Yahoo! were established as online brands but use offline promotional activities to grow their brand awareness.

- *Yahoo Internet Life* magazine is a traditional brand in the sense that the product is marketed in the physical world, but it is also an extension of the online brand.

- Brands such as Egghead.com have completely shifted their product by moving from traditional, offline brands to purely online brands.

- Online brands such as pressplay develop out of a strong offline brand (in this case by the Universal Music Group and Sony Music Entertainment).

- Brands such as Schwab have successfully bridged the gap between online and offline activities.

- Ragu was established offline but uses online promotional activities to grow its brand awareness and loyalty.

It is useful to introduce two further distinctions to the discussion of brands. First is the nature and degree of the transactional aspects of the brand's Internet presence. In Exhibit 12.2, brands are divided into two categories according to whether they were established as a traditional brand or as an online brand. A further distinction is the purpose of the site as solely branding, branding and selling, an intermediary site, or a full e-commerce site. The second dimension is whether the brand is directed at the business-to-business or business-to-consumer market.

	Established as Traditional Brand		Established as Online-Brand	
	Branding Online	**Branding and Selling Online**	**Intermediary/ Vertical Portal**	**e-Commerce**
Business-to-Consumer	Ragu	American Airlines	Yahoo!	CDNOW
Business-to-Business	Boeing	Cisco Systems	Avnet	NexPrise

Source: PricewaterhouseCoopers Moneytree Report 2000.

EXHIBIT 12.2   Case Studies of Successful Online Branding Efforts

This categorization of brands illustrates some basic differences in the branding strategies used by online firms. Some brands originated offline and were then extended to the Internet. These brands are using the Internet either solely as a branding vehicle (e.g., Ragu) or to sell products or services as well (e.g., American Airlines). In contrast, brands that originated on the Internet have all been established with some transactional or e-commerce purpose. Their focus has been to sell products directly to consumers or businesses (e.g., CDNow, NexPrise), or act as an infomediary (e.g., Yahoo!, Avnet). In all of these models, branding plays a key role.

How Have the 2Is Affected Branding?

Branding has been fundamentally changed by the interactivity and individualization of the Internet. As noted in Chapter 6, relationships require interactive and individualized communication. The Internet has affected branding by enabling 2I communication with literally millions of customers simultaneously. Never before has it been possible to implement branding strategies that are individualized in content and timing, and that enable consumers to engage in a dialogue with the firm behind the brand. The result is that consumers now have a much richer understanding of the brands they love. Where else can a consumer watch his or her favorite Nike, Budweiser, or Pepsi ad at the click of a mouse—over and over again? In addition, by being able to individualize the brand, consumers are able to develop a more personal relationship with the brand. Sometimes, such as with Nike iD, customers are even able to develop customized products. The 2Is of Internet-based communication help establish and maintain brand meaning in several essential ways (summarized in Exhibit 12.3).

- *Message timing:* The timing of brand-related communications is different on the Internet. By monitoring consumer behavior on the firm's website or an allied website, messages can be directed at the user at the most appropriate time and in the most appropriate way. For example, brand-related messages for Avis or Hertz can be automatically sent to visitors at travel, vacation, or weather sites. Booking a hotel room, buying an airline ticket, and checking the weather at a distant city strongly imply the need for a rental car. In other words, communications can be timed so that they are synchronous with the consumer's needs. This not only makes the message more likely to break through the clutter, but it also has the potential to make the brand the "hero" because it comes to the rescue to solve a customer problem.

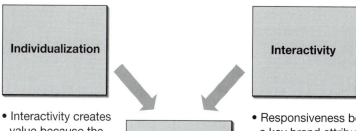

EXHIBIT 12.3   The 2Is and Branding

- Interactivity creates value because the brand is tailored to the individual.

- Customers gain a sense of control with respect to the nature and timing of their interactions with the brand.

- There is a danger that the brand will stray from its core personality.

- Responsiveness becomes a key brand attribute as customers recognize that their concerns are heard and responded to across multiple channels.

- The frequency of interaction is increased—leading to the need to freshen content and target messages to specific usage occasions.

- Customers expect the brand to evolve in response to their needs and desires.

Point–Counterpoint

Should Offline Firms Create New Brands or Use Their Existing Brands?

There is considerable debate in the practitioner community on the value of leveraging an existing brand name into the online environment. Simply put, should companies such as Lands' End, Wal-Mart, American Airlines, and Kmart use their existing brand names in the online environment, or should they create new-to-the-world brand names?

Proponents of the keep-the-same-brand school argue that it takes an enormous amount of time and money to build a strong brand name. People in the venture-capital community claim that it costs $50 million to $100 million to launch a new consumer brand on the Internet. Hence, it makes a great deal of sense to continue using the offline brand name for the online brand. Second, customers who decide to purchase online can be assured that returns and other services can occur offline. Third, it is difficult to uncover interesting new brand names. Fourth, the online and offline brand can have a synergistic effect—one that is greater than either brand operating alone. Finally, target customers will not be confused by brand offerings that appear on new sites (e.g., Kmart brands appearing on BlueLight.com).

Opponents argue that using an existing brand limits the growth of the user base. That is, it is easier for customers to believe that Travelocity or Expedia is the most comprehensive travel site, not their majority stockholders (American Airlines and Microsoft, respectively). Second, existing offline brands "don't get the 'Net." Hence, their user interfaces are likely to be less usable, hip, and interesting next to true dot-com brands. Third, it is possible to sign up more partners—potential competitors, collaborators, and others—when a third-party name is used. For example, General Motors, Ford, and Chrysler selected a new brand name for their B2B exchange.

Also critical is the control that the Internet gives consumers in terms of the timing of interactions. The Internet provides a previously unheard of level of control to consumers who are most interested in the product category in general, and the brand in particular. Interested in sports? By going to NHL.com, NBA.com, or MLB.com, you can dig as deeply as you want into the professional sport of your choice. This thirst for knowledge was not as easily sated in the pre-Internet days. Now sports fans can spend as much time as they want at a site, as often as they want, exactly when they want, all for free. The Internet has given consumers control over their interactions with the brand, and this is likely to strengthen brand connections. Any good relationship requires both parties to have some measure of control.

- *Message frequency:* Firms are now able to communicate with their customers much more frequently. The technology is used by electronic newspapers such as the interactive version of *The New York Times* to send free content to registered users each day. The marginal cost of adding one more subscriber is effectively nothing. The low cost of communicating on the Internet means that firms can (and must) continually update and freshen their content. It also means that the potential for message wear-out is high—if content is stale, consumers will become bored with the site and brand associations will become negative.

  A related issue is information overload. Brands are all about information, but the burning question is "How much is too much?" Consumers can quickly become inundated with messages from firms that communicate just because they can at a low cost.

- *Message content:* Perhaps the most significant impact of the 2Is is on the style and content of the message. The color, graphics, sound, and motion of the Internet give customers the excitement of television with the level of detailed content that might be found in a newspaper or magazine. When the medium is interactive, users are engaged because they actually participate in the choice of what they learn. A recent campaign for a shampoo called Physique by Procter & Gamble found that visitors spent an average of 11 minutes at the brand's website.[4] This compares very favorably with a typical 30-second commercial.

  A second, critical aspect of content is the building of positive brand meanings. By exploiting the 2Is, the firm is linking its brand to very positive attributes related to responsiveness and caring. Brand equity is enhanced to the extent that consumers value services that are customized and responsive to their individual needs. If the 2Is are reliably implemented such that customers learn to depend on the brand, the firm has built a foundation of trust. One of the key benefits of creating brand associations that are based on responsiveness, caring, and trust is that customers are more willing to forgive momentary lapses in service. For example, eBay experienced four service outages in less than a month in the summer of 1999. In one of these instances, eBay webpages were inaccessible for 21 hours. Yet eBay maintained its momentum during 1999, with gross sales more than triple those of 1998.

  One of the key limitations related to content is technology, although this is changing quickly with increased bandwidth, faster processors, and larger disk drives. The time that it takes to load an image, for example, or to watch an interactive product information video or advertisement, can detract from the brand experience. This may be particularly important for brands that are trying to communicate speed, power, and performance. Is it more damaging to have poor web-site performance at BMW's site than at a site that sells clothing?

What Is Brand Equity?

Exhibit 12.4 provides a simple framework for understanding the effects of the brand and brand equity. The exhibit has three basic parts: the brand, customer responses, and benefits (both firm and customer). Brand equity has a wide variety of definitions in the academic literature.[5] According to David Aaker, brand equity is a combination of assets that can be viewed from both the firm's and the customer's perspectives. Put differently, he views brand equity as a combination of consumer responses and benefits. He notes that brand equity is "a set of assets (and liabilities) linked to a brand's name and symbol that add to (or subtract from) the value provided by a product or service to a firm and/or that firm's customers."[6]

Drill-Down

Quotes on Online Branding

"E-branding is more important [than e-commerce]. And it must come first. Because few people will buy your stuff—online or off—unless you are top-of-mind." —Annette Hamilton, Executive Producer, ZDNet

"Brand is the price of entry [to the Internet], not the winning strategy." —Dylan Tweney, InfoNet

"By the time your potential customers log on, they already know what they're look-ing for, and they often know from whom they want to buy it. . . . They're just not lis-tening to branding messages anymore." —Michael Fischler, Principal, The Pubs Group

"Brands stand as comfort anchors in the sea of confusion, fear, and doubt. In dynamic markets, strong brands have more value than ever, precisely because of the speed with which these markets move." —Chuck Pettis, Technobranding

"It took more than 50 years for Coca-Cola to become a worldwide market leader, but only five years for online search engine Yahoo! to gain market dominance. The role of the brand has changed dramatically and has created a vacuum between offline and online brands." —Mark Lindstrom, Executive Director, ZIVO

"A company's website *is* the brand. It's the hub of consumer experience, the place where all aspects of a company, from its annual report to its products to its support, intersect. It's the company in a nutshell, all there in a way that just is not possible in the analog world." —Sean Carton, Carton Donofrio Interactive

A fascinating development of the Internet has been the importance of branding. This is perhaps due to the limited "real estate" that a screen-to-customer interface pro-vides, or to a desire to build consumer-goods companies quickly, or to the percep-tion that this is a winner-take-all environment. Regardless of the reason, it is abun-dantly clear that branding in the e-commerce arena is receiving a great deal of management attention, and that branding is a necessary but not sufficient condition for success. Also, brands serve to add value in each step of the decision process—at prepurchase (e.g., driving traffic to the site), purchase (e.g., erasing doubt), and postpurchase (e.g., assurance).

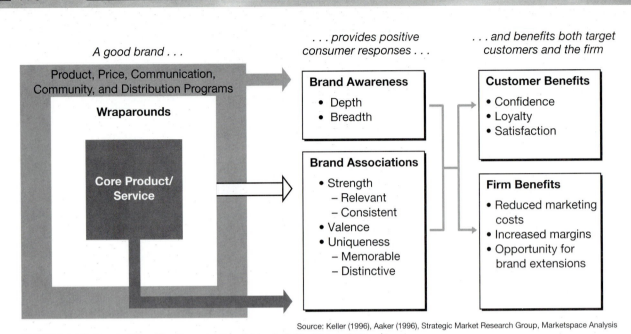

EXHIBIT 12.4   A Simple Conceptual Model for Brand Equity

Other authors tend to focus heavily on customer responses only: "Customer-based **brand equity** is defined as the differential effect that brand knowledge has on consumer response to the marketing of that brand."[7] Here the notion is that brand equity exists when customers react preferentially to the product because of favorable, unique, and strong brand associations. To illustrate, consider two online travel services that are identical in terms of price, customer service, speed of service, travel packages, and all other components with the exception of brand. The extent to which consumers select one site over the other is a measure of brand equity.

Of course, the real world is seldom as simple as the above example would indicate—there are usually multiple ways in which one site differs from another. However, it is clear that brand equity does affect product choice in a variety of contexts. The extent to which consumers associate the brand with experiences, situations, people, ideas, values, or any other source of positive thought or emotion increases brand equity.

Other authors tend to focus only on financial criteria such as the dollar value of the brand. Similar to Aaker's viewpoint, it seems reasonable to divide brand equity into two key components: (1) intermediate customer responses and (2) the benefits to both the customer and the firm. Thus, the framework has three basic parts: the brand, customer responses to the brand (awareness and associations), and benefits (to both the firm and the target customers).

Consumer Responses

Consumer responses can take two broad forms: brand awareness and brand associations. Brand awareness refers to the strength of a brand's presence in the consumer's mind. A brand with high brand awareness (e.g., Monster) is more likely to be recalled—either prompted by an advertisement or unaided by the firm.

Point–Counterpoint

Do Strong Online Brands Matter?

A strong brand can be viewed as essential to the growth of an online business. In particular, with the introduction of so many brands, a strong brand name provides a clear presence in the market. Furthermore, strong brands attract customers, and, hence, in the long run, firms may be able to decrease marketing expenditures once the brand is established. In effect, a strong brand is an instant message that contains a wide variety of associations on the part of target customers. All current online winners have strong brands.

Opponents of this line of reasoning argue that history will prove this argument to be limited. They argue that alliances are the key to locking up a market—and these alliances can be accomplished with strong venture backing. Second, third-party evaluators such as Gomez Advisors and BizRate will increasingly influence consumption—much like *Consumer Reports* does today. However, unlike *Consumer Reports*, the BizRate data are easily available, easy to access, and, hence, can drive consumption behavior during the purchase process. Third, speed to market may be more important than branding. Also, the meaning of brands is changing. Because all experiences are increasingly becoming customized, the meaning of a "mega-brand" is no longer relevant. Finally, while it is true that all winners have strong brands, a number of online losers also had strong brand names.

Brand associations refer to the connections that consumers make to the brand. Consider, for example, the online sporting goods store Fogdog (*www.fogdog.com*). The brand positions itself as "your anywhere, anytime sports store." The wraparounds for Fogdog include high-quality product reviews, a gift center that sorts products by price and category, head-to-head product comparisons, a glossary of sporting terms, advice from category experts, and a generous return policy. The market communications emphasize the benefits of becoming a Fogdog member, including functional (e.g., selection and low prices), symbolic (e.g., buy from the online location that has the best products), and experiential (e.g., faster checkout) benefits.[8] Pricing is consistent with the high-performance, high-quality message. Finally, distribution is selective, with a smaller number of revenue-sharing alliances than some major competitors. All of these marketing activities affect brand associations or perceptions. These associations fall into three categories: strength, valence, and uniqueness.

Strength of Association.   The **strength of association** refers to the intensity with which target consumers link a particular word, phrase, or meaning to a particular brand. Thus, if one were to cue the customer to reflect on the meaning of Fogdog, the customer might say "sporting goods," "high-quality products," "extremely knowledgeable and helpful," "easy place to shop," "too expensive for me," or "great selection." Strong associations tend to be those that are "top of mind" for the customer. Measures of strength include the number of times an association is mentioned, the rank order of the association, and speed of recall. A reasonable hypothesis is that "high-quality products" would be a stronger association to the Fogdog brand name than "California-based company."

Strength of the association is driven by the relevance of the associations to the consumer and the consistency of the branding effort. Target consumers must view the associations to be relevant to their needs and to the product category within which the firm operates. Consistency is the degree to which each element of the brand reinforces the brand intent over time. For example, does the Fogdog symbol reinforce the firm's positioning as a source of high-performance sporting equipment? Is its pricing supportive of its brand positioning? Has it maintained consistency in its advertising? All else being equal, brands that are highly relevant and highly consistent tend to produce strong associations.

Valence.   **Valence** refers to the degree to which the association is positive or negative. Again, consider the Fogdog associations above: "Easy place to shop" is a positive association, "too expensive for me" is a negative association, and "it sells sporting goods" is a neutral association.

Uniqueness.   **Uniqueness** captures the degree to which the association is distinct, relative to other brands. "Extremely knowledgeable and helpful" is an association that Fogdog would like for its own brand and not for competing brands (see Exhibit 12.5). Unique or distinctive brand associations are likely to be more memorable for consumers.

Firm and Consumer Benefits

The customer-based view of brand equity indicates that consumers respond differently to brands they know. The extent of this difference depends on the degree of brand knowledge and the uniqueness, strength, and favorability of brand associations. The benefits to the firm that result from brand equity can be usefully divided into factors related to growth and those affecting profitability.[10]

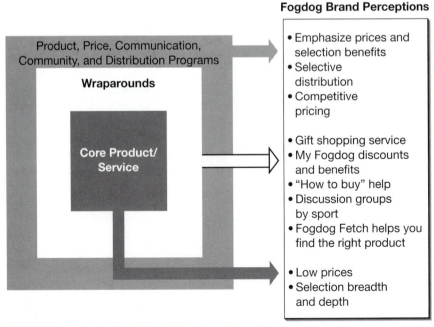

EXHIBIT 12.5   A Model of Fogdog Branding

Drill-Down

The "Mo Factor"

Phil Carpenter, in his book *eBrands*, contends that "the strongest brands are like landslides. As they begin to pick up speed, they gain mass, then more speed, then more mass, until soon little can stand in their way."[9]

The power of the "mo factor" (a term frequently used at Excite, the well-known Web portal company, with "mo" being short for momentum) is indisputable. Publicity is generated in any way possible to communicate the momentum behind the brand. This can take many forms—the announcement of cobranding or revenue-sharing alliances, the number and growth of the subscriber or user base, and, if possible, hitting profitability targets. Firms such as Onsale, Amazon, and eBay make regular announcements to let investors, consumers, and prospective partners know that they have the mo factor.

Carpenter notes that momentum is critical for online brands. Awareness is increased, and consumers may view the brand more positively as a result of its apparent success. At the very least, the buzz that is created drives interest and exploration. Momentum also encourages other online firms to seek alliances, and potential competitors to think seriously about whether there is room for them in the category. Investors and venture capitalists might take a second look as well. Momentum is a very attractive thing to have on your side when you are online.

Drill-Down

Brands That Reflect Consumer Values

Bressler and Grantham argue that Internet brands can be formed not on the basis of product features or associations, but on shared values. They define values as broad tendencies of group members to prefer one state of affairs over another. These preferences are rarely articulated, although they are immediately recognized when someone violates one. Instead, values are reflected in consistent patterns of behavior within society. In the United States, these values include:

- Individuals should determine their own destinies.
- Individuals should control their social and physical environments.
- Actions should be judged in a moral light.
- Authority or "bigness" should be viewed with suspicion.
- We should have as many choices as possible.
- Anything can and should be improved.
- The future should be better than the past.

Given that values are a common bond, companies can attract customers that share a specific value or value set. Bressler and Grantham believe that Apple has been successful, in part, because it has expressed core values through its advertising. They note that other companies such as Disney and QVC have been able to form strong Internet communities because of the values expressed by their brands. Perhaps the most important brand value of all, the authors argue, is trust. Without trust, customers will not be able to get beyond dealing with technology (which they never trust completely) to dealing with a company they know. One of the examples they offer is of Amazon.com aligning itself with American Express through advertising. By including American Express in its ads, Amazon.com leveraged the trust consumers had in this well-known brand.[53]

Strong brands increase the brand's ability to attract new customers and resist competitive activity. These advantages are created because consumers feel greater loyalty toward high-equity brands. Loyalty exists because consumers value the brand and what it represents to the extent that they may ignore, or even reject, new alternatives that are functionally superior. In this sense, brand equity is a reflection of a connection between the customer and brand. This connection leads customers to evaluate the brand differently than they evaluate competing brands. Brand equity implies that consumers are emotionally and psychologically attached to the brand.

A second way in which strong brands promote growth is through their ability to be extended to new products and markets. A brand extension is a strategy in which the firm uses an existing brand name to introduce a new product. Some of the basic advantages of extending a brand include:[11]

- *Reducing customers' perceived risk.* Having a well-known brand name associated with a new product enables consumers to immediately categorize the new product on its likely quality and characteristics. If a brand is trusted, this trust will transfer to a new product carrying the brand.

- *Increasing trade acceptance.* Wholesalers and retailers are more likely to stock and promote a brand extension because of the greater likelihood of consumer acceptance.

- *Increase promotional efficiencies.* The firm will not have to spend as much money on advertising because awareness and favorable associations already exist. One study found that the average cost of advertising as a percentage of sales for brand extensions was 10 percent, versus 19 percent for entirely new brands.[12]

- *Avoid costs related to new brand development.* Developing a completely new brand is costly and time consuming, and there is no guarantee of success.

Brands with strong equity should also command a price premium, and consumers should have a more inelastic response to price increases when brand equity is strong.[13] Price inelasticity means that a price increase will result in a smaller decrease in demand than the same price increase for a low-equity brand, all else being equal. These price premiums must, of course, be judged by consumers to be in line with the perceived value of the brand.

Returning to Exhibit 12.4, brand equity produces benefits for both customers and the firm. Customers experience a variety of benefits that translate into revenue growth, increased margins, and lower marketing costs for firms. For these reasons, it is critical that firms consider the ways in which they can leverage marketing programs to develop strong brands.

It is important to note that brand equity can also have its drawbacks, particularly when firms try to enter new markets or change their business model. Consider the case of Napster, an online firm that developed software for downloading and swapping music files for free via the Internet. In 1999, five major music companies (AOL Time Warner, Bertelsmann, EMI, Sony, and Vivendi Universal) sued Napster, alleging that the software company was engaged in copyright infringement. A court ruled in 2001 that Napster had to shut down its operations while the lawsuit proceeded.[14]

Since the court-ordered closure, a variety of competitors such as Kazaa, LimeWire, and Morpheus sprang up to take Napster's place. The music industry has also launched its own subscription-based services such as Universal and Sony's pressplay, but these services offer a fraction of the selection that was once available on Napster. In May 2002, Bertelsmann announced that it would buy all of Napster's assets and redesign the firm's business model. Bertelmann forgave $85 million in loans to Napster and invested $8 million to pay off the company's creditors. In June 2002, Napster filed for Chapter 11 bankruptcy. Company executives planned to use the protection from creditors afforded by Chapter 11 to reorganize and launch a subscription-based service.

Will the Napster brand help Bertelsmann's new service be more successful? On the one hand, Napster is a well-known brand name; at the peak of its popularity, Napster had more than 60 million registered users. On the other hand, the company was viewed as a technology that gave the power to the people, yet those same people might feel betrayed now that the brand is no longer associated with a grass roots movement. Also, it is questionable whether Napster will attract the right kind of customers—that is, those who are willing to *pay* for music downloads. However, Bertelsmann may be able to exploit the name by selling advertising, and by acting as a paid intermediary for artists who wish to bypass the traditional record company to retailer channel.

Measuring Brand Equity

As noted previously, brand equity can be measured directly in terms of the brand's ability to enhance market outcomes. The following are online and offline examples of direct measures of brand equity:

- A recent study found that Internet retailers with strong customer awareness, such as Amazon.com or CDNow, were able to charge prices that are 7 to 12 percent higher than those of lesser-known retailers.[15]

- One study evaluated brand equity by comparing the prices of twin automobiles. Twins are cars that are manufactured to the same specifications, but are branded differently. After controlling for differences in advertising, actual product quality, and other factors that might affect resale value, the study found that, for example, a compact car would have a market value of approximately 5 percent more if it carried the Mitsubishi rather than the Dodge name.[16]

- Marlboro has achieved a leadership position in the tobacco industry because of its brand equity. In their analysis of the relationship between cumulative advertising investments in the U.S. tobacco industry between 1967 and 1989, Slywotzky and Shapiro found that based on Philip Morris's cumulative advertising spending over the 22-year period, Marlboro would have had a market share of approximately 14 percent if it were an average brand. However, the equity in the Marlboro brand led it to capture a 27 percent share.[17]

However, focusing exclusively on outcomes can be misleading because so many factors affect a brand's success. Many research firms offer rankings of "best" brands based on overall site traffic, unique visitors, or time spent per visit. For example, Nielsen/NetRatings provides a listing of the top 10 brands at home and at the office each week (*www.nielsen-netratings.com/news.jsp;* see Exhibit 12.6). The issue is the use of the term "brand." In these reports, the term brand means "business" rather than only brand equity. Site visits are not just driven by the brand, but are created by all aspects of the offering—content, product or service offerings, pricing, advertising appeals, etc. These rankings are not just about the brand—they are reflections of the firm's overall marketing strategy.

Ranking of the Most Visited Web Brands								
Top Ten Brands, at Work			Top Ten Brands, at Home			Top Ten Brands Overall		
Brand	Unique Audience (000)	Time Per Person	Brand	Unique Audience (000)	Time Per Person	Brand	Unique Audience (000)	Time Per Person
Yahoo!	33,068	2:25:31	Yahoo!	60,654	1:37:00	Yahoo!	78,427	2:16:22
Microsoft	32,516	0:15:46	MSN	55,932	1:02:54	MSN	73,854	1:37:32
MSN	32,119	1:54:45	Microsoft	51,594	0:12:35	Microsoft	70,109	0:16:34
AOL	19,892	0:40:34	AOL	47,356	0:28:19	AOL	60,475	0:35:31
Google	18,777	0:28:35	Google	23,126	0:15:54	Google	33,929	0:26:39
Amazon	15,953	0:15:40	eBay	21,189	1:36:32	Lycos Networks	32,902	0:22:30
Lycos Networks	14,902	0:26:09	Lycos Networks	20,618	0:17:01	Amazon	31,807	0:15:41
eBay	14,248	1:41:04	Amazon	19,544	0:12:44	eBay	30,398	1:54:40
CNN	12,630	0:36:43	About Network	13,702	0:11:40	About Network	22,469	0:16:22
MapQuest	11,156	0:13:56	Netscape	13,002	0:22:19	CNN	22,103	0:28:28

Source: Nielsen/NetRatings. Top Ten Internet Brands. Month of August 2002. This data is based on audience measurement of more than 50,000 U.S. panelists who have home Internet access, and more than 7,000 U.S. panelists who have work Internet access.

EXHIBIT 12.6 Top 10 Internet Brands at Home and Work

Other measures of brand equity or value are indirect, and focus on the associations consumers have with the brand. The usual approach to understanding these associations is to ask consumers for verbal descriptions or "protocols." Understanding only consumers' verbal associations is incomplete, however, because many associations are nonverbal. Indeed, research suggests that the vast majority of the stimuli that reach the brain are visual, with no corresponding verbal description.[18] Further, many brand associations are difficult to articulate because they are based on sensory perceptions (i.e., memories of tastes, smells, sounds, or tactile sensations). A similar argument can be made for emotional or affective impressions. Finally, some associations are unconscious and so consumers find it difficult to share them with researchers. Therefore, a critical issue for managers is how to measure brand associations.

One author has suggested a methodology for understanding brand associations beyond what consumers are willing or able to verbalize. Magne

Supphellen recommends the following process for understanding a brand's core equity:[19]

- *Principle 1:* In-depth interviews are needed to dig deeply into respondents' memories. Although focus groups are appropriate for the study of social reactions, they are no substitute for in-depth elicitation procedures.

- *Principle 2:* A portfolio of techniques is needed—no single technique is adequate. Complementary techniques interact with each other to stimulate respondents' abilities to access and verbalize memories, and overcome their unwillingness to share them with the researcher. A portfolio of techniques helps respondents access memories of all kinds—verbal, visual, sensory, emotional—and associations that typically lie below the conscious level. A multimethod approach might also reduce the potential for respondents to censor thoughts or ideas that they think might be socially unacceptable to the interviewer.[20]

- *Principle 3:* Research findings should not be accepted uncritically. Validation of brand association findings can be achieved using multiple techniques including structured and unstructured projective methods, in-depth interviews, and surveys. Finding the same associations with more than one method adds confidence to the results. A second approach is to validate the creative insights of one or a few respondents on the larger respondent pool. This strategy is beneficial because typically only a few respondents have exceptional insights into the brand and are able to fully articulate their feelings. Validation might also take the form of follow-up surveys using inputs from depth interviews. These surveys can produce quantitative insights into how one brand compares to another, and how brand associations relate to purchase behaviors.

A number of techniques are valuable in measuring brand associations. Each of these methods can be used to implement the three principles identified above.

- *Thought listing.* The default technique for brand associations is some form of thought listing. The technique is very simple. Respondents are given a brand name and are asked to list all of the thoughts or words that come to mind. The words that are "top of mind" are assumed to be the strongest associations. Words or associations that are listed most frequently are thought to represent the essential elements of the brand. However, as noted earlier, this approach is too simplistic to be used on its own.

- *Visual techniques.* Techniques such as the moodboard and Zaltman's metaphoric elicitation method are visually based. In the moodboard technique, respondents are asked to select pictures from magazines or newspapers to reflect how they feel or think about a brand. Then, respondents use the pictures to create a collage, which they are then asked to interpret. The researcher derives the relevant associations from an analysis of the words that respondents use to describe and explain the collage. The ZMET is a variation on the moodboard technique, the difference being that respondents are given cameras to take pictures that form the basis for the collages.

- *Projective techniques.* Projective tasks are useful because they provide respondents with the freedom to distance themselves from their answers or thoughts. When faced with an ambiguous task or situation, respondents are thought to "fill in the gaps" with their own perceptions and attitudes. Projective tasks allow respondents to express their true feelings, even if they are threatening or undesirable, because they are asked to report on "the nature of the external world," rather than about themselves. For example, respondents might be asked to evaluate how a typical person might feel or react in a certain situation. Other techniques include asking respondents to describe the brand in terms of another object such as a tree, celebrity, vegetable, etc.[21]

- *Sentence completion.* Although some might argue that sentence completion is a projective technique, it is a very structured variation of this approach and therefore warrants separate consideration. A sentence completion task might be used to understand consumers' feelings and associations with the Travelocity brand. Consumers might be asked to complete a series of sentences such as: "I use Travelocity only when I _____ ." Answers such as "don't have a lot of time" or "when I care about price" would be favorable associations that could then be probed more deeply. Other sentences might include: "The type of person who shops at Travelocity is _____" and "Travelocity is _____." Each question can generate insights that might not be forthcoming in a free-association task.

- *Depth interviews.* In a depth interview, the researcher asks individual respondents open-ended questions and probes deeply into their memories, with the goal of developing a rich understanding of the respondent's perception of the brand. To overcome the top-of-mind associations that are likely to be the most accessible, researchers can use a snowball technique, in which the first associations are used as a basis for pursuing deeper connections. For example, if a respondent indicates that he or she associates eBay with "fun," the researcher might ask her to explain what she means by fun. If the respondent says that she enjoys interacting with other eBay users, the researcher might then inquire about the types of people she has met and the types of interactions she has had. This process continues until the researcher feels that he or she has a rich understanding of consumers' brand associations. Additional probes might be directed at the types of situations that respondents have encountered regarding the brand, and the feelings that were evoked.

- *Rating scales.* The use of established rating scales can help quantify brand images. For example, asking respondents to indicate their level of agreement or disagreement with scales developed to measure emotions can help them express feelings that are difficult to articulate. Other rating scales, such as Jennifer Aaker's brand personality scale, can provide a structured starting point, one that can be compared across multiple brands. The brand personality scale asks respondents to rate the brand on five dimensions: sincerity, excitement, competence, sophistication, and ruggedness.[22]

It is fair to say that understanding brand associations is a complex and difficult task. However, the techniques identified here are critical to a full understanding of the brand. It is interesting to note that the value of a brand lies entirely in the minds of consumers—if consumers forget the brand, its value is lost. Executives at Coca-Cola are fond of saying that if all the firm's physical assets were destroyed, the management team could go to a bank the next day and borrow $100 billion to rebuild the company.[23]

Marketing Programs to Build Brand Equity

Brand perceptions are affected by all interactions between the firm and its customers. The firm has the potential to enhance brand equity through website design, the brand name and logo, the types of services that are offered, and cobranding arrangements, to name just a few. The next section elaborates further on the price, product, promotion, and distribution strategies that affect brand equity. The section is not comprehensive, but rather focuses on some of the key issues facing firms that are striving to create strong brands in an increasingly online world.

Pricing Program

Consumers' perceptions of the brand are affected by various aspects of the firm's pricing program. Is the brand priced high, medium, or low? In some instances, consumers may infer that quality and price are related—the higher the price, the better the quality. Price has been found to signal higher quality in situations where three requirements are met: (1) consumers are not able to assess quality easily, (2) high quality is demanded, and (3) a sufficiently large percentage of the market is able to assess quality and is willing to pay a higher price for it.[24] These criteria apply to product categories such as wine, consumer electronics, appliances, videotapes, and consulting services.

A second issue is how often the brand is on sale. Frequent discounting is likely to have a negative impact on brand equity because it communicates undesirable brand characteristics such as "it's made by a firm that doesn't plan very well" or "they must have trouble selling the brand at its regular price" or "it's a discount brand and so it's not suitable for a gift." A related issue is the depth of the discount given to the brand. Large discounts exacerbate the negative conclusions that consumers might reach about a brand because of price discounts.

A third issue is the product line pricing strategy. Marketing consultants Al Ries and Jack Trout argue that one of the worst strategies multiproduct companies can undertake is to market products at different price levels under the same brand name.[25] They argue that scotch consumers are confused by Johnny Walker Red and Johnny Walker Black because of the different quality and price levels of the red and black sub-brands. Johnny Walker Black is a premium priced brand that is aged at least 12 years; Johnny Walker Red is a less expensive brand. When someone orders a "Johnny Walker," others are not quite sure whether he or she is a drinker of premium or average scotch. This confusion is particularly deadly for brands that are seeking exclusive or prestigious positions.

Product Program

The brand's product strategy has obvious implications for brand equity. The benefits provided by the product (or service) are what consumers are buying; if the product is poorly designed, the long-term effect on the brand will be negative—no matter what the advertising, promotion, distribution, and/or pricing strategies. Regardless of what else the firm does in the marketing realm, it is critical that it deliver value to consumers. To do so, firms must periodically improve the brand to keep consumers interested and to support its positioning.[26]

One of the most fundamental aspects of product design that affects brand perceptions is quality—a product's degree of excellence or superiority. The following seven dimensions of quality are thought to apply to a wide variety of products:[27]

- *Performance* is the capacity of the product to carry out its primary function. For an online newspaper, performance might be measured in terms of the timeliness, accuracy, and depth of coverage on important news stories. For a personal computer, performance might be measured by processor speed, size of memory, video capabilities, and disk space.

- *Features* are characteristics of the product that supplement its primary function. An MP3 player's features include the ability to customize player settings, a randomized play option, and a mute button.

- *Reliability* is the probability that a product will function well for a specified time period. Reliability can also be measured as the mean time between failures, or the time before the first failure.

- *Conformance* is an engineering term that relates to the degree to which a product's design and operating characteristics meet established standards. At JustFlowers.com, conformance might be measured by the degree to which the delivered flowers are consistent with a predetermined standard of color or aroma.

- *Durability* can be defined as the useful life of the product.

- *Serviceability* is the ease with which a product can be serviced or upgraded. This is an important aspect of many products purchased online because of the absence of face-to-face technical support. For example, consumers are more likely to purchase a computer from an online vendor if they can easily repair or service the machine themselves.

- *Aesthetics* is how the product looks, feels, smells, and sounds. In the case of website design, this is an important part of the brand experience. How can the brand be high quality if its website is not pleasing to the eyes and ears?

An interesting study in the consumer durables industry provides direct support for the importance of product quality as a component of value. David Curry studied the appliance industry over a 20-year period to assess the relationship between product quality and market share.[28] Using *Consumer Reports* data as an objective measure of quality, he found a strong relationship between value (defined as product quality divided by price) and market share. His findings suggest that consumers tend to reward firms that provide the best value. In turn, a brand that consistently offers exceptional value (high quality at a low price) should be viewed very positively.

Distribution Program

The channels used to distribute a product can have a significant effect on brand equity and sales success. As discussed in the distribution chapter, each type of channel intermediary offers a different value configuration to consumers. Channels that provide superior value should enhance the brand equity of the brands that they carry. Further, specific intermediaries within a category can have different capabilities and offer dissimilar levels of customer service. A specialty brand such as Rolex would want to distribute only through retailers that are capable of presenting their brand and products in the best possible light. Every retailer that handles the brand should provide a high level of customer care in terms of return policies, warranty handling procedures, pricing, and advertising support.

A second important way in which the distribution strategy can affect brand equity is through the number of retailers. If the firm attempts to use an extensive distribution system, the brand may be affected negatively because extensive distribution increases competition among retailers, and this places a downward pressure on price. As identified previously, a significantly or frequently discounted price can have a negative effect on brand perceptions. Also, greater price competition produces lower margins for retailers and generates fewer profits to support the brand. As a result, retailers are less likely to invest in cooperative advertising, point-of-purchase materials, and sales training. The same downward pressure on prices, margins, and brand support occurs when the firm uses multiple channels to reach the same customer segment.

A major distribution issue is that brands can "fracture" when they are available both online and offline. Home Depot, for example, is known for its vast selection and its knowledgeable salespeople. It is very difficult for the firm to replicate this same brand on the Internet. For one thing, it is very difficult to make the approximately 50,000 different stock keeping units (or SKUs) found in a typical store available online. Further, Home Depot cannot offer the same access to knowledgeable staff online as it does in the store. Although presenting different messages online and offline breaks a cardinal rule of branding—the need for a consistent message—it may be inevitable under some circumstances.

Promotional Program

Promotion is the "voice" of the brand, and it is fundamental to brand equity.[29] Promotion includes all forms of communication designed to inform, remind, or persuade target customers. The most critical aspect of promotion in branding is the "unmatchable message" that is consistently communicated.[30] Messages such as GE's "We bring good things to life" and Visa's "Everywhere you want to be" are examples of strong messages that point to the essence of the brand (innovation and acceptance, respectively). These messages must be reinforced over time, and across all forms of communication. Below are a few of the ways in which online promotions can build brand equity.

- *Banner ads.* A banner ad is an advertisement placed on a website that is linked to the advertiser's own website. Banner ads have traditionally included text and graphic images but many now include animation and sound. Banner ads provide the opportunity to present the brand to target consumers, and often include a very simple message that reinforces brand meanings or associations.

- *Interstitials.* Meaning "in between," an interstitial is an advertisement that appears in a separate browser window while you wait for a webpage to load. Interstitials are like banner ads, but are more likely to contain animation and detailed graphics and therefore have greater potential to create awareness and communicate brand meanings. On the downside, some users find that interstitials are intrusive because they demand attention (if even just to close them) and they slow access to destination pages. Click-through rates are as high as 5 percent[31] (10 times the average for banners), but costs are higher, too.

- *Sponsorships.* Sponsorships can vary from a simple sponsorship of an e-mail list to much more sophisticated site-sponsorship deals. The advantage of sponsorships is that they can help to build a sponsor's brand by presenting it within the context of the sponsored site and by creating value for visitors to that site.

- *E-mail.* Junk mail, or spam, is an extremely common marketing tool because e-mail lists can be readily available and cheap. More recently, opt-in mail has become popular. It is offered by companies such as Yesmail (*www.yesmail.com*), which allow advertisers to send e-mail messages to a group of people who have indicated an interest in receiving e-mails about that type of product or service. Yesmail has built a database of 8 million users, all of whom have opted to receive e-mails about topics of interest to them. Yesmail claims that its e-mails result in a response rate between 10 and 15 percent.

- *Coupons.* Companies such as Cool Savings (*www.coolsavings.com*) offer their members discount coupons that they can print out and then use for both online and offline retailers. Coupons can be an attractive marketing mechanism because they encourage product trial, and they are a way of selectively discounting prices to the most price-sensitive customers (those that are willing to go to a website and print out a coupon).

The advent of the Internet has meant an increase in the number and complexity of branding communications. Although the Internet offers many new avenues to communicate with and persuade consumers, it can also lead to inconsistencies in the messages that are heard or seen by consumers. For example, firms often use different advertising agencies to handle their online and offline branding efforts, and this increases the likelihood of inconsistent communications.[32] The design and maintenance of a website requires a combination of technical and creative skills that many full-service ad agencies have not had until recently. Further, many organizations have tended to look at websites as a separate aspect of the promotional mix. In the rush to establish an online presence, some companies have forgotten about the need to link the Internet experience to their brands' heritage. The results can be branding confusion (see Exhibit 12.7 for building brand equity).

Media fragmentation is a further barrier to consistent branding efforts. As Chapter 9 identifies, online levers include viral marketing, permission marketing, banner ads, loyalty programs, and serial marketing. These approaches have been added to an already complex array of offline media, including television, radio, newspapers, outdoor, magazines, and direct mail, not to mention consumer and trade sales promotions. The difficulties associated with integrating the firm's branding strategy across media are significant, especially considering the differences that exist in the nature of the brand message that can be represented in each medium. For example, can the same message be communicated in a black and white newspaper ad and a full-color, streaming video on the Web?

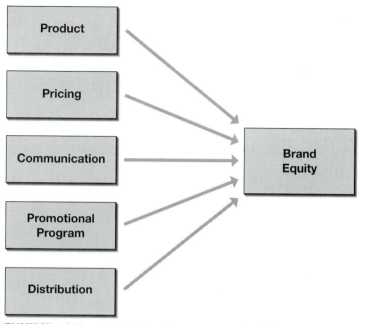

EXHIBIT 12.7 Marketing Programs to Build Brand Equity

Each of the marketing program elements (i.e., price, product, promotion, and distribution) has the potential to affect brand perceptions in terms of prestige, quality, and value dimensions (summarized in Exhibit 12.7). It is important to note, however, that the brand is sometimes affected by other factors that are beyond the scope of management control. For example, eBay has been criticized for some high-profile auctions for kidneys, votes in a presidential election, phony art, and Ku Klux Klan memorabilia.[33] Although it is difficult to imagine that eBay can monitor the more than 5 million items that are listed for auction, and the more than 600,000 that are added every day, many consumers perceive them to be ultimately responsible for what is bought and sold on their site.

A Seven-Step Branding Process

The **seven-step branding process** is an analytical and creative process that leads to the most appropriate marketing programs and activities. This simple, managerially relevant approach to branding is summarized in Exhibit 12.8.

Step 1: Clearly Define the Brand Audience

Chapter 3 focuses on the need to clearly specify the offering's target customers. It can be argued that a larger number of customer segments can be effectively addressed in the online compared to the offline environment. This is due to a number of factors, including the firm's ability to reconfigure its storefront in a real-time fashion for each customer.

Drill-Down

The 11 Immutable Laws of Internet Branding

Al and Laura Ries, father and daughter marketing authors and consultants, suggest that Internet branding differs from traditional branding in 11 distinct ways.[34]

Law #1—The Law of Either/Or: Companies can treat the Internet as either a medium or a business, but not both. If the Internet is a business, it must start from scratch and invent a totally new name. If the Internet is a medium, then it is acceptable to use the existing name.

Law #2—The Law of Interactivity: Interactivity is critical to every website. The authors argue that the secret to branding on the Internet is to present the brand in a way that allows customers and prospects to interact with it.

Law #3—The Law of the Common Name: Al and Laura Ries argue that the most important marketing decision on the Internet is what to name the product. In order to reach a website for the first time, a user must usually type in a word. They write that one of the worst names to select is a common noun such as car, cooking, auction, or wine, because they do not relate to anything unique.

Law #4—The Law of the Proper Name: Brands should be proper nouns that are short, simple, suggestive of the category, unique, alliterative, shocking, and personalized.

Law #5—The Law of Singularity: Firms should avoid being second in their category at all costs. Although No. 2 brands have the chance to survive and prosper in the offline world, this is not the case for Internet brands because of the direct distribution for most products and services. In the offline world, distributors and retailers have a vested interest in supporting the second or even third brands to balance the power of the No. 1 brand, but this is not the case when direct distribution is used.

Law #6—The Law of Advertising: Internet brands need visibility in the offline world to survive and prosper. Online brands that are not advertised through traditional media will soon be forgotten by most consumers. All brands need to be visually reinforced on a daily basis.

Law #7—The Law of Globalism: The Internet is a global medium that does not respect national borders. Building an Internet brand requires a global outlook that accounts for international perceptions of your home country's strengths, government regulations, and language issues.

Law #8—The Law of Time: Not only do firms need to be first, but they must execute quickly and in a focused manner.

Law #9—The Law of Vanity: Companies that are successful in one area soon move into other areas. However, if a brand is extended to products that are inconsistent with its heritage, it will not be successful. Customers do not change their perceptions of the brand just because the firm wants them to. Brands must remain consistent with customer perceptions.

Law #10—The Law of Divergence: Although most pundits argue that the Internet, television, and computers will converge, Reis and Reis take the opposite tack. They assert that divergence is consistent with the "laws of nature," and cite the failure of convergent products such as airplane/automobiles, combination VCRs/TVs, and washer and dryer units.

Law #11—The Law of Transformation: In business, there is never only one way to do things. The Internet will transform many industries, including financial services, catalog retailers, classified advertising, traditional postal services, and traditional retailing.

Overall, the authors provide a provocative view of branding, and competing, on the Internet.

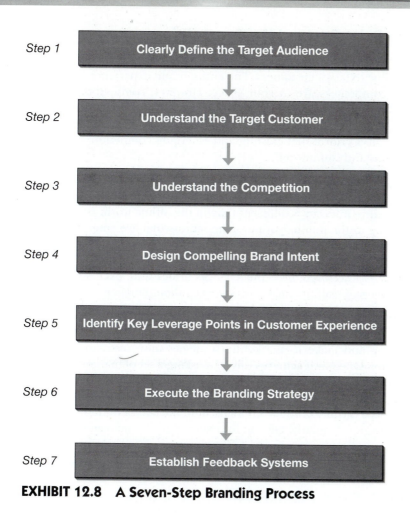

EXHIBIT 12.8   A Seven-Step Branding Process

Step 2: Understand Target Customers

From the broad description of the target customer, it is frequently useful to describe a composite prototypic customer who can bring the target segment to life. Try to describe the prototype in terms of her lifestyle, what she talks about, her favorite sports, what she watches on television, what type of job she has, where she currently shops, etc. This exercise can provide real insights into the design of the Internet experience.

Both online and offline environments require deep understanding of customer behavior. Indeed, firms building brands exclusively in one environment still need to be aware of consumer behavior in the other environment. As noted in Chapter 15, it is clear that a great deal of information can be collected by click-stream data in the online environment; however, this information is not sufficient to infer the attitudinal, interpersonal, and emotional factors that affect consumption choices and experiences. Hence, a blending of traditional and online research is often necessary.

Step 3: Understand the Competition

The competitive environment is also critical given the need to provide superior value to target customers. The entire brand experience is tough enough if no competitors are in your space. However, competition in the online world is incredibly intense. It is not unusual for a firm to develop a clear business plan only to have new competitors emerge prior to the launch date. Hence, it is critical that existing and emerging competitors are understood and constantly monitored.

Competitors must be evaluated in both online and offline environments. The online environment is distinctive in two respects. First, the degree of competitive intensity is different than in the offline world (specifically, this is referring to the number of new competitors that are emerging both within the product category and across product categories). Second, it is much easier to analyze competitors given the emergence of sources such as Hoover's Online (*www.hoovers.com*), the U.S. Securities and Exchange Commission (*www.sec.gov*), and financial sites such as Yahoo! Finance.

Successful firms place a tremendous emphasis on understanding their competitors. Nike, for example, often uses role-playing to stimulate creative thinking and make its marketing strategies more resistant to competitive behavior. One way it achieves this is by asking a set of marketing managers to take the role of a key competitor and develop strategies that will defeat Nike within a product category. This approach creates outside-the-box thinking and keeps the marketing team focused on the competition when developing its strategies. Similarly, GE ran an exercise for its managers in 1999 called "destroyyourbusiness.com" that forced managers to think about where they were most vulnerable to new-economy competitors.[35]

Step 4: Design Compelling Brand Intent

The brand intent brings to life the value proposition or cluster. Value propositions or clusters tend to focus on the high-level customer benefits. Here, firms are looking for a description of how the brand should be interpreted from the customer's viewpoint. The intent should be both clear (i.e., easy to understand) and compelling (i.e., provide positive brand associations). The search engine Google was founded in 1998 by Larry Page and Sergey Brin, two Stanford Ph.D. candidates who developed a new technology designed to find information on the Internet. The firm's mission is to "organize the world's information, making it universally accessible and useful," and its brand intent is simple: "Google helps users find the information they're looking for quickly and effectively." The brand intent is compelling because it communicates benefits that are essential to the search engine category. Everything on Google.com speaks to simplicity, ease of use, and product performance.

While brand intent is important in both online and offline environments, there is a greater opportunity to individualize the brand online. In general, brand intent tends to be segment-focused in the offline environment, while online brands can be individualized. Google can be used at three different levels. The first level is the general search, where users simply type in a search term. The second level is a more specialized search within a specific category of interest such as arts, sports, business, and health. Finally, at the third level, Google users can set preferences in terms of language, search result formats, and content blocking.

One issue facing online marketers is the potential for brand fragmentation due to too much individualization. If individualization leads to distinct performance levels or user experiences, the types of associations consumers have with the brand may be significantly different. To effectively build a brand, it is critical that there are some brand attributes that are nonnegotiable or essential. The core of Google.com is simple and effective searching—values that should be common across all customers, regardless of their search strategy. Because these values form its core, Google should avoid any additional features that would add complexity. It should also avoid undertaking revenue-sharing alliances that might lead to the perception that its search engine is biased or restricted in any fashion.

Step 5: Identify Key Leverage Points in Customer Experience

This step requires the firm to move from the strategic notion of brand intent to the tactical notion of marketing levers—prices of products, customer interface, mix of online versus offline communications—that will activate the customer. The goal is to create the brand intent in the most efficient and effective manner. Consumer research is necessary to identify and evaluate the levers that are most important in motivating consumption.

The customer decision process involves prepurchase, purchase, and postpurchase decisions in both the online and offline environments. In the offline environment, it is the retail salesperson or the telephone customer service representative who guides the customer through the buying process. In the online environment, the store can be reconfigured—much like a chess match—to guide or direct consumers. It is a more subtle form of selling.

Step 6: Execute the Branding Strategy

There are several principles that should guide the execution of the branding strategy. Consider the following:

- *Execute with integrity.* Executing with integrity refers to the quality of the implementation choices—namely, the extent to which the firm provides a clear, trustworthy message. It also means that the firm must be able to deliver on the promise made by the brand. For example, in the offline world, *USA Today* is known for its delivery of colorful, easy to digest, interesting, and entertaining news. When *USA Today* went online in April 1996, it remained true to its brand by offering similar content but also took advantage of Internet technologies. Although initially the company experienced many difficulties and setbacks,[36] it learned from its mistakes and, by 1997, had the largest unduplicated online audience for a print publication.[37] The integrity of the *USA Today* brand is supported by the delivery on the brand's promise in both offline and online versions.

- *Execute consistently.* The branding strategy must be reinforced through associations that are consistent across marketing program elements. Think of the branding strategy as the way the firm teaches consumers about the brand. In order to ensure that consumers learn what is most appropriate, the firm must reinforce its message across the entire marketing program to create a distinct and recognizable brand personality. Thus, a prestigious brand requires a premium price, exclusive distribution, a quality product, and a promotional strategy that includes a sophisticated appeal, high-end media, and appropriate media.

- *Execute patiently.* Strong brands take time to develop. In the offline environment, brands historically require long-term investment. On Internet time, this may be weeks rather than decades; most of the well-known Internet brands have been introduced since 1995. Regardless of the time line, the message must be consistent over time. It is also clear that each consumer can have a slightly modified experience with the brand—given the interactive nature of the Internet. Hence, while both environments attempt to be consistent, the interactivity of the Internet allows customers to experience the brand in unique ways, while still respecting the brand's essence. Careful investment in the core aspects of the brand, patience, and the ability to focus on the long run are critical.

- *Execute flexibly.* A final consideration in executing the brand strategy is to remain flexible enough to be opportunistic. Monster.com always attempts to be one of the first to try particular types of communications (e.g., Super Bowl advertising, blimps) in its category. Opportunism typically occurs at the segment level in the offline environment and at the individual level in the online.

Step 7: Establish Feedback Systems

Branding strategies rarely work out exactly as planned. Market communications sometimes have unintended effects. Competitors may react differently than expected by increasing their advertising budget, changing their message, or cutting price. New competitors may enter the category, or old ones exit. The economy might dramatically improve or weaken. For these and a variety of other reasons, it is important to have regular feedback systems in place.

Strong brands tend to remain strong because they are continually monitored and evaluated.[38] Brand audits in the form of focus groups, other consumer research methods, and an inventory of marketing approaches are used to assess the brand's health. Tracking studies are also used to provide updated information about the brand and its performance. The critical objective of tracking studies is to predict the future of the brand based on its current trajectory. Of course, in some ways brands can be monitored more quickly and more precisely in the online environment. Sophisticated tools exist to track customer responses to the brand, marketing communications, and marketing.

Although the seven-step branding process applies equally well to online and offline brands, there are some significant differences between online and offline brand building. Some of the key differences are summarized in Exhibit 12.9.

Branding Element	Offline	Online
1. **Clearly Define the Brand Audience**	• Limited to a manageable number of segments to prevent inconsistent messaging	• Could include larger number of segments based on values or interests rather than demographics
2. **Understand Target Consumers**	• Requires thorough understanding of environment, desired purchase, and usage experience	• Requires thorough understanding of desired purchase and usage experience in both the offline and online environments
3. **Understand the Competition**	• Requires monitoring of competitor advertisements and activities	• Competitor advertisements and some activities can be directly observed online
4. **Design Compelling Brand Intent**	• Brand intent (desired positioning) designed to address the needs and beliefs of target segments	• Greater opportunity for customization of key messages
5. **Identify Key Leverage Points in Customer Experience**	• Buying process is typically a simplified representation of customer segment behavior with static leverage points	• Buying process can be more dynamic and flexible
6. **Execute the Branding Strategy**	• Strong, positive brands are built up over time • Image reinforced through variety of offline media • Marketing strategy includes plan for sequenced growth and adjustment of brand based on changing customer needs • Building brand awareness requires significant investment • Building brand loyalty takes time offline, especially because early customer receptivity to brands is difficult to assess (and usually involves market research)	• Online interactions bring in added concerns of security and privacy • Limited familiarity with online brands makes fostering trust more difficult • With the ability to customize, one customer's brand image may be different from another customer's brand image • Customization for multiple segments and opportunity for early recognition of the changing customer requires a corresponding tailoring of brand intent • Building brand awareness requires significant investment, especially for those competitors who are not first in their category online • Brands have the potential to generate loyalty more quickly, especially if customers are targeted effectively
7. **Establish Feedback Systems**	• Collecting and analyzing customer feedback is more time-consuming	• Sophisticated tools exist for tracking online; allow for anonymous, interactive, quick feedback

EXHIBIT 12.9   Similarities and Differences in Offline Vs. Online Branding

Two Case Studies of Online Branding

Two case studies of online branding—one for Citibank Online and one for CBS MarketWatch.com—are developed below. In order to understand the branding process and to show how branding can be differentiated on the Internet (an equally important topic), these brands are compared with so-called average performers in the product category.

Case Study One: Citibank Online

Citibank Online provides an excellent example of a bricks-and-mortar company that was able to increase brand recognition and cement customer loyalty by successfully extending its brand online (see Exhibit 12.10 for the homepage of Citibank Online). Citibank is a part of Citigroup, the largest financial services company in the United States, and is continually expanding its online offering by providing banking, payment, discount brokerage, and credit products on its online banking platform.

Citibank Online was not the first Internet banking site. In 1997, Citigroup created the e-Citi business unit to develop the electronic delivery of financial services and e-commerce solutions to its customers. Since its inception, e-Citi has used the Internet and related technologies to create content, extend delivery channels, and customize its services to its worldwide client base in a private and secure manner.

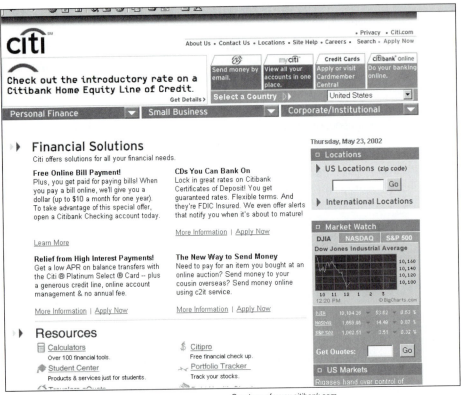

Courtesy of *www.citibank.com.*

EXHIBIT 12.10   Citibank Online

A key to Citibank's online success has been the strength of the Citigroup brand, and its ability to deliver an array of financial services to a worldwide customer base. Citibank delivers to its online customers a "one-stop shop" of financial products and services. These services are accessible using a single login and password and include:

- MyCiti (which gives online customers the ability to aggregate their accounts, enabling a customized one-stop interface)

- C2it (which enables person-to-person payments via e-mail)
- Cititrade (which is an online discount brokerage)

In addition to the aforementioned services that are unique to Citibank Online, the site provides online customers access to their credit card accounts and banking services, and to savings and checking accounts. Citibank is committed to the little things that increase customer ease of use. For example, when existing customers apply for an additional deposit account, their application is pre-filled with the information already gathered by the bank on previous applications. Also, no additional signature is needed for the account to be processed.

Citibank's online strategy and brand are tightly aligned with its offline objectives: to be a customer's primary source of financial and insurance services and, in turn, increase the profitability of the company. Its online offering not only supplements its services for its branch-based clientele, but also serves as an additional medium for branding while reducing the need for costly branch transactions. In its spring 2002 Internet Banking Survey, Gomez ranked Citibank Online the No. 1 overall online banking service.

Comparison with "Average Performer." Exhibit 12.11 compares Citibank Online with Chase's website on the seven-step process of brand building. Again, keep in mind that Chase is by no means the worst performer in the category. Indeed, Gomez ranked the site 12th in online banking (rankings were based on ease of use, customer confidence, on-site resources, relationship services, and overall cost). In order to interpret Exhibit 12.11, it is first necessary to understand the key at the bottom of the exhibit. One can think of the circles as a visual way to express a five-point scale in which a clear circle (one-point score) is a rating of poor performance and a completely black circle is the highest rating (five-point score).

It takes a very lengthy discussion to highlight each and every point illustrated in Exhibit 12.11. Hence, this section focuses only on the most important lessons. A quick visual scan of the exhibit illustrates that Citibank Online systematically outperforms Chase on almost all of the relevant elements. On four of the elements, Citibank Online receives a "very high" score, while Chase received consistently lower scores. By examining particular framework elements, it becomes clear that Citibank substantially outperforms Chase in several ways. With respect to the target audience, the Citibank website targets first-time users as well as its existing clients, while the Chase site appears more suited to the existing client. The Citibank Online site is more user-friendly for first-time online users as well as the bank's existing 500,000 online customers. The website provides an animated tour of the site, and overall the site is cleaner, exhibiting four generally titled categories for the consumer to choose from. In contrast, the Chase site is more text-laden and cluttered. The tour of the site is less customer friendly, and again, it is loaded with text and requires the user to expand exhibits for them to be read. The targeted audience is clearly the existing user.

As far as understanding the target customer, the Citibank site offering is continually being expanded by new financial products and services. The site is oriented toward customer needs rather than products or services. The first major heading is "financial solutions," and it focuses on customer needs such as lowering mortgage payments and saving money for college. In terms

Key Elements	Online Branding Best-in-Class *Citibank Online*		Comparison *Chase*	
	Rating	Rationale	Rating	Rationale
1. Clearly Define the Brand Audience	● (very high)	• Specifically targets consumers with a financial supermarket website. Users can apply and access banking services	◑ (moderate)	• The site is a mixture of small business and personal banking products. This may be confusing for customers
2. Understand the Target Customer	● (very high)	• Constantly anticipates and innovates to meet the needs of the customer; offers a full range of banking and financial services; good use of color and graphics	◕ (high)	• Tends to provide only banking services instead of a full financial services offering
3. Understand the Competition	● (very high)	• The company has developed a one-stop shop for consumers, making available a variety of financial products	◑ (moderate)	• The site provides the consumer with banking services available online and through Web-enabled devices
4. Identify Key Leverage Points in Customer Experience	● (very high)	• The website allows the customer to customize the site and provides information on financial products, a wide variety of banking services, cash incentives, and security	◑ (moderate)	• Chase allows customers to see most loan and deposit accounts online, although personal loans are currently viewable. Doesn't offer same level of ease of use as Citibank Online
5. Design Compelling and Complete Brand Intent	◔ (low)	• Focus, streamlining, and ease of use of website all convey Citibank's message of customer needs first	◔ (low)	• Unclear target segment causes lack of clarity with brand intent
6. Execute the Branding Strategy	◔ (low)	• Trust fostered in the offline word carries over into the online world • Although constantly innovating and adding new financial products and services, the site enables a convenient customer banking channel	◑ (moderate)	• Trust fostered in the offline world carries over into the online world, with extensive information for members on privacy and use of provided information • Different product offering depending on geography
7. Establish Feedback Systems	◑ (moderate)	• Convenient online contact information and telephone numbers provided for 24/7 service	◑ (moderate)	• A more cumbersome approach, with telephone numbers listed separately; customers must select product category for question first

○ = very low   ◔ = low   ◑ = moderate   ◕ = high   ● = very high

EXHIBIT 12.11   Citibank Vs. Chase: Assessment of Key Branding Elements

of understanding the competition, Citibank has developed online products and services that others in this space do not offer. While Chase offers many of the same banking products, it is clear that it is only matching the standard online bank offering.

Overall, Citibank Online provides a more consistent brand image and online product offering compared with Chase. Citibank Online presents a consistent branding message to its existing banking client as well as first-time online banking consumers. It has provided consistent technology and customer-facing innovation since 1997. Finally, with respect to brand recognition, the Citibank Online site receives high marks for relevancy, distinctiveness, consistency, and memorability (see Exhibit 12.12).

Case Study Two: CBS MarketWatch.com

CBS MarketWatch.com (see Exhibit 12.13) is a good example of an online company that has succeeded in branding in both online and offline environments. The CBS MarketWatch.com website offers headlines of

| Key Elements | Online Branding Best-in-Class Citibank Online | | Comparison Chase | |
	Rating	Rationale	Rating	Rationale
Relevant	●	• One-stop shop for online banking and financial services • Customer can personalize the website • Security is prominently mentioned	◐	• Offers only banking services • Information is dense on this virtually all-text site • Security is prominently mentioned
Distinct	●	• Offers existing clients a highly personalized experience (customization) • Offers a broad range of banking as well as financial services and tools	◔	• Allows applicants to make initial deposits • Balances in real-time to reflect transactions
Consistent	●	• Citibank provides the same services to all customers regardless of geography	◔	• Residents outside of California do not have access to all online services
Memorable	◔	• Provides a unique service others cannot offer (in terms of personalization and breadth) • Smart Deals section is the only animated page feature, aside from starting the demo, and alerts the customer to timely bank offerings	◔	• Lack of online/offline message association fails to create a cohesively memorable brand for the consumer

○ = very low   ◔ = low   ◐ = moderate   ◕ = high   ● = very high

EXHIBIT 12.12   Citibank Vs. Chase: Assessment of Key Brand Attributes

business news stories, which are linked to more information. The site also allows visitors to track a personal portfolio, be alerted to particular types of news stories, access company and industry mutual fund research, and link to other financial services. These features are free of charge. Other site offerings include MarketWatchLive (a service that provides streaming real-time quotes, customizable screens, scrolling tickers, and stock price alerts delivered via e-mail, pager, or mobile phone) and My eSignal (which provides real-time quotes and news for up to 20 U.S. stocks and is available for use on Web-enabled mobile phones). Both services require a monthly fee.

In addition to its Internet offerings, the company produces CBS MarketWatch Weekend, a television program scheduled on 117 CBS television stations in 128 markets, reaching over 80 percent of the country. The MarketWatch editorial staff also provides daily business and economic reports on CBS television and radio network news programming. MarketWatch's financial news radio network is heard on 106 stations.

Source: *www.marketwatch.com*. Used with permission.

EXHIBIT 12.13   CBS MarketWatch.com

Overview of Branding Efforts.   CBS MarketWatch.com was launched in 1997 as a joint venture between CBS Broadcasting Inc. and Data Broadcasting Corp. According to Media Metrix, CBS MarketWatch.com is the leading interactive financial news site on the Internet, with an online reach of 6.2 percent and 4.77 million unique users in August 2000. To achieve these numbers, CBS MarketWatch.com allied itself with numerous companies, the most important of which are CBS and *The Financial Times;* together, the two companies have a 34 percent equity stake in CBS MarketWatch.com. These close relationships add to the company's credibility and provide additional media outlets through which to disseminate CBS MarketWatch.com's content, as well as allow the company to utilize the long-established brands of CBS and *The Financial Times*.

With an eye to future customer needs and the technology they will use, CBS MarketWatch.com allied itself with AT&T Corp., Palm Inc., Omnisky Corp., Sprint PCS, and 3Com Corp. in order to provide services over handheld as well as wireless devices, making it easier for customers to access content. To continue its geographic and brand expansion, CBS MarketWatch.com made an agreement with Asiacontent.com that enabled it to develop and maintain country-specific websites throughout Asia.

Comparison with "Strong Competitor." Exhibit 12.14 compares CBS MarketWatch.com to Bloomberg.com on the seven elements of branding. At first glance, it is apparent that CBS MarketWatch.com is outperforming Bloomberg.com on three of seven elements—although the gaps in performance are not as wide as those between Citibank Online and Chase. Indeed, Bloomberg.com is strong in a number of areas, including customer focus (particularly the professional investor) and competitive focus. It is moderately weaker on the interactive nature of the site and the compelling nature of its brand intent. Similar to CBS MarketWatch.com, it is clearly willing to innovate and offer its customers numerous channels to access content.

Exhibit 12.15 compares CBS MarketWatch.com with Bloomberg.com on four brand recognition criteria. Both brands are similar on relevancy; however, CBS MarketWatch.com slightly outperforms Bloomberg.com on the other categories, receiving very high marks for distinctiveness, consistency, and memorability.

The Effects of Brand on the Four Key Stages of Customer Relationships

Up until this point in the chapter, the emphasis has been on understanding brands and the marketing programs or activities that can be used to build them. This perspective has viewed the brand as an outcome of the activities undertaken by the firm. A second perspective is that brands interact with the other marketing levers to affect customer relationships. This section argues that, if used properly, brand equity can enhance the effects of all other marketing levers on buyer–seller relationships. The fundamental point is that high-equity brands increase consumers' responsiveness to price, product, promotion, and distribution programs. As a result, firms with high-equity brands create customer awareness, exploration, and commitment with lower investments than their low-equity competitors. The presence of a strong brand enhances positive marketing activities and minimizes the downside of negative occurrences in the environment (e.g., product tampering) or marketing mistakes. These effects are summarized in Exhibit 12.16.

Key Elements	Online Branding Best-in-Class CBS MarketWatch.com		Comparison Bloomberg.com	
	Rating	Rationale	Rating	Rationale
1. *Clearly Define the Brand Audience*	●	• Specifically targets the mass consumer marketplace	●	• Targets both the mass consumer market and the professional investor, its historic client
2. *Understand the Target Customer*	●	• Constantly anticipates and innovates to meet the needs of the customer, both online and offline	◔	• Tends to be an innovator in the industry, especially for the professional investor segment
3. *Understand the Competition*	●	• Although a late entrant to this space, it quickly matched its competitor's offering • Through licensing and numerous media channels, it has surpassed its competitors as measured by "reach"	●	• Started this innovative service with own proprietary hardware targeting the investment professional • The site and offline services provide investment information as well as a small portion of the site devoted to general news and lifestyle issues
4. *Identify Key Leverage Points in Customer Experience*	●	• Credibility (CBS and *The Financial Times*) • User-friendly and familiar website format • Disseminates content through numerous online and offline channels	●	• Provides financial information for any type of investor • Very user-friendly task bar with links to topics on life, markets, charts, money, and media
5. *Design Compelling and Complete Brand Intent*	●	• Focus, formatting, and ease of use of website all convey CBS MarketWatch.com's message of customer needs first	◔	• Website clearly targets professional investor segment
6. *Execute the Branding Strategy*	●	• Trust fostered in the offline world carries over into the online world • Although constantly innovating new technologies and features (e-Newsletters), stays true to providing financial information to the consumer marketplace	◔	• Trust fostered in the offline world carries over into the online world on a text-intensive site
7. *Establish Feedback Systems*	○	• Not available on the website	○	• Not available on the website

○ = very low   ◔ = low   ◑ = moderate   ◕ = high   ● = very high

EXHIBIT 12.14   CBS Marketwatch.com Vs. Bloomberg.com: Assessment of Key Branding Elements

Key Elements	Online Branding Best-in-Class *CBS MarketWatch.com* Rating	Online Branding Best-in-Class *CBS MarketWatch.com* Rationale	Comparison *Bloomberg.com* Rating	Comparison *Bloomberg.com* Rationale
Relevant	●	• Up-to-date news and financial information • Personalized information through research tools and e-Newsletter • Information available to consumer through a pervasive multimedia network	●	• Offers up-to-date information, with an emphasis on financial information • Offers information through numerous media channels
Distinct	●	• Provides familiar, newspaper-like format for website • Consumers can access content through traditional media channels	◑	• Online and offline content offering is standard for the industry
Consistent	●	• Portrays a consistent image through online and offline channels • Commentators have a financial celebrity status, providing features online and offline	◕	• No key messages online associated closely with the offline campaign (e.g., no featured commentary; however, strong tie-ins with radio and TV branding)
Memorable	◕	• Provides a unique service others cannot offer (in terms of credibility, personalization, and reach) • Online and offline offerings are complementary	◑	• Online and offline offerings are complementary for the professional investor segment in particular

○ = very low ◔ = low ◑ = moderate ◕ = high ● = very high

EXHIBIT 12.15 CBS Marketwatch.com Vs. Bloomberg.com: Assessment of Key Brand Attributes

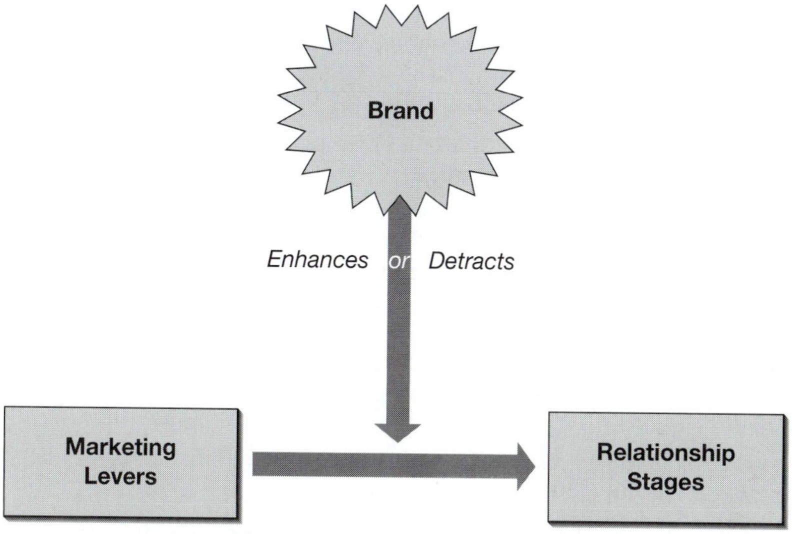
Brand
Enhances or Detracts
Marketing Levers
Relationship Stages

For advertising, a brand can enhance awareness.

EXHIBIT 12.16 Brand as a Moderating Variable

Awareness

As noted earlier, awareness is a critical component of brand equity. Consumers must be aware of a brand for equity to exist. Further, awareness of the brand is needed before a buyer–seller relationship can develop. Below are some of the key ways in which the brand interacts with marketing levers to increase awareness.

- *Offline advertising.* A recent survey of Internet users found recall scores of 78 percent for Amazon.com, 76 percent for Monster.com, and 74 percent for Oxygen.com.[39] Advertising well-known and well-liked brands such as Amazon, Monster, or Oxygen should be more effective because those brands are already known by the target market; breaking through the clutter and communicating their messages should require fewer repetitions.

  The advantages of using existing brands in creating awareness for brand extensions—new products (or websites) that are introduced with an existing brand name—are very clear. Developing a new brand name is very expensive and risky. The cost of introducing a new brand in some consumer markets has been pegged at $50 million to $100 million.[40] Introducing a website or new product with an existing brand name leverages consumers' existing brand awareness and knowledge. The bottom line is a reduction in the expenditures needed to introduce the innovation and build customer relationships.

- *Web price discount.* Some consumers may interpret a price discount as a sign of lower quality or a lack of brand popularity. A strong brand can both overcome these perceptions and enhance the attractiveness of the discount. A discount on a high-equity brand is less likely to be perceived as a sign of poor quality because of the preexisting, strong, and favorable brand associations. Further, customers are attracted to the discount offer because of their awareness and favorable brand beliefs.

- *Increased number of channel intermediaries.* A key measure of brand equity is the willingness of other firms to enter into cobranding or revenue-sharing alliances. Strong brands are appealing to prospective partners because of their effects on consumer responses. In turn, increasing the number of channel intermediaries will have a greater impact on awareness with a high- versus low-equity brand.

- *Online billboards.* Banner ads are likely to provoke greater curiosity and interest among users when they are for a high-equity brand. The banner ads that are the most successful are those that are of interest to the consumer. This interest is related to both the nature of the product category and the reputation of the company as expressed by the brand.

Exploration/Expansion

Strong brands help stimulate consumer interest that in turn leads to exploration and expansion. Brands that are familiar and hold positive associations for consumers can be leveraged to stimulate exploration through several marketing program elements.

- *Direct mail.* According to one consumer study, approximately 46 percent of the public sees direct-mail offers as a nuisance, and 90 percent considers them an intrusion.[41] A critical issue, then, is trying to create enough consumer interest to avoid having a direct-mail piece thrown away. The perceived value of direct mail should be higher with a high-equity brand. Customers are likely to read and respond to a direct-mail piece because of their preexisting attachment to the brand and the company behind it.

- *Targeted price promotions.* A recent study indicates that price elasticity is higher for brands that have large market shares.[42] In other words, a price discount on a valued brand will have a larger effect on market share than the same price discount on an unknown or low-equity brand. Moreover, as discussed earlier in the chapter, there are situations in which consumers will infer quality from price. A price discount, therefore, can signal that the product or service is of a low quality. Brand equity should counteract this effect, resulting in greater interest in the price deal.

- *Efficient site structure.* Creating an efficient site structure will enhance exploration, but only to the extent that the user believes the site is worth exploring. A high-equity brand should increase exploration by affecting expectations about site content. Visitors at well-respected sites such as MP3.com, Yahoo!, iVillage, and E*Trade explore because not only is it easy to do so, but also because they expect value in both the products and services that are offered.

Commitment

Perhaps the most critical element of building brand commitment is trust. Trust is particularly important for products such as financial services where consumers must rely on the firm behind the brand to maintain security, privacy, and confidentiality. Brands such as Visa, American Express, Citibank, and Schwab stand out in this area. Also important is the psychological and emotional connection that customers have with the brand. Being committed to a firm can be accelerated by a strong brand personality—that is, "the set of human characteristics associated with a brand."[43] Consumers should be more committed to brands that reflect their current or desired self-concept. Below are some of the ways in which the brand interacts with marketing levers to create commitment.

- *Volume discounts.* Consumers and business buyers should be more willing to stock up on high-equity brands. Consumers may view volume discounts on low-equity brands with suspicion ("Is there something wrong with the sale merchandise?"). Or, as discussed previously, a discount on a low-equity brand may affect quality perceptions ("It can't be that good a deal if they have to discount it."). In either case, volume discounts on high-equity brands are likely to evoke larger volume purchases than the same level of discount on a low-equity brand. In turn, larger volume purchases can translate into greater commitment to the relationship.

- *Personalized pages.* The likelihood that customers will take advantage of website customization features or capabilities is directly related to the value of the brand. In the first instance, the customer must trust the company behind the brand before he or she will register to take advantage of the website's customization features. Strong brands are likely to create favorable expectations relative to customer privacy, secure computing, and corporate responsibility. A further effect of brand on user

Drill-Down

Brand Loyalty

Shot in gritty black and white, the scene is bleak: A young child, his expression blank and humorless, stares into the camera and declares, "I want to be forced into early retirement."

Remember the ad? Even though it first aired during the 1999 Super Bowl, Monster.com is betting that you do. Like many Internet players, Monster.com has embraced old-school branding for its new e-commerce model, investing heavily (to the tune of $60 million) in the notion that name recognition will translate into page hits, revenue, and ultimately staying power as a powerhouse online brand. But despite the commercial's success—it was seen by some 100 million people, and still enjoys buzz as a best-of-breed dot-com ad—Monster.com is hardly home free. According to a pair of intriguing new studies, when it comes to establishing and maintaining dominant brands on the Web, many companies—even ones that break fast out of the branding gate—may face a bleak scenario of their own.

The first problem: The vast majority of Internet branding initiatives to date seem to have left consumers distinctly underwhelmed. A recent Harris Interactive poll revealed that while respondents were well-acquainted with a few new-economy superbrands— Amazon, eBay, and Egghead topped the name-recognition list—they were unable to name a single Web retailer in the insurance, fitness, or online electronics categories, despite the slew of advertising for Buy.com, Netmarket, and other companies that fit the bill. "The sheer lack of penetration in the minds of most Americans is really stunning," said Ben Black, director of business development at Harris Interactive.

Still, Julia Resnick, product manager for the company's eCommercePulse division, said, "From our perspective, we look at unaided brand awareness among websites and there seems to be a correlation between brand awareness and high performance. It's kind of a chicken and egg thing, though. I don't think branding alone is what's causing the success, but it's really interconnected with performance."

If a company establishes its brand successfully, that means it has conquered the branding problem and is here to stay, right? Maybe not. A study done by Peter Golder, a marketing professor at New York University's Stern School of Business, re-examined a 1923 benchmark NYU study of top brands in 100 product groups and found that only 23 were still leaders in 1997. "I'm not here to bash brands," Golder said. "I certainly agree that they're important. What my study suggests is that the staying power of brands is a lot less than what people may believe."

In the dot-com world, he said, the lack of staying power is particularly relevant because Internet companies try to build brand awareness quickly in a busy marketplace. Golder suggested an alternative tack: "In the Internet environment, there's confusion over brand awareness versus brand equity. I think the primary emphasis of too many Internet companies is on just getting people to be aware of their name, but it's the equity that resides in the brand that ensures success."

So, if you can get consumers to your site but have difficulty filling orders or providing customer service, you can kiss those branding dollars goodbye. Golder said, "If the customer's experience at the site is consistent with your advertising message, then branding works. If it's inconsistent, it'll ruin whatever efforts you've made."

If awareness is bolstered with equity, it's time and money well spent. "With branding, people build associations. If the entire usage experience for the customer reinforces those good associations, then you'll have staying power in an Internet environment that's constantly evolving," said Golder.

commitment is that customers must believe that the brand will provide value on an ongoing basis (e.g., product and service quality). Without this belief, personalization will not necessarily lead to commitment.

This same logic is likely to apply to the effect of brand on permission marketing, customer loyalty programs, customer service initiatives, and so forth. To the extent that the brand is known and has positive associations, the firm is likely to receive differential payoffs in terms of customer commitment.

- *Loyalty programs.* The value of being a member of a loyalty program should be a direct function of brand equity. The value of being associated with a brand that is well known, popular, and prestigious should be more highly valued by customers than the same level of recognition from a low-equity brand. Some research supports this perspective. One study found that the greater the perceived attractiveness of a group, the stronger the psychological attachment to it and the greater the willingness to undertake behaviors that support the group.[44]

Dissolution

A strong brand should help the dissolution stage in two respects. First, a high-equity brand will soften the potential backlash against firms that disengage from unprofitable or undesirable customers. When the firm withdraws services, raises prices, or cuts marketing expenditures, some customers are bound to have hard feelings. These customers might be puzzled or even hurt over the change in the relationship. A strong brand may help to assuage these negative feelings, even though the relationship has ended. A second benefit is that some customers will remain despite the fact that the firm has demonstrated its desire to terminate, or at least redefine, the relationship. Customers are less likely to exit after a reduction in service because of their psychological and emotional connection to the brand. Firms benefit by reducing marketing expenditures, hopefully changing unprofitable customers into profitable ones.

- *Discontinue pricing discounts.* Customers who have very strong and favorable brand associations are more likely to remain with the firm despite a removal of price discounts than customers who do not perceive the value of the brand. Even at a higher price, high-equity brands can provide greater value than competing brands that are functionally equivalent or even superior. The firm retains customers despite a price increase (i.e., the removal of a price discount) because of the intrinsic value of the brand.

- *Reduce advertising expenditures.* Prior investments in advertising reduce the speed at which brand awareness and knowledge decay. As a result, customers maintain brand loyalty. One study seems to support the importance of brand equity in retaining customers when advertising expenditures are reduced. In a study of more than 1,000 advertised brands, mostly repeat-purchased consumer goods, the author found that lower advertising spending is a successful strategy only for stronger brands.[45] Weaker brands lost share when they underspent on advertising, whereas stronger brands maintained or grew their market share despite similar spending levels.

- *Identify "departing friends."* High-equity brands should be better able to identify and track customers who exit. As a result, the firm can more quickly implement customer care programs that allow it to retain customers who have become disenchanted or simply bored with the relationship.

Drill-Down

Brand-Building Websites

Aaker and Joachimsthaler argue that a website is often a significant part of a brand-building program because it can communicate information and associations, and leverage other aspects of the brand strategy.[46] One of the key benefits of a website—relative to other media—is that it is a controlled environment. Customers choose to enter the site directly by typing the URL, or indirectly through a Web link. Further, the users decide where they go and how long they stay, and so they are likely to be involved in the process and attend to the brand message. The authors identify five recommendations about how firms can create a brand-building tool through the Web.

- *Create a positive experience.* The website should: (1) be easy to use to avoid user frustration and confusion, (2) provide a reason for a visit through information, entertainment, transaction capability, or social experience, and (3) exploit the unique aspects of the media related to personalization, interactivity, or speed.

- *Reflect and support the brand.* The brand strategy should be the driver for Web design rather than the desire to be edgy. The authors note that the Hallmark website promotes the brand's core of helping people express their feelings and "touching the lives of others." The brand identity should be supported in the look-and-feel of the site (e.g., romantic, rugged, sophisticated) and be consistent with the values and lifestyles of those in the target market.

- *Look for synergy with other media.* The Internet is only one aspect of the brand's entire communication strategy. It is critical that the Internet not be viewed as an independent medium with its own personality. The authors recommend that firms think of the website as a flagship store, much like Nike-Town locations or L.L.Bean's store in Freeport, Maine. The goal of these outlets is to communicate the essence of the brand, and to showcase the brand for customers and retailers. They also note that advertising, sponsorships, promotions, and publicity should be used to bring consumers to the site. In turn, the website can be leveraged to provide information that is richer, more graphics-intense, and timely than can be found elsewhere.

- *Provide a home for the loyalist.* The website should provide a place for loyal customers—those who are highly involved in the product category and who are committed to the brand. They argue that the loyalists need to know everything possible about the brand and its heritage. They identify with the brand, and have a strong emotional attachment to it that makes them very loyal and enthusiastic advocates. However, their continued support requires an ongoing investment in meeting their needs.

- *Differentiate with strong sub-branded content.* Aaker and Joachimsthaler argue that while functional content can often be copied, firms can benefit from branded features or components. Examples include branded recommendation services (e.g., Travelocity's Road Warrior), personalized advice (e.g., from the Tide Stain Detective), and rich category content (e.g., the L.L.Bean Park Search that allows site visitors to see pictures of parks, forests, and wildlife reserves).

- *Reduce customer care.* Brands can even maintain customer ties when service features or options are removed. Again, the relationship is often held together by much more than just the functional connections between buyer and seller. If customers have an emotional attachment to the brand, they may be willing to accept less value to maintain the relationship. The strength of the brand may also reduce consequences such as negative word-of-mouth through e-mail, chat rooms, and bulletin boards.

In each of these examples, the brand is not the primary lever that moves the customer from one stage to the next. Rather, the brand works in conjunction with a lever to either enhance the lever's positive effects or minimize the deleterious effects of providing less value to the consumer.

eBay Branding

In 1997, eBay founder Pierre Omidyar went to Benchmark Capital for help with his online auction company. Although it was growing at 40 percent a month with 30 percent margins, he needed a professional manager to steer the business. Benchmark identified Meg Whitman as the ideal candidate and invited her to fly across the country to talk with them about joining the management team. The night before her trip, she called up the auction site on her home computer and was appalled at what she found: "The site was in black and white, and the typeface was a basic courier. The branding was confused, with eBay on one page and AuctionWeb on another," Whitman said. [The company was called eBay and the website was called AuctionWeb, but both brands appeared on the site.] "I couldn't believe I was flying 3,000 miles for that."[47]

When Meg Whitman joined eBay, there were at least 150 other online auction companies. Unlike eBay, many of them did not charge for listings. However, eBay had already created strong brand equity. This explains why eBay's trading volume and profitably were on a steep trajectory while people had a large number of choices, many of which were lower-priced alternatives.

Walking through the seven steps of the branding process helps reinforce the qualities responsible for eBay's strong brand in the eyes of buyers, sellers, and investors alike.

1. Clearly Define the Brand Audience. eBay defines itself as "the world's online marketplace." This wording is incredibly inclusive. It incorporates both sellers and buyers who wish to engage in online commerce regardless of where they are geographically. Not only can anyone visit eBay to conduct online commerce, but they can also go to any one of many of its global varieties more tailored to the tastes and norms of those individual markets while retaining many of the branding elements of the original site.

2. Understand the Target Customer. eBay has paid close attention to the needs of its buyers and sellers. Many features and elements of the eBay experience and brand are the direct result of eBay listening to its customers and implementing changes to its site. eBay continually monitors bulletin boards and invites feedback from its users. It even brings its most frequent users to its San Jose headquarters to solicit their views. Ultimately, it incorporates many of its customers' suggestions into the eBay experience and uses them to enhance the overall user experience.

3. Understand the Competition. eBay constantly monitors the competition and continually updates and modifies its strategy to match its competitors. Oftentimes eBay has been on the forefront of defining the online auction experience, as in its use of listing fees to filter out low-value/high-volume sellers.

4. Design Compelling Brand Intent.   eBay's message of "the world's online marketplace" reinforces breadth of service. In this industry, size does matter. For sellers, more buyers mean more customers; for buyers, more sellers mean greater selection. Like Google.com, the eBay website reinforces simplicity, ease of use, and product performance to both sets of customers. eBay's brand intent is individualized: Browsers can easily window shop, purposeful shoppers can find what they need, and sellers can almost always find a customer if their offering is worded and presented properly.

5. Identify Key Leverage Points in Customer Experience.   eBay incorporates many services that enhance the online experience, such as site personalization and easy browsing. However, the focus has always been on building audience as a way of enhancing the most important aspect of the experience: the sale. Introducing a fixed-price element to the original auction format is one example of eBay clearly hitting upon an important leverage point. Less than one year after its introduction, 19 percent of all sales revenue came from the fixed-price format.

6. Execute the Branding Strategy.   Using the examples cited in the chapter, eBay has done the following:

> *Execute with integrity.* The integrity of eBay's brand lies in its creating a safe, simple, compelling online experience for its buyers and sellers. It has maintained these qualities as it has matured and expanded into complementary product categories and markets.
>
> *Execute consistently.* In all of its brand extensions, eBay has maintained a common look-and-feel as well as a greater user experience, including policies and procedures. Someone moving from one eBay platform to the next will have a remarkably similar user experience. The main difference would be the content.
>
> *Execute patiently.* Strong brands take time to develop. eBay began its life as AuctionWeb and evolved into eBay. Similarly, eBay Premier may change into a cobranded site with live-auction stalwart Sotheby's, giving eBay more credibility with the traditional auction set and Sotheby's a greater foothold with the online masses.
>
> *Execute flexibly.* eBay has remained open to emerging opportunities, as evidenced by its launch of eBay Motors. Look for eBay to take advantage of more opportunities as markets and customer needs continue to evolve.

7. Establish Feedback Systems.   eBay stays in close touch with its users through multiple channels. It monitors its message boards, continually keeping its finger on the pulse of its community. By doing so, the company is able to make subtle changes rapidly, ensuring a consistent brand perception. eBay also maintains a feedback loop with its Voices sessions and even through eBay University. By staying in touch with its customers online and offline, eBay takes control of its brand image.

Key Branding Elements and Brand Attributes for eBay Vs. Amazon for Online Auction Services

Exhibit 12.17 assesses the performance of eBay versus Amazon, a key online competitor, for each of the seven steps of the branding process. This section examines only the most important lessons from this analysis. A quick overview of the figure indicates that for online auctions, eBay is generally outperforming Amazon on most of the branding elements. It is important to note that the comparison is only for online auctions, and not branding in general. Clearly, Amazon is one of the most powerful brands on the Internet.[48] The question is, "Is the brand appropriate for online auction services?" eBay gets rated with top performance in all seven elements, compared with just three elements for Amazon.

The following points summarize some of the key differences between eBay and the Amazon auction site.

- With respect to the brand name itself, the meanings and associations of Amazon and eBay are quite different. eBay has consistently focused on its ability to enable individuals to easily do business with one another, and on its ability to foster community.[49] Although Amazon executes extremely well in customer service and support, its traditional customers do not necessarily share these interests.

- AuctionWatch.com rates eBay lower than Amazon on services and fees, customer support, and design and functionality, yet eBay dominates Amazon on market share. One explanation for this is the momentum and market size that eBay was able to capture before it faced competition. Capturing a large market share leads to greater competition for products, higher bids, and sellers becoming more likely to post their goods with eBay. The result is greater attractiveness to buyers, which reinforces the competition for products. A second reason that early market share has benefited eBay is that sellers create their reputations (i.e., their brands) within the eBay community. Sellers learn to trust them, and this increases the likelihood of bidding and high prices.

- eBay has been highly consistent in building its brand. Whereas eBay is only in the auction business, Amazon's heritage has been in books and CDs. Amazon's expanded product line now includes toys, video games, and home improvement products. Amazon has also introduced a free e-card service and zShops, where small independent merchants can do business under the Amazon.com brand name. These strategies have the potential to dilute Amazon's brand equity. On the positive side, Amazon does reinforce its auction service associations via a link to Sotheby's. However, Sotheby's is not a mass market brand that will attract a large volume of new buyers. The eBay brand is much clearer and easier to understand for the majority of consumers.

- eBay has been innovative, but consistent with its cobranding strategies. For example, in 1999, eBay was involved in a 10-day auction of the first BMW X5 sport utility vehicle in the United States. The winning bidder received the automobile two weeks before the car would be available in U.S. showrooms, and proceeds of the auction were given to a charitable organization.[50] It has also established alliances with Saturn (for inspection of used vehicles sold on the site), the NFL (to sell top-end memorabilia), and Warner Bros. (to establish integrated online auction sites throughout its various sites).[51]

In terms of key brand attributes, both companies have very strong brands (see Exhibit 12.18). eBay is the No. 1 brand for online auctions, while Amazon is the No. 1 e-brand. Recent studies have pegged Amazon's awareness at

Branding Element	Rating	eBay
1. *Clearly Define the Brand Audience*	●	• Mass market
2. *Understand the Target Customer*	●	• eBay continually monitors bulletin boards, interacts with users, and even brings frequent users to San Jose headquarters to solicit their views[1]
3. *Understand the Competition*	●	• eBay has continually updated and modified its strategy to match its competitors
4. *Identify Key Leverage Points in Customer Experience*	●	• eBay incorporates many enhancement services (for example, shipping services through its partnership with Mail Boxes Etc.). However, the focus is always on building audience as a way of enhancing the most important aspect of the experience: the sale.
5. *Design Compelling Brand Intent*	●	• Message of "the world's online marketplace" underlines value to buyers and sellers. In this industry, size does matter. More buyers equals more competition for items and higher selling prices
6. *Execute the Branding Strategy*	●	• Clear strategy: eBay is only in the business of online auctions. • Branding alliances have been consistent with mass market approach and solid image of eBay (AOL, Disney). • eBay has vigorously defended its turf against auction aggregators such as Auctionwatch.com, which enable users to monitor multiple actions simultaneously. • Message has consistently focused on eBay as an auction company where users can buy or sell almost anything. • eBay focuses branding efforts on heavy users—serious collectors and small dealers. It advertises in niche publications and commercial magazines and also participates in trade shows.
7. *Establish Feedback Systems*	●	• eBay provides a unique service others cannot offer (in terms of personalization and breadth). • Smart Deals section is the only animated page feature, aside from starting the demo, and alerts the customer to timely offerings.

continued

60 percent of U.S. adults (or, as reported earlier, 78 percent of Internet users), making it the No. 1 e-commerce brand.[52] Further, both brands are highly relevant because their offerings directly address the needs of buyers and sellers. In addition, Amazon offers a host of other products and services that increase site traffic, but not necessarily to the auction side of the business. The clarity and strength of the eBay brand have helped to ensure that the firm maintains its over 70 percent market share,[53] not only in the face of very strong and capable competition from Amazon but also from a host of other firms such as Yahoo!, Excite, MSN, Bid.com, and 321Gone.

Rating	Amazon
◐	• Mass market, but traffic to the site is limited by Amazon's traditional appeal to book and CD customers.
●	• Amazon is one of the most customer-centric firms on the Internet. The firm invests heavily to make the firm responsive to customer needs related to personalization and ordering convenience, as well as in fuzzy-logic search engines that help customers search more effectively.
◔	• Amazon entered the online auction category in April 1999, nearly four years after eBay entered. Amazon entered with a site that was "remarkably similar to eBay's."[2] The imitative strategy indicates an awareness and understanding of the market leader's strategy.
●	• Features such as "A–Z Guarantee" designed to underwrite the risks of online buying and selling. Also, is rated higher on services and fees, customer support, site design and functionality, than eBay.[3]
◐	• Message of "Bid to Win! Value Guaranteed" communicates value to buyers (low prices and guaranteed value), but not to sellers.[4]
◐	• Association with Amazon is confusing. • Investment in and association with Sotheby's strengthens image as auction house, but probably only in the premium market. Other alliances in drugstore, auto, jewelry, etc., solidify retail image but do little to support auction brand.
●	• Lack of online / offline message association prevents the creation of a cohesive and memorable brand.

[1]Green, Heather. 1999. The e.biz 25, *Business Week Online*, 27 September.
[2]Bunnell, Mark. 2000, *The eBay phenomenon*. New York: John Wiley & Sons, 157.
[3]Auction Ratings, 2001. *AuctionWatch.com* 6 January.
[4]Amazon.com 1999 Annual Report. Seattle: Amazon.com

○ = very low   ◔ = low   ◐ = moderate   ◕ = high   ● = very high

EXHIBIT 12.17   eBay Vs. Amazon.com Auctions: Assessment of Key Branding Elements

Key Attributes	Rating	eBay	Rating	Amazon Auctions
1. Relevant	●	• eBay brings together buyers and sellers within a fun, safe exchange environment. The brand delivers on its promise.	◑	• The brand is highly relevant for books and CDs, but less so for auctions.
2. Distinct	●	• eBay is a distinct brand. The brand is unique because it provides a highly functional marketplace, and a positive exchange community.	◕	• Amazon is a distinct brand in terms of its service quality and association with books and CDs. However, it is not a distinct brand in the auction category, on some of the attributes that are most important to buyers and sellers (i.e., user base and sense of community).
3. Consistent	●	• Very consistent execution across media and over time.	◑	• Inconsistent to the extent that the brand has been extended to multiple categories.
4. Memorable	●	• A highly memorable brand that is synonymous with online auctions.	●	• A highly memorable brand that is almost synonymous with online commerce.

○ = very low   ◔ = low   ◑ = moderate   ◕ = high   ● = very high

EXHIBIT 12.18   eBay and Amazon.com Auctions: Assessment of Key Brand Attributes

Summary

1. What is a brand? What is brand equity?

According to the American Marketing Association, a brand is a "name, term, sign, symbol, or design, or a combination of them intended to identify the goods and services of one seller or group of sellers and to differentiate them from those of the competition." The term *product* simply describes the general category of the good, while *brand* refers to all aspects that relate to identity.

Brand equity has a wide variety of definitions in the academic literature. David Aaker argues that brand equity is a combination of assets that can be viewed from both firm and customer perspectives. Put differently, he views brand equity as a combination of consumer responses and benefits. Kevin Keller defines customer-based brand equity as the effect that brand knowledge has on consumer response to a brand. Here, the notion is that brand equity exists when customers react preferentially to the product solely because of favorable, unique, and strong brand associations.

2. What are the consumer responses that make up brand equity?

Consumer responses can take two broad forms: brand awareness and brand associations. Brand awareness refers to the strength of a brand's presence in the consumer's mind. A brand with high brand awareness is more likely to be recollected—either prompted by an advertisement or unaided by the firm. Brand associations refer to the connections that consumers make to the brand. These associations can usefully be categorized in terms of strength, valence, and uniqueness.

3. **What are some of the most significant ways to measure brand equity?**

Researchers recommend that marketers measure consumer perceptions with a combination of techniques such as depth interviews, focus groups, thought listing, visual techniques, projective techniques, and rating scales. Complementary techniques interact with one another to stimulate respondents' abilities to access and verbalize memories, and overcome their unwillingness to share them with the researcher. A portfolio of techniques helps respondents access memories of all kinds—verbal, visual, sensory, emotional—and associations that typically lie below the conscious level.

4. **How are marketing programs used to create brand equity?**

Very broadly, brand perceptions are affected by all interactions between the firm and its customers. The firm has the potential to enhance brand equity through website design, the brand name and logo, the types of services that are offered, cobranding arrangements, etc.

5. **What is the seven-step branding process?**

The seven steps are as follows:

Step 1: Clearly Define the Brand Audience. Branding strategies will be ineffective without a clear specification of the target audience for the offering.

Step 2: Understand Target Customers. From the broad description of the target customer, it is frequently useful to describe a composite prototypic customer who can bring the target segment to life.

Step 3: Understand the Competition. The competitive environment is also critical given the need to provide relative or superior value to target customers.

Step 4: Design Compelling Brand Intent. The brand intent brings to life the value proposition or cluster. Value propositions or clusters tend to focus on high-level customer benefits. Here, firms are looking for a description of how the brand should be interpreted from the customer's viewpoint.

Step 5: Identify Key Leverage Points in Customer Experience. This step requires the firm to move from the strategic notion of brand intent to the tactical notion of marketing levers—prices of products, customer interface, mix of online versus offline communications—that will activate the customer.

Step 6: Execute the Branding Strategy. Principles of good execution include integrity, consistency, patience, and flexibility.

Step 7: Establish Feedback Systems. Branding strategies rarely work out exactly as planned, and so it is important to have regular feedback systems in place.

6. **How do brands interact with other marketing levers to affect buyer–seller relationships?**

The brand interacts with the other marketing levers to affect customer relationships. If used properly, brand equity can enhance the effects of all other marketing levers on buyer–seller relationships. The fundamental point is that high-equity brands increase consumers' responsiveness to price, product, promotion, and distribution programs. As a result, firms with high-equity brands create customer awareness, exploration, and commitment with lower investments than their low-equity competitors. The presence of a strong brand enhances positive marketing activities and minimizes negative occurrences in the environment (e.g., product tampering) or marketing mistakes.

1. Choose three websites. Critique the websites using the components of the seven-step branding process. For example, do you think that the firms clearly defined the target audience before they designed the site? Does the site suggest an understanding of consumers and how they want to use the site? Is there compelling brand intent? Have they executed consistently?

2. How would you measure the brand equity of an online brand? Develop a short survey and give it to three friends or acquaintances. How would you assess the results?

3. Write a brand positioning statement that you think best describes a well-known online brand. Evaluate the effectiveness of the branding strategy. Is the positioning statement positive, strong, and unique? Compare the statement you develop to ones that are developed by other students in your class. Are the statements the same or different? Why? What are the implications for the firm's branding strategy?

Key Terms

brand

brand equity

strength of association

valence

uniqueness

seven-step branding process

Endnotes

[1]Opatow, Lorna. 1985. Creating brand names that work. *The Journal of Product Innovation Management* 2:254–259.

[2]Keller, Kevin Lane. 1993. Conceptualizing, measuring, and managing customer-based brand equity. *Journal of Marketing* 57:1–22.

[3]See, for example, Henderson, Pamela W., and Joseph A. Cote. 1998. Guidelines for selecting or modifying logos. *Journal of Marketing* 62:14–30.

[4]Webber, Alan M. 2000. Trust in the future. *Fast Company* September, 210.

[5]Keller, Kevin Lane. 1998. *Strategic brand management*. Upper Saddle River, NJ: Prentice-Hall, 43.

[6]Aaker, David. 1996. *Building strong brands*. New York: The Free Press, 7–8.

[7]Keller, Kevin Lane. 1998. *Strategic brand management*. Upper Saddle River, NJ: Prentice-Hall, 43.

[8]Functional benefits capture the intrinsic advantages of the product. They tend to be correlated with the features or attributes of the product. Symbolic benefits relate to social approval and personal expression. Experiential benefits relate to what the product feels like to use, and tends to capture various sensory pleasures. See the following article for further elaboration: Park, Choong W., Bernard J. Jaworski, and Deborah J. MacInnis. 1986. Strategic brand concept-image management. *Journal of Marketing* 50(4):135–145.

[9]Carpenter, Phil. 2000. *eBrands: Building an Internet business at breakneck speed*. Boston: Harvard Business School Press, 9.

[10]Lewis, Ian M. 1993. Brand equity: Or why the board of directors needs marketing research. ARF Fifth Annual Advertising and Promotion Workshop, 1 February.

[11]Keller, Kevin Lane. 1998. *Strategic brand management: Building, measuring, and managing brand equity*. Upper Saddle River, NJ: Prentice-Hall.

[12]Smith, Daniel C. 1992. Brand extensions and advertising efficiency: What can and cannot be expected. *Journal of Advertising Research* November–December, 11–20.

[13]Simon, Hermann. Dynamics of price elasticity and brand life cycles: An empirical study. *Journal of Marketing Research* 16:439–452.

[14]For more information see Abrams, Charles. May 20, 2002, Commentary: Bertelsmann gets a bargain. CNET News.com, and also Hu, Jim, Napster: Gimme shelter in Chapter 11, *CNET News.com*, 3 June, 2002.

[15]Smith, Michael D., Joseph Bailey, and Erik Brynjolfsson. 2002. Understanding digital markets: Review and assessment. In *Understanding the Digital Economy*. Erik Brynjolfsson and Brian Kahin (eds.), Cambridge: MIT Press.

[16]Sullivan, Mary W. 1998. How brand names affect the demand for twin automobiles. *Journal of Marketing Research* 35:154–165.

[17]Slywotzky, Adrian J., and Benson P. Shapiro. 1993. Leveraging to beat the odds: The new marketing mindset. *Harvard Business Review* September–October, 97–107.

[18]Zaltman, Gerald. 1997. Rethinking market research. *Journal of Marketing Research* 34:424–437.

[19]Supphellen, Magne. 2000. Understanding core brand equity: Guidelines for in-depth elicitation of brand associations. *International Journal of Market Research* 42:319–338.

[20]Fisher, Robert J. 1993. Social desirability bias and the validity of indirect questioning. *Journal of Consumer Research* 20:303–315.

[21]Durgee, Jeffrey F., and Robert W. Stuart. 1987. Advertising symbols and brand names that best represent key product meanings. *Journal of Consumer Marketing* 4:15–24.

[22]Aaker, Jennifer L. 1997. Dimensions of brand personality. *Journal of Marketing Research* 34:347–356.

[23]Morris, Betsy. 1996. The brand's the thing. *Fortune* 4 March, 72–78.

[24]Tellis, Gerard J. 1986. Beyond the many faces of price: An integration of pricing strategies. *Journal of Marketing* 50:146–160.

[25]Ries, Al, and Jack Trout. 1982. *Positioning: The battle for your mind*. New York: Warner Books.

[26]Quelch, John A., and David Harding. 1996. Brands versus private labels, fighting to win. *Harvard Business Review* January–February, 99–109.

[27]Garvin, David A. 1987. Competing on the eight dimensions of quality. *Harvard Business Review* November–December, 101–109.

[28]Curry, David J. 1985. Measuring price and quality competition. *Journal of Marketing* 49:106–117.

[29]Keller, Kevin Lane. 1998. *Strategic brand management: Building, measuring, and managing brand equity*. Upper Saddle River, NJ: Prentice-Hall.

[30]Slywotzky, Adrian J., and Benson P. Shapiro. 1993. Leveraging to beat the odds: The new marketing mindset. *Harvard Business Review* September–October, 97–107.

[31]Cavoli, Brian. 1999. What really is beyond the banner. *http://adsonline.about.com/aa062199.htm*.

[32]Neuborne, Ellen. 1999. Why famous brands often "fracture" when they hit the web. *Business Week* 12 April.

[33]Lazarus, David. 2000. eBay's Winning Bid. *San Francisco Chronicle* Online 31 August.

[34]Al Reis and Laura Reis. 2000. *The 11 Immutable Laws of Internet Branding*, New York, Harper Business.

[35]Cairncross, Frances. 2000. Survey: E-management—The shape of the new e-company. *The Economist* 11 November, s37–s38.

[36]Anonymous. 1996. USA TODAY Online: How not to do it. *Advertising Age* 26 February.

[37]USA TODAY Online. Case No. 9-598-133. Boston: Harvard Business School Publishing.

[38]Keller, Kevin Lane. 2000. The brand report card. *Harvard Business Review* January–February, 3–10.

[39]Anonymous. 2000. Ad spending doesn't equal brand awareness. Cyberatlas.internet.com 29 June.

[40]Brown, Paul. 1985. New and improved. *BusinessWeek* 21 October, 108–112.

[41]Goerne, Carrie. 1992. Direct mail spending rises, but success may be overblown. *Marketing News* 2, 6.

[42]Mulhern, Francis J., Jerome D. Williams, and Robert P. Leone. 1998. Variability of brand price elasticities across retail stores: Ethnic, income, and brand determinants. *Journal of Retailing* 74:427–446.

[43]Aaker, Jennifer L. 1997. Dimensions of brand personality. *Journal of Marketing Research* 34:347–356.

[44]Fisher, Robert J., and Kirk Wakefield. 1998. Factors leading to group identification: A field study of winners and losers. *Psychology & Marketing* 15 January, 23–40.

[45]Jones, John Philip. 1990. Ad spending: Maintaining market share. *Harvard Business Review* January–February, 1–7.

[46]Aaker, David A., and Erich Joachimsthaler. 2000. *Brand leadership*. New York: The Free Press.

[47]Abrahams, Paul and Barker, Thorold. 2002. ebay, the Flea Market That Spanned the Globe. *FT.com* 11 January.

[48]Collura, Meredith, and Lynda A. Applegate. 2000. Amazon.com: Exploiting the value of digital business infrastructure. Case No. 9-800-330. Boston: Harvard Business School Publishing.

[49]Lenatti, Chuck. 1999. Interview with eBay CEO Meg Whitman: Auction mania. *Upside*, 4 June. (available at *http:// www.upside.com/texis/mvm/story?id537541f8d0*).

[50]Wice, Nathaniel. 1999. BMW auctioning first new SUV on eBay. Time 29 October (available at *http://www.time.com/ time/digital/daily/0,2822,33387,00.html*).

[51]Kuchinskas, Susan. 1999. Eh, what's up eBay? *Adweek* (Eastern Edition), 29 March.

[52]Reis, D., Truong, V., and Towbin C. E. Unterberg. 1999. Amazon.com October 13 (available from Investext, *www. bschool-investest.com*), p.4.

[53]Dwyer, David, and Tim Albright. 2000. eBay. Salomon Smith Barney Inc. 7 November.

[54]Bressler, Stacey E., and Charles E. Grantham, Sr. 2000. *Communities of commerce*. New York: McGraw-Hill, 297.

Designing the Marketspace

Matrix

Substantial planning is required to ensure that the marketing plan will successfully advance customers from awareness to commitment. Because no one set of levers can apply to every marketing problem, and because every plan will have slight variations in segmenting, targeting, and positioning, the Marketspace Matrix is not a hard-wired circuit path for marketing plan design.

Instead, the matrix must be crafted to meet the individual needs of the firm and the customers it seeks. Thus, the matrix is more akin to clay being shaped on a pottery wheel than a kiln-fired pot. Skilled hands and basic design principles shape clay into a pot in the same way that a marketing team can use the principles provided in this chapter to mold the matrix into a powerful marketing tool.

QUESTIONS

As you read this chapter, please consider the following questions:

1. What is a buyer–seller relationship? How can these relationships vary?

2. Why is integrated lever selection important in a marketing plan?

3. How did eBay's application of the Marketspace Matrix change over time?

4. What are the four categories of principles for lever selection?

5. What are the key principles for lever selection within the Marketspace Matrix?

Introduction

Marketing textbooks have typically provided an encyclopedic view of marketing. They often specify a list of standard components but make little effort to either integrate the components or provide a framework for selecting marketing levers. Unfortunately, the most challenging part of creating a marketing plan is choosing and integrating the levers. This chapter's objective is to help firms build a marketing plan within the context of moving customers through the relationship stages. In order to assist marketing managers in their tasks, this chapter provides the following two aids to marketing-campaign development:

- A brief guide to considering the integration of levers in the context of advancing customers through the stages and building buyer–seller relationships
- A list of 10 principles designed to help marketing teams select appropriate levers when designing a Marketspace Matrix

This chapter is divided into the following sections:

A Consumer Perspective: The Marketspace Relational Matrix. This section briefly examines buyer–seller relationships in the context of the Marketspace Matrix and the relationship stages.

The 2Is. This section examines the role of individualization and interactivity across all categories of marketing levers.

Using the Marketing Levers to Establish and Maintain Customer Relationships. This section provides a user's guide to the levers in the context of the relationship stages, with the aim of helping firms think about which levers to pull to create an integrated, customer-centric marketing campaign.

Designing the Marketspace Matrix. This section presents the Marketspace Matrix, a framework for identifying the most appropriate marketing levers to move customers through the relationship stages. The section also presents 10 principles that a firm can use to select levers when building a Marketspace Matrix as a critical component of its marketing plan.

eBay Example. This section describes the evolution of eBay's Marketspace Matrix.

A Consumer Perspective: The Marketspace Relational Matrix

A relationship is a bond or connection between the firm and its customers. This bond may be strong, weak, or nonexistent, and it can be based on logic or emotion. An example of a logical bond is a realization that the customer simply cannot get a better product elsewhere. However, strong bonds typically have an emotional dimension as well—think of your relationships with family and friends. Buyer–seller relationships can be strong, but generally they are not as powerful as the connections we have with people who are close to us. Buyer–seller relationships are based on exchange, where each party expects, or perhaps even demands, value for what is given (i.e., money for products).

The greatest potential for strong buyer–seller relationships exists when the product is an important part of consumers' lives. For example, the automobiles, clothing, jewelry, and vacations we choose are often highly symbolic of who we are. Consequently, a relationship with a particular brand is useful because it helps simplify and reduce the risk associated with purchase decisions. Buyer–seller relationships are also more likely with some types of consumers because they are naturally more interested in a product category.

Firms want relationships with their customers, as long as they are cost-effective relationships. Some customers are not profitable enough to warrant customer relationship management investments. However, customers who are not connected to the firm in some way view each transaction as an independent event. These customers have no loyalty or commitment. In contrast, customers who have a relationship with the firm tend to feel good about remaining loyal, are not as likely to seek out competitive offerings, and actively promote the firm to others. Also, existing customers are willing to pay higher prices because they value noneconomic aspects of the relationship. Firms can use various quantitative methods to assess customer profitability and the value of marketing investments in relationship building.

Over time, some customers will cease to be profitable by any measure. At that point, firms should take steps to dissolve the unprofitable relationships. Firms must understand that not all committed customers are equal, and relationships that bring no benefit to the firm should be dissolved.

By crafting a Marketspace Matrix (see Exhibit 13.1) that takes advantage of the 2Is, firms should be able to build more profitable customer relationships.

The 2Is

The Internet's combination of individualization and interactivity allows firms to choose levers that can move customers through the relationship phases faster and more effectively than ever before possible. This potential demands that firms leverage the 2Is across matrix design as much as possible in order to advance customers to the commitment stage. Furthermore, the

---

Drill-Down

Amazon.com's Pricing Experiment

Between May 2000 and September 2000, Amazon.com tested a dynamic pricing strategy that varied prices of products by determining the profile of existing consumers. Amazon attempted to maximize prices to optimize its margin. Regular customers with a history of buying products were believed to be more likely to pay more, and therefore were charged more for products. The Internet has enabled e-retailers to gauge the shopping habits of consumers with the use of online tracking tools to increase profits from an existing pool of customers. Amazon attempted to test dynamic pricing with its 23 million customers.

In one instance, a customer paid $24.49 for a DVD version of the movie *Titus*. The next week, he went back to Amazon.com and saw that the price had jumped to $26.24. Once he cleared his computer of any identifying data, Amazon gave him the "new customer" price of $22.74. Other cases have revealed price variances of up to $10 for DVDs such as *The X-Files: The Complete Second Season* and more than $50 for a Diamond Rio MP3 player.[1]

This pricing strategy could have played out much differently if not for the discussions on message boards and forums such as DVDTalk.com. Consumers were comparing notes, perplexed by their shopping experiences at Amazon. Confusion became outrage as customers discovered what was going on. A spokesperson stated that the experiment "was done to determine consumer responses to different discount levels" and denied implementing a dynamic pricing strategy. After eventually admitting the use of dynamic pricing, Amazon.com swore it would never happen again.

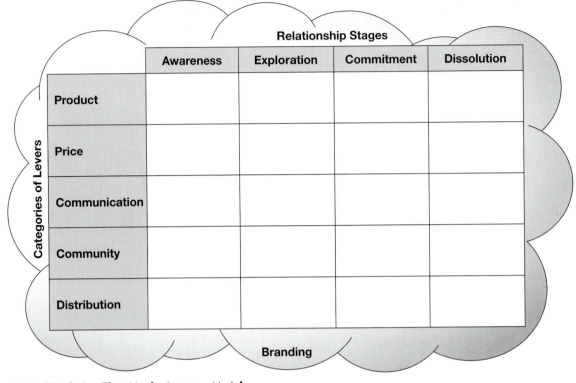

EXHIBIT 13.1   The Marketspace Matrix

2Is allow firms many new possibilities to maintain commitment with their customers.

The 2Is affect each category of levers differently, but the end results—more successful advancement through the relationship stages and improved possibilities for commitment—remain consistent across all levers (see Exhibit 13.2).

Product.   Individualization of user pages (the customer-specified attributes and features lever), such as Yahoo's personalized pages, sustains commitment by providing information that users want. It also increases switching costs: Once users tailor a page, they are less likely to do it at a competitor's site as well. Individualization also spurs users to move from awareness to exploration. For example, a customer considering a pager may discover the Motorola brand. That person can then enter the exploration/expansion stage when considering the possibilities that Motorola offers as a mass-customized product—including a broad mix of colors and features. Individualization, expressed through the mass-customization product lever, makes this possible.

Pricing.   Targeted price promotions, which can be both individualized and interactive in the form of a permission e-mail, can advance users from exploration/expansion to commitment by giving them a price incentive to make the purchase. CDNow sends e-mails to previous customers offering them dis-

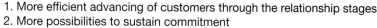

Branding

Result

1. More efficient advancing of customers through the relationship stages
2. More possibilities to sustain commitment

EXHIBIT 13.2   The 2Is

counts on CDs selected by collaborative filtering—that is, CDs that it thinks the customer will want based on previous purchases and purchases made by other customers. The offers almost always involve a price promotion. Thus, targeted price promotions can serve to advance users to the commitment stage and keep them there once they buy.

Communications.   Interactive, targeted banner ads are a classic example of the 2Is' influence on communications levers. Banner ads can be targeted at particular segments, and the interactivity of a banner ad allows a user to move from awareness to exploration just by clicking on it.

Community.   In the case of eBay, the strong, vibrant community sustains buyers' commitment by ensuring a constant supply of a wide range of goods. In turn, the large number of shoppers benefits sellers by driving up auction prices. The eBay community rating system aids the movement of buyers from exploration to commitment by reducing transaction risk. (Sellers with good feedback ratings can generally be trusted to accurately describe and promptly ship the purchased goods.)

Distribution.   Interactivity allows for tight linkages between suppliers and buyers, which can facilitate a collaborative relationship that results in benefits in logistics, inventory planning, and responsiveness. Interactivity in distribution greatly aids the implementation of just-in-time production. For example, Dell's interfacing with suppliers allows Dell to drastically reduce its parts inventory by sharing ordering information and forecasting information. Suppliers can use this information to generate the same inventory savings with their own suppliers, thus benefiting all firms in the supply chain.

Using the Marketing Levers to Establish and Maintain Customer Relationships

As explained throughout this book, a typical relationship is thought to progress through four basic stages: awareness, exploration/expansion, commitment, and dissolution. It is clear, however, that not all customers pass through all four stages, and firms can have important, profitable customers who do not have a commitment to the firm. Further, firms can invest in a wide range of tactics or levers to establish and maintain relationships with consumers (see Exhibit 13.3).

The goal of the Marketspace Matrix is to help firms take an integrated, customer-centric approach to Internet marketing. Marketing managers are responsible for deciding which levers to use, when to use them, and how much to invest in each one. From this perspective, the role of the marketing manager is very similar to that of an investment manager. Managers of mutual funds, for example, must decide which investments to make on behalf of their clients. They try to develop investment portfolios that match the risk and return preferences of their target clients.

Marketing managers make investments in each type of lever to best achieve the firm's marketing objectives—is the objective to increase market share, maximize growth, maximize profitability, or become a market leader? Each of these objectives has different implications for the investments in marketing levers. From a relationship perspective, Internet marketers can think of either increasing the number of customers and moving them toward commitment, or increasing the commitment of existing customers in order to maximize retention. In any case, the firm should utilize the Marketspace Matrix to choose and plan the implementation of marketing levers.

The Marketspace Matrix

Fundamentally, the Marketspace Matrix can visually outline two important, related concepts. First, it provides a starting point for formulating an effective marketing campaign. Second, as shown as Exhibit 13.4, it provides a comprehensive description of the marketing levers available to advance users through the stages. Consider how the levers are used in each of the four relationship stages:

Awareness. Levers that create awareness can be categorized as either direct or indirect. Direct levers are those that are communication-based and are typically under the control of the firm. Advertising and sales promotions are the best examples of direct awareness levers—very simply, firms increase awareness by spending more money or spending it more effectively. Indirect levers, in contrast, include all other levers that stimulate third-party communications that create awareness. A product, community, distribution, or pric-

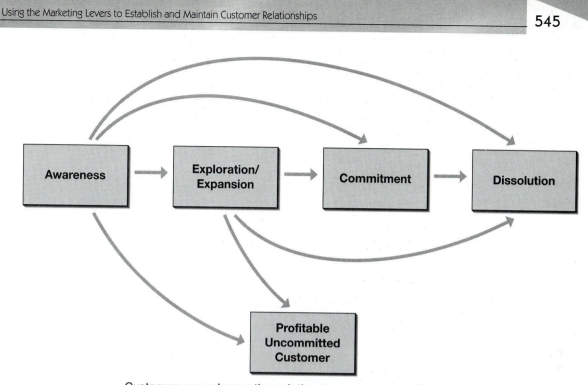

Customers can advance through the stages in several different ways

EXHIBIT 13.3 Moving through the Relationship Stages

ing lever that is novel, for example, will often gain the attention of journalists who then write about the innovation in magazines or newspapers. Word-of-mouth effects work in a similar way. A terrific price promotion has the potential to stimulate tremendous awareness through C2C communication.

Exploration/Expansion.   Levers that facilitate exploration typically provide some incentive for an initial website visit and subsequent investigation of the site. A targeted price promotion, for example, enhances the likelihood that someone in the target market will visit a site for the first time. Once the user arrives at the site, exploration can be facilitated by a functional site that is easy to use and has useful content. For example, exploration is enhanced by the promise of valuable information or an entertaining online experience. Linkages to other sites of interest, collaborative filtering that presents relevant products and services, and a feeling that the site is trustworthy all facilitate exploration and create site "stickiness."

Commitment.   As discussed throughout the book, relationships are based on a buyer–seller bond or connection. Creating commitment is therefore about establishing and maintaining this bond within an exchange relationship. As discussed in Chapter 6, commitment is enhanced by levers that encourage both parties to contribute to the relationship. The seller does this by offering a product or service that provides superior value. The buyer's commitment can then be elevated when the seller facilitates a C2C community that is connected to their offering. The seller can also provide ancillary services such as e-mail services and chat rooms that motivate customers to visit frequently, and offer individualization capabilities. Also important is frequent communication from the firm that encourages a two-way dialogue between the buyer and seller. The buyer must feel that he or she has a voice and that the firm is responsive to it.

Relationship Stages

Categories of Levers	Awareness	Exploration/Expansion	Commitment	Dissolution
Product	• Packaging	• Attributes and features • Fulfillment • Mass customized product • Breadth of inventory • Additional functionality • Packaging • Availability of complementary products	• Customer-specific attributes and features • Postsales support • Incremental allocated benefits • Customer enabling community • Upgrades • Customer relationship management • Customer care	• Customer care
Price	• Click-through promotions • Web referral promotions • Bricks-and-clicks promotions • Web price discounts • Bundle • Frenzy pricing • Prestige • Price as a sign of quality • Hi-lo • Dynamic pricing (as a novel approach—group buying, C2C) • EDLP	• Targeted promotions • Future price promotions • Justify prices • Loyalty programs	• Tiered loyalty programs • Wide variety of pricing plans • Become evangelists (affiliate) • Profit enhancing programs • Volume discount promotions • Targeted promotions • Future price promotions • Fairness • Subscription • EDLP • Dynamic pricing (group buying, C2C) • Two-Part pricing	• Discontinue pricing promotions • Reconfigure loyalty programs • Decrease profit programs
Communication	• Television • Magazines • Radio • Yellow Pages • Telemarketing • Billboards/outdoor advertising • Online billboards (banners/buttons) • Search engines • E-mail • Viral marketing	• Television • Radio • Newspapers • Packaging • Loyalty programs • Customer service • Interactive online billboards lending to website • Links from search lead to website • E-mail with information and link to website • Viral marketing leading to website and/or download • Website • Serial marketing	• Permission marketing with targeted offers • Loyalty programs • Customer service • Permission e-mail • Personalized pages	• Terminate direct marketing
Community	• Outline community benefits clearly and early on in the process • Anticipate and readily answer questions and concerns, quickly establishing a sense of trust • Establish a call for action and further exploration	• Make community exploration easy through efficient site structure • Show everyone individual attention (e.g., welcoming e-mails, guides for novices, chat conversations for new members, use of CRM marketing to tailor site functionality) • Begin the process of equity creation (e.g., member points and loyalty programs)	• Increase equity building (e.g., through tiered loyalty programs, increased rewards) • Recognize individuals' contribution and participation • Develop members (e.g., through leadership opportunities, community roles—guides or watch-persons)	• Spot departing friends early and find solutions to prevent dissolution • Make the "leaving process" fair and efficient • Seek and listen closely to feedback • Allow the option of returning
Distribution	• Number of intermediaries • Number of channels	• Degree of integration • Number of channels	• Degree of interest • Intermediary type • Number of channels • Internal function	• Elimination of types • Reduction of intermediaries • Reduce integration

Branding

EXHIBIT 13.4   The Marketspace Matrix

Dissolution.   Many of the levers in the dissolution stage are the exact opposite of those in the commitment and exploration stages. Here the levers are undertaken with the express purpose of reducing customer value in order to reduce costs and make it more attractive for undesirable customers to switch to another company. Reducing communication, eliminating service options, and raising prices are all dissolution levers that may be appropriate. In the case of a violation of the buyer–seller relationship norms, some customers may be asked to not return to the seller's site.

The levers available have been discussed in detail in the previous six chapters, and they are comprehensively displayed in the Marketspace Matrix (Exhibit 13.4). This matrix is the starting point for marketing managers, as it is a comprehensive guide to the levers available for advancing customers through the relationship stages. Matrix design will and should change over time, however, as changes to the firm's marketing objectives, competitive set, consumer preferences, etc., evolve. The matrix must adapt to those changes. Effective marketing mixes require a deep understanding of all the levers available in each of the four stages, as well as the environment within which the matrix is developed.

It is important to note that not every lever can be perfectly assigned into one relationship stage or even one lever category. Marketers can apply television advertising, for example, to advance users into the awareness, exploration, or commitment phases. Loyalty programs, while primarily classified as a pricing lever, involve communication and can be considered part of the augmented product. Further, creative marketers will use the levers successfully in ways that are not specified in the Marketspace Matrix. Nevertheless, the Marketspace Matrix provides a comprehensive guide available to the components of the marketing mix.

As the matrix is a newly developed tool, its use will continue to evolve as firms develop marketing campaigns. One potential development is the emergence of patterns of matrix design, which will aid marketing teams across categories of goods or services to pick levers. In the next several years, it is expected that research will emerge on matrix building and design that concludes whether or not patterns exist across categories. For example, a particular marketing mix as reflected in the matrix may be well suited to retail establishments, whereas another mix may serve luxury goods. With a finite number of levers and relationship stages, there may only be several applicable patterns that cover the bulk of marketing programs. The possibility exists, however, that few usable patterns will emerge, because all products have certain unique attributes or because the most effective marketing mix will involve a blanket approach of levers across relationship stages and lever categories.

Designing the Marketspace Matrix

Creating a successful Marketspace Matrix requires careful analysis. Levers need to be selected as part of a comprehensive marketing plan that reflects the segmenting, positioning, and targeting that the firm selects. In fact, these are the first steps to successful matrix design and implementation.

Market Segmentation.   If a firm does not segment the market at all, it is selling one product to all customers at one price using mass promotion and distribution. The advantage of this approach is that both marketing and production costs are likely to be minimized. At the other extreme, firms can market customized products to individuals, or "segments of one." Traditionally, this approach has been used in the B2B space where customers demand unique solutions for sophisticated medical equipment, mainframe computers, or construction services. As noted throughout the book, the Internet has made it possible to target and serve individual customers on a mass scale—a segmentation approach that was previously impossible.

Most firms employ segmentation strategies that fall somewhere between the two extremes identified above. Market segmentation is often based on customer characteristics such as demographics, geography, psychographics, or customer responses such as attitudes, needs, and behaviors. Segmentation approaches must be meaningful in the sense that they explain customer behavior, and actionable with respect to the firm's ability to identify and reach customers in the segment.

Target Marketing.   As discussed in Chapter 3, market segmentation is motivated by a desire to maximize the impact of the firm's marketing resources. Once the firm has segmented the market, it must decide what segment or segments it wants to target. The targeting decision should be based on the degree to which the target markets are attractive, as well as the firm's relative ability to provide value to customers in the target market. This requires that the firm perform a thorough analysis of the firm's resources and capabilities relative to the competition.

It is interesting to note that targeting one segment often leads to the alienation of customers in other segments. Firms that market to multiple segments face this problem on a daily basis. For example, people 18 years old and younger make up the largest segment of Coke drinkers. Advertisements aimed at adults make the brand less attractive to young consumers, yet adults are also an important part of Coca-Cola's customer base. One way that Coca-Cola reduces the potential for consumers in one segment to receive a message that is intended for consumers in a different segment is to use different communication levers.

Positioning.   As discussed in Chapter 3, positioning is about affecting the minds of customers in the target market. The goal is to locate the product in such a way that it is unique relative to competitive offerings, and provides value to the target consumer. Determining your product's position requires that you "get inside the mind of the consumer" through consumer research. The firm must understand the preferences of consumers, and how the firm's products are rated relative to competitive offerings.

Firms have a variety of alternatives to differentiate their products and position them advantageously. For example, products can be differentiated on the basis of quality dimensions such as performance, features, aesthetics, conformance to design standards, durability, and reliability.[2] Services can be differentiated on the basis of such things as delivery, installation, customer support, maintenance, and order processing.

These steps also help to immediately eliminate levers that are inappropriate because they are inconsistent with the firm's desired position, or because they are not appropriate for the target market. For example, a company would not want to use price promotions to attract a segment that is price insensitive. Once the firm completes these three tasks, it can begin to select levers and finalize its marketing plan (see Exhibit 13.5). It is clear that there is no one marketing mix that fits all needs; marketing strategy remains both a science and an art (see the Drill-Down titled " 'Cooking Up' a Marketing Strategy"). Providing a prescriptive list of levers for all marketing teams would not only be impossible, it would contradict the notion that segmenting, targeting, and positioning are important to the design of the Marketspace Matrix. However, several principles do apply to matrix design. The principles are designed to help eliminate the use of certain levers in some situations and lean toward the use of particular levers in other situations.

Principles of Matrix Design

The exciting—and frustrating—part of marketing strategy is that there are usually several ways to reach the same objective. The case studies in this book illustrate that while segmenting, targeting, and positioning provide a frame-

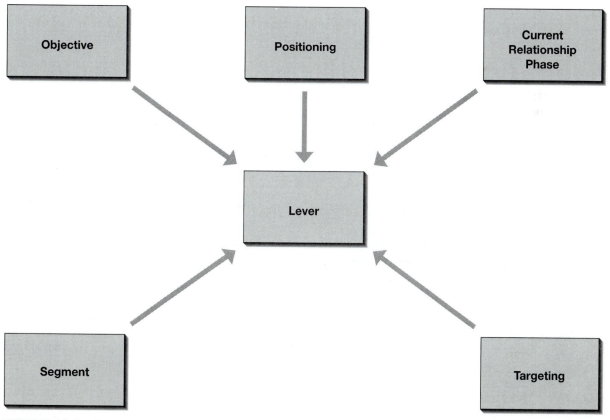

EXHIBIT 13.5   Lever Selection Process

> **Drill-Down**
>
> ### "Cooking Up" a Marketing Strategy
>
> Designing a marketing strategy is both an art and a science. Although there is a formal framework for guiding marketing decision-making, there is also a great deal of creativity and artistry involved. Successful marketing strategies build on a solid analysis and understanding of the environment, but also require imagination and "out of the box" thinking to be highly successful.
>
> To illustrate the matrix design process, we apply these categories to someone who is cooking an Asian dinner. On the analytical side, it is clear that most dishes have a core set of ingredients (just as a marketing strategy includes the core ingredients of price, product, promotion, and distribution elements). The chef begins by identifying the basic ingredients for the dish he is making. For example, the cook might select chicken, carrots, peppers, and soy sauce. Remember, the levers must always match the objective, which in this case is to create a delicious meal. The creative side comes when the chef decides the quantity and ratio of the ingredients in the dish. Too much soy sauce will make the meal too salty; too little will make it bland. Chili peppers will add a bit of spice. The chef must consider the interaction between the ingredients. The soy sauce brings out the flavor of the chicken and the vegetables. The crunchy vegetables contrast with the tender chicken, and the different colors of the carrots, peppers, and chicken create a vibrant palette on the plate. At the end of the process, the chef has created something that can be recognized as a particular type of dish, but it is unique to the extent that he has been creative in preparing and presenting the dish. The same is true of a successful marketing strategy.

work that helps managers identify the optimal mix of marketing levers, there will never be one right answer. There are many strategies and levers that will lead to the firm's goals.

Matrix design is a four-step process that helps marketing managers select and implement appropriate levers. The principles for matrix design span four categories (see Exhibit 13.6):

- Which levers are customers most responsive to?
- Which levers are least likely to generate a competitive response?

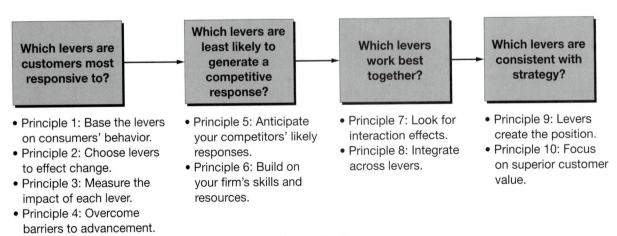

EXHIBIT 13.6 Principles for Marketspace Matrix Design

- Which levers work best together?
- Which levers are consistent with strategy?

Which Levers Are Customers Most Responsive To?

Principle 1: Base the Levers on Consumer Behavior. Understanding consumers is the starting point for any good matrix. For example, the importance of online versus offline distribution channels varies dramatically by product category. Greenfield Online and Target Management found that 38 percent of 13- to 19-year-olds in the United States usually buy active wear and athletic apparel in department stores. Fourteen percent preferred specialty stores, and 14 percent chose full-line sporting goods stores. Only 2 percent of teens prefer to shop online for athletic apparel. Retailers that target the teenage apparel consumer would be well advised to emphasize offline distribution levers. In contrast, retail sales of books are predominately online, with a ratio of $1 online for every $0.68 spent through traditional channels.

The importance of understanding consumer behavior when designing the marketing levers can also be illustrated for durables such as automobiles. A consumer might typically become aware of a new model by viewing a manufacturer's television advertisement. She may then visit a company website or call a toll-free number to get more information, and review independent publications and online sources. Further information-gathering takes the form of a dealership visit and a test drive. The consumer wants to experience and evaluate the new model firsthand and to ask questions in real time. Online companies such as MSN Autos (formerly CarPoint) understand that few people will purchase a car without a test drive, and so instead of trying to sell the visitor online, it refers customers to local dealers who have the customer's choice of automobile. MSN Autos has tailored its system to ensure that potential car buyers get the right information at the right time via the right communication channel.

Principle 2: Choose Levers to Effect Change. In the Marketspace Matrix the focus is on moving consumers through the relationships stages. Because each lever will have a different impact on consumer perceptions and behaviors depending on their relationship stage, it is important to specify exactly what it is you want the lever to accomplish. For example, a firm might want to move a customer from the exploration to the commitment phase. With this understanding, the levers that are most likely to establish a bond with the customer become more obvious. Without a clear idea about what type of change is desired, any lever will do.

Amazon.com demonstrates how the type of levers that are used are directly related to the behavioral change that is sought. Given Amazon.com's need to stimulate impulse purchases, the focus is on levers that encourage this behavior. Amazon's 1-Click ordering capability (see Exhibit 13.7), allows users to purchase without much deliberation. Also, its collaborative filtering stimulates impulse buying by suggesting products that are likely to appeal to a customer based on prior purchases and purchases made by other patrons with similar buying profiles. Also, its "buying circle" function provides information about what others in their peer group, company, community, etc.,

Barrier

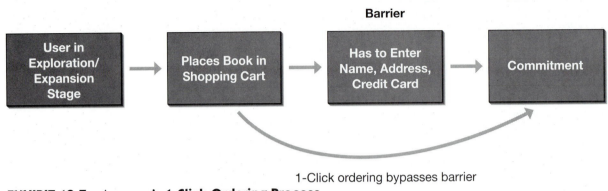

EXHIBIT 13.7 Amazon's 1-Click Ordering Process

are buying. These levers are designed to overcome resistance to the sale by simplifying information search, reducing risk, and making purchases quick and easy.

Principle 3: Measure the Impact of Each Lever. Firms must constantly evaluate the degree to which the levers that have been selected are performing effectively. Competitive reactions, changing customer preferences, implementation problems, and other factors will cause levers to increase or decrease in effectiveness. Further, because each lever differs in the extent to which it affects awareness, exploration, commitment, and dissolution, the measurement process should include multiple metrics. Again, the point is to invest in levers that have the greatest impact on the consumers, and therefore on profitability.

To illustrate the importance of this type of information, a recent study found that search engine positioning (SEP) is the most cost-effective marketing lever available. By one author's calculations, given a $150,000 investment, SEP outperforms other popular online marketing strategies by about 10 to 1.[3] Here's how the three most popular types of online media stacked up against SEP on one important metric—click-through rates:

- Banner ads, at $11 per thousand impressions, bought 13,636,363 impressions with an industry standard 0.3 percent click-through rate at a cost of $3.66 per visitor.

- E-mail marketing, at $450 per thousand outbound e-mails, bought 333,333 recipients with an industry standard 5 percent response rate at a cost of $9 per visitor.

- Keyword buys, at $30 per thousand impressions, bought 5 million impressions with an industry standard 1 percent click-through rate at a cost of $3 per visitor.

The same $150,000 investment in a comprehensive search engine positioning campaign produced a cost per website visitor of just 40 cents across six very different clients. The research does not say that firms should not use banner ads, e-mail marketing, or keyword buys. The research does, however, illustrate the importance of gathering information about the productivity of various levers so the firm can maximize the impact of its matrix. (See Drill-

Down titled "Amazon.com's Pricing Experiment" for another example of how firms understand the impact of each lever.)

Principle 4: Overcome Barriers to Advancement.
Marketing planners must understand what prevents people from moving from one stage to another. The obstacle that stands in the way of advancement should be the target of a lever. Unless the firm overcomes the barrier, the customer or segment will not advance to the next relationship stage.

The handheld-device market is a networked-economy example of this principle. Palm Inc. has been the dominant player in this space, with 60 to 75 percent of the market, (depending on the research group calculating the numbers). This dominance has led to third-party applications for Palm's devices, making them more useful (this is similar to what happened with Microsoft and its dominance in the PC operating-system market). Companies such as Handspring, another handheld manufacturer, simply cannot ignore this dominance. As a result, Handspring has adopted the Palm operating system for its devices. This enables Handspring users to use existing Palm applications (a product lever). Handspring is also able to compete and build awareness using a pricing lever. Handspring devices are cheaper and can often surpass the product functionality of Palm's devices, thus moving customers along the relationship stages without creating the extra barrier of forcing customers to adopt a new operating system.

In an online/offline example, Lands' End, a direct merchant, invited patrons to visit a mobile scanning facility where their body shape was scanned into a computer. When customers visited the Lands' End website, they could access their scanned models and use them to try on clothing. Because one of the primary barriers to purchasing clothing via mail order or the Internet is concern over whether the clothes will fit, this lever could have been a tipping point. This added functionality required an expansion of the customer's relationship with Lands' End, but the customer-specific attributes would have potentially rewarded such a commitment by providing better purchases and fewer returns. The effort proved to be a failure because customers did not care for the often-unflattering scans; women especially resented the fact their hips looked too large. Lands' End ended the campaign when the technology supporting the scanning process could not be improved.

Which Levers Are Least Likely to Generate a Competitive Response?

Principle 5: Anticipate Your Competitors' Likely Responses.
Marketing takes place within dynamic competitive environments. No strategy is ever "set in stone" because direct competitors often respond to your initiatives. In other instances, new entrants can attack with completely new business models. A firm must be able to adapt its matrix to respond to changes in the market, and reallocate its resources in response to these discoveries. What works at one point in time may not work six months later.

A recent study analyzing Procter & Gamble's (P&G's) value pricing strategy in the United States from 1990 to 1996 found that changes in P&G's advertising and promotions strategy ultimately had a negative effect on its market share, largely because of competitive response. The authors found that during that period, P&G made major cuts in deals and coupons, and substantially increased advertising across its product line. The likely goal was to maintain or increase market share while increasing profitability. However, competitors reacted to P&G's strategy by lowering prices and offering trade deals to opportunistically increase market share. Their reaction could be predicted by the degree that their own share and profits were affected by P&G's strategy. Competitors also responded differently due to firm-specific effects, such as whether they competed with P&G in multiple markets and the size of their operations. The authors determined that P&G lost market share in large part because of competitive responses.[4] Overall, P&G was not successful in maintaining or gaining market share because of competitive response.

Principle 6: Build on Your Firm's Skills and Resources. Each firm has a set of skills and resources that reflect the ability to develop successful marketing strategies. To the extent that these skills and resources are unique and superior to those of competing firms, the firm can differentiate itself. For example, superior R&D capabilities might enable the firm to design products that better meet the needs of consumers, or that are easier and cheaper to manufacture. Similarly, close relationships with channel intermediaries will enable the firm to get the product to market more quickly, and locate it in a better shelf position within the store. Of course, it is not enough to have superior skills and resources. The firm must translate these superiorities into advantages that are recognized and valued by consumers. The bottom line is that by using levers that are most consistent with the firm's superior skills and resources, competitors will not be able to imitate or leap-frog the strategy and so the advantage will be sustainable for a longer period of time.

An illustration of the importance of matching the firm's marketing levers with its skills and resources is provided by TiVo Inc. TiVo sells a device that enables television viewers to control exactly what they watch on television and when they watch it (see Exhibit 13.8). The personal video recorder (PVR) can record up to 60 hours of television programming, and pause and replay live TV. TiVo has created over 150,000 subscribers on the basis of a strategy that recognizes the firm's limited resource base. On the offline side, TiVo has partnered with Sony and Philips to gain their expertise in manufacturing the physical product. On the online side, TiVo has relied on viral marketing (more than 90 percent of its existing customers were extremely satisfied with the product) and incentives to stimulate current users to market the product on the firm's behalf. For example, in December 2000, TiVo offered existing subscribers $50 if they converted two new consumers to the service.[5]

Which Levers Work Best Together?

Principle 7: Look for Interaction Effects. Many levers have a much larger impact on consumer behavior when they are used in concert with another lever. Consider the following examples:

EXHIBIT 13.8   TiVo Website

- *Advertising lever interactions.* Making an improvement to virtually any marketing lever will have a bigger payoff when it is advertised or promoted. Having a price cut alone may result in an overall increase in business, but cutting price and using advertising as well is likely to have a much bigger effect. Similarly, improving product design, changing and adding distribution channels, or initiating a promotional campaign will all likely have a bigger impact on consumer behavior.

- *Branding interactions.* As discussed in the branding chapter, the brand interacts with every other marketing lever such that the higher the equity, the greater the impact of the levers that are used with it. Strong brands require less advertising, promotion, or distribution investments compared with weak brands. They also demand higher prices and greater customer loyalty.

- *Communication channel interactions.* There is a potential interaction effect between the advertising vehicle that is used and the message that is delivered by the firm. Simply put, choose your channel, and you have already made a choice about what you are saying. A company that advertises in *Town and Country*, for example, will be perceived as targeting an affluent audience with fairly conservative values. Here, the image of the magazine interacts with the message to enhance perceptions of the brand that is being advertised.

- *Product interactions.* A recent study of marketing alliances examined the interaction between product type and the advertising appeals used in a joint marketing effort.[6] By product type, the authors mean whether the companies market products that are used together (e.g., belts and pants) or offer similar benefits (e.g., cleaning supplies). By advertising appeal, the authors mean whether the advertising campaign focuses on what is unique about the products in the ad, or what makes them similar to other products in their respective categories. The study finds that firms are always better off aligning themselves with another firm that markets a complementary product, and they benefit even more when advertising appeals emphasize what is unique about their products.

As the examples suggest, some combinations of levers have stronger effects when they are used together with one or more other levers than when they are used independently.

Principle 8: Integrate Across Levers. Selected levers must be integrated as well, to create consistency and help generate the desired effect. The chosen levers should reinforce each other to maximize the effect of the marketing plan (see Exhibit 13.9). Remember that every interaction between a firm and its customers is an opportunity to affect customer perceptions. If a firm fails to provide a consistent message through one or more communication channels or points of interaction, consumers will be confused and perhaps alienated.

While this is true in the offline world, the characteristics of the Internet make it possible to modify and expand this traditional principle. On the Internet, the choice of medium can be not only the message, but also the product. Consider E*Trade. The E*Trade website not only symbolizes affordable trading for the mass market, but it is also an integral aspect of the E*Trade service. Customers can customize their stock lists, research the companies, and make investment decisions. Thus, the E*Trade website does more than just convey a message about cheap trading—it delivers the product.

One example of an integrated marketing campaign is the launch of the new Snak-Stix version of Kellogg's venerable Pop-Tarts brand in August 2002.[7] The firm, faced with stagnant cereal aisle sales, is launching the new product with an integrated marketing push that has both online and offline components. The brand itself is being revitalized with a bold new color (blue) and a more progressive shelf appearance. New variations of the frosted candy bar-like form will be offered, including cookies and cream, caramel chocolate, and double chocolate. The TV advertising campaign will tout a "whole new attitude" in snacking to teens, and will be cross-promoted with Kellogg cereal brands, sampling, event marketing, and online ads. All of the levers work together to provide the target market with a very clear understanding of the new product and the value it provides.

Which Levers Are Consistent with Strategy?

Principle 9: Levers Create the Position. If an organization chooses to position its offering in a certain segment of the market, the marketing levers must support that choice. As a result, some levers can be ruled out as inapplicable, and others will appear more attractive. American Express, for example, promotes one of its high-end products, the Platinum Card, by

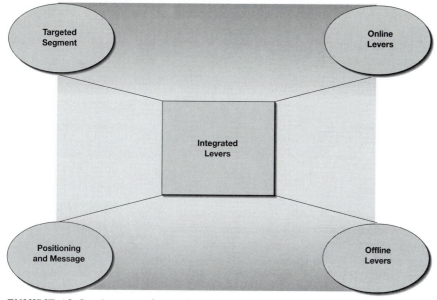

EXHIBIT 13.9   Integration of Levers

sending potential customers a personal invitation. The invitation emphasizes aspects that are consistent with the positioning of the card: prestige, exclusivity, and unique services for the frequent spender. American Express would probably not find it cost-effective to promote the Platinum Card by advertising in *People* magazine.

While this principle may seem obvious, companies sometimes overlook it. A few years ago, Burger King made an implicit positioning choice by offering flame-grilled hamburgers and high customization (customers could request no mayonnaise or extra pickles, for example). However, most of the hamburger chain's marketing focused on price and size, mentioning larger portions and discounted burgers. Price promotions were frequent, and the products included giant burgers and extra drinks. Eventually, the chain realigned its marketing campaign with its offering and started promoting better-tasting, customized burgers and a higher-quality experience.

Principle 10: Focus on Superior Customer Value. It is important to remember that the overarching goal of the matrix is to position the product to provide superior customer value. Providing superior value means customers perceive that the firm's product has unique attributes that are important to them. Unless firms can provide something that is different from competitive offerings and valued by consumers, the firm is in a commodity market where price competition dominates. In competitive markets, firms that provide superior customer value capture higher market shares and profits.

Superior value means providing customers with exceptional functional, symbolic, and hedonic benefits (see Exhibit 13.10). A website such as Barnes & Noble.com offers a very functional service—fast, efficient transactions and products with low prices. As a result, the hedonic value of shopping at Barnes & Noble.com is enhanced—shoppers get what they want with no muss and no fuss. From a symbolic perspective, Barnes & Noble.com shoppers have a shopping experience that is well worth sharing with other consumers: "I bought the latest bestseller at a low price, and it only took me five minutes!"

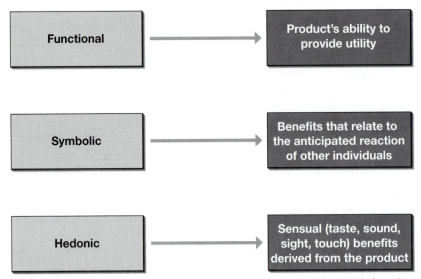

Functional	➡	Product's ability to provide utility
Symbolic	➡	Benefits that relate to the anticipated reaction of other individuals
Hedonic	➡	Sensual (taste, sound, sight, touch) benefits derived from the product

EXHIBIT 13.10 Functional, Symbolic, and Hedonic Explained

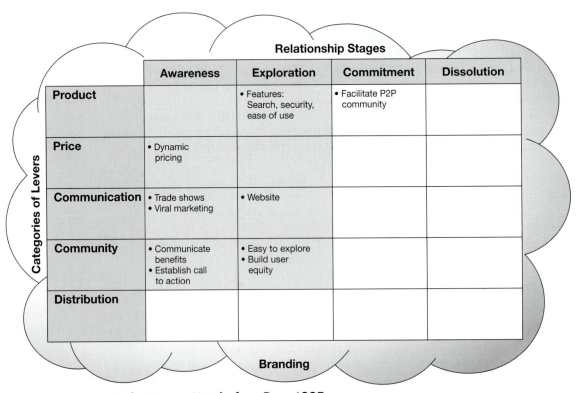

Relationship Stages

Categories of Levers	Awareness	Exploration	Commitment	Dissolution
Product		• Features: Search, security, ease of use	• Facilitate P2P community	
Price	• Dynamic pricing			
Communication	• Trade shows • Viral marketing	• Website		
Community	• Communicate benefits • Establish call to action	• Easy to explore • Build user equity		
Distribution				

Branding

EXHIBIT 13.11 Marketspace Matrix for eBay, 1995

eBay Example

The eBay case illustrates how a Marketspace Matrix differs over the life of a highly successful online firm. This section describes the evolution of eBay's matrix design. It is important to note that not every principle applies in every situation, and some principles will necessarily be weighted more than others.

The Evolution of eBay 's Marketspace Matrix

eBay in 1995

eBay provides a logical first example of the Marketspace Matrix in action. Exhibit 13.11 represents eBay's marketing mix when the site launched. Many of the cells are blank—a firm cannot focus on generating commitment until at least some users advance to the exploration/expansion stage, nor can it necessarily afford to pull levers in every category. In the case of eBay, which was founded to support a hobby, the use of television advertising, for example, made no sense. Moreover, since the product—an online auction service—was completely new, its brand had little value. Yet eBay, even in its nascent phases, developed levers in nearly every category.

Awareness.   Early on, eBay created awareness through its novelty and success. eBay was the first convenient and entertaining online shopping environment. While dynamic pricing was common in the offline world, applying it in an Internet-based engine that anyone around the world could access was a major insight. The system benefited both sellers, who could easily reach a global audience, and buyers, who would be able to virtually scour shops they might have never been able to visit otherwise. The low cost of hosting Internet auctions made it easier for sellers and buyers to participate as well. eBay immediately captured the imagination of millions of consumers.

The firm benefited from word of mouth via both online and offline communication channels. It also promoted the site through viral marketing as well as by outlining the benefits of joining the community. Of course, as the number of users increased, the site became more valuable to all its users. Buyers were able to find a greater variety of goods, and sellers had more people to buy their products. Last, eBay kept a strong presence at trade shows to teach consumers about the auction service and attract the customers most likely to be interested in using the service.

Exploration/Expansion.   eBay's exploration/expansion levers are concentrated in one key area: the website itself. By creating an easy-to-use search engine and a community that users could explore without difficulty, eBay could convert visitors to customers. As eBay gained customers, the growing community fostered exploration and expansion. As more sellers signed on, eBay developed an increased number of distribution channels. The larger number of sellers advanced users into the exploration/expansion stage simply because there were more items to browse and bid on.

Commitment.   eBay relied primarily upon the enabling community product lever to advance users into the commitment phase. The quality of the community correlated directly to the quality of the eBay product, and proved to be the most effective tool in the early days for advancing users to the commitment stage and keeping them there.

eBay in 1998–1999

Once eBay had advanced a significant number of users into the exploration/expansion phase, the firm needed to move its focus to sustaining commitment (for which levers affected by the 2Is proved perfect). As the firm's needs changed, so too did its Marketspace Matrix (see Exhibit 13.12). eBay began to utilize more levers, and the additions were concentrated in two places—the commitment column in the matrix became heavily utilized, as did the community row. eBay also sought to drive awareness and exploration among new users, but the firm designed the bulk of the new levers to advance users to the commitment stage and keep them there.

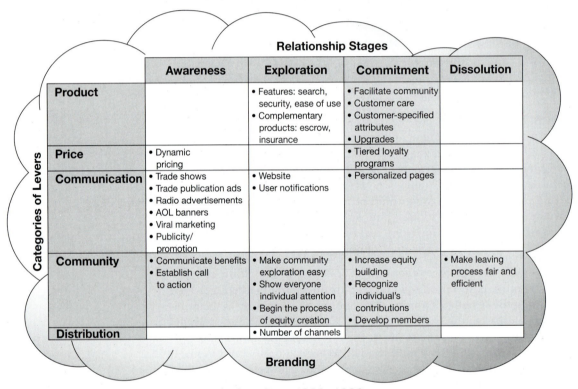

EXHIBIT 13.12   Marketspace Matrix for eBay, 1998–1999

Awareness.   eBay began its first major advertising campaign in late 1998. This included strategic alliances with online partners such as AOL and the now defunct Go.com to drive awareness through banner ads and sponsorships. The auction company also started a radio and print campaign with the "You just might find it on eBay" slogan, and sponsored the auction of famous memorabilia to generate free media exposure and promote the eBay brand as the leading online auction source.

Exploration/Expansion.   eBay focused on enhancing the product by adding new attributes and features to the service, including new categories for goods (such as electronics, computers, and stamps and coins), faster searching, and promotional options. For example, sellers could pay extra to have their items featured on the eBay homepage or to highlight their offerings with a yellow band. eBay also began offering complementary products, such as insurance and an escrow service, to protect buyers from fraud after the sale. The service also improved its e-mail notification service to inform buyers when they were outbid, along with a daily e-mail reminding them of the status of all items they were bidding on.

eBay also enhanced its community offerings. First, many of the product improvements made the community easier to explore. Second, eBay built important mechanisms for equity creation, including the Feedback Forum, which allowed buyers and sellers to rate each other, and thus allowed members to evaluate whether they wanted to deal with a particular user based on the community's recommendations. eBay also built user forums to discuss issues and answer user questions. Thus, veteran eBay users would answer the questions of new and old users alike. This fostered community norms and standards that further served to make the eBay experience reliable and trustworthy, despite the large number of disparate users. Finally, these forums also allowed eBay to show users individual attention—especially since many questions would be answered in minutes. These community levers, which allow for both personalization and interactivity, also served to advance users into the commitment phase. As users received positive feedback, for example, they had little incentive to start using another auction service.

Commitment. eBay's community enabling consistently advanced users toward commitment, and then helped sustain that commitment. Customer care was also an important product lever for the firm; eBay tied individualization and interactivity to all its customer care functions. The site provided personalized pages to allow buyers and sellers to track their auctions, and special customized pages for its power sellers. Moreover, eBay constantly tried to upgrade the software to sustain the enormous user and traffic loads that it endured at peak hours. Occasionally, the system crashed, but eBay was available 362 days per year or more, which translates into 99 percent reliability.

eBay also instituted loyalty programs to reward its best customers. Top sellers could earn the "power seller" rating, which gave customers confidence that a particular seller was consistently trustworthy. Moreover, less frequent users could earn ratings symbols that marked them as customers who had received large numbers of positive reviews (including colored stars that were attached to user names and indicated tiered levels of positive feedback).

These tiered loyalty programs effectively increased member equity in the eBay community. They further recognized individuals' contribution and participation on eBay. Finally, these programs developed members as leaders and guides of the eBay community. Thus, eBay utilized every community lever available in the commitment, exploration/expansion, and awareness phases.

Finally, eBay began improving distribution options for its customers by partnering with firms like iShip, to help buyers estimate shipping costs.

Dissolution. eBay needed the ability to dissolve the relationship with customers who damaged the community—sellers who accepted bids (and money) and then never delivered the merchandise, and buyers who bid and never paid. eBay relied on its community and Feedback Forums to dissuade other users from dealing with the miscreants, but when necessary, eBay itself banned users who violated the community's norms. The process generally proved fair and efficient.

A significant pattern emerged in the Marketspace Matrix. eBay's marketing mix focused heavily on the commitment column and the community row—these two focal points represent the key to eBay's success.

eBay, 2000–Present

Resting on its laurels, however, is not an option when investors expect constant growth. Having nearly perfected its community and ability to retain customers, eBay requires new buyers and sellers to continue its impressive history of growth. eBay has pursued an international strategy, both through building international sites and acquiring competitors; but to increase its core business in the United States, eBay continues to improve its service. Moreover, eBay has stepped up its efforts to advance new users into the awareness and exploration/expansion phases of the relationship (see Exhibit 13.13, which shows the levers eBay has applied most recently to focus on these stages).

Relationship Stages

Categories of Levers	Awareness	Exploration	Commitment	Dissolution
Product		• Features: search, security, ease of use • New Auction categories • Complementary products: escrow, insurance, PayPal	• Facilitate P2P community • Customer care • Customer-specified attributes • Upgrades	
Price	• Dynamic pricing • Promotions to encourage new product adoption	• Buy it now! • Promotions to encourage trial	• Tiered loyalty programs	
Communication	• Trade shows • Trade publication ads • Radio advertisements • AOL banners • Viral marketing • Publicity/promotion • Television ads	• Website • User notifications • Television ads	• Personalized pages	
Community	• Communicate benefits early • Establish call to action	• Make community exploration easy • Show everyone individual attention • Begin the process of equity creation	• Increase equity building • Recognize individual's contributions • Develop members	• Make leaving process fair and efficient
Distribution		• Number of channels		

Branding

EXHIBIT 13.13   Marketspace Matrix for eBay, 2000–Present

Awareness.   The most notable change is that eBay launched its first television advertising campaign late in 2000. Instead of the multimillion-dollar branding campaigns other dot-coms launched in 1998 and 1999, eBay waited until its brand had become established as the world's leading online auction service to start using television ads. Moreover, eBay has been promoting its ancillary services, including the recently acquired PayPal for auction payment purposes. This enables anyone with an e-mail address to send or receive payment, and it supplies eBay with a back-end revenue stream. In early 2001, eBay offered free listings to sellers who accepted eBay Payments as a way to generate early adopters to the service. This move was in keeping with eBay's desire to develop its non-auction, value-added, revenue-generating services.

Exploration/Expansion. eBay continues to expand its product categories, and now has special sections for real estate and cars. These new categories attract new users to the site. eBay has also launched a new pricing option for people who are uncomfortable with auctions. By adding a "Buy It Now" button, sellers can offer buyers a fixed price, eliminating the uncertainty of the regular bidding process. This encourages users who might not otherwise participate in the eBay community to join in and buy products.

eBay also continues to augment its offerings; for example, the company struck a deal to provide discounted UPS shipping to all eBay users through Mail Boxes Etc. franchises. eBay has also launched a seller's assistant, which allows sellers with multiple listings to manage their merchandise more efficiently. Last, of course, eBay has heavily promoted its eBay Payments service, another complementary product offering.

The Marketspace Matrix clearly illustrates a firm's marketing mix. Selecting levers across the matrix does require planning, and the next section illustrates the principles for lever selection.

eBay's Application of the Principles

eBay's series of Marketspace Matrices exemplifies the matrix principles previously enumerated. Not every principle applies in every situation, and some principles will necessarily be weighted more than others.

Which Levers Are Customers Most Responsive To?

Principle 1: Base the Levers on Consumer Behavior. Many of the features and elements of the eBay experience and brand are the direct result of eBay listening to its customers and implementing changes to its site. eBay continually monitors bulletin boards and invites feedback from its users. It even brings heavy users to its San Jose headquarters to solicit their views. Ultimately, it incorporates many of its customers' suggestions into the eBay experience and uses them to enhance the overall user experience.

One of the areas that eBay continually monitors is the "miscellaneous" auction category. eBay refers to this category as its R&D lab, because it is where eBay users push the boundaries of what can be sold on the site. It is in the miscellaneous category that eBay first began selling automobiles, real estate, and computers. eBay's product design is a direct result of monitoring and understanding consumer behavior.

Principle 2: Choose Levers to Effect Change. eBay did not start a massive, national advertising campaign until it had developed both its community and its website. By waiting, eBay ensured that when users moved from awareness to exploration, they would come to a vibrant community with an effective website that promoted advancement to the next stage. Driving users to a nonfunctional site with few products for sale would have been a waste of money. Instead, eBay timed the application of the levers appropriately.

Principle 3: Measure the Impact of Each Lever.   Recently, joint market research by Accenture and eBay found that merchants often earn up to twice as much by selling their liquidation stocks on eBay instead of through traditional liquidation channels. For example, the study found that PCs with a liquidation value of $36 could be sold on eBay for between $80 and $130.[8] Based on this research, eBay and Accenture are planning to invest in a new service, dubbed "Connection to eBay." The new service aims to give retailers, manufacturers, and distributors a more profitable way to sell excess or discontinued inventory.

Principle 4: Overcome Barriers to Advancement.   Buyers and sellers will not use the site unless it is easy to use and safe. By developing its website, enhancing searches, and constantly augmenting its product, eBay has chosen product levers designed to make it easy for people to move from awareness to commitment. A specific example is eBay's Feedback Forum. Before a bid is made, prospective bidders have the opportunity to evaluate a seller's transaction history to see how previous bidders have rated the experience of buying from him or her. After each transaction, users have the opportunity to add to the other party's profile, giving positive points for appropriate behaviors and negative points for inappropriate ones. Sellers who do not play by the rules are suspended from trading.

Which Levers Are Least Likely to Generate a Competitive Response?

Principle 5: Anticipate Your Competitors' Likely Responses.   The shift in lever selection patterns over time reflects eBay's responsiveness to the competitive environment. For example, by heavily investing in commitment levers in 1998–1999, eBay solidified its user base. But by 2000, competition dictated the need for both a stronger brand and the attraction of new users. Adding television advertising helped promote eBay to a whole new generation of potential buyers and sellers, and preempted eBay's competitors.

Principle 6: Build on Your Firm's Skills and Resources.   Television advertising is something that eBay can undertake much more easily than its smaller competitors, because eBay can spread the significant costs of a television campaign over a larger number of transactions. This is one type of promotion that cannot be easily duplicated by online competitors, and it helps eBay sustain market-share dominance. Other types of levers that are affected by eBay's relative scale include the ability to invest in and continually update product design, to provide the widest assortment of items for sale, and to become the low-cost provider. Once self-perpetuating scale advantages are achieved, smaller competitors find it increasingly difficult to compete.

Which Levers Work Best Together?

Principle 7: Look for Interaction Effects.   eBay has taken advantage of interaction effects between various levers. For example, eBay entered into a co-branding agreement with Visa in April 2000.[9] EBay agreed to promote Visa as a primary payment option. The agreement allowed eBay to accept Visa debit and credit cards as payment for small-volume sellers. The payment processing fees on Visa transactions were temporarily waived to encourage new users.

This is a win-win situation for both Visa and eBay because the branding and promotional levers are consistent with the advantages of both brands. Visa is the brand that is "everywhere you want to be," and so partnering with one of the most dominant online businesses is important to maintaining that position. Similarly, eBay wants to ensure that its customers have the convenient purchasing options they want, and to strengthen its brand. The alliance with Visa does both. In addition, at least for the trial period, it stimulates demand for eBay because there is no cost to sellers to use the card. The Visa co-brand interacts with the eBay brand, as well as the price promotion, to generate superior returns for eBay.

Principle 8: Integrate Across Levers. eBay has developed a very integrated approach to its levers. In developing a mature and sustainable sense of community, for example, eBay has stressed consistency across people, process, cultural, and technological characteristics. It has emphasized the development of a large number of core users who participate in the community on a frequent basis. Efficient communication processes have been developed to facilitate member interactions. The development of a strong culture has been promoted through a clear mission and the development of a clear community hierarchy (e.g., through the Feedback Forum). Finally, the technologies that are used within eBay are supportive of the desired outcomes. The result is a community that has rapidly matured and that contributes a great deal to the value of eBay's offering.

Which Levers Are Consistent with Strategy?

Principle 9: Levers Create the Position. eBay's position as "the world's online marketplace" is reinforced through every lever. Each one emphasizes simplicity, ease of use, and product performance for both buyers and sellers. As the No. 1 general auction service on the Internet, buyers and sellers alike recognize that eBay is where the action is. Individuals and businesses interested in selling their goods think of eBay first, because of its integrated strategy. The integration is clear from the branding, product, price, community, promotion, and distribution levers. Whether you are a potential, new, or existing user, eBay provides a consistent, integrated message across every point of interaction and over time. Each lever works in concert with the others to create a clear eBay personality.

Principle 10: Focus on Superior Customer Value. All of the levers that have been discussed underline the value that eBay provides for its customers. eBay creates a strong sense of community among its users; the site's community-based culture is reminiscent of the early days of traditional commerce in which face-to-face transactions were commonplace. eBay encourages users to invest in their relationship with the firm. eBay offers individualization options for keeping track of transaction histories, and encourages users to evaluate other buyers and sellers through the Feedback Forum feature. Finally, eBay is a well-designed service that stimulates repeat interactions. eBay knows that by creating a superior offering it attracts more buyers and sellers, which in turn increases the value delivered to its customers.

1. What is a buyer–seller relationship? How can these relationships vary?

A relationship is defined as a bond or connection between the firm and its customers. This bond may be strong, weak, or nonexistent, and it can be based on either logic or emotion. An example of a logical bond is a realization that the customer simply cannot get a better product elsewhere. However, strong relationships typically have an emotional dimension as well—think of your relationships with family and friends. Buyer–seller relationships can be strong, but generally they are not as powerful as the connections we have with people who are close to us. Buyer–seller relationships are based on exchange, where each party expects, or perhaps even demands, value for what is given.

2. Why is integrated lever selection important in a marketing plan?

Integrated campaigns ensure that levers complement one another and thus drive customers through the relationship stages more effectively.

3. How did eBay's application of the Marketspace Matrix change over time?

eBay first focused on advancing users into the awareness and exploration/expansion stages. The next phase of its matrix involved building community and sustaining commitment. Once the community was established along with a large user base, eBay again returned to bringing new users into the community through the awareness and exploration/expansion phases.

4. What are the four categories of principles for lever selection?

- Which levers are customers most responsive to?
- Which levers are least likely to generate a competitive response?
- Which levers work best together?
- Which levers are consistent with strategy?

5. What are the key principles for lever selection within the Marketspace Matrix?

Principle 1: Base the levers on consumer behavior.

Principle 2: Choose levers to effect change.

Principle 3: Measure the impact of each lever.

Principle 4: Overcome barriers to advancement.

Principle 5: Anticipate your competitors' likely responses.

Principle 6: Build on your firm's skills and resources.

Principle 7: Look for interaction effects.

Principle 8 : Integrate across levers.

Principle 9: Levers create the position.

Principle 10: Focus on superior customer value.

1. Try to describe the Marketspace Matrix of a firm you admire. Identify all of the ways in which the firm has contacted you or interacted with you. Assess its strategies on the basis of the principles we have listed in this chapter. Does the firm's Marketspace Matrix help you understand why you admire the firm? Explain.

2. Pretend that you are an entrepreneur who wants to go online in a category of your choice. What would your Marketspace Matrix look like? Which levers would you emphasize and why? How do these levers differ from those used by firms that are well-established in the market? You will need to visit existing firms to assess their strategies.

3. Assess eBay's strategy from 1995 to the present. Can you update the strategy to the time you are reading this text? What is eBay doing differently? Do you agree with its current strategy?

[1]Streitfeld, David. 2000. The cutting edge: Focus on technology. *Los Angeles Times,* 2 October.

[2]Garvin, David A. (1987), "Competing on the Eight Dimensions of Quality," *Harvard Business Review*, November–December, p 101–109.

[3]Marckini, Fredrick (2002), "Search Engines Deserve More of Your Dollars," *B to B, Chicago*, June 10, Vol 87, Issue 6.

[4]Ailawadi, Kusum L., Donald R. Lehman, and Scott A. Neslin (2001), "Market Response to a Major Policy Change in the Marketing Mix: Learning from Procter & Gamble's Value Pricing Strategy," *Journal of Marketing*, 65 (January), 44–61.

[5]Zoglio, Michael and Luc Wathieu (2000), TiVo, Harvard Business School Case (9-501-038), Jan. 8, 2001.

[6]Samu, Sridhar, H. Shanker Krishnan, and Robert E. Smith (1999), "Using Advertising Alliances for New Product Introduction: Interactions Between Product Complementarity and Promotional Strategies," *Journal of Marketing*, 63 (January), 57–74.

[7]Reyes, Sonia (2002), "Kellogg set to Pop new product, packaging, ads," *BrandWeek*; New York, May 20, 2002, Vol 43, Issue 20, page 5.

[8]Webb, Maynard (2002), "eBay, Accenture to Link Consumers to Manufacturers' and Retailers' Inventories," *Electronic Commerce News*; Potomac; May 13, 2002, Vol 7, Issue 10.

[9]Anonymous (2000), "EBay Marketing Agreement to Promote Visa," *Card News*, Potomac; Apr 5, Vol 15, Issue 7.

CHAPTER 14

Designing the Marketing Program for *The Lord of the Rings*

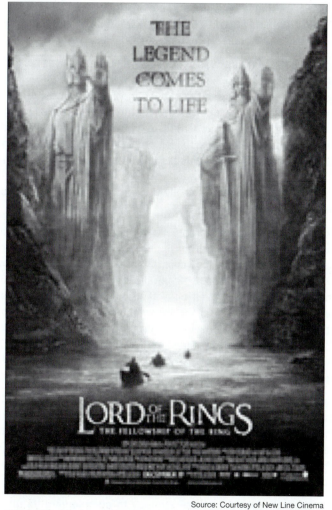

Source: Courtesy of New Line Cinema

EXHIBIT 14.1   "The Lord of the Rings" Theatrical Poster

With substantive input from Heather Kuehnel

In December 2001, New Line Cinema released the first of three films based on the *Lord of the Rings* trilogy by J.R.R. Tolkien. The film, titled *The Lord of the Rings: The Fellowship of the Ring*, won four Academy Awards (from 13 nominations) and garnered more than $313 million at the U.S. box office[1] and more than $860 million worldwide.[2] The movie hit theaters in December 2001, but the initial marketing campaign began two and a half years earlier, with the launch of the official website (*www.lordoftherings.net*) in May 1999. That was also the only place where the first previews were viewable when they were first released in April 2000. Demand was so high that more than 1.7 million copies of the preview were downloaded in 24 hours,[3] and the resulting coverage by print and broadcast media resulted in millions of dollars of promotional value.

By every measure, the integrated marketing efforts for the film proved invaluable in creating momentum for New Line's broader marketing program. Among the online marketing milestones: Online ticket sales accounted for 8.25 percent of the opening weekend's box office receipts; the website won *PR Week*'s New Media Website of the Year award; and the online tactics were the subject of feature articles in *Wired Magazine*, *The New York Times*, *The Wall Street Journal*, *Entertainment Weekly* and *The Los Angeles Business Journal*.

The *Lord of the Rings* trilogy was written by J.R.R. Tolkien in 1954, and more than 100 million copies of the books have been sold. Peter Jackson, who directed the film, said he had always wanted to see a film version of the literary classic, but that it was not until the latter part of the century that he realized the technology existed that would allow him to film his own vision of Tolkien's Middle-earth. A widespread interest in all things Tolkien created a unique business opportunity. New Line Cinema could support Jackson's broad vision, its risk mitigated by a strong consumer following that wanted to see the story brought to the screen. And consumer interest was especially in one profitable segment, young males who attend movies frequently.

Simultaneously producing all three films at once (one for each novel in the trilogy) would require a larger upfront financial commitment than producing one film at a time. It would also, however, streamline the production process and would yield lower overall costs. No studio had ever produced multiple films simultaneously without a proven box-office hit to launch the series, and New Line had never produced a project approaching this scale. The budget for the three films was a hefty $270 million, though it would have been much higher if not for the decisions to shoot the three films simultaneously and to film the entire series in New Zealand, which provided the disparate scenery and visual resources required for the production in one place.

Current entertainment economics favor franchise or sequel products. The return on investment for licensing, merchandising, and distribution are usually higher when consumers are already aware of the product. Also, sponsors often seek to align themselves with brands that have been adopted in the public consciousness. For these reasons, these products enjoy a competitive advantage over nonfranchise products.

New Line used an unusual release strategy to complement its unusual trilogy project. For three years in a row, it would open a film over the December holidays. This ensured momentum for the property, as the short time between releases allowed audiences to anticipate the journey of the film characters. Additionally, it created a highly charged, compressed timeline for the videotape and DVD releases. Those summer releases would create momentum for the next theatrical marketing window.

The purpose of this chapter is to give an integrative summary of the concepts of this book by using this extremely detailed and effective online marketing program as an example. Emphasis will be placed on the Marketspace Matrix and the use of marketing levers to move consumers through the relationship stages.

QUESTIONS

Please consider the following questions as you read this chapter:

1. How should a firm define its goals for each of the relationship stages? How did New Line Cinema define these goals?

2. How did New Line Cinema tie its marketing plan to the "Lord of the Rings" brand?

3. What online levers did New Line Cinema use in "The Lord of the Rings" marketing plan?

4. What offline levers did New Line Cinema use for "The Lord of the Rings?"

5. How successful was the integration of offline and online levers?

6. How do the 2Is affect the choice of marketing levers?

7. Is an online marketing campaign always appropriate?

8. Why was the "Lord of the Rings" campaign so effective?

Introduction

The marketing campaign for the first film, *The Lord of the Rings: The Fellowship of the Ring* (which we will often call *The Lord of the Rings* during this chapter), is a good case study of how a firm plans the relationship stages for several reasons:

- The interactive campaign used an impressive mix of traditional and creative online levers.
- It developed mutually beneficial partnerships.
- It maintained message consistency between online and offline mediums, extending its reach and frequency.
- It advanced customers through the relationship stages and brought a large number of people to the commitment stage.

This chapter is divided into the following sections:

The Lord of the Rings *Brand.* The section gives background on the *Lord of the Rings* brand, including an overview of the trilogy and the worlds of brand licensing and merchandising.

Market Research and Marketing Strategy. This section addresses the primary and tertiary targeting for the marketing program. Segmentation between online and offline consumer groups is addressed, along with marketing strengths and challenges for positioning *The Lord of the Rings*.

Marketing Mix, Targeting and Timing. This section discusses the elements that affect the choice of marketing levers for delineating relationship stages, as well as the timing of marketing communications for each segment.

Planning the Relationship Stages. This section discusses the connection between the relationship-stage framework and the formulation of a marketing plan. The marketing objectives for each of the four relationship stages are defined, then related to how each were defined in the *Lord of the Rings* marketing campaign.

Online Levers in the Lord of the Rings *Campaign.* This section presents an in-depth analysis of the online levers that New Line Cinema applied to promote *The Lord of the Rings*. The levers are discussed by relationship stage, from awareness to dissolution. Levers that cut across stages are also discussed.

Offline Levers in the Lord of the Rings *Campaign.* The section enumerates and examines the offline levers used in the *Lord of the Rings* marketing plan.

The Success of the Lord of the Rings *Campaign.* The chapter concludes with a synopsis of the marketing plan for *The Lord of the Rings: The Fellowship of the Ring* and assesses the firm's strategy for moving customers through the four relationship stages, with particular attention paid to online levers.

Framing the Market Opportunity: The "Lord of the Rings" Brand

The *Lord of the Rings* trilogy presented New Line Cinema with a challenging business prospect: to develop unique programming while weighing the economics and potential profits. It had no model to emulate—never had there been sequels filmed in their entirety without an initial success at the box office. It needed a successful first release to avoid a diminishing domino effect on the second and third films. To mitigate risk, the property was sold in advance in international markets. Specifically, the development costs, and risks, were shared by international distributors in return for the rights to distribute and market the film in their territory in coordination with the U.S. release date. As with any major theatrical release, there were ancillary revenue factors, including pay-per-view, cable and network television, merchandising and licensing (including video games).

John Ronald Reuel Tolkien's trilogy has influenced generations of readers worldwide and continues to captivate new fans. Tolkien's 500,000-word trilogy is a classic story of a heroic quest set in a time of uncertainty in the land of Middle-earth. It is a tale of good and evil pitted in a struggle over the fate of mankind.

The future of civilization rests in the fate of the One Ring, which has been lost for centuries. Powerful forces are unrelenting in their search for it.

But fate has placed it in the hands of a young Hobbit named Frodo Baggins (played by Elijah Wood in the movies), who inherits the Ring and steps into legend. A daunting task lies ahead for Frodo when he becomes the Ringbearer—to destroy the One Ring in the fires of Mount Doom where it was forged.

Tolkien admirers compared him favorably with Milton, Spenser, and Tolstoy. His English publisher, Sir Stanley Unwin, speculated that *The Lord of the Rings* would be more likely to live beyond his and his son's time than any other work he had printed.[4]

W.H. Auden summed up the enduring nature of Tolkien's work in his 1954 review of *The Fellowship of the Ring*: "Lastly, if one is to take a tale of this kind seriously, one must feel that, however superficially unlike the world we live in its characters and events may be, it nevertheless holds up the mirror to the only nature we know, our own; in this, too, Mr. Tolkien has succeeded superbly, and what happened in the year of the Shire 1418 in the Third Age of 'Middle-earth' is not only fascinating in A. D. 1954 but also a warning and an inspiration. No fiction I have read in the last five years has given me more joy than *The Fellowship of the Ring*."[5]

The Tolkien "brand" has extended beyond publishing to include a worldwide licensing and merchandising program, including a 1986 Broadway dramatization and a 1978 animated film of the trilogy. Tolkien licensees have produced a large range of merchandise, including collectibles, toys, and games.

Market Research: Defining the Target and the Message

The goal of movie marketing, of course, is ticket sales. Standard research objectives are to identify key audience segments and to determine messaging that will drive them to the box office.

In the case of *The Lord of the Rings*, the strategy was to start with the core audience of devoted Tolkien fans and then work out to the broadest audience possible as the release date approached. This allowed for maximum online leverage as the earlier groups supported the campaign and therefore broadened the audience. Each group moved through the relationship stages at different times, which helped build momentum through evangelism and online buzz.

Early research determined that the primary audience for general marketing was moviegoers between the ages of 13 and 54, with an emphasis on males. This audience may not have read the books, but may have heard of them. The core, preexisting *Lord of the Rings* fans were primarily males between the ages of 18 and 34 and likely to be Internet users. This audience would be likely to frequent the studio's website, *www.lordoftherings.net*. Therefore, online marketing could be used as a direct, low-cost method to reach this valuable audience.

Drill-Down

"The Lord of the Rings": The Segmenting, Targeting, and Positioning Process

The marketing strategy for *The Lord of the Rings* encompassed a broad scope of activities: promotions, tie-ins, movie trailers, and online community. These levers would help move customers through the relationship stages. Before employing any of these, however, New Line needed to segment its market. This would determine how (and to whom) to best promote *The Lord of the Rings*.

The segmentation process used by motion picture companies typically uses standard demographic variables like age and gender. As New Line segmented and targeted its markets for *The Lord of the Rings*, it determined that the core segment would be viewers aged 18 to 34, due to both that group's large potential revenue base and its likelihood of embracing the movie's epic/adventure themes.

The Lord of the Rings, however, was capable of appealing to far more moviegoers than those in the target segment. The trilogy of books is a literary classic, and *The Lord of the Rings* had already become a strong brand in its own right, even securing references in popular music throughout the 1960s and 1970s. New Line understood that *The Lord of the Rings* would attract viewers aged 13 to 54. The challenge then became one of positioning: How could it make the message broad enough to appeal to the widest feasible range of segments, yet be targeted enough to catch the attention of individual groups?

New Line's answer to the problem was an integrated marketing campaign that leveraged many offline and online strategic partnerships. Central, distinct positioning supported both the campaign and the partnerships. New Line's trailers and own promotion of *The Lord of the Rings* focused on overall messages of good versus evil and an epic struggle for the salvation of mankind. This positioning attempted to blanket a broad range of target segments.

For more targeted messages, New Line used a series of strategic partnerships to reach specific demographics and segments. Several key partners were consistent with the traditional image associated with a literary classic, including *National Geographic*, The American Library Association's Teen Read Week, Tolkien publisher Houghton-Mifflin, and the online arm of *The New York Times*.

Other partnerships broadened the reach and targeting for the property. Burger King promoted the film with an aggressive campaign in the month prior to release. E! Online created editorial content for 18 months prior to the first film's release and targeted younger women, a more elusive audience segment for New Line.

The positioning message for *The Lord of the Rings* was more effectively tailored and marketed to specific segments (e.g., educated readers) through strategic partnerships and more specific ad placement (e.g., point-of-purchase book racks and tailored cable programming). Additionally, much of the cost for this subsegmentation, targeting, and positioning was not borne by New Line. Strategic partners usually take responsibility for creating tailored advertising messages and reaching specific segments. Ultimately, New Line's approach to the integrated marketing campaign and strategic partnerships revolved around a distinct central positioning and effectively promoted the *Lord of the Rings* brand to the entire range of targeted segments.

Business/Marketing Strategy

Corporate and Business Unit Strategy

Corporate Strategy: About New Line Cinema.   Founded in 1967, New Line Cinema is a leading independent film producer and distributor. The company developed as a niche player that targeted underserved audience segments, and relied heavily on word-of-mouth and grass-roots marketing. From early productions, including the *Nightmare on Elm Street* horror series and the *Teenage Mutant Ninja Turtles* franchise, New Line grew by nurturing new film-makers and creating films that traditional studios would not undertake. Its roster includes David Fincher's *Seven* and Paul Thomas Anderson's *Boogie Nights* and *Magnolia*, as well as more traditional films such as *The Mask, Dumb and Dumber, The Wedding Singer, Rush Hour,* and the *Austin Powers* series.

After its acquisition by Turner Broadcasting in 1994 and Turner's acquisition by Time Warner in 1997, New Line began to produce more competitive, larger-budget productions. This led to the production of the *Lord of the Rings* trilogy.

New Line was uniquely suited to develop *The Lord of the Rings*, partly because of a corporate culture that was extremely supportive of the independent development process. Few studios would have given a filmmaker like Peter Jackson the autonomy and creative freedom to film such an ambitious project more than 7,000 miles away from corporate oversight.

New Line licenses its films to ancillary markets, including cable and broadcast television, as well as to international venues. The company, which is now a subsidiary of AOL Time Warner, operates several divisions, including in-house theatrical distribution, marketing, home video, television, acquisitions, production, licensing, and merchandising units.

Business Unit Strategy: About the Interactive Marketing Department. The Interactive Marketing department is a four-person unit of the Theatrical Marketing department. In line with overall strategic objectives, its goal is to drive moviegoers to the box office through the use of online publicity, promotions, advertising, and content-based aggregation vehicles (including websites, syndicated promotional units, and marketing partnerships). As a business unit, it focuses on finding ways to integrate interactive initiatives among the parent company and the multiple online and offline divisions of AOL Time Warner, taking advantage of the broad distribution mechanisms that the umbrella corporate resources make possible.

The Interactive Marketing department at New Line was a good match for the sensibilities of *Lord of the Rings* audiences, having created successful community programs and viral campaigns for projects that appealed to disparate audience segments.

Marketing Strengths and Challenges for "The Lord of the Rings"

When assessing the landscape of the marketplace and determining the marketing strategy, it is beneficial to first determine the strengths and challenges of the brand.

In this case, the benefits were clear early on. There was strong early film awareness, according to National Research Group, an entertainment market-research firm. It found that *The Lord of the Rings* was many consumers' first choice for a movie to see during the 2001 Christmas season—even six months prior to the release.[6] The film had something for everyone, which translated into multidimensional marketing capabilities. The action sequences would appeal to younger males, while the romantic aspects would appeal to females. Research showed that up to one-third of moviegoers had read at least some part of Tolkien's trilogy and had an interest in the film. Further, another one-fourth of moviegoers were aware of the novels but had not read them.

Among the benefits for online marketing possibilities was that the core fan base tended to be very active online, providing a great opportunity for viral marketing. Further, secondary fans were active seekers of entertainment information.

Building a website with depth and breadth would make it possible to please various audience segments through a buffet-style approach. Hard-core science-fiction and *Lord of the Rings* fans could get behind-the-scenes information about the film's production, while others could explore the film's Middle-earth setting and its various creatures and cultures.

The built-in audience also presented a challenge. The core fan base who loved the books would not automatically embrace any film. In fact, the Internet could be a liability if the core fans turned against the film—bad buzz travels fast online. The challenge was to instill trust early on in this ready fan base.

Marketing Strategy

As mentioned in the Chapter 3, strategy construction is not always done through a perfectly defined sequence of steps. For New Line Cinema, early audience research created the foundation for the segmentation portion of the marketing strategy. Afterward, it was important to further define each segment, identify subsegments, and determine their unique value with regard to the Internet. Targeting and timing were essential and proved to be a key factor in getting the most leverage out of the plan.

Once the "who" and the "when" (segmentation and targeting/timing) were established, the positioning of the film needed to be examined for online/offline continuity and audience appeal. For *The Lord of the Rings*, the overall positioning could be broken down and, in a sense, customized for each audience segment for maximum appeal on the Internet. Once a good understanding of the segments, the timing, and the positioning was established, the process of choosing the most effective levers for the marketing mix began.

Segmentation. The potential audience varied in demographics and psychographics. As discussed previously, the core, pre-existing *Lord of the Rings* fans were targeted separately from general moviegoers.

Targeting and Timing. While the basic goals of awareness, exploration, commitment, and dissolution remain the same across all audience segments, the specific objectives and the timing of the execution will be different for each group. Developing a clear set of goals for each group simplifies the selection of levers later and allows each lever to be customized to the objective at hand. The timing of the relationship stages is key in building effective relationships with consumers.

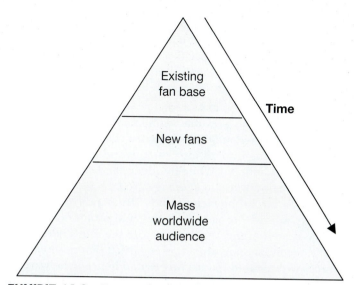

EXHIBIT 14.2   Expanding the Base

- *Core* Lord of the Rings *Fans.* These fans would eventually become evangelists for the movie, so it was important that the tactics for that group begin early. New Line needed to instill trust and assure them that the movies would be high-quality adaptation of the books. Early marketing focused on online awareness to build the base community and gain trust. The initial goals were to create evangelism to carry through to the next audience segment, and to encourage viral marketing to drive campaign momentum. Additional objectives included community building through close coordination with fan websites and established Tolkien groups.
- *Tier 2 (Secondary) Fans.* To broaden the audience beyond the core fans, New Line used specific promotions to appeal to additional audience

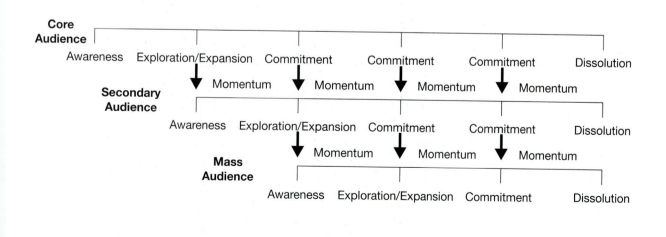

EXHIBIT 14.3   Targeting and Timing

segments. Internet marketing permitted a long-lead, low-cost delivery platform to build relationships through distinct editorial content, which appealed to each group specifically. The timing of these segments would affect the broader audience as additional messaging was introduced near the imminent release of the product.

- *Mass Worldwide Audience.* The mass audience was targeted through multiple media formats and by previous online marketing awareness and expansion efforts directed at other segments. (Evangelism by core groups drove messaging into offline channels and served as awareness levers with broad audiences.) While frequency and consistency of marketing efforts were important in keeping core fans and secondary fans excited, recency was a strong factor in box-office choices by the mass public. This explains why broad advertising and promotional programs were so concentrated in the weeks just before the film's release. With core fans and secondary fans already on board at that point, all available resources were geared toward broader audiences who were ready to plan their weekend entertainment or buy movie tickets. Viral marketing gave credibility and value to the movie's hype, while broader online support from national promotional partners and licensees served as reach vehicles. The mass audience requires compressed movement through the relationship stages. Supporting partner efforts and offline channel support helped to drive momentum and achieve the objective.

Positioning.   Once the audience segments were defined, the positioning of the film had to be decided, with the offline and online positioning working together to provide campaign consistency. The best positioning for the film was determined to be a visually stunning action/adventure with a classic good-versus-evil story that focuses on a ring with great powers. Communications about the plot would focus on the ring—that the ring has powers, that there is a fight for possession of the ring, and that the ring must be destroyed in order to save the world. The marketing needed to communicate that the film would deliver compelling action and epic adventure, coupled with impressive technical effects including the settings, the landscape, the costumes, and the creatures.

Although the positioning was to remain consistent between offline and online communications, the ability to customize for various segments online did allow for slight variations. Both online and offline individual advertising campaigns were tailored for male and female audiences.

Online Marketing Mix.   New Line Cinema utilized at least 25 online levers—some creative, some traditional—to advance customers through the relationship stages. While some clearly applied to only one relationship stage, others cut across multiple stages. The latter will be discussed in their primary categories and will be noted in other sections.

> *Viral Marketing.* New Line took advantage of the fact that *Lord of the Rings* fans would want to spread news about the film trilogy. The studio's viral marketing effort formed the core of its community-based levers and became a powerful tool for generating awareness. The first

Lord of the Rings newsletter sent by the studio generated over a click-through rate of more than 50 percent, but the viral component was equally impressive: More than 25 percent of recipients forwarded it to friends.

Partnerships. New Line found many firms that were eager to co-brand with a *Lord of the Rings* property, and partnerships that New Line developed, such as the AOLTW Roadrunner cable partnership, proved to be a win for both parties.

Shared Content. New Line provided content to a wide variety of websites, most of it "advertorial"—part advertisement, part editorial. Such sharing increased the reach and frequency of the promotional content New Line created for the movie.

The 2Is. A large number of the Internet-based levers used in the *Lord of the Rings* marketing plan, such as downloadable viral content, took advantage of the medium's individualization and interactivity. The result was measurable success in moving Internet users from awareness to commitment, as illustrated by the high number of downloads and viral assets accessed by users on the official website.

The offline marketing campaign also employed a variety of traditional levers, and was notable for several reasons:

Consistency with the Brand. New Line's advertisements and partnerships consistently reflected the spirit and sensibilities of Tolkien, his characters, and the larger theme of good triumphing over evil. Partners shaped their campaigns to align with the style of the film marketing and to embrace the message of working to benefit the community and helping others.

Partnerships. Like the online component, the offline part of the marketing plan relied heavily on mutually beneficial partnerships.

Saturation. The marketing plan generated significant reach and frequency by using multiple communication levers.

Consistent Call to Action: All offline advertisements referred users to *www.lordoftherings.net* or the America Online keyword "Lord of the Rings."

Pricing

Because film production and distribution is a mature industry that has an established pricing model, New Line Cinema did not implement pricing initiatives specifically for *The Lord of the Rings*. Therefore, we will examine pricing issues across the industry.

While there is strong competition among movie studios to drive customers to the box office, the pricing structure is not solely in the hands of studios. Individual theater chains, called exhibitors, share in box office receipts and are involved in determining what consumers will pay. Most consumers are aware that movies are becoming increasingly costly to produce and market. Additionally, in recent years, many exhibition chains have been forced into financial reorganization as a result of offsetting costs associated with building to meet consumer demand while carrying the prior costs of antiquated

---

Drill-Down

Driving Marketing Momentum with an Online Event

Objectives

In April 2000, New Line Cinema launched the first preview footage of *The Lord of the Rings* exclusively on the film's official website (*www.lordoftherings.net*). There were three objectives for this promotional campaign:

1. To show the early adopters that the films would be of high quality and to instill confidence for the product among the most important and critical fan base.

2. To "give something to the fans," as per the request of the film's director, Peter Jackson.

3. To drive awareness and online buzz for both the movie and the official website.

The online launch preceded any other marketing efforts by New Line and was supported only by online, grass-roots efforts.

Execution

New Line Cinema asked webmasters and editors of fan websites to promote the event. Fansite promotional servicing was established via daily e-mail alerts, which included countdown images and accompanying promotional text, sent each evening at midnight to Tolkien site webmasters. This allowed webmasters to be directly tied to the launch event, while the distribution timing created an engaging challenge to be the first to update their websites. The intention was to coordinate a global countdown to the launch of exclusive Internet preview footage of the film on April 7, 2000.

Results

Coordinating the power of the community resulted in a historic event with several milestones:[7]

- More than 1.7 million downloads of the preview footage within 24 hours
- More than 6.6 million downloads within the first week
- More than 10 million downloads within 21 days

These results were outstanding, considering the previous record holder was the fourth installment of the *Star Wars* franchise. The preview for *Star Wars, Episode I: The Phantom Menace* was downloaded 1 million times in 24 hours, 3.5 million times within the first week, and 8 million times within 38 days.

The online launch proved valuable to New Line Cinema by creating momentum for the broader marketing program. The online event received print coverage in *Newsweek*, *The New York Times*, *The Wall Street Journal*, *USA Today*, and the *Los Angeles Times*, and broadcast coverage on CNN, MTV, *Access Hollywood* and the E Entertainment Network. The resulting millions of dollars of promotional value helped to solidify major offline promotional partnerships.

---

exhibition facilities. Most theater chains garner the majority of their revenue from weekend screenings; on weekdays, many operate at a loss.

Movie studios and exhibitors divide the revenue from each ticket sale according to a pre-negotiated rate. Exhibitors also derive significant profits from concessions sales (popcorn, candy, food, and soda). Neither studios nor exhibitors support broad consumer admission discounts; however, discounted rates for seniors, students, and matinee showings are standard.

Exhibitor loyalty programs such as AMC's Movie Watcher program attempt to tie frequent moviegoers to a specific theater chain by offering benefits including discounted or free concession items. Discounted or free admission is only occasionally offered.

In contrast to theaters' established pricing, the associated home-entertainment and ancillary products have variable pricing. DVD and videocassette titles that are slated primarily for rental are traditionally priced higher than those expected to have high consumer sales. Books, soundtracks, and licensed merchandise all employ varied pricing methods that are based on their individual business models.

Customer Experience

Most users of the studio's *www.lordoftherings.net* website are in the commitment stage. Of course, a broad range of other consumers visit, but this quote from a feedback e-mail sent six months before the first film's release is typical: "Thanks for the great website. I especially enjoyed the frame-by-frame breakdown of the trailer. I can't wait to see this movie! I already plan to see it at least twice. Some of the greatest heroes in all literature are in those novels."

In planning the appropriate online *Lord of the Rings* experience, New Line Cinema faced a challenge: How would it engage the core fans without discouraging novices? Those newcomers could feel excluded if the website sent the message that one needed to have read Tolkien to enjoy the film.

To integrate the online and offline experience, New Line took traditional offline assets and repurposed them to leverage Internet strengths. For example, the website featured frame-by-frame breakdowns of the theatrical trailer as individual images and photo galleries that allowed downloading.

Exhibit 14.4 articulates the stages that New Line Cinema utilized for the *www.lordoftherings.net* website. User groups could move through the relationship categories at their own pace, depending on the timing of offline exposure and individual on-site interaction.

Stages	Special "Metrics" for *The Lord of the Rings*
Experiencing Functionality	• Trailer and video materials readily available for viewing • Navigation is simple and clear for downloads, community, and cast and crew information • Easy signup for e-mail and promotions on homepage • Direct links for actions including ticketing shop and merchandising
Experiencing Intimacy	• Website visitors articulate the value they derive from the site experience • Consumers trust the information they find on the site • Strong community develops within site areas • E-mail interaction allows for forwarding to others or linking to the official website
Experiencing Evangelism	• Strong evangelical support from the user base • Trailer and new content postings are seeded throughout community areas as well as on other sites and posting boards • Creates a strong sense of consumer ownership of the brand • The website becomes a trusted friend

EXHIBIT 14.4　Stages of Desired Experience

While it was imperative for New Line Cinema to embrace evangelists early—this group, primarily made up of core fans, was its most important segment—it also needed to avoid overexposing the property. To determine the level of activity and interest among the early-adopting evangelists, New Line showed the first preview footage of *The Lord of the Rings* exclusively on its website. The preview was downloaded 1.7 million times in 24 hours, showing the power of the fan base. Additional indicators included active evangelist involvement in building and sharing content. This was evident by the growth of websites highlighting or dedicated to Tolkien and the movies. An initial review found approximately 300 fan sites; the number grew to more than 300,000 sites by the time the first film was released.

Additionally, evangelists can become quite factious. It was important that New Line support all groups and websites without giving undue preference to some. And though New Line's strategy included supporting evangelists by revealing behind-the-scenes information, it was necessary to request that they not release key plot elements or materials that might cause other evangelists or consumers to think that the movie's entertainment value had been spoiled.

The dynamic component of any marketing campaign—and certainly this one—involves the capability to continuously recalibrate and optimize messaging. Reviewing website logs for customer traffic patterns revealed high-usage areas and gave clues for eliminating inefficiencies and guiding development. One example: Website logs showed that the most popular features on the website, after the movie preview, were downloadable screensavers and background images. New Line dramatically increased the production of screensavers and all downloadable elements, and highlighted these elements in e-mail newsletters. Also, streamlining traffic patterns based on customer experience helped manage the planned four-year editorial content rollout.

Customer Interface

While the online campaign for *The Lord of the Rings* required alignment and consistency with the offline campaign strategy, the official website for the film posed unique challenges. Consumers in the awareness stages visited the website and were advanced to the exploration/expansion stage. The objective was to create an interface that simultaneously speaks to disparate audiences but appeals to consumers who may each encounter the website at different levels in the relationship stages. It was essential that when consumers in an advanced stage virally introduced new users to the official website, the site would not be off-putting to these novices. However, the site had to offer rich, robust experiences for consumers in each relationship stage.

This was accomplished by giving the consumers control of information flow and by using the 7Cs Framework. The goal was to engage visitors with inviting, entertaining top-level messaging. Alignment of context and content would spur consumer exploration and keep engagement high. Compelling messaging and relevant content would rapidly inform consumers of specific production information, and ideally trigger evangelism and commitment.

Context.   The website employed a highly visual style and needed aesthetic and functional balance. Photography, video, and audio materials were incorporated in a highly interactive interface with topic-based content branching that gave consumers control over their individual experience. In contrast to

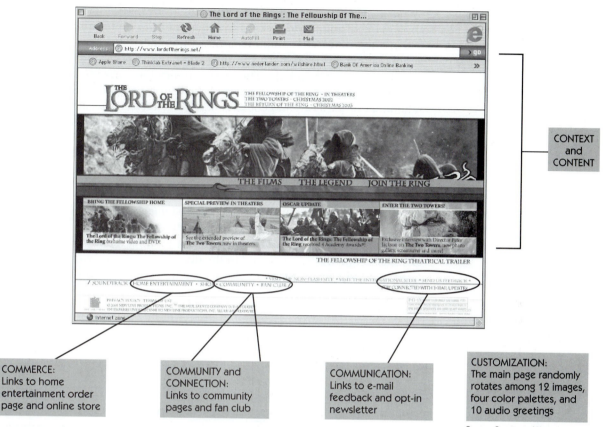

CONTEXT and CONTENT

COMMERCE: Links to home entertainment order page and online store

COMMUNITY and CONNECTION: Links to community pages and fan club

COMMUNICATION: Links to e-mail feedback and opt-in newsletter

CUSTOMIZATION: The main page randomly rotates among 12 images, four color palettes, and 10 audio greetings

Source: Courtesy of New Line Cinema

EXHIBIT 14.5 The 7Cs of the Official Website

many Tolkien websites, the official website used warm colors and light backgrounds for an inviting look-and-feel. The layout and design had to result in intuitive navigation so that it would appeal to many cultures as it was translated into multiple languages.

Content. The content focused on the filmmaking process and the craft and artistry that were employed in this creative process. It included a wealth of visual and descriptive elements, including thousands of photographs, on-set video, and audio interviews.

Community. The official website was developed as both an information resource and a community aggregation point. Co-branded bulletin boards (with partners Lycos, Netscape, and ICQ) had hundreds of thousands of frequent, registered posters. Community was promoted even to those who were not in front of a computer through a wireless community area created through Upoc, a mobile marketing company. It sent text messaging for cellular or handheld delivery to more than 20,000 wireless subscribers, allowing them to choose from multiple movie and Tolkien topics. Wireless consumers could also download *Lord of the Rings* ring tones and icons from cellular carrier VoiceStream.

Customization. There was little customization on the official website. Consumers could sign up for newsletters, wireless updates, or communities, but the marketing effort did not require consumers to register or take any other action to simply enjoy the website.

Communication.   The official website employed several methods to create an ongoing dialogue with users. Firm-to-user e-mail communication was one major communication component and continually reinforced the other six design elements. Consumers who subscribed at the official website received e-mail newsletters regularly. These communications provided value to subscribers by informing them of new website features before other consumers. Additional promotions and contests were directed solely to subscribers, who numbered more than 500,000 by the first film's release. User-to-firm e-mail, facilitated by a feedback link on the homepage, was reviewed by New Line's interactive marketing department and often was instrumental in shaping content development and streamlining customer experience.

Two-way, user-to-user instant messaging was possible through partnerships with ICQ and AOL Instant Messenger. New Line also used a unique instant-messaging technology for this film. An "intelligent agent" called Ring-Messenger was preprogrammed with thousands of responses to a wide array of possible questions. It resulted in the dissemination of key marketing messages while still giving a high-quality consumer experience. This deployment was one of the first fully functioning intelligent agents to go beyond simple automated responses.

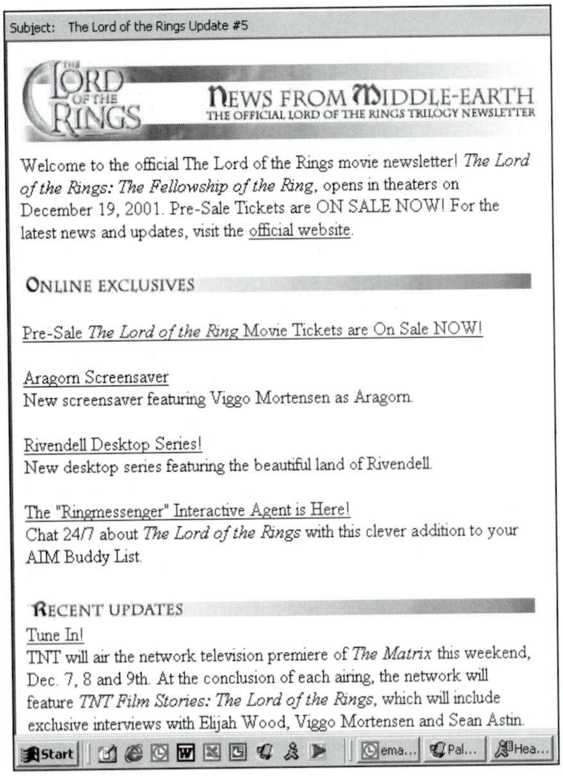

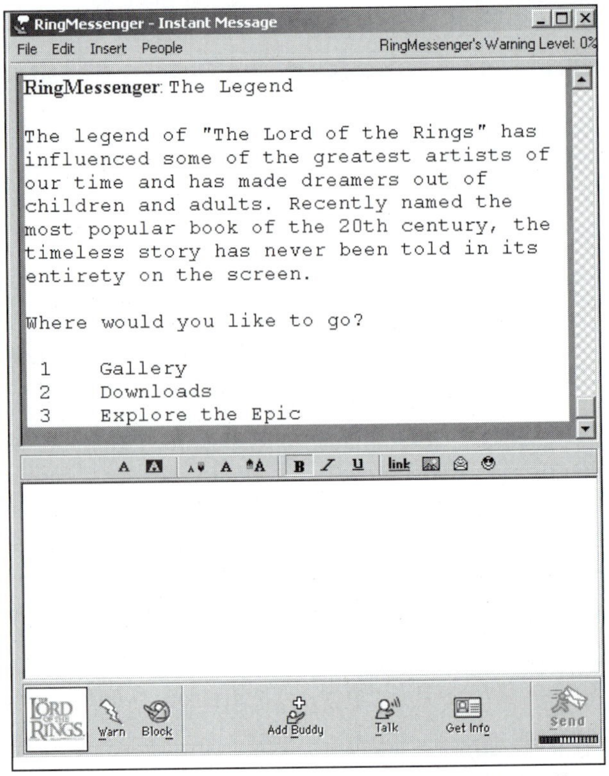

Source: Courtesy of New Line Cinema

EXHIBIT 14.6   Communication: E-Mail and RingMessenger

Connection. The *www.lordoftherings.net* website relied heavily on its relationships with other websites and its positioning as a member of a larger community. The fan-friendly approach was based on New Line's positive track record with fan groups and in the need to develop and maintain online community support. The implementation required commitment from New Line, but surprised fans embraced the opportunity to have an open dialogue with the studio. The official website linked to fan websites, partner websites, and licensees.

Commerce. The website supported several e-commerce initiatives, but the most important was with Moviefone, its partner in selling movie tickets. A link from the homepage went to show times and direct ticketing. Other homepage links directed consumers to the official online store for licensed merchandise sales, an online auction, and an official fan club. E-commerce was included on a consistent basis and integrated into all outreach, affiliate, and direct marketing efforts.

Drill-Down

Is an Interactive Campaign Always Appropriate?

Amid all the buzz and excitement about online advertising and the potential for making campaigns interactive, is there a danger of getting caught up in trying to apply this kind of marketing to cases where it might not be as effective as other marketing communications methods? There are certainly some important considerations to keep in mind before investing valuable resources in an ambitious online campaign.

First, how does the personality of the product match up with the Internet? Products that are seen as cutting edge, for example, match well with the environment of the Web. Other offerings, such as house-cleaning supplies, have less of an Internet marketing feel about them. The entertainment industry is a leader in using the Internet for marketing communications, yet even within the specific category of motion pictures, all are not created equal in terms of Web marketability. The Internet has evolved into an environment where flashy science-fiction and action movies constitute the sweet spot for online marketing—much more so, for example, than romantic or dramatic movies.

While the fit of the offering and the Internet environment is a key consideration, the most important factor is the target audience. Studies show that women tend to use the Internet in a more utility-oriented manner than men do. Women are more likely to go to the Web with a purpose, accomplish their objective, and log off. Men, on the other hand, are more likely to be Web surfers and traditionally have been easier to entice through entertainment-oriented marketing communications. However, marketers are making efforts to level the gender gap by designing marketing messages that are targeted toward harder-to-reach demographics, including women.

For *The Lord of the Rings*, New Line Cinema chose E! Online as a marketing partner primarily because it offered an effective way to reach women online.

Simply putting a marketing message on the Web does not necessarily mean that the target audience will flock to it. Some groups are much easier to reach than others. Considering how the offering's personality matches up with the environment of the Internet and the target audience will help manage expectations and direct the marketing strategy.

Drill-Down

"Lord of the Rings" B2B: International Localization and Translation

Development of the business-to-business strategy for servicing international distribution partners with website assets required proper brand management, planning, and coordination.

New Line Cinema released *The Lord of the Rings* in international markets through a series of distribution agreements with companies that would independently market the property in their respective territories. New Line supports international partner marketing by servicing of domestic marketing materials, brand strategy assistance, and promotional partner planning and integration for each market. New Line Interactive Marketing supports worldwide partner objectives by distributing domestic theatrical marketing website materials and providing support for localization and customization for each territory.

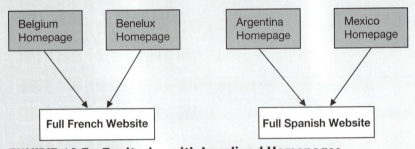

EXHIBIT 14.7   Territories with Localized Homepages

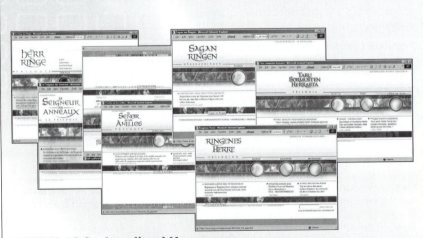

EXHIBIT 14.8   Localized Homepages

For the online brand management of *The Lord of the Rings*, it was imperative to create a global, multilingual footprint that permitted distribution partners to participate with a localized event website. However, customer experience was paramount in online planning, and it was essential to have one global customer-interface style guide. Planning was also required to avoid cross-territory confusion with duplicate websites in the same language. This necessitated that there be only one website per language, although several territories may share the same language. The solution was to create a method for multiple territories to have localized homepages while sharing a unified overall website.

continued

For timely global distribution of marketing materials, an online asset FTP (file transfer protocol) system permitted simultaneous asset distribution for localization. A detailed schedule of development timelines and launch dates were coordinated with each territory. Due to the intense fan interest in *The Lord of the Rings*, all development and FTP areas were secured, and approvals of translated websites were conducted under tight security and management.

This coordination allowed the website to launch in 10 languages, with additional territories joining based on their marketing plans. Certain territories did not have the staff or resources to meet the aggressive translation schedule for editorial content. Based on an analysis of partner territories' marketing needs, it was determined that distributors could choose to develop the entire website or go with a limited customized option. This permitted each territory to choose the strategy that best fit its individual market. Marketing partners that did not have resources were still permitted and encouraged to have a translated homepage, themed localized events, and partner promotion areas in addition to translated territory-specific news and community areas.

International partner websites generated significant traffic. Prior to the launches of the partner websites, approximately 25 percent of the traffic to the official U.S. website was from international visitors. This number dropped to less than 10 percent once major markets had their own active online presence. In January 2002, the German distributor received more than 3 million page views to its *Lord of the Rings* website. Additional territories that benefited from unique local Internet campaigns included the Scandinavian territories, France, Japan, Australia, and England.

Point–Counterpoint

Is Purchasing a Ticket Effectively Dissolution?

Point of View 1

Movie studios' marketing plans should not plan to dissolve relationships with customers who purchase tickets. Instead, the purchase should be viewed as a commitment, and the objective should be to maintain the commitment, which can lead to:

- Viral marketing through positive word of mouth
- Merchandise sales
- Home-entertainment sales (which will be extremely important for the *Lord of the Rings* trilogy in the coming years and should generate significant revenue)

Moreover, the databases of e-mail addresses from online campaigns for successful movies can be helpful in future permission-marketing campaigns. Movie customers are unlikely to be unprofitable long-term customers. They do not meet any of the standard criteria for dissolution, and there is no reason to model them in those terms.

Thus, the goal of commitment stage in a movie's marketing plan should be the consumer's ticket purchase. If ancillary revenues cannot be generated from that customer, the relationship will effectively dissolve itself. While consumers may want to dissolve the relationship after seeing a movie they did not enjoy, there is no reason for studios to encourage them to do so. With Internet marketing campaigns that generate substantial e-mail lists for permission marketing, there is every reason to keep commitment strong to maximize the value of those lists. E-mail lists were used for *The Lord of the Rings* to encourage repeat viewings and also for the announcement of the DVD release. A post-release online survey on the *Lord of the Rings* website revealed that 64 percent of respondents who saw the film "definitely" planned to see it again while it played in theaters. Due to recent compression between the theatrical and video release windows to maximize profits, there is a case to be made against considering dissolution as sound business approach.

continued

Point of View 2

Purchasing a movie ticket constitutes dissolution, from the perspective of a movie studio. Because the vast majority of a movie's revenue typically comes from one-time ticket sales, studios view their customer relationships as effectively terminated upon purchase of the ticket and the viewing of the movie. A user's interaction with the brand after purchasing a ticket is, with few exceptions, essentially irrelevant.

The commitment phase's objective is only to drive intent to buy a ticket. Moviegoers need to have enough of an understanding of the movie to want to see it. Perhaps they will even evangelize it by encouraging friends to view the movie, too. But once the ticket is purchased, the studio does not need to pull any more levers or manage the relationship because, from its perspective, the relationship has ended.

Some might argue that video/DVD rentals and the possibility of sequels means that the relationship should not be considered dissolved. But because the length of time between theatrical and video releases has traditionally been six months or longer, one can argue that the whole cycle needs to be repeated to ensure a large take at the video stores.

New Line Cinema employs the first point of view. It does not consider a ticket purchase as dissolution, and instead attempts to maintain consumer commitment for ongoing product and home-entertainment sales. Additionally, e-mail databases based on proper permissioning are cross-marketed for similar genre initiatives to drive the exploration/expansion stage for related products.

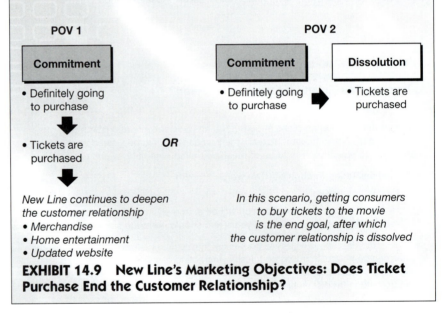

EXHIBIT 14.9   New Line's Marketing Objectives: Does Ticket Purchase End the Customer Relationship?

Design of the Marketing Program

Planning the Relationship Stages

The first step in developing a marketing plan within the context of the relationship stages is to define objectives for each stage. While the basic goals of awareness, exploration, and commitment remain the same across all plans, the specific objectives for individual campaigns will vary. Developing a clear set of goals for each phase simplifies the selection of levers and allows each lever to be customized to the objective.

The online marketing objectives for each phase should provide a path to advance customers to the next phase and take advantage of the 2Is. New Line Cinema's integrated campaign for *The Lord of the Rings* achieved both objectives. Its interactive and individualized components actively managed the movement of users from awareness to commitment.

Awareness.   The *Lord of the Rings* films benefited from pre-existing awareness due to the popularity of the book series. New Line Cinema utilized this awareness, but also targeted a broad consumer market to reach new customers. Awareness of the film went from 36 percent to 85 percent between March 2001 and November 2001. New Line's definition of awareness had three basic points:

- *Recognition.* Consumers should recognize the *Lord of the Rings* brand. Meaning, they should have heard of it before, and know that it is associated with a book and an upcoming film. While the book proved important in developing awareness, levers that allowed reach and frequency of communication were even more critical.
- *Consciousness/Knowledge of the Brand.* Taking brand recognition to the next level, potential moviegoers should be concious of the brand and knowledgable about the film's characters and key themes. Broad themes from the book were exploited as key positioning elements. These components were introduced (through language such as "the epic comes to life") to raise interest levels.
- *Eminence of Product.* Consumers need to understand that J.R.R. Tolkien is considered one of the greatest writers of all time and that the *Lord of the Rings* trilogy was voted "book of the century" in a 1999 poll by Amazon.com. Tolkien's stature as the father of the fantasy genre provided one of the most significant components of the awareness definition for people already familiar with the *Lord of the Rings* franchise.

In short, potential customers reached the awareness stage when they realized that they could see the movie version of *The Lord of the Rings.*

Exploration/Expansion.   The objectives for exploration/expansion focused on attraction, communication, and the development of expectation, which can be segmented into six categories:

- *Understanding.* Moviegoers learn more about the *Lord of the Rings* plot, setting and characters. They discover the lands and cultures of Tolkien's Middle-earth. On the official website, this represents consumers interacting with the primary content areas.
- *Active Learning.* Moviegoers find out more about the movie, including cast members and plot details. On the website this includes expansion into deeper content modules, which focus on the making of the film, or the website map.
- *Desire.* Consumers now begin to consider buying a ticket to see the movie. For those who have not had prior exposure to the books, it may also drive an interest in reading the trilogy.
- *Intent.* Because the online campaign began more than two and a half years before the movie premiered, New Line Cinema created anticipation and commitment among consumers far in advance.

- *Familiarity.* Consumers became extremely familiar with the franchise. This led to increased interaction with the *Lord of the Rings* marketing levers, especially the online components.
- *Spreading the Word.* Moviegoers ask their friends if they know about *The Lord of the Rings*, which leads to awareness generation in those groups.

Users who fail to find interest in the *Lord of the Rings* plot or the technical aspects of the production will naturally dissolve their relationship with the film. New Line Cinema succeeded in generating exploration/expansion in its relationship with moviegoers by building their expectations up to the point where they felt they had to see the film.

Commitment.   Commitment to *The Lord of the Rings* was evident through three possible components:

- *Community.* Consumers become members of groups and posted on websites, developing content based on the films. This high level of interaction with marketing levers increased evangelism.
- *Evangelism.* Many committed *Lord of the Rings* fans recruit others and shepherd them through the awareness stages.
- *Purchase.* Customers finally buy tickets. This is the crucial objective, because ticket sales represent a key percentage of revenue generated by the film.

New Line Cinema selected levers to promote all three of these goals. The studio provided considerable input into the relationship, especially in terms of online content. Levers used to generate commitment also tended to be durable, not one-time promotions.

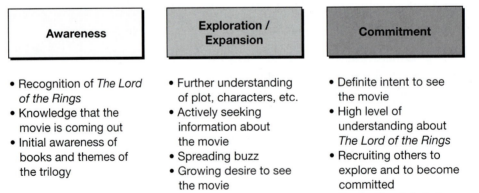

EXHIBIT 14.10   New Line's Objectives across the Relationship Stages

Once its objectives are determined, the marketing team needs to select appropriate levers—both online and offline—to meet those objectives across each relationship stage. Continuing with the *Lord of the Rings* example, this section now turns to a discussion of the online, interactive marketing campaign. Attention will also be paid to offline levers, because of the following reasons:

- The relationship-stages framework works for both online and offline marketing plans; the traditional offline marketing levers function perfectly within the context of this framework, which this campaign demonstrates.
- The *Lord of the Rings* campaign relied on integrated online and offline levers; thus, a discussion of only the online levers would paint an incomplete picture.
- Integrated online and offline plans will generally be more successful than plans that rely on one set of levers.

The "Lord of the Rings" Integrated Plan

New Line Cinema utilized many creative and traditional levers to meet the objectives of its marketing plan. Some applied to only one relationship stage; others cut across multiple stages. The latter will be discussed in their "primary" categories, but noted in other sections.

The plan employed more than 25 online levers, along with more than 25 offline levers. Many of the Internet-based levers took advantage of the 2Is: individualization and interactivity. The result was measurable success in moving Internet users from awareness to commitment.

We now give an overview of the online and offline levers that New Line Cinema used, divided by relationship stage.

Building Awareness with Online Levers

America Online

New Line Cinema's parent company, AOL Time Warner, also owns the flagship America Online Network, the world's largest Internet service provider. Additionally, New Line worked with multiple AOL Web properties to maximize exposure across and beyond the company's substantial network user base, which numbered 32 million subscribers in December 2001. AOL also derived substantial benefits from this campaign: Exclusive *Lord of the Rings* content was released solely through AOL, AOL MovieFone, and other AOL Time Warner online outlets.

The overall focus of the partnership with AOL was to move consumers into the awareness and exploration stages, but it also had the interactive ability to move them into commitment. The different components involved three categories of levers, combined with the individualization and interactivity of AOL.

The Lord of the Rings was prominently highlighted on the AOL welcome screen and in AOL's entertainment section. Additionally, an America Online keyword (Lord of the Rings) gave visitors a one-stop area with links to reviews by other AOL users, news stories about the film, the official website, and, of course, Moviefone, where those now intent on seeing the film could purchase tickets. Users were always one click away from show times and locations via AOL's Moviefone service.

This component of the AOL campaign clearly demonstrates the power of the second I, interactivity. New Line Cinema and AOL designed the promotion of *The Lord of the Rings* in AOL's major content areas to bring customers

Drill-Down

Corporate Synergy: New Line Cinema and AOL

New Line Cinema, a division of AOL Time Warner, was able to leverage unique synergy opportunities in promoting The Lord of the Rings.

Offline exposure through television and print promotion played a key role in driving awareness for the movie. An exclusive debut of the *Lord of the Rings* trailer in September 2001 on the WB Network's *Angel* helped increase awareness in the television show's young female audience. The TNT Network, Time Warner Roadrunner Cable, and Turner Sports leveraged awareness for varied demographics through *Lord of the Rings* broadcast interstitials tied to complementary programming. Immediately prior to the film release, the AOL Time Warner publication *Entertainment Weekly* featured the stars of the movie in a five-cover collectible series that both drove awareness for readers but also allowed the magazine to take advantage of the commitment level of many loyal *Lord of the Rings* fans who collected the entire set. Another company property, Warner Bros. Music, released the movie's soundtrack.

Online, New Line worked with multiple AOL properties to maximize exposure to the network's 32 million subscribers (as of December 2001). Online awareness generated across the AOL flagship service and its Web properties group was expanded via highly accessible levers like an America Online keyword "Lord of the Rings," which was displayed in most offline marketing. New Line provided content—including photos from the set, movie trailers, and screensavers—for syndication across all online service areas, which permitted AOL members to interact with *Lord of the Rings* materials without leaving their preferred website.

The movie was highlighted on the AOL welcome screen and in AOL's entertainment section, and also on AOL Web properties including Moviefone, Netscape, and ICQ in an effort to generate online awareness through online ads, editorial content integra-

continued

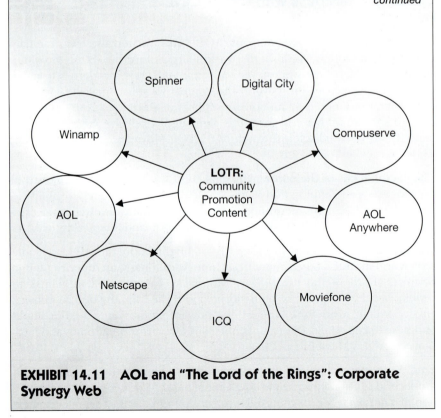

EXHIBIT 14.11   AOL and "The Lord of the Rings": Corporate Synergy Web

tion, and e-mail. While Moviefone generated widespread awareness for *The Lord of the Rings* among frequent moviegoers, awareness was also driven across other key demographics through placement on the Netscape homepage and entertainment sections, community bulletin boards on ICQ and Netscape, and a custom *Lord of the Rings* ICQ client "skin" application. AOL online awareness support extended to other Web properties and business units as well, including AOL Music in its promotion of the movie's soundtrack, and CompuServe's inclusion of *The Lord of the Rings* in its entertainment area and syndication of substantial amounts of content developed by New Line. The Search for the Ring sweepstakes employed all AOL Web properties in a unified promoiton, and the AOL service's welcome screen featured a pop-up ad for advance tickets.

AOL and New Line combined their efforts by making a full range of licensed products for the films accessible in the network. New Line promoted the Shop@AOL effort from outside the AOL network via top-level linking from the New Line store on the official website.

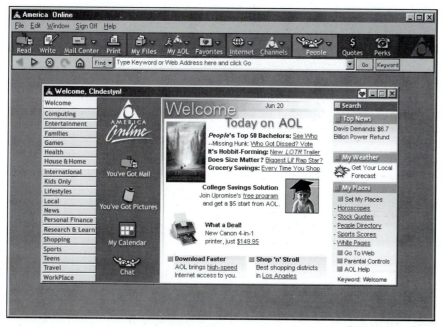

Courtesy of *www.aol.com*

EXHIBIT 14.12   AOL Homepage

into the awareness stage. Millions of users see AOL's welcome screen each day. Those who were interested could click through and quickly enter the exploration phase, perhaps by reading a review or downloading and viewing the movie trailer. The AOL content campaign moved users into the awareness stage, but it was also able to leverage interactivity to allow users to move into exploration and commitment simply and easily.

AOL Web Properties

AOL Moviefone.   Moviefone is the leading online source of movie show times and tickets. The service lets telephone or Internet users enter their zip code and receive information about what movies are playing in their area. Many theaters even allow users to purchase advance tickets. Moviefone was a great fit for the *Lord of the Rings* campaign because research showed that Moviefone users were heavy moviegoers. Its average user attends six times as many movies a year (31.2) as the average American (5.2).[8] Further, 76 percent of its users had attended a movie in the past 30 days.[9]

The Lord of the Rings received substantial promotion, including banner ads, on the Moviefone website. Additionally, hundreds of thousands of promotional e-mails were sent to Moviefone users during the film's opening week. The e-mails contained active links to buy tickets, see the film's trailer, or visit the film's official website.

Moviefone's e-mails, which are delivered to recipients on an opt-in basis, are a textbook illustration of the 2Is at work. First, e-mail recipients tell Moviefone what types of movies they like to see. In other words, they are a self-selecting audience; people who want to see only children's films, for example, would not receive information on *The Lord of the Rings*. Second, e-mails are customized geographically, so moviegoers receive show times only for films playing at theaters near them—making the e-mail highly functional and more likely to be read.

Moreover, the e-mail messages are themselves interactive. Users can move from awareness to exploration by clicking to view the movie's trailer or visiting the *Lord of the Rings* website, or jump directly to commitment by clicking a link that allows them to purchase tickets. Clearly, the Moviefone e-mails show how interactive marketing based on the 2Is can move users from awareness to commitment faster than previously possible.

Netscape.   The Netscape portal, which has more than 40 million registered users[10] and is a division of the AOL Web Properties group, provided strong support to New Line Cinema through promotions that included the Netscape homepage, Netscape entertainment, and broad promtion in targeted areas across its website. Netscape also became an integral community partner by hosting and moderating community bulletin boards dedicated to the trilogy. This added value to both websites: Netscape created promotional programs that drove consumer awareness of the *Lord of the Rings* bulletin boards, and New Line linked to the bulletin boards from the official website.

ICQ.   AOL ICQ is an instant-messaging service with more than 100 million users worldwide. Forty-eight percent of its users are between the ages of 18 and 34.[11] ICQ proved to have high penetration and adoption within the core *Lord of the Rings* fan community. In addition, the members of the ICQ development team were fans of the books and wanted to work with New Line to promote the films. This passion and interest carried great weight with New Line's management team. Many companies saw *Lord of the Rings* partnerships as a business arrangement, but the partnerships that were developed out of a shared vision and commitment were of the highest value to New Line and forged an organic connection with the property.

ICQ supported the property by creating a custom "skin" application, an interchangeable visual interface, unique sound themes and an exclusive *Lord of the Rings* promotional area. ICQ also became a community partner, hosting official bulletin boards and giving the community effort significant promotional support. ICQ programs eventually delivered more than 500 million impressions in support of the film's release.

EXHIBIT 14.13 Moviefone: Content Integration

Netscape and ICQ community integration also supported the commitment stage. This aspect is highlighted later in the chapter in the Drill-Down titled "Community as a Key Lever to Commitment."

Additional Levers. AOL support extended to other Web properties and additional business units. Editorial and advertising programming included promotion of the *Lord of the Rings* soundtrack on AOL Music and a *Lord of the Rings* radio station on AOL Spinner/WinAmp.

CompuServe, which has more than 3 million subscribers accessing its content, communication features, and forums, included *The Lord of the Rings* in all service areas for entertainment and used content that was developed by New Line Cinema and syndicated to multiple AOL editorial and content areas.

AOL Digitial Cities, a collection of city guides, highlighted local promotions for the property, including bookstore events and local talent appearances.

Other AOL Promotions

Search for the Ring Sweepstakes. The AOL Web Properties group worked with New Line to develop a promotion called the Search for the Ring sweepstakes. The interactive sweepstakes gave Web surfers nine chances to win

Lord of the Rings memorabilia and collectibles. The sweepstakes was featured on a number of AOL's popular Web brands, including Netscape, Compu-Serve, Moviefone, MapQuest, AOL.COM, WinAmp/Spinner, Instant Mes-sanger, and Digital Cities. It relied on "RingMessenger," an interactive agent that participants added to their instant-messaging Buddy List, to dispense clues on the location of the hidden rings. Each week, a ring graphic was hid-den on one of the seven websites. The RingMessenger also gave information on the movie, including links to the website for video clips, interviews with the cast and crew, and links to show times and ticketing on MovieFone.

Source: Courtesy of *www.aol.com*.

EXHIBIT 14.14   AOL Search for the Rings Sweepstakes

AOL Service Tie-In.   In addition to the movies and entertainment sections, AOL also promoted *The Lord of the Rings* heavily in all major content areas of its service. During the two weeks prior to theatrical release, AOL launched a pop-up ticketing promotion from its welcome screen. The pop-up screen linked users to Moviefone's *Lord of the Rings* page, which offered online ticketing, clips from the movie trailer, and links to related content on AOL.

Source: Courtesy of *www.aol.com.*

EXHIBIT 14.15   AOL Welcome Pop-Up Advertisement

America Online Network:

- AOL Keyword "Lord of the Rings"
- AOL Welcome, What's New, AOL Today
- AOL You've Got Mail and AOL Celebrity Voices
- AOL Live event with cast
- AOL Entertainment: Cinemaniacs, Celebrities, Coming Soon and Now Playing
- Cannes media event coverage
- AOL Computing Channel: *Lord of the Rings* screensaver promotion
- AOL Men: "Fantasy Women" gallery
- AOL Women: "The Men of *Lord of the Rings*"
- Teens: Feature on Elijah Wood
- AOL Plus: Featured movie on Tower and main movie feature on Entertainment
- AOL Community
- People Connection
- Groups@AOL
- *Lord of the Rings* Group special feature
- AOL Invitations
- *Lord of the Rings* holiday cards of different characters

EXHIBIT 14.16   "The Lord of the Rings" on AOL

Fan Sites

New Line worked closely with fan groups and webmasters of Tolkien websites. These groups created editorial content dedicated to the movies daily. While these groups were already at the commitment relationship stage, their evangelism created awareness in other groups and generated positive buzz through news coverage of their evangelistic activities. New Line provided fan sites with promotional content for their websites and interacted with webmasters continually. It also invited fan webmasters to press activities and film premieres and routinely gave them access to filmmakers and others involved with the films.

As previously mentioned, active fan involvement in building and sharing content about the films encouraged the growth of websites focused on Tolkien and the movies. The 300 fan sites in 1999 grew to more 300,000 by the release of the first film. Key drivers for this explosion in activity were the enthusiasm of the fans and the heightened awareness of *The Lord of the Rings* due to early marketing initiatives. Additionally, publisher Houghton Mifflin reported dramatic increases in sales of the trilogy. All-time book sales doubled, from 50 million to more than 100 million, in the years between the announcement of the films' production and the release of the first film. The interest of new recruits, committed fans, and film enthusiasts combined to create an extremely active user base and high levels of user-generated content.

New Line Contests

New Line Cinema ran a large number of contests on a wide spectrum of websites. The contests gave away merchandise including *Lord of the Rings* T-shirts and posters, and were accompanied by substantial promotional content. Contests were used as an awareness lever to attract users' attention. By providing *Lord of the Rings* content to various websites, New Line also enabled an exploration/expansion lever that could be experienced without visiting an external site. New Line conducted contests on high-traffic portals as well as more targeted websites. Promotions were an effective tool to efficiently target secondary demographics. For example, the teen websites Alloy.com and Bolt.com were selected as entertainment websites with a predominantly young female audience.

Besides generating awareness for the movies, the contests also captured entrants' e-mail addresses and provided an opt-in checkbox that users could click to receive messages about future movies or the home-entertainment release of *The Lord of the Rings*. With this database of eager moviegoers, New Line can target moviegoers based on their past habits and generate awareness for future movies. Moreover, personalized and interactive e-mail is more likely to spur users to jump into the exploration and commitment phases, so proper management of the opt-in e-mail lists should result in effective, low-cost marketing campaigns in the near future.

Online Magazine Promotions

New Line aggressively sought out publicity in online magazines, ranging from the online versions of *People* and *TV Guide* to smaller, less prominent publications. It sent press releases and made the movie's stars available for photo shoots and interviews. It arranged online chats with major portals and targeted websites. These efforts helped New Line increase its reach among Internet users. While saturating the vast space of the Web is difficult, *The Lord of the Rings* had a presence on nearly all major Web properties.

Because viewers could easily access articles about the film, this content served as a lever for both awareness and exploration. The interactivity of online magazines allowed readers to easily continue their exploration by linking to the official website.

Drill-Down

Building Awareness with NYTimes.com

New Line's partnership with NYTimes.com, the website of *The New York Times*, was a unique project developed by a major national newspaper and an entertainment property. The resulting promotional website (*www.nytimes.com/tolkien*) launched two months before the theatrical release of the first film.

Audience Target

NYTimes.com's audience is slightly more educated, affluent, and older than the average Internet user. Research showed that the website's readership is about 55 percent male and that 53 percent of users had attended a movie in the last 30 days.[12] Similar to those who read the offline version, this group of upscale adults was very valuable to New Line because of their role as opinion makers and influencers.

Objective

The NYTimes.com promotion relates to a key component of the Marketspace Matrix: The credibility of the channel matters. The audience coming into contact with the features and content of the *Lord of the Rings* promotion on NYTimes.com is far more likely to accept the property as a product they can trust. The promotion acts as an endorsement. The primary objectives for the NYTimes.com promotion were to drive awareness among intellectual opinion makers and influencers and to enhance credibility for the brand.

Executing the Campaign

NYTimes.com was in a unique position to work with New Line Cinema on the *Lord of the Rings* trilogy due to its archives of editorial content. Its mini-site on NYTimes.com featured W.H. Auden's original *Times* review of the first book in the trilogy, *The Fellowship of the Ring.* The site also contained *Times* reviews of the second and third books and other Tolkien-inspired productions, including the ill-fated 1986 Broadway version of the trilogy and Ralph Bakshi's 1978 animated feature.

Content offered on NYTimes.com's Tolkien site leveraged interactivity with specific features, such as the audio file of J.R.R. Tolkien reading from the trilogy's second book, *The Two Towers*, as well as the complete first chapter of *The Fellowship of the Ring* and a slide show of cover art and illustrations from rare editions of the books. The deep, Tolkien-specific content was valuable to the *New York Times* audience and to the core *Lord of the Rings* fans who became regular visitors to the website.

New Line Cinema was the sole sponsor of the mini-site and developed content to supplement the archived materials. The high degree of relevancy of the materials that New Line provided gave exclusivity and timeliness to the promotion and helped the *Times* to give this mini-site offline exposure in the daily newspaper, creating a high level of integrated messaging.

Campaign Effectiveness

The campaign included a high level of brand and content integration and was considered valuable to the NYTimes.com readership. The newspaper delivered significant offline promotion of the online campaign. The Tolkien mini-site received more than 1.5 million page views, and the CEO of New York Times Digital, Martin Nisenholtz, called it one of the *Times'* most successful efforts at integrating online and offline material.[13]

Building Awareness with Offline Levers

Movie Trailers

New Line introduced *The Lord of the Rings* to moviegoers with trailers that played in theaters across the nation. Trailers are commonly used as a lever to build awareness. They can be shown before movies that attract a similar target audience in order to increase the impact of the promotion.

TV Commercials

In its television commercials, New Line adopted a similar strategy and tone as used in the movie trailers. The television campaign focused on the film's epic nature and classic good-versus-evil theme. Due to the trilogy's large cast of characters and multiple story lines, the first wave of commercials introduced the major principal characters.

Radio

In its radio promotions, New Line selected stations with listeners that fit the same demographic as *Lord of the Rings* fans. The goal was to generate awareness and buzz among those who were highly likely to become paying customers at the box office.

Outdoor Ads

Outdoor ads, which appeared on billboards, buses, and telephone booths, also aimed to build awareness about the movie. Some were sponsored by partners such as domestic electronics partner JVC.

Print Ads

The Lord of the Rings showed up in numerous magazine and newspaper ads. In fact, after television commercials, newspaper ads received the largest budget allocation. The print ads also promoted awareness.

Retail Point-of-Purchase Displays

Publisher Houghton Mifflin designed new book covers that used images from the films. This point-of-purchase display presence built brand awareness in stores around the world. As the media campaign for the movie broadened, the retail presence escalated to take advantage of heightened awareness. Additionally, the movie's website address was placed on all reissued covers, which promoted exploration. Consumer purchases of the books signified commitment and, in some cases, viral marketing.

Partnerships and National Promotions

In choosing partners, New Line Cinema was sensitive to matching brand personality, so that fans of the books worldwide would not feel the brand was denigrated. New Line's partners hoped to benefit from the ad dollars the studio would spend and increase the equity of their brand with the millions of Tolkien fans. As a result, companies were willing to pay for partnership marketing, promoting their own products while building awareness for the movie.

The media dollars from tie-in partners permitted New Line to concentrate its own dollars on specific demographic groups and spread the promotional spending throughout the holiday season. The result was a campaign that easily made it past the clutter to gain high exposure.

Burger King. Burger King Corp. created a global marketing program spanning more than 10,000 restaurants featuring *The Lord of the Rings*. The $30 million campaign launched around Thanksgiving 2001 and provided broad reach with an adult-targeted sweepstakes and collectibles offer. Burger King also designed awareness programs to target the Hispanic community. All Burger King packaging carried the address for the official movie website, and an online sweepstakes was created for the Burger King website.

Burger King consumers who purchased *Lord of the Rings* collectibles—including light-up glass goblets and the youth-targeted "Ring of Power" toys—signified a level of commitment and viral marketing. Sean Astin, who plays the hobbit Samwise Gamgee in the movie, said just before the movie opened, "I was talking to a friend of mine. He said: 'You'll never guess who was on my fries.' I was like: 'Really? I was on the fries? Cool!' "[14]

JVC Electronics.   JVC parnered with New Line to establish a comprehensive, co-branded marketing program that promoted JVC consumer video products and the theatrical release of *The Lord of the Rings*. JVC was the exclusive electronics partner for the theatrical release of the first film.

The joint marketing campaign kicked off with the unveiling of a billboard in New York's Times Square. JVC and New Line Cinema also collaborated to create sweepstakes, bounce-back couponing, and bundling opportunities, which included a limited-edition DVD player with co-branded packaging and featuring a custom compilation DVD version of LOTR behind-the-scenes footage. The co-branded packages were available starting in September 2001 to support awareness in retail locations. Consumers who purchased the product and viewed the behind-the-scenes footage would enter into the exploration/expansion phase. As with the Burger King promotion, JVC packaging carried the official website's address.

Barnes & Noble.   Bookstore chain Barnes & Noble partnered with New Line to establish in-store and online programs to support the film release and book sales. Both companies leveraged the branding impact of theatrical images emblazoned on the new covers of the trilogy. In-store events and book signings with the cast and filmmakers were coordinated with the film's publicity schedule and with the release of new books including *The Fellowship of the Ring Visual Companion* and *The Lord of the Rings Official Movie Guide*. Barnes & Noble stores had prominent point-of-purchase displays, and in-store video monitors played film trailers and behind-the-scenes footage.

Barnes & Noble and New Line also sponsored the American Library Association's Teen Read Week, which featured community events nationwide.

American Library Association and Teen Read Week.   New Line Cinema joined American Library Association for its annual Teen Read Week in October 2001. Program goals and branding encouraged teens to "Read for the

Source: Courtesy of New Line Cinema.

EXHIBIT 14.17   "The Lord of the Rings" Book Covers

Fun of It" and to "Make Reading A Hobbit." Bookstores nationwide participated, with Barnes & Noble joining as an official sponsor. Schools and libraries received posters featuring *Lord of the Rings* characters reading. This targeted a secondary, youth-based component of the general awareness strategy.

Television Promotions: The WB Network.   In September 2001, The WB Network joined with New Line to become the exclusive network to air the premiere of a new theatrical trailer. The trailer aired during the broadcast of *Angel*, a show chosen to drive awareness among young women. The WB promoted the trailer extensively, which helped develop awareness.

New Line Cinema partnered with other network television and cable outlets to create unique, targeted programming to support the release of *The Lord of the Rings: The Fellowship of the Ring*. Other networks that aired awareness initiatives include TNT Network (vignettes during the film *The Matrix*), Time Warner Roadrunner Cable (on-air promotion of online sweepstakes), Starz Encore (on-air vignettes), Turner Sports (on-air mention of online sweepstakes), and MTV (inclusion in a half-hour special highlighting holiday films during the program *Movie House*). Television "promos" like these aimed to drive awareness; however, when consumers watched one of the specials, it moved them to the next relationship stage. For this reason, television programming will be discussed later in this chapter in the exploration/expansion and commitment sections.

Long-Lead and Fast-Breaking Campaigns: Magazines, Newspapers and TV Programs   Long-lead and fast-breaking magazine, newspaper, and television programming offers the ability to coordinate levers in rapidly timed succession. These opportunities should be coordinated for online exploitation as well. Long-lead magazine promotions included stories that appeared more than one year before the release of the first film, such as an exclusive *Vanity Fair* photo shoot of the cast in character in New Zealand. As the December 2001 release moved closer, magazine covers were arranged on monthly and weekly publications, including *TV Guide*'s series of four collectible covers and a five-cover series on *Entertainment Weekly*. While editorial content does function as an awareness lever, consumers who interact with the materials move to the exploration/expansion stage.

Strong awareness across consumer segments was driven by newspaper features and appearances by cast members and filmmakers on talk shows including *Late Show with David Letterman, Today, Live with Regis and Kelly* and MTV programs. Additionally, press junkets encouraged local journalists to interview the cast and filmmakers for local broadcasts.

Online Levers that Encourage Exploration/Expansion

Official Website
New Line Cinema's official movie website (*www.lordoftherings.net*) was the earliest marketing element and a focal point in its strategy to establish a dialogue with the most important segment of its customer base. Because the website address was branded in all physical media, it created a call to action for consumers to interact with the brand, which clearly represents the exploration/expansion stage.

Online Levers	Offline Levers
• AOL welcome page • Moviefone • ICQ • Netscape • Spinner • Winamp • Digital City • Compuserve • AOL service tie-in • Fan websites • New Line contests • Online magazine promotions • NYTimes.com	• Movie trailers • TV commercials • Radio • Outdoor ads • Print ads • Retail point-of-purchase displays • Partnerships and national promotions • Burger King • JVC • Barnes & Noble • American Library Association—Teen Read Week • Television promotions—The WB Network • Long-lead and fast-breaking campaigns: Magazines, newspapers and TV programs • TV programming and special promotions

EXHIBIT 14.18   Levers for the Awareness Stage

The homepage's links encouraged Tolkien experts and neophytes alike to navigate deep into the website. For the uninitiated, it was essential to have an interface and editorial style that encouraged exploration and did not suggest that previous knowledge of the brand was necessary. The visually based homepage with continuously rotating promotional content units encouraged visitors to "explore Middle-earth." Users could click on a map of Middle-earth and find out about its various cultures, creatures, and lands in a simple, entertaining way. Additional levers that used content and promotional elements created for the official website are described below.

AOL Keyword "Lord of the Rings"

New Line Cinema provided content for AOL's proprietary network. Any AOL member could enter the America Online keyword "Lord of the Rings" to get to a customized *Lord of the Rings* page with links to the official website and features within AOL brands, including Moviefone, AOL Entertainment, Movies, Music, Spinner, Winamp, Computing, and the AOL Parenting, Women, and Men channels.

AOL Moviefone had exclusive photos from the set, as well as a downloadable movie trailer. Additionally, New Line repackaged a large quantity of content from its official website, including cast lists, story summaries, and production notes, so that AOL members could enjoy this material without leaving the AOL service.

The AOL keyword system also set up an effective distribution channel for other promotions created by New Line and its partners. So not only could New Line leverage AOL's 32 million members, but it also enabled partners to take advantage of AOL's efficiency as a distribution channel. The AOL keyword was branded on all media developed by New Line, receiving the same placement as the official website address. The keyword also served as

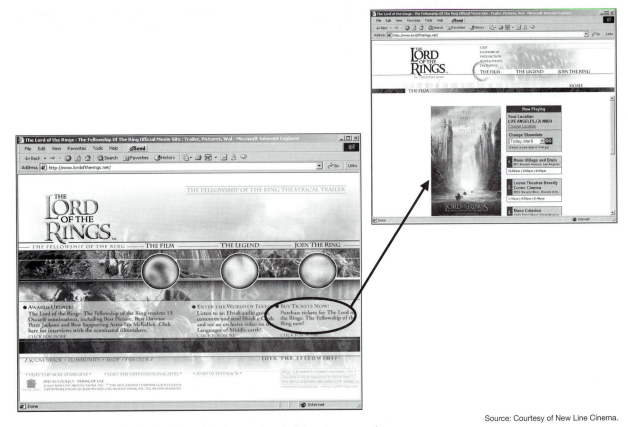

Source: Courtesy of New Line Cinema.

EXHIBIT 14.19   Official Website (www.lordoftherings.net)

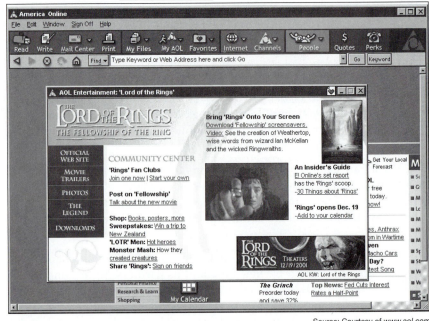

Source: Courtesy of *www.aol.com*.

EXHIBIT 14.20   AOL Keyword "Lord of the Rings"

an important vehicle within AOL for exploration/expansion of the *Lord of the Rings* franchise. Users who were already aware of the brand could find more information and links to commitment-generating promotions.

Syndicated Content

New Line Cinema provided *Lord of the Rings* content to websites in order to make these affiliate sites more interesting to fans and to foster exploration and expansion. Trivia contests, which included photo galleries and video clips, drove millions of page views for partners and moved consumers beyond initial relationship stages. The consumer could interact with the *Lord of the Rings* materials while remaining on the original websites.

Programs and contests facilitated awareness as well as exploration and expansion by connecting to deep content areas. One successful contest was an early promotion with AOL that included awareness and exploration levers. The promotion offered a chance to win a trip to Cannes and attend a party with the *Lord of the Rings* cast and filmmakers at a castle in the French countryside. The contest garnered over 100,000 entries and helped build a newsletter database by including an opt-in box on the entry form.

EXHIBIT 14.21   AOL Promotion: Win a Trip to Cannes

Source: Courtesy of *www.aol.com*.

By sharing the content it had already developed for its own website with a wide range of partners, New Line increased the content's reach and frequency. Of course, partners also provided links to the official website. In effect, this "syndication" effort gave potential moviegoers more opportunities to expand their relationship with *The Lord of the Rings*.

E-Mail Marketing

New Line's e-mail marketing campaign promoted ongoing exploration/expansion with tailored, content-based messaging that was relevant to the campaign and to subscribers. The homepage of the official website invited visitors to "join the fellowship by staying connected with e-mail updates."

Beginning in summer 2001, monthly e-mails alerted users to website enhancements, breaking news, cast and filmmaker interviews, and video features. In the months before the film release, the frequency increased and newsletters also included alerts for partner product launches, national events, and special promotions and cast appearances.

It is important to note that the goal of this e-mail campaign was not to monetize the consumer, but rather to promote exploration/expansion. The global online strategy was to give consumers value through the e-mail programs. Not until the first movie was released in December 2001 was there a request for consumer action—to attend the movie. At that point, New Line wanted subscribers to progress to the commitment stage.

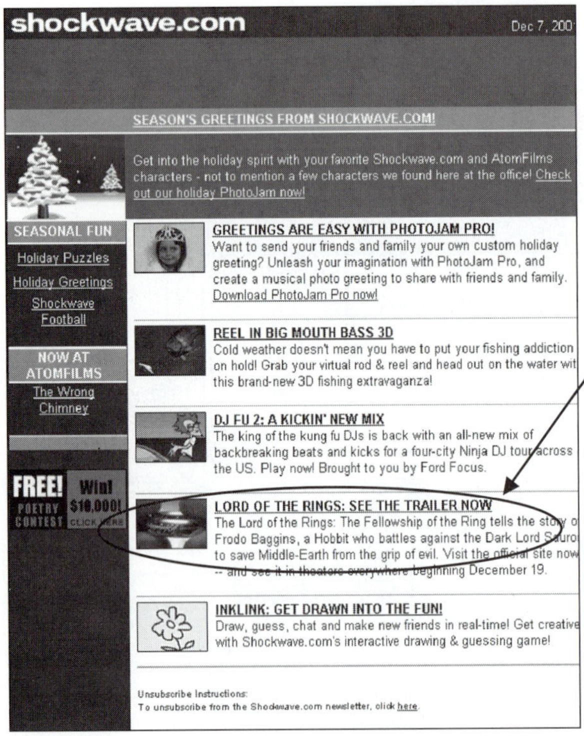

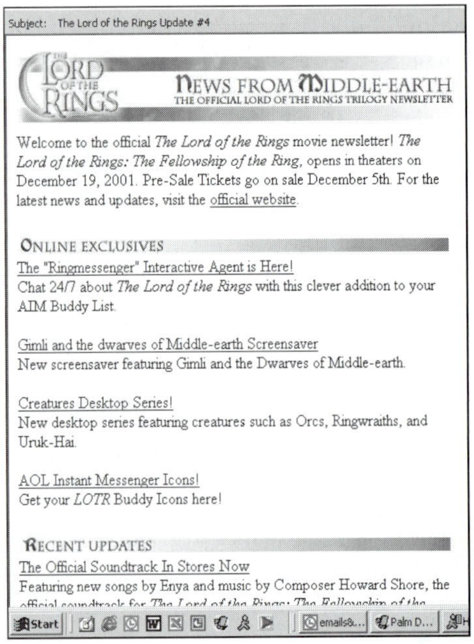

Source: Courtesy of *shockwave.com* and New Line Cinema..

EXHIBIT 14.22   E-Mail Marketing

Apple QuickTime

New Line hosted all *Lord of the Rings* trailers on Apple's QuickTime website, a leading supplier of Internet-based video streaming. QuickTime offered a link to download and view the trailer. People perusing the QuickTime website were likely to be looking for Internet-based video, making this an effective lever for exploration/expansion.

Couponing for In-Theater Sweepstakes (Offline to Online)

New Line created a nationwide in-theater promotion called "One Sweepstakes to Rule Them All." The promotion was advertised on more than

6 million cups, popcorn bags and popcorn tubs. On their own, those containers served as awareness vehicles. However, the call to action—to enter the contest—drove exploration and expansion by sending consumers to the official website to enter. The contest lasted from November 2001 until February 2002 and drew more than 300,000 entrants.

Drill-Down

E! Online Promotion: "Force of Hobbit"

New Line Cinema partnered with E! Online, the website for the cable network E! Entertainment Television, for a series of features that let audiences follow the development of a motion picture with an insider view. The online partnership gave New Line maximum coverage to an elusive, predominantly female demographic. The editorial content in the monthly features drove exploration and expansion with this difficult-to-reach audience in a highly trafficked, qualified environment that otherwise would have required significant advertising resources.

The arrangement with E! Online resulted in having an E! Online journalist in New Zealand throughout production. The journalist created monthly reports from the set and during postproduction, exploring the entire process from a behind-the-scenes vantage point.

The E! Online coverage began in November 1999 and represented a significant investment of time and resources by E! Online. The resulting editorial features offered in-depth coverage of key filmmaking disciplines.

Target Audience

New Line wanted to develop a partnership to broaden the film audience and to reach young women, who were determined to be a secondary but key audience. E! Online's audience was 61 percent female, and 63 percent of E! Online users were between the ages of 18 and 34 and had attended a movie in the last 30 days.[15]

Objective

Because early traffic to the official website was predominantly from men aged 18 to 34, New Line needed to reach women. Additionally, E! Online was an attractive partner due to its anchor editorial partnership with America Online's flagship service, which also had a high index among female moviegoers. (The E!/New Line partnership was developed in the summer of 1999 and preceded the AOL Time Warner merger that brought New Line under the AOL umbrella.) This early editorial integration into the AOL service was an important business initiative for New Line and *The Lord of the Rings*.

Executing the Campaign

The promotion gave E! Online exclusive editorial access to the New Zealand set for more than a year and a half before the release of the film. The promotion was fashioned to permit an early view into the production of an epic motion picture. The journalist and E! Online editors would create monthly reports, working closely with New Line to develop an editorial calendar that would create momentum and heighten consumer exploration of the content. New Line promoted the features by highlighting the coverage on the official website, and the studio gave E! online access to movie premieres and key promotional events. Examples of E! Online editorial production features:

May: Cannes Film Festival coverage
June: Locations
July: Sound
August: Christopher Lee profile (Saruman)
September: Casting; profile of extras coordinator

continued

October: Music/Howard Shore, the composer for *The Lord of the Rings*

November: Profile of writers

December: Fellowship ensemble reflect on upcoming release

January 2002: Motion capture, a key component of computer graphics where actors movements are recorded digitally to build complex visual film effects.

February 2002: WETA Digital, the special-effects house in New Zealand

E! Online benefited from an audience influx upon posting the monthly coverage. Each month, loyal *Lord of the Rings* fans immediately devoured new features the moment they hit the Internet. The viral promotion of the E! Online coverage was another benefit; many fan websites established permanent links to E! Online.

Campaign Effectiveness

E! Online's *Lord of the Rings* coverage averaged more than 700,000 page views per month, with a total of 17 million page views before the release of the first movie. The editorial coverage drove significant exploration and expansion, particularly in the months immediately preceding the release. During that time, the *Lord of the Rings* coverage generated 34 percent of all page views in E! Online's features/specials area, and it ranked as one of the 10 most popular features on the website.

Offline Levers that Encourage Exploration/Expansion

Prominent Magazine Coverage

As mentioned when we discussed awareness levers, *The Lord of the Rings* made the cover of many popular magazines. The covers promoted awareness, but the full-length articles also gave consumers an opportunity for exploration and expansion. Such articles typically gave the movie's story line and spotlighted the main characters. Prominent coverage included covers of *Entertainment Weekly*, *TV Guide*, and *American Cinematographer*, as well as feature articles in *Newsweek* and *Premiere*.

Television Programs

Also mentioned with the awareness levers, broadcast networks promoted awareness through occasional promotions, but consumers who actively tuned in for dedicated programs triggered the exploration lever. Several programs were even targeted enough to move viewers to commitment. Television networks with shows that served as exploration and expansion levers included E! (half-hour special with cast interviews), Fox (half-hour special called *Quest for the Rings* with cast and filmmaker interviews), FX Network (rebroadcast of Fox's *Quest for the Rings*), MTV (half-hour special with behind-the-scenes footage and interviews), and National Geographic (a special called *Beyond the Movie: The Fellowship of the Ring* that traced the influences of J.R.R. Tolkien's trilogy).

Houghton Mifflin

New Line Cinema benefited from book publisher Houghton Mifflin's efforts to drive readership in three relationship stages. As noted in the awareness section, point-of-purchase displays offered impression-based branding for the film through the new book covers. Branding the official website address on all publications gave consumers a way to learn more about the film. Consumers who purchased the books moved to the exploration/expansion stage and were highly qualified for the commitment stage.

Houghton Mifflin also published movie tie-in books that proved invaluable as promotional assistance for New Line. Copies of *The Fellowship of the Ring Visual Companion* and *The Lord of the Rings Official Movie Guide* were used by the studio as premiums with press and influencers, which also provided value to Houghton Mifflin.

ALA Promotion: Teen Read Week

The American Library Association's Teen Read Week primarily drove awareness. However, anyone who participated in the national program or attended events moved to the exploration/expansion stage.

Offline References to the Website

Another way in which New Line encouraged customers to reach the exploration/expansion stage was by channeling them from offline awareness to the *www.lordoftherings.net* website. All offline advertising referred to the official website so that curious consumers could deepen their *Lord of the Rings* experience. Additionally, as mentioned in many of the descriptions of awareness levers, the website branding was included in partner programs. (See Exhibit 14.23 for levers of the exploration/expansion stage.)

Additional Levers

New Line launched *The Lord of the Rings* with high-profile premieres on several continents. The world premiere in London was a star-studded event that garnered worldwide attention. The lavish after-party and red carpet ceremony received significant broadcast exposure and front-page coverage in entertainment publications. New York City and Wellington, New Zealand, hosted additional premieres.

Online Levers	Offline Levers
• Official website	• Prominent magazine coverage
• AOL Keyword "Lord of the Rings"	• TV programs
• Syndicated content	• Publisher Houghton Mifflin: New book covers for *The Lord of the Rings*
• E-mail marketing	• ALA Promotion: Teen Read Week
• Apple Quicktime	• Offline references to the website
• In-theater sweeps	• Movie trailers
• E! Online promotion	• PR coverage

EXHIBIT 14.23   Levers for the Exploration/Expansion Stage

Gaining Commitment with Online Levers

LordoftheRings.net

In addition to being a key lever for the exploration and expansion phase, the official website provided many tools that generated and sustained commitment to the *Lord of the Rings* brand.

Downloads

Downloadable files brought the *Lord of the Rings* experience to users' computer desktops and personal digital assistants (PDAs). These products kept the movie fresh in consumers' minds and sustained commitment in those

Trailers: Moving Consumers through the Stages

Timing has a direct effect on the relationship stage of marketing levers. Based on prior exposure, demographic, psychographic proclivity to be converted to a product, and other factors, customers will move through the relationship stages at various times, even when experiencing the same marketing materials.

Movie trailers illustrate this concept perfectly. New Line Cinema released the first *Lord of the Rings* footage in April 2000—and showed it only online. This drove extremely high usage from an audience who had been targeted as the core demographic (age, gender, etc.) and psychographic (values, beliefs, attitudes, etc.). Additionally, publicity about the massive number of downloads on the day the trailer was released—including coverage on CNN and in major newspapers—reached a mass audience. For fans of the *Lord of the Rings* book trilogy who had not heard about the film version, this trailer generated awareness. For those who did know the film was in production, it transitioned them into exploration/expansion—and, in many cases, commitment.

In January 2001, the first theatrical trailer was released globally. This event created a large offline publicity push, as it coincided with the completion of principal photography in New Zealand for all three films. For general audiences, this was the first visual media impression of the series of films, and it represented the awareness stage. For core fans, this point represented exploration/expansion. For those who waited in line overnight at theaters to see the trailer the next day, it was commitment. This event also leveraged and compounded another lever, community, as it was the first time that fans of the property were exposed to it in a cohesive, group situation. On Memorial Day weekend in 2001, the first full-length theatrical trailer was released. Again, this single lever represented various relationship stages, based on each audience member's previous exposure. This release would be the first mass exposure to the property and would function as awareness. In September 2001 a more developed full-length trailer was released, and the campaign's momentum kept building. This trailer was during the television show *Angel* on the WB Network in an effort to drive awareness among young women. The extensive promotion that the WB gave to the exclusive broadcast helped reach this difficult-to-target group.

The media campaign in the month before the film's release represented the final stage of timing and used broader-reach vehicles to drive awareness, exploration, or commitment for each consumer group. It helped to solidify commitment for those in the exploration/expansion phase and to quickly seed awareness through reach and frequency for other groups. It also encouraged consumers already in the commitment stage to act as evangelists. This added exponential exposure and generated awareness and exploration in other consumer groups.

After the film's release, New Line used a theatrical trailer for the second film, *The Lord of the Rings: The Two Towers*, to create commitment for the trilogy. Immediately after the Academy Awards in March 2002, New Line attached a 3½-minute segment of *The Two Towers* to the end of the first film, which was still running in thousands of theaters around the world. The core audience returned to theaters to view the added footage, thus continuing their commitment, while consumers who were seeing the film for the first time were exposed to these materials which would create exploration/expansion, if not commitment, based on their affinity for the first film.

who were excited about the movie even before it was released. After the release, these free downloads helped sustain interest in the franchise and encouraged viral marketing that supported DVD and videocassette sales. Examples of these downloads include:

Drill-Down

Community as a Key Lever of Commitment

A multilevel community plan was a key component of the *Lord of the Rings* marketing strategy. New Line chose to embrace the existing Tolkien "eco-system" and build upon established community efforts as an organic model, instead of trying to assert undue community influence in those areas. This generated goodwill, gave New Line a high level of acceptance within the established community, and facilitated acceptance for the property as a whole. Additionally, new communities would be created and nurtured to expand the reach and cater to a wider audience.

This required direct involvement on a strategic level in positioning the brand in community areas, but any interaction necessitated careful placement and had to be preceded by gaining the trust of the individual community outlets. In creating new communities, the brands and aggregators were chosen based on a demographic and psychographic match with primary audiences and brand objectives. All new efforts were to expand communities and not displace other groups. Stewardship of new community areas was open to influence by evangelists, who were encouraged to populate the areas. This permitted a more dynamic environment and allowed for an organic integration with existing community programs.

Initial community efforts were heightened by the April 2000 launch of the Internet-only preview footage, which received a colossal online response. Disparate fan groups and communities rallied around the first look at the film. Each community segment analyzed each frame of the trailer and went to great lengths to create individual shot-by-shot breakdowns of hundreds of images from the two-minute footage. Each image was discussed in painstaking detail, and this dialogue would travel and cross-pollinate communities.

Timing is a key component in the community strategy. Proper planning is required to shepherd consumers through the three levels of community—nascent, formative, and mature—toward any business objective. In the following examples, the three levels of community are included in the explanation of the community efforts employed by New Line Cinema.

1. Groups and clubs were created. Members from established community groups on disparate fan sites were encouraged to populate them. In 1999, clubs created by New Line on the Lycos network had more than 40,000 members.

   Level of Community: Nascent Level. Prior to the first film's release, New Line developed wireless communities that were nascent due to the limited consumer adoption of technology. Wireless activity included user subscription to *Lord of the Rings*-related SMS (text) notification services, which provided daily information updates . These services also notified subscribers of benefits and wireless couponing, which was employed upon release of the film. New Line promoted its wireless community in fall 2001, and there were more than 20,000 active members by the first theatrical release. Because the aggregate number of domestic consumers subscribed to wireless data services was limited, as a marketing objective it was too early to expect broad domestic reach via wireless community development.

2. New Line developed community bulletin boards on Netscape and ICQ. New Line could have created bulletin boards on its own website, but chose Netscape and ICQ as community aggregation points because of their large number of users and the high level of support and promotion those websites agreed to give their *Lord of the Rings* community areas. The users of those sites had demographics and psychographics that matched the movie's target audience. In return for supporting The *Lord of the Rings* communities, the websites were promoted by New Line's official film website.

   Three community partners—ICQ, Netscape, and a new wireless community—were integrated into the official website. ICQ proved a solid choice as it had developed a popular instant-messaging client with accompanying community

continued

bulletin boards, forums, and chats. More than 450 million ICQ clients had been downloaded, and an average of 12 million ICQ users launched the client daily. New Line worked with ICQ to create custom *Lord of the Rings* sounds schemes, a custom client interface, and message boards.

While ICQ targeted a slightly younger audience (48 percent were aged 18 to 34), Netscape's audience was slightly older (68 percent were aged 25 to 54), which meant a broad range of users would be reached between the two. Further, Netscape offered more than 40 million registered members who use the portal to check personalized information and access their e-mail.

The third key community partner was a wireless community that was jointly developed and promoted by AOL Wireless, VoiceStream, and Upoc. Visitors signed up to receive movie news and participate in discussions via their mobile phones. This community was not only provided with SMS trivia and information about the film, but wireless promotional coupons were also sent to the 20,000 users to redeem for a gift when they saw the movie at a Loews theater.

Level of Community: Formative Level. NLC timed the deployment of new community initiatives based on the marketing plan and finding the intersection between the business goal and targeted consumer interest levels. The communities were adopted as key levers and supported by New Line's marketing efforts. In shepherding Netscape and ICQ bulletin boards and developing community messaging with partners who provided a logical bridge with specific demographic/psychographic audiences, NLC was able to quickly develop formative-level communities.

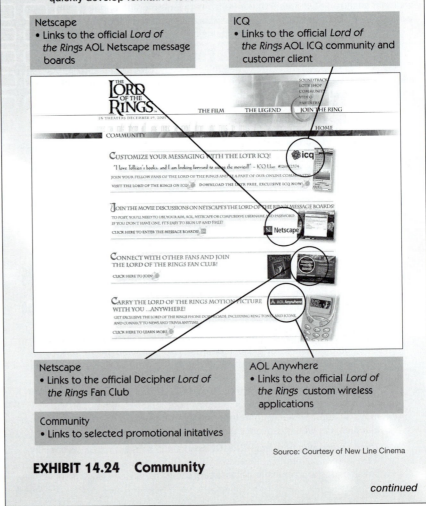

Netscape
- Links to the official *Lord of the Rings* AOL Netscape message boards

ICQ
- Links to the official *Lord of the Rings* AOL ICQ community and customer client

Netscape
- Links to the official Decipher *Lord of the Rings* Fan Club

AOL Anywhere
- Links to the official *Lord of the Rings* custom wireless applications

Community
- Links to selected promotional initatives

Source: Courtesy of New Line Cinema

EXHIBIT 14.24   Community

continued

3. New Line Cinema supported unrelated fan-sponsored community areas as well. This gained credibility with its most important audience—also the most resistant and cynical group—and drove dialogue about the movies. A hands-off approach turned fans into supporters by allowing disparate subcommunities to move through the exploration/expansion phases until they became confident in the product and moved to the commitment stage.

Level of Community: Mature Level. New Line took an open-minded approach to *Lord of the Rings* community efforts by supporting off-site community efforts and participating in partnerships and guerilla community groups that were not controlled by New Line. The idea was that an open dialogue would show good faith with marketing-resistant communities and build trust between the fans and the studio.

The mature communities had three shared characteristics as their foundations. There was a constant thirst for information, and the groups were extremely active. The continuous posting of images, video, and fan-created content generated excitement among disparate groups who were all in the commitment stage. Additionally, most members of the group had read the trilogy of books. Many had read the books dozens of times, which resulted in a strong common bond.

EXHIBIT 14.25   Wired Magazine Cover

Drill-Down

Communities and Positioning: Are All Communities Appropriate to Your Brand?

New Line chose not to promote role-playing communities or to overdevelop these elements on its official website. The roots of the role-playing communities are based in fantasy, and in initial film-positioning studies it was deemed detrimental to expand the audience for the films by embracing fantasy. Instead, epic themes and the power of the individual to affect an ultimate outcome were chosen as actionable positioning elements that proved to generate interest from consumers.

While it had a strong desire to support existing *Lord of the Rings* communities and to prove the quality of the feature film to various Tolkien fan groups, New Line did not want to create any appearance of exclusivity around the property. It was important to prove the integrity of the filmmakers' vision and their attentiveness to the Tolkien text; however, to put undue focus on the written text could be off-putting to consumers who might feel it was a prerequisite to read or understand the books to enjoy the film.

Screensavers.   New Line Cinema provided free screensavers with *Lord of the Rings* images. (Screensavers prevent damage to computer monitors by rotating the images that appear on the screen during idle time.) The screensavers helped maintain commitment in their users, and also advertised the movie to people who walked by the computer, particularly in office environments.

Wallpaper.   Electronic wallpaper displays a pattern or image on a user's computer desktop. Much like screensavers, wallpaper sustained commitment and also served as free advertising.

Ticketing
In the two weeks prior to the theatrical release, New Line tied into advanced ticketing initiatives through direct-sales e-mail campaigns. The e-mail programs accounted for the online presale of 15,000 tickets. The homepage of the official website allowed consumers to enter their zip code and either buy tickets directly through AOL Moviefone or find out where the film would be playing in their area. This offer also functioned as a reminder that the movie was coming to theaters soon.

In addition to fostering exploration and commitment, the interactive components of the official website provided opportunities for interaction between the user and the brand that helped move users from the awareness stage to the exploration stage. The 2Is, which were inherent to the website, also helped drive users from exploration to commitment. While the 2Is made the website effective, the wide variety of material on the website and the array of partnerships also proved essential in driving exploration and commitment.

Shop@AOL
AOL joined New Line in creating a major initiative to offer consumers a full range of licensed *Lord of the Rings* products. It was a more wide-reaching vehicle than New Line's own general online store, as it was highly promoted as a place to buy *Lord of the Rings* merchandise on AOL's flagship service in addition to the Internet Web properties group. New Line promoted the Shop@AOL effort and included top-level linking from the New Line store on the official website.

AOL Wireless and VoiceStream

New Line partnered domestically with AOL Wireless to offer a wireless "community" in association with partner Upoc, a service that builds mobile communities by allowing users to send messages to any kind of mobile phone or two-way pager. The communities develop based on subscription, similar to an e-mail newsletter. For the *Lord of the Rings* situation, the mobile component allowed the content to be created and accessed continuously. This promotional integration was a good use of the 2Is, as the community allowed individualistic two-way messaging and consumers could download and adopt exclusive ring tones, phone icons and screensavers in association with AOL and New Line telecommunications partner VoiceStream. Consumers who interacted within wireless community areas or adopted *Lord of the Rings* content on their mobile phones had a level of commitment that indicated it was highly probable they would attend the film.

Amazon.com

Amazon.com heavily promoted *Lord of the Rings* books and created cul-de-sac areas to feature licensed products, which were specific areas within Amazon that were dedicated to *The Lord of the Rings*. Amazon clearly believed this promotion would benefit its business, as a 1999 Amazon readers poll listed the *Lord of the Rings* trilogy as the most important work of the last century. Amazon.com also highlighted the film's opening in its weekly movie e-mail, which was delivered to more than a million subscribers.

Additional Levers

Additional commitment levers include the previously mentioned community partnerships with Netscape and ICQ. These partner areas were jointly promoted by the partner and the official website. Also, Warner Brothers Music created an online area that could be accessed via the enhanced portion of the CD of the movie's soundtrack. This area gave committed users exclusive content and allowed non-exclusive access to those in the exploration/expansion stages.

Gaining Commitment with Offline Levers

Merchandising

The movie version of the trilogy spawned a broad range of licensed products. Consumers who bought *Lord of the Rings* toys, watches, T-shirts, and other merchandise certainly showed a high level of commitment to the movie and the brand.

Houghton Mifflin Books

As noted previously, Houghton Mifflin published movie-specific tie-in books that were invaluable as promotional premiums for members of the press and key influencers. Also, consumers who purchased the books, *The Fellowship of the Ring Visual Companion* and *The Lord of the Rings Official Movie Guide*, were committed to the brand.

Theatrical Trailer (Fall 2001)

Timed for specific segments, the final theatrical trailer in fall 2001 moved consumers in the exploration/expansion stage to the commitment stage.

Drill-Down

The Official Film Website and Its Role in Commitment

Positioning for the official website required a balance between broad appeal and targeting. It would be a resource for all consumers, but also needed to offer value to each segment. The objective was to create an interface that speaks to disparate audiences but individually appeals to consumers at different levels in the relationship stages.

The website for the *Lord of the Rings* trilogy had one of the earliest online marketing leads ever for an entertainment property. It launched at the address *www.lordoftherings.net* two-and-a-half years before the theatrical release of the first film.

Target Audience

The core audience for the early marketing campaign was the dedicated base of Tolkien fans. This group, primarily males aged 17 to 24 with additional members aged 18 to 34, was extremely vocal and Web savvy. It became imperative to create an early online destination for the films because the fan base began promoting the theatrical production of the films from the moment it was announced.

Objective

The official website was not developed solely to service the fan base. It would become imperative in later marketing efforts that the official website not seem to "speak to the converted." However, this Drill-Down will focus on the early launch of the website and the early need to service the core fan demographic. For the initial website launch, there were several objectives:

1. New Line needed to set up an online destination from which to position the property. The fans had been quite passionate about the trilogy, and there was a need to keep the brand from being marginalized by grass-roots positioning, which had the best intentions but could be detrimental to broader marketing efforts.

2. New Line felt it was important to create an open dialogue with the fans. Other studios traditionally do not work with fan websites due to the high level of interaction required. New Line believed in engaging the fan base and not assuming a superior position.

3. New Line correctly assumed that this passionate group would serve as both the best evangelists for the property and also the most vociferous critics. It was imperative to gain the trust of this group and to have an open dialogue. This proved helpful in later efforts when the fans realized and accepted New Line's efforts as genuine. Webmasters and fan groups regularly had contact with the Internet marketing team, extending well outside office hours.

Executing the Campaign

In managing and maintaining the commitment level of the growing *Lord of the Rings* user base, New Line created partnerships for online community development that included bulletin boards and wireless community functionality. Additionally, New Line supported online grass-roots efforts and tried to drive online evangelism from the website into offline community activity. These efforts solidified the official website as a primary momentum driver for the broader studio marketing program.

The official website provided a vast quantity of content to invigorate evangelists. Exclusive video content that deeply explored the production process was themed to the creatures, cultures, languages, and lands of Middle-earth. The website also helped cement commitment to the trilogy by offering screensavers, downloads, and other tools to allow users to adopt *The Lord of the Rings* and experience the brand regularly.

continued

Campaign Effectiveness

The official website was extremely effective at developing and maintaining the ongoing commitment of the core fan base. Acquisition for direct marketing programs exceeded a half-million users by theatrical release and continued to rise sharply after the release. Website polling confirmed New Line's assertion that website users were evangelists for the brand. Polls showed 82 percent of respondents having read some or all of the *Lord of the Rings* trilogy and 93 percent "definitely" recommending the film to a friend. In fact, 64 percent planned to see the film again in theaters, and 92 percent said they would probably buy the DVD or videocassette.

The staggered timing of the trailers allowed New Line to target frequent moviegoers early and move them toward commitment.

Sci-Fi Channel Special: "Cinema Beyond: A Passage to Middle-earth"

Television programming tailored to specific demographics can drive commitment and also encourage evangelism. In this case, an hour-long program created for core fans, *Cinema Beyond: A Passage to Middle-earth*, aired on the Sci-Fi Channel multiple times in the two weeks leading up to the theatrical release of *The Lord of the Rings*.

Conventions (Comicon)

New Line supported fan events and conventions as outlets for driving evangelism and to gauge commitment levels. Attendance at these events indicated an intent to see the film and was an effective tool for tapping into the thoughts of the fans.

Warner Bros. Soundtrack

The movie soundtrack, which included a new song by Enya, was released by Warner Bros. Records just before the film's premiere. A music video for the song "May It Be" was also created. The soundtrack was a marketing lever to promote further interest in the movie, and it was highly probable that consumers who purchased the soundtrack would see the film.

Online Levers	Offline Levers
• Official website	• Merchandising
• Screensavers	• Houghton Mifflin tie-in books
• Wallpaper	• Theatrical trailer (fall 2001)
• Ticketing	• Sci-Fi Channel special, "Cinema Beyond: A Passage to Middle-earth"
• Shop@AOL and Shop.newline.com	• Conventions (Comicon)
• AOL Wireless and VoiceStream	• Warner Bros. soundtrack
• Amazon	

EXHIBIT 14.26 Levers for the Commitment Stage

New Line Cinema clearly drove people to purchase tickets, which was the ultimate objective of the commitment stage as defined in the marketing plan. Moreover, New Line provided substantial opportunities for evangelism. The

2Is played a crucial role in this phase by enabling a high degree of personalization and interactivity. Finally, by partnering with AOL Moviefone, the studio also generated interactive opportunities for ticket purchases.

Dissolution

As mentioned in the Point–Counterpoint titled "Is Purchasing a Ticket Effectively Dissolution?" movie studios' marketing plans should not plan to dissolve relationships with customers who purchase tickets. In this particular case, New Line viewed ticket purchase as commitment, and the objective was to maintain that commitment. If ancillary revenues cannot be generated from a committed customer, the relationship will effectively dissolve itself.

A visual summary of the marketing campaign can be found in Exhibit 14.27, and its Marketspace Matrix is pictured in Exhibit 14.28.

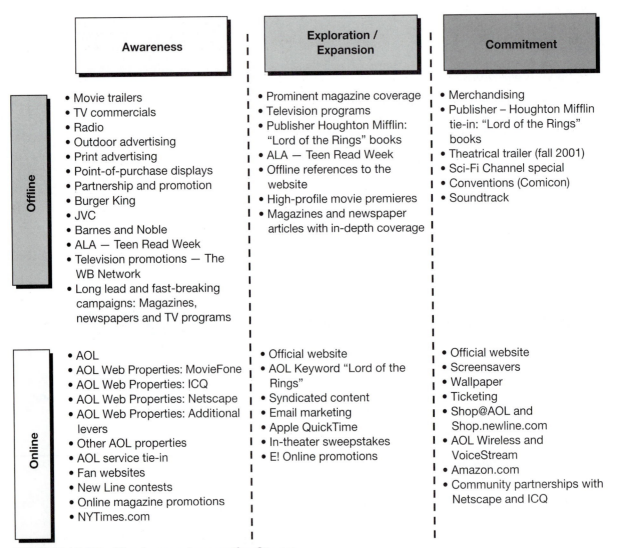

Awareness	Exploration / Expansion	Commitment
Offline		
• Movie trailers • TV commercials • Radio • Outdoor advertising • Print advertising • Point-of-purchase displays • Partnership and promotion • Burger King • JVC • Barnes and Noble • ALA — Teen Read Week • Television promotions — The WB Network • Long lead and fast-breaking campaigns: Magazines, newspapers and TV programs	• Prominent magazine coverage • Television programs • Publisher Houghton Mifflin: "Lord of the Rings" books • ALA — Teen Read Week • Offline references to the website • High-profile movie premieres • Magazines and newspaper articles with in-depth coverage	• Merchandising • Publisher – Houghton Mifflin tie-in: "Lord of the Rings" books • Theatrical trailer (fall 2001) • Sci-Fi Channel special • Conventions (Comicon) • Soundtrack
Online		
• AOL • AOL Web Properties: MovieFone • AOL Web Properties: ICQ • AOL Web Properties: Netscape • AOL Web Properties: Additional levers • Other AOL properties • AOL service tie-in • Fan websites • New Line contests • Online magazine promotions • NYTimes.com	• Official website • AOL Keyword "Lord of the Rings" • Syndicated content • Email marketing • Apple QuickTime • In-theater sweepstakes • E! Online promotions	• Official website • Screensavers • Wallpaper • Ticketing • Shop@AOL and Shop.newline.com • AOL Wireless and VoiceStream • Amazon.com • Community partnerships with Netscape and ICQ

EXHIBIT 14.27   The Levers Across the Stages

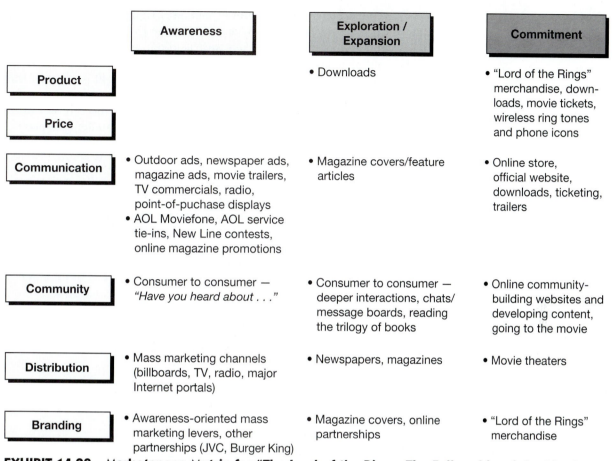

EXHIBIT 14.28   Marketspace Matrix for "The Lord of the Rings: The Fellowship of the Ring"

The Success of the "Lord of the Rings" Campaign

Measured by box-office receipts, the marketing plan for *The Lord of the Rings: The Fellowship of the Ring* was a stellar success. In addition to strong ticket sales, the movie also delivered value for its promotional partners. Buzz about *The Lord of the Rings* seemed to be ubiquitous for most of November and December 2001. Industry tracking showed an awareness level of 94 percent among moviegoers during the week of its release. More than 59 percent of moviegoers declared a "definite interest" in the film. (For male moviegoers over the age of 25, the number jumped to 70 percent.)

In theater exit polls on opening day, more than 50 percent of the audience said the Internet was one of their sources for information on the film.[16] Considering that Internet spending accounted for less than 2 percent of the marketing budget, online marketing had a phenomenally high return on investment, and gained customers at a much lower cost than offline marketing. (New Line Cinema's budget for *The Lord of the Rings* had a higher Internet marketing budget allocation than is typical for other New Line films.)

New Line's efforts converted online buzz into significant advance ticket sales, with direct e-mail programs accounting for 15,000 online ticket pre-sales.[17] More than 1.3 million tickets were sold online in December 2001.[18] Further, online ticket sales accounted for 8.25 percent of the opening weekend's sales.[19] According to theater exit polls, more than 40 percent of the opening weekend's audience said they learned about the movie from the Web. Furthermore, 50 percent of male moviegoers said the Internet campaign drove them to the box office, and one-third of the audience reported seeing an online advertisement.[20]

In the awareness stage, New Line generated substantial recognition for the epic nature of the property. It established the pedigree of the brand and made customers understand that the quality of the production would match the trilogy's literary value. In the exploration/expansion stage, moviegoers were able to learn about the characters, cultures, and languages of Middle-earth, and New Line provided tools to help people inform their friends about the movie. In the commitment stage, the studio made it easy to see the film, to evangelize it, and to continue the commitment stage by reading the books or listening to the soundtrack.

Six factors leading to success:
Offline and online partnerships
Reach and frequency on the Internet
The 2Is
Viral marketing
Good message
Complementary levers

EXHIBIT 14.29   The Success of "The Lord of the Rings"

The marketing plan's success was the result of six factors:

- *Offline and Online Partnerships.* Partners wanted to be associated with the *Lord of the Rings* brand (and the demographic that the property reached), and New Line wanted to increase its reach and frequency across all media formats, online and offline. The number of partnerships New Line Cinema struck significantly expanded the reach and frequency of the campaign.

- *Complementary Levers.* New Line applied a large number of levers to creating awareness, the bulk of which were offline levers. For the commitment phase, the plan's focus switched to online levers. In all stages, however, New Line integrated online and offline levers to maximize the overall effect of advancing customers through the stages.

- *Reach and Frequency on the Internet.* New Line Cinema leveraged its relationship with corporate parent AOL Time Warner and its flagship AOL Internet service, gaining access to its more than 30 million users. New Line also reached out to nearly every major Internet property to generate awareness for *The Lord of the Rings*. AOL and the other online partners derived substantial benefits, while the studio generated tremendous reach and frequency across many demographic groups by using a wide array of online and offline levers. Integration significantly enhanced the number of ad impressions delivered.

- *The 2Is.* New Line Cinema developed personalized and interactive tools that kept customers interested in the franchise and ensured that they would purchase tickets. The studio also used its partnership with Moviefone to make it easy for customers to find out where the movie was playing and to purchase tickets online. Because the offline levers tended to be less interactive, they were tied to the very interactive official website, *www.lordoftherings.net*. The power of the offline levers to advance customers through the relationship stages increased dramatically when augmented by the online levers. This online/offline integration propelled customers through the stages in a way that a non-integrated plan could not.

- *Viral Marketing.* Users could choose from a multitude of ways—both novel and traditional—to promote the movie to their friends. Viral marketing was integrated into various online levers in a way that stayed true to the *Lord of the Rings* brand while encouraging users to "send this page to a friend," "send this e-mail to a friend," or send their friends an e-card with their favorite character.

- *Good Message.* New Line Cinema found a good message and stayed with it: The *Lord of the Rings* brand represents the valiant struggle of good over evil.

Summary

1. How should a firm define its goals for each of the relationship stages? How did New Line Cinema define these goals?

The marketing objectives for each relationship stage should provide a clear path to advance customers to the next stage. A successful Internet marketing plan will not only draw on levers that lead users into a particular stage, but it will also drive users from stage to stage by taking advantage of the 2Is. New Line Cinema's integrated campaign for *The Lord of the Rings* achieved both of these objectives, and made use of both interactive and individualized components to ensure a vigorous plan that actively managed the movement of users from awareness to commitment.

2. How did New Line Cinema tie its marketing plan to the *Lord of the Rings* brand?

Many people already had significant awareness of J.R.R. Tolkien's book trilogy. New Line worked hard to build on that existing popularity, and carefully crafted all marketing efforts to maintain the brand's integrity. The look-and-feel of the ads reinforced the epic nature of the books, and partners were chosen according to how well they fit with the property.

3. What online levers did New Line Cinema use in the *Lord of the Rings* marketing plan?

Online levers included AOL tie-ins, a wide variety of contests, online magazine promotions, the official website (*www.lordoftherings.net*), syndicated online content, customized homepages, online ticketing, and website downloads.

4. What offline levers did New Line Cinema use for *The Lord of the Rings*?

Offline levers included movie trailers, TV commercials, radio ads, outdoor ads, print ads, point-of-purchase displays, partnerships, magazine covers and articles, free promotional products, the musical score, offline references to the website, and merchandising.

5. How successful was the integration of offline and online levers?

Efforts to integrate the offline and online levers used in the marketing campaign were highly successful. This was due in large part to the consistent use of similar themes and style across all levers. The online and offline levers worked together to give consumers a consistent experience with the *Lord of the Rings* brand. Many of the offline levers directed consumers to online sources where the experience could be deepened.

6. How do the 2Is affect the choice of marketing levers?

The 2Is have a significant effect on the choice of marketing levers because they enable the customer relationship to progress and deepen very quickly. New Line leveraged the power of individualization and interactivity wherever possible, and tied less interactive offline levers to the very interactive official website. The power of the offline levers to advance customers through the relationship stages increased dramatically when augmented by the 2Is of the online levers.

7. Is an online marketing campaign always appropriate?

An online marketing campaign is often very effective at moving customers from awareness to commitment. A strong online campaign, however, is not always appropriate. How well the offering "fits" with the Internet is an important consideration. Firms need to understand the target customer group. If that group is not online, an online campaign will not be effective.

8. Why was the *Lord of the Rings* campaign so effective?

The *Lord of the Rings* campaign was effective for a number of reasons. First, New Line established clear and proper objectives and employed the 2Is to deepen the customer experience and move consumers to the commitment stage. Online and offline levers were well integrated and worked together. Also, the campaign stayed true to the *Lord of the Rings* brand and the classic, timeless message of Tolkien's work.

Endnotes

[1] Box Office Charts, *www.Variety.com*, July 2002.

[2] Cumulative Box Office Charts, *www.Variety.com*, July 2002.

[3] Lyman, Rick. 2001. Movie Marketing Wizardry: "Lord of the Rings" Trilogy Taps the Internet to Build Excitement. *The New York Times*, 11 January, B1.

[4] J.R.R. Tolkien obituary. 1973. *The New York Times*, 3 September.

[5] Auden, W.H. 1954. "The Fellowship of the Ring" book review. *The New York Times*, 31 October.

[6] Unless otherwise cited, awareness tracking data is derived from proprietary research reports from National Research Group (NRG), *http://www.nrg.com/*.

[7] Download statistics provided by Akami Technologies Inc., which hosted the trailer. *http://www.akamai.com/en/html/about/press/press110.html*.

[8] Motion Picture Association of America, December 2001.

[9] @plan Inc., Spring 2002 Release.

[10] @plan Inc., Spring 2002 Release.

[11] @plan Inc., Spring 2002 Release.

[12] @plan Inc., Spring 2002 Release.

[13] Special Report on Interactive Marketing. *Advertising Age*, 18 Novermber 2002.

[14] Ian Markham-Smith. 2000. Lord of the Rings films and products set to out-magic even Harry Potter. *International Market News*, December 28. *http://www.tdctrade.com/imn/imn190/films05.htm*.

[15] @plan Inc., Spring 2002 Release.

[16]National Research Group reporting. December 2001.

[17]Combined proprietary reporting from Fandango.com, Movifone.com and Movietickets.com.

[18]Combined proprietary reporting from Fandango.com, Movifone.com and Movietickets.com.

[19]Box Office Charts. *www.variety.com*, July 2002.

[20]National Research Group reporting. December 2001.

Leveraging Customer Information Through

Technology

This section focuses on how technology, in the form of customer information systems, plays a critical role in reducing the uncertainty associated with managerial decision making. This section focuses on three important customer information processes: marketing research, database marketing, and customer relationship management. Marketing research has been used often and effectively in evaluating and targeting markets, as well as in supporting strategic marketing-mix decisions; database marketing, with strong roots in direct marketing, has been used frequently and effectively in customer acquisition; and customer relationship management is concerned primarily with retention-related activities. There are five stages in each of these processes: problem definition, data collection, data organization, data analysis, and data utilization.

Customer Information Systems

Effective customer-centric marketers make, and then act on, three major types of decisions. First, they evaluate markets, strategically decide which ones to target and penetrate, and then go after them. Second, they learn about the details of target market consumers, devise strategies and tactics to acquire customers, and then go get them. Third, they assess the long-term profitability of each customer, decide which ones to retain, and then go about keeping them (see Exhibit 15.1).

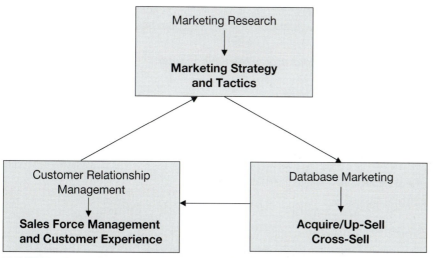

EXHIBIT 15.1   Customer-Centric Marketing Process

To reduce the uncertainty associated with these decisions, and to increase the likelihood of desired outcomes through better decision-making, marketers seek out information about the makeup and nature of markets and consumers, such as demographics, lifestyles, behaviors, and preferences. The Internet is a great source for this information, offering direct interaction among consumers and organizations. Electronic technology is another good tool for enhancing decision making by virtue of its ability to record, maintain, and quickly process vast amounts of information.

Co-authored by Bruce D. Weinberg and Craig Thompson

The objective of this chapter is to give an overview of processes for obtaining, organizing, analyzing, and utilizing customer-relevant information that can reduce the uncertainty associated with each of the three major types of decisions, and thereby support better managerial decision-making and firm performance (see Exhibit 15.2). Marketing research, database marketing, and customer relationship management (CRM) will be discussed in this context.

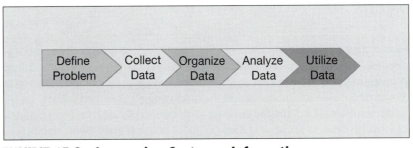

EXHIBIT 15.2   Leveraging Customer Information

QUESTIONS

Please consider the following questions as you read this chapter:

1. What is marketing research?

2. What is the framework of marketing research?

3. What are marketing research data-collection methods?

4. How do online methods compare to offline methods?

5. What research is best done through the Internet?

6. What are the implications of international Internet marketing research?

7. What is database marketing?

8. What is the purpose of customer relationship management?

9. Why should firms develop customer information systems?

Introduction

The organization of the material in this chapter emphasizes an overarching framework for leveraging customer information in Internet marketing (see Exhibit 15.3). First, emphasis is placed on the implementation sequence of each decision, as it is done in practice. Second, most would agree that the stages of each process involve problem definition, data collection, data organization, data analysis, and data utilization. Third, marketing research has been used often and effectively in evaluating and targeting markets, as well as in supporting strategic marketing-mix decisions; database marketing, with strong roots in direct marketing, has been used frequently and effectively in customer acquisition; and the lion's share of managing a relationship with a customer involves retention-related activities.

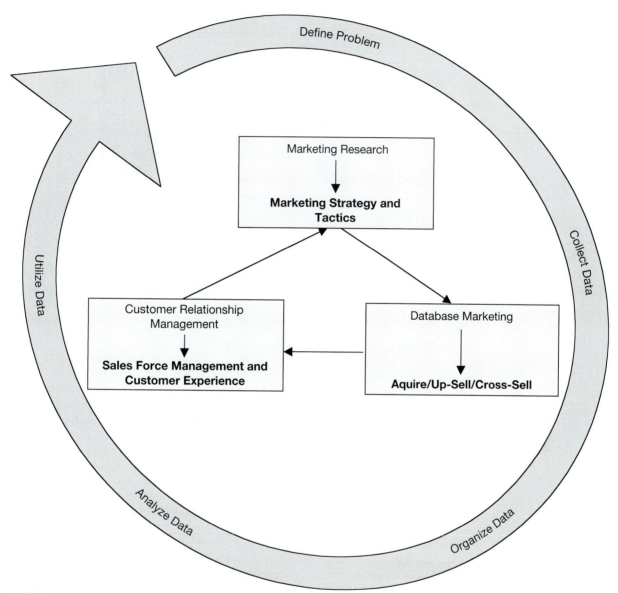

EXHIBIT 15.3   Customer Information System

Marketing Research

In the past, marketing research was a slow, labor-intensive, and costly task that was often outdated before it was even finished. The Internet has given marketing research a new image by enabling researchers to slash costs by more than 90 percent and reduce turnaround time from months to days. With estimates that 765 million people will be online by 2005, Internet marketing research has the potential to become one of the most powerful tools for gathering marketing information.

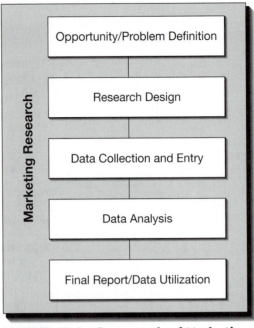

EXHIBIT 15.4   Framework of Marketing Research

What Is Marketing Research?

Marketing research is the study of the requirements of distinct markets, the acceptability of products and services, and the methods of developing new markets. It is a systematic and objective process used to collect, organize, maintain, analyze, and present information about a specific market in order to identify and define marketing opportunities and problems. Marketing research connects marketers with their customers, consumers, and the public (see Exhibit 15.5).

A market is any established means by which the exchange of goods and services takes place. It implies trade that is transacted with some regularity and regulation, and in which some competition is involved. A market can be as broad as an entire industry (such as telecommunications) or a segment of an industry (such as wireless telecommunications), or as specific as a market niche within that segment (such as wireless application protocol, or WAP).

Marketing research helps companies to understand and meet consumer wants and needs by providing constructive information about the quality and usefulness of their products and services. Companies also rely on marketing research to determine if consumers will accept new products or services; it is less expensive to conduct marketing research than to introduce a product or service that fails.

Marketing research employs surveys, tests, and statistical studies to analyze consumer trends and forecast the size of a market (see Exhibit 15.6 for additional uses). Regardless of the objective, all marketing research has the goal of obtaining data that allow companies to make better-informed decisions. If the data obtained are reliable, the result will:

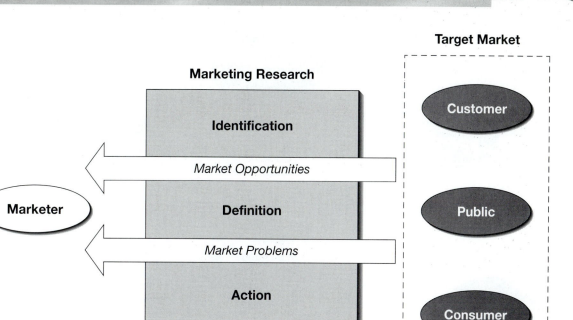

EXHIBIT 15.5   What is Marketing Research?

- Improve the quality of decision making
- Guide communications with current and potential customers
- Identify potential opportunities in the marketplace
- Minimize business risk by uncovering prospective problems
- Create benchmarks and track progress
- Evaluate overall success

Define Problem

In Chapter 2, opportunities and problems were evaluated in the broad context of a marketing strategy. Here, opportunities and problems are evaluated on a micro-level, in the context of a marketing research plan. To evaluate potential business opportunities, a marketing researcher must carefully investigate the source of an opportunity or problem—only then can a determination about the proper type of study be made. To do this, the researcher must have a fundamental understanding of the underlying change that led to the need for additional information in the first place. Further, it is imperative that the researcher understands the environment in which the problem or opportunity originated in order to ensure the results produced by the study are feasible.

The term "environment" implies anything from corporate culture to legal, financial, and technical constraints. For example, a marketing research study might indicate that a wireless telecommunications company needs additional

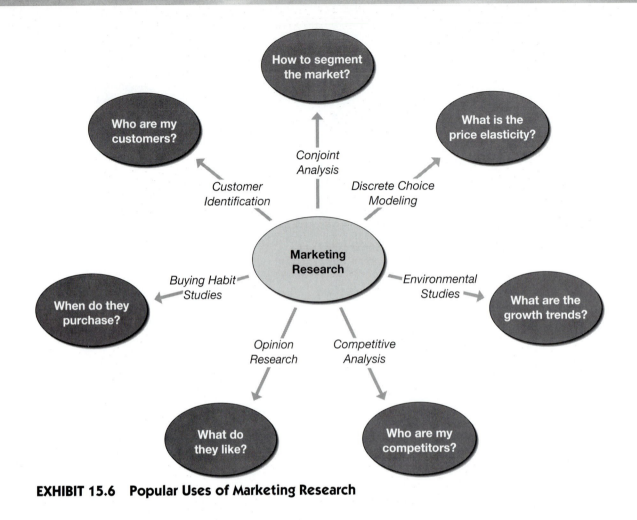

EXHIBIT 15.6   Popular Uses of Marketing Research

third-generation (3G) spectrum in order to provide new services and expand existing services. Yet if the company already has the maximum spectrum allowed by the government, the study is of no value because the solution is not feasible. As a part of the opportunity- or problem-identification step, a researcher must perform a cost-benefit analysis before undertaking any marketing research. This step requires weighing the potential benefits of the marketing research study against the costs of such a project. In practical terms, the problem- or opportunity-identification step requires the researcher to state the project's objectives in a list, figure, or descriptive paragraph. From there, the researcher must refine the objectives until a comprehensive set of research questions is articulated. Exhibit 15.7 gives an example of proper problem or opportunity identification.

Unfortunately, researchers often underestimate problem or opportunity identification—or circumvent it entirely. They either do not understand the problem at hand or do not allocate sufficient time and resources for this step. Instead, they simply select the type of information they want to investigate, which is akin to treating the symptoms of a disease instead of its cause.

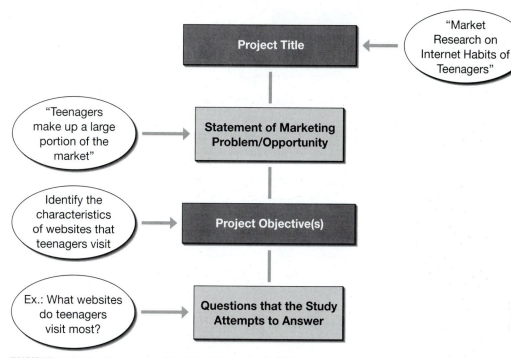

EXHIBIT 15.7   Opportunity/Problem Definition

Research Design

The research-design step is like the blueprint of a house; it is what the researcher uses to make all crucial decisions about the study. First, the researcher must decide what type of study to conduct. Depending on the problem-identification step, the researcher makes a selection from exploratory research design or from conclusive research design (a combination of causal research design and descriptive research design; see Exhibit 15.8).

Exploratory research emphasizes gaining ideas and insights about a problem, attempting to answer "why," "how," and "when" questions. It helps break broad, vague problems into smaller, more manageable statements. Exploratory research is an effective design when the objectives of the study are to gain intelligence and ideas of why certain things are happening—for example, why some Internet companies are failing while others are thriving. It is often used when a problem has not been clearly defined or its scope is unclear, because it allows the researcher to become familiar with the problem and to generate testable hypotheses. Exploratory research determines the best research design, selection of subjects, and data-collection methodology, although its use is limited.

Conclusive research is used to answer "how often" and "how many" questions. It follows a formal research design process and provides reliable data for drawing conclusions or making decisions. Often, it is quantitative in nature. Conclusive research provides a reliable picture of a population by using a valid research instrument, and it tests hypotheses in formal research.

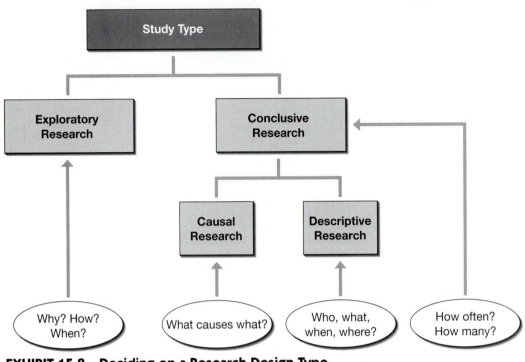

EXHIBIT 15.8   Deciding on a Research Design Type

There are two major categories of conclusive research: descriptive and causal. In **descriptive research**, the researcher determines the frequency with which something occurs or how separate events are related. It provides information about the population or universe under study (the elements within a given group about whom data are required) by describing the who, what, when, where, and how of a situation. It does not provide any information about what causes things to occur. Observations and surveys are the two most common types of descriptive research.

If the researcher needs to know what causes a specific behavior, occurrence, or motivation, then **causal research** is appropriate because it establishes a relationship between variables and focuses on determining a cause-and-effect relationship. In order to determine the cause, the researcher makes an assumption about which variable is causing the change in another variable and then changes that variable while holding constant all other variables (either in an experiment or statistically). Causal research is complex and affected by factors that researchers cannot always control, such as people's attitudes. Experimentation, computer simulation, and econometrics are the research methods used to explore the cause-and-effect relation between variables.

After determining the type of study to conduct, the researcher must decide whether to use secondary research, primary research, or a combination (see Exhibit 15.9). **Secondary research**—information previously collected and published—is the easiest, fastest, and least-expensive option. As discussed in more detail in the next section, secondary research may be a study, a census, a set of newspaper articles, or any data that are available on the Internet. In the past, researchers did secondary research in libraries, spending

hours searching through reference books, magazines, and newspapers articles. The Internet has fundamentally changed the way researchers conduct
secondary research. With reduced costs (and close-to-zero marginal costs),
researchers can search the Internet, quickly covering the entire globe if
necessary.

Primary research is information the researcher must collect for a specific
purpose, and is necessary when secondary research does not exist. Primary
research methods include conducting surveys, questionnaires, focus groups,
and interviews to create market data. Much as it did for secondary research,
the Internet has had a revolutionary impact on primary research, as it allows
a researcher to collect data via Internet surveys or though e-mail.

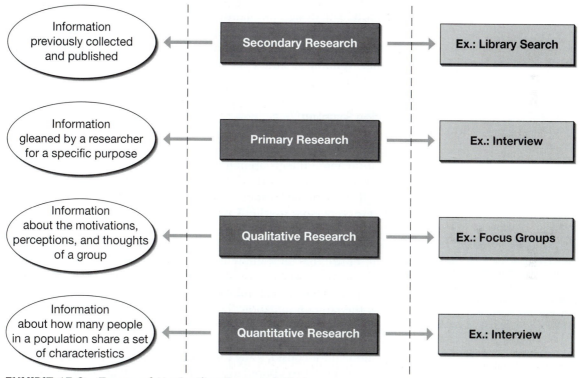

EXHIBIT 15.9   Types of Marketing Research Data

Overall, there are two basic types of research data: quantitative and qualitative (see Exhibit 15.9). Before determining which type is needed, the
researcher must review what problem the study attempts to answer: a "why"
or a "how many" question. If it is "why," then qualitative research is appropriate; if it is "how many," then quantitative research is the right choice. The
methods of collecting and analyzing each data type are quite different, and
it is often impossible to ascertain the answer to both "why" and "how many"
with only one form.

Qualitative research provides an understanding of customer attitudes about
products or services. Focus groups, both offline and online, are used more

than any other qualitative method to obtain key information about the motivations, perceptions, and thoughts of a target group or groups. Other qualitative methods include in-depth interviews, small discussion groups (dyads, triads, or minigroups), customer intercepts, quality function deployment, product testing, mystery customer research, and the voice of the customer.[1]

Researchers use quantitative research to establish benchmarks (e.g., market size to estimate business potential and measure the size and importance of market segments), obtain statistically valid responses from a target audience (or population), and measure the result of programs. The main reason for conducting quantitative research is to learn how many people in a population have, or share, a particular characteristic or group of characteristics—in other words, to determine the relationship between one thing (an independent variable) and another (a dependent or outcome variable) in a population. The design of quantitative research methods facilitates accurate and reliable measurements that permit statistical analysis and allow researchers to create models that predict whether someone holds a particular opinion or would act in a certain way based on an observable characteristic.[2]

Population Sampling

Because the purpose of conducting marketing research is to develop an understanding of a market or segment, it is vital that a researcher gather information about the group in question. In many cases, it is either impossible or not feasible to work with the entire target population. For example, a study of national attitudes toward online purchases that requires surveying every person in the United States is neither economical nor practical. Rather, sampling is used to obtain responses from a representative segment of the population of interest, which are then extrapolated onto the entire market. Simply interviewing friends, or those who shop only on Saturdays, will not result in reliable data for the entire population. Sampling involves carefully selecting a representative, random sample from the target population. The sample must be large enough to accurately mirror the characteristics of the target population and must be selected at random. If the sample is not representative and random, then a researcher cannot consider any forecast derived from that research representative for the subject population. Questions such as "How big is a representative sample?" and "How many subjects does the researcher need to include in his study?" are important considerations for the marketer designing a study.

What Research Is Best Accommodated by the Internet?

Given the enormous growth of the Internet, in terms of both subscribers and content, researchers might be tempted to use Internet-based research for all research tasks. The Internet is primarily an enabling tool that affects the data collection step and revolutionizes the reporting phase. The use of the Internet as a data-collection tool and research delivery mechanism has made it possible for researchers to conduct marketing research more quickly and less expensively. A cautious researcher, however, will avoid this approach; Internet marketing research works for many situations, but not all.

There are no fixed rules about what tasks can or cannot be addressed through Internet-based research. Ultimately the researcher must make the final decision on where best to obtain data. In making this decision, the researcher should follow some basic guidelines (see Exhibit 15.10).

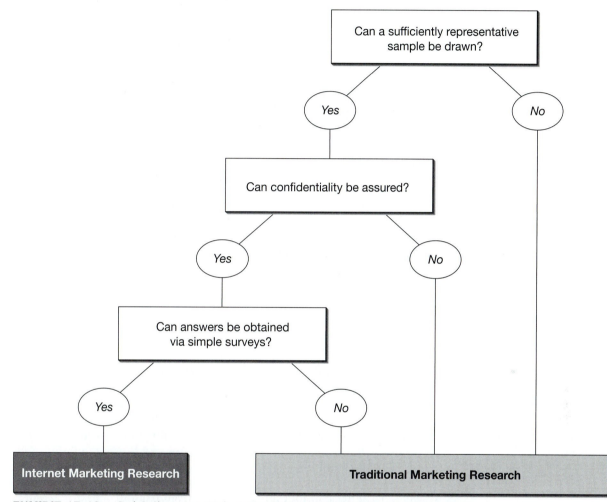

EXHIBIT 15.10   Guidelines on Using the Internet for Marketing Research

First, and probably most important, is the question of a representative sample. Can the Internet be used to draw a representative sample from the target population? A main consideration in answering this question is a sampling concept called sample selection bias. A **sample-selection bias** is introduced when a particular segment of the target population is ignored in the sampling process. Consider a study that attempts to monitor the hours per week a person spends on the Internet. For this, a banner is placed on an Internet portal and everyone who uses the portal must complete the questionnaire. The sample selection bias occurs by excluding everyone who did not start Web surfing through this particular portal. A researcher also must evaluate how representative the online population is for the specific research project. There is no need for everyone in the target population to be online; however, the researcher must ensure that the target market has a large enough Internet user base to prevent the introduction of a sample selection bias.

The second criterion in evaluating the usefulness of the Internet for a project is confidentiality. As a rule, if any of the material is confidential, the Internet is not recommended because researchers do not have proper control over the distribution of the material. A more appropriate research method for confidential material is the personal interview, at a central location.

Third, in the design phase of the marketing study, a researcher must consider the complexity of the interview process. The Internet is better suited for short, simple, unambiguous surveys and questionnaires. If a project calls for complex questioning, an offline interview will yield a higher quality of data. It is recommended that anything that takes longer than 15 to 20 minutes to complete should be conducted offline.

In addition to these three criteria, it should be mentioned that the Internet has also enabled international marketing research projects. Historically, these projects have been extremely complex to administer and prohibitively expensive. With the Internet, however, researchers can communicate with market participants around the globe. The barriers of databases with incomplete addresses, lost international mail, time delays from mailing, and expensive and time-consuming travel have all been reduced. Consequently, international marketing research has become a new marketing research topic. To do effective international research, the researcher must also consider two additional aspects particular to this kind of marketing research: translation and culture.

First, it is important that in-country experts translate multilingual research, because a textbook understanding of a language does not properly capture the required nuances, and one country's use of a word might differ slightly from another country's use. Second, multicultural research requires a careful review of the cultural tastes, preferences, and taboos in each participating country. For example, in the United States and Europe, opinion polls about state dignitaries are commonplace, and newspapers and magazines frequently print them. Yet it is highly unlikely that an opinion poll about the royal family of Thailand would ever be conducted there, and most certainly it would never be published.

The guidelines above are not all-inclusive, and the researcher should use past experience and common sense when deciding whether to use the Internet for data collection. Moreover, to avoid any unpleasant surprises, it is highly recommended that a researcher become familiar with a test site before conducting any research. A test site will reveal any ambiguity and will give the researcher an idea of any preempted completion.

Collect Data

Once a research plan has been developed, the researcher begins data collection. A researcher can select from a number of offline and online collection methods. This section describes the most popular offline and online mar-

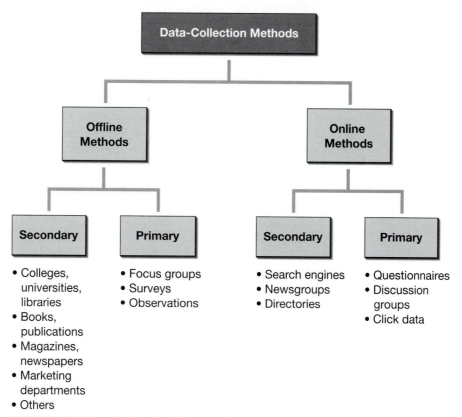

EXHIBIT 15.11   Marketing Research Data-Collection Methods

keting research tools and discusses their advantages and disadvantages. Exhibit 15.11 provides an overview of these tools.

Secondary Research Methods

As mentioned in the previous section, secondary research material is information that has been gathered by other parties and has been made available for public use. The most well-known sources of secondary data are published statistics, published texts, media (e.g., documentaries), and personal documents. Other sources include:

- Past marketing research surveys
- Other surveys
- Census information
- Publications
- Focus group reports
- Written, verbal, or video information

There are many reasons to rely on secondary research, and this option should be investigated prior to undertaking primary research. Secondary research is less expensive, readily accessible, and the best way to examine large-scale trends. Often it is the only resource available, especially for historical information. Moreover, a researcher can use it to plan the collection of primary data, to define the population, and to select the sample for primary research.

There are also problems with secondary research that must be recognized. First, the availability of data may be limited or nonexistent, and thus primary research is required. Second, the relevancy of the secondary research material must be established. Are the units of measurement the same? Is the definition of classes appropriate? Are there time-related problems? Finally, the accuracy must be validated. Was the researcher competent? What was the motivation of the researcher? Did the researcher have any bias?

Until a few years ago, offline secondary research was the most popular research method. Students and researchers alike spent countless hours browsing through research material in libraries and other research facilities. Although the Internet is slowly eliminating this method of research, it remains the only way to obtain information that is not available online. Over time, secondary offline methods should become obsolete. With more than 50 million webpages already online, this virtual library is growing at the rate of 10,000 pages a day.[3] It is becoming commonplace for researchers to explore the Internet for existing data before visiting the library or conducting primary marketing research.

There are three general places to conduct secondary Internet marketing research: the Internet (usually with the aid of search engines), newsgroups, and directories. Newsgroups are much like chat rooms, but conversation generally does not occur in real time. The largest newsgroups are international, with hundreds of participants and tens of thousands of regular readers. Finally, there are a number of directories available on the Internet that researchers can access. Although the Internet has a tremendous amount of resources, there are strengths and weaknesses that the researcher must understand in order to use the Internet profitably.

Search Engines.   Search engines are essential for any type of research. They provide fast and thorough worldwide searches on a multitude of topics. If the data exist, a search engine will likely find it. Some of the more popular search engines include:

• AltaVista	• Google	• Northern Light
• Ask Jeeves	• Hotbot	• Search
• Dogpile	• LinkMonster	• Surfpoint
• Excite	• Lycos	• Yahoo!
• Go	• Mamma	• WebCrawler

One should not expect to receive free, high-quality data with a simple inquiry on a search engine, as few companies that sell data can afford to give it away. However, many marketing research companies have a corporate webpage, and search engines can be a good starting point for checking on the availability of published reports.

The most vexing problem of search engines, or information drawn from webpages, is information overload. There is a tremendous amount of information and the researcher cannot control the quality of the information, much of which is contradictory.

Newsgroups. Newsgroups are not a recent phenomenon—indeed, they were around long before the Internet became popular. However, they have become a popular category for secondary marketing research on the Internet. Also known as Internet discussion groups, a newsgroup is essentially a message board. Discussions start when someone posts a question or comment on a site and other members reply. Still others reply to the replies. The discussion forms a chain of related postings called a "thread."

There are thousands of Internet newsgroups on a broad range of topics. The primary advantage a newsgroup has over a search engine is that search engines provide links to webpages owned by companies or individuals. These webpages might present a biased viewpoint based on the objective of the webpage designers. Newsgroups, on the other hand, usually represent a free, unfiltered discussion about a particular topic, and can serve as both a secondary and a primary research tool. For secondary research, newsgroups provide a valuable source of data by a number of participants. For primary research, a researcher can use newsgroups to collect information on particular issues.

Directories. The Internet is also host to a large number of directories. The topics covered are diverse, and access to most of these directories is free. Popular in this category are the online equivalents of yellow and white pages. The availability is not limited to the United States, but includes many other countries as well. Directories are becoming increasingly accurate and can provide an excellent starting point for a researcher examining a directory-related issue.

Offline Primary Marketing Research Methods

Offline and online primary research are discussed in two separate sections. Although primary research methods are similar, the difference between offline and online methods is considerable and warrants greater distinction.

Before the advent of the Internet, primary research was at the center of marketing research. Although far from being phased out, offline methods are slowly being replaced, in full or in part, by online alternatives. The major reasons for this shift are time and money. Traditional research is expensive, and corporations elect to use it for only the most crucial business decisions. Moreover, there is a direct tradeoff between time and money—the shorter the deadline, the higher the price. If the budget is small, the project likely will require more time and may not be as thorough. This necessary tradeoff is particularly detrimental for fast-moving industries, such as e-commerce, or industries with short business life cycles.

For many research projects, offline marketing research is still a valuable and effective data-collection method. A researcher opting for primary research via an offline method can choose from one of three major categories—focus groups, surveys, or observations—or combine any of the three.

Sidebar

Online Secondary Research
Every time a person accesses the Internet, information about that person is collected. This information can be captured on any number of websites and includes data such as how the user arrived at a particular site, what the user viewed while at the site, who the user communicated with while at the site, and where the user went after leaving the site.

Over the past few years, companies such as Planet-Feedback and Opion have developed new marketing research businesses designed to capture what is said about companies online and to determine customer trends as they are emerging. Both companies, through their proprietary technology, scan Internet discussion boards for consumer opinions about companies and their goods and services. In this setting, customers speak freely in an open dialogue. Opion attempts to identify opinion leaders by analyzing how the leader's phrasing spreads through a group. The company does not track a user through the use of cookies or IP addresses; it simply tracks the buzz such users create and uses this buzz to predict trends before they become widespread. PlanetFeedback attempts to sort these conversations by product and product attributes to help companies market and improve their products. *Note: Planet Feedback acquired much of Opion's technology and intellectual-property assets in August 2002.*

Focus Groups.   Focus groups are an assembly of people (often six to nine) who meet at a predetermined location. The group session is led by a monitor who follows a script; the session lasts about one or two hours, and often is videotaped or audiotaped. This type of group is particularly useful for qualitative research, as it can be used to solicit ideas, feedback, and constructive evaluations of products, issues, and future promotional ideas. To assure a representative sample, there should be a minimum of two groups scheduled per target market.

Focus groups bring out users' spontaneous reactions and ideas and provide useful insights on group dynamics and organizational issues. However, because the reactions and ideas are spontaneous, they merely assess what subjects say they do. Because there are often major differences between what people say they do and what they actually do, focus groups should be supplemented by observations.

Surveys.   Surveys are popular for quantitative research projects to answer the why, how, and who of a particular problem. They are most useful when attempting to substantiate a hypothesis, prove a theory, minimize risk, or obtain reliable samples for projecting trends. Trained professionals usually develop surveys and distribute them to research participants in person, over the telephone, or by mail.

Personal, or in-home, interviews are most useful in situations where the interviewer wishes to observe reactions, to probe, or to clarify answers. Generally, interviews are scheduled in advance with participants, resulting in a high survey completion rate. Interviewers can use visual displays and control the sampling of the target population. However, in-home interviews are costly, time-consuming, and suffer from interviewer bias. Interviewer bias is the contaminating effect of the interviewer's opinion, expectation, or general lack of objectivity.

Telephone interviews are less costly than personal interviews and have a relatively good geographical reach. However, telephone interviews can be problematic; often, people are not willing to cooperate. Even if they do consent, their time is limited, so a survey cannot be too long. It is best not to use telephone interviews for complex issues that require extensive explanation.

Surveys conducted by mail provide wide geographic distribution at a relatively low cost. The interviewer is eliminated, along with any interviewer bias. The anonymity of participants can be assured, and respondents can answer at their leisure. However, accurate mailing lists are hard to obtain, and thus the responses are not necessarily representative of the population. Again, the length of the survey must be limited because few people are willing to spend a lot of time and energy completing a questionnaire. Consequently, mail surveys usually get sufficient coverage for a first set of questions and limited or no coverage for ensuing questions. This is commonly referred to as question-order bias. Finally, mail surveys cannot guarantee a specific total sample.

Observations.   Observation research is the systematic process of recording the behavior of people, objects, and occurrences without questioning or communicating with them. Observational research addresses a problem inherent in both surveys and focus groups: biased information. As mentioned above, research subjects often provide biased information about themselves if asked directly. Observation research provides information that is more accurate in that there is no direct communication with the subject, but an observation of actual behavior. There are two basic groups of observation research: naturalistic and obtrusive.

A researcher using a naturalistic approach observes subjects as they interact in their natural environment. For example, sitting on a nearby bench and watching children playing at a playground is a **naturalistic observation**. Observing a subject being interviewed through a one-way mirror is another example. The key to natural observation is that the observer in no way interferes with the behavior or actions of the research subjects. **Obtrusive observation** is just the opposite. Here, the researcher joins the observation group, and each member knows his or her role. An example of obtrusive observation is the Division of Motor Vehicles representative sitting next to a test taker during an on-road driving test.

Although observation research addresses a number of undesirable features of surveys and focus groups, it is among the most difficult data-collection techniques. Observers must undergo significant training in observation methodologies, particularly on how to report their findings.

Online Primary Research Methods

Until a few years ago, a high-quality primary marketing research study took considerable time, effort, and money to complete. An average study would take at least three months, and often much longer, from start to finish. For example, telephone interviews of individuals would cost a sponsor around $60 per interview. Given the representative sample requirement, an average study could cost over $100,000 to complete.

The rapid growth of the Internet, however, has created opportunities for collecting worldwide primary research data. Online survey costs have dropped to approximately $0.25 per person, representing a 99 percent savings. Moreover, rather than intercepting people in a mall or going door to door and asking people to complete a questionnaire, online researchers literally have the capability to reach millions of individuals at the click of a mouse. Marketing researchers widely believe that the impact of the Internet on marketing research is comparable to the impact that the high penetration rate of telephones had on telecommunications in the late 1950s. Already, a large number of marketing research firms, think tanks, and corporations take advantage of the new data-collection method. For instance, CNN.com features a daily opinion poll on its webpage, examining current political and social debates.

How the role of the Internet in marketing research develops in the long run, however, remains to be seen. The key challenges of this new medium are quality and acceptance. Quality is of critical importance; research suppliers strive to collect quality Internet data. This is not a trivial task. Acceptance is similarly important, as only time will tell whether clients are willing to embrace the Internet as a reliable alternative to traditional marketing research methods.

The research tools for Internet-based marketing research fit roughly into three categories: questionnaires, discussion groups, and click data. Questionnaires tend to be more useful for qualitative research, where the researcher is trying to determine the "who" (Who made a decision?) and the "what" (What did he or she decide?). Discussion groups are more suited for qualitative research that answers the "why" (Why was that decision made?) and the "how" (How was it made?). Click data are most appropriate when the researcher does not want to interfere with behavioral patterns.

Questionnaires. Questionnaires are a collection of graphical user interfaces (GUIs). Depending on the researcher's goals and preferences, one interface might work better than another (see Exhibit 15.12). There are no fixed rules on which interface works best. Once the researcher has identified the type of online questionnaire to be used, the questionnaires must be programmed using Java, HTML, or any other programming language, and then posted on a secure Internet website. Researchers steer traffic to the website and encourage Internet users to participate in the survey by using banner ads on selected websites, direct e-mail invitations, and telephone and mail invitations. Listed below are some questionnaire interfaces.

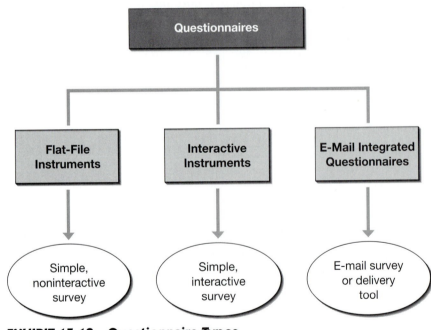

EXHIBIT 15.12   Questionnaire Types

- *Flat-file instruments.* Flat-file instruments (FFIs) are Web-based interfaces consisting of a simple questionnaire that is posted on a secure webpage. Examples of FFIs are the daily surveys posted on CCN.com. The defining characteristic of an FFI is a limited number of questions presented in a noninteractive format. Some FFIs are software-enabled to display automatic statistical updates. That is, as soon as a user submits his answers, statistical feedback compares them with the answers of all previous respondents. One advantage of the FFI method is that surveys are easily designed and programmed. Particularly convenient are surveys posted on a regular basis. Also, given the limited number of questions, they are user-friendly and do not require much time to complete. A drawback of an FFI is the limited number of questions that can be posed, as well as the lack of interactivity. Consequently, an FFI is best suited for situations in which researchers want to frequently poll the market with a limited set of questions at a low cost.

- *Interactive instruments.* Interactive instruments are upgraded versions of FFIs. They are almost the same as FFIs except they have interactive capabilities, which means a researcher can use responses to past questions to pose future questions. An interactive survey that is well-known to graduate students in business administration is the Graduate Management Aptitude Test (GMAT). Although not online, the computer version of the GMAT selects the level of difficulty of future questions based on the responses of previous questions. Interactive questionnaires are complex to design and implement, and thus are recommended only for experienced users and when interactive capability is important.

- *E-mail integrated questionnaires.* E-mail is often used for conducting Web-based surveys. First, instead of posting a questionnaire on a webpage, e-mail can be used to distribute questionnaires to participants. To date, e-mail questionnaires have been used mainly for studies involving smaller, more homogeneous groups.[4] Researchers seem not to use e-mail surveys for larger or international projects. At least one study suggests that this is an untapped market, and concludes that e-mail–integrated questionnaires can provide "adequate data for the study of online populations . . . [and] may provide richer data about online behavior than postal mail surveys."[5] E-mail also can be sent to invite people to participate in a survey and provide them with a link and password, if necessary, to the site that contains the questionnaire. Finally, e-mails can be used for reminder messages to those who have not completed a survey, or as a thank-you message to those who have.

Regardless of the type of online survey used, a researcher must decide on a number of logic features that he or she wants to include in the questionnaire. The list below provides a selection of popular logic features.

- *Password control.* This feature controls who completes a survey and excludes anyone who does not fit the profile of the research subjects. For example, Wells Fargo Bank might want to investigate the customer satisfaction of its online customers. To limit the respondents to Wells Fargo Bank customers, it could make the questionnaire available only to individuals who are currently logged in to its system by requiring a user name and password.

- *Answer reduction.* This feature shows only answer choices that respondents either picked or did not pick as an answer to a previous question.

- *Answer and question randomization.* Survey respondents tend to answer a first set of questions carefully, and then skip through or omit the remaining questions. To get an approximately even exposure to all questions, researchers often randomize the display sequence of question or answer choices.

- *Answering requirement.* This option requires survey participants to answer a predetermined number of questions before being able to submit the survey. The predetermined number of questions could include all questions or only a subset.

Similar to traditional offline survey design, effective questions are key to any questionnaire. However, when designing online questionnaires and questions the researcher has additional decisions to make. The Internet is best suited for the following three types of questions: (1) single-response, dichotomous, or multichotomous questions; (2) scaled questions; and (3) paired-comparison or tradeoff questions (see Exhibit 15.13).

Single-response, dichotomous, or multichotomous questions are questions that ask the respondent to select from one, two, or several responses. "Pick your income range," followed by a list of five income categories, is an example of such a question. Because the user completes the survey online, it forces the respondent, via programming language, to pick one and only one answer from the list.

Scaled questions are similar, except that they rank the importance of an item on a nominal or ordinal scale. "On a scale from one to 10, with one being the lowest and 10 the highest, how do you rank the importance of monthly performance reviews?" is a sample of this type. Again, this ensures that a respondent pick one and only one option from the list. "Which kind of car do you prefer—a Porsche or a Mercedes-Benz?" is an example of a paired-comparison or tradeoff question. This type of question also allows respondents to select only one answer.

Questions that are somewhat suited for online questionnaires, but not necessarily recommended, are those that require multiple comparison, multiple response, or a ranking. "What car brand do you prefer—Lexus, Porsche, BMW, or Mercedes-Benz?" is an example of a multiple comparison question. "Choose one or more locations from the above list" is an example of a multiple response question. "Rank from one to 10, with one being the lowest and 10 the highest, the importance of these 10 concepts" is an example of a ranking question. These types of questions add complexity to the design and programming of the questionnaire, increase respondent error, and reduce participation rates.

Finally, open-ended questions, such as "In 100 words or less, what do you think of personal Internet use in the workplace?" are not well suited for the Internet. They require extensive typing by the respondent, therefore yielding low participation rates.

In addition to considerations about the type of questions to ask, researchers must keep in mind the following three rules when drafting an online questionnaire:

1. Ask only simple questions.

2. Ask only questions that can be answered.

3. Avoid leading questions; do not try to sell a product or lead the respondent in a certain direction.

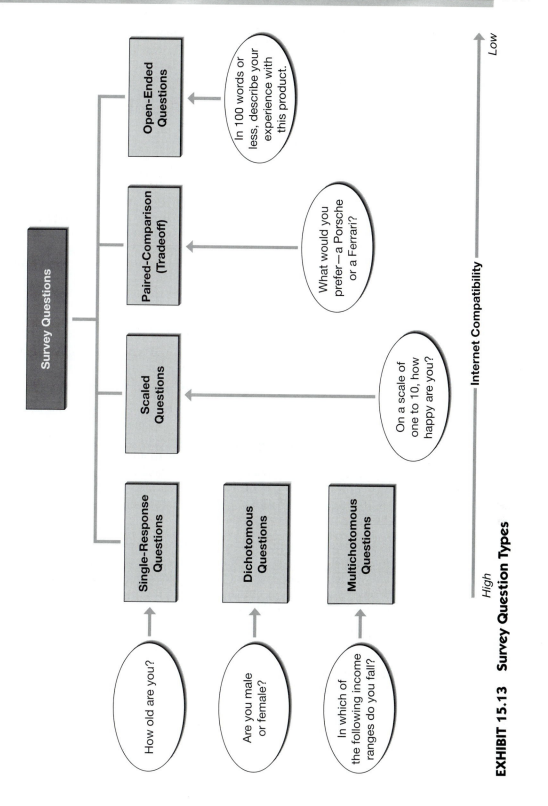

EXHIBIT 15.13   Survey Question Types

Discussion Groups.   As with questionnaires, discussion groups come in many variations. They range from a more open forum, such as chat rooms, to closely monitored sessions, such as focus groups. As mentioned previously, discussion groups can serve as a secondary research tool if the discussion is monitored by an observing party, or as a primary research tool if a number of questions are posed and participants' responses elicited.

Online chat groups or chat rooms allow individuals to interact using typed messages. America Online's chat rooms are some of the most popular on the Internet. AOL features chats about a number of topics, and users can select which discussion they want to join. Although chat rooms create interactivity among participants, they are of only marginal use for marketers. Chat rooms are not sufficiently formal and cannot provide high-quality research data. Unless researchers are simply interested in getting an idea of what the market might think about a topic, they should avoid chat rooms.

The Internet also provides an excellent foundation for conducting online focus groups. Usually consisting of six to nine participants, online focus groups are held in a virtual facility that only selected participants can access, via a personal computer and an access code. Online focus groups last from one to two hours and usually are monitored to keep the group focused.

The main advantage of online focus groups is that they can be controlled better than chat rooms, in at least two respects. First, they consist of recruited participants rather than a self-selected group; for example, when investigating the response to a new medical treatment, an online focus group might consist of a number of experts in the field (an expert-user panel). Second, due to their size, focus groups are more easily monitored than chat rooms. Thus, the researcher has more control over the quality of the data obtained from focus groups.

Compared with their offline counterparts, online focus groups represent a substantial cost savings as participants can log in from almost anywhere in the world without travel and lodging expenses. Moreover, participants receive compensation only for the time they spend in the focus group, not for travel time. Due to the reduced time requirements, scheduling an online focus group is also easier.

Click Data   This is an increasingly prominent data-collection tool. Click data are collected by tracking an Internet user's moves through a website or even across websites, which yields information about his/her preferences. Click data are the online equivalent of observational data. In most cases, the Internet user is unaware of any tracking. This makes click-data research highly controversial.

A number of methods exist to collect click data. One method is user tracking. Internet advertising company DoubleClick, for example, tracks an individual's steps through various websites via the use of "cookies" and advertisements in their researcher network. Click data can also be collected through site tracking. Although not nearly as detailed as user tracking, site tracking records information such as:

- Names of visiting host computers
- Countries from which users are visiting
- Internet protocol addresses of visitors
- Traffic volume by hour
- Search engines that were used or the referring webpage
- Average load time
- Type of operating system used by the visitor
- Total hits per visitor by day or month

The advantages of click data can be summarized in two words: cheap and easy. The only cost associated with click data is obtaining the necessary software to collect the data, although sometimes this software is free. However, a researcher must carefully review whether click data will work for a specific research task. One obvious drawback of click data is that they provide only information about users visiting one webpage or a number of webpages in a larger network. Thus, unless the researcher focuses only on obtaining information from this population or has reason to believe that this population is representative of the target population, click data might yield biased results.

The Internet has become an important source for marketing researchers. Web-based marketing research has revolutionized the industry and has mitigated time and cost concerns that researchers have struggled with for decades. However, online methods come with a different set of limitations, which must be taken into consideration by the researcher (see Exhibit 15.14).

Decision Factor	Offline Method	Online Method
Cost	High	Low
Turnaround time	Slow	Quick
Effort	Labor-intensive	Labor-nonintensive
Data quality*	Medium	High
Researcher control	High	Low
Sampling	Accurate	Inaccurate
Sample-selection bias	Controllable	High to uncontrollable**
Delivery/illustration	Limited	Unlimited
Interviewer bias	High	Low
Geographical coverage	Limited	Unlimited
Anonymity guarantee	High to medium	Low to medium
Ethical issues (privacy)	Low	High

*Quality of data is defined here as ease and timeliness of data collection and entry.
**As the Internet becomes ubiquitous, this issue is becoming less important.

EXHIBIT 15.14   Comparison of Offline and Online Marketing Research Methods

Organize Data

A critical step in marketing research is collecting the data and organizing the data for analysis. If the researcher designs the study carefully, this step is purely mechanical and simply executes the steps outlined previously. However, whether done mechanically through scanning technology, or manually by a data-entry person, data entry can result in mistakes—some of them irreparable. Data cleaning is of utmost importance, as the analysis is only as good as the quality of the data. Data cleaning should be done manually by at least two people, followed by a final computerized error check, before the data are submitted for analysis.

Analyze Data

The objective of the data-analysis step is to gain insight into the collected data and make forecasts or predictions based on the results. The researcher has a number of analytical procedures available to him (see Exhibit 15.15), ranging from simple tabulations to complex econometric models.[6] Below is a brief summary of typical analytical procedures.

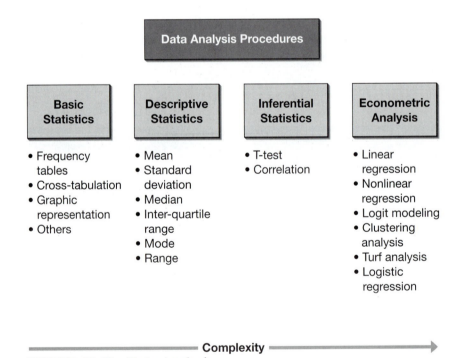

EXHIBIT 15.15   Data Analysis

- *Frequency tables.* A simple way to analyze the collected data is to display then in the form of a table, counting all the possible responses to a question and the percentage of respondents who gave each response.

- *Cross-tabulation.* Cross-tabulation combines two or more categorical variables into one table to show frequencies and percentages. It is an extension of frequency tables, but instead of displaying the count and percentage for each variable, it does it by categorical variable.

- *Graphic representation.* Line charts, pie charts, bar charts, and two- and three-dimensional figures are all examples of graphic representations.

- *Descriptive statistics.* Although slightly more advanced, descriptive statistics make use of statistical measures to describe the characteristics of a population. Measures include central tendencies, mean, median, and mode, and corresponding measures of variability, standard deviation, interquartile range, and range.

- *Inferential statistics.* These statistics draw inferences about a sample or population through either hypothesis testing or estimation.

- *Econometric analysis.* Many modeling techniques can be applied to marketing research data. These techniques require advanced econometrics and are outside the scope of this book.[7] Common types of econometric analysis include linear and nonlinear regression analysis, logit modeling, clustering analysis, turf analysis, and logistical regression.

Validation

Validation is a crucial step in any marketing research study. Also known as a "face test," validation is a test of common sense, and answers the question of whether the results of the study seem realistic. Validation tests are usually divided into two overall categories: internal and external. **Internal validation** tests ensure that there are no abnormalities in the study results. For example, in a study in which the researcher wants to examine the effect of pricing levels on demand, the researcher would assume that the higher the price, the less the demand for that good or service. An internal validity check would test for this expectation to hold. However, if demand goes up when the price increases, and there is no logical explanation for that phenomenon, the study will have failed the internal validity test.

Similarly, **external validation** tests compare the outcome of the study to external sources that are known to be true. For example, in a study that forecasts the penetration rates of the Internet, one could forecast the penetration rate for the year 2000 and then compare the forecasts to information for that same year. If the forecast and the actual figure differ significantly, the study would have failed the external validity test.

Utilize Data

The last step in a marketing project is the summarization of the findings in a formal report. The report should focus on key statistics that are clearly presented in understandable language. A researcher should refrain from confusing charts and industry jargon. Many research reports also tend to include an overload of information that is not relevant to the reader. A completed report should provide companies with information about the study market segment, and help management make decisions about how to approach and communicate with existing and potential customers.

The Internet has drastically affected marketing research, especially the availability of research reports and other secondary data sources. In the past, research reports were distributed via magazines, newspaper articles, textbooks, or industry conferences. Now, the Internet enables these reports to be distributed quickly and inexpensively to a wide audience.

Zoomerang Example

Recently, a colleague was invited to participate in a Zoomerang survey about jewelry styles and jewelry-buying preferences. She logged onto the survey website and completed the survey within 15 minutes. The survey began when she clicked on a link sent in an e-mail to her, and then entered the provided password.

The survey was easy to follow. The first questions established basic demographics (age, income, zip code, etc.) and her jewelry-buying habits (purchase jewelry for self, buy jewelry at a mall store, etc.). After two short screens of these questions, perhaps no more than 10 questions total, the next series of screens showed pictures of various pieces of jewelry. For example, she was shown a set of rings made of different materials (yellow gold, white gold, combinations of white and yellow gold, etc.) and asked to select the style she liked best. After going through several dozen picture sets, the survey concluded with a few additional questions regarding price. After completing the survey, she was entered into a drawing for a prize. When she tried logging back on to the site to study the survey further, the password no longer worked, nor did the back button on the browser.

Evaluating the survey according to the framework in this section, we can surmise the company sponsoring the research study was interested in the buying habits of jewelry shoppers and was likely interested in whether the styles being shown were attractive to people who buy jewelry. Referring back to Exhibit 15.7, it appears the study was trying to answer the question, "What styles does our target market like, how likely are they to buy those styles, and at what price?"

After observing the survey format, the research type was likely a conclusive research study. In more detail, the survey was seeking primary quantitative research. One concern of surveyors might have been that the population that shops and buys jewelry online is not necessarily the best population to determine the most popular styles. Our colleague mentioned that she had filled out an online profile that is kept on file with Zoomerang, and that they contact her via e-mail when they need a particular sample that matches her demographic, thus the invitation e-mail and password. This approach seemed similar to telemarketers or catalogers who target consumers based on zip codes.

In assessing the questionnaire, first let us review Exhibit 15.10. It appears that a representative sample could be drawn using the Internet, that the site was protected, that the back button on the browser was disabled, and that the survey was straightforward and easy to use. By these measures, using the Internet for this survey was appropriate.

Database Marketing

Not too long ago, customer attentiveness was the rule rather than the exception in buyer and seller exchange events. Vendors would interact frequently with their customers, and as a result got to know them. This knowledge base made it easier for them to "push the right buttons" and satisfy them. For example, consider a shopping experience of a fictitious Mrs. Schwartz:

> Herbie invited Mrs. Schwartz's son to his seventh birthday party. Not knowing his taste or his hobbies, Mrs. Schwartz set out for Avril Toy to buy him a gift. As she entered the store, the shop owner, Mr. Avril, greeted her. "I'm looking for a toy that a 7-year-old boy might like," Mrs. Schwartz told him. Mr. Avril showed her a few items, but she was still unsure what to buy. Mr. Avril then asked a key question: "Could you tell me something about the birthday boy, so maybe I could recommend something?" Mrs. Schwartz replied, "Herbie will be seven and—." Before she could finish her sentence, Mr. Avril interjected, "Pardon me, but is the birthday boy Herbie Smith?" It so happened that Mr. Avril lived next to Herbie, his own kids played with Herbie and his siblings, and several other parents had already purchased birthday gifts for Herbie at his store. He proceeded to tell her about Herbie's interests, and informed her of what other people had already purchased for him. Within a few minutes, Mrs. Schwartz had purchased a gift for Herbie that she felt was something he did not own and would enjoy, and that no one else would be giving him for his birthday.

Mrs. Schwartz felt that she'd received exceptional service at Avril Toy. She felt that her individual needs were understood, attended to, and satisfied. The x-factor was a merchant, Mr. Avril, who was armed with important knowledge that allowed him to provide personal service.

Such service is not the norm today. Rather, standardized and impersonal service has become fairly standard. Manufacturers lost touch with individual consumers. They focused on scaling production, communication, distribution, and market knowledge in order to increase value and profits. This approach helped to drive down prices for consumers, and delivered respectable profits to firms. However, the mass-produced exchange process left consumers feeling that many of their personalized needs were not being recognized. The term **Mrs. Schwartz** can be used to represent these alienated consumers who wish to have their needs understood and satisfied.

Relatively recent advances in computer and Internet technology have enabled marketers to more easily obtain and utilize meaningful individual-level consumer information, and to reconnect with customers, as part of the marketing process. **Database marketing** has the potential to augment the mass-produced approach with increased attentiveness, customization, and efficient spending, which would increase utility for consumers—and profits for organizations—when carried out effectively.

Note that the concept of database marketing is not new. Local merchants such as Mr. Avril, who existed long before the invention of computer databases, practiced a similar type of marketing. Processes at the heart of database marketing are obtaining meaningful individual-level consumer information, respecting consumers' privacy, analyzing this information to estimate consumer response to various offers, and making marketing decisions based on this expected response. The primary difference between Mr. Avril's type of database marketing and today's version of it is the capabilities of available support tools.

Define Problem

In database marketing, four general types of objectives exist: (1) identifying prospects, (2) qualifying prospects, (3) acquiring a customer through the sale of a good or service, and (4) managing a relationship with a customer.[8]

Identifying prospective customers, or leads, is important to both B2B and B2C marketers. Sales leads may be identified through available lists or through interactive phenomena such as website or e-mail newsletter registration. This becomes very important if the cost of a field sales call is high and when marketing infrequently purchased products such as automobiles, real estate, and insurance. Prospects become qualified leads when they indicate an authentic intention to buy, through processes such as visiting a retailer's website, requesting more information in response to an e-mail newsletter, or signing up for a free product trial offering through a website. When a qualified lead is available through an interactive channel, the opportunity exists to increase communication, learn more about a prospective customer, and develop a prepurchase relationship.

As in direct marketing, selling is a frequent objective of database marketing. For example, Amazon.com registrants may review several daily personalized "gold box" promotional offers for products that are available at specially discounted prices for up to one hour after being viewed. When a consumer makes an initial purchase and establishes a relationship as a customer, database marketing may be used effectively to manage this relationship. This is discussed in greater detail in the section on customer relationship management.

Planning a Database Marketing Program

The elements of a database marketing program plan are similar to those in a corporate strategy or marketing plan (see Exhibit 15.16). The details of each component of this process are not discussed here because many of them are covered in the chapters on strategic and marketing planning. However, one key aspect of the plan that is different, and is described here, is database planning considerations, which include database development, utilization, and enhancement.

When developing a database, the first important reality to keep in mind is that the database will "only be as powerful as the data it houses."[9] Therefore, it is critical to:

- Identify customer-related data that can effectively support decision making
- Develop procedures for obtaining and entering these data into the database
- Determine how these data and information will be retrieved
- Define who will have access to the database

It is also important to carefully plan how and when a database will be utilized, and to anticipate opportunities for updating or enhancing a database.

Enhancement refers to the incorporation of additional data, typically from outside sources, in order to better understand prospects or customers, and to better predict their response to marketing actions. These data could be classified along the lines of any segmentation scheme, such as demographics, psychographics, or behavior. For example, a retailer or manufacturer could enhance its database of current customers or website registrants with psychographic data on their athletic or cultural interests.

I.	Marketing objectives
II.	Market analysis
	A. Customer analysis and segmentation
	B. Competition
	C. Environment
III.	Offer and market fit
IV.	Assessment of performance with similar programs
V.	Communication strategy
	A. Targeting and positioning
	B. Unique selling proposition
	C. Media and list decisions
	D. Message strategy
VI.	Database requirements
	A. Development
	B. Utilzation
	C. Enhancement
VII.	Program budget
VIII.	Timeline
IX.	Accountability

EXHIBIT 15.16   Database Marketing Program Plan

Database Marketing Decision Variables

The primary decision variables or levers in a database marketing program are the offer, creative, media, timing, and customer service. The offer is composed of the product, relevant purchase terms (such as price, payment terms, or discounts) and the product's positioning. The creative lever includes considerations for copy, layout, design, fidelity such as video or sound, functionality such as degree of interactivity, and elements of personalization such as addressing the target consumer by name. The media decision pertains to the channel(s) for distributing an offer, such as e-mail, website, and instant messenger, as well as traditional channels such as telephone and postal mail. The timing variable includes decisions on when, and how often, to deliver an offer. For example, a retailer may decide to have a pop-up notice about a free shipping promotion appear every time a person directs his or her browser to the retailer's website homepage. Or, a retailer may elect to vary the delivery of an e-mail offer to an individual based on the frequency of that person's behavior, such as visiting the website, abandoning a full shopping cart, or viewing the webpage of a particular product.

Customer service is also an important database marketing program decision variable; it can be a major determinant in customer satisfaction, particularly in situations where the physical products offered by competitors differ very little, or when the shopping process itself is important to consumers, which is the case in many online buying situations.[10] This decision involves selecting the types and levels of service activities or options to be used for facilitating a purchase by a consumer. Some types of customer service include the availability of service agents, product information, opportunities to try or test the product, offer guarantees, and fulfillment-related aspects such as payment, shipping, and order-process monitoring.

The level of customer service is determined by the variety and intensity of each type of service option made available. For example, Lands' End service agents are available via toll-free telephone numbers, e-mail, and online chat. Macromedia allows prospective customers to download 30-day free-trial versions of its software products, including those that retail for thousands of dollars. L.L. Bean accepts product returns when consumers are anything less than 100 percent satisfied. Amazon.com e-mails order confirmation and processing information, and enables consumers themselves to monitor the order process, including shipping. Neiman-Marcus will immediately arrange for pickup and delivery of a product that was delivered in defective condition.

Collect Data

In order to develop a meaningful understanding, or form a reasonable composite, of a prospect or customer, marketers need to acquire data on them. Ultimately, the collective data should enable the marketer to more efficiently acquire, or serve, customers that will, through their response, satisfy performance criteria detailed in the marketing plan, such as revenues or profits. Database marketers consider lists as sources of these data. A list is a collection of data that correspond to identifiable individuals, commonly by name and contact information such as address, who may be potential targets of a database marketing program.

Sources of Lists

Customer data may come from either internal or external sources. Internally generated data result from a direct relationship with a person. For example, tracking website visit behavior, dialogue from an e-mail or chat interaction with customer service, purchase transactions of a registered website member or affinity cardholder, or posts to an organization-controlled discussion forum.

External data may be from three different types of lists. **Response lists** consist of individuals or organizations who have an identifiable product interest, such as golf equipment, and have responded favorably to a marketing offer. A favorable response is traditionally a purchase. However, it may include other responses, such as website or e-mail service registration. For example, Hotmail users and Edmunds.com registrants could be included on response lists for each of these services. A **compiled list** is an amalgamation of multiple lists that contain data on individuals who possess at least one characteristic of interest. The data may be compiled from public sources such as voter registration or census records, or from private sources such as sweepstakes, health clubs, and magazines. A **house list** contains data on customer responses for that specific organization.

List Processing

After selecting a list, a marketer does not immediately distribute an offer to each name on the list. Possessing a list of people and information for contacting them directly, such as an e-mail or physical address, may not be sufficient for effectively delivering an offer to, or contacting, a prospect or customer. **List processing** is a set of procedures for preparing a list for distribution. The main components of list processing are nixie elimination, duplicate elimination, and list suppression.

A list should be cleaned of entries with incorrect addresses and of nixies, which are list entries that contain "undeliverable" addresses. If a person appears more than once in a list, then duplicate entries should be eliminated so that only one offer is distributed to each person, assuming that this is intended. Delivery should not be made to individuals who have requested that their names be suppressed from contact lists—for example, through the Direct Marketing Association's Mail Preference Service, Telephone Preference Service, or E-Mail Preference Service.[11] The term merge/purge is commonly used to describe the combined processes of eliminating duplicates and suppressing list names. Finally, offers should be delivered to individuals who are qualified and likely to provide a response that will satisfy objective criteria of the database marketing program.

Privacy

Information privacy is an individual's ability to control the terms under which personal information is acquired and used. U.S. consumers are highly concerned about privacy issues, and this concern will likely increase as the ability of technology to capture, store, access, share, and process personal information improves.

It is critical that the privacy requests of individuals be honored, given that (1) obtaining information about, and interacting with, customers is at the heart of database marketing; and (2) not respecting a consumer's privacy is a major trustbuster that could significantly reduce the likelihood that a consumer would respond positively to a program offer.

Organize Data

It is critical to identify customer-related data that can effectively support decision making, develop procedures for obtaining and entering these data into the database, determine how these data and information will be retrieved, and define who will have access to the database.

The foundation of database marketing is the establishment and updating of databases for the purpose of supporting managerial decision-making, particularly those databases related to customer acquisition and retention. Many organizations already collect, and have access to, customer data, and may have numerous physical databases. This does not necessarily mean, however, that these organizations have a database that is focused on supporting customer acquisition and retention decisions. A firm should take a consumer-centric approach in establishing a database.

Establishing a Database

When establishing a database for purposes of database marketing, conceptualize each prospective or current customer as a vector of data within the database (see Exhibit 15.17). The content of a **customer vector** should consist of information that may be useful in supporting marketing decisions with respect to acquiring or retaining that customer, or perhaps other customers who are similar or related in some meaningful way. It is not necessary that the data actually be stored in this way. However, it is important to envision the organization of the database in this way when establishing one.

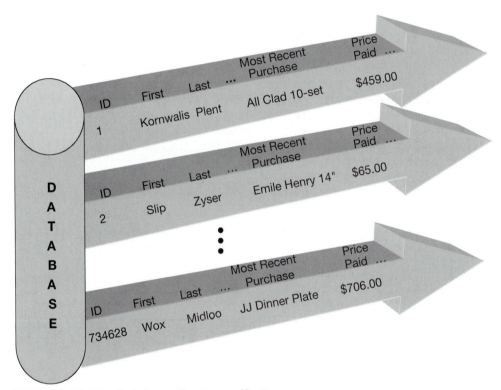

EXHIBIT 15.17   Database Customer Vectors

Next, take an inventory of available data that currently support customer acquisition and retention decisions and processes, and then enter these data, in spirit, into each individual's vector. Ideally, these data will: (1) describe consumers along characteristics such as demographics and lifestyles; (2) report on their transaction history, including information such as products purchased or returned, the date and time of the transaction, expenditures, and discounts applied; (3) inform on the details of customer-firm interactions at contact points, such as click-stream data, when navigating a website, customer inquiries through customer service, and word-of-mouth in online forums; and (4) maintain consumer response to database marketing offers, including items such as offer details, timing, and response.

Updating a Database

As detailed in the section on collecting data, additional information about customers in a database may be obtained from either internal or external resources. In the case of updating a database, it is interesting to consider the effort required in obtaining these data. Winer discusses a 2x2 framework (see Exhibit 15.18) that involves analysis along dimensions of customer interaction (direct and indirect) and interaction frequency (frequent and infrequent).[12]

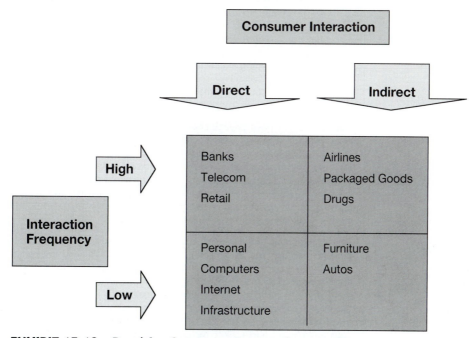

EXHIBIT 15.18   Provider-Consumer Interaction Matrix

Organizations that have frequent direct interaction with consumers, such as supermarkets or drugstores, are most easily disposed to updating their customer database vectors. Alternatively, organizations that have infrequent indirect interactions with their customers, such as automobile manufacturers, need to work relatively hard to obtain new customer information. Firms that have infrequent direct interactions and those that have frequent indirect interactions fall somewhere in between these two extremes. The main point of the framework is that, unless a firm has frequent direct interactions with a customer, it will have to work harder in building its database.

Firms that have to work harder should conceive of tactics or programs that would create more direct interaction, such as e-mail newsletters, contests, and registration-required online content (see the Drill-Down titled "MIT's Auto-ID Program"). For example, the online edition of *The New York Times* is free, but registration is required in order to read complete articles. A registered user's click streams can be tracked.

Analyze Data

The ultimate focus of analysis in database marketing is estimating consumer response to an offer and the expected profit of alternative database marketing programs. This is traditionally done through a process of list segmentation, along with economic analysis of expected revenues and costs.

Drill-Down

MIT's Auto-ID Program

Packaged goods manufacturers, among others, may soon have more direct contact with their customers thanks to researchers of the Auto-ID Center at MIT. The researchers have devised electronic transponders, or "smart tags," that can be attached directly to products and connect them to the Internet. With these tags, consumers could load up their carts and have their credit cards charged automatically after passing through a checkout equipped with special detectors programmed to read and process each tag. These digital dog tags would assist with supply chain issues, such as keeping shelves stocked with products wanted by consumers. In addition, they might also help reduce theft. Corporate sponsors of this research include a variety of leading firms such as Procter & Gamble, Kimberly-Clark, Gillette, Pepsi, Wal-Mart, Target, Tesco, and ACNielsen.

Consumers may have privacy concerns about the use of these tags. First, each product purchased with a credit card could be tracked. At the present time, a credit card company may know how much a consumer spends at a retailer. With smart tags, the credit card company could also know the precise composition of each basket of goods. Second, a variety of sources could gain access to, and use, the information. Retailers and manufacturers, if they cooperate, could obtain the purchase data. Government agencies may demand access to the information under certain conditions. Will no purchase remain private?

Third, the location of these items could be tracked, subject to placement of detectors that can read the tags. At the present time, the detectors need to be within a few feet of the tag in order to read its signal. If, however, the receiving technology could be embedded cheaply in wired or wireless networks, then the precise location and movement of all owned items could conceivably be coordinated. Manufacturers could use this information to learn more about, or interact with, their customers. The government could conceivably use this information to set or enforce policies. For example, litter could be tracked back to the purchaser, who could subsequently be fined.

The smart-tag system is being tested in some Wal-Mart stores. Costs for mass use of such a system, however, are currently prohibitive—the variable cost for each tag is estimated at 50 cents. The target cost for practical usage is 5 cents.

List Segmentation

List segmentation is used to associate individuals with various types of possible responses, such as favorable (buy) and unfavorable (not buy). List segmentation consists of applying segmentation to a list. That is, each person is placed into a distinct group or category. The groups are commonly based on response or characteristic variables that are related to response behavior. Practically, it is a process for determining to whom a particular type of offer should be distributed. It is not assumed that everyone on a list will receive an offer, as some individuals could be categorized into segments for which a less than desired response may be predicted, such as no purchase.

In addition, not all individuals may see the same offer, as various segments may respond differently to different offers. At the greatest extreme, each person would comprise a unique segment with its own estimated response, such as probability of purchase, expected dollar value of purchase, or lifetime value. Distinct offers could be created for each type of expected response, or other decision criteria, such as profits.

Though consumer response could be estimated at the individual level, it is not assumed that segmentation schemes with group sizes of one are optimal— even when anticipated response for every individual is unique. Other aspects of the marketing process may play a significant role in determining a final segmentation solution, such as operations or network effects. Suppose that every single person on a list had a unique color preference for a bicycle; it may not be optimal, however, to satisfy the ideal color preference for each person due to paint limitations. Or suppose that each person had a unique reservation price for a compact disc and that each person's reservation price was greater than variable cost. It could therefore be optimal to provide each person with a unique offer price. If offers were transparent, however, this could quickly turn into a fiasco, with buyers feeling that they were treated unfairly. An Amazon.com experiment with differential pricing created significant ire among its customers when those customers discovered they were being charged different prices for similar products.[13]

The ultimate objective of list segmentation is to identify people to whom an offer, when made, will result in profit, and to save resources by not contacting those who are unlikely to result in a profitable transaction or relationship.

Segmentation Variables

Traditional classes of variables, such as demographics and psychographics, are useful in list segmentation. Three classic behavioral variables used in database marketing are recency of last purchase, frequency of purchase, and monetary purchase(s) expenditure, collectively referred to as **RFM.** Recency of last purchase is represented by the number of consecutive offers/contacts or months since the last purchase. Frequency of purchase is commonly represented by the number of previous purchases or the proportion of offers/contacts that resulted in a purchase. Monetary amount is typically represented by the total or the average dollar expenditure. Ultimately, whether a variable is used in list segmentation depends on its availability, its costs, and its expected usefulness.

Segmentation Techniques

In the end, segmentation techniques are used to develop a response-related score for each person, and to categorize individuals into segments. In many instances, these scores reflect an individual's probability of purchase, expected dollar expenditure, or lifetime value. It is also important to identify the characteristics that define each segment, as this can provide efficiencies in future list acquisition and target decisions. The scores, or the segments, are used to determine (1) whether to distribute an offer to an individual and (2) the type of offer that should be distributed to each person.

Multiple Regression.   Multiple regression is a widely understood and easy to interpret statistical technique. In list segmentation, it is used to develop a scoring formula that can be used to predict the response to a particular criterion, such as lifetime customer value. A series of independent variables, typically consumer characteristics, are used to predict a dependent variable, typically a behavioral response of some type.

Multiple Discriminant.   This technique is somewhat similar to multiple regression in that it yields a scoring equation. It differs from regression, however, in that the dependent variable is categorical, and predictions are made for the likelihood of membership in each group.

Logistic Regression. Logistic regression is used to develop a scoring equation that predicts the likelihood of each type of response. Logit models are multiplicative and nonlinear (as opposed to multiple regression models, which are additive and linear).

Cluster Analysis. Cluster analysis considers input variables associated with an object and forms distinct groups of like objects, referred to as clusters. In segmentation, clusters would be considered the segments. The object may be a person. However, it may also be many other phenomena, including a geographic region or even a zip code.

Automatic Interaction Detection (AID). AID is a cluster-like technique that uses categorical variables and determines segments based on interaction effects. This technique tends to require a large amount of data, and has relatively large amounts of error. Few consider it the best technique to use for segmentation. Some use it to identify significant interactions, and then use this information in some other type of technique—for example, multiple regression.

Chi Square Automatic Interaction Detection (CHAID). CHAID is similar to AID, except that it allows for more than two levels of a variable.

Neural Networks. Neural network analysis was devised to emulate the process of the human brain, in that the association between input and output is determined through a learning process. It is assumed that processing elements, or neurons, are interconnected with weighted connections, or synapses, in a series of layers. The number of layers in the network and the weights of the connections are what is determined in the learning process. This technique was designed for pattern recognition in complex systems, and to produce robust solutions where input data are imprecise. It considers a variety of consumer characteristics (inputs) and responses (outputs) to learn which patterns of characteristics result in each type of response. The analysis is much like a "black box" in that the inner-workings of network analysis are difficult to comprehend in a meaningful way. In terms of segmentation, the analysis is used to classify individuals into particular segments, such as the contact group and the do-not-contact group.

Measurement

The criteria for segmenting a list, targeting customers, and defining offers for customers can vary widely. The most commonly used measures are those involving revenues or profits. The concept that serves as the foundation for a variety of measurement approaches is **customer lifetime value** (CLV). A customer's lifetime value is a firm's expected total net present value of profit from all direct interactions and exchanges with that customer. The value is based on forecasts of that customer's total stream of revenues in all interactions involving an exchange, less the total stream of costs in interactions, which are typically those for acquisition and service.

Computing the CLV can be complex. However, the overall process, which involves identifying important revenue and cost factors and important customer behaviors and realities over time, can actually clarify sources of profitability—and, in turn, effectively guide decision making with respect to acquiring, retaining, and managing a relationship with a customer. For example, some factors that could affect revenue over time are the number of purchases, the types of items purchased, and the price paid for each item. Models involving terms that reflect these factors could then be used to do "what if" analysis, and to identify potentially more profitable strategies for managing a relationship with a customer.

Measuring CLV has enabled managers to consider a variety of other decision-making criteria, such as return on investment. Most important, this measure helps organizations identify the types of customers that they can and cannot serve profitably at the current time, the types that are highly desirable and that they should pursue, the types that they should avoid, and how to act on this information.

Testing Potential Database Marketing Programs

A traditional tenet in database marketing is to test a program unless it has a high likelihood of success. Testing could be related either to the key program decision variables or the type of person to target. Particular attention should be devoted to important aspects of a program for which a high degree of risk and uncertainty is present.

Hypothesis testing is commonly done. This process involves identifying the decision variables to be investigated; defining the criterion on which the test will be performed, such as cost to acquire a customer or response; formulating the hypotheses to be tested; designing the test; selecting the significance level at which to perform the test; determining the sample size; setting the decision rule for accepting or rejecting the null hypothesis; performing the test; analyzing the results; and then making a decision for each variable being tested.

As in any testing situation, the greater the number of variables or aspects of a variable to be tested, the greater the cost of testing. Sometimes costs in testing can be reduced through good experimental design—for example, identifying situations in which a fractional factorial design would suffice.

Utilize Data

In database marketing, customer acquisition is the goal that drives how data are analyzed, interpreted, and applied. For marketing purposes, the data are helpful in making typical marketing-related decisions, such as segmentation, targeting, positioning, pricing, and promotion. Differences are likely to exist, however, in the approach to interacting with prospective or current customers. As awareness of differences among consumers increases, so too will the opportunities to provide distinct offers to consumers. This, in turn, can generate more profits. At the extreme, the implications of this are significant. Each person would represent a segment of one, could be targeted with a unique offer, and would be willing to pay more for an offer that was tailored just for them.

A key benefit of database marketing is that other functional areas, such as sales, finance, and manufacturing, could utilize the same database information to aid their own decision making. In addition, the customer information could improve cross-functional decision making. For example, marketing could identify the marketing costs and utility associated with various product offerings for each person, operations could determine the production costs for all possible product offer scenarios, sales could estimate the costs of selling, customer service could approximate the long-term care implications, and finance could project profitability and return on investment.

UNCB Example

Established in 1853, the local Union National Community Bank (UNCB) in Mount Joy, Pennsylvania, is a small bank that provides friendly small-town customer service. When large financial institutions, such as FleetBoston Financial, moved into the area, UNCB discovered that customer expectations about banking products and services had changed, and they began losing customers. They tried to stem the tide by reducing loan rates and fees, and by increasing interest rates for deposits. This competitive strategy, however, was ineffective.

The bank invested $250,000 in a database marketing and customer relationship management (CRM) system in order to get back on track, to go after additional market segments, and to improve business operations. It stored customer information in a single data warehouse, and used software to more easily view and analyze customer account activity. The system was able to compute profitability for each customer based on the frequency, revenue, and cost associated with various behaviors, such as banking with a teller, an ATM, or the Internet. Customer profitability was used to segment the market. This allowed the bank to shift from treating everyone the same to treating customers differently based on their value.

This led to strategic changes in UNCB's banking fees and rates. All customers were still treated very well. Customers in high-value segments, however, were treated with extra special care. Tactics were devised for increasing profits from low-value segments, such as directing them to lower cost electronic banking, and selling them higher revenue products. The early returns on investment looked promising. The bank realized a benefit of $1 million, and noninterest income and profits increased by 50 percent and 35 percent, respectively.

Customer Relationship Management

The most valuable baseball card in the world is the extremely rare T206 Honus Wagner. This card was distributed with tobacco in 1910. Honus Wagner demanded that production and distribution of his "tobacco" card be halted early in its production run because, as the most popular legend has it, he was opposed to cigarette smoking. Others, however, have argued that he was opposed to its production because he was not compensated for use of his likeness. Baseball card authorities believe that approximately 50 versions of the T206 Honus Wagner remain in existence.

- In 1985, a mint-condition T206 Honus Wagner baseball card was worth $25,000.
- In 2002, it was worth $1,260,000. The same card, only in fair condition, was worth $78,000.

CRM Lesson No. 1: Take care of your valuable investments, which in marketing are your profitable customers.

Not all customers, however, will be like a T206 Honus Wagner. Dwight "Doc" Gooden broke onto the major league baseball scene in 1984 and by the end of the 1985 season was considered the most dominant pitcher in baseball.

- In 1985, a mint condition 1984 Topps Dwight Gooden baseball card was worth $70.
- In 2001, it was worth 1 cent.

CRM Lesson No. 2: Select your investments wisely. Not all customer acquisitions will be worth it.

Traditionally, marketers have focused more of their actions and expenditures on acquiring customers than on retaining them. Experts report, however, that placing increased emphasis on **customer retention** can significantly impact marketing efficiency and profitability. Management experts Reichheld and Sasser found that "firms can boost profits by almost 100 percent by retaining just 5 percent more of their customers."[14] Desatnick showed that it costs five times more to acquire customers than to retain them.[15]

The Internet and advances in technology have created increased opportunities for maintaining one-to-one dialogue and contact with each customer. During the 1990s, the CRM industry grew quickly, reaching $22 billion in 2001.[16] That number is expected to reach $47 billion in 2006.[17]

Define Problem

Customer relationship management is concerned with three primary directives. First, organizations need to learn about their customers at the individual level, and respect their differences. This will enable firms to recognize the customers with which it is likely to have a profitable relationship and provide indicators for best serving each one. Second, organizations need to formulate strategies for sustaining relationships with profitable or potentially profitable customers. Third, tactics for advancing relationships with customers by creating more value for them need to be devised and put into action. These activities should, in turn, generate a more valuable customer— for example, through cross-selling or up-selling, positive word-of-mouth, and referrals.

Ultimately, customer relationship management is about generating loyalty among customers who are, or will become, profitable. It is also about abandoning relationships with customers who are not, or are unlikely to become, profitable. Practitioners would be wise to employ great care in dissolving relationships with less desirable customers because some dissatisfied customers will share their experiences with others. Consumers are much more likely to spread negative word-of-mouth than positive word-of-mouth.

Collect Data

Organizations can learn more about, and better serve, their customers by facilitating interactions with them. In *Permission Marketing*, Godin asks, "Does every single marketing effort you create encourage a learning relationship with your customers? Does it invite customers to 'raise their hands' and start communicating? Once people become customers, do you work to deepen your permission to talk with those people?"[18] Interactions allow buyers and sellers to continue their contact and communications, which are extremely important elements in healthy and meaningful relationships.

Mechanisms that support customer- or company-initiated contact are an important part of CRM. Simplifying access to an organization, and the benefits it offers, increases the likelihood that a customer will reach out to an organization when engaged in any stage of the buying process, such as searching for information or making another purchase. The opportunities associated with these interactions, particularly obtaining information about a customer's beliefs, attitudes, and behaviors, can give a firm competitive advantage. The learning process associated with better understanding a customer includes recording important elements of an interaction, adding interaction records to other stored information, and analyzing these data.

Customer information based on a touch between a customer and the firm may be collected through touchpoints. The broadest definition of a touch is when a firm encounters information generated by a customer, or when a customer encounters information generated by a firm. A customer viewing a billboard, for example, would be considered a touch.

Touchpoints are the mediums, vehicles, and/or locations through which organizations and customers interact. The greater the number of, and access to, touchpoints, the greater the likelihood that organizations and consumers will keep in touch and continue their market-related "conversations."[19] The ideal, theoretically, would be a never-ending touch. However, the best practical approach is to enable interactions that will likely yield valuable customer information or behavior, through feasible touchpoints.

Relevant touchpoints for Internet marketing include all offline and online forms, such as stores, kiosks, websites, e-mail, chat, telephone, online forums, national offline events such as eBay Community Conference Live, and loyalty or reward programs such as Mobil's Speedpass.[20] Relevant information about the context of a touch, consumer behavior and response, and relevant firm behavior and response from each interaction should be recorded and added to a customer's vector in a database.

Most of these touchpoints are discussed in detail in other chapters of this book. E-mail, however, is discussed here. E-mail has emerged as an extremely important touchpoint. In fact, many believe it is the most important online marketing medium, given its recent adoption and usage rates. E-mail can be classified by whether a firm is using it to initiate contact with a customer or to respond to a contact initiated by a customer.

Firm-Initiated E-Mail

There are four major uses of e-mail for initiating contact with a customer: announcements, special offers, invitations, and newsletters. Announcements provide information about an organization's makeup, practices, partnerships, and the like. They tend to include material that can impact a customer, such as new policies. For example, prior to an NBA basketball game between the Boston Celtics and the Orlando Magic at Boston's Fleet Center, Ticketmaster.com distributed information about "new Fleet Center security procedures" (see Exhibit 15.19). E-mails are also effective for distributing information about special offers, such as a clearance sale event. Hanna Andersson, for example, regularly e-mails customers about special sales (see Exhibit 15.20). E-mail invitations tend to be for events, such as attending webcasts or conferences, or participating in community events or marketing research. Newsletters are distributed on a regular basis, include content that is not necessarily of an immediate sales nature, and are useful to a subscriber (see Drill-Down titled "E-Newsletters that Work").[21]

Drill-Down

E-Newsletters that Work

Michael Katz, dubbed a leader in e-mail marketing by the Peppers & Rogers Group,[22] is the author of a book called *E-Newsletters that Work*.[23] At Blue Penguin Development, where he serves as "chief penguin," Katz writes a bimonthly e-newsletter called "Michael Katz's E-Newsletter on E-Newsletters." [24] Below are insights about e-newsletters gleaned from conversations with Katz and from his book.

An e-newsletter, also known as an e-zine, is one of the best marketing tools to come along in recent years. It is important to first define an e-newsletter. Simply put, it is a glorified e-mail that one sends in bulk to subscribers; that's it. There are three components of an e-newsletter: (1) content (what one writes about, and how one writes about it), (2) formatting/layout (how the content is organized, including fonts, graphics, sections, and links), and (3) delivery/list management (how to add, subtract, and manage the names on a subscriber list, as well as what's involved in getting the newsletter out the door efficiently).

E-newsletters are forwardable, linkable, measurable, archivable, and interactive. They can increase lead generation and cross-selling, raise customer lifetime values, initiate or continue a two-way dialogue with customers, position a firm or person as an expert, and hypercharge existing marketing efforts. Variable costs are extremely low, and fixed costs are easy to control.

E-newsletters have become wildly popular, particularly in the B2B area where folks receive, and promptly delete, about a dozen inbox-cluttering e-newsletters per day. In fact, there is a lot of clutter out there. Fortunately, prospects and customers tire quickly of the self-promoting, in-your-face brand of e-newsletter. Organizations can write e-newsletters that break through the clutter and strengthen relationships over the long term by providing useful, relevant information presented in a clear, genuine voice.

According to Katz, there are three main principles for writing effective e-newsletters.

Principle No. 1: Words Trump Everything Else Every Time

"Grab a copy of *To Kill a Mockingbird*, by Harper Lee. The 1961 winner of the Pulitzer Prize is as fresh and engaging as it was 40 years ago. Now compare it to the last paperback mystery you bought when you were stuck at the airport. Notice anything? Why is one so much more memorable than the other? Is it the binding? The cover art? The paper quality? The distribution network that delivered the books to the store? No, no, no, and no.

"It all comes down to the words. The text of *To Kill a Mockingbird* scrawled on the back of a restaurant napkin would be a more interesting read than a beautiful, high-quality book filled with junk. At the end of the day, content is what matters.

"Obvious? Maybe, but the value of quality words is frequently and almost universally ignored in the world of e-newsletters. Conversations among businesspeople are overwhelmingly dominated by discussions of tracking, formatting, list management, and other logistical aspects of e-newsletter production. Go to e-newsletter business seminars, read business articles about e-newsletters, or listen to the e-newsletter vendors talk about what matters, and content almost never makes it to the top of the list.

continued

"There's nothing wrong with talking about these things, but it's a waste of time if the content of your e-newsletter isn't great. So when you think e-newsletter, think *To Kill a Mockingbird*. At the end of the day, words are the only currency."

Principle No. 2: Love the One You're with

"The primary reason that e-newsletters are so powerful is that they provide a systematic means for growing and maintaining relationships. It's not because they're cheap or trackable or archivable or clickable or forwardable, although they certainly are all those things. It's because they give you a vehicle for connecting with the people who purchase or are likely to purchase your product or service, month after month after month.

"If you write your company newsletter with a focus on enhancing the relationship between you and your readers, you will stand head and shoulders above your competition, most of whom are missing this point entirely, and who (whether they say it out loud or not) view their e-newsletter as an inexpensive way to send direct mail to their house list. When it comes to developing an effective e-newsletter, everything you do—from the way you speak to your readers, to the topics you select to write about, to the way you manage requests to be taken off your mailing list—should reinforce your relationship with your readers."

Principle No. 3: To Thine Own Self Be True

"A few months ago, I attended a local business meeting where I didn't know anybody. After a few minutes of wandering around, I began talking to a man named Mark, who owned his own executive coaching business. Terrific guy: warm, friendly, smart, and easy to talk to. As it turned out, Mark was just about to launch an e-newsletter, and upon learning what I did for a living, he asked if I would mind taking a look at it. I said sure, send it over.

"What a shock. The newsletter, although filled with useful information and insights, was completely without Mark's personality. It was dry, dull, and uncomfortably formal. It was missing the one thing that made Mark stand out in my mind: his vibrant personality. I sent the newsletter back to Mark suggesting some changes, and, in particular, encouraging him to 'speak' to his readers in the same genuine way he welcomed me into the meeting the previous week. He did, and what a difference!

"Look, many of us were taught to write very formally, and in business writing in particular we write as if we are appearing in front of a Senate subcommittee on the importance of being serious in the workplace. Don't do that. E-mail is an informal, one-to-one medium, and the stuff that plays well in *The New York Times* reads like dust online. Be yourself, and give your readers as much of that self as you can in every newsletter."

General principles for effective e-mail marketing pertain to the recipient, the e-mail components, and the response. The Association for Interactive Media's Council for Responsible E-Mail[25] has developed six resolutions for responsible e-mailers:

1. Senders must not falsify a domain name or use a nonresponsive IP address without implied permission from the recipient.

2. Senders must not falsify the e-mail subject line to deviate and mislead recipients from the message content.

3. E-mail messages must include the option to unsubscribe from receiving future e-mails, or valid and responsive contact information of the sender, list manager, or list owner.

4. Marketers must inform recipients of the marketing purpose for using their e-mail address.

5. E-mail addresses must not be harvested with the intent to send bulk unsolicited commercial e-mail without a consumer's knowledge or consent.

6. Sending bulk unsolicited commercial e-mail to an e-mail address without a prior business or personal relationship is objectionable, where a business or personal relationship is defined as any previous correspondence, transaction activity, customer service activity, personalized marketing message, third party permission use, or proven offline contact.

Before you attend the BOSTON CELTICS Vs ORLANDO MAGIC, we wanted to make you aware of the new Fleet-Center Security Procedures.

As we begin another exciting season of FleetCenter events, we remind you that bags, backpacks, luggage, coolers, parcels, briefcases and like articles will be strictly prohibited from the FleetCenter. Binoculars are permitted, but please no cases.

All guests will be subject to search, at the FleetCenter's discretion, of their person and/or possessions (including women's handbags of normal size which may be allowed entry after such search). Patrons with prohibited articles will be turned away at the entrances and no storage or "check-in area" will be provided for such items. Enforcement with be without exceptions.

We're confident that these added precautions are prudent and will be welcomed and understood by everyone. We ask that you please forward this information to anyone who may be going to future FleetCenter events or games. If you have further questions, please go to http://www.fleetcenter.com/tickets_boxoffice.htm or contact your local Ticketmaster Charge by Phone.

Thank you and enjoy the game!

Source: Courtesy of Fleet Center.

EXHIBIT 15.19   E-Mail Describing New Fleet Center Security Procedures

---

Dear Hanna Friend,

If you love a good sale, now's the time to check out all the new specials at hannaAndersson.com!

Go to our sale section for terrific savings on current season items such as Wiggle Pants, Jeepers Creepers, Cozy Flannel Dresses, Cargo Pants in Twills or Cords and Women's Dresses, as well as of past season items! Click the link to go directly to the sale section. http://www.hannaAndersson.com/saleavailability/?MAIL=FALL01

We hope you enjoy the savings,

Hanna

We at Hanna believe we are sending this e-mail with your permission. If you feel you have received this message in error, please click the link below and accept out apologies for the intrusion. You will be removed from this list promptly.

Source: www.hannaanderson.com. Used with permission.

EXHIBIT 15.20   Hanna Andersson Specials E-Mail

The Recipient. A recipient will first decide whether to open an e-mail. E-mail perceived as uninvited (aka spam) is highly unlikely to be opened. A permission-based e-mail, however, has a reasonably high likelihood of being opened. Permission can be obtained directly or indirectly—for example, through a third-party source that keeps e-mail address lists of individuals who have agreed to receive e-mail from particular vendors.

The E-Mail. Keep in mind that e-mail is conversational in nature. E-mails constructed with this principle in mind tend to be most effective. The purpose of an e-mail communication, stated in the subject line, should be clear—the recipient will decide whether to open the e-mail or delete it in a matter of seconds. When sending e-mails for the first time, personalization should be considered. For example, an e-mail alerting a baseball card collector to a new Honus Wagner card up for auction might include the recipient's name in the subject line: "Bruce, there's a mint T206 Honus Wagner up for auction."

The content of the e-mail itself should be readily apparent. On average, it is best to keep sentences to less than two lines, and paragraphs to less than five lines. A lengthy soliloquy can work well in theater, but it is rarely effective in an e-mail. Also, if the reason that the recipient might be interested in the contents of the e-mail is not clear to the recipient, then the odds are low that the e-mail communication will do much for either the customer or the firm.

Response. The objective of sending an e-mail is to provide additional value to a customer, which in turn should result in greater profits for the organization. Before sending an e-mail, it is important to test not only message content or the makeup of an offer, but also format and other communication issues. The latter includes testing variables pertaining to (1) the subject line, such as length and word selection; (2) the body, such as the greeting, sentence length, number of paragraphs, use of color, which links to include, and number of links to include; and (3) distribution decision variables such as timing and frequency.

Metrics for consumer response should also be measured. Common behaviors to measure are whether an e-mail was opened, whether a reply was made, whether an e-mail was forwarded, whether a link to a website was clicked, and any subsequent website behavior such as product search or purchase.

Customer-Initiated E-Mail

There are three primary ways in which organizations tend to respond to e-mail: through automation software, through people, or through a combination of automation software and people. **E-mail automation systems** assist with receiving and sending e-mails, including formatting and distributing them. Artificial-intelligence–based natural language processing is used for direct replies, or to route an e-mail to a particular person who would then provide a direct reply. In general, the natural language process involves parsing an e-mail for key words, and then using this analysis to classify it for action.

When e-mail volume is high, these types of systems can provide great value. For example, they can classify an e-mail and distribute it to the appropriate person based on criteria such as capacity utilization or area of expertise among customer service providers. Errors in classification by the software can be identified in this type of process because people will read the e-mail before a reply is sent.

E-mail marketing experts do recommend caution, however, when using an autoresponder to send a reply that is based purely on natural language processing. E-mail automation systems can be programmed to identify specific patterns, and they can be effective in responding to e-mails that fit known patterns—particularly when the e-mail sender is required to use a form or self-classify the nature of an inquiry. Problems can easily arise when an e-mail does not fit a predefined pattern, or is parsed poorly. A customer's trust in a relationship can be damaged when a sender finds a reply to be unresponsive, that is, leads to an evaluation such as "That's not what I was asking about," "This reply is useless," or "Were they even listening to me?"

The principles behind an effective reply are age-old and straightforward. First, an organization should communicate that it heard the customer and understood the purpose of the e-mail. Second, the reply should address the purpose of the e-mail to the best of the firm's ability. For example, suppose that a Rolls Royce owner sent an e-mail to the company asking about the availability of Rolls Royce key cases—at a time when, unbeknownst to the owner, Rolls Royce key cases were out of production. Possible responses by Rolls Royce included: (1) not replying; (2) indicating that Rolls Royce sells some accessories; (3) indicating that Rolls Royce key cases are no longer produced; (4) indicating that Rolls Royce key cases are no longer produced, and recommending how one might obtain one, such as through a Rolls Royce owners' group; or (5) indicating that Rolls Royce key cases are no longer produced, and then offering assistance in finding one in the marketplace.

Opportunity in Online Community

Online communities are great places for consumers to obtain honest and helpful information that is tailored for their specific needs. It is also an important touchpoint through which firms can learn about, and remain in contact with, customers. Small vendors and individual sellers have caught on to this. Large institutions, however, have not delved deeply into the opportunity because it is a difficult effort to scale.

There is a great need for CRM online community tools. While e-mail provides direct contact between a firm and its customer, this type of touchpoint is unlikely to reveal everything about a customer. Customers reveal different aspects about themselves in different social contexts, such as communities. The potential value in leveraging a community experience in order to better serve customers is tremendous. The opportunity to create and provide tools to realize this potential is similarly outstanding.

Organize Data

Data organization refers to the process of grouping database records—that is, customers—for review, analysis, or utilization. The key part of this process is identifying the key consumer characteristics that would provide material insight into serving a customer, such as those used in segmentation.

Customers may be organized along company-centric and customer-centric dimensions. Company-centric cuts of the data would be based on how employees are organized to serve customers. For example, managers may organize by customer size, geography, products, or brand. Customer-centric dimensions are defined by customer preferences, perceptions, states, or purpose such as preferred touchpoint(s), trust in an organization, loyalty or strength of a relationship, or role in the buying process.

It is common for firms to organize around company-centric dimensions, and to then condition data based on customer-centric elements. For example, account executives may be organized to serve large, medium, and small accounts in a particular geographic region. Data would be organized into these three groups and then made accessible to each type of account executive. Each account executive could then condition the customer data by customer-centric variables, such as relationship strength and preferred touchpoint. This organization could be used in turn to support an action-oriented decision, such as determining which customers to contact first and how to contact them about a new product offering.

Analyze Data

CRM analysis revolves around the state and value of a relationship. Emphasis is placed on measures such as satisfaction, loyalty, share of customer, and customer lifetime value, in addition to common measures of marketing performance such as revenues, profits, and market share.

Satisfaction

Customer satisfaction is based on cumulative experiences related to a firm and its offerings. A positive relationship exists between customer satisfaction and profitability.[26] That is, the greater a customer's satisfaction, the greater the likelihood that a consumer will be disposed to behave favorably toward a firm.

Customer satisfaction with an organization, as modeled by the creators of the American Customer Satisfaction Index, is a function of a customer's perceived quality, perceived value, and expectations.[27] Perceived quality is based on a consumer's most recent consumption experience. Perceived value is the perceived level of product quality relative to the product price. Customer expectations, in essence, reflect the customer's predictions about the organization's ability to deliver quality in the future. The level of customer satisfaction affects the degree of customer loyalty.

Loyalty

Loyalty is a "deeply held commitment to rebuy or repatronize a preferred product/service consistently in the future, thereby causing repetitive same-brand or same brand-set purchasing, despite situational influences and marketing efforts having the potential to cause switching behavior."[28] It is an attitudinal state that is a function of value, trust, and commitment within supplier-customer relationships.[29]

Loyalty is frequently determined by patterns of repeat purchase behavior, although attitude-based models have highlighted three stages of brand loyalty: cognitive (think), affective (feel), and conative (do). The ultimate state of loyalty is one in which the consumer views the product as being in accord with his or her social identity, and could not feel whole without it.[30] For practical purposes, however, it is reasonable to estimate loyalty with measures based on recent purchase experiences, such as probability of purchase, frequency of purchase, and likelihood of spreading positive word-of-mouth.

The main benefits of having a perfectly loyal customer—that is, one who purchases only from one firm—are the decreased costs associated with service and support over time and the customer's decreased price sensitivity.

Share of Customer

Share of customer is an individual-level metric that is similar in nature to the market metric of market share. A firm's share of customer is the percentage of total expenditures made by that customer on the firm's products in a particular product category. Suppose Raymond spends an average of $300 per month on concert tickets, and that $240 of this is on tickets to Jimmy Buffett concerts. In addition, suppose Jane spends $1,000 per month on concert tickets, $240 of which is for Jimmy Buffett concerts. This means that Jimmy Buffett's share of Raymond's and Jane's concert-going expenditures would be 80 percent ($240/$300 x 100) and 24 percent, respectively. Share of customer can also be measured on other scales, such as product class.

The focus on share of customer, rather than share of market, is important. First, the process of CRM emphasizes serving individuals rather than markets. Therefore, a metric that pertains to a consumer rather than a market is consistent with the process. Market share is a market-level metric that reveals market performance; customer share is a customer-level metric that reveals customer performance. Second, share of customer can identify opportunities that may be masked when using market-level analysis. Raymond and Jane would be classified in the same way given their identical expenditures on Jimmy Buffett concerts. Customer share analysis would suggest, however, that Raymond and Jane should not be classified similarly, as her share of Jimmy Buffett concert viewing (24 percent) is significantly less than that for Raymond (80 percent). Jane has a lot more upside potential that may be worth pursuing. Share of customer directs organizations to learn more about, and focus their efforts on, individual customers.

Utilize Data

The marketing significance of customer relationship management is its customer-centric focus. In general, organizations using CRM are attempting to employ a marketing philosophy that begins and ends with establishing and maintaining mutually beneficial relationships with customers.

While this is a sound strategy in theory, it is not always so sound in practice—a fact reflected in the flagging health of the CRM industry in 2002. Providers and adopting firms assumed that CRM was a hardware and software system that, after being installed, would make them instantly customer-centric in mind and actions. This is similar to assuming that the installation of word-processing software on a computer will instantly make someone a great writer. (See Point/Counterpoint titled "Is CRM More Appropriately a Domain for Information Systems or for Marketing?")

Point–Counterpoint

Is CRM More Appropriately a Domain for Information Systems or for Marketing?

Information System Point: The Internet created a new channel through which companies could directly interact with their customers. Customer relationship management systems that came to the fore during the 1990s were promulgated by information technology-based efforts. Software modules were developed to optimize important functions and decision making that involved interaction with customers, such as sales force management, marketing automation, channel management, and customer service. Technology systems streamline customer interaction-focused operations delivering lower costs, greater customer satisfaction, and higher profits. These systems are complex and require expertise in technology and process flow, certainly the domain of IT departments and personnel. CRM is now a $20 billion-plus industry that highlights the importance of retaining customers and dealing with them on a one-to-one basis.

Marketing Counterpoint: Current CRM providers believe that their systems offer turnkey solutions to managing relationships with customers. Unfortunately, customer focus is not something that is turned on with a switch. Organizations need to understand what it means to be customer-centric in order to be customer-centric. The majority of CRM implementations fail. Like dot-com retailers that erroneously thought that having an Internet presence would somehow lead people to shop online, CRM providers underestimated the importance of marketing principles in serving both internal and external customers. Managing the marketing process with customers, including the utilization of customer information, falls in the marketer's domain. Developing technology tools to support this effort is the domain of information systems.

Tools and architecture, such as information technology-based CRM systems, can indeed promote and support the utilization of customer-centric marketing. Firms need to realize, however, that effective implementation of CRM requires people who understand the process of being customer-centric and can effectively manage a relationship with a customer. Nevertheless, technology has made great contributions in CRM, at the very least by increasing its awareness. The next steps in the evolution of effectively managing customer relationships will involve developing CRM literacy and skill in application, and applying the wisdom learned from both failures and successes.

CRM systems have been designed by providers (such as Siebel, SAP, Epiphany, and Chordiant) to support marketing automation, sales force automation, customer service, customer interaction, and customization. These components can be useful in acquiring and retaining customers. The major emphasis in relationship management, however, is retaining customers. Postpurchase activities that lead a customer to buy again, or buy more, from an organization need to focus on learning more about a customer.

Best Buy Example

Best Buy, the $19.6 billion leading electronics retailer, is focused on being a customer-centric organization. Best Buy has spent more than $20 million on customer relationship management systems in order to learn more about its customers, to provide better customer service, and to retain its customers.

The company wants to leverage this information so that each customer feels they are remembered, and to provide each customer with personalized attention and effective service.

Best Buy's objective is to have a single customer view when serving an identified customer. The company integrates customer information from a variety of touchpoints, such as in-store checkout, in-home repair, customer service call center, and customer service e-mail. Suppose a consumer who purchased a computer in the store calls a consumer relations representative with a question about compatibility while reviewing a software item on the Best Buy website; the consumer relations representative will see which system the customer purchased and use this information to provide assistance.

Transaction data are also used to target customers with new offers or cross-sell. For example, Best Buy might e-mail a photo printer special to customers who have signed up to receive e-mail offers and also own a digital camera. Best Buy also computes lifetime customer value for each customer. This information is used to classify customers by profitability, which in turn can impact the types of offers customers receive, such as discounts. CRM appears to be paying off for Best Buy, as customer satisfaction, profitability, and sales rates from database marketing programs have all shown increases.

eBay Example

Department-store pioneer John Wanamaker famously complained over 100 years ago that half his advertising was wasted—he just didn't know which half. Marketers have come a long way since then, aided by multiple data-gathering techniques, sophisticated computational models, and the vast computing power available to them via personal computers. The Internet has been perhaps the most incredible data source (and, potentially, the most valuable diagnostic tool) of all. Huge virtual warehouses full of product and customer data have been created over a few short years.

How does eBay, sitting atop one of the largest repositories of customer data, respond to this treasure trove of information? eBay has responded in several ways. One of these is through the creation of a marketing research arm called the Consumer Insights and Analysis Group. Its director, Richard Rock, a Stanford MBA graduate with a year's experience working for online directory company WhoWhere, was responsible for creating the first customer valuation models for eBay. By poring over its customer data, eBay is able to determine who its most valuable customers are and focus its energies on meeting their needs. To accomplish this, eBay measured loads of data and conducted detailed analyses. Armed with this information, eBay could then implement programs and promotions catering to the most valuable customer segments, extracting the greatest value from its growing customer base for its efforts.

Teasing out the gold nuggets from the piles of informational dirt is no small challenge. "There is a lot of promise in data management," says Rock, "but most companies are drowning in data, and that's the biggest obstacle."[31] With over 800 items listed and over $17,000 in gross revenue recorded per minute, eBay's data pool is enormous. Sifting through it to find out what can be learned is a top priority for eBay.

CEO Meg Whitman's tenure at Procter & Gamble has influenced her management of eBay. Like P&G, eBay places a great deal of value on information. All of eBay's category managers (similar to P&G's brand managers) live and breathe by their data. This emphasis on information and its value to the firm is one thing that kept eBay alive during the dot-com flameout.

eBay's vice president of marketing, Michael Deering, emphasizes the importance that eBay places on its data. For example, he has tried to understand customer behavior by tracking how prospective buyers respond to promotions on the site. In mid-2001, eBay marketers gained the ability to see their data in a more user-friendly way. Reams of data came alive off of spreadsheets, with information captured in pie charts, graphs, and tables. Suddenly, it became much easier to use the data to make management decisions. After having their data in this new format for four months, eBay marketers were able to greatly improve the efficiency of eBay's front page. With one of these spreadsheets in hand, Deering could "tell you that our winter sports promotion rocked, and that 'baby's first holiday' didn't. I can tell why, and I won't promote it again."[32] Exhibit 15.21 shows an eBay promotion for Mother's Day, which was designed after conducting marketing research.

Market research tells eBay's marketers that perfume, flowers, and jewelry are particularly compelling around Mother's Day. Acting on this information, they prominently feature a Mother's Day promotion on the site highlighting these categories.

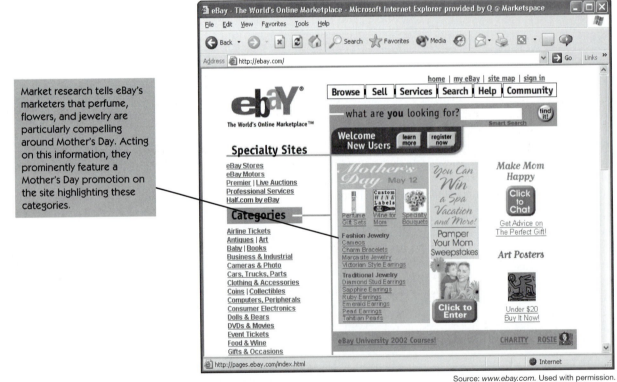

Source: *www.ebay.com*. Used with permission.

EXHIBIT 15.21   eBay Promotion for Mother's Day

eBay Member/Seller Perspective

The popularity of online auction sites, particularly eBay, has created a need for research tools that can be used to inform auction strategies. These tools can be used to make auction selling decisions based on completed auction information, to construct and post new auctions, to manage active auctions, and to support post-auction activities such as winner notification and invoice processing. The former is done by downloading into an analytical engine, such as an electronic spreadsheet, the values of important auction variables such as auction item, final selling price, start and end times of auction, number of bids, and rating of seller.

A number of organizations offering tools for sellers, as well as buyers, have emerged. ChannelAdvisor[33] serves established manufacturers and retailers such as IBM, Kodak, Intel, and Motorola. Andale Research[34] says that it can "take the guesswork out of selling online" by researching important selling issues such as product prices, when to post an auction, and the length of an auction. It offers services for personal sellers and corporate sellers, with monthly subscription fees starting at less than $10 per month. HammerTap[35] sells eBay auction research software for less than $200.

Summary

1. What is marketing research?

Marketing research is a tool that helps companies understand and meet consumer wants and needs. It provides information about the quality and usefulness of products and services so that companies can determine if consumers will accept a product or service. Marketing research helps to eliminate the introduction of products or services that have a high likelihood of failure. Failure is extremely costly to both companies and consumers, as companies ultimately attempt to pass on losses to consumers.

2. What is the framework of marketing research?

The marketing researcher must follow a series of steps before undertaking a study. These steps include defining the opportunity or problem and determining the type of research design necessary to address the opportunity or problem. When developing the research plan, it is important for the researcher to make decisions about what population to sample, as well as how to collect, organize, and analyze the data. The marketing researcher will use the research findings to guide or determine marketing or product strategy.

3. What are marketing research data-collection methods?

Marketing research data collection can be done offline or online, using either secondary or primary research methods. With offline secondary research, researchers visit libraries and similar institutions and search the available material for information about a selected topic. If this search yields no results, a researcher can use offline primary research—for example, organize a focus group, draft a survey, or directly observe the subjects. Primary research, particularly offline, is very resource-intensive. Thus, a researcher might first consider online secondary research if nothing else is readily available. With online secondary research, the researcher surfs the Internet looking for data on the study topic. Researchers can also conduct primary research online using an online focus group, online survey, or click data. Finally, researchers can always combine offline and online methods. Although there are no fixed rules determining which method is best, the researcher can apply a set of guidelines, together with common sense, to determine which data-collection method is best for a specific project.

4. How do online methods compare to offline methods?

Offline and online methods each have advantages and disadvantages. Offline methods are expensive and labor-intensive, but may be more reliable. Online methods reduce the turnaround time and the cost of a project. The primary drawback of the online method is the difficulty of drawing a random and representative sample, thus avoiding sample-selection bias.

5. What marketing research is best done through the Internet?

Internet-based marketing research works best for projects in which a representative sample can be drawn from the population, there is no issue with confidentiality of the data, and the topic is sufficiently simple that it can be communicated to the research participants via a short, straightforward survey.

6. What are the implications of international Internet marketing research?

The Internet enables researchers to obtain data from around the globe. This requires that surveys or other research tools are properly translated, and that questions are tailored to reflect local tastes, preferences, and taboos.

7. What is database marketing?

Database marketing consists of obtaining meaningful individual-level consumer information, analyzing this information to estimate consumer response to various offers, and making marketing decisions based on this expected response. The strong interest in database marketing is due to its potential to augment a mass-marketing approach with a one-to-one approach that promises increased attentiveness, customization, and efficient spending, which would increase utility for consumers (and profits for organizations) when carried out effectively.

8. What is the purpose of customer relationship management?

Traditionally, marketers have focused more of their actions and expenditures on acquiring customers than retaining them. Emphasis on customer retention, however, can have a significant impact on marketing efficiency and profitability. Customer relationship management is a philosophy and a process that emphasizes customer retention. The Internet and other advanced technologies make feasible the implementation of sophisticated CRM solutions, which focus on maintaining a one-to-one dialogue and contact with each customer.

9. Why should firms develop customer information systems?

Effective marketers use market and customer information to inform, and reduce the uncertainty associated with, managerial decision-making. Customer information is power, and customer information systems enable firms to leverage this power.

Activities for Students

1. Managers at a consumer electronics company have to assess the market potential for high definition television (HDTV). Using secondary research methods, determine the size of the U.S. market for HDTV. What is the size of the worldwide market for HDTV? Be sure to note your sources.
2. Based on favorable preliminary marketing research, the consumer electronics company decides to enter the HDTV market. Develop a research plan that would help the company determine the features it needs to include in its offering to be competitive in this market.
3. Develop a survey/questionnaire that would help an Internet service provider (ISP) determine what features are most desired by both existing and potential customers.
4. Identify an organization that uses database marketing or customer relationship management systems. Interview individuals within the organization who use these systems to support decision making. Assess the benefits, payoffs, challenges, and weaknesses of these systems. Do you believe that the organization is customer-centric in its approach to serving markets and customers?
5. Think about situations in which you received excellent customer service. In addition, think about instances in which firms thought they were providing you with great customer service, but in fact you found little or no value in their actions. Describe these situations, and explain why you perceive each service act as valuable or valueless. Given this, what do you believe makes for great customer service? How could firms use your insights to deliver great customer service?
6. Subscribe to several e-newsletters on topics, or from firms, of interest. Which parts of each e-newsletter did you find valuable, and why? Conversely, identify e-newsletter issues, particularly content issues, that you found less than desirable. Explain why you did not value them. Consider factors such as formatting, frequency, and personalization in your response.
7. Place an item up for auction on eBay. Prepare a write-up that details your selling experience. Include such details as item description, auction start date and time, auction end date, initial bid price, type of auction, whether reserve was selected, bid history, the URL of auction, any relevant e-mails, etc. Include a snapshot of your auction page after your auction is completed and any post-auction details such as payment, shipping, and feedback. It is recommended that you participate as a "serious" bidder in at least one auction prior to carrying out this exercise.

exploratory research	internal validation	list segmentation
conclusive research	external validation	recency, frequency, monetary (RFM)
descriptive research	Mrs. Schwartz	customer lifetime value
causal research	database marketing	customer retention
secondary research	response list	customer relationship management
primary research	compiled list	touchpoints
sample-selection bias	house list	e-mail automation system
naturalistic observation	list processing	share of customer
obtrusive observation	customer vector	

[1]See, for example, *http://www.nop.co.uk/*.

[2]See, for example, StatSoft, Inc. 2001. Electronic statistics textbook. Tulsa: StatSoft. *http://www.statsoft.com/textbook/stathome.html*.

[3]Petska, Karen, and Egil Juliussen. 1999. *Computer industry almanac*. Computer Industry Almanac, Inc.

[4]Smith, C. 1999. Casting the Net: Surveying an Internet population. *Journal of Computer-Mediated Communication* 3, no. 1.

[5]Sheehan, Kim Bartel, and Mariea Grubbs Hoy. 1999. Using e-mail to survey Internet users in the United States: Methodology and assessment. Journal of Computer-Mediated Communication 4, no. 3.

[6]A number of textbooks exist on this topic, and those interested in more detail should refer to specific textbooks on statistical and econometric analysis for an in-depth review. See, for example, Greene, William H. 1999. *Econometric analysis*, 4th ed. Upper Saddle River, New Jersey: Prentice Hall.

[7]Ibid.

[8]Roberts, Mary Lou, and Paul D. Berger. 1999. *Direct Marketing Management*. Upper Saddle River, NJ: Prentice-Hall, 9.

[9]Jackson, Rob, and Paul Wang. 1997. *Strategic Database Marketing*. Lincolnwood, IL: NTC Business Books, 83.

[10]Berry, Leonard. 1999. *Discovering the Soul of Service: The Nine Drivers of Sustainable Business Success. Free Press*.

[11]See *www.the-dma.org*.

[12]Winer, Russell S. 2001. A Framework for Customer Relationship Management. *California Management Review* 4:89-105.

[13]Cox, Beth. 2000. Amazon.com Owns Up to a Mistake. Online at *http://www.internetnews.com/ec-news/article.php/4_471541*.

[14]Reichheld, Frederick F., and W. Earl Sasser, Jr. 1990. Zero Defections: Quality Comes to Services. *Harvard Business Review* 5:105–111.

[15]Desatnick, Robert.L. 1988. *Managing to keep the customer: how to achieve and maintain superior customer service throughout the organization*. San Francisco, CA : Jossey-Bass**.**

[16]Sinha, Debashish, and Beth Eisenfeld. 2002. *CRM Services Market Size and Forecast, 2001–2006*. Gartner. Report #ITES-WW-MS-0111.

[17]Ibid.

[18]Godin, Seth. 1999. *Permission Marketing: Turning Strangers into Friends, and Friends into Customers*. Simon & Schuster.

[19]Locke, Christopher, Rick Levine, Doc Searls, and David Weinberger. 2001. *The Cluetrain Manifesto: The End of Business as Usual*. Perseus Books.

[20]See *www.speedpass.com*.

[21]newsletter resources at *www.interniche.net/partner/sales/ezinedirectories.htm.*

[22]Peppers & Rogers Group. 2001. *Email Marketing: Reaching Customers and Driving ROI*. Insight Report. Norwalk, CT.

[23]*www.ENewsletterBook.com.*

[24]*www.BluePenguinDevelopment.com.*

[25]*www.imarketing.org.*

[26]Anderson, Eugene W., Claes Fornell, and Donald R. Lehmann.1994. Customer Satisfaction, Market Share, and Profitability: Findings from Sweden. *Journal of Marketing* 3:53-66.

[27]Fornell, Claes, , Michael D Johnson, Eugene W Anderson, Jaesung Cha, and Barbara Everitt Bryant. 1996. *Journal of* Marketing 4:7–18.

[28]Oliver, Richard L. 1999. Whence Consumer Loyalty. *Journal of Marketing* 1:33–44.

[29]Buttle, Francis, and Jamie Burtin. 2002. Does Service Failure Influence Customer Loyalty. *Journal of Consumer Behaviour.* 3:217–227.

[30]Oliver, Richard L. 1999. Whence Consumer Loyalty. *Journal of Marketing* 1:33–44.

[31]Green, Heather. 1999. The Information Gold Mine. *BusinessWeek.* 26 July.

[32]Brown, Eryn. 2002. How Can a Dot-Com Be This Hot? *Fortune,* 21 January.

[33]*www.ChannelAdvisor.com.*

[34]*www.Andale.com.*

[35]*www.HammerTap.com.*

Evaluating the Marketing Program

So, how did the marketing program do? That question is the focus of Part VII. Because the business unit is heavily concerned with financial performance, we focus this section principally on the new-to-the-world online matrix and the need to emphasize "integrated" customer metrics along with financial metrics and marketing implementation metrics. In particular, we review the basic customer metrics in the offline world and the new metrics in the online world, and we show how these metrics need to be combined to provide a clear picture of how customers are reacting to the firm and its offerings.

Metrics

This chapter focuses on how companies can assess the performance of their Internet marketing programs. Most companies routinely review financial benchmarks such as sales and profits. To determine marketing performance, managers also use a core set of metrics that measure the health of the customer base and its contribution to profits. To assess how each marketing program element builds the customer base, they will use a set of more specific metrics relevant to the particular element. This chapter proposes an integrative approach, combining online and offline marketing metrics appropriate to each of the four customer relationship stages. Some of the challenges, complexities, and pitfalls of tracking customer behavior across offline and online environments are discussed within this context. The chapter concludes by applying the discussed concepts to eBay.

QUESTIONS

Please consider the following questions as you read this chapter:

1. Why should managers be concerned about metrics?

2. What are the characteristics of good metrics?

3. Why do marketing managers need financial, customer-based, and implementation metrics?

4. What are the strengths and weaknesses of the traditional hierarchy-of-effects model?

5. What are the stages of the integrated hierarchy-of-effects model? How do they relate to the four stages of a customer relationship?

Introduction

This book has examined the key objectives in creating a successful Internet marketing program and, subsequently, the key elements in creating an effective interface design. This chapter focuses on **metrics**—the performance indicators that reflect the health of the business and, in particular, whether the marketing program is on course.

The main purpose of this chapter is to propose an approach that measures and integrates both online and offline customer metrics. The chapter starts

---

Co-authored by Katherine Jocz. With substantive input from Javier Colayco, David Bennion, Craig Thompson, and Yannis Dosios.

with a review of why good metrics are important, continues with an overview of traditional financial metrics used to track bottom-line performance, and then introduces the topic of customer metrics. Next is a discussion of our integrative customer metric model, which emphasizes the importance of capturing online and offline customer metrics across the four customer relationship stages. These key customer metrics are based on both practice and academic research. The chapter continues with a discussion of metrics for websites and other marketing program elements. It then explores some of the challenges and pitfalls of tracking customer behavior across offline and online environments. The chapter concludes by examining eBay's customer metrics through the different stages of a customer's auction experience.

Why Metrics Matter

Metrics represent the performance targets of the company. They provide vital feedback to the firm, which enables quick confirmation of success or the immediate identification of corrective actions needed, such as changes in processes, strategy, or product offerings. Furthermore, the act of specifying concrete goals with precise measurements can help senior managers clarify their strategic priorities and set clear directions for other managers. Clearly documented performance targets can go a long way toward communicating the particular goals and strategy of a company throughout the organization.

Metrics help increase accountability at different levels within the organization. That is, general performance measures such as sales growth and amount of sales are likely to have companywide accountability. On the other hand, specific measures related to website usability can be tied to the interactive design function, while customer service metrics can be tied to the customer service department. Frequently, metrics are linked to the performance appraisal system. If the metrics are tied to the reward system, then they have substantial weight behind them. At the same time, choosing the wrong set of metrics, such as metrics that drive behavior toward the wrong objectives or metrics that can be artificially manipulated, can be very damaging. The right metrics can help align individual objectives, functional or departmental objectives, and companywide strategic activities.

Take General Electric, renowned for its focus on setting and achieving measurable goals for its various business units. At GE, metrics are used to manage projects and people at all levels of the organization. CIO Gary Reiner has achieved cost savings amounting to hundreds of millions of dollars through careful monitoring of procurement costs.[1] This is how a recent news article described the system:

> Reiner also reins in costs on the little things. Using his 'digital cockpit,' a piece of software that provides real-time access to 'mission-critical jobs,' Reiner can monitor how quickly the help desk is responding to calls. If the response time exceeds a prescribed standard, the system automatically fires off an e-mail to the appropriate group of people asking that the situation be addressed. If the problem isn't fixed, more e-mail goes out to an ever-wider number of people until the response time is brought back to normal levels.[2]

What Is a Good Metric?

Firms use a number of metrics, each appropriate for a specific purpose. The characteristics shared by good metrics are that they are easily measurable, interpretable, robust, generally accepted, and linked to desired business outcomes.

Easily Measurable

By definition, a metric is measurable. However, some measures are much more difficult to collect and use than others. Management may prefer to use metrics that can be derived from existing systems and processes such as the firm's accounting or inventory control systems. In other cases, capturing metrics data may require the setup and maintenance of systems and procedures that require significant capital investment and human resources.

Speed of data collection is another consideration. If what is being measured fluctuates a great deal over time, the associated metric should be one that can be tracked frequently and quickly. An analogy is daily temperature: Readings taken two days a year are not particularly informative about any other days that year, or about the year's overall temperature. One advantage of online metrics is that they can easily be captured and tracked on a nearly continuous basis.

Some outcomes are easier to translate into metrics than others. Traditional financial metrics are relatively straightforward and easy to acquire, while more qualitative metrics can be difficult to specify and to obtain. How does the firm translate the desired outcome of customer satisfaction with its website into a metric? Should it ask a general question such as, "How satisfied are you with the website?" Or should it ask a series of questions about satisfaction with the website's usability, content, products, ease of use, and so on, and then aggregate these measures into a customer satisfaction index? How can the firm induce a representative sample of customers to supply the necessary information?

Interpretable

Metrics should be readily interpretable and have an agreed-upon meaning within the domain in which they are being used. A case in point: The concept of stickiness, or length of visitor time on a website, makes perfect sense as a measure of success for eBay. However, the same measure is ambiguous at best in the case of American Airlines. Frequent travelers want to book tickets, cash in travel vouchers, and check frequent-flier mileage. The last thing these travelers want is to stay on the website for an extended period of time. In this case, a high amount of time spent on the website and a high number of page views would probably be a measure of a frustrated consumer rather than an interested one. On the other hand, stickiness could be indicative of a committed, satisfied customer who stays on the website to check out a number of alternative itineraries. The point is: Interpretable, unambiguous metrics are needed in order to make relevant comparisons.

Robust

A robust metric applies equally well across different business units or products and over time. It is also resistant to minor variations in the way the data is collected. That is, a change in the metric reflects a change in the outcome it is measuring, not a change in the meaning of the metric or a change in the measurement procedure.

Generally Accepted

Generally, outside stakeholders in a business are most comfortable with the reporting of hard numbers related to revenues, margins, number of customers, and other readily quantifiable numbers. Not as highly valued are the softer measures of customer perception such as brand awareness or customer satisfaction. Even so, more credibility is attached to metrics of this type that are collected using standard definitions and procedures than to metrics that are unique to a particular firm. Purchasing metrics from third-party vendors can increase credibility and acceptance and also allow benchmarking and comparisons with other firms in the industry.

During the dot-com era, new metrics such as the number of hits or number of visitors to a website were considered a relevant and appropriate metric of business performance. In the long run, however, analysts, investors, and others continued to rely on traditional metrics such as number of customers and revenue per customer.

Linked to Desired Business Outcomes

Some metrics directly measure a key business outcome. Others measure performance aspects linked to key outcomes. Such metrics can provide managers with an early warning system or set of diagnostics that allow for corrective actions to be taken if needed. Rayport and Jaworski introduced the **Performance Dashboard**, a framework for assessing the strategic health of a company.[3] The Performance Dashboard encompasses the following elements:

1. The magnitude of the opportunity a company is seeking to address
2. The viability and sustainability of the firm's business model
3. The customer outcomes
4. The effectiveness of the company's branding and implementation
5. The company's financial performance

When examining the causes of a company's poor financial performance, managers need to look at all of these metric categories for potential answers. For example, a company may have an effective and efficient marketing strategy, but may do a poor job of delivering a product and providing after-sales support, thereby turning away customers, revenues, and profits.

The Marketing Metrics Framework

Of the Performance Dashboard metrics listed above, the financial metrics, customer metrics, and branding and implementation metrics best capture a firm's marketing performance. Taken together, they enable managers to understand the drivers of a firm's performance in the marketplace. Exhibit 16.1 shows these three categories of metrics for assessing marketing performance relative to objectives. **Financial metrics** measure bottom-line results and are at the most aggregate level. Next, **customer-based metrics** capture marketing's performance in building customer-based assets that translate into financial results. Finally, **marketing implementation metrics** assess how well each element of the marketing program performs in terms of building customer assets.

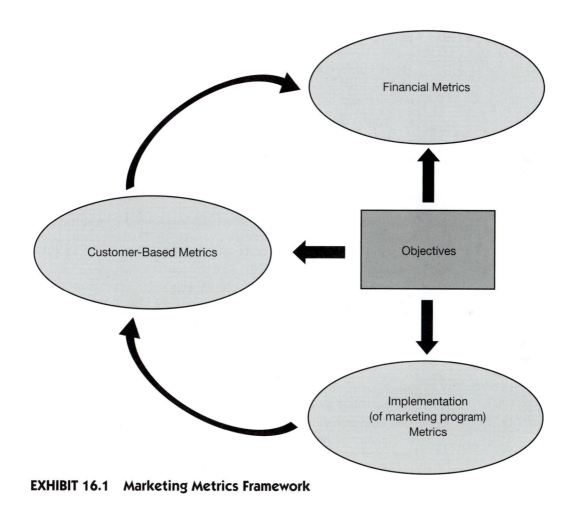

EXHIBIT 16.1   Marketing Metrics Framework

Consider just one set of linkages between financial, customer-based, and implementation metrics: Share prices take into account earnings per share; earnings per share reflect profits; profits depend on revenues and costs; revenues derive from product sales; product sales depend on the number of customers and the number of purchases per customer; the number of purchases per customer depends on customer satisfaction with the product; satisfaction with the product is affected by product quality, and so forth. By analyzing these types of linkages, managers can take actions to improve overall financial results.

The remainder of the chapter will review the overall performance metrics most relevant to marketing management and then focus on the customer-based and marketing implementation metrics.

Financial and Other Metrics of Overall Marketing Performance

Financial Metrics

Marketing managers use a small set of metrics to monitor the bottom-line performance of a product or business unit. These generally accepted measures include:[4,5]

- Sales
- Revenue
- Gross margins
- Profits
- Marketing spend

Financial measures reflect strategic choices from the most recent planning period and, to some degree, an accumulation of all previous planning periods. Hence, Amazon's most recent financial performance is a function not just of the past 12 months but of all the years since its launch in 1995. Typically, targets for these metrics are expressed in comparison with previous periods, e.g., a 10 percent increase in sales over the previous year. Financial measures were once stated annually, and then quarterly, but today's information systems allow financials to be reported at ever-shorter intervals. Following five years of work on improving internal processes, Cisco Systems can now close its books in a day.[6]

Financial measures are used by chief executives of the company, and are also weighed and analyzed by the investment community. Though they are extremely influential, one shortcoming of financial metrics is that they are at a very general level and are "backward looking." In other words, they offer managers little guidance about specific factors that influence financial outcomes or how to achieve better results in the future.

Performance Relative to Competitors

In addition to comparing current performance to current objectives and performance in previous periods, marketing managers commonly assess performance relative to competitors. Examples of these metrics include:

- Market share
- Relative return on investment

Market share has been criticized by Porter and others when used as the primary goal for a business.[7] The dot-com boom saw many companies striving to achieve market share at all costs, regardless of the expense of acquiring customers or of subsidizing the cost of delivering products or services. Nevertheless, market share is a useful benchmark of performance and an indicator of potential power in the marketplace.

For all three categories of metrics—customer-based and implementation metrics as well as financial metrics—managers can gain a more accurate picture of performance by making relevant comparisons to competitors. Selectively benchmarking against best-practice companies from different industries can provide additional insight.

Customer-Based Metrics

The marketing department is responsible for developing and implementing strategies that create value for customers. In turn, creating value for the customer creates value for the firm: Customer purchases are the ultimate source of cash flow in a business. Thus, metrics that capture the current and expected future value of the customer base are essential for evaluating marketing performance.

The most obvious customer-based metrics are objective, quantitative measures of customer outcomes, such as number of customers or number of purchases per customer. These are key indicators of marketing performance and can be directly linked to financial results. In addition, marketers rely heavily on subjective measures of customers' responses to the firm's marketing activities, such as brand knowledge or satisfaction, to understand the processes leading to purchase and repeat purchase. How does the senior marketer accurately interpret and best use each of these indicators? How should online metrics be combined with offline metrics? These questions are at the heart of customer-based metrics for Internet marketing.

Hierarchy-of-Effects Model

For the past 50 years, marketers have used the **hierarchy-of-effects model** to explain the stages that a customer moves through to purchase goods or services. Although this model is often inappropriately restricted to marketing communication specialists, it is a simple way to understand how a customer must be educated, informed, and "transitioned" in order for sales to occur. At each stage in the model, different metrics are used to track customers' attitudes, knowledge, or behavior.

Exhibit 16.2 shows the conventional, yet simplified, hierarchy-of-effects model applied to the four customer relationship stages.[8] The customer moves through a seven-step process:

1. Awareness
2. Knowledge
3. Attitude
4. Purchase intent
5. Purchase
6. Postpurchase
7. Loyalty

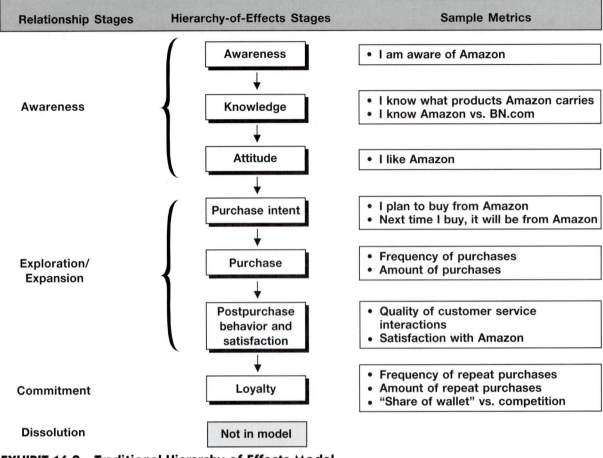

Relationship Stages	Hierarchy-of-Effects Stages	Sample Metrics

Awareness

Awareness → • I am aware of Amazon

Knowledge → • I know what products Amazon carries / • I know Amazon vs. BN.com

Attitude → • I like Amazon

Exploration/ Expansion

Purchase intent → • I plan to buy from Amazon / • Next time I buy, it will be from Amazon

Purchase → • Frequency of purchases / • Amount of purchases

Postpurchase behavior and satisfaction → • Quality of customer service interactions / • Satisfaction with Amazon

Commitment

Loyalty → • Frequency of repeat purchases / • Amount of repeat purchases / • "Share of wallet" vs. competition

Dissolution

Not in model

EXHIBIT 16.2   Traditional Hierarchy-of-Effects Model

The hierarchy-of-effects model's simplicity has a number of advantages. First, it is intuitively appealing. Managers can easily comprehend the value of the different metrics at each step and can easily put together a scorecard of how they compare to the competition on each measure. Second, in the market communications and market research area, the measures and tracking systems have become quite routine—and hence, standardized across firms. Thus, it is easy to purchase services in the open market to track one's performance. Finally, it provides a wealth of important diagnostic information on where customers are being either lost or "hooked" on the product. For example, it is quite interesting to know that 75 percent of your target customers know of your brand, know of your brand features, have positive attitudes about your brand, have strong predispositions to buy, yet do not actually purchase the product. This evidence would suggest that a firm should focus on the coverage of the distribution outlets rather than more advertising. The key point is that knowing the specific stage where the problem is (e.g., lack of brand awareness in the awareness stage) enables the manager to more precisely target an intervention.

Practice-Based Problems with the Hierarchy-of-Effects Model

Where does the model fall short? The hierarchy-of-effects model appears to be simple, straightforward, and easy to implement. It provides managers with clear diagnostic measures that can be directly linked with specific interventions. The problem is that most of the measures rely upon questioning target customers about their attitudes or behavior, rather than directly observing their behavior. Let us assume for the moment that customers are honest and truly attempt to provide the best answers to questions. Even with this assumption, problems can occur for a variety of reasons—customers can have difficulty recalling brands, have a lack of introspection on their own shopping behavior, and, more frequently, may just not know the answers to many behavioral questions.

Online Hierarchy-of Effects-Model

Online customer metrics can draw on the wealth of data that can be unobtrusively collected on customer behavior. Yet while the online metrics offer a more precise set of measures on behavior, one also needs to consider what is lost when one shifts away from the attitude, knowledge, and predisposition measures to pure behavioral data. For a comprehensive understanding of its customer base, a firm needs to track both subjective measures of the consumption process—as articulated by customers—as well as the objective behavioral tracking and outcome measures.

Exhibit 16.3 shows the steps of the online hierarchy of effects. This figure illustrates a process with the following sequence:

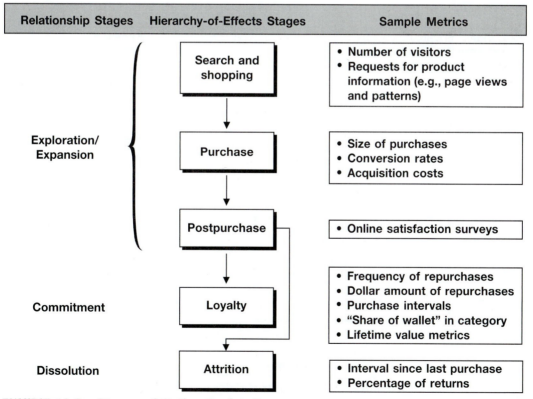

EXHIBIT 16.3   Stages of Online Buying Process

1. Search and shopping

2. Purchase

3. Postpurchase

4. Loyalty

5. Attrition

Clearly, there is a shift from "asking the customer" to "watching the customer." The focus is squarely on measures that reflect behavior rather than attitudes or perceptions.

Integrated Model of Customer Metrics by Relationship Stage

Combining the offline and online metrics that apply as a customer moves through the relationship stages results in Exhibit 16.4. The first and second columns reflect the traditional hierarchy of effects and the online hierarchy of effects, respectively. The last column shows that these can be combined quite easily. The chart reveals a simple point. Traditional approaches rely heavily on customer perceptions (e.g., attitudes, knowl-

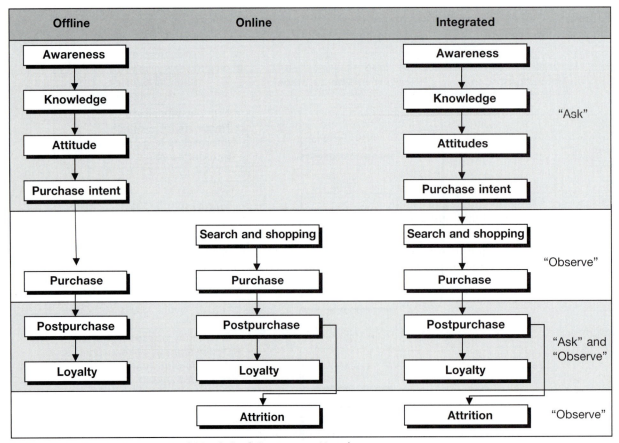

EXHIBIT 16.4   An Integrated Model of Customer Metrics

edge, behavioral intent) while the online methods rely heavily on behavior (see Exhibit 16.5). Does this mean online methods are better? Not at all. If one wants to find out why customers decide to visit or about their experience on a website, the easiest thing to do is to ask them. Moreover, the perceptual data often reveal very specific information about where the market communications programs fail (e.g., consumers were aware of a site, but were not knowledgeable about the type of inventory being sold, indicating that the market communications do not need to focus on general awareness but rather on knowledge building relative to other websites). The key point is that both sets of data are needed, and hence, the integrated model is the most appropriate way to think about measuring and tracking the customer base.

Before discussing the key metrics used for each of the relationship stages, it is important to make several observations about the hierarchy-of-effects models shown in Exhibits 16.2, 16.3, and 16.4. First, the sequence from awareness to loyalty is just one possible ordering of effects. For instance, consumers may not have well-formed knowledge or attitudes about a product until after a trial purchase. Second, managers often track the metrics from a previous customer relationship stage throughout subsequent stages. Thus, it is common to track attitudes or knowledge even when metrics on purchase behavior are available. Third, managers will likely choose a subset of metrics to focus on. They will seek to eliminate those that give redundant information and focus on the metrics that best explain the overall performance outcomes discussed previously.

Awareness Stage

In the awareness stage, the customer is becoming aware of and gaining knowledge about the product or brand. The customer is also developing attitudes toward the product or brand. Attitudinal measures may reflect the consumer's emotional responses, preferences, or affection for a particular brand. Metrics at this stage are best gathered by directly questioning customers. When this is impractical, marketers use proxy measures such as computing the number of viewers exposed to a commercial or counting the number of visitors to a website. Typical metrics are awareness, knowledge, and attitude. Perceived differentiation or preference can also be used.

Awareness. A prerequisite for purchase is awareness that the product exists. It can be measured by prompted or unprompted recognition of the product or brand.

	Online	Offline
Prepurchase Attitude and Knowledge	Strong	Weak
Search and Actual Shopping Behavior	Weak	Strong
Purchase and Loyalty	Moderate	Strong

EXHIBIT 16.5 Strengths and Weaknesses of Online and Offline Metrics

---

Drill-Down

How Firms Track Integrated Customer Metrics

Given the current economic environment, it is not surprising that e-commerce companies are trying to increase the profitability of their marketing efforts. Firms are increasingly developing initiatives to track company-specific customer metrics across channels, creating one-to-one marketing campaigns, and gathering customer-centric data to gain customer insights. This data collection is a vital tool in the development of targeted marketing strategies.

To maintain a competitive advantage in accurately measuring customer behavior, companies are realizing that they must gather integrated customer information—data that encompasses online and offline behavior. In order to develop this integrated customer relationship management capability, companies are employing the services of CRM software companies and application service providers.

CRM software companies such as Chordiant, E.piphany, and Blue Martini deliver online tools and software solutions that gather and develop market intelligence for their clients. These companies enable the information-gathering systems within a company's call centers, online sources, and sales data to be combined and analyzed to determine what a client is looking for in a relationship with a company. By developing this customer insight, a company can then create unique marketing initiatives aligned with customer preferences, building a deeper relationship with the targeted customer. Some firms also manage the data for their clients. These providers aggregate a company's digital data from the company and third-party sources and develop reports tailored to customer needs.

The most common service provided by the majority of these firms is to gather data from several sources—including advertisement initiatives, click streams, and transactions—and combine and analyze them. The trick for companies is using the right metrics to measure and profile their customers, and then marketing and selling to the more profitable individuals.

Knowledge.   This metric assesses a consumer's understanding of the product's benefits, features, and performance relative to competing products.

Attitude.   Attitude refers to the degree to which the customer likes a particular brand or product.

Perceived Differentiation or Preference.   These metrics assess competitive advantage. A consumer may know and like the product but see little difference between it and competing products.

Exploration/Expansion Stage

This relationship stage encompasses purchase intent and search, purchase, and postpurchase behaviors. As with the awareness stage metrics, purchase intent is measured by directly querying consumers. Data and metrics for search and purchase behaviors are rather straightforward. For both search and purchase behavior metrics, observation is preferred over questioning. In this regard, online marketing has an advantage over offline marketing. Similar to direct-mail marketers, online retailers have access to data on the number of customers, purchases per customer, **conversion rate**, and **acquisition cost** per customer. These metrics allow marketers to compute profitability per customer. Postpurchase metrics include both attitudinal and behavioral metrics. These metrics are good indicators of future customer behavior.

Purchase Intent. Questions to measure purchase intent are typically framed in a way that asks customers to project their behavior in the future. A typical question for target customers would be, "If you were to buy books today, which bookstore would you use?" Or, "On your next shopping occasion, would you shop at Tower Records or Sam Goody?" Research suggests that this behavioral predisposition is a stronger predictor of eventual behavior than the attitudinal or knowledge measures. Hence, market research firms will typically track behavioral predisposition in the absence of objective purchase data.

Number of Visitors. For online marketing, one metric of exploratory behavior is the total number of unique visitors to a website. A visit typically refers to a given person's visit to the website (but in practice is measured as the number of uniquely identified computers that visit a website in a given period). Related metrics are number of new visitors, repeat visitors, or registered visitors.

Requests for Product Information. Online marketers can collect this metric of exploratory behavior by analyzing such statistics as pages requested on websites or responses to e-mail messages. Requests to call centers or the sales force are other sources for this metric.

Number of Customers. This important metric is most easily tracked by marketers who have customer databases (e.g., direct marketers, online marketers, or marketers with loyalty programs). In addition to metrics on the total number of customers, other important diagnostics are measures of the number of new customers and the number of customers relative to the target segment (sometimes referred to as penetration rate).

Purchases per Customer. Another important metric in the purchase stage is purchases per customer. Marketers will want to look at the number of purchases per customer over time and the distribution of purchases across customers. The classic 80/20 rule—that a firm tends to get 80 percent of its revenue from 20 percent of its customers—has not changed, but the ability of firms to understand, target, and support the customers within that 20 percent segment has improved. There are hosts of potential purchase behavior data. These data can be subjective (e.g., data gathered through questions like, "When was the last time you purchased books?") or objective (e.g., dates of purchase, dollar amount of purchase, overall purchase history, share of book purchases across retail channels). Offline firms have a mixed record of purchase tracking. Some firms constantly track these important measures; others do not.

Acquisition Costs. The cost of acquiring a customer is another critical metric that can be directly tied to profitability. Typically, this is measured by examining the number of purchasing customers relative to the amount of communications dollars in a particular medium. For example, if one paid

$500,000 for banner ads or sponsorships on AOL, and 1,000 customers could be directly linked to these communications (because the customers clicked through a banner ad and bought an item for sale), then the cost per acquisition of a single customer would be $500.

Conversion Rate. This metric assesses the conversion of prospects into customers. Conversion rates are critical for the firm because they can easily be tied to increased profitability and cash flow. Consider, for example, Exhibit 16.6, originally proposed by J. William Gurley in a *Fortune* article.[9] The chart illustrates that a small improvement in conversion rates has a large increase in revenue.

	Conversion Rate		
	2%	4%	8%
Advertising Costs	$10,000	$10,000	$10,000
Visitors	5,000	5,000	5,000
Transactions	100	200	400
Cost/Transaction	$100	$50	$25
Revenue	$10,000	$20,000	$40,000
Marketing/Revenue (%)	100	50	25

Note: Average transaction size = 100%
Source: Gurley, J. William, 2000. The most powerful metric of all. CNETNews.com, 21 February
URL: *http://www.news.com/Perspectives/Column/0,176,403,00/html?tag=st.ne*

EXHIBIT 16.6   The Power of Conversion Rates

Satisfaction. Postpurchase attitudes track the customer's immediate response to the purchase experience. This is usually tracked as a general satisfaction measure or a set of specific satisfaction measures with respect to the individual aspects of the buying experience. Typical questions to gain such measures might include, "Were you satisfied with the selection and the sales support?"

Commitment Stage

If there is one overwhelming truism in marketing, it is that loyal customers are often the most important and profitable customers. Thus, one of the key metrics to examine is indicators of loyalty—these include traditional metrics such as **retention rate**, frequency of repurchase, "**share of wallet**," and the newer metric of **customer lifetime value**.

Repurchase Rates. A steady or increasing rate of repurchase is a good indicator of commitment. It is important to realize that purchase rates averaged across customers can mask a very different trend from that revealed by tracking specific individuals or segments. For example, a declining purchase rate among your oldest customers or your biggest spenders is a warning sign of future sales decreases that may not show up in average statistics.

Retention. Retention rates measure the percent of customers who continue to purchase your products. Similar to repurchase rates, retention at the individual customer level is more indicative of commitment than changes in the total number of customers over time. (Firms with high churn rates could simply be acquiring new customers as the old customers are leaving).

Share of Wallet. This metric represents a marketer's share of the customer's overall purchases for the same type of product and is another indicator of loyalty. Thus, while it is important for Amazon.com to know that it has a regular, predictable customer who buys $400 worth of books a year, Amazon would also like to know that the customer buys $100 worth of books per year elsewhere. In that case, the customer purchases $500 worth of books per year, of which $400 is from Amazon. Hence, Amazon's share of wallet is 80 percent.

Lifetime Value. Customer lifetime value is an estimate of the long-term profitability of an individual customer. Such estimates are generally based on measures of acquisition costs, current profitability, and assumptions about future repurchase rates and purchase amounts. A recent study showed how the current and future customer base of a company could be valued using a customer lifetime value framework along with forecasts of the growth in the number of customers. The same study showed that improvement in retention rate has a very large impact on customer value, more so than the same percentage improvement in acquisition costs or margin.[10]

Dissolution Stage

The dissolution stage is marked by consumers leaving the customer base—in other words, a cessation of purchases, expressed as **attrition rate**. Potential indicators of dissolution are low scores on the satisfaction and repurchase rate metrics discussed earlier, as well as high levels of complaints and high levels of returns. Such metrics are useful in forecasting future weaknesses in the customer base and for designing interventions to retain valued customers.

Attrition Rate. This metric assesses the rate at which customers leave. While seemingly straightforward, in practice analysts use estimation techniques to distinguish an infrequent customer from a customer who will never return.

Percentage of Returns. A high level of returns can signal impending dissolution. This metric should be compared against relevant benchmarks. For instance, there could be a higher return rate for merchandise purchased online compared to merchandise purchased in physical stores.

Number of Complaints. The number of complaints is a behavioral measure that can indicate dissatisfaction leading to dissolution.

Internet Marketing Program Implementation Metrics

The integrated set of metrics discussed in the previous section show the current and expected profitability of the customer base. The metrics link directly to the financial measures used by top management to assess the marketing performance of the business. They also indicate at which steps of the customer

Testing for Trust

Arguably, the driving force behind consumers' repeat business is their trust in a given firm. If a firm's products meet a consumer's expectations, are delivered on time, and include good customer service, then trust develops and will drive further sales. Why, then, has such an important variable for driving financial success not been established as an explicit metric for measuring consumer behavior? And how does a firm test for trust?

The difficulty of such an endeavor quickly becomes clear: Trust means different things for different people and different websites. For some websites, trust means that prices will be competitive. For others, it means that products are guaranteed. For a shopper, it may mean that customer concerns are quickly addressed.

While a consumer's measure of trust in a firm and its services might be hard to capture in an interview or survey, there are proxies that can reasonably capture trust. Such proxies, usually tied to loyalty metrics, were mentioned in the chapter: frequency of purchase, percentage of "true loyalists" (those who shop only at one store), etc. Presumably, a consumer's trust is reflected in repeat buying behavior—firms that do not establish trust with customers will generally not have many repeat customers.

While there is no perfect measure for gauging trust, these proxies provide adequate methods of testing. Given that trust, repeat business, and loyalty are critical ingredients for a firm's success, these proxies need to be followed closely.

relationship the marketing program is performing well and where corrective actions are needed. However, they are usually not sufficient to assess the performance of individual marketing programs or elements, or to indicate what specific actions should be taken to improve performance.

In a recent article, Frank Mulhern noted:

> Much of marketing today is defined by, and acted on, in terms of the marketing mix variables. In practice, the marketing manager's function is to manage the variables represented by the 4Ps. The use of customer databases to measure individual customer profitability helps shift the emphasis from managing marketing mix variables to managing customers . . . . In this manner, customer profitability analysis plays a central role in data-driven relationship marketing and individual customer-based marketing communications.[11]

Fortunately, a wealth of potential metrics is available to help managers diagnose the effectiveness and efficiency of their marketing program. This section describes a number of metrics frequently used to assess firms' websites and their degree of offline/online integration. It also suggests some of the key metrics that may be used for product, price, communication, distribution, and community.

Tracking too many measures is time-consuming and potentially confusing. Criteria for selecting the metrics to use include the importance of the element that is being measured to achieving marketing objectives and whether a change in the metric is associated with a change in one of the customer-based metrics. For instance, if a website is intended to appeal to a narrow set of repeat customers, then tracking the number of website hits may not be as useful as tracking visits from registered users.

Website Interface

There are various approaches to measuring the performance of a firm's website. One approach uses internal data from the website to arrive at performance metrics. For example, a firm might evaluate itself against competitors in terms of number of website visitors or the amount of time it takes for pages to download. Another approach is to survey customers about their experiences with the website, either through a questionnaire placed on the website or through a third-party provider.

Behavioral Metrics

Firms can observe—through click-stream data—the exact pattern of a consumer's navigation through a site. These click-stream data can reveal a number of basic data points on how consumers interact with websites. Metrics based on click-stream data include, but are not limited to:

- The number of page views (i.e., the number of times a particular page has been presented to a visitor)
- The pattern of websites visited, including most frequent exit page and most frequent prior websites
- Length of stay on the website
- Dates and times of visits
- Number of registrations filled out per 100 visitors
- Number of abandoned registrations

- Demographics of registered visitors
- Number of customers with shopping carts
- Number of abandoned shopping carts

Exhibit 16.7 provides definitions of common metrics based on click-stream data.

To interpret such data properly, managers try to benchmark against other companies. For instance, consumers seem to visit their preferred websites regularly—even checking back to the website multiple times during a given session. Indeed, the probability that a website has been revisited during a session is approximately 90 percent.[12] Thus, while consumers tend to home in and become loyal to a small number of websites, they tend to revisit those websites a number of times during a particular session.

Attitudinal Metrics

Numerous scales have been developed to measure consumers' perceptions of website quality.[13] Typically, consumers are surveyed regarding their evaluations of quality or attitudes toward various dimensions of the website. Scores on these dimensions are then combined into an overall rating. Again, such metrics are most useful when compared to competitors' ratings or one's own score at different points in time.

Offline/Online Integration

Firms are just beginning to develop metrics to measure the degree to which offline/online operations are integrated. One type of metric assesses the integration of internal business processes and operations supporting online and offline operations. Examples would include:

- Customer service integration—the ability of staff to help equally with online or offline service and to access integrated databases of customer histories
- Cross-platform look-and-feel similarity—consistency of online environment and physical cues such as advertising and packaging

Another set of metrics tracks offline and online interactions with customers and prospects. Marketing communications or inquiries by prospective customers in one channel may result in sales through the other channel. Thus, a clear challenge for metrics is to account for all the multiple influences on a particular customer. Other challenges include developing metrics for the experiential aspects of offline/online integration. Sample metrics are:

- Cross-platform sales, upselling, and cross-selling
- Perceived ability of the customer to move seamlessly between online and offline at any phase of the purchase cycle
- Customer service costs online versus offline

Product

A key set of metrics is the attractiveness of the firm's current product offerings relative to competitive offerings. As an indicator of future revenues, many businesses also track metrics for innovativeness. Innovativeness metrics

Tracking Generic Online Metrics
Online metrics are useful both in the generic and at the firm-specific level. While firm-specific metrics help measure a firm's own progress (by, for example, tracking how its website becomes more "sticky"), generic metrics help answer the question, "Better compared to what?" Generic metrics can yield industry and competitor data for simple but useful benchmarking exercises. They can also provide important user and market data, gleaned from the actions of millions of Internet users. These aggregate metrics provide benchmarks and guidance for more effective decision making.

Many popular sources track a number of generic metrics regarding various industries, users, and markets. Such metrics—like the number of unique visitors for a set of websites or an industry, rankings of stickiest sites, and other metrics that track market or demographic trends—can provide not just competitor information but useful projections for possibly lucrative trends. Firms that provide this data include comScore Media Metrix, Nielsen//NetRatings, Forrester, eMarketer, and AdResource. They often offer both free and paid reports, with the latter usually being more specific by industry or market.

1. Visitor Metrics

Unidentified Visitor	A visitor is an individual who visits a website. An "unidentified visitor" means that no information about that visitor is available.
Unique Visitor	A unique visitor is one who can be recognized and counted only once within a given period of time, usually between a half-hour and an hour. An accurate count of unique visitors is not possible without some form of identification, registration, or authentication.
• Session visitor	A session ID is available (by cookie or token) or inferred (by incoming IP address plus browser type), which allows a visitor's responses to be tracked within a given visit to a website.
• Tracked visitor	An ID (e.g., cookie) is available which allows a user to be tracked across multiple visits to a website. No information, other than a unique identifier, is available for a tracked visitor.
• Identified visitor	An ID is available (by cookie or voluntary registration), which allows a user to be tracked across multiple visits to a website. Other information (name, demographics, possibly supplied voluntarily by the visitor) can be linked to this ID. Another way to obtain an identified visitor ID is to develop a Web gateway or panel (e.g., Web TV or PC Meter) that captures a complete record of a visitor's behavior.

2. Exposure Metrics

Page Exposures (page views)	The number of times a particular webpage has been presented to visitors in a given time period, without regard to visitor duplication.
Site Exposures	The number of visitor sessions at a website in a given time period, without regard to visitor duplication.

3. Visit Metrics

Stickiness (visit duration time)	The length of time a visitor spends on a website. Can be reported as an average in a given time period, without regard to visitor duplication.
Raw Visit Depth (total webpages exposure per session)	The total number of pages a visitor is exposed to during a single visit to a website. Can be reported as an average or distribution in a given time period, without regard to visitor duplication.
Visit Depth (total unique webpages exposure per session)	The total number of unique pages a visitor is exposed to during a single visit to a website. Can be reported as an average or distribution in a given time period, without regard to visitor duplication.

4. Hit Metrics

Hits	When visitors reach a website, their computer sends a request to the site's computer server to begin displaying pages. Each element of a requested page (including graphics, text, interactive items) is recorded by the site's server log file as a "hit." Hence, a single page with multiple graphics can be counted as multiple hits since each graphic is counted as a separate hit. Given that page designs and visit patterns vary from site to site, the number of hits bears no relationship to the number of pages viewed or visits to a site and so are generally regarded as an inaccurate form of measuring traffic.
Qualified Hits	A further refinement of hits, qualified hits exclude less important information recorded in a log file (such as error messages, etc.). While qualified hits provide a better idea of traffic volume than overall hits, this figure is still not an accurate assessment of actual number of users.

EXHIBIT 16.7   Frequently Used Website Metrics

are particularly relevant for firms whose product strategy is to be a leader or early adopter in bringing products to market. Possible product metrics include:

- Attractiveness—for example, perceived quality, product features, sales per item
- Innovativeness— for example, number or percent of new products, revenue from new products

Pricing

As discussed in Chapter 8, firms may choose any one of several pricing goals and strategies. Appropriate pricing metrics will vary accordingly. In addition, most firms monitor the extent to which actual prices vary from the standard list prices and the results of promotional pricing with metrics such as:

- Percent sold on discount
- Incremental sales from promotions

Communication

Effective communications reach the desired target audience, convey functional or emotional product benefits, and stimulate a desired action. For each of these types of outcomes there are metrics tailored to track the performance of particular communication media, such as advertising (see Exhibit 16.8), public relations, promotions, direct mail, and so on. Many

---

Drill-Down

Choosing Metrics for Target.com

Assume that Bob Ulrich, chairman and CEO of Target Corp., a national discount retailer, wants to understand the value of Target.com to the company. What key marketing metrics can he use to monitor the website's effectiveness?

He could begin by choosing appropriate metrics for each of two customer segments: consumers who want to buy Target's products online, and consumers who want to learn more about Target's products before purchasing them at a Target store.

For the online shoppers, relevant metrics would include the conversion rate of visitors to purchasers and the number of purchases per customer. For a more accurate picture of the value of the website, it would also be helpful to know the incremental sales due to the website—in other words, what percentage of the consumers who purchased online would have purchased offline if that was their only option?

For the offline shoppers, a metric that relates online search to offline purchases is needed. One possibility would be direct tracking—say, if Target could correlate redemption of online coupons with offline sales. Another possibility would be to develop a metric based on exit surveys conducted at Target stores. Questions might include: Have you ever used Target.com? How did Target.com influence your purchases today? How do you use the Target.com website? Of the purchases that you made today, what percentage would you *not* have made if you had not visited Target.com?

After analyzing the revenues produced by Target.com, Ulrich would then want to look at website click-stream metrics and perhaps usability studies to see if improvements could be made to the website's effectiveness.

companies turn to market research firms or other third parties to track specialized metrics. Following are a few representative metrics:

- Audience coverage (reach, frequency, click-throughs on banner ads)
- Awareness and attitudes
- Lead generation

1. Exposure Metrics		Banner/Page/ Site Frequency	The number of times unique visitors were exposed to a banner or visited a page or website.
Impressions (exposures, ad views)	Number of times an ad banner is downloaded and presumably seen by visitors. One impression is counted each time an advertisement is delivered by a Web server.		
		Effective Frequency	The number of exposures needed for an ad to become "effective." In mass-media models, advertisements require a certain amount of exposure before they can be deemed effective. Research has indicated that less than three exposures will not allow adequate recall. Too many exposures can be inefficient—after seven, eight, or 10 exposures, improved recall is incremental.
Gross Impressions	The sum of all media exposures (number of people or homes) disregarding duplication.		
CPM	Cost per thousand impressions (or exposures). The cost to serve 1,000 impressions through a given website.		
2. Reach and Frequency Metrics			
Reach	The number of unduplicated people or households that will be exposed to an advertising schedule at least once over a specified period of time	Effective Reach	The number of people who are exposed to an ad at the effective frequency.
		3. Other Metrics	
		Ad Click-Through (ad click rate)	The percentage of visitors who were exposed to a banner, clicked on the banner, and then were exposed to a target ad in a given time period, without regard to visitor duplication.
Banner/Page/ Site Reach	The number of unique visitors exposed to a banner or who visited a page/site in a given time period.		
Frequency	The number of times that an individual is exposed to a particular advertising message in a given period of time.	Cost Per Inquiry	The cost to generate an inquiry in direct-response advertising, such as banners. Calculated by the total cost of the direct-response advertisement divided by the number of inquiries it generates.

EXHIBIT 16.8   Frequently Used Online Advertising Metrics

Community

Because community members tend to be the consumers most involved with the marketers' products, metrics on community can be a useful leading indicator of future business performance. When community is viewed as an adjunct to or offshoot of the marketing program (e.g., a community fostered by an automobile manufacturer), the outcome of most interest to managers is the influence of the community on consumer buying decisions. For businesses where community is central to the business model (e.g., the chat rooms on BabyCenter.com), a broader range of metrics would be used. Data for community metrics can be gathered through website click streams and observation. Examples of metrics are:

- Number of members
- Frequencies of positive and negative comments
- Ratio of "actives" to members, or of "super-actives" to members

Distribution

As discussed in Chapter 11, two primary considerations in distribution channels are efficiency and effectiveness. Efficiency metrics assess the costs and complexity of providing products and services to consumers through the distribution system. Effectiveness metrics describe the ability of the distribution system to perform functions that create value for customers. In addition, many firms monitor the quality of their relationship with channel partners. Sample metrics include:

- Distribution costs (e.g., inventory costs)
- Distribution coverage (e.g., access to target market segments)
- Value provided to end customers (e.g., speed, price, convenience, information)
- Satisfaction of channel members

Branding

The strength of a firm's branding can be measured in terms of the leverage it provides the firm in the marketplace. A strong brand should enable companies to command a price premium, obtain extra support from distributors, or gain acceptance for brand extensions (i.e., new products with the same brand name). The strength of a company's brands can also be measured in terms of customers' perceptions. As described in more detail in Chapter 12, metrics of brand equity include the following:

- Price premium and margins relative to competition
- Brand extension opportunities (e.g, number of extensions, marketing cost to introduce them)
- Customer evaluation (e.g., brand awareness and strength, valence and uniqueness of brand associations)

Complexities and Challenges in Online Metrics

At this stage, it is clear that Internet marketing provides a wealth of information—including click-stream data from websites and customer history data from databases—that can reveal the entire cycle of consumption, from initial visits to loyalty. These data are easily stored, and software is readily available to "mine" the data. So where do online metrics fall short?

Are Relevant Data Being Used?

The most obvious problem is that most companies do not actually analyze and take action on the data. Many do not even examine their log files. It is also apparent that one needs to carefully think through the applicability and meaningfulness of the data that are analyzed. For example, three metrics often used carelessly are stickiness, page views, and conversion rates. The problems with interpreting stickiness, or length of time on the site, as a measure of customer experience were discussed earlier.

The metric of page views is another one that can be misleading. Consider this metric in regard to a Lands' End catalog, either offline or online. A large number of page views mean several things: (1) the customer is casually browsing through the catalog to see what types of clothes could be most appropriate for various family members; (2) the customer is unable to find suitable merchandise; or (3) the customer recalls buying items in a previous shopping trip and wants to purchase the same staple clothing such as socks, shirts, and underwear. If the consumer is simply browsing, then a large number of page views is desirable. He or she is shopping and finding the experience useful and fun. If, however, the customer is "goal directed," then he or she wants to find the right pair of blue socks and order them. A small number of page views would be best for this consumer.

Conversion rates can also be misleading when considered in isolation. Yes, a business wants high conversion rates. However, it wants high conversion rates from the most preferred customers—the ones who supply the cash flow, provide great word of mouth, and perhaps even use a limited amount of firm resources (such as follow-up phone calls or e-mails for service). Additionally, knowing who is a likely converter can be as important as the overall rate. Results of one retail study indicate that frequent visitors have a higher conversion rate (16.6 percent) than infrequent visitors (11.1 percent).[14] Equally important, a related study shows that consumers exhibiting certain changes in frequency behavior (e.g., consumers who visited infrequently, then became more frequent visitors) are more likely to buy. Hence, it was clear that "momentum" shoppers—those whose between-visit times become shorter—had the highest conversion rates and were the most likely to respond to targeted marketing.[15]

The most important message here is that all metrics must be tied directly to business strategy. One site may target stickiness, while a second may target conversion rates of frequent visitors. Even the level of the targeted metric—such as stickiness—must be tailored to the particular site. Further, target levels may vary for different customer groups. For instance, American Airlines has a very specific goal for the time it should take to book a first-class domestic fare by phone. A longer time is associated with a less efficient process. The same is true for the website. Target metrics are established to move the highest value customers through the experience as quickly and efficiently as possible.

How Does One Capture the One-Time Buyer More Effectively?

Evidence suggests that about 30 percent of online retail customers buy once and do not return.[16] How does one learn enough about these types of customers to increase the probability that they will someday return? Quite possibly the firm needs to focus not only on the customer experience at the original point of contact (the retail store or the online store) but also on recapturing customers through effective cross-promotion activities. Hence, for a one-time purchaser through a retail store, it may be most appropriate to attempt to stimulate new demands in other channels. Even with good database integration, metrics on one-time or very infrequent buyers are apt to be sparse.

Are Metrics Integrated across Channels?

A recently completed study on channel cannibalization provides interesting evidence that supports the synergistic effect of multiple channels. In particular, one central finding was that people's gathering of information online seems to increase purchases in other channels. For all five product categories in the study, online information searches tend to increase traditional retail purchases. Moreover, the magnitude of these effects appears to be substantial. In contrast, however, newspaper and magazine information searches do not appear to substantially increase online purchasing.[17] So, though an offline search in physical stores does not appear to stimulate online sales, it appears that online activities stimulate offline sales.

Grainger, an industrial goods supplier, found this to be true. It discovered that when long-term customers whose purchase amounts had stabilized began to actively use the Grainger website, their sales tripled compared with long-term customers who did not access the Web.[18] If Grainger had not had a cross-platform integrative database, it could not have observed these effects. Consumer goods firms that sell through retailers or distributors tend to be at a disadvantage in this respect compared to service firms and B2B firms.

Who Is the Advocate for Integrative Customer Metrics?

This chapter describes a framework for blending various metrics into a single set of integrated metrics. However, putting together a set of integrated metrics is not easy. The issue is not always whether the data are available, but whether time constraints or organizational constraints keep senior mangers from specifying the right set of customer metrics. Given current organizational structures, it is frequently the case that no single department or group plays the role of "voice of the customer" across all channels. What happens is that the customer experience is maximized within a particular channel, but the overall customer experience—the experience across all channels—is not maximized.

One solution is customer experience councils. Dell Computer integrates customer behavior into its e-business strategy across platforms. Its internal research revealed that there were specific drivers of loyalty: order fulfillment, product performance, and post-sale service. Dell narrowed its focus to these three areas to enhance an integrated customer experience.[19]

Are Marketing Costs Accounted For?

The cost of acquiring customers online can be considerably higher than acquiring them offline. For example, according to one study, the customer acquisition cost is 20 percent to 40 percent higher for an online apparel customer than it is for an offline customer.[20] The only way a company can make a profit is by maintaining customers who make repeat purchases over time—the average amount customers spend generally increases as they become more familiar and comfortable with the site. According to the same study, repeat online retail customers spend more than twice as much after a two-year relationship with a website than during the first six months of the relationship. The study concludes that an online retailer needs to keep a customer for 1.1 years before it breaks even.

It is clear that companies that do not succeed in motivating their customers to return to their websites are likely to face significant losses. Companies need to work hard to earn customer loyalty. Among other things, they need to make their sites easy to use and navigate, they need to deliver reliably and punctually, and they need to offer timely and comprehensive customer support. Strong performance in these areas can translate into strong financial results. At the same time, investments in improving the customer experience are expected to pay off in terms of both greater efficiencies in serving customers and better customer retention. A study of online retailing found that 56 percent of retailers reported online profits in 2001 compared with 43 percent in 2000, with profits driven by "continued performance improvements in marketing efficiency, an increase in the number of repeat online buyers, and tighter expense control" as well as overall market growth.[21]

There was a time when profits did not seem to matter to dot-com businesses. Clearly, those times have passed. Before the Nasdaq slump in spring 2000, it was standard practice for companies to spend more than 100 percent of their revenue on marketing. The Super Bowl telecasts in 1999 and 2000 were dominated by dot-com advertisements whose costs approached or exceeded $2 million per ad.

Profitability, however, has once again become important. As a result, companies have slashed their marketing expenses. Yet successfully marketing to prospective customers remains critical. Companies are therefore trying to find more refined and cost-effective ways of reaching new customers. For example, many companies now use targeted e-mail marketing, which has a minimal cost and can return a click-through rate that is 8 percent higher than untargeted e-mail.[22] Others resort to a careful selection of affiliates. Whatever their choice of marketing strategy, companies are realizing that careless spending on marketing can quickly lead to poor financial results that today's market is not likely to tolerate.

eBay Example

When thinking about metrics by which the eBay site should be measured, it is important to note certain nuances of the online auction segment. In this section, eBay's metrics (looking primarily at the original United States version of eBay and not its international versions such as eBay France) are analyzed across the following stages: search and shopping, auction, post-auction and loyalty. This example examines key questions that eBay can ask about its customers, the specific metrics to track their behavior, and the types of analyses that can be performed (see Exhibit 16.9). eBay's financial metrics are discussed later in the example.

Stages	Customer Metrics	Implementation Metrics
Search and Shopping	• Number of unique visitors • Number of repeat visitors • Number of registered users	• Website: Number of page views, length of stay (stickiness), pattern of sites visited • Community: Number of users on My eBay
Auction	• Number of auctions user participates in • Average dollar amount per auction • Average dollar amount per product category	• Website: Time spent inside auction • Product: Conversion to "Buy It Now" feature; length of auction • Communications: Conversion to "E-Mail a Friend" • Distribution: Profitability per seller
Post-Auction	• Percentage of returns • Online satisfaction surveys • Auctions won vs. lost	• Community: Replies to feedback, number of fraud reports • Website: Transactions finalized vs. dropped
Loyalty	• Frequency of auction participation • Interval since last auction • Share of auctions (identify competitors)	• Distribution: Items sold vs. not sold

EXHIBIT 16.9   Online Tracking—eBay Customer Metrics

Search and Shopping

Using visits metrics is one way to assess the size of eBay's customer base. This can be expressed in a number of ways. eBay ranks No. 8 among all websites in unique monthly visitors from work and at home in the United States[23] (see Exhibit 16.10). Looking at daily numbers, eBay has 5.5 million unique daily visitors, almost 26 percent of the entire online community (see Exhibit 16.11). That is roughly 25 percent of Yahoo!'s daily unique visitors and 16 percent of AOL's numbers. While eBay and Amazon have the same number of unique monthly visitors, eBay has over twice as many unique daily visitors, which indicates that eBay has a higher visitor return rate than Amazon. Looking only at the online auction segment, it is immediately evident that eBay dominates the field. It gets over 26 times more unique daily visitors than second-ranked uBid.com (see Exhibit 16.12). In fact, eBay has more unique daily visitors than uBid has unique monthly visitors.

eBay is one of the 10 most visited websites.

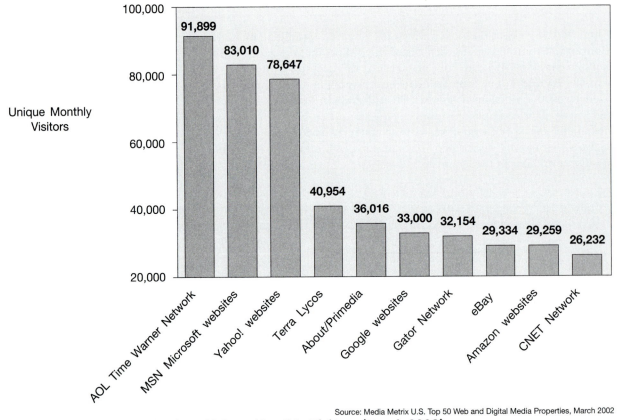

Source: Media Metrix U.S. Top 50 Web and Digital Media Properties, March 2002

EXHIBIT 16.10   eBay Metrics—Unique Monthly Visitors (March 2002)

The number of registered users provides an indication of the company's ability to convert browsers into likely buyers (see Exhibit 16.13). eBay has more than 42 million registered users, more than 9 percent of worldwide at-home Internet users.[24] Given that the majority of those users are in the United States, and that eBay still does the majority of its business there, it represents more than 37 percent of U.S. Internet users.

To assess the effectiveness of the site, the next step is to examine factors thought to influence user behavior:

One quarter of all Web users visit eBay.

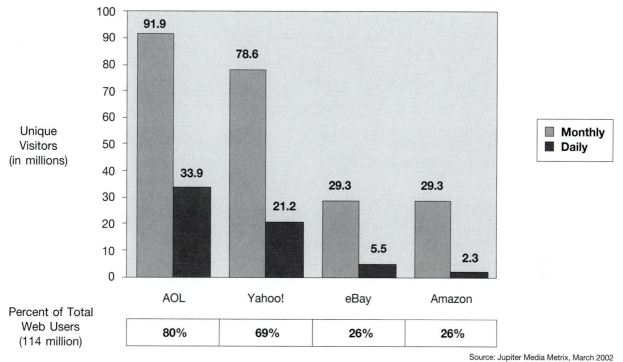

Source: Jupiter Media Metrix, March 2002

EXHIBIT 16.11   eBay Metrics—Unique Monthly and Daily Visitors (March 2002)

eBay has more visitors than all other auction websites combined.

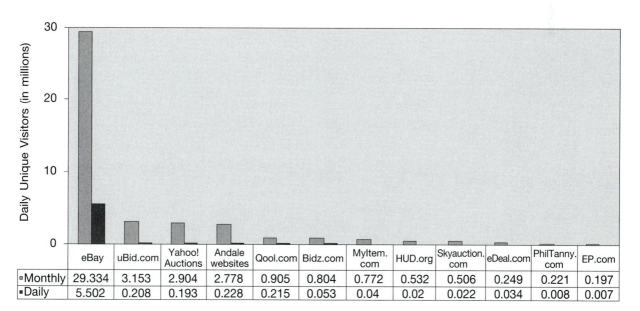

	eBay	uBid.com	Yahoo! Auctions	Andale websites	Qool.com	Bidz.com	MyItem. com	HUD.org	Skyauction. com	eDeal.com	PhilTanny. com	EP.com
▪Monthly	29.334	3.153	2.904	2.778	0.905	0.804	0.772	0.532	0.506	0.249	0.221	0.197
▪Daily	5.502	0.208	0.193	0.228	0.215	0.053	0.04	0.02	0.022	0.034	0.008	0.007

Audience size for all auction sites with reportable traffic: 32.6 million monthly unique visitors
6 million daily unique visitors

Source: Jupiter Media Metrix, March 2002

EXHIBIT 16.12   eBay Metrics—Unique Daily Visitors to Auction Websites (March 2002)

eBay's registered user base has doubled or almost doubled every year.

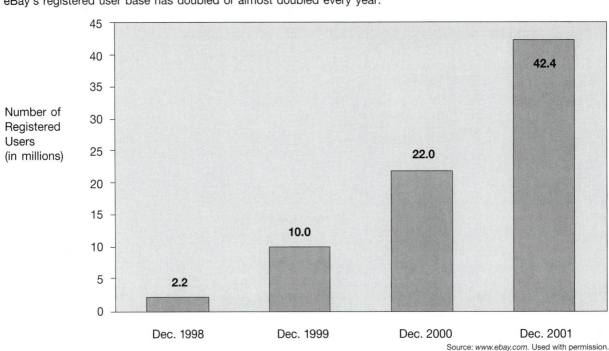

EXHIBIT 16.13   eBay's Registered-User Evolution

Source: *www.ebay.com.* Used with permission.

- What do users browse for at the website?
- How do users browse the website?
- How broadly and deeply do users browse the website?
- How long do users browse the website?

Notice that "browse" is used in each question. At this stage, eBay is interested in how users navigate the website. Click-stream patterns help answer all of the "what" and "how" questions posed above. For instance, eBay would profit immensely if it could identify that a significant percentage of its user base goes from the homepage to the search engine (implying that users usually come for a specific purpose) but then resort to the Help page (perhaps the number of items returned is too large and diverse).

The number of pages viewed per day is a good indicator of how much the users interact with the website. eBay could look at the number of unique pages viewed per day to get a sense of the breadth of a typical user session. This could indicate that either people are doing lots of window-shopping or, conversely, they are having trouble navigating the site. This highlights an easily overlooked aspect of metrics: While the Internet can generate large amounts of data, firms have to be careful about drawing conclusions from the information.

To answer the question about how long the user interacts with the website, eBay could use the stickiness measure previously discussed in this chapter. As a rule of thumb, eBay wants the user to spend as much time as possible exposed to the content within the virtual borders of the website. More content means more auctions, more items, more opportunities to bid, and increased attractiveness of the website.

eBay ranks well in terms of stickiness (see Exhibit 16.14), with slightly more minutes spent per user per day than Yahoo! but somewhat less than AOL, although the comparison with AOL is distorted because many people use AOL.com for e-mail and stay on the website for long periods of time. Compared to other online auction websites, eBay does extremely well. Its users stay almost three times as long as uBid users do and more than four times as long as Yahoo! Auctions users. Because people spend more time on eBay, auction sellers there have a greater chance of having their goods viewed than on any other online auction site.

eBay rates high in "stickiness."

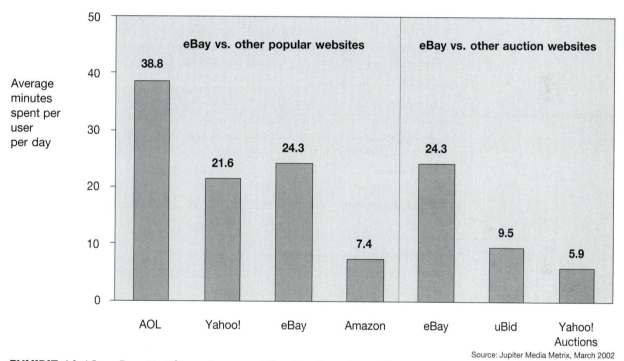

EXHIBIT 16.14 **eBay Metrics—Average Minutes Spent per User per Day**

Source: Jupiter Media Metrix, March 2002

Auction

At the auction stage eBay can determine each user's profitability and the specific conversion rate for buyers and sellers. These metrics are critical, as they are tied to eBay's overall profitability and cash flow. At this stage, eBay is able to assess the appeal of its auction format and test variations. In addition, eBay can look at a variety of other metrics to gauge the quality of its marketing implementation:

- How profitable are our sellers/items/categories?
- How well are our communications working?
- How can we capitalize on targeted marketing?
- How can we tailor and personalize our users' experience?

- How are new features doing?
- How can we forecast the market for different auctions?

After analyzing the number of auctions and the dollar amount attached to each one, eBay would be able to tailor the website for individual needs—perhaps by providing quick links to the most desirable areas of the website, focusing on the items or the price range in which the user usually bids. For instance, if one user tends to bid often on Lakers tickets, eBay could tailor a homepage that links directly to sports-related auctions or give him the options of creating a personal website focusing on sports or basketball.

Conversion rates are obviously important for eBay. Conversion rates typically chart the percentage of visitors who become customers. (For example, a 10 percent conversion rate states that 10 out of 100 visitors will buy something.) Thus, knowing what percentage of the registered user base frequently posts items, the average dollar amount attached to items, and thereby the average profit margin on each auction is crucial. Also, knowing the percentage of items that do not sell (because the reserve is not met or other reasons) can help determine the level of satisfaction of eBay's sellers.

Knowing the success rate for new features such as "Buy It Now" would give eBay a sense for where the market is going in terms of desired features. eBay found that in its first year of existence, 19 percent of all sales revenue came from the fixed-price format, indicating a definite desire for those kinds of transactions.

Post-Auction

eBay would likely want to answer the following questions at this stage:

- How satisfied are our users?
- How effectively do we retain customers compared with our competitors?
- How does fraud affect the business?

By answering these questions, eBay would be able to analyze its effectiveness in maintaining a happy community (along with methods such as keeping constant track of the Feedback Forum). Also, knowing how often and when the user returns to eBay helps determine the level of loyalty.

To respond with speed and efficiency to market needs, eBay should execute online satisfaction surveys and be attentive to users who do not consider certain transactions completely successful. Along those lines, eBay needs to focus on the fraud metric, particularly as its community grows substantially.

The time spent inside each auction would give eBay a sense of how interested the user is in auctions overall. The number of auctions won and lost would indicate the general degree to which the user is committed to winning an auction. (A highly committed user adds value to the seller and eBay alike by driving auction prices higher.) A bidder may look at the number of bids for an individual item. For instance, when a user gets a list of auctions for the Palm M505, she may look at the number of current bids. In general, the greater the number of bids, the greater the interest in the auction and the greater the competition.

Loyalty

At this stage, eBay is seeking answers to questions such as:

- How loyal is our community?
- What "share of wallet" do we attract?
- Do users post at multiple auction sites?
- Who are our competitors?
- What are the barriers to loyalty or "exclusivity"?

By analyzing the frequency with which users participate in auctions, eBay can identify a pattern of interaction. This metric is important because, when crossed with the frequency of visits, it can indicate users' loyalty to the website.

In addition, identifying the other websites that users visit gives eBay a good sense of its competitors. Furthermore, if those competitors do not rely solely on auction interactions, that is helpful information about what kind of transactions attract the target market.

eBay Financial Metrics

It is important to examine some key financial metrics for eBay and link them to the company's customer initiatives. This section focuses on two categories of financial metrics: (1) revenue and (2) cost and profitability.

Revenue

eBay has experienced significant growth in its net revenues over the years, from $41.4 million in 1997 to $224.7 million in 1999 to $748.8 million in 2001.[25] During that period eBay made some important acquisitions (such as Butterfield & Butterfield and Kruse Inc. in May 1999), but the company's increases in revenue were driven not by the newly acquired companies but almost entirely by increased use of eBay.[26] This was reflected in the growth in the number of registered users, the number of listings, and merchandise sales. This indicates that the company's investment in marketing, website design and usability, and customer support are paying off. That said, net revenue per registered user has dropped, from $121 in 1997 to $22.50 in 1999 to $17.25 in 2001. The company's explanation: As the number of users grows, there is an increase in users who make practical and one-time purchases, bringing down total average spending per user.

Cost and Profitability

In order to make its website more user-friendly and to support its customers, eBay has made significant investments, including design changes and an expansion of the company's customer-support and website operations departments. A two-year effort to bolster its infrastructure is reflected in an increase in the cost of net revenues as a percentage of net revenues, from 20.3 percent in 1997 (before the effort) to 25.6 percent in 1999 (when it began) to 18.0 percent in 2001 (when it finished).[27] At the same time, the company increased its spending on sales and marketing in order to build its registered user base from less than 500,000 in 1997 to 10 million in 1999 to 42.4 million in 2001. Sales and marketing costs as a percentage of net revenues increased from 37.8 percent in 1997 to 42.8 percent in 1999 and then decreased to 33.9 percent in 2001 as eBay's brand equity helped establish it as the online auction market leader.[28]

Still, relative to the tremendous growth in the company's user base, the increase in sales and marketing spending has been low. This can be attributed to one of eBay's greatest strengths—customer acquisition through referrals. More than half of its customers are referred to the website by other users. "If you just do the math off our quarterly financial filings, you see that we are spending less than $10 to acquire each new customer . . . the reason is that we are being driven by word of mouth," said the company's CEO, Meg Whitman.[29] Furthermore, the cost to maintain and support referred customers is lower than for customers acquired through other marketing methods, because referred customers tend to go to the people who referred them to answer their questions.

Looking at overall profitability, eBay's net income as a percentage of net sales dropped from 17.1 percent in 1997 to 4.8 percent in 1999. This was due in part to the increase in sales, marketing and customer support described above, as well as to an increase in product development costs, aimed at expanding the company's user and listing base. However, it rose to 12.1 percent in 2001 as eBay hit its stride and began to leverage its brand and enter new markets. It remains to be seen if eBay can continue the upward trend in its net income margins, but eBay remains one of the most notable online companies to have sustained rapid growth while remaining profitable during this period.

Summary

1. Why should managers be concerned about metrics?

Metrics drive organizational behavior in a number of ways, including helping to clarify strategic objectives, communicating the strategy, tracking performance, increasing accountability, and aligning objectives.

2. What are the characteristics of good metrics?

Good metrics are relatively easy to measure in a timely fashion. They are unambiguous, easy to interpret, and robust. (In other words, a change in the metric reflects a change in the outcome it is supposed to measure.) In addition, metrics need to be generally accepted by business stakeholders and linked to the desired business outcomes.

3. Why do marketing managers need financial, customer-based, and implementation metrics?

Each set of metrics gives managers information on different aspects of performance. Financial metrics assess the bottom-line performance of the business. Customer-based metrics measure the health of the business's customer assets. Metrics that measure the implementation of the marketing program explain what actions need to be taken to strengthen the customer base and, ultimately, the financial results.

4. What are the strengths and weaknesses of the traditional hierarchy-of-effects model?

The hierarchy-of-effects model appears to be simple, straightforward, and easy to implement. Yet most of its measures rely upon questioning target customers about their behavior rather than direct observation of their behavior.

5. **What are the stages of the integrated hierarchy-of-effects model? How do they relate to the four stages of a customer relationship?**

The stages of the integrated hierarchy-of-effects model are related to the four relationship stages as follows:

- The awareness stage includes awareness, knowledge, and attitudes.
- The exploration/expansion stage includes purchase intent, search and shopping, purchase, and postpurchase.
- The commitment stage includes loyalty.
- The dissolution stage includes attrition.

Activities for Students

1. Select an online company and recommend a set of marketing metrics for it. Consider how you would evaluate the performance of the business against its objectives and how you would try to improve performance.
2. Select a well-known offline company that has established an online presence. What set of metrics would you use to evaluate its online/offline integration? How would you obtain these metrics?
3. From public sources (including magazines, newspapers, or companies such as comScore Media Metrix), collect comparative statistics on at least five metrics and 10 companies. What do these metrics tell you about the marketing performance of these companies? What are the strengths and weaknesses of these metrics?

Key Terms

metrics	marketing implementation metrics	retention rate
Performance Dashboard	hierarchy-of-effects model	share of wallet
financial metrics	conversion rate	customer lifetime value
customer-based metrics	acquisition cost	attrition rate

Endnotes

[1]Black, Jane. 2002. The cultural key to net gains. *BusinessWeekOnline*. April 15. (*http://www.businessweek.com:/print/technology/content/apr2002/tc20020415_9527.htm?mainwindow*).

[2]Ibid.

[3]Rayport, Jeffrey F. and Bernard J. Jaworski. 2001. *E-commerce* New York: McGraw-Hill/Irwin.

[4]Ambler, Tim and Debra Riley. 2000. Marketing Metrics: A review of performance measures in use in the UK and Spain. Centre for Marketing Working Paper, London Business School.

[5]Winer, Russell S. 2000. What marketing metrics are used by MSI members?, Marketing Metrics, Report No. 00-119, Marketing Science Institute, Cambridge, MA.

[6]Woerner, Stephanie. 2002. Networked at Cisco. Teaching Case #1, Center for eBusiness, Sloan School of Management, Massachusetts Institute of Technology. July 20.

[7]Newing, Rod. 2002. Crucial importance of clear business goals. FT.com. July 5.

[8]While the stages may vary with a particular author, they generally include prepurchase, purchase, and postpurchase stages corresponding to the first three of our stages.

[9]Gurley, J. William. 2000. The one Internet metric that really matters. *Fortune* 141 (5): 392, 6 March.

[10]Gupta, Sunil, Donald R. Lehmann, and Jennifer Ames Stuart. 2001. Valuing customers. Report No. 01-119, Marketing Science Institute, Cambridge, MA.

[11]Mulhern, Francis. 1999. Customer profitability analysis: measurement, concentration, and research directions. *The Journal of Interactive Marketing* 13 (1), Winter, 25–40.

[12]Montgomery, Alan L., and Christos Faloutos. 2000. Using clickstream data to identify world wide web browsing trends. Working Paper Series, Carnegie Mellon University, 13 February.

[13]In May 2002, Naveen Donthu collected over twenty different scales, listed on his website at *http://www.gsu.edu/~mktnnd/webevalcites.pdf.*

[14]Moe, Wendy, and Peter S. Fader. 2000. Capturing evolving visit behavior in clickstream data. Working Paper Series, Wharton Business School, August.

[15]Moe, Wendy, and Peter S. Fader. 2000. Which visits lead to purchases? Dynamic conversion behavior at ecommerce sites. Working Paper Series, Wharton Business School, August.

[16]Fader, Peter, and Bruce Hardie. 1999. Repeat buying in cyberspace. Presented at Institute for Operations Research and the Management Sciences, November 8.

[17]Ward, Michael R., and Michell Morganosky. 2000. Online consumer search and purchase in a multiple channel environment. Working Paper Series, Department of Agriculture and Consumer Economics, University of Illinois, Urbana, 29 September.

[18]Reichheld, Frederick F., and Phil Schefter. 2000. e-Loyalty: Your secret weapon on the Web. *Harvard Business Review* July–August, 107.

[19]Ibid.

[20]Ibid.

[21]E-commerce—color it green. 2002. *Internetnews.com*. June 12. *http://www.internetnews.com/ec-news/print/php/1364481.*

[22]Email: An effective marketing tool. *123 Jump*, February 27, 2001.

[23]Media Metrix U.S. Top 50 Web and Digital Media Properties.

[24]Nielsen//NetRatings estimates the global online access population (from home) to be 461,964,794 (*http://www.nielsen-netratings.com/hot_off_the_net_i.jsp*).

[25]eBay 10-K.

[26]Ibid.

[27]Ibid.

[28]Ibid.

[29]Reichheld, Frederick F., and Phil Schefter. 2000. e-Loyalty: Your secret weapon on the Web, *Harvard Business Review* July–August.

Contributing Authors

Katherine Jocz is a thought leader and director of academic relationships for marketspaceU at Marketspace, a Monitor Group company. Her areas of expertise include brand management, innovation, service quality, marketing research, and marketing metrics. Before joining Monitor she was vice president of research operations at the Marketing Science Institute. Previously she held positions in communications and publications at Bolt Beranek and Newman and Massachusetts Institute of Technology.

Ms. Jocz has published articles in *Marketing Management* and is the editor of several volumes. She served on the *Journal of Marketing* editorial review board for 12 years and has also been a board member of the Association for Consumer Research, a member of the U.S. Census Advisory Committee, and a frequent reviewer, panelist, and program committee member for American Marketing Association conferences and Public Policy and Marketing conferences.

Bruce Weinberg is an associate professor of marketing and e-commerce at Bentley College's McCallum Graduate School of Business. He is an expert in online consumer experiences, and analyzes them from a marketing and customer satisfaction perspective. In his Internet Shopping 24/7 Project he immersed himself in studying online shopping as a participant observer by retail shopping exclusively online for one year.

Professor Weinberg earned his Ph.D. at the MIT Sloan School of Management and his bachelor's degree in Mathematics/Computer Science at Boston University. He has served on the faculty at Northwestern's J.L. Kellogg Graduate School of Management, Boston University, Babson College, and Tufts University's Fletcher School of Law and Diplomacy. Professor Weinberg has received awards for both teaching and research. In 1997, he received the MSI/H. Paul Root Award from the American Marketing Association for the "most significant contribution to the advancement of marketing practice" for the paper "Premarket Forecasting of Really-New Products," published in the *Journal of Marketing*. His publications have appeared in the *Journal of Marketing, Journal of Marketing Research, Journal of Interactive Marketing, Marketing Science Institute* and *Advances in Consumer Research.*

His research and teaching have been featured or covered in books and media such as *The Wall Street Journal*, MSNBC, NPR, and *Business 2.0. Inc.* magazine dubbed him "The Netty Professor."

Jon Davis joined Marketspace in 2001 as a member of the R&D team. He has worked on a variety of projects, including the development of a series of case materials on AOL Time Warner and several of its media properties. He also serves as the publisher of marketspaceU.com, which provides textbook support for adopting undergraduate and graduate school faculty.

Mr. Davis's background is in the publishing industry. Before joining Marketspace, he worked for the new-media division of Universal Press Syndicate. As director of business development, he was in charge of expanding the reach of its leading online word and puzzle game franchise currently marketed under The Puzzle Society brand. Mr. Davis previously worked for Creators Syndicate, where he designed and managed its two-pronged online launch: Creators.com offered time-delayed syndicated content for free while paying customers such as Washingtonpost.com received same-day delivery of syndicated comic and editorial features. Mr. Davis also worked for an AOL Greenhouse company creating and managing content for the online service. He began his publishing career in circulation for Times Mirror magazines, working on *Ski*, *Skiing*, and *Popular Science.*

Mr. Davis received his bachelor's degree in anthropology from Brown University in 1989 and his MBA from Carnegie Mellon in 2000, with concentrations in marketing and strategy. He enjoys bicycling, especially with his wife on their 1964 Schwinn tandem bike purchased on eBay.

Kate Bernhardt is a media professional with more than 25 years of experience in the production and business sides of film, TV, multimedia, and the Internet. An award-winning producer/director/writer of many nationally and internationally recognized projects, including PBS science and arts programs, Ms. Bernhardt left the world of film and television in the early 1990s, intrigued by the power and challenge of new media. Ms. Bernhardt was a key team member in creating groundbreaking multimedia biographies and was a pioneer in several Web content ventures. She is especially drawn to issues of information architecture, usability, and customer-centered design, and has had extensive hands-on experience developing Web content and commerce initiatives. Currently, Ms. Bernhardt leads the video department at Marketspace. She is a member of the Writer's Guild of America, east, and a former president of the New England chapter of Women in Film and Video, a national organization of media professionals.

Craig Thompson is the director of academic content for marketspaceU at Marketspace. He has worked on a variety of projects, from contributing to the group's textbook efforts and case development to managing the development of accompanying teaching materials for the texts on the marketspaceU.com website.

Mr. Thompson's background is in engineering consulting. Before joining Marketspace, he worked for a number of consulting firms designing bridges, university campus expansions, urban redevelopments, and numerous projects in the private sector.

Mr. Thompson received his bachelor's degree in engineering from the University of Cincinnati, and his MBA and a master's degree in international project management from Washington University in St. Louis. While at Washington University, Mr. Thompson assisted faculty with courses at the graduate and executive levels in the areas of economics, strategy, corporate finance, negotiations and conflict management, international business, and organizational behavior and design.

A

acceptance   Willingness to embrace the Internet as a reliable alternative to traditional marketing research methods.

acquisition cost   The cost of marketing programs to attract new customers, often expressed as cost per newly acquired customer.

actionable segmentation   Segmentation that allows companies to make informed decisions about a potential offering.

administrator-to-user value   Examples include newsletters, mailing lists, supervised chats, and offline events.

affiliate marketing   Agreement between two firms that directs users of one firm's website to an affiliated firm's website in exchange for a fee.

alignment   The process of coordinating a firm's goals, resources, activities, and implementation to achieve its strategic goals.

asynchronous communication   Delayed communication, where the time between a message being sent, read, and replied to can vary greatly. Examples include message boards (bulletin boards) and mailing lists.

attraction   The degree to which the firm's offering is perceived to be more desirable than the offerings of competing firms.

attrition rate   Percentage of existing customers who have stopped being customers in a specified time period.

auctions   Auctions come in many different varieties. The underlying foundation of auctions is a pricing mechanism that engenders competition between buyers in a manner that allows the buyer with the highest product reservation price to purchase the item.

augmented product   A product that incorporates attributes that provide additional benefits beyond the core benefit.

awareness   A stage in a relationship in which the the parties recognize each other as possible exchange partners.

B

banner ads   A boxlike graphic image used on a web page to display an ad.

basic product   The mimimum product, or set of product attributes, needed to provide the core benefit.

beachhead positioning   The target segment is a subsection of the larger, offline segment. The positioning is similar but might be focused toward the smaller customer group.

beachhead targeting   For BAMs entering the online market, involves targeting a portion of their targeted offline segments online.

blanket positioning   For BAMs entering the online market, their targeting segment does not change and the appropriate positioning is fairly straightforward.

blanket targeting   For BAMs entering the online market, involves targeting the same online segments as the firm targets offline.

bleed-over positioning   The target segment is composed of both old and a new type of customer. The positioning would resemble the offline offering, but also make the online offering attractive to new types of customers.

bleed-over targeting   For BAMs entering the online market, involves targeting both a portion of their offline segment and part of a new segment.

brand   A symbol such as a name, sign, symbol, color, or design, or a combination of them designed to identify the goods and services of one seller and to differentiate them from those of the competition.

brand equity   From a customer perspective, brand equity is defined as the differential effect that brand knowledge on consumer response to the marketing of that brand. Brand equity requires that consumers are both aware of the brand, and have associations that are unique, valued, and strong.

bundling   The strategy of selling two or more products as part of a package. Pure bundling is a strategy where products are sold only as a bundle. Mixed bundling is a strategy where products are sold both individually and as a bundle (bundle price is generally lower than the sum of the individual product prices).

C

causal research   Causal research is complex and affected by factors that researchers cannot always control, such as people's attitudes. Experimentation, computer simulation, and econometric methods are the research methods used to explore the cause-and-effect relation between variables.

channel effectiveness   The degree to which a distribution system performs functions that create value for consumers.

channel efficiency The amount of resources required by a distribution system to make a product or service available for consumption or use.

channel power The ability of one channel member to influence another.

coercive power The ability to withhold resources if the partner does not act in accordance with its wishes.

cognitive and emotional elements The customer's intellectual and emotional reactions to a site.

collaboration The process of working jointly or cooperatively with other channel members.

commerce The transactional capacity of a site—the sale of goods, products, or services.

commitment A stage in a relationship in which the parties feel a connection in the sense of an obligation or responsibility to each other.

communal relationship A purely altruistic relationship, with each party focused on meeting the needs and wants of the other(s) in the relationship.

communication The dialogue that unfolds between the website and its users. This communication can take three forms: firm-to-user (e.g., e-mail notification), user-to-firm (e.g., customer service request), or user-to-user (e.g., instant messaging).

community A set of interwoven relationships built upon shared interests.

complementary product A product whose use enhances the benefits provided by another product.

conclusive research Research used to answer "how often" and "how many" questions. It follows a formal research design process and provides reliable data for drawing conclusions or making decisions. Often, it is quantitative in nature (i.e., it can be quantified and summarized). Conclusive research provides a reliable picture of a population by using a valid research instrument, and it tests hypotheses in formal research.

connection The network of formal linkages between the site and other sites.

content All digital subject matter on a website.

context A website's aesthetics and functional look-and-feel.

conversion rate The percentage of prospects or visitors who become customers.

co-opetition Occurs when companies are both competitors and collaborators.

core benefit The fundamental benefit that a customer seeks in a product.

cost per click-through Media cost based on the number of viewers following a hyperlink within an ad.

cost per thousand impressions (CPM) Media measurement unit describing the cost of delivering 1,000 impressions. An impression is a measure of the opportunity to see a message by a user.

cost per transaction Media cost based on the number of transactions generated.

customer decision process An organizing framework that looks systematically for unmet or underserved needs.

customer experience A target customer's perception and interpretation of all the stimuli encountered while interacting with a firm.

customer lifetime value A firm's expected total net present value of profit from all direct interactions and exchanges with a customer until death does them part.

customer relationship management A marketing process focused on retaining customers and based on decision making that revolves around better understanding existing customers, identifying customers with whom to maintain a relationship, and implementing tactics to maintain and advance customer relationships.

customer vector A database record that contains every bit of information retained about a customer.

customer-based metrics Metrics intended to measure the performance and health of a company's customer assets.

customer-centric marketing communication A concept of marketing communications that recognizes that customers have many choices about what media and communications they engage with and thus the need for marketers to present relevant communications at appropriate times and places.

customization A site's ability to modify itself to—or be modified by—each user.

D

database marketing A marketing process for acquiring customers that involves obtaining meaningful individual level consumer information, respecting consumers' privacy, analyzing this information to estimate consumer response to various offers, and making marketing decisions based on this expected response.

descriptive research Research that determines the frequency with which something occurs or how separate events are related. It provides information about the population or universe under study (the elements within a given group about whom data are required) by describing the who, what, when, where, and how of a situation.

direct competitors Rivals within the same industry that offer a similar or competing product.

dissolution A stage in a relationship in which one or both parties exit.

distribution channel A system of organizations involved in the process of making a product or service available for consumption or use.

dynamic market A market where prices are fluid. Auctions and exchanges are examples of dynamic markets.

dynamic pricing A pricing environment in which prices are fluid, not fixed. In most pricing environments, prices are relatively fixed due to the "menu costs" associated with changing prices. The Internet allows prices to be changed at relatively low prices.

E

elders Long-time regulars and leaders who share their knowledge and pass along culture.

elements of the customer experience The key factors that constitute the customer experience.

e-mail automation system A system that assists with receiving and sending e-mails, including formatting, and distributing e-mails.

encounter element The customer's reaction to a site on various occasions.

enduring involvement A strong interest in a product or service category over an extended period of time.

e-newsletter A glorified e-mail that one sends in bulk to subscribers, typically on a regular basis.

equity building The process of creating value within a community through increasing levels of participation. The process begins in the expansion stage.

exchange relationship A relationship based on the giving of one thing in return for another.

exclusive distribution A distribution strategy that employs a limited number of outlets or points of access.

experience hierarchy The evolution of the customer's experience over time.

expert power The ability to influence based a channel member's expertise or skills.

exploration A stage in a relationship in which the parties consider the possibility of exchange. The

customer may investigate the website, seek out third-party evaluations (e.g., *Consumer Reports*), and initiate trial purchases.

exploratory research Research that emphasizes gaining ideas and insights about a problem, attempting to answer "why," "how" and "when" questions. It helps break broad, vague problems into smaller, more manageable statements.

external validity Tests that compare the outcome of the study to external sources that are known to be true. For example, in a study that forecasts the penetration rates of the Internet, one could forecast the penetration rate for the year 2000 and then compare the forecasts to information for that same year. If the forecast and the actual figure differ significantly, the study would have failed the external validity test.

F

financial metrics Metrics that capture the revenues, costs, profits, and bottom-line performance of a business.

fit and reinforcement Fit refers to the extent to which each of the 7Cs individually supports the business model. Reinforcement refers to the degree of consistency between each of the Cs.

frequency The average number of times an ad is delivered to a viewer during a given time period.

H

hierarchy-of-effects model A group of models positing multiple stages in an individual's purchase process, from awareness through postpurchase.

hybrid value Value created through releasing trapped value while creating new-to-the-world value.

I

impact In the context of marketing communications, the value of an individual exposure in a specific medium based on the likelihood of

recipients to respond positively to the communication.

indirect competitors Companies in other industries that produce similar or competing products or services.

individualization The degree to which firm-customer interactions are tailored or customized to the individual user.

infomediary A category of online firms that bring together buyers and sellers to facilitate puchasing decisions. Examples of infomediaries include portals, virtual communities, and transaction aggregators.

integrated marketing communications A concept of marketing communications that recognizes the added value of planning and executing a variety of communications tools—e.g., advertising, direct response, sales promotion, and public relations—in a seamless, integrated fashion to achieve maximum impact.

intensive distribution A distribution strategy that employs the maximum possible number of outlets or points of access.

interaction An act temporarily linking two individuals at a very basic, noncommittal level where trust plays a marginal role.

interaction intensity The frequency with which the parties in a relationship make contact.

interactive communication Communications and media where information exchange is bidirectional between recipients and senders.

interactivity The degree to which a two-way flow of communication or dialogue occurs between the firm and customer.

intermediary type The specific form of channel member that is employed in the channel.

internal validation Tests that ensure that there are no abnormalities in the study results. For example, in a study where the researcher wants to examine the effect of pricing levels on demand, the researcher would assume that the higher the price, the less the demand for that good or service. An internal validity check would test for this expectation to hold.

interstitials ads   Ads that appear between two website content pages.

involvement   The importance or relevance of an object, idea, or behavior to the consumer—the extent to which it relates to consumers' values, interests, or needs.

L

leaders   Volunteers, contractors, and staff who keep the community running.

legitimate power   Power that is based on contractual agreements that specify the terms and responsibilities of a channel relationship.

lifetime value   Total net profit of a customer over the entire expected length of relationship.

M

market   Any established means by which the exchange of goods and services takes place. It implies trade that is transacted with some regularity and regulation, and in which some competition is involved.

market opportunity analysis   A systematic tool for determining the viability of a new venture or initiative.

marketing implementation metrics   Measurements of the performance of the business's marketing program.

marketing mix/marketing program   Focuses on the implementation of marketing strategy using product, price, promotion, and distribution channel levers.

marketing strategy   The process of identifying market segments (segmentation), choosing an attractive segment consistent with the firm's resources and goals (targeting), and strategically communicating the product's benefits to the target segment (positioning). The goal is to leverage the company's

resources to meet its strategic and financial goals.

marketspace   The digital equivalent of a physical-world marketplace.

marketspace matrix   A framework for identifying the most appropriate marketing levers that are designed to move customers through the relationship stages.

mass communication   Communications and media that reach a broad audience but with little or no opportunities for differentiation and targeting.

meaningful segmentation   Segmentation that explains customer behaviors, offers insight into motivations, and defines customer relationship to products and/or services.

Metcalfe's Law   States that the usefulness, or utility, of a network equals the square of the number of users—in other words, the more users on a network, the more useful the network is to those users.

Mrs. Schwartz   Representative of all consumers who want to be heard and understood in order to have their needs better satisfied.

N

naturalistic observation   Subjects are monitored as they interact in their natural environment.

new opportunity positioning   Involves repositioning the offering entirely—attempting to capture the attention of a completely new segment.

new opportunity targeting   For BAMs entering the online market, involves targeting an entirely new segment online.

new-to-the-world value   Previously unknown offering(s) that represent entirely new markets or functionalities.

novices   New members who need to learn the ropes and be introduced into community life.

O

objective element   The customer's experience of a site's basic functionality.

obtrusive observation   Here, the researcher joins the observation group, and each member knows her role. An example of obtrusive observation is the Division of Motor Vehicles representative sitting next to a test taker during an on-road driving test.

offering   Any new initiative, product or service designed to bring an opportunity to the end user (i.e., the customer).

opportunity nucleus   A set of unmet or underserved customer needs.

outsourced content   Site content that has been licensed from third parties, such as newsfeeds or stock ticker reports.

P

perceived element   The customer's unique interpretation of a site.

Performance Dashboard   A set of metrics comprising five categories: business opportunity, business model, customer outcomes, branding and implementation, and financial.

permission marketing   When customers agree to share personal information in exchange for receiving targeted marketing communications.

personalization   Personalization and customization both refer to the ability to provide products and services tailored to individual customers. With personalization, the user is passive and the marketer decides how to tailor the product. With customization, the customer requests desired product features and characteristics.

physical goods   Tangible materials and objects that have economic utility or satisfy an economic want.

portals   A Web navigation hub such as Yahoo! or Lycos.

positioning   Allows companies to stake claims about their products in the minds of their target segment, letting companies communicate distinct advantages over competing strategies.

positioning plan Involves the implementation of a positioning strategy through the following steps: (1) Identify actual product positioning, (2) Determine ideal product positioning, (3) Develop alternative strategies for achieving ideal product position, (4) Select and implement the most promising alternative, and (5) Compare new actual position with ideal position.

power The ability to affect the behavior of another person or organization.

price differentiation Usually results when firms create value added options for relatively homogenous products. These value-added components allow firms to achieve price differentiation.

price discrimination The pricing practice of charging different prices to different people for the same product.

primary research Information that the researcher must collect for a specific purpose. It is necessary when secondary research does not exist. Primary research methods include conducting surveys, questionnaires, focus groups, and interviews to create market data.

product An offering that can be exchanged to satisfy a need or want; includes goods and services.

product life cycle The concept that a product or product category passes through different stages of sales growth and profits, e.g., introduction, growth, maturity, and decline.

product portfolio The set of products that a business offers for sale.

Q

qualitative research Provides an understanding of customer attitudes about products or services. Focus groups, both offline and online, are used more than any other qualitative method to obtain key information about the motiva-

tions, perceptions, and thoughts of a target group or groups. Other qualitative methods include in-depth interviews, small discussion groups (dyads, triads, or mini-groups), customer intercepts, quality function deployment, product testing, mystery customer research, and the voice of the customer.

quality When referring to Internet data, the degree to which the data are accurate, useable for research purposes, and timely.

quantitative research Research that establishes benchmarks (i.e., market size to estimate business potential or volume and to measure the size and importance of market segments), obtains statistically valid responses from a target audience (or population), and measures the result of programs. The main reason for conducting quantitative research is to learn how many people in a population have, or share, a particular characteristic or group of characteristics—in other words, to determine the relationship between one thing (an independent variable) and another (a dependent or outcome variable) in a population.

R

random An event in which all outcomes are equally likely, as in the testing of a blood sample for the presence of a substance.

reach The total number of unique viewers who see an ad during a given time period.

reactions to stimuli element The customer's response to brand and design.

real-time communication Immediate communication, where messages are sent, read, and replied to immediately. An example is online chat.

recency, frequency, monetary (RFM) Three classic behavioral variables used in database marketing: recency of last purchase, frequency of purchase, and monetary purchase(s) expenditure.

referent power The ability to influence because of the firm's reputation or brand equity.

regulars Established members who are comfortably participating in community life.

relationship A bond between individuals expressed by commitment, intensity, and trust.

relationship norms Patterns of behavior that are expected of the parties to a relationship.

relative element The aggregate of the customer's prior experience and the source of the customer's evaluation of the current experience.

resource system A discrete collection of individual and organizational assets and activities that when taken together, create organizational capabilities that allow the company to serve customer needs.

retention rate The percentage of customers who are repeat customers.

reward power The ability of one channel member to offer another a benefit for complying with a request.

S

sample selection bias Introduced when a particular segment of the target population is ignored in the sampling process.

satisfaction A judgment about the extent to which an exchange firm met or exceeded each party's requirements.

secondary research Information previously collected and published—it is the easiest, fastest, and least expensive data-collection method.

segmentation The division of a product market into subunits of consumers who are similar in what they value within the product category, or in terms of their cost to serve, or characteristics that make them accessible to a particular marketing program.

selective distribution A middle-of-the-road strategy in which the firm seeks a balance between making the product as widely available as possible and controlling availability.

sensory element The customer's reaction to offerings that relate to the senses: sight, taste, smell, touch, hearing.

service An action performed by one party for the benefit of another party; most services involve physical goods as well.

seven-step branding process An analytical and creative process that leads to the most appropriate marketing programs and activities for branding.

share of customer An individual level metric, similar in nature to the market metric of market share, that equals the percentage of total expenditures made by a customer on a firm's products in a product category. Share of customer can also be measured on other scales, such as product class.

share of wallet The percentage of a customers' purchases of your product versus the customer's total purchases of the product.

situational involvement A temporary interest in a product or service category that usually occurs only when a person is undertaking a particular purchase or consumption activity.

stage-gate process A structured process for new product development that comprises multiple stages with a decision point between each stage on whether to move forward to the next stage.

static market A market where prices are relatively unchanged. Retail outlets generally employ static market type of pricing strategies.

strength of association The intensity of the associations consumers have with a brand. The stronger the associations, the more reliably consumers will link them to the brand.

T

tailoring Site customization that is initiated and managed by a firm.

targeting The process of evaluating market segments for overall attractiveness, and choosing segments that are consistent with the firm's marketing strategy and capabilities. In evaluating attractiveness, firms should focus on a segment's size and growth, structural attractiveness, and growth.

touch point A medium, vehicle and/or location through which organizations and customers interact.

traditional retailer A business whose sales come primarily from sales to final consumers.

transaction aggregators Firms that facilitate buying and selling by creating links between interested parties. Examples include Auto-by-Tel and Travelocity.

trapped value Potential value that can be unlocked by creating more efficient markets, enabling easier access, or disrupting pricing power.

trust A belief that the other party is reliable and will fulfill his/her obligations.

U

uniqueness The degree to which the associations consumers have with a brand are different from assocations they have with other brands. Uniqueness is a function of both the memorability and distinctiveness of the associations.

user-to-administrator value Examples include subscription fees, activity fees, content fees, and commission fees.

user-to-user value Examples include user-generated content, distribution of digitizeable goods, conversation and relationships with other community members.

V

valence The degree to which the associations consumers have with a brand are positive rather than negative.

value system An interconnection of processes and activities within and among firms that creates benefits for intermediaries and end consumers.

virtual communities Internet firms that facilitate interactions between online users who have a common interest. Examples include Fray.com, habbo.com, and Geocaching.com.

virtual shopping mall Aggregators that provide linkages to mutiple online retailers.

visitors People without persistent identity in the community.